The 1991 Census User's Guide

Edited by
Angela Dale and Catherine Marsh

London: HMSO

© Crown copyright 1993
First published 1993

ISBN 0 11 691527 7 ✓

HMSO publications are available from:

HMSO Publications Centre
(Mail, fax and telephone orders only)
PO Box 276, London, SW8 5DT
Telephone orders 071-873 9090
General enquiries 071-873 0011
(queuing system in operation for both numbers)
Fax orders 071-873 8200

HMSO Bookshops
49 High Holborn, London, WC1V 6HB
(counter service only)
071-873 0011 Fax 071-873 8200
258 Broad Street, Birmingham, B1 2HE
021-643 3740 Fax 021-643 6510
Southey House, 33 Wine Street, Bristol, BS1 2BQ
0272 264306 Fax 0272 294515
9-21 Princess Street, Manchester, M60 8AS
061-834 7201 Fax 061-833 0634
16 Arthur Street, Belfast, BT1 4GD
0232 238451 Fax 0232 235401
71 Lothian Road, Edinburgh, EH3 9AZ
031-228 4181 Fax 031-229 2734

HMSO's Accredited Agents
(see Yellow Pages)

and through good booksellers

Foreword

Censuses of population usually take place every 10 years. One of my 19th century predecessors was responsible for three of them. In these days of shorter job tenure not every Registrar General gets one. I did; and in doing so I became very conscious of two things — the long historic tradition of which the census is a part, and the enormous range and complexity of a census — the complexity of its planning, of the field work, of the data handling systems, of the resulting statistics, and of the uses to which those statistics are put.

The history of census taking has been admirably summarised in 3½ pages in this guide. This is a fascinating subject in its own right, shedding many interesting lights on the social, economic, and even constitutional development of our country. Moreover today's census can only be fully understood in its historical context, because one of the most important purposes of a census is to track changes over time. For this reason the by-word of successive Registrars General has been evolution rather than revolution. And it is significant that when, in 1992, we consulted users about the form and conduct of future censuses, few of the respondents saw a case for radical change.

Nonetheless, evolution has produced major changes since 1801, when the main customer was the national government; the main object was to test the proposition that the population was getting too big for the country to support without substantial imports of food (it wasn't); and the census questions were few and their coverage, by today's standards, narrow. Today, many national data can be produced with sufficient accuracy from sample surveys. One of the main justifications for modern censuses is that they are the only source of reliable and comparable local statistics. The questions are wide ranging. Modern technology has made it possible to cross-tabulate the results in myriad ways, and to present them in geographical detail whose fineness is constrained only by considerations of confidentiality. And the results are used by more and more people from more and more walks of life for an ever growing number of purposes. The demand for information is such that the Registrars General have to decline requests to include some topics simply in order to keep the burden of householders within acceptable limits.

It would be easy, no doubt, for users to overlook the compromises which we have to make, and to blame us for not meeting some particular need. Users may also fail to appreciate the full potential of what we do provide, or can provide on request. A statistician's recurring nightmare is that people will use and interpret statistics without properly understanding their sources, provenance and limitations. This guide deals clearly and expertly with these issues, and many more. It will be an invaluable aid to understanding of the 1991 Census and its results.

It will be evident to any reader that the guide has not been a simple undertaking. I should like to express my appreciation, and that of my colleagues, the Registrars General for Scotland and Northern Ireland, of the splendid job which Angela Dale and Catherine Marsh have done.

PETER WORMALD
Registrar General for England and Wales

Contributors

Robert Barr
Department of Geography
University of Manchester
Manchester, M13 9PL

Keith Cole
Manchester Computing Centre
University of Manchester
Manchester, M13 9PL

Paul Compton
School of Geosciences
The Queens University
Belfast

Angela Dale
Social Statistics Research Unit
City University
Northampton Square
London, EC1V 0HB

from 1.9.93:
Census Microdata Unit
University of Manchester
Manchester, M13 9PL

Chris Denham
Census Division
Office of Population Censuses and
  Surveys
St Catherine's House
10 Kingsway
London WC2 6JP

Robin Flowerdew
Department of Geography
Lancaster University
Lancaster, LA1 4YB

Anne Green
Institute for Employment Research
University of Warwick
Coventry, CV4 7AL

Catherine Marsh (late)
Census Microdata Unit
University of Manchester
Manchester, M13 9PL

Richard Wiggins
SSRU, City University
Northampton Square
London, EC1V 0HB

Contents

Page

14   Whither the census?
Angela Dale

In Memoriam — Catherine Marsh

Cathie Marsh was still working on this book when she died of cancer on January 1st 1993. Over the last decade Cathie developed a keen interest and formidable expertise in census-taking in general and, in particular, the developments leading up to the 1991 Census in Britain.

Cathie's involvement with the census can be traced from work on the history of the census, published in 1985, to her major involvement with developments for the 1991 Census. In 1986 the Census Offices asked the ESRC to provide comments on proposals for the 1991 Census. Cathie was a member of the ESRC Research Resources and Methods Committee at this time and of its Working Group on the 1991 Census. As part of this Working Group, Cathie organised a survey of academics to get their views on the topics to be included in the census, on census geography and on access to census microdata, the results of which were published in Marsh *et al.* (1988). This provided the starting point for Cathie's pioneering work to obtain the release of anonymised samples of microdata from the 1991 Census. From 1987 Cathie was a key participant in discussions with the Census Offices and later took over the chair of an ESRC subgroup on the 1991 Census with the specific aim of making the case for the release of samples of microdata from the 1991 Census. She co-ordinated the production of a major document which set out the arguments for the Samples of Anonymised Records. The document included not just an assessment of the research value to be gained from such samples, but contained a detailed statistical assessment of the disclosure risks that could be incurred through their release. This latter assessment was vitally important in persuading the Census Offices that the risk of disclosure was negligible. The work was published in 1991 in the *Journal of the Royal Statistical Society, Series A* (Marsh *et al.*, 1991a). Cathie's pioneering work in assessing risks of disclosure was recognised internationally, and in particular by an invitation to present a paper at the conference of the International Statistical Institute in Cairo in September 1991 (Marsh *et al.*, 1991).

The case for samples of microdata from the census had previously been made during the 1970s but had been abandoned, largely because of uncertainty over whether such data could be considered a statistical abstract under the 1920 Census Act. The credit for getting microdata back onto the political and research agenda and winning the case for them must be attributed in very large part to Cathie's vision, determination and sheer hard work. Cathie was a firm believer in the value of empirical enquiry and she saw the census as, in many ways, the most complete account of the population and its social condition. It was therefore essential that the use of census data for research purposes should be maximised, and the SARs played a vital role in promoting this. Having won the battle to achieve the SARs, Cathie was then awarded funding from the ESRC and the Joint Information Systems Committee (JISC) to establish the Census Microdata Unit at the University of Manchester to house and disseminate them. It is a cruel irony that she did not live to see the release of the SARs and has not been able to carry out any of the research plans that she had developed for the SARs.

Cathie's work and interest was not confined to academic spheres. Her paper in the *Journal of the Market Research Society* on the applications of the SARs in marketing research was awarded a medal for the best paper in 1991 (Marsh, 1991). At the time of her death Cathie was also involved in work with local authorities to estimate the impact of the 1991 Census undercount at local level. She had been responsible for a seminar on 'The validation and uses of census data' jointly organised by the Royal Statistical Society and the Social Research Association and held on November 24th, 1992. This was largely concerned with the undercount in the 1991 Census and Cathie made an eloquent contribution in which she set out a series of possible causes of the census undercount and suggested the means by which they should be further investigated.

This book arose from a desire to bring together into a single volume information about the 1991 Census and the various forms of output, to ensure that census data achieved the widest possible use. Cathie was an inspiring force behind the book and, through her influence, it has turned into a more substantial and more valuable publication than would otherwise have been the case. As well as playing a major editorial role, Cathie wrote four of the chapters. Chapter 5 (Privacy, Confidentiality and Anonymity in the 1991 Census) and chapter 12 (The Samples of Anonymised Records) were largely finalised before her death. Chapter 1 was almost completed and additions and alterations have been made only to round off unfinished themes. Cathie was still working on chapter 6, part II until just before her death. Although some additions and deletions have been made, mainly in response to comments by OPCS, the rationale for the chapter, the arguments contained within it, and, indeed, the bulk of the text, all came from Cathie.

If this book is able to play a part in persuading more people to examine the evidence for themselves, and to increase the use made of census data by social scientists, then it will be a fitting tribute to Cathie's passionate belief in the power of rigorous analysis and rational argument in furthering the ends of social science.

References

Marsh, C. (1985) 'Informants, respondents and citizens', in M Bulmer (ed) *Essays in the History of British Sociological Research* Cambridge: Cambridge University Press

Marsh, C., Arber, S., Wrigley, N., Rhind, D. and Bulmer, M. (1988) 'The view of academic social scientists on the 1991 UK Census of Population: a report of the Economic and Social Research Council Working Group', *Environment and Planning (A)*, Vol. 20, 851-889

Marsh, C., Skinner, C., Arber, S., Penhale, B., Openshaw, S., Hobcraft, J., Lievesley, D. and Walford, N. (1991) 'The case for samples of anonymised records from the 1991 Census', *Journal of the Royal Statistical Society (A)*, Vol. 154, 305-340

Marsh, C., Dale, A. and Skinner, C. (1991) 'Safe Data versus Safe Setting: Access to Customised Results from the British Census' *Bulletin of the International Statistical Institute, Proceedings of the 48th Session* Cairo September 1991

Marsh, C. (1991) 'Microdata from the 1991 Census of Population in Britain: applications in marketing research', *Journal of the Market Research Society*, Vol. 33, No.1, 275-284

Acknowledgements

A great many people have contributed to this book. The greatest debt is owed to OPCS who have provided most of the raw material upon which the book is based. In particular, Chris Denham has provided extensive help, information and comments at every stage of the book and takes major credit for checking the accuracy of the information provided and improving the editorial process. Any remaining inconsistencies or unintentionally misleading statements are those of the authors and editors. We are also very grateful to David Pearce, Bob Armitage, Ian Golds and Andy Teague for providing additional comments on draft material and supplying additional information. Linda Street, Terry Russell and their staff from the Titchfield office gave up a great deal of time to explain the intricacies of the fieldwork and census processing. Frank Thomas from the General Register Office (Scotland) has also provided invaluable comments and information, particularly on aspects relating to Scotland. Lastly, but by no means least, a huge debt is owed to Pat Broad of OPCS Information Branch who has had the difficult job of steering this volume through to publication. Pat has been a constant source of good advice and calm organisation and we are greatly indebted to her.

Additionally acknowledgements are due to a large number of people who have provided help with particular chapters: Alan Holmans of the Department of the Environment for comments on chapter 2; David Martin of Southampton University for comments on both chapters 3 and 9; Keith Cole for supplying the data for Table 4.4. and Figure 4.7; Tracey Schofield for compilation of the raw material for tables 5.1 and 5.2; Patrick Heady of OPCS for considerable assistance and advice on chapter 6, parts I and II; Steve Simpson of Bradford City Council for comments on chapter 6, part II; John Roberts, Malcolm Campbell and Virginia Knight of Manchester University Computing Centre and Steve Simpson of Bradford City Council for help with chapter 8; Lak Bulusu and Andrew Teague of OPCS, Glen Everett of the Employment Department, Keith Dugmore of MVA Systematica and Keith Cole for assistance with chapter 10; Chris Skinner at the University of Southampton for his advice on sampling errors and Robin Flowerdew for help in specifying the geographical areas for the 2 per cent individual SAR in chapter 11; Isobel Macdonald Davies of OPCS for comments on chapter 12; Phil Rees of Leeds University for additional information on SAS for Northern Ireland for chapter 13.

We would like to thank the following for kind permission to reproduce copyright material: the Controller of Her Majesty's Stationery Office (maps 3.1-3.3, which are reproduced from the Ordnance Survey 1:10000 and 1:2500 maps); OPCS (figures

1.2, 2.1-2.2, 4.1-4.5, 6.1-6.3, 8.1-8.4, 10.1-10.3, map 11.1 and appendix A); the Trustees of the British Museum (figure 1.3); the Daily Sport (figure 1.1); Solo Syndication & Literary Agency Ltd (figure 5.1); The Geographical Journal (map 9.1); Oxford University Press (maps 9.2 and 9.6); Centre for Urban and Regional Studies, University of Birmingham (map 9.3); the Geographical Association (map 9.4); the University of Edinburgh (map 9.5); Pergamon Press Ltd (map 10.2).

We would also like to thank the ESRC who provided funding towards the production of this book under the ESRC/JISC Initiative on the 1991 Census.

The editors are responsible for the final content and balance of the text and any mistakes or omissions that have been made. The content of each chapter reflects the views of the authors and editors and the opinions expressed are not necessarily those of the Census Offices of the UK (OPCS, GRO(S) and CO(NI)).

ANGELA DALE and CATHERINE MARSH (late)
April 1993

Abbreviations List

AMF	Area Master File
CODOT	Classification of Occupations and Directory of Occupational Titles
CVS	Census Validation Survey
EC	European Community
ED	Enumeration district
ESRC	Economic and Social Research Council
GBF-DIME	Geographic Base File-Dual Independent Map Encoding
GHS	General Household Survey
GIS	Geographical Information Systems
LBS	Local Base Statistics
LGD	Local government district
LLMA	Local Labour Market Areas
LS	OPCS Longitudinal Study
NHSCR	National Health Service Central Register
OA	Output Area
OPCS	Office of Population Censuses and Surveys
PED	Pseudo enumeration district
PES	Post-Enumeration Survey
POA	Provisional Output Area
SAR	Samples of Anonymised Records
SAS	Small Area Statistics
SED	Special enumeration district
SEG	Socioeconomic group
SMS	Special Migration Statistics
SOC	Standard Occupational Classification
SSA	Standard Spending Assessment
SWS	Special Workplace Statistics
TIGER	Topologically Integrated Geographical Encoding and Referencing
TTWA	Travel-to-work-areas
UN	United Nations

Introduction

The 1991 Census provides the most authoritative social accounting of people and housing in Britain. The population targeted is universal: all present, or usually resident in the country on census night, along with a count of housing. Comparable statistics are generated for very fine geographical areas. The twenty or so questions in the census can be cross-classified to provide powerful statistical insights into the social conditions of the population and its housing. The decennial census is, furthermore, a unique source for studying social change, forming the longest running social account of the population. So valuable is the exercise that this form of periodic stock-taking of a nation's human resources is now conducted in most countries in the world.

The British census is conducted compulsorily by Act of Parliament, and strict guarantees regarding the confidentiality of the data and the anonymity of respondents are given to all, which affects the form of output that can be produced. Nonetheless, the 1991 Census broke new ground by making available a wider range of products than ever before while at the same time strengthening various aspects of its confidentiality protection.

The purpose of this book is to provide a guide to the 1991 Census, to its conduct and to the products available, assisting the reader wherever possible in identifying and obtaining access to census data in the form most appropriate to their needs. The book is intended to be of value to all census users, and aims to cover the complete range of products from the census. It is not, however, meant to replace the documentation produced by the Census Offices which will always be the definitive source of information about the census. For this reason the book does not contain the technical detail of Census Office documents. Rather, the Guide is intended to be accessible to the relative newcomer to the census and to give an overview of the entire census process and the outputs available to users, in a single volume.

To assist those coming newly to the census we have tried, as far as possible, to avoid the use of jargon and acronyms, although this has not always been easy! We assume that the reader is likely to use the book for a range of purposes and may not read through chapters sequentially. Therefore, each chapter is designed to stand alone and, intentionally, there is some overlap between chapters. Because of the interrelationship between chapters, extensive cross-referencing has been used to help readers navigate their way around the book. A full indexing system has also been used.

Inevitably in a book such as this, there is a tension between providing the basic 'facts' of the census operation and placing these in a more considered context.

Individual chapters vary in the extent to which this balance is struck, reflecting both the material being covered and also the perspective of the author. Nonetheless, each chapter should contain basic information about the topic under discussion. A further tension is introduced by the need for early publication. The importance of getting the book into the public domain as quickly as possible has meant that, in some cases, work within the Census Offices is still in progress and final outcomes cannot be reported. This is particularly true for the work on the coverage and quality of the Census, and of some of the guidance on statistical points. Further contact points at the end of each chapter and full referencing should enable the reader to pursue any unresolved issues and to obtain further detail if needed.

The census is not just another social survey; its sheer size puts practical constraints on what is possible. Readers who wish to make intelligent and appropriate use of census data need to gain a good understanding of how the enterprise is conducted. In any data collection process, a series of decisions have to be taken about what topics should be covered, how questions should be worded, which response categories used and which editing rules applied. Different decisions produce different data, as the various census tests make clear. Other processes also influence the data collected, especially the way in which the fieldwork is organised and the efficiency and skill of the enumerators. It is therefore essential for the careful census user to be aware of the details of the process of data collection.

Although the focus of this book is on the 1991 Census, it is also important to place it in the context of its recent predecessors. A large number of users of the 1991 Census will also have used the 1981 and 1971 data. It is therefore important to be aware of the situations where comparisons across censuses are possible, and those where differences cause problems. Changes between censuses relate not just to the topic and wording differences, but also to the geography of the census and to the population base. In chapter 2, the reader will find a general discussion of the content and factors influencing change over previous censuses, and in chapter 4 more detail is given on the process of fieldwork and data entry. The topic of census geography is covered specifically in chapter 3. Part I gives a detailed description of the geography of the 1991 Census, indicates the process of development over past decades and also suggests some possible future developments. Part II provides a commentary on the current census geography and draws some comparisons with the US.

The census is founded on Acts of Parliament which give it a statutory basis — most notably in the 1920 Census Act which gives the authority for a census to be conducted, and the 1991 Census (Confidentiality) Act. It is also increasingly founded on European Community (EC) law, including the harmonisation of census activities. In addition, the United Nations (UN) co-ordinates census activities over a wider area than the EC. Ultimately, however, the census is dependent on the acceptance and trust of the public, and therefore both real and perceived issues of confidentiality must be discussed. In chapter 5 the reader will find a comprehensive account of the various ways in which the Census Offices meet their obligations to respect the confidences contained in the census forms.

Following discussion on the context of the census, and the process of data collection and construction, chapter 6 is concerned with the coverage and quality of the data and how this is measured. The success of the census enterprise has traditionally been evaluated by a survey in which a small sample of areas is checked shortly after the census and a sample of households interviewed in greater depth by more experienced staff. Such a Census Validation Survey was conducted in 1991, and chapter 6 Part I contains a description of its methodology, comparing it with similar exercises in other countries, and presents some preliminary findings. However, in 1991 it seems likely that the level of undercount was substantially greater than had been estimated in other post-war British censuses, and also that the Census Validation Study did not successfully capture the majority of those who were missed. Part II of chapter 6 therefore explains how the figures from the Census and the Census Validation Survey can be reconciled with the Registrar General's mid-year population estimates. It also considers how any potential undercount might affect the user of census data.

The emphasis in chapters 1 to 6 is therefore on understanding the process of data construction. This provides the underpinning for the subsequent chapters which are concerned with outputs from the census and how they can be used. The 1991 Census has the greatest ever range of outputs available, and is probably richer in this respect than the output from any other census in the world.

Opportunities are provided both for individual level analysis of cross-sectional and longitudinal data, as well as for the analysis of very small areas. Chapters 7 to 12 take each of the census outputs in turn and provide an introduction to the form and organisation of the data, the research potential offered, problems or pitfalls for the unwary user, software available for analysis and contact points for access and further information.

Chapter 7 provides an introduction to census output as users sometimes find it hard to know precisely where to find particular pieces of information. Chapter 8 deals with the Small Area and Local Base Statistics, the content of which has virtually doubled since 1981. Use of the improved geographical base of the census — digitised boundaries for all census areas and links to postcodes — in mapping and spatial analyses is discussed in chapter 9. Aggregate census data are also available in the form of origin-destination matrices showing flows to work and moves from one year previously; these special workplace and migration files form the subject of chapter 10.

The next two chapters deal with the two forms in which microdata are available from the 1991 Census. Cross-sectional samples of anonymised records are being produced for the first time, and made available for importing to the user's own hardware and software environment. The background to the development and the detail of the files available is given in chapter 11. The linked census records in the Longitudinal Study now provide data over a 20-year time span — 1971, 1981 and 1991 — and offer very exciting possibilities for studying social change at the individual level, as chapter 12 points out. Both types of data will make detailed analysis of census data at the individual and household level much richer than was possible in previous censuses.

Two chapters conclude the volume. While the focus of all the other chapters in this volume is the census in Great Britain, many users will wish to make statements about the United Kingdom. Since censuses in Northern Ireland are conducted under a different statute than in Great Britain, and various aspects of both content and procedure differ somewhat, we have included a chapter specifically on the Northern Ireland census. Finally, we take a look at the future for population censuses in Britain and elsewhere, and the pressures on census offices around the world to adopt new ways of counting their population. Just because something has been done in a particular way for 200 years does not mean that it will continue in that way.

1   An overview

Catherine Marsh

1.1 WHY WE NEED CENSUS-TYPE INFORMATION

Modern bureaucratic societies are organised on principles that presuppose the availability of accurate information on the population and its characteristics. As later sections discuss, important decisions such as the amount of revenue receipt from government depend upon the availability of accurate information on population and housing, not just nationally but also at the local level.

Accurate and detailed information at a local level can be obtained in a number of different ways. What determines the choice of a census? One of the fundamental requirements of modern society is an accurate count of population at a local level. Whilst sample surveys are routinely used by government to provide information on a wide range of topics (for example, employment, health, family income) they are by definition sample surveys, with associated sampling errors; they are not able to supply accurate information at a local area level and are voluntary with typical response rates of around 80 per cent. Such surveys cannot, therefore, provide the accurate local level population accounting that is required by modern day society.

Nonetheless, the model of a compulsory census that covers the entire population is not universally adopted. Some European countries which keep an accurate population register and make it a legal requirement for all residents not only to be registered but to record a change of address, have used this as a source of information in preference to conducting a census. Denmark's 1991 Census was entirely register based, but some countries (Sweden and Belgium) use a combination of information from registers and a census questionnaire whilst the Netherlands uses data from registers and sample surveys (Langevin, Begeot and Pearce, 1992).

The time interval at which this complete and universal information is collected has also to be decided. If the census is to be of value then it must be repeated at sufficiently frequent intervals, but, offset against this is the cost of census taking and the burden on the public. In chapter 6 (II) we discuss how the British government uses registration data to provide annual estimates of population, taking the census as a benchmark. Both over time and across different countries, the most frequent interval for censuses has been 10 years; some countries use 5-year intervals (e.g. Australia and Canada) and others rather more irregular intervals, but less than 10 years (e.g. France). In recent decades the statistical offices of the European Community and the United Nations have imposed greater conformity on the timing of census-taking and a decennial census has become the norm.

1

In the UK and in many other countries, the census thus produces a near-complete snapshot of the population and its housing at 10-year intervals. In order to achieve an acceptable level of coverage the census has to be compulsory and this, in turn, demands that the public are given firm assurances of confidentiality. The importance given to maintaining the confidentiality of census data precludes the release of any data relating to identifiable people. But, as we shall see in chapter 11, Britain has, for the first time, taken the step of releasing samples of *anonymised* records relating to individuals and households from the 1991 Census. The USA, Canada and Australia also release similarly anonymised records, although this route has been less vigorously pursued within the European countries. The compulsory nature of the UK census also means that the topics covered must be generally acceptable to the public and, because the census form is designed for self-completion, it must be relatively straightforward.

1.2 THE LEGAL FRAMEWORK TO THE BRITISH CENSUS

Censuses in Great Britain are conducted with statutory authority, which means that proposals must be put to, and approved, by Parliament. Prior to 1920, each individual census required an Act of Parliament. The 1920 Census Act gave the Registrars General for England and Wales and Scotland the *general* authority and duty to conduct censuses in the whole or any part of Great Britain at intervals no shorter than every five years. In fact, the provision for a quinquennial census has only been used once — in 1966 when a 10 per cent sample census was held. Reports on a census have to be laid before Parliament.

Although the primary legislation is the 1920 Act which enables censuses to be taken, it is necessary, in addition, to make an Order in Council (secondary legislation), directing that a particular census is taken. The Order is laid before Parliament giving the date when the census will be taken and the persons by whom and with respect to whom returns are to be made; it also sets out the broad topics on which questions will be asked. In addition, for each census, Regulations must be drawn up and laid before Parliament. These set out in detail the manner in which the enumeration should be carried out, and the duties of the enumerators and census officers (OPCS and GRO(S), 1988). Directives agreed by the European Council of Ministers on both the content and the timing of censuses are mandatory unless a member state obtains a derogation (Langevin, Begeot and Pearce, 1992).

Protection against misuse of the data is given by Section 8 of the 1920 Act (see chapter 5). When Section 2 of the Official Secrets Act 1911 was repealed, it was necessary to enact the Census (Confidentiality) Act of 1991 in order to reinforce the confidentiality of personal census information and to prescribe penalties for anyone working on the census enterprise who broke that confidence.

1.3 ADMINISTRATIVE RESPONSIBILITY

Responsibility for the conduct of censuses in the UK is divided between the Office of Population Censuses and Surveys (OPCS) in England and Wales, the General Register Office (Scotland) (GRO(S)) and the Census Office (Northern Ireland) (CO(NI)). We shall for ease refer to OPCS and GRO(S) collectively as 'the Census Offices' in this volume.

The Northern Ireland census is discussed fully in chapter 13.

Censuses separate to that of the UK were carried out in the offshore islands of Guernsey, Alderney, Jersey and the Isle of Man which are not subject to UK or EC legislation on censuses. Except for Jersey, which held its census on 10 March 1991, these censuses were conducted at the same time as the United Kingdom, although output is not harmonized with that for the rest of the British Isles. For further information see the *Census Newsletter,* No. 26, June 1993.

1.4 THE PRACTICALITIES OF CONDUCTING THE CENSUS IN BRITAIN

The 1991 Census took place on 21 April 1991. It was the 19th decennial census to have been conducted in a series which began in 1801. The only interruption came during the Second World War, when a system of national registration temporarily replaced it as a basic population count.

The census is centrally financed by Government and cost about £135 million in 1991. In unit terms, however, the census enterprise is cheap — around £2.50 per head (over 10 years). Although the census fieldwork and processing requires a very considerable mobilisation of staff over a short time period (for more details see chapter 4), the planning stage is very long and detailed. The geographic base

Figure 1.1 'Better not make it this Sunday Dave, my husband would have to put you on his census form!' (*Daily Sport*, 18 April 1991).

is planned well in advance following considerable consultation (see chapter 3) and all the published output is preplanned, again following consultation with users (see chapters 7 and 8). A series of 1991 Census User Guides, available from OPCS long before any data were published, gave the outlines of all tables planned (see chapter 7) as well as details of the Small Area Statistics and Local Base Statistics (see chapter 8).

1.4.1 The population base

The population can be enumerated either on the basis of where people happen to be at a particular point in time, or on the basis of where they usually live. Although historically the British census used the former basis, in recent decades it has used a combination of the two. It requires householders to fill in information about any person who was present on census night and also about all those usually resident in the household (figure 1.1). Additionally, visitors are asked to give their usual place of residence. This allows a number of different population bases to be calculated, as chapter 2 explains.

One way in which the census provides a comprehensive picture of the population, unparalleled by any other data collection activities, is in its coverage of the

Table 1.1

Population present in institutions and other communal establishments in England and Wales, 1851, 1931 and 1981

1851 — Inmates and staff in public institutions		1931 — Inmates and staff in institutions		1981 — Population present on census night not in private households	
All persons	**271,006**	**All persons**	**890,434**	**All persons**	**1,206,930**
Barracks	48,567	Workhouses	128,233	Hotels and boarding houses	209,546
Workhouses	125,430	Other poor house		Hospitals/homes — other	
Prisoners	26,726	institutions	80,652	psychiatric	140,883
Lunatic asylums	18,141	Homes for the insane	182,130	Hospitals/homes — other	273,008
Hospitals for the		Homes for the cripples	3,804	Homes for the old and	
sick	10,053	Homes for the blind	4,343	disabled	205,362
Asylums and other		Homes for the deaf and		Children's homes	27,834
charitable		dumb	2,810	Educational establishments	90,029
institutions	42,089	Homes for inebriates	294	Prison department	
		Hospitals (including		establishments	43,471
		naval and military)	193,052	Defence establishments	96,649
		Convalescent and		Civilian ships, boats, barges	3,811
		nursing homes	54,920	Hostels and common	
		Prisons	10,976	lodging houses	44,742
		Reformatories	12,586	Miscellaneous communal	
		Naval, military		establishments	58,208
		barracks,		Campers, persons sleeping	
		Royal Navy ships	166,593	rough, etc*	13,387
		Other ships	45,567		
		Inland boats and barges	4,484		

* Includes caravans and other non-permanent buildings with all enumerated persons usually resident elsewhere.

Source: *Population Trends*, 1981, vol. 48, p.39.

population which does not reside at a private address. Residents of communal establishments and those without a fixed address at all formed around 1.5 per cent of the population in 1991; they include some of the most underprivileged people in British society, yet they are not covered in the continuous government surveys which use the postal address file as their sampling frame, or indeed in any household survey which involves interviewers seeking information at private households. The census has historically been the only reliable source of information about the institutional population (table 1.1), and can be used to construct a fascinating social history of the gradual changes in the numbers and types of total institutions in which people live.

In 1991, as a response to requests from organisations for the homeless and other consultations, a special effort was also made to enumerate people sleeping rough. The details of this are presented in chapter 4.

1.5 SIZE AND COMPLEXITY

The sheer scale of the Census enterprise is hard to convey other than by citing various indicators. Some 118,000 enumerators were employed in 1991 to distribute and collect forms; with the addition of supervisory, managerial, coding and processing staff, it is estimated that at the peak of work one in 400 people were employed on the census (Mahon and Pearce, 1991). Twelve miles of shelving were needed to house the forms at the input processing stations (figure 1.2). Both fieldwork and processing are discussed in detail in chapter 4.

The size of the operation also dictates that the fieldwork stage must be well tested and robust. The whole system has to work in the hands of staff most of whom have had very little time to gain experience in the process. As the census is held at only 10-year intervals it is essential that no major mistakes are made. The similarity in the form of the census each time is not just for reasons of continuity, but because there is a tremendous need to abide by the dictum 'if it works, don't fix it'! Changes between censuses are (ideally, but not always in practice) subject to elaborate testing, and the lead time is long: forms of census wording for the 1991 Census were tested in 1987.

A further consequence of the size of the census is the use of sampling to avoid the need to code fully all items on the census forms. For those items which are considered 'hard to code' (mainly those which generate a high proportion of written-in answers), only a 10 per cent sample is fully coded. The way in which the 10 per cent sample of households and residents in communal establishments is drawn is described fully in chapter 4.

The importance of having a tried and tested system makes the census an inherently conservative enterprise. Users can often be infuriated by the apparent lack of responsiveness of the Census Offices to what seem to be eminently sensible suggestions for change, failing to realise just what is at stake if things go badly wrong. In fact, as we shall see in chapter 4, one very small error in the editing algorithm for input processing in 1991 caused a delay of five months in producing results for the first county, although some of this time was subsequently recovered.

The size and complexity of the census also requires considerable information and publicity to ensure that the public know about it and the reasons for conducting it. Despite being compulsory, the success of the census is dependent upon the good will and cooperation of the public.

**Figure 1.2   Storing the 1991 Census forms at the Regional Processing
Office at Hillingdon, Glasgow**

Public enquiry units were set up in 1991 in England and Wales and in Scotland to deal with a large number of written and telephone enquiries. The England and Wales unit received 210,000 phone calls and almost 3,000 letters between the end of March and the end of May 1991. Over the same period Scotland received over 6,400 phone calls and some 240 letters. In both England and Wales and Scotland just over 40 per cent of the phone calls were to say that census forms had not been collected and a further 20 per cent saying that a form had not been delivered. Field staff were given this information by the enquiry units.

1.6   CHOICE OF DATE FOR THE CENSUS

The year in the decade in which the census is held has remained unchanged (apart from the 1939 National Registration and the consequent dropping of the 1941 Census) since the first census of 1801. The choice of date of the census, however, retains some flexibility. Picking one day only for enumeration is essential for an accurate count to be made. The goal is to identify a day which maximises the following factors: the number of people at their usual place of residence; continuity with previous censuses; reasonable weather and daylight hours; the avoidance of dates of local elections and possible dates for national elections; delivery of key census results to the required timetable. After the first few censuses, which were conducted in June, conventional wisdom suggests that a date in April achieves this goal best and is in line with the EC directive for censuses to be held between March and May.

One of the issues in selecting the date for recent censuses has been the treatment of students, who make up the largest group of people who are away from home for a substantial part of the year. In 1971, census day was held in the vacation, while in 1981 it was in term-time. As a result, many university towns were unable to make reliable estimates of changes in their usual resident population, and all areas were affected to some extent. In 1991, when the census date fell during the vacation for most students, form-fillers were, for the first time, explicitly instructed to include students as residents at their parental home and also to give their term-time address.

The inclusion of a new question on the term-time address of students will, if continued in the future, help remove a major ambiguity about intercensal change but makes this aspect of population comparisons between 1981 and 1991 very tricky.

1.7 NEW TOPICS IN 1991 AND CONTINUITY BETWEEN CENSUSES

The 1991 Census also introduced new questions on limiting long-term illness, ethnic group and central heating; it reintroduced a question on weekly hours worked and provided a count of dwellings. These new topics and questions are covered in detail in chapter 2, which also highlights other changes from past censuses.

There is an inherent tension in the decisions over introducing new topics and dropping old ones, between reflecting changing needs for information whilst retaining comparability with previous censuses. Chapter 2 discusses in more detail some of the pressures and constraints over what topics should be included in the census. Despite efforts by the Census Offices to retain continuity where possible, the decennial snapshot approach is vulnerable to the vagaries of what else is happening in the economy at that point in time. In both 1981 and 1991, levels of unemployment were particularly high, for example, and in 1991 the housing market was also depressed, a fact that must be remembered by users wanting to make intercensal comparisons of economic activity levels.

1.8 WHAT THE CENSUS IS USED FOR

Whilst a number of different sources are used to monitor change at a national level, or to record small area populations, the census is *the* benchmark. It is *the* baseline for the mid-year estimates of population. These then form the fundamental input to various types of resource apportionment. Revenue is distributed to local districts and to health authorities using a complex formula largely based on a head-count of the population but also using the characteristics of the population — most of which are drawn from census information.

Because it covers everyone, the census also enables small-scale local estimates to be made in a comparable form. These are then the inputs to many different types of planning process. Many agencies use them for planning services of various kinds to the community. Local social services departments use numbers of elderly people when planning the level of service provision, whilst numbers of children are used by education authorities to forecast schooling needs. The training agencies use the information on the higher educational qualifications of the population in their skills audits in different localities. The central Department of Transport and the planning departments in local authority districts make extensive use of information about means of transport to work. The new question on long-term health problems will provide additional information for those responsible for providing local health services.

Whilst these are the two most basic reasons for taking a census — to recalibrate population estimates and to provide government with consistent information at a local level — the census is also widely used by many other sectors of the economy. The retail sector uses demographic information in the census to map area profiles when it is considering siting new outlets. A great deal of academic research is based upon census products.

The census is also the gold standard against which many aspects of social surveys are judged, and sometimes on which they are based. Most social surveys have two-stage sample designs, selecting first a representative sample of small areas in which to concentrate interviewing. The stratification for the list of areas is almost universally done by ordering in terms of various census characteristics. Attempts to validate the representativeness of sample surveys use the census to check the basic demographic profile of the respondents selected. The best information about the characteristics of non-respondents to sample surveys in Britain has been obtained by using the census to trace non-respondents to the government continuous surveys, such as the General Household Survey and the Family Expenditure Survey. From such studies we know, for example, that sample surveys are often biased against the elderly, single person households, and ethnic minority households (Rauta, 1985; Redpath, 1986). In short, high quality survey work, far from being an alternative to censuses, could not take place without a high quality census.

Population censuses, however, have a very long history and, in Britain, there are some important milestones which mark the way to the 1991 Census. The following section reviews the background to censuses in general and the British census in particular.

1.9 HISTORY OF CENSUSES AND CENSUS TAKING

The Bible gives us several examples of quite early people counts; for example, the fighting strength of the children of Israel at the Exodus was ascertained by a count of all males of 20 years and upwards made by enumerators appointed for each clan. Similar activities can be documented in ancient Persia, China and Egypt. However, the word 'census' is a Latin word, and it is the Romans who placed the activity of counting the people on a regular footing. Under the constitution of Servius Tullius, a count of the citizens of Rome, in six separate classes, was to be undertaken by public officials ('censors') appointed specially for the task. Each family was enumerated, along with their wealth and property, including land, livestock, slaves and freedmen. The purpose of this activity was explicitly one of apportionment; the division of the population into classes and centuries for administration and taxation was done on the basis of population numbers and wealth. As the republic grew, the function of the censors grew increasingly important. The act of counting the population took on an increasingly ceremonial role as well as practical, and one of the commonest ways of becoming a citizen of Rome was to be enumerated at the quinquennial census. Whilst many bureaucratic societies have, in the past, used a census to count how many soldiers they could call up, or to assess the base for taxation, modern censuses have more than a bureaucratic goal: accurate population bases form the heart of valid social science and social policy.

The dividing line between these ancient activities and modern censuses is the uncoupling of the process of counting from the process of taxation or military conscription. When a count is being done for a specific administrative purpose, the results can be seriously contaminated. In 1711, a census was conducted in China for the purpose of levying a poll tax, and enumerated 28 million people. Forty years later, when a count was undertaken for the relief of distress, 103 million were enumerated! While this is an extreme example, headcounts for explicitly administrative purposes must always be suspected of bearing the hallmarks of the purposes for which they were undertaken.

Modern census taking began when enquiries were undertaken solely for the purpose of ascertaining population size, whether within geographical or economic subdivision. The hallmark of whether any particular enquiry should count as a 'modern' census is whether the results of it were published: the earlier administrative headcounts were not conducted for purposes of general enlightenment, so there was no reason to publish the results.

There is debate about where the origin of this modern impetus is to be found. One centre of early activity in population counting was Scandinavia where Sweden conducted a census in 1749, followed swiftly by Finland and Norway. These counts were thought to have been stimulated by the devastating effect of the Great Northern War (1700-21) on the male population of the country. However, these early 'censuses' were, in fact, special tallies of existing systems of population registration rather than special purpose enquiries as such.

France also can claim an early entry into the counting game; like Britain until the Glorious Revolution, it had a 'hearth tax' which led officials to count the number of houses as early as the 14th century. France instituted compulsory registration and publication of population figures in the 17th century, and in one of her colonies (later Quebec), such periodic enumerations were conducted between 1665 and 1754, thus leading Quebecois to claim paternity of census taking.

1.9.1 Census taking in the USA

'No taxation without representation' had been the touchstone of the American colonists in their battles with Britain, so it is not surprising that the USA should provide one of the earliest and best examples of modern census taking. There was a debate at the convention which drew up the constitution about whether each state should have equal representation in Congress or representation according to its size of population. The solution was the creation of two chambers, in one of which (the House of Representatives) representation was to be proportional to population. Envisaging rapid changes in relative populations, the convention enshrined in the constitution the provision for a census to be conducted every 10 years in order to

Figure 1.3 'Overpopulation'
Source: Cruikshank's Comic Almanack, 1851

verify the population count; 'No capitation or other direct tax shall be laid unless in proportion to the census or enumeration of inhabitants hereinbefore directed to be taken' (OED). Federal census taking began in 1790, classifying the population as free or slaves, the free as white or non-white, the white as males or females and the males by age! It continued every 10 years thereafter. Unlike Europe, where fears about the size of the population provided most of the impetus to census taking, political representation was at the heart of the decision to establish a US census; it is interesting to note that this issue is still at the heart of modern discussions about adjusting the census for the undercount.

1.9.2 The background to the British census

In 1753, a 'Bill for taking account of the Number of People and of the total Number of Marriages, Births and Deaths' was proposed by a private member in the House of Commons. Its principal opponent was William Thornton, MP for York, who viewed such an enumeration as 'totally subversive of the last remains of English liberty', tantamount to the establishment of a police state, while handing out important information to Britain's enemies. He declared that any enumerator who came his way would receive 'the discipline of the horse pond' (quoted in Taylor, 1951, p.715). However, the more sober arguments in favour won sway. Had the Bill not been timed out in its passage through the House of Lords, Britain would have been the first large European country to conduct a census.

It was another half century before legislative momentum gained sufficient strength to bring a further proposal back to the House. Concern about rate of population change fuelled demands for a census in Britain as it had done in Scandinavia, but the predominant fears were of excess population growth rather than population decline. Such fears, especially that the population might be growing too fast among the 'feebler' elements of society (the poor, the intellectually degenerate, or even the Irish) were a recurrent theme among census takers and social statisticians throughout the 19th and early 20th century (figure 1.3).

By the beginning of the 19th century, Britain's population was growing rapidly. Malthus published his famous *Essay on the Principles of Population* in 1798 in which he argued that population had a tendency to grow exponentially while food supplies only increased arithmetically. Although no-one seems explicitly to have referred to Malthusian ideas in the debate in Parliament, food supplies relative to population were clearly an important issue for a country which had been seven years at war with France and which had just suffered a disastrous harvest.

In 1800 John Rickman, clerk to the House of Commons, outlined 12 arguments for having a census, ranging from general intellectual goals of the Enlightenment, to precise and utilitarian aims (Rickman, 1800). As many of these arguments are still current today, they are briefly listed below:

(1) The intimate knowledge of any country must form the rational basis of legislation and diplomacy.

(2) An industrious population is the basic power and resource of any nation, and as such its size needs to be known.

Table 1.2

Topic coverage of the Census of Population, England and Wales, 1841-1991

	1841	1851	1861	1871	1881	1891	1901	1911	1921	1931	1951	1961	1966	1971	1981	1991
Age	✓	✓	✓	✓	✓	✓	✓	✓	✓	✓	✓	✓	✓	✓	✓	✓
Sex	✓	✓	✓	✓	✓	✓	✓	✓	✓	✓	✓	✓	✓	✓	✓	✓
Marital status		✓	✓	✓	✓	✓	✓	✓	✓	✓	✓	✓	✓	✓	✓	✓
Birthplace		✓	✓	✓	✓	✓	✓	✓	✓	✓	✓	✓	✓	✓	✓	✓
Nationality	✓	✓	✓	✓	✓	✓	✓	✓	✓	✓	✓	✓				
Ethnic group																✓
Usual residence												✓	✓	✓	✓	✓
Migration												✓	✓	✓	✓	✓
Economic position				✓	✓	✓	✓	✓	✓	✓	✓	✓	✓	✓	✓	✓
Journey to work													✓	✓	✓	✓
Occupation	✓	✓	✓	✓	✓	✓	✓	✓	✓	✓	✓	✓	✓	✓	✓	✓
Place of work									✓	✓	✓	✓	✓	✓	✓	✓
Industry									✓	✓	✓	✓	✓	✓	✓	✓
Qualifications												✓	✓	✓	✓	✓
Fertility								✓			✓	✓		✓		
Marriage duration								✓	✓	✓	✓	✓		✓		
Housing (number)	✓	✓	✓	✓	✓	✓	✓	✓	✓	✓	✓	✓	✓	✓	✓	✓
Rooms (number)						✓	✓	✓	✓	✓	✓	✓	✓	✓	✓	✓
Tenure												✓	✓	✓	✓	✓
Household amenities											✓	✓	✓	✓	✓	✓
Cars													✓	✓	✓	✓
Infirmity		✓	✓	✓	✓	✓	✓	✓								
Limiting long-standing illness																✓

(3) The number of men required for conscription to the militia in different areas should reflect the area's population.

(4) Similarly, there are defence reasons for wanting to know the number of sea-men.

(5) The production of corn needs to be planned and thus it is essential we know how many people need to be fed.

(6) A government anxious to increase total 'felicity' needs to know the number of marriages and the factors affecting them. [Rickman was convinced that population growth and human happiness accompanied each other.]

(7) The true size of the population, even after the effects of war, is probably far bigger than the usual estimates, and knowledge of this would 'be the most consoling gratification to every lover of his country'.

(8) In a time when many fear the disaffection of the people, doing a census would improve the Government's image as setting out to promote the public good.

(9) A census would generally encourage the social sciences to flourish.

(10) It might encourage improved methods of property counting which would be useful for the operation of the land tax.

(11) The life insurance industry would be stimulated by the results.

(12) There is wide consensus among those writing about the state and politics of the need for a reliable estimate of the population.

Whether any modern government would be persuaded that census taking was an effective means of good public relations management is perhaps doubtful, but most of the reasons put forward by Rickman still hold good today.

Rickman persuaded Abbott, a member of parliament, to introduce a Private Member's Bill to conduct the first census; interestingly the arguments for the census focused principally on the need to assess food requirements accurately after the disastrous harvests of 1800. Yet there is no doubt that the general climate created by Malthus' essay on population provided the backdrop for the first English census which took place in 1801.

The first four censuses in England and Wales were conducted by Overseers of the Poor, whose suitability for the job was doubted both by opponents and eventually also by its organisers (Drake, 1972). In Scotland the early censuses were conducted by Schoolmasters. As can be seen from table 1.2, the contents of the first four British censuses were quite sparse; the first census recorded inhabited houses in the area and families that inhabited them, uninhabited houses, persons by sex (other than members of the armed forces), and persons employed in a fourfold division of occupational groups.

Developments of census methodology have repeatedly been the occasions for a leap forward to be taken in social science methods. We have become so used to the sophistication of today's methods of information collection that we often forget how hard it was for our predecessors to work out some of the basic tools of their trade. The idea of producing standardised forms for recording information, for example, did not occur naturally; it was not until 1831 that special schedules were issued to enumerators to aid them in recording, and special sheets were issued to them to help them keep a tally using the 'five-bar gate' method (Mills, 1987). The following paragraphs trace the development of the census in England and Wales.

The 1841 Census is generally seen as the first 'modern' census (History of the Census of 1841; Nissel, 1987) because it moved from a system whereby enumerators compiled summary returns to a system where a separate schedule was provided for each householder and the names and characteristics of each household member were listed. The 1841 Census was also the first to count the population at a single time point — Sunday 6 June. This method of counting the population was made possible by using the machinery set up within the new General Register Office for the compulsory registration of births and deaths. The field force of local registrars, which provided the apparatus to conduct this new type of census, represented a bureaucracy whose interest in the exercise was principally accuracy. However, there were not enough registrars to undertake a census in which a schedule had to be completed for each householder, and therefore the important decision was taken to ask householders to fill in their own forms. Enumerators were recruited to hand out and collect in the forms: a method which has continued for 150 years but which was revolutionary in the mid-19th century, and a testimony to how far mass education had penetrated by the 1840s. The idea that social research should be aimed at the subjects of research — that investigators should trust respondents to provide accurate information rather than rely on the second-hand testimony of expert witness and informants — is another major contribution to social science first introduced for the census (Marsh, 1985).

The real showpiece of mid 19th-century English democracy and the social statistics movement, however, was the census of 1851 which coincided with the year of the Great Exhibition. The 1851 Census was organised by William Farr and Horace Mann, with a subcommittee of the London Statistical Society to help prepare for it, as there had been for the 1841 Census (see *Journal of the Statistical Society of London*, vol. 111, April, 1840, pp.72-102). The 1851 Census was the first to ask exact age and the first to ask marital status and relationship to head of household. A major introduction, due to the far-sightedness of William Farr, was a question on occupation, for which 332 different occupations were recorded and grouped into classes. This formed the basis for the Registrar General's social class schema, still in use in the 1991 Census. The classification of occupations was also used with the newly available registration details on deaths to provide information on occupational mortality (Nissel, 1987). The 1851 Census scored another first by producing two volumes of tables relating to the districts and sub-districts of England and Wales devised for the registration system, as well as maps showing the density of population and distribution of people by occupation (Nissel, 1987).

Whilst output from successive censuses increased and became more sophisticated, the next major milestone was not until 1911 when the punched card was introduced for processing census returns. Hollerith had won a competition to provide a mechanical means of analysing the 1880 US Census, which used punched cards. Without this, data analysis would not have been completed before the 1890 Census.

Use of the punched card enabled mechanical sorting and gave a further boost to the production of census output. However the 1911 Census was also unique in that it introduced questions on fertility within marriage. In contrast to the first census in 1801 which was informed by Malthusian concerns, the fertility questions in the 1911 Census were triggered by a falling birth rate.

The 1961 Census formed a further milestone because it introduced sampling at the time of enumeration. Ten per cent of households were given a longer form to complete which contained questions on economic activity, education and household composition. In the event, this turned out to be less than successful because enumerators were reluctant to issue a long form to those who might find it difficult to complete. This experiment has not been repeated, although there is evidence from other countries that it can be achieved with considerable success. Instead, subsequent censuses have sought full information from all households and then processed a 10 per cent sample for those questions such as economic activity and education which are time-consuming to code. The 1961 Census was also the first to use a computer to process the returns. The General Register Office used the computer of the Royal Army Pay Corps in Winchester, although it acquired its own computer for the 1966 sample census.

Subsequent chapters make reference to developments in more recent censuses.

1.10 CONCLUSION

This chapter has considered the development of the census over time and the way in which the needs of different kinds of society influence not only whether a population count is conducted but the way in which it is done, and how the results are made available. Nonetheless, over recent decades there has been a remarkable convergence in census taking throughout the world. Both the UN and the EC have provided an impetus to the harmonisation of content and timing. There have also been many parallel developments in the way in which census output is made available, although there are also some interesting differences which relate to national perceptions of freedom and authority. These issues will be picked up and discussed in more detail in the final chapter.

2 The content of the 1991 Census: change and continuity

Angela Dale

2.1 INTRODUCTION

There is an unyielding tension in the collection of census data between change and continuity. As social realities change, this must be reflected in the questions asked and the definitions used, otherwise the census will become fossilised and lose its relevance. On the other hand, one of the main uses of the census is to make comparisons over time — to record shifts in the population, changes in the occupational structure, changes in housing. Table 1.2 in chapter 1 shows the extent of continuity over time in the topics covered; but changes in classification schemes, in boundary definitions, and in question wording all mean that comparability is often difficult and sometimes impossible. This problem is accentuated by the fact that there is usually an interval of 10 years between censuses. The speed of change in society is such that there is inevitably a requirement to alter the categories used to code information, or to alter question wording in recognition of changed assumptions and meanings.

The purpose of this chapter is to provide an overview of the content of the 1991 Census in the context of changes that have occurred over the years, but with particular reference to that between 1981 and 1991 and, in some cases, 1971 and 1981. The chapter is concerned with two areas: the population base of the census and the topics included in the census. The geographical areas used in the census are covered in chapter 3 (I) and special aspects of census geography are discussed in chapter 9. Much of the material in the chapter is drawn from *1991 Census Definitions* (OPCS and GRO(S), 1992b). However, the chapter does not attempt to replicate or summarise that volume. Rather, it aims to discuss those areas that are judged to be of particular interest or where there has been significant change between censuses.

With minor exceptions, the 1991 Census included all the topics in the 1981 Census and added three new questions for individuals: ethnic group, limiting long-term illness and term-time address of students, whilst weekly hours worked was reintroduced; it also included a new question on central heating in the household amenities section. A number of other answer categories were updated: for example, tenure, economic position and relationship in the household. Additionally the method used to count household spaces provided a count of dwellings which was not available in 1981.

2.2 WHAT DETERMINED THE COVERAGE AND CONTENT OF THE 1991 CENSUS?

A range of different factors vie in affecting what is and is not asked in a census and of whom. Firstly, there are the statutory requirements, discussed in chapter 1, which lay upon the Registrars General the requirement to conduct a decennial census. Additional to the national requirements, the Council of Europe Directive of May 1987 (Langevin, Begeot and Pearce, 1992) required that the 1991 Census covered 'certain demographic, economic and social characteristics of individuals, households and families at national and regional level'.

In deciding exactly what topic areas are covered, a number of other forces come into play. Firstly there are the requirements of central and local government and other users for information on, for example, the demographic structure and housing situation of the population. The British Census Offices conducted a very wide consultation exercise, with all census users, before the 1991 Census. Secondly, there are the constraints of privacy and burden on respondents (see chapter 5) and the self-completion nature of the questionnaire that limits what can be asked. Thirdly, there are limitations of cost; each question requiring a response by all household members added about £50,000 to the cost of the census, assuming the simplest question with one key stroke depression. Decisions over topics to be included also take into consideration the availability of information from other sources, particularly the large, continuous government surveys. Finally, the precensus tests (see chapter 4) are used to pilot proposed topics and a number are rejected at this stage because, for a variety of reasons, they are considered unworkable.

The Statistical Office of the United Nations makes regular reports on the *Principles and recommendations for population and housing censuses*. Applications of these recommendations for Europe are considered by the Working Group on Population Censuses of the UN Economic Commission for Europe with the intention of obtaining maximum comparability within Europe. Priest points out the difficulties of trying to reconcile historical and international comparability. He concludes 'one of the challenges that makes the work of the statistician exciting is the challenge to accommodate conflicting objectives' (Priest, 1987, p. 272).

Table 2.1 shows the extent to which 'basic' topic items are included in the censuses of EC countries. The only basic items not asked in Britain in 1991 were: availability of a kitchen, source of water supply and the age of housing. A set of tables, specified to maximise comparability between member states, are required to be deposited with the European Commission. These are quite simple compared with the output from the British and other national censuses. The tables are published in a report by the Statistical Office of the European Community some time after the decennial round of censuses.

There are a further set of topics which are recommended by the UN and, amongst these, there is much greater variation between EC countries. In the 1990 round of censuses, the UK was the only EC country to ask ethnic group, whilst none of the EC members asked about income, despite the UN recommendation (Langevin, Begeot and Pearce, 1992) and the fact that it is asked in the USA.

Table 2.1

Inclusion or exclusion of basic topics from the United Nations recommendations in the nine countries carrying out conventional censuses

Characteristics	Topic	Excluded from Census
Demographic	Sex	None
	Age	None
	Marital status	None
	Country of birth	None
	Citizenship	Ireland, UK
Geographic	Place of usual residence	None
	Place of residence at prior reference date	Belgium
Economic	Type of current activity	None
	Occupation	None
	Industry	None
	Status on employment	None
	Place of work	Spain
Education	Educational attainment	None
Household and family	Relationship to reference person	None
	Tenure status	None
Housing units	Type of ownership	Belgium, Spain, France
	Type of living quarters (conventional dwellings and communals)	None
	Occupancy status	Belgium, Luxembourg
	Occupancy by more than one household	None
	Number of occupants	None
	Number of rooms	None
	Kitchens	France, Ireland, UK
	Water supply system	France, Luxembourg, UK*
	Toilet facilities	None
	Bathing facilities	None
	Type of heating (central heating)	None
Building	Type of building	None
	Period of construction	UK

* Included in Northern Ireland.
Source: *Population Trends* 1992, vol. 68, pp. 33-36.

2.2.1 Questions not in the 1991 Census

Whilst this section is primarily concerned with those questions included in the 1991 Census and how they differ from previous censuses, it is worth outlining briefly those topics which were mentioned in the 1988 White Paper on the Census (OPCS and GRO(S), 1988) as considered for inclusion but rejected. These were: age of building; access to a telephone; receipt of social security benefits; income; main language spoken in the home and ability to speak English; the speaking, reading and writing of Celtic languages throughout Great Britain; the means of travel to place of education; address five years before the census; qualifications obtained at school or through experience; occupation one year before census; second jobs; and smoking. These topics were not included either because the case was not considered strong enough, or because tests showed that the quality of information would not be good enough, or because it was considered that the questions would place too great a burden on the public (see chapter 5).

Decisions have to be made not only about the topics to include in the census, but also who is to be included; that is, how to define the *population base*. The following section reviews some of the alternatives and then describes the population bases used in the 1991 Census.

2.3 POPULATION BASE AND DEFINITIONS: WHO SHOULD BE COUNTED?

There are two basic methods of enumeration: first, to ask each household to enter on the census form everyone *present* on census night, irrespective of where they usually live, and secondly to enter on the form everyone *usually resident*, irrespective of whether they are present or absent from that address on census night (Redfern, 1981).

For most purposes, the *usually resident population* is of greatest interest, for example, in assessing housing needs or the use of health services. In Britain, however, we have no formal way of attributing usual address and, in some cases, there is likely to be uncertainty as to whom should be entered on the census form. Historically, Britain has recorded the *population present on census night* whilst (since 1931) also recording each person's usual address. Since 1961 (in that census for a sample only) households have additionally been asked to enter anyone *usually resident in the household but away on census night*. From this information it is possible to measure the usually resident population in two ways:

(1) by redistributing visitors (those enumerated but not usually resident) back to their *home areas* (as given in the usual address question) but, for practical reasons, not back to individual addresses;
(2) by counting the people recorded on the forms as *usually resident*.

These two methods of establishing the usually resident population give slightly different figures. The first method will miss a member of a household absent abroad on census night, as s/he will not be enumerated in the census. The second method would include a household member out of the country on census night, but misses entire households who are absent from home on census night.

19

In recent British censuses the first method (recording everyone present on census night) has been amended also to include absent usual residents — if someone else was present in the household. The problem of 'wholly absent households' encountered by the second method has been addressed in the 1991 Census by asking such households to complete, voluntarily on their return, a census schedule, or by imputing selected characteristics of those wholly absent households who did not complete a form (see below and chapter 4).

In 1981, some 700,000 households, containing an estimated million people, were *wholly absent,* that is households in which someone was usually resident but no person was present in the household on census night, and the residents of such households were excluded from the enumeration at their usual addresses. These absent households and the people usually resident in them were omitted from the majority of 1981 Census tabulations, despite the fact that many were enumerated as visitors at some other address in Great Britain (see table 6.10 in chapter 6 (II) for a comparison with 1991). To transfer back visitors to their areas of usual residence at an early stage of processing would have significantly delayed output, and to link visitors back to individual households would have been difficult and costly.

The following sections discuss the population bases used in the 1991 Census.

2.3.1 The population counted in 1991

As in 1971 and 1981, the 1991 Census counted all persons present on census night and also all persons usually resident, whether present or absent on census night in households. (In communal establishments only those present were counted.)

In 1991 two main population bases were defined for statistics about people: (i) *the population present base* and (ii) *the usually resident population (topped-up present/ absent) 1991 base (residents).*

(i)   *The population present*
     This included the total population enumerated, including visitors from elsewhere in Britain and also from overseas. This base was consistent with the population present base used in 1981.

(ii) *The usually resident population (topped-up present/absent): 1991 base (residents)*
     This base was new in 1991. It included the usually resident (present/absent) 1981 base (see (iii) below); usually resident members of wholly absent households where a form was voluntarily returned; estimated usually resident members of wholly absent households where no form was returned (values are imputed) and households with residents but where no contact was made (values are imputed). This second base formed the usually resident, or resident population base most commonly used in 1991 Census output.

To facilitate comparisons with 1981, a further population base was defined:

(iii) *The usually resident population (present/absent): 1981 base*
     This conformed to the 'usually resident population' base used in the 1981 Census and included residents enumerated in households and communal estab-

lishments and also absent residents from households with at least one person present in the household. It excluded wholly absent households.

This base was used in some 1991 Census tables to facilitate comparisons with the 1981 resident population base, although such comparisons will be affected by the different level of people missing from this base (see chapter 6 (II), table 6.10). Comparisons are also affected by differences in the way in which students are categorised. The 1991 base categorised as economically active all students in employment or seeking work in the week before the census, whilst the 1981 base defined all students as economically inactive.

(iv) *The usually resident population (transfer) base: alternative 1981 base.*
This was not used for standard output from the 1991 Census and is not therefore discussed here. It is, however, shown in figure 2.1 in order to provide a complete picture of the relationship between the 1981 and 1991 population bases. Figure 2.1 shows the interrelationships between these bases diagrammatically.

Figure 2.1 Inter-relationship of population bases

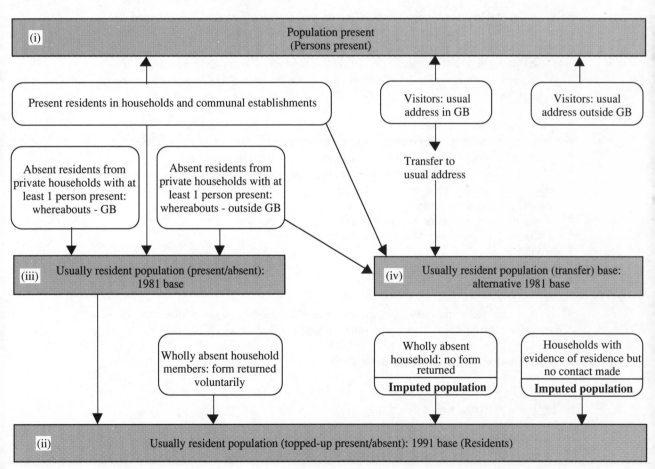

Source: *1991 Census Definitions*, OPCS & GRO(S), 1992b, p.8.

2.3.2 Term-time address of students

In the 1981 and 1991 Censuses the form-filler was advised: 'for students and children away from home during term time, the home address should be taken as the usual address' (notes for question 7, 1991 Census form). In 1981, for students on vacation and at home at the time of the census, there was no information collected on term-time address. This was incompatible with the Registrars General's annual estimates for local and health authority areas which take the student's term-time address as the usual one. The possibility of carrying out the 1991 Census in term-time was considered, in order to provide comparability with the estimates. However, it was decided that the census would then be too close to the local elections in early May 1991. As an alternative, the 1991 Census asked form-fillers whether a student's or school-child's address of enumeration was the term-time address. If not, they were asked to state the term-time address. This information was used to prepare a national matrix of ward of usual residence by ward of term-time address, which was used to redistribute students for the Registrars General's annual estimates.

2.3.3 Population bases used in output

Each census table has a population base, the members of which are arranged in counts in the table. The base may be all *people present or resident*, but is also often a subset, for example, people resident in households. Output from the 1991 Census also used population bases which are defined around units other than people. A list of those used is given below. Definitions are given later in this chapter under the relevant subheading.

- Households with residents
- Households with people present but no residents
- Household spaces occupied by a household, or unoccupied
- Dwellings — structurally premises (a building or part of one) designed for occupation by a single household
- Families of resident persons
- Units of non-permanent accommodation
- Units of converted or shared accommodation
- Rooms
- Cars available to households
- Communal establishments

As in previous years, the 1991 Census made a distinction between households and communal establishments. These and other definitions are discussed below.

2.3.4 Population and household definitions

Household
In 1991 a household was defined as:

(i) one person living alone; or
(ii) a group of people (who may or may not be related) living, or staying temporarily, at the same address, with common housekeeping.

As in 1981, enumerators were instructed to treat a group of people as a household if there was any regular arrangement to share at least one meal (including breakfast) a day, *or* if occupants shared a common living or sitting room. The occupants of one-room accommodation or of a caravan (or other non-permanent accommodation) were treated as a single household.

In 1971, instructions to enumerators required that the condition of common housekeeping or sharing a meal each day should be met. The change in instructions in 1981 resulted in a reduction of about 108,000 households (0.6 per cent) between 1971 and 1981 (Todd and Griffiths, 1986). A large proportion of these losses were concentrated in the privately rented furnished sector, resulting in a reduction of 17 per cent in the number of such households identified in 1981 using the 1981 instructions as compared with identification using the 1971 instructions. In fact, the change in instructions followed a change in practice in the field, and therefore the actual difference may have been rather less.

Head of household

For statistical purposes the census tabulations take as 'head of household' the person who is entered as Person No.1 on the household schedule (OPCS and GRO(S), 1992b, section 6.49), although the instructions ask for the head or joint head of household to be entered first on the census form. Analysis of the OPCS Longitudinal Study (see chapter 12) showed that, in 1981, 97.3 per cent of married household heads were male.

Communal establishments

Communal establishments are defined as those in which some kind of communal catering is provided. This definition covers a very wide range of institutions, including long-term homes for disabled people, general hospitals and special hospitals, prisons, army barracks, university halls of residence, boarding schools, hotels and hostels. Campers and persons sleeping rough are included in tables on communal establishments. Service families living in married quarters are enumerated as private households. For sheltered housing, the criterion used for classification as a communal establishment is that less than half the people in the housing have their own separate accommodation with facilities for cooking their own meals. Chapter 4 discusses the way in which communal establishments were treated in the fieldwork.

There is an important distinction to be made between visitors to communal establishments and those for whom this was their usual address. Question 7 on the form used in communal establishments requested 'If you usually live here, please tick "This address". If not, tick "Elsewhere" and write in your usual address'. Students and school children were specifically directed to give their home address as their usual one. For those living in homes and hospitals which took patients mainly on a long-stay basis, the communal establishment was normally the usual address. If there was doubt, the rule was that a person who had been in the same hospital or home for six months or more counted it as their usual address. All those enumerated in hotels and homes and hospitals taking residents or patients on a short-term basis (e.g. general hospitals, maternity homes), were classified as visitors to the communal establishment and the usual address was taken as that given in response to question 7. For other institutions such as psychiatric hospitals and prisons, the 'six month' rule applied.

A further distinction amongst those enumerated in communal establishments related to the position in the establishment. This enables staff living in all types of communal establishments to be distinguished from patients or inmates, although separate families were not identified in communal establishments.

In general, the categorisation of communal establishments was consistent with 1981. However, there has been an expansion in the number of major categories in 1991 to 18, providing additional distinctions between National Health Service or local authority hospitals and homes, and private hospitals and homes. The 18 major categories, distinguished in the Local Base Statistics and County/Region Reports and table 3 of the *Communal Establishments* volume (see chapter 7, section 7.3.7) are:

- NHS hospital/homes — psychiatric
- NHS hospitals/homes — other
- Non-NHS hospitals — psychiatric
- Non-NHS hospitals — other
- Local authority homes
- Housing Association homes and hostels
- Nursing homes (non-NHS/LA/HA)
- Residential homes (non-NHS/LA/HA)
- Children's homes
- Prison Service establishments
- Defence establishments
- Education establishments
- Hotels, boarding houses, etc.
- Hostels and common lodging houses (non-LA)
- Other miscellaneous establishments
- Persons sleeping rough
- Campers
- Civilian ships, boats and barges

In 1981, people sleeping rough and those camping while on holiday were included together in the output under the heading 'vagrants and campers'. In 1991 people sleeping rough were subject to a special enumeration and are identified as a separate category in output.

2.3.5 Enumeration of those sleeping rough

Concern in a number of quarters over the apparent rise in homelessness led to a special exercise in the 1991 Census to count those sleeping rough on census night. Census Officers attempted to recruit field staff from charitable organisations for the homelessness to help with the enumeration. Sites were identified before the census by voluntary organisations, local authorities and churches. Altogether 1,312 sites were listed, all of which were checked by local Census Officers. However, because of changed circumstances and the fact that the list was up to 12 months old, only 453 sites were being used on census night by people sleeping rough. This special count included only those sleeping in the open air or in tents at the predefined sites; it excluded those in shelters, hostels or squats. The count did not include those sleeping rough elsewhere who were identified by enumerators. The special exercise found 2,845 people sleeping rough in Great Britain; a breakdown by local authority areas in England and Wales is given in an *OPCS Monitor* (1991c). This was a preliminary count and the final figures are published in table 3 of the *County Reports, Part 1* (see chapter 7, section 7.2.1) and in the *Report for Great Britain, Part 1* (chapter 7, section 7.2.7). Final national figures are not available at the time of writing.

The Census Validation Survey (see chapter 6 (I)) was restricted to households because of the difficulty of recontacting the highly mobile populations not in households, even a few weeks after the census, and it does not, therefore, provide a way of checking the coverage of this enumeration. However, the inclement weather on census night and the fact that only prelisted sites were visited, are both factors likely to have affected the count of numbers sleeping rough.

2.4 CENSUS TOPICS

The aim of the rest of this chapter is to provide some background information on the topics included in the 1991 Census schedules, and to highlight differences in question wording or definitions with previous censuses, particularly 1981. It also provides a context for detailed discussion of particular topics in later chapters. All classifications given are those used in census output. For a full and complete definition of all the 1991 topics it is necessary to consult *1991 Census Definitions* (OPCS and GRO(S), 1992b).

An overview of the contents of the 1991 Census is given in chapter 1 (table 1.2) and appendix A replicates the full 1991 Census forms for both private households and individuals living in communal establishments such as hospitals or hostels. Reference will be made in the text to the question and section numbers in the census schedules.

2.5 QUESTIONS ASKED OF EACH HOUSEHOLD IN THE 1991 CENSUS

2.5.1 Postcode of enumeration

Whilst names and addresses are recorded on the census schedule, they are not entered into the computer. However, in 1991 for the first time in England and Wales, the *postcode* of each address was collected and entered into the computer. Postcodes provide a common geographic base for statistics from various sources and the very numerous 'building blocks' of unit postcodes provide potential flexibility in computing output areas (see chapter 3). Their inclusion also meets one of the recommendations of the Chorley Committee (Committee of Enquiry into the Handling of Geographic Information,1987) and opens the way to benefiting from the advances in Geographic Information Systems (GIS) that have come into operation since the 1981 Census. Some examples of this are given in chapter 9. In England and Wales, postcodes are the *alternative geographic base* for 1991 Census output; in Scotland as in 1981 (and retrospectively for 1971), postcodes are the *geographic base* for output. Chapter 3 (I) gives full information on the geography used in the 1991 Census.

2.5.2 Dwellings

The 1991 Census included a count of dwellings. This forms a key statistic in assessing the size of the housing stock. A dwelling is defined as 'a building or part of a building that forms separate and self-contained accommodation designed to be occupied by a single family or household' (Whitehead, 1988, p. 19). For most households living in houses or purpose-built flats their dwelling is easy to identify, but it poses special problems in multi-occupied houses. Identifying the extent to which dwellings are shared is particularly important in estimating the future demand for housing.

Procedures for identifying dwellings in multi-occupied houses have varied over the years. In the 1971 Census, the concept of privacy was used to decide whether or not households shared 'household space'. A household space described 'the totality of all the rooms used by the household for living purposes, together with areas such as halls, landings, passages and stairs which are necessary for movement between such rooms and for, but not only for, access to that household's living accommodation' (OPCS, 1983a, section 2.3). Where households shared a household space — either by sharing rooms or sharing the space needed to gain access to rooms — they were deemed to share a single dwelling. (Note that bath/shower and WC were omitted from this definition.) However, where households shared access solely to get to their own accommodation, for example, sharing a common entrance from the street, this was deemed not to impinge upon their privacy and dwellings were not counted as shared. This definition of shared household space led to confusion in multi-occupied houses where a household might occupy the top floor of a multi-occupied property and, although having no separate front door, did not share circulation space by virtue of the fact that other residents had no need to use the top floor. In 1971 such a household space was counted as a separate dwelling and was considered to be self-contained; this produced a situation where three households could be sharing the same building, two classified as sharing a dwelling and one classified as not sharing.

In the 1981 Census steps were taken to avoid the complex procedure for identifying a dwelling during enumeration. A question asked whether a household's rooms (not counting a bathroom or WC) were enclosed behind their own front door inside the building. This was designed specifically to overcome the problem identified in 1971 and to give a measure of self-containment. The 1981 Census did not include a count of dwellings as such, but allowed an estimate to be made from data on household spaces (OPCS, 1981).

The 1991 Census reverted to a direct count of dwellings which were defined as 'structurally separate accommodation' (OPCS and GRO(S), 1992b, section 5.6). A dwelling was shared where a household had a shared entrance from the street *and* was not self-contained. Accommodation was not self-contained if 'to move from your room(s) to bathroom, WC or kitchen facilities you have to use a hall, landing or stairway open to other household(s)'. Where there was only one such household in a shared house, bungalow or flat, the accommodation was classified as an 'unattached household space'.

Although, conceptually, a dwelling forms a third level, in addition to the household and the person, summary variables for people who share the same dwelling are not computed in standard output. By contrast, in France, information is collected for three units, hierarchically arranged — the building, the housing unit (the occupants of a housing unit form a household) and the person (Redfern, 1981).

2.5.3 Dwelling type and household space type

The 1991 Census recorded much fuller information on type of accommodation (Panels A and H2 on the Household Schedule) than in 1981. The enumerator was asked to distinguish whether the household's accommodation, if it was a whole house or bungalow, was detached, semi-detached or terraced. This information was collected in Scotland in 1981 but not in England and Wales. Households occupying the whole of a purpose built flat or maisonette were classified by whether it was a commercial building or not, whilst accommodation in converted or shared housing was distinguished by whether there was a shared or separate entrance into the building and by

Table 2.2

21-category output classification of household space types, 1991 Census

Household space type	Panel A code	Accommodation code (H2)	Bath/shower and inside WC (H4)
Accommodation in permanent buildings			
Unshared dwellings — purpose built			
1 Detached	2	-	-
2 Semi-detached	3	-	-
3 Terraced	4	-	-
4 Purpose built flat in residential building	6	-	-
5 Purpose built flat in commercial building	5	-	-
Unshared dwelling — converted			
6 Flat — separate entrance to building	7	3	-
7 Flat — shared entrance into building	8	3	-
8 Flatlet — separate entrance to building	7	1	-
9 Flatlet — shared entrance into building	8	1	-
Unshared dwelling — not self-contained			
10 Flat	7	4	Exclusive use of both
11 'Rooms'	7	4	Not exclusive use of both
12 Bedsit	7	2	-
13 Unoccupied	7	4	Not known
Shared dwelling — not self-contained			
14 Flat	8	4	Exclusive use of both
15 'Rooms'	8	4	Not exclusive use of both
16 Bedsit	8	2	-
17 Unoccupied	8	4	Not known
Unattached household space — not self-contained			
18 Flat	8	4	Exclusive use of both
19 'Rooms'	8	4	Not exclusive use of both
20 Bedsit	8	2	-
21 Unoccupied	8	4	Not known
Non- permanent accommodation (22)	1	-	-

Source: *1991 Census Definitions,* OPCS & GRO(S), 1992b, pp. 17-18.

the type of accommodation (H2). However, the key to identifying multiple occupancy in the 1991 Census was the 'building bracket' — a marking which enumerators made in their Record Books (see chapter 4) to indicate household spaces which were in the same building.

Information on dwellings has been used to produce a classification of dwelling types (table 2.2) that also provides a count of the number of household spaces within a shared dwelling.

A full classification of household space types is shown in table 2.2. In some tables this is collapsed to 16 categories by combining 'shared dwellings — not self-contained' with 'unattached household spaces — not self-contained'.

Self-containment of household spaces

The concept of self-containment is defined differently in the 1991 Census in comparison with 1981 and this, in turn, differed from 1971.

In 1981, in England and Wales, a household space with two or more rooms was defined as self-contained where its rooms (not including a bathroom or WC) were enclosed behind its own front door. A household space where an entrance from outside the building was shared with one or more other household(s) was self-contained if it had its own front door inside the building. Household spaces of only *one room* were defined as self-contained if they had *exclusive* use of a bath and inside WC. For 1991, the definition was changed to require the rooms *and* kitchen facilities, bath and shower, and inside WC, to be contained behind the 'private' door. In Scotland, the most closely corresponding question in 1981 was on 'shared access' to the household accommodation.

As discussed above in the context of sharing, in the 1971 Census self-containment hinged upon an absence of the use of shared circulation space, that is, space which the household had to share with others in order to move between its own rooms. Because of these changes in definition with successive censuses it is not possible to make precise comparison between 1971, 1981 and 1991 statistics on self-contained accommodation.

Number of rooms

The 1991 Census continued the established question which asked the form-filler to count the number of rooms which the household has for its own use. The question explained which type of rooms to count and which not to count — for example, 'small kitchens under 2 metres (6 feet 6 inches) wide'. Used in conjunction with the number of persons in the household, the number of persons per room can be calculated, thereby providing a measure of overcrowding or under-occupancy. Overcrowding is one of the measures used to calculate the amount of spending which local government is allowed to make. It is also widely used in defining areas of multiple deprivation.

The census makes no attempt to record the different uses of rooms. In Scotland only, where post-war censuses have shown a greater degree of over-crowding than in England and Wales, in both 1981 and 1991, a measure of overcrowding was used that took into consideration the composition of the household in terms of their age, sex and marital status. This *occupancy norm* was based on a comparison of the total number of rooms which the household was considered to need, compared with the number of rooms available. Rooms entitlement was calculated according to the formula below.

A one-person household is assumed to require only one room. Where there are two or more residents it is assumed that they require one room (as a common room) and, for each of the categories below, one additional room (as a bedroom):

- two married people of opposite sex
- each other person aged 21 and over
- each pair aged 10–20 of the same sex
- each pair formed from a remaining child aged 10–20 with a child aged under 10 of the same sex
- each pair of children aged under 10 remaining
- each child unable to form a pair

The recording of number of rooms is notorious for the wide variation between that perceived and recorded by the form-filler and that recorded more objectively by an

Table 2.3

Changes in definitions of kitchens and rooms from 1961 for England and Wales

Definitions of kitchens from 1961

1961	Kitchens included only if used regularly for meals or as living rooms or bedrooms
1966	All kitchens were included
1971	Kitchens less than 6ft wide excluded
1981	Kitchens under 2m (6½ft) wide excluded
1991	Kitchens under 2m (6½ft) wide excluded

Definitions of rooms in 1971, 1981 and 1991

1971 Do not count:
Kitchens less than 6ft wide
Bathrooms and toilets
Sculleries not used for cooking
Closets, pantries and storerooms
Landings, halls, lobbies or recesses
Offices or shops used solely for business

Note: a room divided by a sliding or fixed partition counted as two rooms but one divided by a curtain counted as one.

1981 Do not count:
Small kitchens under 2m (6½ft)wide
Bathrooms and WCs
Offices or shops used solely for business

Note: a room divided by a sliding or fixed partition counted as two rooms but one divided by a curtain counted as one.

1991 Do not count:
Small kichens under 2m (6½ft)wide
Bathrooms
Toilets
Do count:
Living rooms
Kitchens at least 2m (6½ft) wide
All other rooms in your accommodation

interviewer in the post-enumeration survey. This forms the topic of a fuller discussion in chapter 6 (I). Benjamin, writing in 1970, says 'The count of rooms always causes difficulty' (1970, p. 43). The *1981 Census post-enumeration survey* (Britton and Birch, 1985) found a gross error rate of 28.6 per cent, with nearly half the disagreements relating to the inclusion or exclusion of the kitchen. Although from 1971 there has been reasonable consistency in the definition of a kitchen, the need for the form-filler to judge whether the kitchen is above a minimum width provides a major source of inaccuracy.

Table 2.3 summarises the changes in the instructions, since 1961, for determining whether or not to count a kitchen and for counting the total number of rooms. Simplification since 1971 reflects recognition of a reluctance by the public to read long, detailed instructions.

Tenure

A question on tenure was first introduced in the 1961 Census and made a distinction between owner-occupied and rented; and, if rented, whether private, from a local authority, with a business, or by virtue of employment.

The 1991 Census introduced a distinction between buying and owning outright and dropped the 1981 Census distinction between freehold and leasehold owner-occupation. Leases of less than 21 years were included with the 'renting' categories in 1991. An additional category of renting from a New Town, Development Corporation (or Commission), or Housing Action Trust was added to the renting section in England and Wales, whilst Scotland identified a New Town Development Corporation and also renting from Scottish Homes. The tenure of a dwelling is derived from the tenure of the occupying households. Where there was more than one kind of household tenure in a dwelling the following priority order was used (OPCS and GRO(S), 1992b, section 5.51):

1 Owner occupied — owned outright
2 Owner occupied — buying
3 Rented from a housing association
4 Rented from Scottish Homes
5 Rented from a New Town
6 Rented from a local authority
7 Rented privately — unfurnished
8 Rented privately — furnished
9 Rented with a job or business

Amenities

Since the 1951 Census this question has changed and developed to reflect the amenities which were the subject of government policies for housing improvement. In 1971 the question covered a cooker, a kitchen sink, hot water supply, bath or shower, an inside flush WC and an outside flush WC. In 1981, cooker, kitchen sink and hot water supply were dropped because they were almost universally present. In 1991 a separate question on an outside flush WC was dropped and added was a question on central heating (including night storage heaters, warm air or under floor heating) and whether it was available in some or all rooms. Questions on the use of a bath or shower and inside WC distinguished between exclusive use and shared use with another household. The absence of exclusive use of basic amenities remains an important indicator in the allocation of resources.

Central heating formed one of the basic topics recommended for the 1990 round of censuses in the European Community (Langevin, Begeot and Pearce, 1992) and was asked by all nine member states which carried out conventional censuses. The only recommended basic housing topic not asked in Britain was source of water supply.

Occupancy type: households

From information given on completed forms as recorded by the enumerator, the type of occupancy of residential accommodation fell into one of the following categories:

- Households with residents
  - enumerated with person(s) present
- Absent households
  - enumerated
  - imputed
- Vacant accommodation
  - new, never occupied
  - under improvement
  - other
- Accommodation not used as main residence
  - No person present
    - second residences
    - holiday accommodation
    - student accommodation
  - Persons enumerated but no residents
    - owner-occupied
    - not owner-occupied

Derelict buildings were not recorded unless there was evidence that someone was living there. Second residences were defined as company flats, holiday houses, and other types of accommodation which were *known* to be the second residences of people who had a more permanent address elsewhere and which were not occupied on census night.

Accommodation in permanent buildings which was let for holidays, for example, self-catering flats, was defined as *holiday accommodation* only if it was unoccupied on census night. Accommodation where people were present on census night but there were no usual residents was assumed to augment the count of either second homes (if it was owner-occupied) or holiday homes (if it was not owner-occupied). *Student accommodation* was defined as accommodation which was unoccupied on census night but was occupied *entirely* during term-time by one or more students. In some cases it was difficult for enumerators to distinguish between a second residence or holiday accommodation and student accommodation.

In comparison with 1981, there were only two changes in 1991. Firstly, in 1981 student accommodation was included as *second residences* and not separately identified; secondly, the 1991 Census had an additional category for *absent households* where data were imputed.

Occupancy type was also derived for dwellings. For multi-occupied dwellings the occupancy type was chosen according to a priority order that put household spaces with residents first.

Floor level in Scotland

In Scotland, where more than a third of households live in purpose-built flats, but not England and Wales, the 1991 Census had an additional question on floor level, as in 1981. The 1991 question differed from that in 1981 by asking the lowest floor on which *any* of the household's living accommodation was situated. In 1981, the question was concerned with the floor on which the entry to the household's accommodation was situated.

Cars and vans

The 1991 question was the same as that asked in 1981: '.... the number of cars normally *available* for use by you or members of your household (other than visitors)'. Tick boxes distinguished none, one, two and three or more. It is important to note that the question was not about car ownership as such, and the same car could possibly be 'available' to more than one household. Responses to this question are used to show the areas where private transport makes the most demand on road space and to indicate areas where people are most likely to be dependent on public transport. Access to a car or van may be associated with mode of travel to work, discussed in chapter 10.

2.6 QUESTIONS ASKED FOR EACH PERSON AND CODED FOR ALL PERSONS

2.6.1 Name, sex and date of birth

Although there were slight differences in the wording of the instructions to the form filler, the information requested was essentially the same as in 1981.

The first full census to ask date of birth rather than age was that of 1971. Checks on the way in which age had been recorded in earlier censuses revealed a tendency to anticipate birthdays and a minor degree of preference for particular numbers (Benjamin, 1970). The addition of date of birth in 1971 also paved the way to establishing the OPCS Longitudinal Study which draws a sample based upon date of birth (see chapter 12).

2.6.2 Marital status

The marital status question asked in England and Wales was unchanged from that in 1981. In Scotland, however, the 1981 question did not distinguish between first and subsequent marriages. For England and Wales and Scotland the 1991 Census expanded the tick box for 'single' to 'single (never married)'. This may have decreased the number of divorced or widowed people who reported themselves as 'single'. The marital status question referred to the legal status; relationship within the household formed a separate question, coded for only the 10 per cent sample and is discussed below.

A tendency to under-report divorce and for single women with children to describe themselves as widowed had been revealed in the 1961 Census (Benjamin, 1970). By comparison, the 1981 Post-Enumeration Survey showed gross error rates on marital status to be less than 5 per cent; one may assume that divorce and birth of a child outside marriage had become much more socially acceptable by that time.

2.6.3 One-year migration

The identification of a 'migrant' was based on answers to the questions on usual address (question 7) and address one year ago (21 April 1990) (question 9). The 1991 question was unchanged from the 1981 Census. Information on five-year migration was asked only in the 1971 Census. It is important to remember that information represents net migration over a one-year period and ignores any other moves during the year. Moves within the year before the census, away from and then back to the original address, will not be recorded either.

The following categories were identified in the 1991 Census output:

(a) *A migrant within one year of the preceding census* was a person who had a different usual address one year ago from that given at the 1991 Census. In tables of migration flows, the usual address at census provided the *area of destination* and the usual address one year ago the *area of origin.*

(b) *A migrant household* was a household whose head was a migrant.

(c) *A wholly moving household* was a household all of whose resident members aged one year and over were migrants with the same address (defined as the same unit postcode) of usual residence one year before the census. Children aged under one on census day 1991 were included as members of wholly moving households.

(d) *The resident population* used in tables in the *Migration* volumes was defined according to the topped-up present/absent base. *A migrant resident* in an area was a resident in the area who was resident at a different address one year before census.

For migrants, the usual address at census was coded to the enumeration district or output area, whilst usual address one year ago was coded to postcode and then translated into wards or into a higher level via the Central Postcode Directory (see chapter 3, section 3.1.5).

The type of move, for example whether within a defined area, or to a defined area, was also derived along with the distance moved, grouped into six categories (or 14 categories in the Sample of Anonymised Records — see chapter 11). Chapter 10 contains much greater information about the migration data from the 1991 Census and explains in some detail the various sets of migration tables which are available and how they may be used.

2.6.4 Country of birth

Country of birth has been a regular question in the census since first appearing in 1841. The 1991 Census provided tick boxes for England, Scotland, Wales, Northern Ireland, Irish Republic and elsewhere. If 'elsewhere' was ticked, then the form filler was asked to supply the *present* name of the country in which the birthplace now is. These responses were then coded to about 100 categories. The full country of birth classification is given in table 1 of the *Ethnic Group and Country of Birth* volume (see chapter 7, section 7.3.4) and a slightly collapsed version in table 7 of the Local Base Statistics. In other tables more abbreviated versions are used, although in the non-tabular forms of census output — the Samples of Anonymised Records (see chapter 11) and the OPCS Longitudinal Study (see chapter 12) — a much fuller classification is retained and is available for use in multivariate analysis subject to confidentiality considerations.

2.6.5 Ethnic group

The 1991 Census was the first to include a question on ethnic group. The Census Offices conducted an extensive consultation and testing exercise before including this question; chapter 4 contains further information on the process of developing the question. The 1991 Census provided nine tick-boxes and, for two of these, asked for further information to be written in. The coding frame used was based on the seven precoded categories plus a further 28 derived from the written descriptions given in the 'Black — Other' and the 'Any other ethnic group' boxes and from any multi-ticking of boxes. The full question is reproduced in appendix A (question 11 in the census form).

For most output, the full 35 codes (see annex B of *1991 Census Definitions*) are condensed into 10 categories. These are:

- White
- Black — Caribbean
- Black — African
- Black — Other
- Indian
- Pakistani
- Bangladeshi
- Chinese
- Other groups — Asian
  — Other

For 5 out of 6 Small Area Statistics (SAS) tables only 4 categories are used:

- White
- Black
- Indian, Pakistani and Bangladeshi
- Chinese and other groups

A count of the members in each of the 35 categories for local authority districts is given in table A of *Ethnic Group and Country of Birth*.

Responses to a 1989 census test were used to construct the coding frame for the ethnic question. The allocation of specific written answers was updated during data processing. The post-enumeration survey carried out on the 1989 ethnic question test found that, overall, 87 per cent of respondents had given a single ethnic group with which there was no detectable problem. Ten per cent of respondents had omitted to answer the question whilst 3 per cent gave answers that involved more than one code, or were ambiguous. In the 10-category classification shown above, the 'Other groups — Other' category contains all those coded North African, Arab or Iranian, Asian/White, British; and also Black/White when written in under 'Other ethnic group — mixed origins'. It also includes all other written-in answers under 'Any other ethnic group' that have no code allocated to them, including nonsense answers. It is not, therefore, possible to make any inferences about the ethnic origins of the 'Other groups — Other' category which makes up 0.5 per cent of residents of Great Britain. Where no answer was given, imputation was used as described in chapter 4.

2.6.6 Limiting long-term illness

This question, new in 1991, provided information on the general incidence of morbidity, and was not concerned with specific illnesses, health problems, handicaps or disabilities as such. The actual question wording was:

> Does the person have any long-term illness, health problems or handicap which limits his/her daily activities or the work he/she can do?'
>
> Yes, has a health problem which limits activities
> Has no such health problem

The instructions on the form specifically requested the inclusion of problems due to old age. The question applied to all individuals included in the census.

From pre-census tests (see chapter 4) it was found that long-term illness as recorded by this question correlated well with use of services such as GP consultations and with in-patient and out-patient visits to hospital. The information provides a simple, but nationally comparable, indication of the need for health and personal social services for the long-term sick both nationally and within local and health authority areas. It provides the only source of nationally consistent information available at local level. The question also provides information on the household composition, age structure and housing circumstances of people with long-term illnesses. Chapter 4 discusses the development of the question.

Although information on health has not been asked in recent censuses, between 1851 and 1911 the census was used to collect information on various sorts of disability (e.g. deaf, dumb, blind). This practice was discontinued as the figures were thought to be unreliable (Whitehead, 1988).

2.6.7 Household composition

The 1991 Census used two approaches to deriving household composition variables. The first took only the answers which were 100 per cent coded. The second used additional information on *relationship in household*, coded for the 10 per cent

Table 2.4

Household composition and household dependant types

Household composition type		*Household dependant type*	
1	No adults, all dependent children	1	Household with no dependants
	One adult (male)		Households with 1 dependant, aged:
2	Aged 65 or over with no dependent children	2	0– 4
3	Aged under 65 with no dependent children	3	5–15
4	With 1 dependent child	4	16–18
5	With 2 or more dependent children	5	19 up to pensionable age
		6	Pensionable age and over
	One adult (female)		
6	Aged 60 or over with no dependent children		Households with at least 2 dependants
7	Aged under 60 with no dependent children		Age of youngest dependant 0–4 and age of oldest:
8	With 1 dependent child	7	0– 4
9	With 2 or more dependent children	8	5–15
		9	16–18
	Two adults (1 male, 1 female)	10	19 up to pensionable age
10	One or both of pensionable age with no dependent children	11	Pensionable age and over
11	Both under pensionable age with no dependent children		Age of youngest dependant 5–15 and age of oldest:
12	With 1 dependent child	12	5–15
13	With 2 dependent children	13	16–18
14	With 3 or more dependent children	14	19 up to pensionable age
		15	Pensionable age and over
	Two adults (same sex)		
15	One or both of pensionable age with no dependent children		Age of youngest dependant 16–18 and age of oldest:
16	Both under pensionable age with no dependent children	16	16–18
17	With 1 or more dependent child	17	19 up to pensionable age
		18	Pensionable age and over
	Three or more adults (male(s) and female(s))		
18	With no dependent children		Age of youngest dependant 19 up to pensionable age and age of oldest:
19	With 1 or 2 dependent children	19	19 up to pensionable age
20	With 3 or more dependent children	20	Pensionable age and over
	Three or more adults (same sex)		
21	With no dependent children	21	Age of youngest dependant pensionable age and over
22	With 1 or more dependent children		

Source: *1991 Census Definitions* OPCS & GRO(S), 1992b, sections 6.45 and 6.52.

sample, to establish the relationship of each household member to the 'head of household', taken in the census processing as the person in the first column of the census form.

This section deals with the two household composition variables derived using 100 per cent coded information. The first, *household composition type*, was derived from the age, sex and marital status of household members and the second used age, sex, marital status and also information on limiting long-term illness and economic position to derive *household dependant type*. Table 2.4 shows the categories of both variables; the classifications are collapsed in some census tables.

The *head of household* was defined as the person entered in the first column of the form, provided that person is 16[1] or over and usually resident at the address of enumeration. A *dependent child* was defined as: a person aged 0-15 in a household, or a person aged 16-18, never married, in full-time education and economically inactive. (This definition differed from that used in the 1981 Census for the 100 per cent processed household composition variable by adding the extra qualification 'and economically inactive'. The 1981 definition also included persons aged 19-24, never married and classified as a student.) An *adult* was any person who was not a dependent child.

The classification of households into *household dependant type* was defined in terms of *dependants* and *non-dependants* in the household. A *dependant* was either a dependent child, or a person who had both a long-term limiting illness *and* whose economic position was either 'permanently sick' or 'retired'. A *non-dependant* was a residual category defined as any person who was not a dependant.

These household composition variables make no reference to relationship within the household, which was coded only for the 10 per cent sample. It does not, therefore, make use of information on cohabitation.

2.6.8 Welsh and Gaelic languages

A question on the Gaelic language was first asked in Scotland in 1881 and on the Welsh language in Wales in 1891. These questions were continued in the 1991 Census. In consultation for the 1991 Census, some users in England expressed a requirement for a question on language, other than English, usually spoken in the home. Others asked for a question on Welsh and other Celtic languages in England. With the exception of Ireland, other EC countries did not ask a question on language, although in the US, especially with the growth in numbers of Hispanics, the use of a language other than English at home is asked, whilst Canada, with two official languages, asks the language first learned in childhood, the language spoken at home and ability to speak both English and French.

In Wales the following question applied to all people aged three years and over: 'Does the person speak, read or write Welsh?' with tick boxes as appropriate

In Scotland the question was slightly different in form: 'Can the person speak, read or write Scottish Gaelic?'

2.6.9 Economic activity

The 1991 Census asked all people aged 16 and over to record information on economic position in the week before the census, for example, whether in employment, retired, at school or in full-time education (question 13). Also, for those working for an employer, question 13 asked whether they worked full-time (more than 30 hours a week) or part-time. The question also made the important distinction between an employee and the self-employed, distinguishing for the latter between those employing others and those not. Whilst the question had more pre-coded response categories than in 1981, it provided similar basic information.

---

[1] A very few households where there were no usual residents over 16 (e.g. with a relative temporarily looking after orphaned children) have heads aged under 16, and notes show how these are treated in particular tables.

Figure 2.2 Lifestage classification

53. Residents aged 16 and over in households

Lifestage category		ALL PERSONS		All household heads	
a		In a 'couple' household	Not in a 'couple' household	In a 'couple' household	Not in a 'couple' household
		b	c	d	e
CLEVELAND					
Aged 16 - 24	No children aged 0 - 15 in household	7,699	34,877	2,505	3,156
	Child(ren) aged 0 - 15 in household	6,328	20,571	2,223	3,073
Aged 25 - 34	No children aged 0 - 15 in household	14,625	17,187	7,043	7,091
	Child(ren) aged 0 - 4 in household	28,261	5,527	13,602	3,880
	Child(ren) in household, youngest aged 5 - 10	11,350	3,878	4,774	2,887
	Child(ren) in household, youngest aged 11 - 15	1,297	1,137	522	599
Aged 35 - 54	No children 0 - 15 in household	26,319	49,764	12,368	28,120
	Child(ren) aged 0 - 4 in household	8,564	4,577	5,375	2,564
	Child(ren) in household, youngest aged 5 - 10	16,508	7,975	9,223	4,609
	Child(ren) in household, youngest aged 11 - 15	9,409	14,455	4,930	7,927
Aged 55 - pensionable age	Working or retired	12,885	10,390	9,051	8,120
	Unemployed or economically inactive (but not retired)	10,331	9,707	6,190	7,026
Pensionable age - 74		34,319	26,952	15,126	21,608
Aged 75 and over		9,335	17,200	5,683	15,328

Source: *1991 Census County Report: Cleveland (Part 1)*, OPCS, 1992, Table 53, p. 262.

Table 2.5

Economic position and employment status — output categories

Economically active
    Persons in employment
        Employees
1   Full-time
2   Part-time
        Self-employed
3   With employees
4   Without employees
5   On a government scheme
    Unemployed
6   Waiting to start a job
7   Seeking work
8   Students (included above)

Economically inactive
    9   Students
    10   Permanently sick
    11   Retired
    12   Other inactive

Source: *1991 Census Definitions*, OPCS & GRO(S), 1992b, section 6.65.

Question 13 required all descriptions that applied to be ticked for the twelve possible activities. Any others not listed were written in. Boxes 1-4 (see appendix A) referred to paid work, whilst other boxes referred to government training schemes, unemployment, full-time education, long-term disability, retirement and looking after the home or family.

A maximum of three codes were entered onto the computer file, with 'on a government scheme' and 'in full-time education' taking precedence over other boxes. After this, the three lowest numbered boxes (those most likely to refer to employment) took priority. This gave rise to a 12-fold economic position/employment status classification shown in table 2.5. In the OPCS Longitudinal Study (see chapter 12) all three codes are retained.

Students in category 8 in table 2.5 are full-time students who were also economically active in census week. They were included in the appropriate economic activity category as well as being included in category 8. Students in category 9 were those who did not tick any boxes 1-4 at question 13. A tick in box 5 — Government Training Scheme — took priority over any other box. In 1981, Government training schemes, still in their infancy, were not distinguished, although a box for 'apprentice or articled trainee' was included.

The introduction of a category for economically active students was a change from 1981. It followed International Labour Organisation definitions adopted in the early 1980s. This means that comparisons between 1981 and 1991 need to be made with caution as all students in 1981 were categorised as economically inactive.

2.6.10   Lifestages

Following recommendations from the Market Research Society, the 1991 Census output included a new 'lifestage' classification. This is illustrated in figure 2.2 opposite.

This 'lifestage' classification is being developed in various market research surveys and will allow comparison between the sample survey results and the census 'base line', as well as providing valuable statistics for the commercial users of the Census.

2.7 TEN PER CENT DATA IN THE 1991 CENSUS

This section is concerned with the seven census questions, four of which required mainly a written answer rather than a tick in a box, where coding was done for a 10 per cent sample of households only and a 10 per cent sample of people in communal establishments. These census questions tend to be known as the 'hard to code' items. The way in which the 10 per cent sample was taken is described in chapter 4.

2.7.1 Household and family composition using relationship in household

A second approach to classifying household composition used information on the *relationship in the household* (question 5 on the Household Census form; not asked of people in communal establishments), rather than simply the age, sex, marital status and long-term illness variables used to construct household composition as described in section 2.6.7. The census defined a family as consisting of at least two people who may be either married or living together as a couple and of the opposite sex, with or without never married children, or a parent living with his or her never married child(ren). Other people were defined as not being within a family.

Information on relationship within the household enabled families within households to be distinguished and classified. However, this approach required a reference person within the household to whom the relationship of all others was stated and meant that a family unrelated to the head of household could not readily be distinguished. Forms with two or more persons unrelated to the head of household were referred to editors. They could use such evidence as was on the form (e.g. names, ages and sex) to identify families not related to the head of household.

The census form needed to provide a clear and simple instruction for selecting the first person to list on the form. This was achieved by telling the form-filler to enter first the 'head or joint head of household and then to state the relationship to this person of all others in the household'.[1]

From the responses to question 5 which asked for the relationship of each other person in the household to person number 1, a 17-category classification was produced (table 2.6) which, in turn, was used to group individuals into families and to classify households according to whether they contained families and if so, the number and type contained.

---

[1] The choice of the reference person has implications for the extent to which relationships can be derived in a multi-generational household. By choosing the person with the most kin relationships, information can be maximised (Priest, 1987). For example, in a three-generational household, a person in the middle generation will have explicit linkages both upwards and downwards which distinguish mother from mother-in-law and daughter from daughter-in-law.

Table 2.6

Categories of relationship in household

0	Head of household
1	Spouse
2	Cohabitant
3	Son/daughter
4	Child of cohabitant
5	Son/daughter-in-law
6	Cohabitant of son/daughter
7	Parent
8	Parent-in-law
9	Brother/sister
10	Brother/sister-in-law
11	Grandchild
12	Nephew/niece
13	Other related
14	Boarder, lodger, etc
15	Joint head
16	Other related

Source: *1991 Census Definitions*, OPCS & GRO(S), 1992b, section 7.7.

The 1991 question differed from that asked in 1981 by providing a category for 'living together as a couple'. In 1981, only people who wrote in their relationship as 'cohabitant' or similar were recorded as such and the term 'de facto spouse' was used in the output categories. This is likely to have underestimated the extent of cohabitation. The change in the wording of the relationship question reflected the substantial increase in cohabitation since 1981. In 1981, 5.6 per cent of women aged 20-24 (the peak age for cohabitation) were reported as cohabiting by the General Household Survey. In 1990 this figure was 16 per cent (Smyth and Browne, 1992). The wording change, whilst reflecting changes in social norms, also means that there is a lack of comparability with the 1981 Census.

The edit program for the 1991 Census allowed only couples of opposite sexes to be categorised as 'cohabiting'; where same sex couples were recorded as 'living together as a couple' in the relationship question, this was changed to 'unrelated'. In the months preceding the census there was a campaign by some gay and lesbian organisations to persuade OPCS and GRO(S) to recognise same sex couples in the census output. However, from the experience of the 1989 census test, it was decided that a count of same sex couples would produce unreliable results.

2.7.2 Classifications derived from relationship in the household

In a major advance on 1981, a computer algorithm was used to establish 60 family unit types within households and to allocate individuals to families as appropriate. This detailed, 60-item Family Unit Classification is given in appendix C of the *1991 Census Definitions* volume (OPCS and GRO(S), 1992b). Four basic categories of family are distinguished in statistical output:

(a) *Married couple family*: a married couple with or without their never-married child(ren). This includes couples where no child is recorded within the household.

(b) *Cohabiting couple family*: two persons of the opposite sex living together as a couple with or without their never married child(ren), including cohabiting couples where no child is recorded within the household.

(c) *Lone parent family*: a father or mother together with his or her never-married child(ren).

(d) *No family person*: an individual member of a household not assigned with other members of a family. A household containing, for example, a brother and sister with no parents, would be classified as a 'no family household' containing two persons, as would one containing one or more unrelated people.

Table 2.7

Classification of household and family composition type

Households with no family
1	1 person
2	2 or more

Households with 1 family
    Married couple family with no children
3	Without others
4	With others

    Married couple family with child(ren)
      Without others
5	With dependent children
6	With non-dependent children only

      With others
7	With dependent children
8	With non-dependent children only

    Cohabiting couple family with no children
9	Without others
10	With others

    Cohabiting couple family with child(ren)
      Without others
11	With dependent children
12	With non-dependent children

      With others
13	With dependent children
14	With non-dependent children

Lone parent family
    Without others
15	With dependent children
16	With non-dependent children only

    With others
17	With dependent children
18	With non-dependent children only

Households with 2 or more families
19	With no children
20	With dependent children
21	With non-dependent children only

Source: *1991 Census Definitions*, OPCS & GRO(S), 1992b, section 7.15.

To be defined as a child in a family unit a person had to be second-generation in the unit and single, with no partner or child of the person *apparent* on the census schedule. There was no limit on age, so that a never-married man of 40 living with his divorced mother would be in a lone-parent family. If the same man were divorced, then neither he nor his mother would be part of a family and they would each be classified as a *no family person*. A *dependent* child also had to be in a family in generation 2, and to conform to the definition given under Household Composition in section 2.6.7.

The standard classification, derived from this and used in many of the census tables, is given in table 2.7.

It is particularly important to note that information on *de facto* unions was not used in the 1981 classification of family types. Thus in 1981 a cohabiting couple with one child was classified as a 'lone parent family with others' (the other being the second of the two adults); the effect of this was to inflate the number of one-parent families. Because men were more likely to be nominated as head of household, they rather than their female partners were recorded as the parent of the child. Therefore the number of male one-parent families was particularly inflated (Brown, 1986). By adding a box for 'living together as a couple', the 1991 Census should have largely overcome this problem — although cohabiting couples can only be distinguished for the 10 per cent sample as relationship is only coded for this sample. Nonetheless, it is important to note that in some cases the children will be the natural (or adopted) child of only one member of the cohabiting couple.

Where a family is not related to the head of household, the relationship between family members may be apparent from the further information supplied in the relationship box. This can be checked or supplemented by applying a series of algorithms based upon assumptions, for example, of the minimum age difference between a parent and child.

2.7.3 Employment

In the 1981 Census, employment status was asked as a separate five-category question and was used with other information on occupation and industry to produce an extended classification of employment status. In the 1991 Census there was no question on employment status explicitly. Instead, the economic position question (question 13) was extended to distinguish the self-employed from employees. Other distinctions — managerial or supervisory, with or without employees — were made as part of the coding for the Standard Occupational Classification (SOC), discussed below.

Employment related questions asked of all those aged 16 and over who had had a job within the last 10 years

In 1981, questions on occupation and industry were asked in respect of the job held in the week before census for those currently in paid work and for the last occupation for people out of work, wholly retired or permanently sick or disabled. For some members of this group, the last occupation could have been twenty or more years before and the response was therefore likely to be unreliable. It was also difficult to explain to form-fillers why it was needed. Additionally, information was *not* sought from those who ticked *only* boxes for housewife, full-time education or 'other'.

In recognition of these difficulties, the 1991 Census asked questions on work hours, industry and occupation for *all* those who had held a paid job *within the last 10 years*, irrespective of their current employment status.

Hours worked per week: A question on hours of work was first included in the 1961 Census, but for part-time jobs only. In 1971 it was asked of all jobs but dropped in 1981 when, as an economy measure, only full- or part-time working was recorded as part of the question on economic activity (Redfern, 1981). In 1991, the full/part-time distinction was retained in the 100 per cent economic activity question (13), but, additionally, *usual* number of hours worked in the *main* job was included (question 14) and coded for the 10 per cent sample. Where comparison is needed with the 100 per cent full/part-time distinction, full-time working is defined as 'more than 30 hours' and part-time as '30 hours or less', but more than 1 hour per week.

Occupation: Question 15 in the 1991 Census schedule followed the usual practice of past censuses and asked for the title of a person's job and a description of the usual things that s/he did. Information on place of work or industry was used in the coding if it enabled an occupation to be categorised more precisely, for example by distinguishing a jeweller working in the retail sector from one working in restoration.

The 1991 Census coded occupation to the Standard Occupational Cassification (SOC) (OPCS and Employment Department Group, 1990 a, b, 1991). This replaced the 1980 Classification of Occupations which was used in the 1981 Census which, in turn, replaced the 1970 Classification of Occupations used in the 1971 Census. The SOC aims to classify jobs (as opposed to persons) on the basis of information on the job title and a description of the type of work done. It differs from the 1980 Classification of Occupations by taking no account of the employment status of the person, for example, whether an employee or self-employed. While remaining exactly comparable with over half the 1980 Occupational Coding Groups, it introduces new distinctions within fast growing industries such as information technology and also between those types of work which account for a high proportion of women's employment and which, in the past, have been poorly distinguished. SOC also aims to reduce the proportion of jobs allocated to the residual 'not elsewhere classified' category. The third volume of the *Standard Occupational Classification* (OPCS and Employment Department Group, 1991) describes the relationship of SOC to the 1980 Classification of Occupations and the extent of continuity between the two classifications.

At its most detailed level, direct one-to-one correspondence between the two classifications is preserved for only about 56 per cent of the 1981 reference population, making direct comparison at this level very difficult. The use of operational codes to produce the 1991 SOC (see chapter 4) allows dual coding to the 1980 Classification of Occupation also, thereby facilitating comparison between 1981 and 1991 on the 1980 base. Only a very limited amount of 1991 Census output uses the 1980 classification, although special tabulations (see chapter 7) can be ordered using it.

The SOC comprises:
   9 Major Groups, subdivided into
  22 Sub-major Groups, subdivided into
  77 Minor Groups, subdivided into

317 Unit Groups created from the 3,800 Classification of Occupations and Directory of Occupational Titles.

The Major and Sub-major grouping, used in many census tabulations at small area level, is given in table 2.8.

The 1981 Post-Enumeration Survey (PES) (Britton and Birch, 1985) checked the accuracy of the occupational information in the 1981 Census by classifying the occupational descriptions into the occupational categories of the 350 1980 OPCS operational codes and found differences from the census code in about 25 per cent of cases. This discrepancy may have been due to fuller information being given in the PES, to differences in the coding procedures used in the PES and the Census, or to differences in the accuracy of either the reporting or the coding of occupation. The use of a computerised system of occupational coding in the 1991 Census (described in chapter 4) should reduce coding variability.

In this and other classifications where most tabular output provides only a reduced form of the classification it is important to note that other, non-standard forms of output, often allow access to much fuller classifications. Chapters on the

Table 2.8

Major and sub-major grouping of SOC

1   Managers and Administrators
1a Corporate managers and administrators
1b Managers/proprietors in agriculture and service
2   Professional Occupations
2a Science and engineering professionals
2b Health professionals
2c Teaching professionals
2d Other professional occupations
3   Associate Professional and Technical Occupations
3a Service and engineering associate professionals
3b Health associate professionals
3c Other associate professional occupations
4   Clerical and Secretarial Occupations
4a Clerical occupations
4b Secretarial occupations
5   Craft and Related Occupations
5a Skilled construction trades
5b Skilled engineering trades
5c Other skilled trades
6   Personal and Protective Service Occupations
6a Protective service occupations
6b Personal service occupations
7   Sales Occupations
7a Buyers, brokers and sales representatives
7b Other sales occupations
8   Plant and Machine Operatives
8a Industrial plant and machine operators, assemblers
8b Drivers and mobile machine operators
9   Other Occupations
9a Other occupations in agriculture, forestry, and fishing
9b Other elementary occupations

Source: *1991 Census Definitions*, OPCS & GRO(S), 1992b, section 7.37.

Samples of Anonymised Records (see chapter 11) and the OPCS Longitudinal Study (see chapter 12) indicate the level of detail available from these forms of output.

In the 1971 Census a question was introduced on occupation one year ago. This was intended to provide information on occupation mobility, although it was dropped in 1981 and was not included in 1991. The annual Labour Force Survey (OPCS, 1992d) does, however, include this question.

Industry: For those with a job in the week before the Census and/or within the last 10 years the name of the employer and a description of the employer's business was asked; if self-employed, the name and nature of the business was asked. This was used to code the industry in which the person worked. The name of the employer or business was asked in order to code type of industry more accurately (see chapter 4); it was not stored on computer. Industry is coded to the Standard Industrial Classification (HMSO, 1979) — also used in the 1981 Census. It has 10 Divisions, each denoted by a single digit, shown in table 2.9; each division is divided into 60 Classes, denoted by the addition of a second digit. These are divided further to form 222 Groups and 334 Activities by the addition of third and fourth digits.

Social class, SEG and employment status
Social class based upon occupation: Stevenson introduced the Registrar General's social class schema in the 1920s as a categorisation of occupations that reflected 'the wealth or poverty and the culture associated with class' (OPCS, 1978, p. 2). Over the years the social class categories have changed somewhat, for example the split between non-manual and manual skilled occupations was added in 1971. The number of people in the classes has also changed over time, reflecting the changing occupational structure. In the 1991 Census, the same basic social class schema was retained, but the title was extended to *social class based upon occupation* to make clear that occupation provides the key to the classification. Generally, SOC Unit Groups are allocated in their entirety to a particular class, except where an individual has the employment status of 'foreman' or 'manager'. Persons of 'foreman' status whose basic social class is IV or V are allocated to Social Class III, whilst those of 'manager' status are allocated to Social Class II. Table 2.10 lists the classes distinguished. Further details are given in Volume 3 of the *Standard Occupational Classification* (OPCS and Employment Department Group, 1991).

Table 2.9

Industry divisions

0	Agriculture, forestry and fishing
1	Energy and water supply industries (energy and water)
2	Extraction of minerals and ores, other than fuels; manufacture of metals, mineral products and chemicals (mining)
3	Metal goods, engineering and vehicle industries (manufacturing metals, etc)
4	Other manufacturing industries (other manufacturing)
5	Construction
6	Distribution, hotels and catering (distribution and catering)
7	Transport and communication (transport)
8	Banking, finance, insurance, business services and leasing (banking and finance etc)
9	Other services

Source: *1991 Census Definitions*, OPCS & GRO(S), 1992b, section 7.45.

The extent of discontinuity between social class based on the 1980 Classification and social class based on SOC is, not surprisingly, much less than at the most detailed level. The overall gross measure of discontinuity between the two is given by the proportion of cases that fall into off-diagonal cells when the two variables are cross-tabulated; this is 2.3 per cent, using a 0.5 per cent subsample of occupations drawn from the 1981 Census returns (OPCS and Employment Department Group, 1991, table 3). More than half of this discontinuity is produced by a transfer of cases from Social Class IV to Social Class V. This results from a change in the treatment of domestic workers and cleaners.

Socioeconomic group (SEG): SEG was introduced in the 1951 Census and extensively amended in 1961. It is a non-hierarchical classification which uses both occupation and employment status and aims to bring together people with jobs of similar social and economic status. The categories are given in table 2.10. Information

Table 2.10

Social class based upon occupation and socioeconomic group

Social class based on occupation

I	Professional etc. occupations
II	Managerial and technical occupations
III (N)	Skilled occupations: non-manual
III(M)	Skilled occupations: manual
IV	Partly skilled occupations
V	Unskilled occupations

Socioeconomic group

1	Employers and managers in central and local government, industry, commerce etc. — large establishments
1.1	Employers
1.2	Managers
2	Employers and managers in industry, commerce, etc — small establishments
2.1	Employers
2.2	Managers
3	Professional workers: self-employed
4	Professional workers: employees
5	Intermediate non-manual workers
5.1	Ancillary workers and artists
5.2	Foreman and supervisors
6	Junior non-manual workers
7	Personal service workers
8	Foreman and supervisors: manual
9	Skilled manual workers
10	Semi-skilled manual workers
11	Unskilled manual workers
12	Own account workers (other than professional)
13	Farmers: employers and managers
14	Farmers: own account
15	Agricultural workers
16	Members of armed forces
17	Inadequately described and not stated occupations

Source: *1991 Census Definitions*, OPCS & GRO(S) 1992b, sections 7.5.1 and 7.6.1.

on size of establishment was used to make distinctions within categories 1 and 2. It is obtained by using the Census of Employment lists of employers produced by the Employment Department to look up the name of the employer as given on the census form. (These lists were also used to code industry.)

Further information on the construction of SEGs from the SOC Unit Groups is given in Volume 3 of the *Standard Occupational Classification*. The extent of discontinuity between 1981 and 1991 is 2.0 per cent — slightly less than that for social class — and also arises through changes in the coding of domestic workers and cleaners ((OPCS and Employment Department Group, 1991, Table 4).

Employment status: Generally, employment status came from responses to question 13, which were 100 per cent coded. However, for some purposes employment status was further broken down by hours worked or by manual, non-manual occupations using the 10 per cent data. *Persons on a government training scheme* were classified as economically active and in employment, but the 1991 Census collected no information on the particular scheme. Therefore people on government schemes had no information coded on occupation, industry, hours worked, social class and SEG unless they had held a job in the previous 10 years. *People not in employment* in the week before census day were only included if they had held a job in the previous 10 years.[1]

2.7.4   Workplace and transport to work

Form-fillers were asked to write in the address of the place of work of persons with a job in the week before census day (question 17) and to tick a box to indicate the means of daily journey to work (question 18). Question 17 differed from the 1981 Census only in that members of the armed forces were not required to give their place of work for security reasons. Question 18 dropped the category 'car or van — pool, shared driving' which was included in 1981 as this means of travel to work was no longer considered relevant to Government policy.

Address of workplace
The postcode of the address of workplace was recorded and, through the OPCS Central Postcode Directory (see chapter 3, section 3.2.5), was used to allocate workplace to local authority wards, districts or counties. Where postcodes were missing or incomplete, they were obtained, as far as possible, from the 1989 Census of Employment and other sources and added during coding. Usual address and workplace were used together to produce three main categories of workplace type:

  (i)   resident and working in the area;
 (ii)   working in area, resident outside;
(iii)   resident in area, working outside.

Categories (i) and (ii) together give the total population *working* in the area, whilst (i) and (iii) give the total employed population *resident* in the area. More detailed categories were used in the main output on this topic.

---

[1] Omission of these two relatively small groups from parts of some of the local base statistics and small area statistics necessitates care when making comparisons within the set of tables.

Information on workplace is used to assess the difference between the day-time and night-time composition of localities — important for environmental planning and decisions over the services needed in an area. Information on the numbers and characteristics of people who travel from one area to another to work, together with the means of transport to work and the distance travelled are available in machine readable form as the *Special Workplace Statistics*; chapter 10 provides details of the structure, content and use of these data. Information on location of workplace in relation to that of usual residence forms the basis for deriving *travel-to-work areas*, described in chapter 10. Travel-to-work-areas were first derived following the 1981 Census and were constructed from the commuting patterns of the usual residents of each ward and those who worked in each ward (*Employment Gazette*, 1984).

Daily journey to work
The question on means of daily journey to work referred to the longest part, by distance, of the person's normal journey to work. During the coding of workplace and journey to work, the edit program checked for inconsistencies and imputed alternative values if necessary to maintain consistency. For example, if the workplace had been given as 'mainly at home' the edit procedure ensured that transport to work was coded as 'works mainly at home'.

Distance to work was calculated from the straight line linking the Ordnance Survey National Grid reference of the postcode of residence to that of the postcode of workplace. For England and Wales, the calculation was performed using the National Grid reference of the first address in each postcode, contained in the Central Postcode Directory; the reference was usually given to the nearest 100 m. In Scotland, the references were to the nearest 10 m and were referenced from the centroid of the populated part of the postcode. Where people live away from home during the week their usual address was taken as their home address. This can lead to some anomalous answers when comparing distance to work with means of travel to work.

The distance to work categories used in census output are given in table 2.11.

Table 2.11

Distance to work categories

Workplace stated		
	1	Less than 2 km
	2	2– 4 km
	3	5– 9 km
	4	10–19 km
	5	20–29 km
	6	30–39 km
	7	40 km and over
	8	Workplace at home
	9	No fixed workplace
	10	Workplace not stated
	11	Workplace outside GB

Source: *1991 Census Definitions*, OPCS & GRO(S), 1992b, section 7.7.

Qualified manpower

As in 1981, the 1991 Census asked for details of higher qualifications obtained after age 18: up to three different qualifications by title, subject(s), year and awarding institution. For coding, each qualification was allocated to a six-digit code; the first three digits indicated the type and level of the qualification and the second three indicated the subject in which the qualification was obtained. The awarding institution was not coded but used to improve the accuracy of the coding. Indexes of acceptable and unacceptable qualifications, updated with the help of the Department For Education in England and Wales and the Scottish Office Education Department were used for checking.

In 1971, the qualified manpower question was complemented by asking whether the person had obtained specified school-level qualifications (GCE A-level, equivalent Scottish qualifications, OND and ONC). This was dropped in 1981 as an economy measure and was not revived in 1991.

Answers to the question on higher qualification were used to produce two codes for each qualification: the *educational level* and the *subject group* of the qualification.

Educational level

For the purpose of census tabulations, qualifications were grouped into three levels:

(i) level a — higher university degrees of UK standard

(ii) level b — first degrees and all other qualifications of UK first degree standard and all degrees of higher degree standard (except those classified as level (a), above)

(iii) level c — qualifications that are: general, obtained at 18 and over, above GCE A-level standard; below UK first degree level

Level (c) included most nursing and teaching qualifications, although degrees in education would be mainly classified as level (b). A *qualified* person held at least one qualification at level (a), (b), or (c).

Subject group

The major subject(s) of each qualification a person held was coded using a standard subject classification. This consisted of 10 subject groups and 108 primary subjects. The full classification is given in annex G of the *1991 Census Definitions* volume (OPCS and GRO(S), 1992b).

Unless otherwise stated, census tables used the most recently obtained qualification at the highest level to determine the educational level and subject for each person.

Information from the qualified manpower question provides an assessment not only of the pool of resources held by the population as a whole, but also of the extent to which they are being used and in what kinds of occupation and industry. For example, the numbers of people holding nursing and teaching qualifications who are not in paid employment can provide an indication of the potential reserve pool of labour for those professions.

2.8 INTERPRETATION OF THE 10 PER CENT SAMPLE STATISTICS

The 10 per cent sample is a stratified sample covering one in ten enumerated house-holds and one person in ten enumerated in communal establishments. The method of drawing the 10 per cent sample is covered in chapter 4, together with a discussion of an OPCS evaluation of the 10 per cent sample drawn from the 1981 Census.

In 1991, the Census contains counts for *wholly absent households* who completed a census form voluntarily on their return home and imputed information for wholly absent households who did not return a form. These latter, imputed households, were excluded from the 10 per cent sample because there was no way of imputing reliably the more complex items of census data. Therefore simply grossing up the 10 per cent sample by a factor of 10 does not give figures comparable with published figures for the *total population*. A reliable sample of the total population can only be obtained by multiplying the sample count by a sampling factor which represents the ratio of the 100 per cent count to the sample count. A discussion of the way in which this can be obtained is given in the *Census Newsletter*, No.25, 1993, pp. 15-17, and is also given in chapter 8, section 8.6.5. OPCS will be conducting an analysis of the reliability of the 10 per cent sample and results will be reported in the *1991 Census General Report*.

3   Census geography

I — An overview

Chris Denham

___

Introduction

This chapter provides guidance on the geography of the census in Britain: it describes the geographic base for statistical output from the 1991 Census and also provides some historic background to aid an understanding of the current diversity of census geography within Britain. One theme of the chapter is the development of small area building bricks for release of census statistics, particularly the greater use of postcodes in Scotland in comparison to England and Wales. A further theme is the introduction of coordinate references — as spot references or as digital boundaries — to permit the geographical manipulation of the data. The earlier parts deal with Great Britain as a whole, but later there are separate sections for England and Wales and for Scotland to reflect differences north and south of the Border.

3.1 THE DEVELOPMENT OF CENSUS GEOGRAPHY IN GREAT BRITAIN

3.1.1 Reports for statutory areas: a nineteen census series

From the first census in 1801 results have been issued for statutory areas and other areas defined for administrative purposes. These remain the main geographical base in the census reports. However, the Census Act 1920, makes no mention of the areas for which a census is to be reported. The choice is left to the Census Offices.

The information in census tables is determined by the choice of the geographical base as well as the choice of the attributes covered in the census and the categories into which the attributes are divided. While a great deal of effort goes into the design of census questions and tables to meet users' needs, the production of results only for *statutory* areas would mean that analyses of phenomena that are independent of this base would be impaired.

Census results for areas defined for *statistical* purposes first appeared in the reports of the 1921 Census which gave tables for six 'regions', but these were merely aggregates of existing statutory areas. A further development was the definition of five 'conurbations' prior to the 1951 Census. The conurbations, too, were aggregations of existing statutory areas, grouped to recognise 'functional interrelationships' in large urban agglomerations. In addition, from the time of the 1871 Census, very simple statistics have been published for wards and civil parishes (and from 1801 for civil parishes in Scotland) — small administrative areas which gave more flexibility of aggregation. However, the area base for reports has been inflex-

52

ible and remains so until the present. A sole exception is the use of 'urban areas' defined for 1981 and 1991 Census reports on the basis of land use and population, regardless of administrative boundaries.

Statutory and administrative divisions of the country generally have a hierarchical structure. Many divisions of the country have been made at different times, often unrelated to one another, so that several sets of areas with overlapping boundaries have been reported in each census. In 1901 and again in 1921, reports were prepared for 20 different kinds of area. Although various traditional areas such as ecclesiastical parishes and court areas have been dropped from recent censuses, the area base for the 1971 Census was the most complex ever. It provided statistics for local government areas as defined both before and after reorganisation in 1974 — amounting to some 22 different types of area in all.

3.1.2 Statistics for small areas: developments over five censuses

For the 1961 Census a fundamental change was made in the geographical base: simple, standard statistics were made available for wards and civil parishes and, below them, for enumeration districts (EDs) - the smallest area for the management of enumeration in the census field operation, typically formed of a group numbering between 150 and 250 households. This change meant that the number of areas for which separate statistics were available increased 10-fold (by the provision of ward and parish statistics), or by 40- or 50-fold (by the provision of ED statistics). Not only were statistics for very local areas provided, but the standard statistics could be aggregated for any combination of the areas — the 'building brick' approach.

At first these statistics were known as the *Ward Library*, but then became known as *Small Area Statistics* (SAS) from the 1971 Census, and in the 1991 Census, now that they have two tiers, as the *Local Base Statistics* (LBS) and SAS (see chapters 7 and 8). The geographic coverage of the 1961 Ward Library was incomplete as it was produced only on demand, but the Ward Library from the 1966 Census and the SAS from the 1971 Census covered all wards, civil parishes and EDs. Subsequent developments in the 1981 and 1991 Censuses have strongly reinforced the 'building brick' approach which relies on standard small area statistics to provide geographical flexibility.

3.1.3 Small area geography: the search for a multi–purpose base

The Census Offices have always recognised that the use of EDs as statistical areas is a compromise between the requirements of census field and processing operations and the requirements of users, the latter normally being subordinate in any conflict of priorities.

The use in the census of area bases that are independent of the processes of census-taking first became an issue in the 1960s when Ward Library statistics were introduced. EDs, which are not marked on published Ordnance Survey maps, are often unrelated to other areas recognised by users and are quite ephemeral. EDs, and even wards, are often not a suitable base for data which are not closely related to residential population; for example, the number of people with workplaces in an area. However, as long ago as 1966, the General Register Office (predecessor to OPCS) suggested that a set of permanent small areas should be defined as statistical building bricks for the census. These building bricks would be available for use in other data sets and, preferably, would have geographical references suitable for direct geographical manipulation.

What seemed then to be two contrasting options were available in the late 1960s — the Ordnance Survey National Grid system and the Post Office (predecessor to the Royal Mail) postcode system, although the latter had only recently been launched. With hindsight the options can be seen to be almost entirely complementary: the postcode is provided by respondents and, through directories, may be linked to the coordinate references of the National Grid system, which respondents normally cannot provide, but which allow the geographical manipulation of the data. The early failure to recognise the essentially complementary nature of postcodes and the National Grid has still not been fully remedied in England and Wales.

3.1.4 The National Grid System

The National Grid uses letters and numbers to denote location on the Ordnance Survey maps covering Great Britain. Developed in the years before World War II, it consists of a breakdown of a grid into progressively smaller squares — from the largest with sides of 500 km to the smallest of 100 m drawn on the maps. But 'squares' of a resolution as detailed as 1 m can be read from large–scale maps, providing, at the most precise level, a unique 12 digit reference to any point on the Grid. The west to east coordinates are given first (the easting), followed by the south to north coordinates (the northing). The Grid is the basis of any information from an Ordnance Survey map held in digital form, although the Grid can be transformed to other coordinate systems.

After much discussion in central government, consultation with census users and practical trials in the office and field, it was decided to reference all 1971 Census addresses (and the census data for those addresses) directly to the National Grid. The aim was to produce statistics for populations falling within National Grid squares of 100 m or, in sparsely populated areas, of 1 km. The alternative, considered at the time, was to take the street pattern and segments of streets (for example, London Road, North Side, or even numbers 16 to 58) as the reference base for addresses. Such systems were being developed by the US Bureau of the Census (see chapter 3(II)), but settlement patterns in Britain seemed relatively more difficult to describe in this way.

Also, before the 1971 Census, a trial was conducted in High Wycombe which gave every address a unique National Grid reference to a 1 m resolution, and geographically flexible output was produced from this base. However, it was impossible for confidentiality reasons to release an address 'gazetteer' from the census for general use, nor could it have been updated between censuses. Moreover, contemporary computer power would have been severely tested in using such data on a large scale, and the idea was shelved in favour of grid squares as an output area.

The National Grid was seen as a common spatial base for various sets of data. A combination of characteristics — accessibility, stability and suitability for statistical analysis and automated cartography on the computers of the time — made grid squares seem an attractive areal base for census statistics. Grid squares, however, have serious disadvantages as statistical areas as well as merits. They do not correspond with physical features on the ground nor with administrative boundaries; the population of grid squares varies widely, a problem exacerbated by steps taken to preserve confidentiality.

One of the merits of census statistics for grid squares is that they enable close comparisons to be made between the results of successive censuses, provided that referencing is consistent. In the 1981 Census the initial intention was to reference to 1 km squares throughout England and Wales. Any referencing to 100 m squares was to be done on request. However, grid square referencing was in the end done only in a limited number of areas where it was requested and paid for by customers. In Scotland, in 1981, population and household counts were offered for 1 km squares. No demand for grid square referencing as such emerged before the 1991 Census, and none has been done in the 1991 Census. Use of information referenced by the coordinates of the National Grid is no longer constrained to the simplicity of larger grid squares.

A link between the SAS for EDs (1971, 1981 and 1991) and the National Grid is provided by a grid reference for a point within each ED — sometimes known as a 'centroid' or 'spot reference'. Geographical Information Systems (GISs) are now able to sort such point referenced data into any set of digitised polygons. Such polygons would have to include a reasonable number of EDs for each census to overcome the variability arising from the changing numbers and positions of EDs, but rectangular grids can be used as the polygons.

3.1.5 The postcode system

The second option for a geographic base for the census is the postcode system. The Post Office (now Royal Mail) introduced its postcode system as part of the mechanised sorting of mail. This remains the prime function and the system covers every address in the country to which mail is delivered. The system is now well known to users of statistical information. On average, a unit postcode covers about 15 postal delivery points, with a range of one to around 50 addresses, and a unit postcode may also be assigned to a single large user, for example, a business. A postcode as used by the Royal Mail does not represent an area with defined boundaries, it is merely a delivery point or a string of addresses, grouped to reflect a postman's walk.

Although unit postcodes build up hierarchically into larger areas, for example, the postcode sector, such areas may bear little relationship to administrative or other recognised areas. Nonetheless, because unit postcodes are about a tenth the size of an ED — in population terms — they can be aggregated into approximations of administrative or other areas.

Postcodes are now widely known to the public and can therefore be collected with address information on census forms, other questionnaires, and administrative records. But postcodes are not well mapped and they change over time. They are also the property of the Royal Mail and, whilst the Royal Mail has taken a very generous view on the use of postcodes in various sets of information without requiring any payment, free use cannot be taken for granted. Indeed their future use for statistical purposes rests on the viability and stability of the Royal Mail's coding and mail handling system.

The use of postcodes as a geographical code in the census began with 1981, although there was some retrospective use with the 1971 Census in Scotland. The 1981 Census also marked the start of a divergence of Scotland from England and Wales.

In Scotland, for the 1981 Census GRO(S) mapped the postcodes from information supplied by the Post Office, and the EDs in Scotland were defined as groups of unit postcodes, typically some ten of them. The postcode sector largely replaced the ward as a statistical output area in Scotland, as there was uncertainty about the degree and timing of forthcoming changes in ward boundaries when the Census was planned. The application of postcodes in the 1981 and 1991 Censuses of Scotland is described in section 3.4, below.

In England and Wales, however, as well as in Scotland, postcodes played a futher part in the 1981 Census. They were used for the geographical analysis of addresses remote from the address of enumeration. Respondents to the census were asked to give the postcodes (if known) of their address one year before census day (where different from present usual residence) and of their workplace. Any postcode omitted was added at the processing stage by reference to postcode directories. Statistics on the areas from which migrants had come, and statistics on workplaces, were produced on the basis of wards, or other areas, defined as the aggregates of postcodes approximating to the wards. The application of postcodes in the 1991 Census of England and Wales is described in section 3.3.3, and chapter 10 is about workplace and migration statistics.

The mechanism for the use of postcodes for the geographic coding of data with addresses supplied by the public is a computerised postcode directory — the Central Postcode Directory. For each postcode it gives the ward, district and county in which the first address of the postcode lies, together with a National Grid reference for the first address in the postcode. The directory is regularly updated by the Census Offices.

The Central Postcode Directory

The Central Postcode Directory (CPD) is a computerised directory that links each postcode in the UK to its ward, district, county and National Grid reference. The CPD was created by the Census Offices in conjunction with the Royal Mail. The main purpose of the CPD is to assist in the area coding of data for government and the National Health Service. The first address within the postcode is used to make the linkage and all other addresses with the same postcode are allocated the same ward, district and county. The directory is updated twice a year and is estimated to omit only about 0.1 per cent of postcodes. The Scottish directory also links postcodes to various other area types, for example, civil parishes, localities and inhabited islands, and is maintained by the GRO(S) who, twice a year, supply OPCS with a copy.

Options for the geography of the 1991 Census in England and Wales were evaluated in the period after the 1981 Census. Two were identified — to stay with conventional EDs or to use unit postcodes so that postcodes fitted into EDs. The change to postcodes was considered mainly because they were becoming established as the base for other statistical data sets and because they would introduce a greater degree of flexibility. Unfortunately, unit postcodes had not been mapped in England and Wales — a time-consuming and expensive exercise in which it would have been necessary to find each address in each of the 1.26 million unit postcodes in large-scale maps. The cost and effort of doing so for the census weighed against the benefits of adopting postcodes. The final decision was that traditional EDs should once again form the basis for the census. So postcodes do not fit into EDs. However, in a very limited number of areas, local authorities mapped unit postcodes as the basis of ED boundaries under the 'local requirements' procedure (see section 3.3).

3.1.6 Conclusion

The development of the geographic base for recent censuses, described above, helps in understanding its current diversity and the range of issues which affect it. The main points are: there is no general-purpose area coding and geographical reference system in the public domain nor an organisation to operate such a system; attempts were made to introduce geographic bases before computer systems for them were fully adequate; and funding for the improvement and wider use of postcode geography was forthcoming in Scotland, but not, at a later date, in England and Wales.

3.2 GEOGRAPHY FOR THE 1991 CENSUS

3.2.1 Enumeration: the first objective

The first objective of any census is a complete count of the population, and this requires a comprehensive frame to organise enumeration and translate easily into the varying sets of areas used for output. The collection of the census information is of course centred on recognition of households and communal establishments, but in Britain there is no adequate list (or 'frame') of these *before* a census, and enumeration is organised within bounded districts.

The census of 1841 was the first to divide the country, systematically, into districts in order to provide a more accurate enumeration of the population. Thomas Lister, the first Registrar General of the newly established General Register Office, was responsible for the 1841 Census and took the newly defined 2,193 registration districts and subdivided them into enumeration districts (Nissel, 1987). Each enumeration district was to contain between 15 and 200 inhabited houses, and Lister gave the registrars detailed instructions on how they should decide on the size of each district. Similar use of the Registration system began in Scotland in 1861. This process of division of the country for census operations has been carried forward, albeit with modifications, to the present day.

The collection area in the 1991 Census throughout Britain has remained the enumeration district (ED), although the methods of drawing up the ED were different north and south of the Border. The ED is also the small area 'building brick' for the main output from the 1991 Census in England and Wales, but not in Scotland, where the 'output area' (OA), consisting of unit postcodes, has taken the place of the ED for the first time. However, postcodes were collected for the address of every household in the 1991 Census in England and Wales, and were entered into the computer files of census data to act as an alternative geographic base.

Dividing the country into EDs and marking them on large–scale maps is a major task in planning a census. Each ED is the responsibility of one enumerator who delivers and collects a form at each household within the defined area of the ED (however, a few enumerators may be responsible for a couple of EDs, when one

Figure 3.1 1991 Census output areas

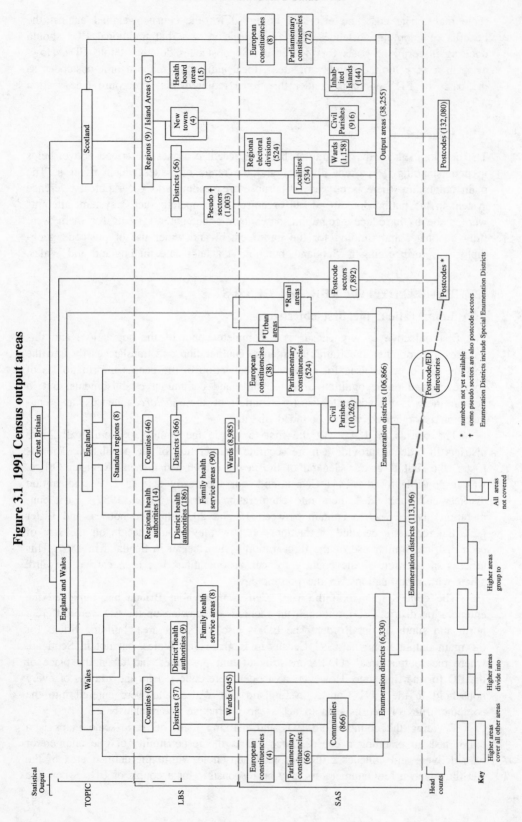

or more is small). EDs cover the entire country without omission or overlap. The fieldwork for the Census is discussed in chapter 4.

Each ED represents a workload that can be performed in the time available, given the circumstances of the area. Wherever possible, its boundaries must follow significant physical features, such as roads and railways. The census forms for each ED are given a unique identification number and are handled as a unit throughout field operations and processing, avoiding the expense and delays of sorting individual forms into areas for output. In addition, where the ED is the area 'building brick' for output, every boundary used in any of the geographical bases for tables must coincide with ED boundaries.

A summary of the geographic base of the 1991 Census in Great Britain is given in figure 3.1. This shows the hierarchies of areas based on the small area 'building bricks', and the differences north and south of the Border.

3.3 ENGLAND AND WALES

The aims of the census geography system were: first, to provide a set of areas to enable enumeration to be carried out; second, to provide a base for administration of the census; and, third, to provide a base for statistical output. The system provided various operational areas used to carry out and manage the census, a base to control the issue and collection of census forms and other documents, a base for the payment of the field staff, and, finally, a base to control processing. The key, linking all these activities, is the 1991 Census *geographic database.*

As the geography system also provides the basic units for output, EDs were designed to nest within a complex set of areas recognised in output. In particular, because of the importance to local authorities of the small area statistics for EDs, and for ad hoc areas built from them, OPCS worked closely with the local authorities — at county and district level — to construct EDs that recognised areas of special local interest. An initial approach to local authorities through a survey of geographical requirements in 1987 showed that many had specific requirements and would like to be consulted about ED planning. Most local authorities were also prepared to supply OPCS with details of new housing and of demolition since 1981 and expected up to 1991 — information needed to estimate enumerators' workloads. Receipt of local boundary requirements and development information was organised in stages between July 1988 and August 1989 to match the progress of ED planning.

3.3.1 Planning the 1991 EDs

The set of EDs used for the 1981 Census formed the base for planning areas for 1991. Changes were kept to a minimum whenever possible, but arose from changes in the intercensal decade: in the number of housing units; the social composition of areas; and statutory boundaries. The main objectives in planning EDs were: to create workloads of a manageable size; to cover all land; to design areas with boundaries which were easy for enumerators to recognise; to meet specifications for minimum size; and to meet special local requirements, as well as to retain as much comparability with 1981 ED boundaries as possible.

There are two types of ED: ordinary EDs, and special EDs (SEDs). The latter are large communal establishments which were expected to contain 100 or more people on census night ('shipping' EDs are a variety of SED). SEDs are separately identified and excluded from the ordinary ED containing the establishment, both at enumeration and for the output of some statistics, although no boundary is drawn around a special ED. They are discussed more fully in chapter 8, section 8.4.1.

The information used to plan EDs was: the 1981 Census boundaries; changes in statutory boundaries since 1981; details of changes in the housing stock since 1981 (obtained from district and county councils); 'weighting factors' derived partly from using 1981 Census Small Area Statistics to identify areas where the time taken to enumerate a household would be longer than average; and a set of maps for each district. The maps used for planning — subsequently copied for the field operation and also supplied as reference maps with statistics — were the Ordnance Survey 1:10,000 maps throughout England and Wales, supplemented in all urban areas by the most up-to-date 1:1,250 or 1:2,500 maps available. Once the information was assembled, the planning of EDs went through six stages discussed in detail by Clark and Thomas (1990).

EDs emerged from planning with an identity number for field purposes, shortened for processing and output purposes. For example:

Field ED number: NF 01FA02, where:

NF = local government (LG) district area ('N' Norwich)
01 = census district number within LG district
FA = electoral ward within LG district
02 = ED number within ward.

Output ED Number: NF FA 02 (the census district number is omitted)

3.3.2 Continuity of enumeration districts: 1971-81, 1981-91

When OPCS contacted census users before the 1981 Census, many asked for 1971 EDs to be used again in 1981 to allow a straightforward comparison. As far as possible, 1971 EDs were retained for 1981. Approximately half were eventually unchanged, but this varied considerably between districts. Where ED boundaries were changed, an effort was made to give 1971-81 comparability at local level by ensuring that the boundary of a group of 1981 EDs would coincide with a group of 1971 EDs, even though, within the group, ED boundaries had changed. The information on comparability was available to users who could re-group areas within the basic framework to local requirements, but a national set of comparable small areas was commissioned by the Department of the Environment — given the name of 'census tracts' — and made generally available.

Contact with users before the 1991 Census produced far less emphasis on the need for geographical continuity, and there had been indications that the 1971-81 census tracts had proved quite difficult to use for large areas. Nevertheless, the same approach, of changing EDs only when necessary, was adopted for 1991, although the degree of direct comparability between the 1981 and 1991 Censuses is less than between 1971 and 1981. Moreover, an equivalent of the 1971-81 census tracts has not been commissioned at the time of writing. The geographic bases for analyses of change between 1981 and 1991 seem likely either to be set up in an ad hoc way at local level or to be done in a broader, more approximate way, through Geographical Information Systems (GISs). For example, information on 1981 and 1991 EDs can be captured through a GIS by their 'spot references' within polygons representing the areas in which change is under study, prior to aggregation of comparable statistics for the sets of EDs.

3.3.3 Postcodes in the 1991 Census, England and Wales

Capture

The postcode of the address of each household was collected in the 1991 Census, as it was in 1981, but the postcodes were put on the computer record for the first time in 1991 and provide an alternative geographic base for census information. Postcodes were also collected for 'remote addresses' (usual residence, term–time address, address one year previously, workplace), as in 1981, for the coding of addresses and information to small areas.

The postcodes of enumeration were checked for validity in the data capture process and, where an error or omission was found, postcodes were either imputed — where the chances of a correct imputation were high (for example, a missing postcode for a household between two others with identical postcodes) — or were inserted from a Royal Mail directory of addresses and postcodes. This process leaves some marginal geographical inaccuracy in the data, and this varies by area according to the rate of missing postcodes and/or the detail of the postcode system.

Uses

The main purposes of having postcodes as an *alternative* base are: first, to allow *exact* statistics to be produced for areas defined in terms of postcodes; second, to prepare a 'matrix' of postcodes and EDs so that non-census information containing postcodes can be allocated to EDs and thereby associated with census characteristics; and, third, to provide 'historic' (1991 Census) information on a postcode basis for comparison with any future census with a postcode base. On the last point, whilst the postcode system is subject to change, it is generally evolutionary change in reaction to a change in the number of mail delivery points (addresses), and it is not the type of sudden or 'catastrophic' geographical change which has been faced by the users of two or more censuses.

Limitations

There is, however, one major problem in having two independent small area bases: the possibility of subtracting — differencing — the numbers for one base from those for the other base to produce statistics which relate to very small numbers of persons or households below the confidentiality thresholds. In large sets of output it is difficult to detect where products of differencing are unequivocably identifiable to a specific small area, and where they are not. The only remedies appear to be either to simplify the statistics released, or to perturb the statistics (to a degree greater than the standard 'blurring' of census small area statistics — see chapter 8), or to increase the population of output areas. All are steps which would diminish the value of having statistics for small areas defined *precisely* in terms of postcodes.

The fuller use of postcodes as an alternative base in England and Wales has been hampered by the lack of maps of unit postcodes and by the lack of any inherent information in the postcode system which gives relative geographic positions. The prospects for a 'map' of postcodes becoming available in the 1990s has increased considerably with the floating by Ordnance Survey of their Address Point product which would give a grid reference to a one metre resolution for every address within every postcode unit, so mapping the postcodes as strings of coordinates (see section 3.9.2).

Products: statistics and directories

Small area statistics for postcode sectors will be aggregated from the census files on the basis of postcodes of enumeration. There is an average of 2,000 households in a postcode sector, and risks to confidentiality through differencing will be very limited. Summary statistics for postcode sectors will also be published to serve the wide use of these areas in business and commerce.

OPCS have produced a 'matrix' associating postcodes to EDs. There are directories produced on a county by county basis linking whole and part unit postcodes to EDs, giving a count of households in each whole or part postcode and a spot grid reference for each postcode. The format is described in the 1991 Census *User Guide 26*. A second phase of directories contains postcodes not captured in the census (for example, those without residential addresses). It may also be possible, if users have a need and will meet the cost, to update the directories as postcodes change by using information obtained for the Central Postcode Directory (see section 3.1.5), but only an approximate link between a new postcode and a 1991 ED could be given, and no household counts could be allocated to new or changed postcodes.

Table 3.1 shows some of the variety of management, statutory and 'statistical' areas built from EDs in the 1991 Census in England and Wales. The 'statistical' areas are non-statutory but are recognised on a systematic basis.

3.3.4 Management, statutory, and statistical areal sets — built from EDs in the 1991 Census

The boundaries of local government and electoral areas are subject to change over time. The Local Government Boundary Commissions keep boundaries of wards and civil parishes under review, whilst parliamentary boundaries are reviewed by the Parliamentary Boundary Commissions. The Census Offices are not committed at the time of writing to producing census statistics for any revised local government areas which may be introduced in the 1990s. The issue of statistics for new areas would depend on the degree to which existing boundaries were replaced by new ones, and on needs expressed by users. County reports for the new areas were produced after the major local government reorganisation in 1974, and summary figures were published for new Parliamentary constituencies after reorganisation in 1983.

Area Index Files

The Census Offices produce index files which give the constitutions of higher level areas in terms of the primary building bricks (either ED or output area). These index files can be used to produce aggregations of Local Base or Small Area Statistics for higher level areas. However, the blurring of the Local Base and Small Area Statistics for confidentiality reasons may distort the figures produced by such aggregations (see chapter 8, section 8.6) and the use of larger building blocks is advisable. The index

Table 3.1

Management, statutory and statistical areal sets, built from EDs in the 1991 Census

Management	Statutory	Statistical (3)
Census area	Country (E&W)	Urban area
Census district	County (1)	Rural area
Enumeration workload	Local government district	Central (statistical) areas in cities
Enumeration district	London borough	(central business districts)
	District electoral ward	New Towns (4)
	Civil parish/community	Special local areas
	(in Wales)	Standard statistical regions
	Regional health authority/	Travel-to-work areas (5)
	district health authority (2)	
	Urban development area	
	Parliamentary constituency	
	European constituency	

Notes on table 3.1

(1) Metropolitan county councils were abolished in 1986 and some of their functions transferred to the metropolitan district councils; nonetheless metropolitan counties are still distinguished in census output to provide continuity with 1981 as a sub-regional area covering major centres of population.

(2) The National Health Service areas came into being in April 1982 following the 1980 Health Services Act. There is therefore a lack of consistency between the National Health Service areas at the time of the 1981 Census and at the time of the 1991 Census. The change in the structure pre and post-1982 is summarised below:

Pre-1982
15 regional health authorities
98 area health authorities
216 health districts

Post-1982
15 regional health authorities

216 district health authorities

Although there are the same number of lower tier authorities both before and after the 1982 reorganisation, 52 of the new district health authorities are in fact the result of amalgamations and divisions.

(3) Statistical areas are defined to meet a variety of needs, but have no statutory basis. They may, however, as with standard regions, be based upon existing administrative areas, and remain relatively unchanged over a number of censuses with their definition known before the census.
A further type of statistical area is defined after the census on the basis of its results, and is likely to change at each census. Urban and remaining rural areas were specifically defined for both the 1981 and 1991 Censuses, after the completion of the census, and were built from groups of individual EDs. Urban areas cover conurbations, cities and towns of all sizes defined on a land use basis so, for example, statistics are available for smaller towns within the larger local authority areas.

(4) The 23 'new towns' of England and Wales had lost their distinctive statutory status before the time of the 1991 census, and are no longer recognised as such by the Census. But New Town boundaries may have been specified and recognised as local requirements (see section 3.3.3). New Towns used to be characterised by rapid growth, high economic activity rates, predominately young populations, and public sector housing. However, these characteristics have been considerably diluted as some New Towns have moved into their fifth and sixth decades of existence.

(5) Travel-to-work-areas are defined after the census by the Employment Department. These are zones which meet the criterion that a given proportion of residents of the area should also work within the area. They are derived by consideration of actual journey to work patterns at ward to ward level, and typically have a centre of employment surrounded by more residential areas. A more detailed description of these is given in chapter 10, section 8.

files also have other applications such as forming an intermediate step to obtaining the postcode constitution of a higher level area from an ED/postcode directory.

For England and Wales, the ED to higher output area index is the Area Master File (AMF). For each standard ED, the AMF contains a record which provides the codes for the various types of higher output area to which the ED belongs. In Scotland, the output area to Higher Area Index File performs the same function. Details of these files are available from the contact points given in section 3.7.

3.4 SCOTLAND

In the 1991 Census in Scotland, output areas for statistics are **not** the same as the areas used for enumeration. This differs from the situation in Scotland in 1981, and also from England and Wales in 1991. This development was facilitated by the use of unit postcodes as building bricks.

Mapping the postcodes in Scotland

Since 1973, GRO(S) has mapped and maintained boundaries to contain the addresses in each unit postcode. The boundaries are drawn so that the entire land surface of Scotland is covered. Each postcode is assigned to an electoral ward, to a civil parish, and to about 15 other area types. The codes for these area types are stored on a postcode directory which is used within and outside GRO(S) to assign postcoded data to larger areas, and as statistical 'building bricks'.

Applying the postcode geography

The postcode was used in the 1981 Census of Scotland in two ways. First, in the planning of workloads for enumerators, estimates of the number of households in each postcode were prepared, and postcodes were assembled into suitably sized EDs. Second, in editing census data, because an ED contained only a given set of post-codes, the postcode on a household form in an ED had to be one of that set, and any not in the set were rejected by the editing process.

Small Area Statistics (SAS) were produced for each ED as in England and Wales, but, in Scotland, an exact association between the SAS and postcoded data from other sources could be made. In addition, to meet an order from the Scottish Office for comparable 1971-81 small area statistics, all 1971 Census records were postcoded and aggregated into 1971 statistics for 1981 EDs, where possible using 1981 SAS table layouts. The resulting reformatted SAS (RSAS) were made available at about the time of the 1981 Census.

Developments for the 1991 Census

The 1981 Census EDs in Scotland, with an average of about 120 households, were about two-thirds the size of those in England and Wales. As part of a wider policy to reduce unnecessary differences in the Census north and south of the Border, GRO(S) decided to plan 1991 EDs from scratch to bring most workloads up to the level of those in England and Wales. Users' requirements for output areas were, first, continuity with previous censuses and, second, greater flexibility than in 1981 for aggregation to ad hoc areas. So 1991 EDs were not adopted as output areas because they would not give continuity with 1971 and 1981, and a decision was taken to create a new form of 'output areas' (OAs).

Constructing Output Areas in Scotland

It was decided that no OA should contain fewer than 16 households and 50 residents — thresholds which apply throughout Britain — but some of the work of defining OAs could only be done once the actual counts of households and residents became available for comparison with the confidentiality thresholds. This phase of the work had to cause the minimum delay to output, and the definition of OAs had two stages. A pre-census phase created *provisional* output areas (POAs) based on the estimated household counts used in ED planning. Then, when actual household and resident counts became known, each POA either passed the confidentiality checks and was confirmed as an OA or failed and was merged with one or more neighbouring POA so that an above-threshold OA was formed.

To select postcodes to form sets of POAs it was necessary to know which postcodes had common boundaries. After consideration of a number of methods, it was decided to digitise all postcode unit boundaries in Scotland (130,000 postcodes from 5,500 maps), and construct a 'neighbouring postcode database' automatically, which had the extra benefit of allowing digitised boundaries of postcodes, OAs and other areas (for example, the 1981 EDs) to be displayed and manipulated by Geographical Information Systems (GISs). The digitising and verification of boundaries was done in-house by GRO(S).

3.5 GREAT BRITAIN

3.5.1 Census geography in conventional and digital forms

The 1991 Census is the third British census in which geographic information has been supplied both as boundaries of census areas marked on large-scale Ordnance Survey maps and in which some geographical information has been supplied in digital form. It is also the third census in which users have created additional digital information at local level.

Uses of digital information

The information provided is *either* in the form of a spot reference locating an area for which statistics are provided *or* in the form of the boundary around the area.

The *spot reference* (a National Grid co-ordinate reference for a spot centrally placed in a small area, either central to the geographic area or weighted towards the centre of population) provides the user with considerable scope for analyses. Some examples are:

- to find the area on a grid referenced map.
- to create point symbol maps (amalgamating data for points where density is high on a smaller scale map), and to create maps where 'contour' lines join points of equal value or show other 'surfaces' expressing the spatial patterns in values at the points.
- to calculate representative distances between areas, perhaps as input to models.
- to link data by nearest neighbouring spot reference techniques.

- to identify the spot referenced data as being within polygons of regular shape (for example, grid squares that can be used for mapping and analysing intercensal change) or with digitised boundaries (for example, catchment areas, flood plains).
- to act as the basis for the calculation of synthetic polygons for use, for example, with shaded area mapping.

A set of *digital boundaries* for census areas, *in addition*, allows the user, for example:

- to calculate area measurements and population densities.
- to derive digital boundaries for higher level areas.
- to prepare precise shaded area maps, ideally where the density of population is relatively even.
- to link with other data referenced to polygons and allow manipulation through Geographic Information Systems.

Census small area statistics are now deficient without both types of digital information, and the products available are described in the following paragraphs.

Boundary products in Scotland

GRO(S) provides boundary information in a number of ways for the areas for which census results are issued. The choice of product depends on, among other things, access to particular hardware and software. Users who wish to handle 1991 output in a similar way to the way they handled 1981 output may buy an output area (OA) by postcode index file, and obtain copies of the maps used by enumerators which show postcode boundaries.

Users with the appropriate hardware and software may purchase and use OA boundaries in digital form. Data for OAs can then be manipulated and displayed with the boundaries for those areas. Digitised unit postcode boundaries may also be purchased. Used with the postcode by OA index file, OA boundaries can be created from the postcode boundaries, as well as boundaries for postcoded data from non-census sources.

Boundary products in England and Wales

OPCS, unlike GRO (S), had no application for digital boundaries in the 1991 Census which would justify the cost of creation at ward and/or ED level, and it could not prepare them for other users on a speculative basis. Nevertheless, OPCS recognised the value of digital information in connection with the census statistics and, in a 1987 survey of geographic requirements, it was found that local authorities covering some half the population of the country anticipated using digital boundaries with 1991 Census statistics. OPCS therefore adopted a policy of facilitating the digitising of census boundaries where this was done by other organisations.

The complete 1991 Census boundaries for England and Wales, down to the most detailed level (ED), have been digitised separately as commercial ventures by two organisations — Graphical Data Capture Ltd (the ED 91 products), and a consortium comprising of the London Research Centre, MVA Systematica, and Taywood Data Graphics (the ED-line product) — and are available from these organisations in a variety of forms. Each organisation has a non-exclusive agreement with OPCS (in respect of the ED boundaries and identities) and Ordnance Survey (in respect of the base maps on which the ED boundaries are drawn) which grants them the right to create digital versions of the Census boundaries and licence their use to third parties.

OPCS loaned the complete set of ED maps at 1:10,000 scale to each organisation without charge in return for a modest royalty when the digital boundaries are supplied to third parties, and also in return for a copy of the boundaries for use in OPCS. Ordnance Survey charged a fee for the use of its maps. In addition, Ordnance Survey was commissioned by the Department of the Environment to produce a digital version of ward boundaries in England at the time of the Census. An agreement was subsequently reached by which Ordnance Survey became an additional partner in the ED-line consortium, with integration of the Ordnance Survey and ED-line boundary sets at ward level.

Users of census statistics who need digital census boundaries may of course also produce versions for their own use from the ED maps supplied by OPCS, provided that they have a licence from Ordnance Survey to cover the digitising of information from the maps. However, although OPCS do not charge for the digitising of census boundaries in such circumstances, the agreement of OPCS and Ordnance Survey must be sought for the supply of such boundaries to third parties.

At the time of writing (October 1992) the following geographical information, in summary, is available in digital form for England and Wales:

- spot National Grid references for EDs and wards, to 10 m resolution for EDs planned at 1:1250 or 1:2500 scale and to 100 m resolution elsewhere, supplied with SAS and/or LBS and included in the standard charge (hectare measurements provided by Ordnance Survey are also supplied with SAS and/or LBS for wards).
- National Grid references for each unit postcode (100 m resolutions for the 'first address' in a unit postcode) are included in the postcode to ED directories (see section 3.3.3); in effect this gives a 'cluster' of unit postcodes spot referenced within an ED, although postcodes split between EDs are only represented by one spot reference.
- the 'ED 91' boundaries for all census areas.
- the 'ED-line' boundaries for all census areas.

OPCS also supplies copies of Ordnance Survey 1:10,000 maps marked with ED, ward and civil parish (communities in Wales) boundaries; larger scale maps can be supplied for densely settled urban areas. A complete set of such maps is on long-term loan to local authorities in return for the information supplied for the planning of the 1991 Census, and sets on microfilm have been supplied for use in universities.

3.6 CONCLUSION

3.6.1 Census geography in the future

There are a number of challenging questions about the future of census geography. Some will be answered as the 1991 Census is used, others will have to be addressed as the next census is planned.

In the shorter term, it will be possible to find out whether the smaller area 'building bricks' in Scotland, and the comparability that they give with 1981 areas, has helped to realise a greater value from the Census in Scotland than in England and Wales. OPCS will also find out whether postcodes are feasible as an alternative geographic base for the census. It will be able to gauge how much of a market there is in England and Wales for 1991 statistics for precisely defined postcode sectors, or whether the directories of postcodes and EDs will give users much of what is required on a 'best fit' basis.

It will also be possible to judge whether the use of digital census boundaries purchased at commercial rates shows an adequate benefit over the use of spot references for the geographical analysis and presentation of the census results. More generally, it will be possible to see how far the use of GIS changes the use of census statistics by increasing geographical flexibility or by helping the integration of data from separate sources. It will also be possible to see whether a GIS approach proves adequate to give 1989-91 small area comparability in England and Wales, or whether exact comparability in some form of census tracts is, after all, required.

The Census Offices will remain open to suggestions of requirements for more documentation on census geography, and for any new products which users would wish to have and which could be produced from 1991 Census information. The implementation of an office-wide geographical support service in OPCS, and the continual development of the postcode base in Scotland, are also likely to lead to new products becoming available during the 1990s.

In the longer term, the Census Offices will be considering, in consultation with users, whether census statistical output areas should be divorced from census operational areas, and whether there is any realistic prospect of offering, or of needing to offer, geographic flexibility based on the locational referencing of individual addresses. The Census Offices are also likely to examine whether a future census operation would need the definition of small areas for enumeration or whether enumeration of pre-listed addresses could satisfy coverage requirements.

OPCS will be particularly concerned to determine whether it would be cost effective to introduce a postcode base into the next census of England and Wales on the Scottish model. But both Census Offices are also likely to examine whether there is a prospect that the geographic base for a future census could be provided more cost-effectively from an external multi-purpose base such as the proposed Ordnance Survey Address Point system.

A final question which concerns all those with an interest in the use of postcodes for information purposes is the continued availability, at affordable costs, of a system which depends primarily on continued use by the Royal Mail, or any successor organisations, in automated letter sorting.

This first part of this chapter has aimed to provide an ordered introduction to census geography. Part II by Robert Barr, is written from the point of view of the census user, raising issues and pointing to inter-connections between geography in the census and other aspects of the census.

3.7 FURTHER INFORMATION AND CONTACT POINTS

A summary of all developments is provided by the *Census Newsletter* produced five or six times a year by the Census Offices and distributed without charge. Names may be added to the mailing list by contacting OPCS Census Customer Services on 0329 813 800 (or for those in Scotland, GRO (Scotland) Census Customer Services on 031 334 4254), from whom prospectuses and other user guides are available.

Census Customer Services	Census Customer Services
Segensworth Road	GRO
Titchfield	Ladywell House
Fareham	Ladywell Road
Hants PO15 5RR	Edinburgh EH 12 7TF

For enquiries about the content of census reports or abstracts, the use of census results and any other general enquiry, please write to Census Division, OPCS at St Catherine's House, or phone 071 396 2024 or 071 396 2248, or write to Census Division, GRO at Ladywell House, or phone 031 314 4217.

For information on:

the ED 91 boundaries contact:
Graphical Data Capture Ltd
telephone 081-346 4959

the ED-line boundaries contact:
a member of the partnership between
the London Research Centre,
MVA Systematica, Ordnance Survey, and
MR-Data Graphics

London Research Centre: telephone 071-735 4250
MVA Systematica: telephone 0483 728051

3   Census geography

II — A review

Robert Barr

3.8 INTRODUCTION

'People Count', proclaims one of the census slogans, and indeed the census of population is concerned primarily with people and the households in which they live. Unfortunately people and households are highly mobile, moving around on a daily, weekly, annual and sometimes longer term basis. The journey to work or school, shopping, leisure, weekends, and holidays away, all affect short-term population patterns. Employment related moves and moving house as families grow, children leave home, or people retire, make up longer term patterns. All of these affect the 'population' — a term that in itself implies both people and place — and while this may be defined in terms of the attributes of the people, for example the school age population, it is more usually a way of describing a place in terms of the number and the characteristics of the people who live there.

In the census, places and people are inextricably linked. While we do not go to the extreme of the Biblical census, of demanding that everyone returns to their birth place, the census does distinguish between people's location on census night and their usual place of residence. As a result, two sets of counts can be produced — the population present, based on actual locations of people on census night and the resident population, based on normal residence (more detailed discussion of these different bases is given in chapter 2). The census also collects other geographic information: address of workplace, students' term-time addresses and address one year ago.

Complex questions are raised in deciding how these geographic variables should be coded. Geographers are concerned with the effect of places on human behaviour (and vice versa). They, and other statisticians, have made the social science community aware that the way in which areas are defined can affect the apparent relationships found between place and social characteristics. The two principal problems are known as the *modifiable areal unit problem* and the *ecological fallacy*. Briefly, the modifiable areal unit problem arises because there is an infinite number of ways of defining sets of areas into which to group people. Each would have different population characteristics even though the underlying characteristics of the individuals in the population were the same. The second problem, the ecological fallacy, is based on the fact that relationships may be found between the characteristics of areas (an association between levels of crime and the presence of a particular ethnic group, for example) which do not exist at the level of the individuals who make up those areas. These two problems are dealt with more fully in chapter 9.

Part I of this chapter provided a description of census geography and set out its aims. This part is devoted to a number of important issues surrounding census geography. It considers the part that geography plays in the planning, administration, publication and analysis of the census. The issues can be summarised (hopefully in a memorable way) as the five 'P's: practicality, privacy, parsimony, public accountability and political control and will be discussed under these headings.

3.9 PRACTICALITY

3.9.1 The construction of enumeration districts in Britain

In order to take the census, it is necessary to identify the population to be enumerated and to divide the workload among a large number of enumerators. In Britain we are fortunate that the country is relatively compact and the population is concentrated largely in the urban areas. We are also fortunate in being one of the best mapped parts of the world with detailed, and relatively up-to-date, large-scale topographic maps available for the whole of England, Wales and Scotland from Ordnance Survey and for Northern Ireland from the Ordnance Survey of Northern Ireland (Harley, 1975).

This makes it possible to divide up the entire land surface into enumeration districts (EDs) each of which is the responsibility of a single enumerator working over a period of about three weeks around census day. The enumerator is responsible for ensuring that everyone within their ED on census night is accounted for. As described in chapter 4, this involves delivering a census form to each household before census night and collecting it afterwards. Enumerators are also responsible for identifying all household spaces in the buildings in their ED by reference to a large scale Ordnance Survey map.

The planning of the ED framework for a census is a large and complicated undertaking. In Part I of this chapter, the consultation process which takes places prior to drawing up boundaries is discussed. While encouraging local authorities and other census users to express their views on the geography of the census, OPCS was responsible for drawing up the ED boundary framework for England and Wales in 1991 and the General Register Office (Scotland) was similarly responsible for Scotland.

ED boundaries have to fulfil many objectives — some essential, others desirable. The three essential characteristics are that they must not cross any statutory boundaries if they are to be used for census output, as in England and Wales; they must create manageable workloads for the enumerators; and they must completely cover the land mass with no districts overlapping or omitted. It is highly desirable that boundaries should be easy for enumerators to recognise, by following features such as roads, railways and rivers. There are other desirable characteristics that ED boundaries should have when used for output: they should meet any special local requirements, they should remain as similar to the boundaries used in the previous census as is practical, they should avoid crossing important non-statutory boundaries and their social characteristics should be as homogeneous as possible. It is never possible to conform to all the ideals. However, EDs have been successfully defined for each census and refined over the decades to make a practical building block for the collection and aggregation of population data.

The definition of EDs in England and Wales was carried out by OPCS in the period running up to the census. Two main products emerged from this process. The first was a 1991 Census *geographic database* (see Part I of this chapter) containing an entry for every 1991 ED. The database is a vital planning and administrative tool for the census. It includes ED identifiers, a number of characteristics of each ED and administrative fields for field management control and payments.

The second product was a set of up-to-date maps for England and Wales at a variety of scales onto which the new ED boundaries and local government boundaries had been marked. A total of some 77,000 base maps were used and about 400,000 copies of these were taken. Having added any available new information about housing stock changes, the new ED boundaries were drawn on the maps. Three different scale Ordnance Survey maps were used for ED planning: 1:10,000 (see map 3.1), 1:2,500 (see map 3.2) and 1:1,250 (example not shown).

The 1:2,500 maps were the ideal ones for enumerators to work with, but the series was more out of date than the others, so enumerators were supplied with the most up-to-date map available.

The planning process for EDs is summarised in section 3.2 of this chapter and chapter 4, section 4.4 describes the process by which a range of sociodemographic factors were used to estimate the workload that an ED would generate. Once defined, EDs were grouped into census districts (each of which was controlled by a Census Officer) for administrative purposes, and were given a unique identifier, the *Field ED Number*, described in part I of this chapter. The EDs that were defined in the planning stages of the census may not correspond perfectly with the output areas for which SAS are available. As explained in chapter 8, it was sometimes necessary to amalgamate EDs if the populations were smaller than anticipated and fell below the confidentiality threshold of 50 persons and 16 households.

The practical aspects of census geography are paramount. If the census was not organised effectively there would be either no data, or the data collected would be of little value. Yet these practical issues are of least interest to the data providers (those responsible for completing the census forms), and the census users. The remaining concerns of census geography are to satisfy them.

3.9.2 Census geography in the United States

Before leaving the practical aspects of defining census management geography, it is interesting to compare Britain with the US. In Britain, at present, it could be argued that no fully adequate or reliable geographically referenced address base exists, (almost certainly, no such base exists for census taking) although the Royal Mail's Postcode Address File (PAF) could become such an address base if it were fully cross referenced with the Ordnance Survey's large-scale maps as is proposed for the Address Point product (chapter 3, section 3.4.4). When Address Point is implemented, and an adequate updating system for it is devised, Britain will have a grid reference to 1 m resolution for every address in the country. This will give census planners the opportunity to draw any boundary they want and automatically generate an address list containing all the addresses within that boundary. That will allow considerably more flexibility both in planning censuses and in exploiting their results.

In the short term, it appears that the ED boundaries digitised for 1991, though of high quality and more than accurate enough for census mapping, may not perfectly enclose every Address Point property centroid for the EDs they describe. For England and Wales, at least, the relationship between the digitised boundaries of EDs and addresses will remain slightly fuzzy until after the 2001 Census. This is not the case in the US where it is possible to match addresses to census areas; in fact the normal definition of a census area in the US is a list of addresses.

In the US, census forms are mailed out to most households and the majority also mail them back. This is only possible because there is an accurate and relatively complete set of postal addresses for the population. This mailshot is augmented by enumerators following up missing forms and by enumeration of special populations such as itinerants. This is arguably a more efficient use of enumerators who can concentrate their time and effort on those respondents who most need it.

The contrast between Britain and the US is significant and important because it not only influences the administration of the census itself, but it also affects the flexibility of the output and the degree to which other data sets can be matched to the census. The history of the search in the US for a reliable address database is interesting and instructive. The absence of a reliable national large-scale map series like the Ordnance Survey maps in Britain led to the need to compile the Address Coding Guide, a comprehensive address register somewhat like the Postcode Address File, specifically for the purpose of facilitating mailed censuses. In order to link the address base to the geography of the census, a mapping system was devised for the 1970 US census. The system, known as GBF-DIME (Geographic Base File — Dual Independent Map Encoding), was initially created only for the metropolitan areas. The basis of the system was a computer file that recorded the characteristics of street segments: a segment is that section of a street between intersections or nodes. For each segment the name of the street was recorded, the start and end nodes numbered and the latitude and longitude of these nodes recorded. The accuracy of this system was relatively easy to check, and it allowed simplified maps to be drawn of the road network. Where administrative or other census boundaries did not follow roads, they were included as segments.

Thus by 1970 the US census had identified a system for defining census 'blocks', which usually corresponded to urban blocks surrounded by streets. This system provided an elegant cross-reference between the address (the most common geographical reference attached to social data), the built environment and the geography of the census and other administrative systems. Given any census block, for example, a set of all its constituent addresses could easily be generated. Conversely, any address could, by a simple look-up operation in the segment table, be correctly located in a census block and approximately located on a map.

This system proved its worth in 1970 and was extended to most urban areas for the 1980 Census, but was then replaced by a new system on broadly similar principles. For the 1990 Census, a comprehensive system known as TIGER (Topologically Integrated Geographical Encoding and Referencing) was created, which aimed to cover the entire country, and which provided a more effective database structure and which was linked to better maps, with the shape of roads and other segments recorded. The TIGER database was incomplete at the time of the 1990 Census. However, data collected in the census have been used to update it. The US Bureau of the Census has set about establishing cooperative arrangements with a

Map 3.1   An example of a 1:10,000 Ordnance Survey map used for ED planning

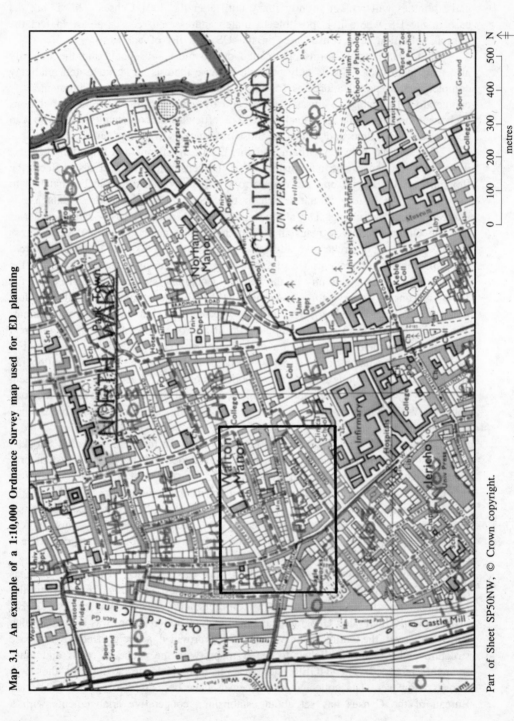

Part of Sheet SP50NW, © Crown copyright.

The map, which covers part of North ward in the City of Oxford, is an *extract* from the 1:10,000 maps which show ward boundaries and names together with ED boundaries (pecked lines) and numbers. The superimposed rectangle shows the area covered by the map 3.2 opposite. The position of boundaries is approximate and they are, for example, drawn to avoid obscuring road names where possible.

Map 3.2 Example of a 1:2,500 Ordnance Survey map used for ED planning

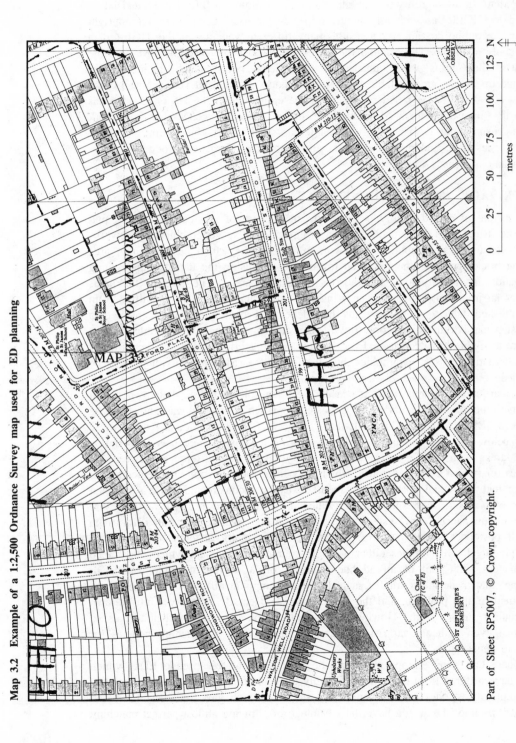

Part of Sheet SP5007, © Crown copyright.

The map, which covers the whole of one ED (FH15) and part of several other EDs in North Ward in the City of Oxford, is an *extract* from the 1:2,500 maps which show ward boundaries and names together with ED boundaries and numbers on the most detailed Ordnance Survey base maps. Where used, the larger scale 1:1,250 maps show similar information.

range of local government bodies throughout the US with the aim of maintaining TIGER as a national geo-referencing base and sampling frame for the census and many other government surveys as well as for routine administrative use.

Perhaps most significantly of all, the US Freedom of Information legislation has led to TIGER, as with all output from US censuses, being placed (copyright free) in the public domain. As a result, many different versions of the TIGER data are publicly available. The original files are available cheaply on CD-ROM from the Bureau of the Census, while enhanced, value-added versions which are more complete and up-to-date are available from some vendors. Simplified versions also exist, such as a $99 CD-ROM based road map of the entire USA. The US experience has shown that investment in a comprehensive and maintainable geographic framework for the census which is made freely available can significantly enhance the use made of the census data, and provide encouragement to many forms of productive cooperation among census users.

3.10 PRIVACY AND CONFIDENTIALITY

The principle of confidentiality is central to the release of any census derived material and it underlies many decisions concerning alternative geographical frameworks for the census. A geographical framework of the census which has minimum area building bricks provides the first step towards anonymising the data by aggregating information from individuals to statistics describing areas. The size of the areas provides an important element in ensuring that individuals cannot be identified from the published tables. As the census has developed over time, and census data processing has become more sophisticated, the size of area for which detailed census data are available has decreased. Ever smaller building bricks offer the flexibility to build alternative census geographies, but also present a risk that individuals may be identified.

A particular problem exists if census users are able to define their own output areas built up of small units such as postcodes (such a system was shown to be feasible by Rhind, 1990). While software can prevent the output of any area whose size is below the confidentiality threshold, a problem exists where users can define several areas which differ only marginally. By taking the difference between the statistics for two user defined-zones, which may differ only by one unit postcode, the data for that individual postcode can theoretically be reconstructed. As a significant number of postcodes correspond to individual properties there is a risk of disclosure in such circumstances. Any system that allowed ad hoc areas to be created from data for unit postcodes would have to prevent such marginally differenced areas from being produced. This implies either a single source of such data which maintained a permanent audit trail of all ad hoc requests, or, a degree of randomisation or 'blurring' that made the results of such detailed attempts at differencing meaningless. The extent of this problem, and the disclosure risk it entails, is not yet fully known and requires further study. However, the emphasis on census confidentiality is so great that even a theoretical risk is taken seriously when establishing policies for access to census data.

There had been a proposal to provide census output for 'pseudo EDs', which would have differed from the actual EDs only to the extent that they would comprise the complete postcodes (rather than part postcodes) which gave the 'best fit' to an ED. Such pseudo EDs would have the advantage of allowing almost perfect matching of address referenced data, but the disadvantage that they would not necessarily be continuous areas and would, in England and Wales, not have known boundaries. Because of the danger that census confidentiality could be breached by differencing, this proposal has been dropped for the 1991 Census. This is discussed further in chapter 9, section 9.2.2.

There are a number of ways in which the release of data for geographical areas may breach the confidentiality of an individual census return, and which must be guarded against. The most obvious is the very small area, where many of the tabulations will have single entries in the cells. The problem of small areas is dealt with by blurring (or modifying) counts and by setting a minimum threshold of households and individuals that must be present before any census data is released for an area. In 1981 that threshold was 25 persons and 8 households; for 1991 it has been raised to 50 persons and 16 households for the SAS and 1,000 persons and 320 households for the LBS. Particular tables may still contain very small cell counts for individuals with an unusual set of personal characteristics. This problem is dealt with either by the suppression of tables with few values or by the addition of random noise to the values of individual cells. Both pose problems for geographical analysis because they provide either an incomplete, or an inaccurate data set for certain areas. Chapter 8 discusses in some detail the effects of perturbation and suppression which affect the analyst. Where the geographical units concerned are census output areas such as EDs or wards the problem is less serious (though sparsely populated areas must be treated with caution). Particular difficulties are caused where very sparsely populated units are used — such as the kilometre grid squares which were used experimentally as output areas for the 1971 Census. The details of how confidentiality is maintained are dealt with in chapter 5.

3.10.1 Problems of geo-referencing census data

Census data are seldom used in isolation and most commercial and research uses of the census involve relating other geographically referenced data, such as health records or details of product purchases, to census data. As mentioned above, this matching is greatly facilitated by the availability of complete address and postcode lists which are cross-referenced by census output area. In the US the Census Bureau developed the Addmatch program (using addresses derived from pre-census listings) which was made freely available to census users for this very purpose; similar developments have not taken place in Britain. The census form included an assurance from the Registrar General that the respondent's name and address would not be entered into the computer; OPCS therefore hold no complete list of addresses generated by enumerators during data collection on any computer. Generating such a list by alternative means — for example as part of a separate recording of addresses and ED identifiers, would be costly. It might also be difficult to convince the public that this would not lead to individual data being released. The absence of an address to ED directory has led to many analytical efforts to generate such an index; these are discussed more fully in chapter 9.

The most detailed geographical index that will be available for 1991 in England and Wales, from which an approximate address to ED directory may be constructed, is the Postcode to ED Directory (chapter 3, section 3.3.3). While census forms have had postcodes recorded on them since 1981 and postcodes of workplaces and previous addresses were used in area coding, in 1991 postcodes for addresses of enumeration as well were entered onto the computer together with other data from the form. The directory allocates each postcode to an enumeration district. Where a postcode is broken by an ED boundary the number of households falling into each of its constituent EDs will be given. Further details of the Directory are given in chapters 7 and 9 and in the 1991 Census *User Guide 26*. In Scotland there will be a postcode-output area index file which gives an exact match between postcodes and Output Areas (see chapter 3, section 3.5.1).

While every possible step is taken to ensure the confidentiality of census data at the level of the individual, there is a way in which collective privacy is breached by the publication of data for areas. The most popular value added products from the census are various sociodemographic classifications. A number of companies such as CACI, CCN, Pinpoint and Infolink use multivariate methods to classify census enumeration districts into 30 or more neighbourhood types based on their social profiles. Most of these profiles enable companies marketing their products, and other organisations such as the health service or police authorities, to relate the service records of their customers to the census profiles of their home areas. While census information is not available at the level of the postcode unit, most of the demographic classifications are produced in such a way that any record with a postcode can be easily associated with the social area classification code. It is important to note that these area classifications are based on the patterns of association of a large number of small area statistics, and the descriptors given to each category simply pick out the most distinctive features.

These profiles are used by marketing companies to target mail shots to areas where a high proportion of the residents may be expected to have an interest in a particular set of products or services. A less desirable use of such classifications — and, indeed, any area level information — is to blacklist areas with particular social characteristics (Openshaw, 1989). People identified as living in particular types of area may be denied credit or insurance or may be subject to special terms for financial transactions. Such policies can be seen as either discriminatory or as prudent business practice. These uses are all based on the premise that area-level classifications can provide a very cheap alternative to obtaining individual level data through a survey. Because of the dangers of making assumptions about individuals on the basis of aggregate information describing the area in which they live, such linkages have a high failure rate in predicting the characteristics of individual residents.

Where special health, or educational promotion schemes need to be well targeted, aggregate information on just two or three key variables — for example, the age and health profile of the area — may provide a better basis for concentrating effort than the social classification schemes.

3.11 PARSIMONY

It is the objective of many statistical procedures to achieve 'parsimony' — the reduction of a large number of observations to a small number of descriptive statistics that summarise those observations. In early censuses this parsimony was achieved by asking few questions, combining the answers in a limited and simple number of ways, and reporting the results for large areas. Many statistics were available only at the county level. The census now generates one of the largest sets of social data available. Although the development of information technology is making the handling of such data sets easier, data sets of this size still create processing and publication problems. By publishing data for places, rather than people, the size of the data set to be handled can be limited to manageable proportions in two ways. The size of area for which data is published can be made large. The number of statistics describing each area can be kept small. The product of the number of places, which can be thought of as the rows in a census data matrix, and individual variables that can be represented, determines the size of this matrix. As technology has improved over time both the number of output areas and the number of statistics available for them has grown. Despite aggregation by area, there is an almost unlimited number of ways in which the responses to census questions can be combined to provide statistics for areas.

We have already seen (Part I of this chapter) that the number of different administrative areas for which census output is produced is prodigious. Yet the administrative divisions in the country do not necessarily match, either in scale or composition, the distribution of the population as reflected by the census. The statistical output areas reflect yet another search for parsimony and homogeneity.

In addition to the statutory and geostatistical areas postcode based areas will be used for output in both England and Wales and Scotland. The details of postcode based output were discussed in Part I of this chapter. In England and Wales statistical output will be provided for postcode sectors which contain an average of some 2,000 households.

Postcodes, if adopted in England and Wales to the same extent as in Scotland may, one day, be the sixth 'P' of census geography. However, at present, they neither reflect administrative boundaries (postcodes cross virtually all statutory boundaries) nor do they reflect social reality or the built environment. They are difficult to identify on the ground, as the system is not designed to fill the available land area, but only to include all delivery points. This can be seen in map 3.3. Scottish ED boundaries also appear far more complex, and less well related to ground features than English or Welsh ED boundaries (except in the few cases where local authorities defined and submitted their own postcode based ED boundaries to OPCS for use in 1991).

The definition of postcodes is delegated by the Royal Mail to local offices and their completeness and accuracy can vary from area to area. While postcodes are generally very stable over time, they can be re-defined at any time to reflect local postal requirements and old postcodes can be re-used sometimes as soon as six months after their withdrawal. Postcodes are fundamentally an organisational tool for the delivery of mail and as such are maintained and controlled by the Royal Mail, which, while happy to see them widely used for statistical, marketing and other purposes, is unwilling to adapt the system to meet other users requirements (Raper, Rhind and Shepherd, 1992).

For planning purposes, postcodes give a good idea of where changes in enumeration workload have taken place (by tracking the growth in postcodes from 1981 to 1991). The postal address and its included, or implicit, postcode is the most commonly used geographical reference. Census data are usually related to data that have been collected, and aggregated, from other sources rather than used in isolation. Service or sales data from both public and private organisations are very frequently postcoded. By going one step further and creating all output areas from unit post code areas, it becomes possible to build a wide range of sizes and configurations of areas all of which relate to the references potential users already have attached to

Map 3.3 An example of an OS map showing boundaries of postcodes and EDs for an area in Scotland

Boundaries

———— postcodes

▬▬▬▬ postcode/enumeration districts

For simplicity, a postcode is labelled only with its inward part, i.e. the last three letters. The outward part for postcodes for most of this map is G69, for the south edge is G71. So, for example, the postcode labelled 7AW is G69 7AW.

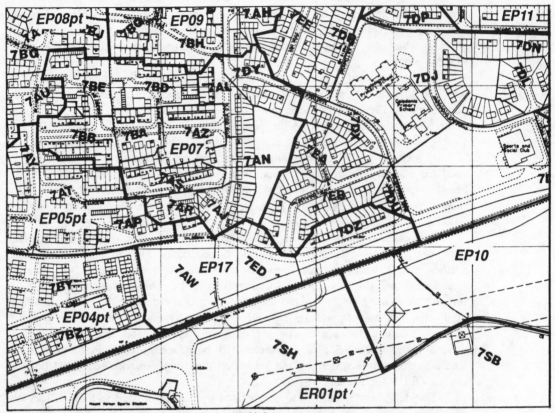

Part of plan NS6763 (scale 1:2500 reduced in size by one third)

© Crown copyright.

Source: *Population Trends,* 1990, vol. 60, p.15.

their data. The spatial imprecision of postcodes is relatively unimportant compared to their wide use and the simplicity of matching to areas based on them. While statisticians and geographers may agonise about the imprecision, most other census users are happy to have easy to use, locality based approximations.

The ideal output from the census would be limited to a user defined set of variables for a user defined set of zones which would make up the smallest data matrix fit for the user's purpose. The adoption of a statutory area-based census geography was initially a tool for the parsimonious production of statistics. Increased data processing capacity has led to the production of a very large census data matrix, from which users can select geographical areas and variables of interest. If the requirements of confidentiality can be accommodated the future holds the prospect of the ultimate in parsimony — a user defined matrix of the minimum size, and exactly specified to meet the user's specific needs.

3.12 PUBLIC ACCOUNTABILITY

The public sector in general, and local authorities in particular, differ from most private enterprises, in that they have a responsibility to provide services to everyone living within their boundaries. A private enterprise has a responsibility to its customers, and to its shareholders, but is not normally publicly accountable for the universality of its provision. Customers in the private sector identify themselves by buying goods or services. Market research may seek to identify additional potential customers, but there is no penalty other than a commercial one for failing to identify the extent of the market. By contrast local and health authorities are funded on the basis of a range of indices, in particular the Standard Spending Assessment (Bennett, 1980). They incorporate census-based estimates of population numbers and census derived factors reflecting the needs of the local population. Organisations such as the Chartered Institute of Public Finance and Accountancy monitor the expenditure of local authorities on a *per capita* basis to ensure that the inputs provided from government sources are being spent efficiently and equitably. The census, and the annual mid-year estimates during the intercensal decade provide the basis for public accounting and, in turn, public accountability.

Census data are published for a range of the administrative areas of local government and the health service. The boundaries are important because resources are allocated to these areas to meet defined social needs and the census provides a vital source of information for those responsible for the allocation of services. The modifiable areal unit problem disappears once statutory boundaries are defined because discussions concerning alternative statistical units become largely academic. An advantage of local authority and health authority boundaries is their relative stability over time. The largest redrawing of local government boundaries since the 19th century took place in 1974 in England and Wales, following the Maud Report on local government reorganisation. In Scotland it occurred a year later following the Wheatley Report. The 1971 Census data were aggregated to both pre- and post-1974 local government areas leading to a total of 22 different types of output area in all.

The Local Government Boundary Commissions examine local authority boundaries from time to time and adjudicate on proposals for change. However, historically, local authority boundaries have proved to be exceptionally stable. This may not be the case during the 1990s as there are proposals for a move from the two tiers of local government, outside the metropolitan counties, to a system based on a single tier. This reorganisation is to be based, initially at least, on local proposals for amalgamations and reallocation of duties, so it is likely to lead to a period of instability before a new administrative map of Britain emerges.

Whilst we have stressed public accountability and public accounting as the reasons for the dominance of the statutory boundaries in census output, such boundaries can, over time, acquire social and economic significance, particularly where radical policies are pursued. The ambition of certain local authorities to become the dominant landlords within their area of jurisdiction, pursued continuously from the 1930s to the 1970s, may become a social reality in the concentration of public housing — and high rates of unemployment — within their boundaries. The effect of such processes are evident from the discontinuity of certain census indicators at an administrative boundary. The conventional problem of the modifiable areal unit (see chapter 9) is one of statistical definition — particular local and central government policies and initiatives can genuinely modify the characteristics of administrative areas even if their boundaries were originally relatively arbitrary. Census data published on a statutory boundary base provide us with a powerful tool to track such changes.

Most, though not all, statutory areas are governed by elected councils or by appointed members of councils that fall within their areas. This political reality is also reflected in the geography of the census.

3.13 POLITICAL CONTROL

The plans for the census are approved, and usually debated, by Parliament, and the reports of the census are laid before Parliament. So Parliament exercises ultimate control over the form and content of the census. Data are published for all the constituencies that elect Members of Parliament, and for the wards that elect County and District councillors. The census provides politicians with a profile of their electorate which enables them to check that their constituents are receiving a fair share of resources from their respective local and central governmental authorities. Politicians are in a key position to ensure public accountability both at an intra- as well as at an inter-authority level. The data provided in the census both for their local authority areas as a whole and for their individual constituencies provide them with a vital tool for this task.

The Boundary Commissions for England and Wales (located in OPCS) and for Scotland (located in the Scottish Office) are required by law to keep the Parliamentary constituencies under review. These commissions use information on the number of registered electors, not census information; however, the Local Government Boundary Commission, responsible for local government boundaries, receives much evidence based on census data, from individuals and organisations who wish to argue for boundary changes.

Electoral boundaries, particularly ward boundaries, are relatively frequently adjusted. It is a general democratic principle that equality of representation involves approximately equal numbers of electors in constituencies of the same type, electing each representative. Population shifts within local authorities lead to a need for the redrawing, or sometimes the amalgamation of electoral wards to establish multi-member electoral units. In contrast, the growth and the decline of the population of administrative authorities does not cause a problem and administrative boundaries have much greater stability over time.

The recommendations of the Boundary Commissions are open to public and political scrutiny and once agreed are placed before Parliament for approval. In the US a much larger range of public officials are elected and boundaries are necessary for municipal, county, state, and national (House and Senate) elections. A reassessment of electoral boundaries is mandatory after each census and the process involves much wider participation than is common in the UK. Final plans for the boundaries of areas returning national politicians are then scrutinised by the Federal Department of Justice before acceptance.

While to the general public the census is seen largely as an administrative exercise, it is also an important tool of democratic government. It is for this reason that, despite the availability of an ever larger number of alternative administrative sources of population data, conventional head count censuses are likely to survive into the 21st century. It is not enough for a census to be effective and accurate, it needs to be seen to be conducted fairly and understandably as so many of our democratic processes are influenced by its results.

3.14 CONCLUSION

The discussion so far has emphasised the general principles behind the definition of, and the need for a geographical framework for the census. The flexibility of the 1991 Census has been enhanced by a finer level directory which will allow unit postcodes to be related to enumeration districts. At the same time as the census SAS were published, two sets of digital boundary files of English and Welsh enumeration districts became commercially available. GRO(S) have digitised, and are selling all boundaries of the Scottish output areas (Part I of this chapter gives details of both). These additional products, and the likelihood that enhanced geographical coordinates may be published for the unit postcodes over the next few years, will provide the scope for much more flexible use of the 1991 Census data than has ever been possible before. The methods, and the potential pitfalls in the application of such methods are discussed in chapter 9. Ordnance Survey have also produced and undertaken to maintain an up-to-date set of digital boundaries for the British statutory areas down to ward level. These promise scope for a dynamic census geography for 1991 rather than one frozen to the boundaries as defined on census day, as was the case in 1981.

The 1991 Census will be seen as one where a large number of incremental improvements to an already tried and tested geographical framework yielded many advantages for census users. It marks, with the availability of the Samples of Anonymised Records, the end of census data constrained entirely by geography. At the same time the flexibility and reliability of the geographical framework for the census has been greatly enhanced. In Scotland it is hoped that considerable investment in a more versatile postcode-based method of defining EDs and output areas will have been entirely paid for by efficiency savings made possible through the enlargement of EDs and the reduction in the number of enumerators and also through sales of digital products and automation of area planning for the next census. The 1990s also mark the beginning of the end of census geography being the result of a series of relatively unrelated ad hoc decennial exercises. OPCS are now examining the possibility of establishing a maintained geographical framework that will meet not only the needs of the census but many other government statistical and administrative requirements.

It is to be hoped that a system of audit that guarantees confidentiality will eventually lead to the adoption of a totally flexible system of handling individual census records that will free census users from the constraints imposed by present systems of geographical aggregation and analysis. In the meantime the geographical framework for the census remains both a strength and a weakness of the entire enterprise.

4 Fieldwork and data processing

Angela Dale

4.1 INTRODUCTION

The foundation of the 1991 Census enterprise and the statutory basis to it have been described in chapter 1. This chapter is concerned with the fieldwork, the subsequent data processing, and the way in which this shaped the final products from the 1991 Census. The chapter provides a context for later discussion on specific forms of output. It aims to highlight the strengths and limitations of the data and to clarify the relationship between the different forms of output. Chapter 6 (I), on the Census Validation Survey, provides preliminary information on the extent to which the Census succeeded in its aim of enumerating the population and suggests, using results from the 1981 Post-Enumeration Survey, areas where the quality of enumeration in the 1991 Census may be least good.

One of the most important requirements of a successful census is to ensure that coverage is complete and accurate and that data are safely and speedily transferred from schedules to computer. The enormity of the undertaking, and the importance attached to producing outputs to a tight deadline within a fixed budget mean that, as far as possible, procedures must be tried and tested. There is little margin for error in such an undertaking and no scope for taking risks. This argues for a conservative approach to changes in data collection and processing procedures between censuses. The use of such innovations as postal delivery and collection and machine reading of forms were evaluated but not adopted in the 1991 Census. However, even after the most careful preparations there can still be problems, as illustrated by the delay in processing the 1991 Census results (see section 4.5.4).

Planning for the 1991 Census began almost as soon as the 1981 Census was completed. Table 4.1 shows the key dates in planning the 1991 Census. Once the effectiveness of the 1981 Census was assessed, a period of preparation for the 1991 Census began, timed so that a Census Order could be laid before Parliament by the end of 1989.

Examples of the long and detailed planning for the Census include the consultation and testing of a question on ethnic group after the decision not to include a question in the 1981 Census (White, 1990); the decision-making process over computing hardware and software for the 1991 Census which began in the mid-1980s; and the search for suitable accommodation to house the data entry process.

Table 4.1

Summary of the key dates in planning the 1991 Census

1981-2	Evaluation of the 1981 Census
1983	Parliamentary announcement of decision not to hold a mid-term (1986) census but to plan on assumption next census would be 1991
	De-briefing of users
1984	Census Offices set broad strategy for planning 1991 Census
	Formation of project groups on specific topics
1985/86	Ethnic group question wording tests
1987	Advisory groups set up (government departments, local authorities, health authorities)
	Consultation with users on geographical base
	Census test (April)
	Parliamentary announcement of decision to continue to plan for census in 1991
1988	Proposed package put together (based on tests and consultation)
	Publication of White Paper setting out government proposals for 1991 Census
1988-90	Consultation with users on form of output
1989	Census test (April)
	Legislation (Census Order) debated
1990	Legislation made — regulations published containing census questionnaire
	Processing dress rehearsal starts
1991	April 21, Census Day

4.2 PRE-CENSUS TESTS

Recent censuses have been preceded by small-scale voluntary field tests of questions and their wording, together with larger scale tests and 'rehearsals' of the whole field operation. The type of development that takes place is discussed below, with particular reference to the ethnic group question and the long-term illness question.

4.2.1 The ethnic group question

This question was the subject of extensive debate and testing. Following the decision not to include a question in the 1981 Census, a Sub-Committee of the House of Commons Race Relations Committee (the Sub-Committee on Race Relations and Immigration) reported in May 1983 with a recommendation that a question on racial or ethnic origin should be included in future censuses, subject to confidentiality assurances and a clear intention that the information would be used to promote programmes against racial discrimination and disadvantage (White, 1990; Sillitoe and White, 1992).

Small-scale tests were carried out in 1985 and 1986 (Sillitoe, 1987) following which the 1988 White Paper, *1991 Census of Population* (Cmnd 430), proposed that a question on ethnic group should be included in the Census provided that a further trial of the question in the 1989 'dress rehearsal' census test was successful. In this respect the question was different from other questions which were firm policy in the White Paper.

The value of the ethnic group question is stated thus:

'The information from the question on ethnic group will enable central and local government and health authorities to allocate resources and plan programmes taking account of the special needs of the ethnic minority groups. It will provide comparisons of patterns of employment, housing and so on of people in different ethnic groups in

85

different parts of the country and this will help identify areas of disadvantage. The information will also help the Government and local authorities carry out their responsibilities under the Race Relations Act 1976.' (White, 1990)

The outcome of the trial is considered under section 4.2.3.

4.2.2 The 1987 census test

The 1987 census test was primarily concerned with testing the field procedures for the 1991 Census. The opportunity was also taken to test some revised or new census questions, but a further test specifically concerned with question wording was held in autumn 1987. (The ethnic group question was *not* included in these tests.) The fieldwork procedures for the 1991 Census had to take account of the increased mobility of the population, the growth of one-person households, second homes and overseas holidays, all of which made it harder to ensure that a complete enumeration would take place (Pearce, Clark and Baird, 1988).

The 1987 test provided a number of positive results. It confirmed that Assistant Census Officers could be effectively used to check the quality of returns from enumerators, and to check the accuracy of an initial listing of properties made by the enumerator. It suggested that the identification of absent households — as opposed, for example, to vacant property — could be improved and that absent householders could be expected to return forms. It also allowed refinements to be made to a weighting system applied to enumerators' workloads and identified improved methods for field payments — about 25 per cent of the total cost of the census.

However, the census test also indicated the possibility of a low response rate, particularly in the inner city areas, and flagged up difficulties experienced by enumerators in locating dwellings. These problems were also raised by the 1989 census test.

4.2.3 The 1989 census test

The 1989 census test represented a dress rehearsal of some of the plans and procedures for the 1991 Census. It also contained the ethnic group question, to test its acceptability with the public. About 90,000 households were covered in three areas of England and three areas of Scotland, chosen to provide a cross-section of the population and of types of housing which would be encountered in the full census.

It tested the methods set up to manage information coming from the field, and identified steps necessary to ensure recruitment of enumerators and the methods of paying them. The data generated by the census test forms were used to test all stages of the data processing system and, in particular, to assess the extent to which postcodes of enumeration could be adequately collected. Only 6 per cent of household forms had an incomplete or missing postcode for the address of enumeration. Those missing could be imputed by an automatic system or by reference to directories.

The way in which enumerators treated the accommodation of unrelated groups of people was also checked — particularly whether it was identified correctly as a household or a communal establishment. It was concluded that where accommodation for such groups was arranged mainly as flats or bedsits, enumerators treated it as such, and it could not therefore be distinguished from other households; where communal catering facilities were present, enumerators treated the accommodation correctly as communal establishments.

One of the main purposes of the 1989 census test was to establish the acceptability of the ethnic question and whether its inclusion affected the overall response rate. The following paragraphs show the type of information which can be gathered in a test, although no other question for the 1991 Census was tested as extensively.

The overall response rate to the voluntary test was 60 per cent — a result in line with the 1987 voluntary test which did not include the ethnic question. However, there was considerable variation in response rates between the sample areas. East Lothian had the highest response rate (89 per cent) whilst the response rate of 42 per cent in Birmingham was of particular concern and resulted in further work to establish the reasons for the low return rate. It was thought to have been influenced by a local Member of Parliament who campaigned against cooperation in the voluntary test. The main source of information on the coverage and quality of the census test was a Post-Enumeration Survey (PES) (White, 1990) which covered both households which had cooperated and those which had not. The PES sample was designed to interview roughly comparable numbers of households containing Black or Asian people and of households containing only White people, and also to interview a substantial number of households where the ethnic question had not been answered or where an answer had been written in (as opposed to the answer categories which could be ticked).

In attempting to establish why households had not taken part in the census test, the PES found that less than 0.5 per cent of the total sample gave the ethnic question as a reason for not responding. Ten per cent of informants, including 23 per cent of Black informants, said they were 'too busy' or 'could not be bothered' to take part in the test, whilst language difficulties prevented 8 per cent of Asians from completing the form. However, census test enumerators failed to contact 17 per cent of eligible households. This high figure explained the 13 per cent of informants in the PES who could not remember the census test enumerator calling. It also indicated that, as in the 1987 census test, enumerators failed to locate a significant proportion of eligible households.

Those who took part in the test were asked if they had any objections to answering any of the questions on the form. Overall, 7 per cent mentioned an objection to the ethnic group question — only 1 per cent higher than those who mentioned an objection to the question on long-term illness and 2 per cent higher than those objecting to the name of employer and address of workplace. However, of those with objections to the question, Black groups were more heavily represented than other groups — 19 per cent in comparison with 7 per cent for Asian and 5 per cent for Whites. The group whom enumerators failed to contact in the test was also asked if they objected to the ethnic group question. The proportions reporting an objection were very similar to those who had taken part in the test.

The PES also provided a measure of the quality of the response to the ethnic group question. Responses which agreed with those established by the interviewer were combined with responses where two or more boxes were ticked but the interviewer judged that a valid answer could be obtained in processing. If these latter were assumed to be 'accurate', then there was a 90 per cent accuracy rate for 'Whites', 85 per cent for 'Blacks', 89 per cent for 'Asians' and 82 per cent for other groups.

On the basis of these results it was concluded that the presence of the ethnic group question was not a significant cause of non-response in the census test and that the level of accuracy was acceptably high. This met the White Paper criteria for inclusion of the question (OPCS and GRO(S), 1988), and it was finally decided that the census would contain the question on ethnic group (OPCS and GRO(S), 1990a, b).

4.2.4 The introduction of a question on long-term illness

Another census topic which was subject to quite extensive testing — the 1987 rather than the 1989 test — was an indicator of health. Central government and local and health authorities already used census information on the age structure of the population to assess the needs for services and the budgets therefore required. It was felt that the 1991 Census would provide a much firmer basis for such assessments, particularly at the local level, if an indicator of illness or disability could be included.

The 1987 census test included two possible question on health, shown in figure 4.1 (Pearce and Thomas, 1990). The first was designed to elicit information about specific disabilities, whilst the second asked about limiting long-term illness and also short-term illness over the past two weeks. The General Household Survey (GHS) had shown that there was a correlation between reported illness and level of use of general practitioner services and hospital out-patient and in-patient services. Two versions of the test form were produced, identical except for having only one of the health questions.

The census test showed that the disability question did not work well. In 21 per cent of cases there was no answer and the follow-up study found that non-respondents were more likely than average to be disabled. Only 30 per cent of those identified at interview as disabled had indicated this on the census test form. It was therefore decided that the quality of information was too poor to use the question in the 1991 Census.

However, results on the long-term illness question were consistent with those obtained from the GHS and seemed to be slightly better than the disability question as an indicator of some form of disability. The question was correctly answered for 91 per cent of persons; 4 per cent were described incorrectly and there was no answer for 5 per cent (Pearce and Thomas, 1990). The short-term illness question worked less well, with less than 50 per cent agreement with the follow-up survey and it was concluded that it would add little to the prediction of health service usage. Therefore only a long-term illness question was included in the White Paper proposals and adopted for the 1991 Census.

The census question was the same as that used in the GHS during the 1980s, with the important exception that the GHS did not add the specific reference to the inclusion of age-related (illness) problems. In comparison with the GHS, the census question may be expected to have included a higher proportion of the elderly who report a limiting long-term illness. Benzeval and Judge (1993) attempted to assess the value of this question by replicating it in the OPCS Omnibus Survey. They confirmed that the age-related qualifier appeared to encourage the reporting of a limiting long-standing illness by those aged 75 and over, but lower rates of reporting were found amongst younger age groups, among both men and women. They also suggested that the limiting long-standing illness question was a weaker predictor of health service when used on its own and much more powerful when combined with information on acute illness. They concluded that best guidance on the relative needs of different areas for health care could be obtained by combining information on limiting long-standing illness with other sociodemographic variables such as age, tenure and car ownership.

Figure 4.1 The disability and long-standing illness questions used in the 1987 wording test

Answers to the remaining questions are not required for children under five years

Has difficulty in:

- dressing him/herself ☐ 1

- bending or lifting ☐ 2

- gripping or reaching ☐ 3

- hearing conversation even if wearing a a hearing aid ☐ 4

- reading newspaper print, even when wearing glasses or contact lenses ☐ 5

8. Does the person have any of the long-term difficulties or disabilities listed?

   Tick all difficulties the person has, **including any that are due to old age.** However, box 8 need not be ticked for persons aged over 65.

   For children aged 15 or under tick if the child has more difficulty than is usual for its age.

   If no difficulties, tick box 9.

Has great difficulty in climbing stairs ☐ 6

Unable to live alone without help from other people ☐ 7

Limited in the paid work, education or training he/she can do because of health problems, disability or handicap ☐ 8

Has none of the problems or disabilities listed above ☐ 9

Answers to the remaining questions are not required for children under five years

8a. Does the person have any long-term illness, health problem or handicap which limits his / her daily activities or the work he/she can do? **Include problems which are due to old age.**

Yes, has a health problem which limits activities ☐ 1

Has no such health problem ☐ 2

b. Over the the two weeks up to and including has the person had any short term illness which kept him/her away from work or education for a day or more, or limited his/her daily activities?

Yes, has had an illness which limited activities ☐ 1

Has had no such illness ☐ 2

Source: *Population Trends* 1990, vol. 61 p. 29

4.3 PUBLICITY FOR THE 1991 CENSUS: 'IT COUNTS BECAUSE YOU COUNT'

Complete and accurate coverage has already been identified as one of the most important objectives of the 1991 Census. To achieve this the public needed to know that a census was to be conducted, to be convinced of its importance and to believe that information given would be treated confidentially. Therefore publicity played a vital role in the execution of the 1991 Census.

The OPCS publicity strategy was developed for the 1989 census test and then carried forward, with appropriate modifications, into the plans for the 1991 Census. This strategy was developed in the context of growing concerns amongst the public about confidentiality and privacy and also in the light of the problems encountered by (former) West Germany in the 1980s — although the constitutional, political and national backgrounds to the problems were particular to West Germany and were not replicated in the UK. These concerns resulted in the 1981 Census in West Germany being delayed until 1987, largely because of public campaigns over privacy and confidentiality, focusing particularly on the use of the census to correct the local registers of population (Langevin, Begeot and Pearce, 1992).

The OPCS publicity strategy identified three areas where particular problems might be encountered and which therefore needed special attention. These were: (1) misconceptions by the public about use of census returns to compile community charge registers, (2) the inclusion of the ethnic group question and (3) difficulty in contacting householders.

In the event, the latter problem turned out to be the most important. The various causes included: reluctance to answer the door, particularly in inner city areas; changing working patterns; an increase in one-person households; and people simply wanting to avoid completing official forms. The latter reason, of course, is also likely to have been associated with worries about the community charge.[1]

The approach used to overcome these problems was to spell out to the public the reasons for conducting a census and to stress the confidential treatment of all information given. This was done using a paid advertising campaign including both posters and television. Free publicity in both national and local media was generated by the newsworthiness of the census. Briefing materials were provided for local authorities, citizens advice bureaux, race relations organisations and other voluntary bodies. Finally, and, as it turned out, probably of greatest effect, were two documents distributed by census field staff — the Advance Round Leaflet and the Information Leaflet delivered with the census form. The Advance Round Leaflet was delivered two to three weeks before census day as part of the enumerators' task to list all buildings in their enumeration districts (EDs) (see section 4.4.3). A subsequent survey showed that nearly 60 per cent of households recalled seeing this. The Information Leaflet, recalled by 46 per cent of households, was translated into 12 languages and also into braille. The total cost of the publicity campaign was some £2.5 million for Great Britain.

4.4 THE 1991 CENSUS FIELDWORK

As in 1981 in England and Wales, a four-tier fieldwork structure was used in 1991 throughout Great Britain: 135 Census Area Managers (CAMs), who managed 2,562 Census Officers, who in turn managed 7,750 Assistant Census Officers who managed the 117,600 enumerators. This is summarised in figure 4.2. Each Census Officer was responsible for a Census District, assisted by about three Assistant Census Officers. The entire country was divided into areas which reflected this hierarchy, with the

[1] An announcement that the community charge was to be abandoned was made by the Prime Minister, John Major, a couple of weeks before the 1991 Census took place.

Figure 4.2 1991 Census field staff, Great Britain

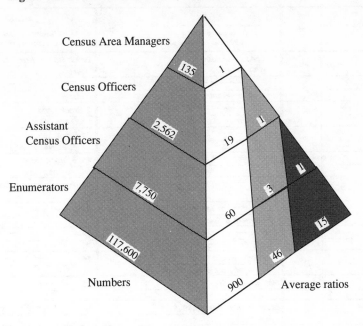

Census Area Managers

Census Officers

Assistant
Census Officers

Enumerators

Numbers

Average ratios

basic geographic unit for census fieldwork as the ED. Most EDs represented the number of households that a census enumerator could be expected to cover within the allocated time, taking account of local circumstances. A few small EDs were grouped to form 'enumeration areas' for field purposes. The planning of EDs as field (and statistical areas in England and Wales) took place during 1990 and is discussed in chapter 3 (I). Once ED boundaries were agreed, they were drawn on large-scale Ordnance Survey maps, copies of which were issued to Census Officers, Assistant Census Officers and enumerators at the start of fieldwork.

EDs in England and Wales were graded into seven categories by expected difficulty of enumeration. The number of households in an ED ranged from 50–120 for the most difficult ED to 175–250 for the most straightforward. The 120,000 EDs in Great Britain were grouped into 2,600 Census Districts. This grouping was designed to give a standard workload: the number of EDs in each Census District ranged from 25–35 for the most difficult to 50–60 for the simplest. The grading of EDs by difficulty allowed payment of a fixed fee to enumerators, although special topping-up payments were also made when more households than expected were found in an ED.

4.4.1 The geographic database (GDB)

Once ED boundaries were agreed, this information was entered into the 1991 Census geographic database (GDB). The database (chapter 3 (I)) contains a record for each ED and provided the base for control of the field management system, the input processing operation, and, finally, the creation of the statistical output. The GDB will be referred to again in following sections.

Figure 4.3 Enumeration Record: Part 1, for listing addresses during the Advance round

Address (Location or Description of Premises - as required)	Code	Address (Location or Description of Premises - as required)	Code	Address (Location or Description of Premises - as required)	Code
8 West Downs Close	P	11 Acacia Avenue / 1st Floor Back	P	Brook House, Brook Lane / Flat 3	P
10 ———"———	P	1st Floor Front	P	———"——— / Flat 4	P
12 ———"———	P	———"——— / 2nd Floor	P	2 Brook Lane / Greengrocers	NR
14 ———"———	P	13 ———"———	P	2a Brook Lane / Flat above Greengrocers	PR
Esso Garage	NR	15 ———"———	P	4 - 8 Brook Lane / Childrens Home	CE
Row of lock-up shops	NR	17 ———"———	P	Brook Lane Primary School	NR
1 Acacia Avenue	P	19 ———"——— / Basement & Ground	P	10 Brook Lane	P
3 ———"———	P	———"——— / 1st & 2nd Floors	P	12 ———"———	P
5 ———"———	P	The Eagle Public House / Corner of Acacia Ave/Brook Lane	NR	14 ———"———	P
7 - 9 Acacia Avenue / Retirement Home	CE	Flat above Pub	PR	16 ———"———	P
11 Acacia Avenue / Basement Flat	P	Brook House, Brook Lane / Flat 1	P	18 ———"———	P
———"——— / Ground Floor	P	———"——— / Flat 2	P	Waste land with Caravan / Board up - being developed?	?

No. of Private residences (P) [26] No. of Partly Residential Premises (PR) [2] No. of Non-Residential Buildings (NR) [5] No. of Communal Establishments (CE) [2]

Source: *1991 Census Field Manual*, OPCS, 1990

Figure 4.4 Enumeration Record: Part 2, for private residences and partly resident premises

Address (Location or Description of Premises - as required)	Panel A Code Building Bracket†	Name No. of persons	Del.	Coll.	Source	No. of rooms	Type of accommodation Lowest Floor	Notes	ACO Completion of form check	Form No.	Box 0 Ticked	Boxes 1 or 2 Ticked	Total on form K + L
A	B	C	D	E	F	G	H	I	1 2 3 4	J	K	L	M
18 Colville Avenue	2	Stevens 7	√2	√2				Not Monday		1	6	1	7
20 ———"——— / Flat above hairdressers	5	Carter 4	√+I	√+I				22/4 - 11am / 24/4 - 5.30pm		2	4		4
22 ———"——— / Basement Flat	7	Mrs Robinson 3	√SR	√				Collect after 6pm / Envelope not used		3	3		3
———"——— / Ground Floor Flat	8	Evans	√ (OTH)	√	3	5	4	No furniture or curtains / Occupied from 20/4 / Collect 24/4		4	2		2
———"——— / First Floor Flat	8	Allen 3	√ABS	√ABS	1	4	3	Entire household away / 19/4 -22/4 - form completed anyway		5		3	3
24 ———"———	3		V (IMP)	V (IMP)	2	8		Neighbour says property / renovated throughout / No change at Collection		6			
18 Colville Avenue / Caravan in back garden	1	Anderson 2	√	√						7	2		2
Nelson House, Colville Avenue / Flat 1	6	Burrows 4	√	√				5 people on form / Mother-in-law arrived / unexpectedly on 20/4		8	5		5
———"——— / Flat 2	6		SEC	SEC	2	5		Owner of property keeps / 1 flat for own use and lets / the others		9			
———"——— / Flat 3	6		STU	STU	2	5		Neighbour says students / live in top flat during term time		10			
Page Totals											22	4	26

* Scotland only
† Multi-occupied only

Source: *1991 Census Field Manual*, OPCS, 1990

For Use at Census Office

4.4.2 Training for field staff

Training for the Census was carried out as a 'pyramid' system: Census headquarters staff giving detailed training to Census Area Managers, who then recruited and trained Census Officers using a standard training package, and Census Officers in turn recruited and trained Assistant Census Officers and enumerators. Staff at each level received detailed written instructions. Enumerators were issued with a *Field Manual* which contained instructions for each stage of the fieldwork. They were also trained to complete a two-part Enumeration Record. Part 1 listed all the addresses identified by the enumerator and Part 2 recorded basic information about each household, including the 'building bracket' used to describe the type of accommodation. Figures 4.3 and 4.4 reproduce fictitious examples of completed Enumeration Records used in the enumerators' Field Manual. They are discussed below.

4.4.3 The Advance Round

The enumerator firstly located and listed on Part 1 of the Enumeration Record all the properties in the ED and delivered an Advance Round leaflet to each address that might be occupied. Instructions to enumerators emphasised the importance of careful planning of routes to ensure that no accommodation was missed, that derelict buildings were noted and that enquiries were made if there was any uncertainty over whether accommodation was residential. Part 1 of the Enumeration Record then provided the first estimate of the number of household spaces in the ED.

4.4.4 Delivery

The Delivery Procedure was designed to ensure that the enumerator called at every residential address in the ED and made contact with all households. Following contact, a census form was left with an adult in each household. For people whose first language was not English, translations of questions, but not the forms, were available in Arabic, Bengali, Cantonese, Greek, Gujerati, Hindi, Punjabi, Somali, Turkish, Urdu and Vietnamese. Enumerators were told to ask their Census Officer for an interpreter if necessary. Any refusals to accept a form when contacted at the delivery stage were passed up the line to the Assistant Census Officer and Census Officer.

If, after having made several calls at an address, an enumerator was still unable to make contact, neighbours might be asked if there were any households in the accommodation and, if possible, the name of the householder(s). A census form was then left for each non-contacted householder.

The address from Part 1 of the Enumeration Record was copied on to Part 2 (column A) at the time of delivery, with any new households added as necessary. During this stage further details were recorded on Part 2 of the Enumeration Record (figure 4.4). Column B of this Record required the enumerator to identify the type of accommodation from the list of 'Panel A' codes (figure 4.5).

At each delivery contact, enumerators took two steps. First, they checked the number of persons in a household and issued a continuation form if there were more people than spaces on the census form. Second, they noted if anyone else (another household) lived at the address. The number of people in each household and the householder's name were recorded in the Enumeration Record (column C) and the enumerator checked when it would be convenient to call back after census day to collect the form. For multi-occupied buildings, more detailed instructions were issued

Figure 4.5   Enumeration Record Codes

Column B   **Panel A Code**

A caravan or other mobile or temporary structure		1
A whole house or bungalow that is	detached	2
	semi-detached	3
	terraced (include end of terrace)	4
The whole of a purpose built flat or maisonette	in a commercial building (for example in an office building or hotel or over a shop)	5
	in a block of flats or tenement	6
Part of a converted or shared house, bungalow or flat	separate entrance into the building	7
	shared entrance into the building	8

Column D & E   **Delivery & Collection Codes**

1 H Form Delivered/Collected	✓
2 H Forms Delivered/Collected	✓2
H Form + I Form Delivered/Collected	✓ + I
Sealed Return Envelope Delivered/Collected	✓ SR
Vacant Accommodation (New)	V (NEW)
Vacant Accommodation (Improved)	V (IMP)
Vacant Accommodation (Other)	V (OTH)
Absent Household – Form Delivered/Collected	✓ ABS
Absent Household – Form not Collected	ABS
Second Residence	SEC
Holiday Accommodation	HOL
Student Accommodation	STU
Refusal at Delivery	RD
Refusal at Collection	RC

Column F   **Source of Information Code**

Householder	1
Neighbour or other reliable source	2
Enumerator	3

Column G   **Lowest Floor (Scotland only)**

Lowest floor level	
Basement	**B**
Ground	**G**
Floor Number	(as appropriate)

Column H   **Type of Accommodation Code**
(if Panel A = 7 or 8)

A one room flatlet with private bath or shower, WC and kitchen facilities.	1
One room or bedsit, not self-contained (to move from the room to bathroom, WC or kitchen facilities they have to use a hall, landing or stairway open to other household(s)).	2
A self-contained flat or accommodation with 2 or more rooms, having bath or shower, WC and kitchen facilities all behind its own private door.	3
2 or more rooms, not self-contained (to move between rooms or to bathroom, WC or kitchen facilities they have to use a hall, landing or stairway open to other household(s)).	4

Source: *1991 Census Field Manual*, OPCS, 1990

to try to ensure that all households were located. The enumerator had to identify each household; record the location of each household's accommodation (e.g. ground floor); check that every household had been found and that all accommodation had been accounted for; complete column B of the Enumeration Record using the appropriate 'Panel A' code to record the type of building; and bracket together all households in the same building. Caravans or other non-permanent structures were only recorded in Part 2 of the Record if they were occupied on census night or they were someone's usual residence.

Anyone aged 16 years or over in a household was entitled to make a separate Individual Return sealed in an envelope, rather than have information entered by the householder on the household form. For anyone who requested it, sealed returns could be sent direct to the Census Officer; this facility had to be offered by enumerators to anyone known to them. The enumerator recorded delivery details in column D of Part 2 of the Enumeration Record.

Enumerators were asked to identify absent households — where all usually resident members of a household were away from their permanent residence on census night and no one else was present. For these absent households, enumerators recorded in the Enumeration Record the estimated number of usual residents, the estimated number of rooms and the type of accommodation. If a member of the household could not be contacted the enumerator was asked to try to obtain this information from a neighbour or other 'reliable source'.

The enumerator was also required to account for unoccupied accommodation and assign it to one of the categories listed in figure 4.5 (columns D and E) covering vacant accommodation, second residences, holiday accommodation and student accommodation. This information was used to code occupancy type (described in chapter 2, section 2.5.3).

Large establishments expected to have 100 or more people present were identified before the census and enumerated as Special enumeration districts (SEDs). In all other cases, enumerators were asked to make the distinction between households and communal establishments. The proprietor or manager of the communal establishment was asked to complete an L form, listing all residents. Individual forms (I forms), with envelopes for their return, were left with the proprietor or manager who was asked to ensure that each resident completed one (see appendix A). Where a person, for example with severe learning difficulties, was unable to complete a form the manager was responsible for ensuring its completion.

4.4.5 Collection

After census night all accommodation was revisited by the enumerator who was instructed to collect or account for every form delivered. The enumerator was responsible for checking that the form had been fully completed, that nobody had been missed off and that absent households, vacant and other unoccupied accommodation had not changed status since delivery. Column E on Part 2 of the Enumeration Record was used to record collection details.

Enumerators were asked to give as much assistance as necessary to complete the form, particularly where the householder was elderly or had difficulties with the form. Any refusals to return a form at collection, or to complete part of the form, were referred to the Assistant Census Officer and Census Officer, who then visited the household concerned.

Where 'absent households' were still away, or had gone away unexpectedly when the enumerator called back, an Absent Household Leaflet was left, with a reply paid Absent Return envelope. Households who subsequently returned home were asked to complete the form on a voluntary basis and post it back to Census headquarters.

At communal establishments, the enumerator was instructed to check that the Individual Returns matched the people listed on the L form.

Where householders had initially refused to accept or complete the census form, cooperation was usually obtained after a visit by the Assistant Census Officer or Census Officer. The remaining cases were referred to Census headquarters in England and Wales, Scotland or Northern Ireland. Solicitor's letters were sent to refusers and these elicited further responses. Finally, a number of cases where evidence was clear cut and satisfied the strict requirements of the newly introduced Police and Criminal Evidence Acts, were prepared for prosecution. About 330 people were finally convicted for failing to complete a census return (Mahon, 1992).

4.4.6 After collection

After collection there was a two-stage check on completeness. First, the enumerator made a further, more detailed, check on the completed forms and, secondly, a random sample was checked by the Assistant Census Officer to ensure the quality of the returns (Clark, 1992). If there was missing information above the acceptance criteria set, the enumerator was instructed to contact the householder to collect the information, either by telephone (if the householder had indicated that this was acceptable) or by another visit. The Census Officers brought together all forms for their area and these were sent to one of the two census processing offices by secure courier service in a predetermined order.

Counts of population and households were compiled immediately after the collection of forms. Enumerators were asked to use the answer to question 6 on the census forms, on whereabouts on census night, to record on Part 2 of the Enumeration Record (columns K, L), the numbers present and absent on census night in each household. These were added together to give ED totals. This information was used to produce the preliminary counts, published in the 1991 Census Preliminary Reports for England and Wales and for Scotland (OPCS, 1991b; GRO(S), 1991).

The preliminary counts are simple head counts of the population recorded as *present* at addresses identified by the Census field staff, and counts of household spaces, whether occupied or not. For Great Britain, 53.9 million people were recorded as present on census night; whilst this figure was very similar to that recorded for census night 1981, it was about 2 per cent lower than an advance estimate of the population present, 'rolled forward' from the base of the 1981 Census. The preliminary count did not include late returns of census forms; neither did it include imputed information for households with whom no contact had been established.

The preliminary counts also differed from the advance estimates because the latter were of usual residents, rather than persons present. Other differences from the advance estimate arose from difficulties in estimating migration to and from Great Britain accurately, from the balance of visitors to Great Britain and absentees from Britain, and from the extent to which the 1991 Census undercounted the population present. This is discussed more fully in chapter 6.

As well as providing the preliminary count, the ED totals were also an important addition to the geographic database (see section 4.4.1). This provided control information on the numbers of people expected to be processed in each ED and other aggregates of EDs. It also recorded whether the ED was the same or different from 1981.

4.5 DATA PROCESSING

The enormity of the census fieldwork was matched by the enormity of the data processing enterprise. As with other parts of the census operation, the processing stages were planned in great detail, building as far as practicable on 1981 experience. The 1989 census test provided a dress rehearsal for much of the processing work.

Processing was divided into two parts: input and output. Input began at the point where completed census schedules were delivered to the processing offices and covered the stages of coding, keying, editing and imputation. As in previous years, not all the census questions were fully (100 per cent) processed. In general those items which were easy to process (mainly tick boxes) were 100 per cent coded and a 10 per cent sample (discussed in chapter 2, sections 2.7 and 2.8) taken for the 'hard to code' items (table 4.2).

After 100 per cent coding for each county and then coding the 10 per cent sample, the data were passed to 'output processing' where derived variables were added, extra output created, and the various kinds of output (for example, Small Area Statistics, Local Base Statistics, Sample of Anonymised Records) prepared and extracted. Figure 4.6 gives an overview of the processing stages. Before input and output processing is described, the computing environment in which this took place is outlined.

4.5.1 Computing environment

As a result of a corporate strategy review in the late 1980s, OPCS decided to move to a database management system which would be used not only for the 1991 Census but also for handling vital registration data. The requirements imposed by the quantity of the data and the confidentiality requirements led to the adoption of Model 204, which runs in an IBM environment and is marketed by the Computer Corporation of America. The mainframe selected was an Amdahl (Model 5990), with SAS (Statistical Analysis Software) as the standard analysis package. However, the requirement to produce tables for the Census Reports could not easily be met by either Model 204 or SAS, and resources were not available to convert TAU — an in-house tabulation package written for an ICL environment — to the IBM environment. The ICL computer which preceded the Amdahl was used to produce all the counted data needed for tabulations, including the Local Base and Small Area Statistics (see chapters 7 and 8). An electronic publishing system took the TAU-generated tables and slotted them into the predesigned format for printed reports (see chapter 7).

4.5.2 Control and monitoring of processing

An innovation for the 1991 Census was the computerised methods of monitoring all stages of the processing system. This provided much greater control so that at any

Figure 4.6   1991 Census processing: input and output stages

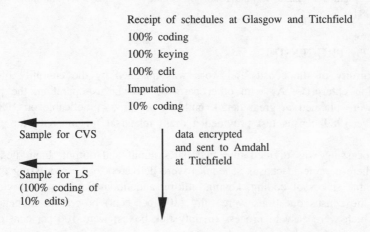

INPUT PROCESSING

Receipt of schedules at Glasgow and Titchfield

100% coding

100% keying

100% edit

Imputation

10% coding

Sample for CVS

Sample for LS
(100% coding of
10% edits)

data encrypted
and sent to Amdahl
at Titchfield

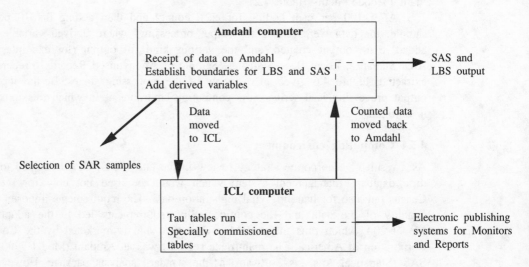

OUTPUT PROCESSING (Titchfield)

Amdahl computer

Receipt of data on Amdahl
Establish boundaries for LBS and SAS
Add derived variables

SAS and
LBS output

Data
moved
to ICL

Counted data
moved back
to Amdahl

Selection of SAR samples

ICL computer

Tau tables run
Specially commissioned
tables

Electronic publishing
systems for Monitors
and Reports

one time information could be automatically generated on, for example, the stage of the 100 per cent edit, the progress being made with coding or keying data, and the tables being run.

4.5.3 Input processing

One of the first tasks, before any data could be keyed, was that of physically storing 23 million census forms weighing some 850 tonnes and occupying 17 miles of shelving. This was met by leasing and refurbishing an old Rolls Royce factory in Glasgow. Data input was then divided between Glasgow (85 per cent of census forms processed) and Titchfield (15 per cent). A total of 2,000 staff were employed on the census processing; most of them for less than a year.

Census schedules were stored in boxes, one for each ED. Each box was labelled and given a bar code — another innovation with the 1991 Census. The bar code provided the means of tracking individual boxes as they passed through the various stages of data input. The bar codes were read by laser pens, or 'wands' (giving rise to the new occupation of 'wander'), with information recorded on microcomputer. This meant that any box of schedules could be instantly located.

Population count and the geographic database (GDB)

Earlier sections of this chapter explained the use of the Enumeration Record to count the total population present and population absent for each ED. When boxes of schedules reached Glasgow or Titchfield, the population keyed for each ED was checked against the figures previously entered into the GDB as a means of quality control. The GDB was used to check the completeness of each ED as it passed through the system. It also contained, for the preparation of output, information on the groupings of EDs into higher level areas such as parliamentary constituencies and European constituencies. Additionally it played a crucial role in assessing whether output statistics met the thresholds required for confidentiality. This is discussed further under output processing.

Coding

All the '100 per cent' questions, most of which had tick boxes for responses, were clerically checked and coded if necessary; any additional answers written in were converted to numerical codes. If postcodes were missing the Royal Mail Postcode Address Directory was used to convert addresses to postcodes. This was done for: enumeration address, usual residence, usual residence one year ago, term-time address and workplace address.

Keying

Once coding was completed, responses were keyed into a network of microcomputers and verified. Data keyed at the Glasgow office were collected into batches of up to 150 EDs, encrypted for security reasons and transmitted across the Government Data Network to the Amdahl mainframe at Titchfield. Data were collected and transmitted automatically, twice a day for each of the six (minimum) counties being coded and keyed at any one time.

4.5.4 The role of editing and imputation[1]

The 1961 Census was the first to use a mainframe computer and, because of this, the first to introduce automated consistency checks into the census processing. However, it was not until the 1981 Census that an automated editing system was introduced to identify missing values and inconsistencies between data items and then to impute consistent values for them and also for any items found to be invalid at the data capture stage. The 1981 Census edit system was based upon work by Fellegi and Holt (1976) for use in the Canadian census; that used in the 1991 Census was a development of the 1981 system.

Full editing and imputation was used only with the 100 per cent data (shown in table 4.2). Whilst the 10 per cent data were edited for consistency, or missing

[1] Much of the material in this section is based upon Mills and Teague (1991).

Table 4.2

The 100 per cent and 10 per cent coded items in the 1991 Census

100% coded

household

- nature of accommodation and sharing
- number of rooms
- tenure

- amenities
- availability of cars and vans
- lowest floor of accommodation (Scotland)

persons

- sex
- date of birth
- marital status
- whereabouts on census night
  (asked in households only)
- usual address
- term-time address of student/schoolchild
- usual address one year ago
- position in establishment
  (asked in communal establishments only)

- country of birth
- ethnic group
- long-term illness
- ethnic group
- Welsh language (in Wales)
- Gaelic language (in Scotland)
- activity last week (whether working, retired,
  looking after home, etc.)*

10% coded

- relationship within household (asked in households only)
- hours worked per week*
- occupation*
- industry of employment (name and busines of employers)*
- address of place of work*
- means of daily journey to work*
- higher qualifications*

* Asked only for those aged 16 and over.

values, the only remedial action taken was to code as 'not stated' those which could not be solved clerically. The discussion below therefore relates solely to the 100 per cent data.

100 per cent prime edit

The main purpose of editing was to identify inconsistencies in the data, for example where date of birth gave an age of three years but employment status was 'working for an employer full-time'. The edit stage used *edit elimination* tables to identify inconsistencies for an individual across seven items:

- age (derived from date of birth)
- marital status
- term-time address
- usual address one year ago
- economic position
- Welsh/Gaelic (Wales/Scotland only)
- position in establishment (if in communal establishment)

Editing was carried out on each ED separately, organised into blocks of up to 150 by county. A *tolerance level* was set for the number of invalid, missing or inconsistent values that could be accepted for each variable. If these tolerance levels were exceeded, then the census schedules for the ED were extracted for clerical checking. However, after a considerable amount of editing had been completed, but before the publication of any results, a manual check identified an error where an estimated 400,000 people had given a particular combination of inconsistent answers which would have led them to be incorrectly classified as students had the error not been identified (Mahon, 1992). This was rectified by software written to identify and correct the incorrect records. The boxed entry overleaf provides an account of the 'student problem'.

Different tolerance levels were set depending upon the type of geographical area. It was expected that inner city areas would have more invalid, missing or inconsistent data than other areas. There were four levels:

- Inner London
- Outer London and metropolitan authorities
- other large urban areas with likely problems of enumeration
- elsewhere

Edit checks were also carried out on household items. In order to check the accuracy of the count of dwellings in the 1991 Census, a special edit and imputation procedure was set up which checked whether a logical sequence of 'building bracket' codes had been recorded by the enumerator. This was only relevant to multi-occupied houses where enumerators were asked to record whether the housing unit was at the beginning of a bracket, at the end, or in the middle. (Multi-occupied buildings must, by definition, include at least two housing units, forming the beginning and the end of a bracket; see section 4.4.4 on delivery of the census forms.) In order that the whole ED sequence of building brackets could be considered, housing units were examined in groups of three. Brackets that were missing at one end (e.g. that started but did not close) were invalid and were imputed if the tolerance level was not satisfied.

4.5.5 Imputation of individual data items

Once the edit had been completed and the tolerance levels satisfied, each ED was ready to have new values created to replace any remaining invalid, missing or inconsistent items. Imputation used the 'hot deck' system, whereby the values imputed were drawn from recently processed cases which had the same values on a set of other, related items. The variable marked for imputation was always that which entailed fewest changes within the individual record.

An *imputation table* (table 4.3) was set up in which the variables used were those which were known to relate closely to the variable to be imputed. Thus tenure, building type and number of residents predict well the number of cars available to a household. Using this example, the cells of the table stored the number of cars available to households for each category. Each county was processed separately and numbers in each cell were drawn *initially* from relationships observed in earlier censuses and census tests. As processing continued, the imputation tables were continuously updated with new values from wholly valid records.

When a record was encountered with a missing value on number of cars, the number in the appropriate cell of the imputation table was used. Because imputation

Error in the edit of economic activity

The 1991 Census form contained a question asking for term-time address of students and schoolchildren (question 8). (The rationale for this question is discussed in chapter 2, section 2.3.2). The census form also asked each person aged 16 and over for their economic activity in the week before the Census. It was anticipated that some people would give seemingly inconsistent answers to the two questions because, for example, a student who was working during the vacation might have ticked 'in employment' and not 'student' — even though the question allowed both to be ticked. Where there was multi-ticking the edit process gave precedence to 'student', but other codes were also retained so that working students could be tabulated as part of the working population as well as students (see section 2.6.9). The editing system was programmed to take a response of 'This address' or 'Elsewhere' in question 8, rather than 'Not a student' from any person aged under 55, as evidence that the person was a student. Any inconsistent answer to the economic activity question was then changed to 'student'. While this sort of inconsistency did occur, it was greatly outweighed by the number of non-students who answered question 8 as though they were students, by ignoring 'Not a student' and ticking 'This address' instead.

The fault was found during a routine data quality check when the number of records which needed editing exceeded the threshold for acceptability and were subjected to a manual check. However, most of the 100 per cent data input processing had already been completed by this stage. Because the effect of the error was to misclassify an estimated 400,000 people from economically active to economically inactive students, it was decided that the problem had to be rectified.

The edit system had not been designed to mark which records were changed during the edit process, so there was no easy way of identifying in the post-edit database the 'real' students from those created by the edit. The solution adopted was to go back to an earlier, pre-edited version of data stored after the forms were coded but before any editing had been done. This data was scanned by computer to identify cases where a person aged 16 or over had ticked 'This address' or 'Elsewhere' in question 8 but had not ticked 'student' in question 13. Such people were deemed to be students if they had said that their term-time address was 'Elsewhere' or if they were young people resident in educational establishments, otherwise they were deemed to be non-students.

Files were then compiled which held the original keyed version of economic activity code and the corrected term-time address code ('Not a student'). These files were matched with the post-edit database and the corrections applied to the records. Checks were carried out to ensure that the corrections did not cause inconsistencies with other data.

In the case of imputed households (absent households not returning a form, 'no contact' households and refusals) there was no pre-edit data from which to pick up corrected values. Therefore printouts of households containing 'students' aged over 24 were produced and decisions were made about which members were *de facto* students through visual inspection of the household composition.

There are likely to be residual statistical effects because it was impossible to identify for certain, even by looking at the census forms, whether a person making the error was a true student or not. The expected effects are:

- counts of economically active students may be slightly low because in any case of doubt the correction system always created a non-student rather than a student
- counts of economically inactive students may also be slightly low, whilst counts of other inactive persons may be slightly high for the same reason
- tables dealing with term-time address will contain slightly too few students resident at, or enumerated at, their term-time address (but the number recorded with a term-time address 'Elsewhere' will be accurate)

The numbers involved in these residual classes are expected to be small; an estimate of the number of 'lost' students will be produced after the processing of the main Census results.

Source: OPCS, 1992e

Table 4.3

Imputation table for cars, as used in the 1991 Census

Tenure	Building type and number of residence															
	Permanent accommodation								Non-permanent accommodation							
	1	2	3	4	5	6	7	8+	1	2	3	4	5	6	7	8+
Owner occupied																
– owned outright	·	·	·	·	·	·	·	·	·	·	·	·	·	·	·	·
– buying	·	·	·	·	·	·	·	·	·	·	·	·	·	·	·	·
Rented privately																
– furnished	·	·	·	·	·	·	·	·	·	·	·	·	·	·	·	·
– unfurnished	·	·	·	·	·	·	·	·	·	·	·	·	·	·	·	·
Rented with a job or business	·	·	·	·	·	·	·	·	·	·	·	·	·	·	·	·
Rented from a local authority, new town, or Scottish Homes	·	·	·	·	·	·	·	·	·	·	·	·	·	·	·	·

Values held in each cell — number of cars from previous households with the appropriate combination of attributes

Source: *Population Trends* 1991, vol. 64, p. 33.

was carried out on a county by county basis on clusters of 50 geographically close EDs (each cluster of 50 EDs formed a census processing unit), small scale geographical variations in the data could be reflected in the imputed data.

4.5.6 The amount of imputation of individual data items

The amount of imputation required is one indication of the overall quality of the data (although incorrect but valid and consistent data would pass through the edit check undetected). Figures are not yet available for 1991, but in the 1981 Census the amount of imputation for most items was below 1 per cent and the main reason was that the information was missing on the census form. In 1981, Inner London was consistently high in the amount of imputation needed as were many of the metropolitan areas. However, some rural areas were surprisingly high on particular variables.

An evaluation carried out after the 1981 Census (Brant and Chalk, 1985) found that the automatic editing system produced accurate results for all items except employment status and was able to correct for non-response bias. In 1981 employment status was the item with the highest amount of missing data. The 1981 question was not repeated in 1991, although the main elements were included in the 'activity last week' question.

4.5.7 The imputation of data for absent households

The 1991 Census included, for the first time, households absent on census night (see chapter 2, section 2.3.1). In the 1981 Census some 700,000 households in Great Britain, containing an estimated 1 million persons, were classified as absent households and the residents were excluded from the enumeration at the usual address (although, of course, many were enumerated elsewhere as 'visitors'). Many were one-person households, known to be over-represented amongst absent households.

The increase in the number of one-person households in recent years and the increase in travel and overseas holidays meant that the number of absent households was likely to be greater in 1991.

Absent households were asked to complete a census form voluntarily on their return home. Where forms were returned in time, they were included in the processing; however, not all absent households returned a form. Some did not return home in time to be included in the processing; others may have chosen not to complete the form voluntarily.

For the latter households who were absent and did not complete a census schedule later, the following information, (which was recorded by the enumerator for all absent households), was used:

- the number of residents
- the number of rooms
- whether the building was self-contained (if in a multi-occupied house)

The 'type of area' was provided by reference to the ED identity.

These four items set the parameters for an 'absent household' reference table in which the table cells contained up to six complete sets of household and personal data for absent households who *did* return forms. At the beginning of processing the initial values in the table cells were taken from the 1981 Census and the 1989 census test. As the processing system encountered completed forms from absent households, the personal and household details were stored in the relevant cell of the imputation table, replacing the oldest household stored. When a non-responding absent household was processed, details (for the fully processed items only) were imputed by copying the most recently stored absent household record which matched on the four key variables. This ensured that small geographical variations in the characteristics of absent households were imputed as accurately as possible.

4.5.8 The quality of imputation of absent households

Absent households have very different characteristics from present households. They tend to be smaller and their members more skewed towards either end of the age distribution — 16–24 or 65 and over. By imputing only values from one absent household to another absent household, major distortions in aggregate values of absent households should be avoided.

Evaluations of imputed absent households from census tests showed that the procedure worked well and that aggregate distributions did not differ significantly from the true distribution for most characteristics.

Non-responding absent households formed about 1.4 per cent of usual residents of England and Wales in the 1991 Census. There was, however, considerable geographical variation in the level of wholly absent imputed households. At county level, the highest rate was 8.85 per cent of usually resident households in Inner London; at the other extreme, 0.93 per cent of usually resident households in Staffordshire were imputed. There was also variation in the percentage of households imputed within counties, most notably between the London boroughs (table 4.4).

Nottinghamshire can be used to provide an example of how the variation in level of imputation decreased as the level of geographical aggregation increased. The county of Nottinghamshire had 1.30 per cent of its resident population imputed — very near to the national average. Of the 8 districts in the county, Nottingham had

Table 4.4

Imputed wholly absent households as a percentage of usually resident households, England and Wales

County code	County	%	District code	London Borough	%
England, metropolitan counties			*Inner London*		
01	Inner London	8.85	01AA	City of London	15.86
02	Outer London	2.82	01AB	Camden	9.90
03	Greater Manchester	2.06	01AC	Hackney	10.34
04	Merseyside	2.28	01AD	Hammersmith and Fulham	8.89
05	South Yorkshire	1.17	01AE	Haringey	7.92
06	Tyne and Wear	1.56	01AF	Islington	7.80
07	West Midlands	2.25	01AG	Kensington and Chelsea	13.75
08	West Yorkshire	1.66	01AH	Lambeth	10.68
			01AJ	Lewisham	6.90
England, shire counties			01AK	Newham	5.64
09	Avon	2.33	01AL	Southwark	9.44
10	Bedfordshire	1.80	01AM	Tower Hamlets	6.31
11	Berkshire	1.94	01AN	Wandsworth	5.94
12	Buckinghamshire	1.39	01AP	Westminster, City of	12.27
13	Cambridgeshire	1.64			
14	Cheshire	1.25	*Outer London*		
15	Cleveland	1.13	02AQ	Barking and Dagenham	1.99
16	Cornwall and Isle of Scilly	1.65	02AR	Barnet	3.19
17	Cumbria	1.20	02AS	Bexley	1.06
18	Derbyshire	1.17	02AT	Brent	6.88
19	Devon	2.04	02AU	Bromley	1.75
20	Dorset	1.64	02AW	Croydon	3.06
21	Durham	1.00	02AX	Ealing	3.78
22	East Sussex	2.87	02AY	Enfield	2.43
23	Essex	1.39	02AZ	Greenwich	3.75
24	Gloucestershire	1.42	02BA	Harrow	1.96
25	Hampshire	1.43	02BB	Havering	1.20
26	Hereford and Worcester	0.98	02BC	Hillingdon	1.96
27	Hertfordshire	1.49	02BD	Hounslow	4.10
28	Humberside	1.43	02BE	Kingston upon Thames	2.24
29	Isle of Wight	1.97	02BF	Merton	2.81
30	Kent	1.61	02BG	Redbridge	1.89
31	Lancashire	1.51	02BH	Richmond upon Thames	2.56
32	Leicestershire	1.44	02BJ	Sutton	1.77
33	Lincolnshire	1.18	02BK	Waltham Forest	4.15
35	Northamptonshire	1.20			
36	Northumberland	1.01			
37	North Yorkshire	1.45			
38	Nottinghamshire	1.67			
39	Oxfordshire	1.53			
40	Shropshire	1.14			
41	Somerset	1.36			
42	Staffordshire	0.93			
43	Suffolk	1.42			
44	Surrey	1.55			
45	Warwickshire	1.13			
46	West Sussex	1.60			
47	Wiltshire	1.31			
Wales					
48	Clwyd	1.35			
49	Dyfed	1.40			
50	Gwent	1.54			
51	Gwynedd	2.18			
52	Mid Glamorgan	1.22			
53	Powys	1.71			
54	South Glamorgan	2.44			
55	West Glamorgan	1.42			

Source: 1991 Census, Crown Copyright.

Figure 4.7 Percentage resident population imputed in Nottinghamshire at county, district, ward and ED level

	Percentage imputed
Nottinghamshire	1.30

Districts

Ashfield	0.68
Bassetlaw	0.57
Broxtowe	0.70
Gedling	0.69
Mansfield	0.62
Newark and Sherwood	0.72
Nottingham	3.03
Rushcliffe	0.73

Wards

Percentage imputed
(lower limit)

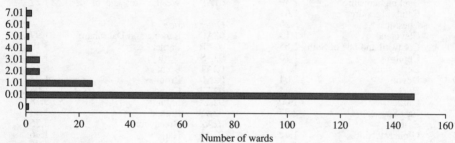

Number of wards

Enumeration districts

Percentage imputed
(lower limit)

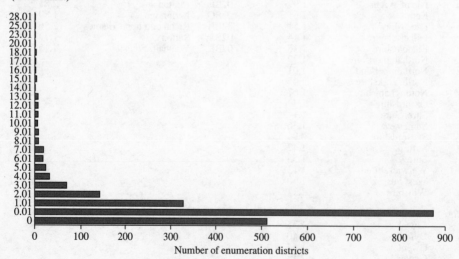

Number of enumeration districts

highest imputation rates with 3.03 per cent and Bassetlaw lowest with 0.57 per cent. At ward level, percentage imputation ranged from zero to 8.49 per cent whilst at ED level, imputation reached 10 per cent or higher in 2 per cent of EDs, but with nearly 25 per cent of EDs recording no imputation. (Figure 4.7.) The Census Validation Survey, conducted in June 1991, checked the quality of imputation for households recorded as absent in the Census (chapter 6 (I)), but results were not available at the time of writing.

4.6 DRAWING AND CODING THE 10 PER CENT SAMPLE

Not all census questions were coded for the entire population. For reasons of economy those which gave a high proportion of open-ended responses, referred to as 'hard-to-code', were coded for a 10 per cent sample only. The 1991 procedure followed closely on that developed for the 1971 and 1981 censuses. The sample was selected during processing from the 100 per cent records. There were three levels of stratification: first each county was treated separately; second, each processing unit of 50 consecutive enumeration districts[1] was treated separately; third, each processing unit was split into strata consisting of 10 households or 10 persons in communal establishments. As no 10 per cent data were imputed for 'wholly absent' households, they were not included in the 10 per cent sample.

The 10 per cent sample, therefore, consisted of one household selected at random from each stratum of ten consecutively recorded households, and a similar sample of persons in communal establishments. Within the blocks of 50 EDs, the strata ran continuously from the first household in the first ED to the last household in the 50th ED and from the first person in the communal establishment in the first ED to the last person in the last communal establishment in the 50th ED. The sample comprised all persons in the sample households, plus the sample of individuals in communal establishments. Unless there were no imputed households in an area, the sample will be less than 10 per cent.

The stratified nature of the household sample tended to reduce the sampling error, but when the 10 per cent sample was used as a sample of individuals this was offset for some variables by the effects of clustering within the household. Persons with particular characteristics tend to be clustered within a household; for example, people with higher qualifications, or people who have migrated together. Sometimes particular characteristics are paired, for example, journey to work by car and journey to work by public transport in a household with only one car available.

A number of evaluations of the 10 per cent sample were carried out following the 1981 Census. Since the methods used for both drawing and validating the sample in 1981 were repeated for 1991 (with the important exception that imputed households, included for the first time in the 1991 Census, were not included in the sample) it is worth recording what was discovered about the methods in 1981. OPCS (1983c) calculated the design effect (the ratio of the true variance of a sample value to the variance calculated on the assumption of simple random sampling) for 168 census characteristics, for each county. For most of the 168 items the square root of the design effect was very close to 1, indicating that there was very little difference

---

[1] Where there were fewer than 50 census processing units left at the end of a county, these were treated as one complete unit.

between the 10 per cent sample and a simple random sample; for a few characteristics this value lay outside 0.9 to 1.1, indicating that the 10 per cent sample differed significantly from a simple random sample. Design effects were low where geographical stratification had a strong effect, for example those travelling to work by tube, and high where characteristics were shared by several members of the same household, for example, 'in a farming occupation' or 'born outside the UK'. Design effects will also be made available for the 1991 Census in early 1994 and can be used to adjust the 10 per cent sample estimates where necessary.

A further evaluation (OPCS, 1985) was carried out on 38 individual and five household items from eight census questions included in the 100 per cent data, to test for bias in these items in the 10 per cent sample. Generally, differences between the 10 per cent sample and 100 per cent data were within the range expected if a simple random sample had been drawn. However, for some relatively rare characteristics which were also clustered within households the sampling distribution was biased. This was much more marked in small areas than in large areas. Skewed distributions were mainly associated with being born outside the UK and having changed address in the year preceding the census; both these characteristics were likely to show clustering within households. For these characteristics in particular, small area sample counts tended to underestimate the true values.

As imputed 'wholly absent' households were excluded from the 1991 10 per cent sample, an estimate for the total population can only be obtained by multiplying the sample count by 10 (adjusting for the design effect if necessary) and then adjusting for the number of residents in imputed wholly absent households on a *pro rata* basis, on the assumption that imputed households had the same characteristics as enumerated households. However, it has already been noted that this assumption is unlikely to hold.

Preliminary advice on estimating 100 per cent figures from the 10 per cent sample is given in the *Census Newsletter* No. 25 (February 1993) and is discussed further in chapter 8, section 8.6.5. Further information will be published by OPCS in *User Guides* later in 1993.

4.6.1 Coding the 10 per cent sample

A brief summary of the coding process for the items in the 10 per cent sample is given below.

- *Hours worked per week* was coded from the number of hours written in by the form-filler.
- *Occupation* was coded to 480 computer codes, which enabled the occupation to be classified according to both the 1981 Classification of Occupations and also to the 374 Unit Groups of the Standard Occupational Classification (OPCS & Employment Department Group, 1991). The coding process checked a number of pieces of information from the forms and then used computer–assisted coding (CACOCC, Census Office in-house software) to assign a code. In some circumstances the information on industry was used to identify which code to use.
- *Industry* was coded using the address of the employer (or business). Both the List of Large Employers (over 25 employees) and the Postcode Address File

were used to locate the employer (or business) as named by the respondent, and establish the industry coding appropriate to the employer (or business). The List of Large Employers was prepared within the Census Offices from information derived from the 1989 Census of Employment. As well as names and addresses of employers (and businesses) it contains the industry code, postcode and size of establishment.

- The *address of workplace* was postcoded for computer-processing and allocated to higher geographical areas using the OPCS Central Postcode Directory (see chapter 3 (I)).
- *Daily journey to work* was captured from either the box ticked or from the coding of written-in replies. Where more than one box was ticked the lowest number was coded. A check for inconsistencies between workplace and journey to work was also made.
- *Qualified Manpower* was coded using a series of OPCS generated-manuals which list the qualifications awarded by all UK colleges and institutes of higher education. There was also a list of qualifications not allowed, and, for overseas qualifications, a manual was prepared from various sources including the British Council.

For occupation, industry and qualified manpower, the codings were written on the schedules and then keyed in. As a general principle, coders had little discretion in making judgments about cases which were unclear; all such cases were referred to supervisors. Information on examples of changes over time in question wording and classifications is given in chapter 2.

4.6.2 Extraction of records for the OPCS Longitudinal Study

During input processing a sample selection program marked the sample of people with birthdates on four dates of each year for the OPCS Longitudinal Study. Chapter 12 explains the basis for the sample. A database for these records was made and the 10 per cent items were specially coded for all those not included in the 10 per cent sample. As with the 10 per cent sample, there was no imputation beyond that done for the 100 per cent items. Once fully edited, derived variables were added for the OPCS Longitudinal Study.

4.7 OUTPUT PROCESSING

Once coding, editing and imputation of the 100 per cent data was complete, they were passed to the second processing stage: output processing. The 10 per cent coded data were similarly passed to output processing after coding was finished. The output database consisted of both the raw data keyed in from forms and also the geographic database (GDB), which provides the key to which of the higher level areas (such as Parliamentary constituencies or European constituencies) each ED fits.

The GDB for England and Wales also held a record of which EDs and wards failed the population size threshold test for confidentiality (see chapter 5) for either the Small Area Statistics or the Local Base Statistics. A failed area was merged with another adjacent area. This is discussed in detail in chapter 8, section 8.5.

4.7.1 Derived variables

In the final output tables only about 16 'prime' variables, as recorded on the census forms, were retained. All others were derived. In deriving a variable an algorithm transforms an input variable, for example date of birth, into an output variable, for example single years of age. About 400 variables were derived in total; of these, 120 were derived for the 100 per cent Local Base Statistics and a further 40 for the 10 per cent Local Base Statistics. A list of all the derived variables and their categories was stored in a PC-based Glossary. For most variables this also holds a copy of the algorithm used to derived the variable, and copies for particular variables can by obtained from OPCS Census Customer Services at Titchfield.

The output database for Great Britain, comprising the raw data, the derived data and the GDB, was some 100 gigabytes in size. At this point all the coding and edit stages were completed and the data were ready for transfer to the ICL mainframe computer for aggregation into counts for tables. Before being passed to the ICL computer, the Samples of Anonymised Records (see chapter 11) were drawn from records in the 10 per cent sample.

Extracts from the output database were moved from the Amdahl to the ICL using cartridges, one county at a time. The tabulation package TAU was used to make the necessary counts. Table parameters were set up well in advance so that the actual production of tables was largely automated with little call on programmers' time. For output to be published in reports (see chapter 7) TAU tables were moved from the ICL computer to the electronic publishing system by a direct network link. The final, electronically-held, camera-ready copy was sent to HMSO for printing and publication.

For output supplied as machine-readable abstracts (see chapter 7), a copy of the counted data was sent back to the Amdahl where it went through the final output stages, one county at a time, to produce, for example, the Local Base and Small Area Statistics (see chapter 8) for customers.

This chapter has provided some background to the way in which census data is collected and processed. Subsequent chapters concentrate on particular output products available to users.

5 Privacy, confidentiality and anonymity in the 1991 Census

Catherine Marsh

5.1 INTRODUCTION

There is an inevitable conflict between two key values in modern society: the right to privacy and the right to information. Neither can be treated as absolute. The state becomes involved, not only as a regulator but as a primary information creator and distributor, in debates about how the balance is to be struck. Census offices in particular have turned to two different mechanisms to try to make compatible the rights of individuals to privacy with the needs of the state and public at large to know. The first and historically prior of the two mechanisms is to ensure that the census is conducted in a safe environment; it is recognised that some people do need to have access to personal data in the course of conducting the census, but various forms of confidentiality pledges and safeguards are given to restrict access to personal census data. With the advent of electronic computing, a second technique has come to the fore, however; if computerised information can be stripped of identifiying information at the storage stage, the anonymity of census respondents can be protected (Marsh, Dale and Skinner, forthcoming).

The British Census Offices take various steps directly to protect the privacy of citizens through controlling the content of the census. They then use both confidentiality and anonymity mechanisms to ensure that the highest degree of security attaches to the data collected. This chapter is therefore organised around these three key concepts. It is not principally concerned with internal procedures; readers who would like a description of how OPCS conducts itself internally with respect to all the data under its stewardship are advised to consult its statement of policy on the topic (OPCS, 1992c).

5.2 PRIVACY

Privacy in the sense of a dignified withdrawal of a person to the social space around him, the realm of intimate family and acquaintances, is a relatively modern concern (Williams, 1976: p.204; Shils, 1979). In feudal times, the social relations of the village were available for all to see, and the modern distinction between public and private was not yet appropriate. As cities developed, the facts of social existence were not so transparent: social relationships became enclosed behind factory and tenement doors, and an increasing number of people worked some distance from where they lived. These developments led to the need for special enquiries to un-cover the realities underlying life in industrial cities. Censuses and social surveys thus appeared and grew with capitalism.

It is arguable that the recent growth of computerised information and the birth of a sector of the economy devoted to data collection and transmission is turning the world back into a global village where the attempt to retain privacy is a forlorn hope. Whatever the future holds, however, there is evident present public concern to maintain privacy and to defend the individual against 'the information gatherers' (Hewitt, 1977). In these circumstances, government sponsored social surveys and particularly censuses are forced to consider what are appropriate subjects to be re-searched, and an attempt is made to restrict topics to those which fall firmly on the public side of the public–private divide.

Unlike many other countries, including the US which enacted a privacy law in 1974, Britain has no specific legislation granting citizens' rights of privacy; the Data Protection Act of 1984 (discussed further in section 5.3.1) does not grant such rights, and fails to provide a legal definition of privacy. Several bills have been proposed and the debate continues, but to date all attempts have foundered; this has in part been through failure to agree about the balance between protecting the privacy of the individual citizen and that of public officials, and in part through a feeling that Britain's libel laws are sufficiently strong to prevent the need.

Census offices work with a sense of what subject matters are fit for enquiry by census and which are deemed too private; they exert a self-denying ordinance which prevents many subjects coming forward for study. One of the factors underlying the changes in census content, shown in table 1.2 (chapter 1) undoubtedly reflects his-torical alterations in sensitivities about particular issues, or perhaps, more accurately, beliefs within the Census Offices about public reactions to topics. We shall consider what is known about public reactions to census content in the last section of this chapter.

There is not, nor ever has been, a question on income in the full British census. Successful income questions are asked on the censuses in Australia, New Zealand, the US and Canada, yet European countries tend to treat income as a taboo topic and none of the EC countries includes a direct income question (Langevin, Begeot and Pearce, 1992; p.36). Census users feel the absence of such a question keenly (Marsh *et al.*, 1988) and have tried to get an income question included on the census repeatedly, but without success. Because of the wide interest shown in the subject, questions on income were asked in both the 1968 and 1969 pre-census tests. The 1968 pre-test found that, not only was it difficult to find suitable questions that would give acceptable reliability, but there was also some hostility from the public (Cushion, 1969). Revised versions of the question were tried in the 1969 test, but it was decided not to ask the question in the 1971 Census (Bulmer, 1979). However, the Census Offices agreed to a follow-up survey to the 1971 Census, on the specific topic of income, but the results, both in terms of response rates to the voluntary survey and in terms of data quality, were not encouraging and have been influential in persuading the Census Offices that income is both politically and technically infeasible for inclusion in a census (Banfield, 1978). In the user consultation before the 1991 Census, a question on the receipt of social security benefits was proposed as an indicator of low income, but it did not receive sufficient support to get as far as pretest. Users therefore put a great deal of effort into constructing surrogate measures, using car ownership and occupational prestige, for example, as indirect indicators of income level. This issue will undoubtedly continue to be debated for censuses in the future.

Another major topic which features in the censuses of many other countries (including Northern Ireland) but not in Britain is religion. There was only ever one voluntary Census of Religion in 1851 which was a census of accommodation and attendance on one particular Sunday rather than an investigation into religious persuasion (Thompson, 1978; Pickering, 1967). It suggested that half the church buildings and 40 per cent of those attending church were Nonconformists. Attempts were made at every subsequent census of population in the 19th century to include a question on religious persuasion, but were blocked by the Nonconformists ostensibly on grounds of conscience and privacy, but probably more because they thought they would not fare so well with a measure based on belief alone (Drake, 1972; pp.15-18). It is doubtful today whether there would be such resistance, although the need for denominational profiles in a much more secular society has dwindled and no one has made a strong case for including a question on religion in the census since 1910. It is the ethnic minorities in Britain, with cultures still often strongly differentiated on religious grounds, who have kept the demand for some aspects of a religion question alive, albeit as subdivisions within the question on ethnic minority status; Muslims, Hindus and Sikhs in particular wanted separate identification in 1991, feeling themselves to be members of different minority groups (Sillitoe, 1987).

The ethnic question itself was for a long time also feared to be too private a subject for inclusion in a British census, despite the fact that the 1920 Census Act specifically includes race as a topic which may be asked on censuses. Nationality had been asked in earlier censuses, but there had been controversy over the inclusion even of the country of birth questions in post-war censuses. A voluntary census test in Haringey in 1979 to test the acceptability of a question on ethnicity for the 1981 Census met with refusal and organised opposition by ethnic minorities who objected both to the idea of asking about ethnicity in principle and to the particular form that the wording took. As a result a decision was taken not to include questions on ethnicity or nationality in 1981 (OPCS, 1980). However, a Subcommittee of the House of Commons Home Affairs Committee on Race Relations and Immigration was appointed to inquire into ethnic and racial questions in future censuses. It reported in May 1983 that there should be a question on ethnic group included in the census, subject to reassurances on confidentiality and a clear objective to develop programmes against discrimination. Further wording tests were conducted in the mid-1980s and careful soundings were taken from the Commission for Racial Equality (Sillitoe, 1987). The result was a form of question which produced technically adequate responses and which commanded the support of the ethnic minority communities in Britain (White, 1990; Sillitoe and White, 1992). It is also probably true to say that the terms of debate about ethnicity in Britain had changed over the decade; ethnic monitoring and the provision of statistics on disadvantage became politically valued goals. The same ethnic minorities who campaigned against the inclusion of the question in 1981 were advocating its inclusion in 1991. Furthermore, in the US and Canada one of the most vigorous debates that takes place about the census concerns which groups shall be statutorily separately identified and thus separately counted.

Another area over which there has been controversy is that of marital and fertility status. The 1971 Census, which collected information on the fertility histories of women, only addressed these questions to married women, on the grounds that to put the same question to unmarried women might give offence (see chapter 13 for similar reasoning over the fertility questions in the 1991 Northern Ireland Census). Even these questions caused some disquiet in the House of Commons, and no fertility questions have been asked in the British census since. The exclusion of a cohabitation category in either the marital status or relationship question prior to 1991 probably originated in a sense of propriety, although once again changing mores and behaviour led to its inclusion in the relationship question in 1991 without any adverse comment.

As with the income question, moral issues about what is an appropriate topic for censuses can get intertwined with technical issues of the quality of the resulting data in other questions. There is an ethnical component to the difficulties of sorting out family relationships in households in a more satisfactory way than at present where only relationship to the head of households (the first person on the form) is established. In order to sort out the family structure within a census household, one would want to ask a question such as 'Whose child is this?' on the census schedule, which could lead to possible embarrassment. Pretests of schedule design which would enable such questions to be asked of all possible relationships in the household were conducted before the 1991 Census, but the results were not sufficiently encouraging to include a multiway relationship question on the main census schedule. Using one fixed reference person in the household — the first named on the form — has the advantage of being both easier to administer and avoiding too much detailed questioning about precise relationships in complex households.

An issue closely related to privacy is that of 'respondent burden' (Sharp and Frankel, 1983); the state, as well as having a duty to keep its enquiries to publicly acceptable subject matters, also has a responsibility not to overburden its citizens with unnecessary form-filling. However, while relieving respondent burden is related to maintaining privacy, it can often be achieved most efficiently by linking sources of existing data together without having to burden the citizen with another enquiry (OPCS, 1992c; p.2). Such linkage is often also perceived to be a threat to privacy in its own right; unfortunately we know very little about how the general public would like the state to balance out these two aspects of privacy.

In order to minimise respondent burden, the census schedule is kept as short as possible. Government departments had to present a positive case to the Census Offices before any question in the 1981 Census was included; continuity for its own sake was not deemed a sufficient argument. As a result, the 1981 Census was the shortest post-war census. A similar procedure in 1991 meant departments had to argue very hard to get the three extra questions onto the 1991 schedule, and some proposed topics, including several questions which had been pretested, were not included.

One obvious solution to the respondent burden problem is to use sampling on the census, and to ask a second set of questions to a random subset of the population so that the burden for no individual is too great. This is a procedure routinely adopted in North America, where the sample is pre-selected from lists of addresses and seems to work well. The British Census Offices had bad experiences of field sampling in the 1961 Census, where the hard to code questions were only asked of a 10 per cent sample of the population (Whitehead, 1983). Unfortunately, although enumerators were instructed to hand out long forms to every tenth household on a strictly random basis, they appear often to have avoided giving the longer form to households where they thought the householders would have difficulty or would be unlikely to fill it in. As a result, the 10 per cent sample was badly biased against large and single-person households. The problem was particularly bad in communal establishments, and Newman (1978a) recounts some amusing stories about how such randomised forms were treated in a forces establishment, whose officers viewed random procedures as most disorderly and set about 'correcting' them.

After this relative failure, census officials were only prepared to consider sampling in the field for the full census of 1971 if tests showed that a reliable mechanism for it could be worked out. A three-stage procedure was elaborated in tests, whereby the enumerator first delivered the short form, then went back to one in 10 households to deliver a long form, and then returned to collect it. Newman (1978a) reports that there were '(v)arious practical difficulties in this procedure which it was felt could not be solved before the census itself was mounted' and sampling was therefore not undertaken. Analysis of test results suggested, however, that the methodology which had begun to be developed did not suffer from the biases of the previous two attempts and a complex interlocking sample was designed for the cancelled 1976 Census. Nonetheless, field sampling has not been proposed since then, although it could offer great potential for reducing respondent burden.

5.3   CONFIDENTIALITY

While the census is, therefore, restricted to topics which are not deemed overly sensitive by the Census Offices, 'it would be prudent to assume that certain topics (e.g. marital, parental or other relationships in a household, ethnic and related topics, employment, qualifications, previous residence) could cause at least embarrassment and possibly actual disadvantage or discrimination' (OPCS and GRO(S), 1991a, p.12). Every effort is, therefore, made to ensure that the information which individuals supply is treated with the utmost care. The need to know principle applies: only those who absolutely need to see the information in the form where it can be linked to individuals gain such access. Moreover, those individuals who have to have access to this information are bound to maintain confidentiality by law.

5.3.1   The legal guarantees

Confidentiality of census responses is protected by section 8 of the Census Act 1920 which was amended by the Census (Confidentiality) Act 1991. Under the terms of the latter Act, it is an offence for any member of the census staff to disclose personal census information to others without lawful authority. Anyone found guilty of an offence is liable to up to two years in prison or a fine (on which no limit is set) or both.

Under section 8 subsection 1 of the 1920 Act, it is an offence punishable by a fine (currently) of up to £400 to contravene the Census Regulations, which, in particular, forbid the use, publication or communication of census information by any person except for defined census purposes, and require anyone having custody of documents containing census information to keep them safe from unauthorised access. In this way, householders and other members of the public who handle census documents are also bound by the confidentiality requirements.

Other legislation also affects the security of census data. Under section 3 of the Public Records Act 1958, people responsible for any type of public record have a duty to make safe arrangements for the disposal of any records important enough to warrant preservation. These records are usually opened after 30 years and are transferred to the Public Record Office at that time, but they may be retained longer if the case is made. In an Instrument of the Lord Chancellor (No. 12 of 20 June 1966), 100 years was prescribed as the period of closure of the decennial census returns. Periods of closure affecting Scottish census data are determined by departments on advice from the Scottish Records Advisory Committee, who have recently kept Scottish rules in line with English practice; (however, 19th century census enumerators books were released before the 100-year period in Scotland). This 100-year period is longer than the 70 years more commonly in force in other countries, but does mean that British historians of the future will eventually be able to gain access to the original schedules, unlike their counterparts in countries such as Australia where the forms are destroyed (Castles, 1991).

The other relevant legislation to consider is the Data Protection Act of 1984 which gives subject-access rights to individuals to discover, challenge and if necessary correct information about themselves which is held on computer files. The Act places obligations on those who record and use any personal data on computers; they must be open about that use and follow sound and proper practices — the Data Protection Principles — set out in a schedule to the Act.

The census databases are subject to the registration provisions of the Data Protection Act, even though names and addresses are not on the computer which holds the main census database. This is because: first, it is possible for the Census Offices to identify an individual to whom the data relate from other information in the Offices' possession; and second, postcodes are entered and might in some rural areas lead to a theoretical risk of identification. However, since the information is held only for the purpose of preparing statistics and carrying out research, it is exempt from the subject-access provisions of the Act.

The passing of this legislation, and establishment of the Office of the Data Protection Registrar, has had other effects on census procedures. It has raised consciousness in the general climate of public opinion about the importance of confidentiality. The eight Data Protection Principles, explained in detail in guideline 4, (ODPR, 1989) set standards which all registered data users, including the Census Offices, must abide by. Furthermore, its permanent staff of officials provide a source of expertise on the holdings of other main databases and can therefore alert the public and government about possible abuses of census information at a small geographical level.

5.3.2 Security in the field and processing

The legal guarantees were communicated to the public in several ways. Assurances about the confidentiality of census information were given to the public in the Registrar General's letter to the household contained on the census form (see appendix A) and in the information leaflets distributed to all households with their form. The specific guarantees given were:

- answers would be treated in strict confidence and used only to produce statistics

- Census Office staff were bound by law to make sure the information given on census forms remained secret and safe
- anyone improperly using or disclosing census information was liable to prosecution; for example, it would be improper for someone to pass on information given to them by a visitor to enable them to complete the census form
- no information about identified people or households would be given to anyone outside the Census Offices in central government or elsewhere, although the form could be produced as evidence in prosecuting someone for refusing to complete it properly
- names and addresses would not be fed into the census computer and
- the census forms would be kept securely within the OPCS and treated as confidential for 100 years.

The advertising campaigns also reassured the public about these same issues, using the slogan: 'Secret and safe'.

On the main 'H' (household) schedule, there was a box for the name of each household member to ensure that the person completing the form remembered to include each member of the household and answered the questions in each column about the correct person (see appendix A). However, any individual could request an 'I' (individual) form if they wanted to keep their personal information secret from the person completing the form, and enumerators also had special envelopes for situations where the respondents did not want the enumerator to see the form or where the household was known to the enumerator. In the event the low level of uptake of these provisions, however, suggests that the public was not greatly exercised about possible threats to their privacy posed by the collection process.

The listing of names and addresses on the forms and in the enumerators' records were principally devices to ensure accuracy of information recording. Recording of full names and addresses enables quality control on the work of the enumerators; in the words of T.H. Lister who planned the first householder census form in 1841: 'The names should be written at length . . . an enumerator may sit at home and make marks and no examiner could detect his errors' (cited in Drake, 1972; p.25). The recording of names and addresses also enabled follow-up surveys to be directed to named individuals and to enable the linking of a sample of records to the Longitudinal Study (see chapter 12); however, such links were done manually and, for reasons of confidentiality and cost, the names and addresses were never entered onto a computer. The opportunity to create a definitive address to enumeration district directory was thereby lost, leaving users with only the ED to Postcode Directory (see chapter 3, sections 3.3.3 and 3.10.1). In the future, the Census Offices could consider the entry of names and addresses and enumeration district identifier onto a separate computer file to create an address to postcode link, although this need may now be met by Ordnance Survey's Address Point directory (chapter 3, sections 3.3.3 and 3.9.2).

Enumerators were required to assure the Census Offices that they understood the legal requirements about confidentiality. Enumerators could not work in or near areas where they lived, or where they were well known, and in the few isolated cases where this happened special arrangements were available to enable respondents to use sealed returns which could not be opened by the enumerator. In particular, no one involved in any way with compiling registration lists for the local authorities for tax-raising purposes could be employed on any part of the census endeavour, and publicity stressed this independence of the 'poll tax'. Enumerators carried authorisation cards, and only duly authorised companions or helpers were permitted.

Appropriate security precautions were taken when collecting the completed material. Security carriers were used to take the forms to one of two processing offices where the computer installations were entirely under the control of OPCS and where all the staff had also given undertakings that they understood the legal requirements of confidentiality placed upon them. While all forms for the area around Titchfield were sent to Hillingdon near Glasgow for processing, all Scottish forms were processed in Scotland. The precise conditions of the processing centres and of the computer arrangements were subject to an independent review and are discussed further in section 5.3.3.

Once the data had been entered, the original forms were transferred to secure storage and will not be released for 100 years. This has happened with every census since householder forms were introduced by the General Register Office in 1841, the only exceptions being the census of 1931, the forms from which were destroyed accidentally and the sample census of 1966 which was destroyed because sample censuses do not get the same legal protection.

5.3.3   An independent security review

As in 1971 and 1981, an independent review of the protection of confidentiality in the computing arrangements for the 1991 Census was commissioned by the Census Offices. For the first time, the review was put out to competitive tender, and was won by the British Computer Society, who had in fact carried out the review in 1981. Their terms of reference were to review the appropriateness and adequacy of any aspect of the computing and related arrangements for the 1991 Census, taking into account the principles of the Data Protection Act, the sensitivity of the information held, the risks of a breach and the costs of precautionary measures. These terms ensured that their main concern was with the arrangements for preserving confidentiality of census information at a stage when it still could potentially be attached to identifiable individuals, rather than with either intrusions into privacy via the census content or the detailed techniques adopted to ensure anonymity in released census statistics.

The Review was forced to cover the intention rather than the practice of census procedures; it was conducted predominantly during 1990, in order to make a report in time to affect census procedures if that was deemed necessary. The Review Team was impressed with the commitment to maintaining confidentiality that they encountered at the highest levels in the Census Offices, and were happy with the careful and disciplined recruitment, documentation and training procedures that had been set in place for all the temporary staff recruited by the Census Offices. The arrangements for splitting up sensitive work with personal data into different tasks which could be performed by different people were particularly commended by the Review Team. However, they were concerned at the prospect of any subcontracted staff being brought into any of the Census Offices, and recommended that all staff should be directly employed.

They considered physical and electronic storage, entry, transmission and processing mechanisms in detail. (None of the details of arrangements or systems were actually reported, to prevent the security review itself becoming of use to any person seeking to crack the system.) They looked carefully at the way in which the forms were collected and taken to temporary Input Processing Stations, reviewing precisely who had access at each stage, satisfying themselves that it was the smallest number of people consistent with accurate processing, checking and correction. Access to the temporary offices was carefully reviewed, from car-parking arrangements to restrictions on where photocopiers could be accessed. They also recommended that the computer holding the main census database should not be connected to any government data or communications networks.

In general, the Review Team reported that 'the arrangements made so far are, in its opinion, fully in keeping with the very high standards of confidentiality required' (OPCS and GRO(S) 1991a, para 13) and that the plans and intentions current at the time of preparing the report also matched up to the standard. The Census Offices accepted all the major recommendations except one; they did not agree immediately to implement automatic electronic screening at the input stations, together with random baggage checks, preferring to keep it under careful review and to implement only if necessary. The BCS Review Team also suggested that there was a case for applying some of the new developments for the 1991 Census to earlier censuses to facilitate intercensal comparisons and thus add value to census data. The cost that census users are prepared to pay, and practical considerations such as changes of computer system may, however, limit the extent to which this is possible.

5.4 MAINTAINING ANONYMITY IN CENSUS PRODUCTS

Increasing power and speed and decreased costs of computing have led to greater data availability but also to new threats to privacy. The public and media are worried that super efficient computers make much cheaper, easier and therefore more likely, the matching of records across databases. Although much of the belief in the great accuracy and efficiency of computer systems seems in practice to be wide of the mark (e.g. Müller *et al.*, 1991), much of the research into data protection measures also assumes that the overlap of information in different files might enable a sufficient number of perfect matches to be performed for a threat to privacy to exist. Various measures are, therefore, adopted to guard against inadvertent disclosure by the Census Offices of any item of census information about an identifiable person. It must be understood in these discussions that such risks cannot be reduced to absolute zero. Anonymisation was argued above to be a compromise between the need of the individual to privacy and the need of the state to know; the precise level of anonymisation is a further compromise, since too much masking of the data can make it useless for research purposes.

5.4.1 Protecting anonymity of data in reports

It is in theory possible to disclose information about individuals by publishing tables with small cell sizes. Imagine, for example, a table of occupation by sex by marital status for a particular small area. If a cell for female, divorced dentists had a frequency of 1, a reader of the table might be able to work out who that dentist was and to know from the table that she was divorced.

The simplest way to prevent this type of disclosure is to restrict the fineness of detail in which census variables are reported, and to group rare categories. Unlike the explicit arrangements for the SARs (discussed below in section 5.4.4), the degree of permitted disaggregation in both published tables and small area statistics is limited by the judgement of Census Office staff. In general, variables with many categories such as age, occupation, qualifications, country of birth, are published in grouped categories in tables. The precise grouping used can often be frustrating for users who might have preferred slightly different categorisations.

Alterations can also be made to cell frequencies in order to mask their true values. There are five techniques for masking potentially identifiable individuals in frequency tables:

- suppressing cells entirely
- perturbing each cell slightly by adding a small amount of random error
- conventional rounding (grouping digits according to a predefined formula)
- random rounding (adjusting frequencies up or down at random)
- controlled rounding which ensures that the sum of rounded entries equals the rounded value of the sum of the unrounded entries (Fellegi, 1975).

For the 1971 Census, a conventional rounding technique was used for all tables based on the '100 per cent' items in published, printed reports, rounding cell frequencies to the nearest 0 or 5 and calculating percentages and rates using the rounded figures (Newman, 1978a; pp.25-27). This injection of a small amount of error in published tables led to many irritations for users where totals did not tally exactly and where percentages rarely summed to 100. Moreover, conventional rounding does not offer a good method of disclosure protection, as it can under certain circumstances be reversed (Cox *et al.*, 1986, p.141). The procedure was therefore dropped from 1981 onward and replaced by the second method (above) of adding a small amount of random error to each cell, but only for tables in reports below local authority area. The US Bureau of the Census, by contrast, uses four of the five above-mentioned techniques in its published output (it does not use conventional rounding) and has a major programme to investigate the complications in data analysis that these procedures give researchers (Cox *et al.*, 1986).

5.4.2 Protecting the anonymity of the Small Area Statistics (SAS) and the Local Base Statistics (LBS)[1]

Perhaps the most sensitive census product is the SAS supplied to customers on repayment. This certainly engendered most of the discussion around the Census Confidentiality Bill. Census data are widely used by the geo-demographics industry as the most reliable source of data enabling small areas to be profiled, but not, of course, as a source of actual names and addresses, a distinction which some members of the public may not fully appreciate. The Census Offices therefore take extra care to ensure that the aggregated information that they release about small areas cannot be used to make precise inferences about individuals in those areas.

---

[1] For ease of reference all discussion refers to the SAS only, except where there are differences between the SAS and the LBS.

The SAS are frequency counts and are therefore in principle capable of protection by each of the five methods mentioned in section 5.4.1. Small cell sizes in tables are much likelier to occur in the machine-readable small area statistics than in the published reports. For this reason they are subject to a disclosure protection procedure which adds a small amount of random noise to the cells of tables. Cole (chapter 8) explores further some of the consequences of its adoption in the SAS. Because of public concern over the way in which firms which already had existing databanks on small areas might be able to use SAS in order to identify people, the rules governing disclosure protection for SAS were tightened up between 1981 and 1991.

In order for statistics for an ED to be given separately in the SAS tables, the population of the ED has to reach a threshold of 16 (8 in 1981) households and 50 (25 in 1981) people in Great Britain. For EDs which fall below this, only the total numbers of persons and households are published. These thresholds are significantly higher than equivalent thresholds used in published data from the US census (Courtland, 1985: 414). In Northern Ireland the thresholds are twice as high as in Great Britain — 32 households and 100 people in the 1991 SAS.

Small area statistics are modified only at levels below the area of local government district and only for the 100 per cent data. SAS tables based on 10 per cent processing are deemed to be sufficiently protected already, as sampling in itself gives a great deal of disclosure protection.

For confidentiality reasons, the process of modification is not fully disclosed by OPCS. In brief outline, the 1991 modification process took place within each district and, for the SAS, modified each cell in the tables by +1, 0 or -1 in a quasi-random pattern. To avoid negative numbers in tables, no adjustment was made to precise zeros in tables. In the case of the LBS, available at ward level but with a finer level of detail than the SAS, the procedure was operated twice so that each count was altered by the addition of a number between -2 and +2.

The modification procedure used with the 1991 Census data differed from that used in 1981 in that the latter first paired EDs within districts before applying the addition of +1, 0 or -1. This pairing did not take place with the 1991 data.

The modification procedure in 1991 operated on a probability basis such that, for the LBS, if 10 cells in a table are being summed, the resulting number may differ from the actual count by as much as ± 20, but there is less than a 5 per cent chance that the difference will exceed ± 4. For the SAS, there is a less than a 5 per cent chance that the sum of 10 cells will differ from the actual count by more than ± 3, although in theory the difference could be as much as ± 10. The size and consequences of the error thus introduced are discussed in detail in chapter 8 where Cole provides some illustrations of the scale of problems that can occur.

5.4.3 Protecting anonymity in the Special Workplace and Migration Statistics

There are two matrices of origin to destination flow statistics available from the census, described fully in chapter 10. The data structure is different to other forms of output, being a series of vast matrices at different levels of geographical aggregation recording how many migration or travel-to-work flows there were from ward to ward, district to district and so on. The possibility of uniqueness in these matrices is very great: most of the cells in the ward-to-ward migration flow matrix are empty, for example.

In the Special Migration Statistics, simple ward flows are given with no restrictions but only disaggregated by age and sex. Interdistrict migrant flows are given disaggregated by other variables which might potentially identify individuals. They are therefore subject to a thresholding rule which stipulates that there must be at least 10 migrants between any two districts before the flow can be disaggregated by marital status, ethnic group, illness, economic position and Gaelic/Welsh speaking, and at least 10 wholly moving households before disaggregation by tenure and economic position of the head of household is allowed.

The Special Workplace Statistics are drawn from the 10 per cent fully coded sample and is therefore subject to no further disclosure.

5.4.4 Protecting anonymity in the Samples of Anonymised Records (SARs)

Anonymity in microdata can be protected by a series of techniques analogous to those used in frequency data. In this section we review the techniques of anonymisation being used on the SARs. The effect of the measures adopted in limiting the amount of information available is covered more fully in chapter 11; in that chapter an attempt is made to quantify the risk of disclosure of personal information through release of the SARs.

Some variables are deemed so risky that they are suppressed before microdata are released. Direct identifiers such as name and address have obviously been suppressed. Precise date of birth has also been suppressed, as have name and address of the employer.

Other variables are only considered to pose a risk to the anonymity of the record if they are released in fine detail. Geography is the most obvious example, as the unit postcode could in theory have been made available on the microdata. A decision was therefore taken only to identify large geographical areas to protect respondent anonymity. On the individual level file, large local districts were separately identified if their population crossed a threshold of 120,000; otherwise they were amalgamated to form larger districts. On the household file, only regional information was given.

With some other variables, the smaller categories have been grouped, either across the entire range of the variable or only at the extremes (a process known as 'top coding'). The rule used to decide the level of detail to be released was to group information categories to a sufficient detail so that, on average, the expected sample count would be at least one for each category of each piece of information for the lowest geographical area permitted on each SAR.

Some justification for restricting attention to the distribution of the univariate categories of each variable in turn was given by Marsh, Dale and Skinner (forthcoming). They demonstrated that the risk of an individual having a unique combination of values of a set of variables could be predicted with a high degree of certainty simply from knowledge of their membership of rare categories of each variable taken singly. The precise cut-off at an expected value of 1 was set at a value sufficiently high to give reasonable protection of anonymity.

The rule was applied to each census variable. Expected counts were obtained by using 1981 Census frequency counts (supplemented by more recent surveys, for example the Labour Force Survey) at the national level for the whole population. To obtain expected counts, the count of 1 per category per SAR area was grossed up to the national level:

$$C = 1/X * (Y/Z)$$

where C = expected count at the national level;

X = sampling fraction ($\frac{1}{50}$ for individual SAR and $\frac{1}{100}$ for household SAR);

Y = national population (56 million);

Z = smallest geographical area population (120,000 for individual SAR and 2.1 million (East Anglia) for household SAR.

Thus 25,000 and 2,700 were the two thresholds used for the individual and household SARs respectively. The precise variables affected by these threshold rules, as well as some additional measures taken to ensure anonymity of categories felt to pose a greater temptation to the malicious hacker for example, politicians and sports personalities, are outlined in chapter 11.

In theory, a small amount of random noise could have been added to certain variables in a manner analogous to the procedure adopted for the SAS. A technique similar to this has been used in the 1990 US Census for example: geography has been subject to a degree of perturbation by switching a small number of similar households between nearby areas (Navarro, Florez-Baez and Thompson, 1990). However, the natural levels of noise in the data, combined with the analytical difficulties of minimising bias to both measures of location and spread by such techniques in a multipurpose file, led to perturbation not being implemented in any form for the SARs.

Finally, as was argued in the previous section, sampling offers a strong source of disclosure protection for sensitive data. It not only reduces the actual risk that a particular individual can be found in the census output, but it probably has its greatest effect by reducing the chances that anyone would make the attempt at identification by this means. The two SARs (a 1 per cent sample of households and a 2 per cent sample of individuals) are sufficiently small to offer a great deal of protection; the samples do not overlap so that the detailed household or occupational information available on the household file cannot be matched with the detailed geographical information available on the individual file.

5.4.5 Protecting anonymity in the OPCS Longitudinal Study (LS)

The OPCS Longitudinal Study (discussed in chapter 12) contains census information linked to other vital statistics such as births, certain illnesses, deaths and so on. Because it contains data that might be considered more sensitive, the principal method used to protecting respondents' privacy in this dataset is to restrict access to it; the records are not released as publicly available microdata, but maintained on the OPCS computer where the strict conditions of access described in section 5.3 above apply. However, as an additional precaution, some anonymisation procedures are undertaken on the LS as well. Because the main method of protecting this dataset is confidentiality rather than anonymity, the results governing such things as fineness of geography permitted can be somewhat more relaxed that on the SARs.

The LS is also a sample of records, and is therefore protected through the sampling mechanism. The dates of birth used to select respondents for the LS are kept a strict secret: if published, people would know (or could find out) who was in the database, and the considerable protection offered to individuals by sampling would be lost. The geographical detail offered on the LS is restricted to local districts, the smallest of which has a population of 20,000. This is smaller than permitted on the SARs, and a choice of geographies is available in the LS (e.g. health districts as well as local authority districts). Beyond this grouping of geography, none of the

Figure 5.1 **'I know the census is supposed to be completely secret, but I am surprised you've only got one toilet in that big house of yours.'**
(Evening Standard 24 April 1991)

Table 5.1

Content of Parliamentary questions* about the census: 1920–1991

	1991	1981	1971	1966	1961	1951	1931	1921
Question content and wording	3	9	9	3	-	2	3	2
Compulsory nature of census, penalties	4	8	-	-	-	1	-	
Confidentiality provisions, safeguards and breaches	14	7	13	2	2	5	1	-
Language: questions, translations	2	7	4	2	-	1	1	-
Recruitment, pay and conditions of employment of enumerators	6	8	10	-	-	6	15	10
Timing, cost, administration of census, printing, etc.	6	3	9	3	-	5	6	16
Timetable for publication, or availability of tabulations	6	10	7	4	6	3	8	7
General questions about need for or responsibility for the census	-	-	2	-	1	3	-	2
Other — miscellaneous	19	7	9	2	1	3	3	1
Total	56	55	71	16	10	28	38	37

* Questions relating to census matters that were reported in the *Hansard* volumes for the House of Commons in the year preceeding census year, the year of the census and the year following.
Source: Bulmer, 1979, p 168 for years up to 1971; *Hansard,* House of Commons for 1981 and 1991.

grouping and top coding of variables necessary on the SARs has been done. Age is available directly in yearly bands without top coding, and, although researchers would never be allowed to see the finer grain birth date information, its existence makes possible the definition of different age-groupings such as yearly bands of children approaching school age each September.

Anonymity in the LS is protected by a manual screen of all tables and statistical summaries produced from the database to ensure that they do not threaten disclosure of information about identifiable individuals. Because the database cannot be transported to another machine, nor accessed directly by outsiders to OPCS, these sorts of checks and controls are possible. They would pose too much work for OPCS if they were to be undertaken entirely by them, so preliminary screening of users and requests is performed through the Social Statistics Research Unit at City University, whose work and role is described more fully in chapter 12.

5.4.6 Conclusions on anonymisation techniques

The growth of electronic computing has made possible these and other new methods of preserving the privacy of individual respondents while enabling researchers to get more value from expensively collected census data. The area of disclosure protection has received growing interest in the 1980s and 1990s; readers wishing a review of the recent literature should consult the proceedings of a conference organised by the International Statistical Institute devoted to the topic (ISI,1992). New techniques of this kind have an important role to play in ensuring that respondents' anonymity is objectively better secured. It is important that the professional social science community understand how these techniques work and their role in preserving privacy. However, it is probably the case that they play little part in reassuring the lay public about the security of the confidentiality guarantees given in the census; indeed, there is a danger that such techniques may contribute to the mystification of the process of census taking and reporting. It is to the important topic of public perceptions of confidentiality risks that we now turn.

5.5 PUBLIC PERCEPTIONS OF CONFIDENTIALITY

Having rehearsed the careful ways in which the Census Offices maintain the confidentiality of the identifiable information entrusted to them, we conclude this chapter by considering whether the public is impressed or not. The rapid development of information technology has led not only to the greater possibility of misuse of personal data and difficulty in maintaining anonymity, but it has also led to heightened public and media sensitivity to issues connected with privacy, as the BCS Review Team noted (OPCS and GRO(S), 1991a; para 29), and as the cartoon in figure 5.1 illustrates.

In this section we shall first consider the climate of public opinion as reflected by the views of Members of the House of Commons in the questions they ask about the census. We shall then consider what systematic evidence (beyond cartoons) can be gleaned about the opinions of the general public.

5.5.1 Debates in Parliament on the census

Politicians can have an important influence on the census. The call by some Members of Parliament in 1971 for a boycott of the census had a fine (albeit small) influence on census response. In the preparation for 1991, certain MPs kept the topic of using postcoded census data in the public eye, and fears about the census wording tests led one Birmingham MP to advocate boycotting the test census in 1989 (Pearce and Thomas, 1990).

However, it is important to know how widespread such concerns about confidentiality were among politicians. Trends in the attitude of politicians towards the census can be obtained by consulting the parliamentary record, *Hansard*. Table 5.1 traces Parliamentary interest in the census by reporting a content analysis of Parliamentary Questions relating to census matters.

The figures for questions surrounding the 1991 Census only include questions asked up to June 1992. The rise in the number of questions concerned with privacy and confidentiality is clear. Prior to 1971 very few questions related to these topics, but since then confidentiality has become the single biggest issue of concern with the census in the eyes of Members of the House of Commons. Inspections of the content of the questions reveals concern over the activities of the geodemographics industry in particular.

5.5.2 Public concerns about census privacy

Ironically, privacy and confidentiality do not seem to be major factors governing responses to surveys. People seem either not to hear the guarantees given to them on the doorstep or not to read the assurances provided, and even if they do hear them, fail to believe them; such are the general conclusions of research in the US (Singer 1978; National Research Council 1979).

Evidence from Britain suggests that the British are if anything even worse informed and less trusting about census matters than the US public. We are fortunate to have access to survey data collected by the Gallup organisation in Britain three months and one month prior to the census, and similar questions asked one month prior to the census in the US by the Gallup Organization Inc; the results are shown in table 5.2.

The answers to questions (a) and (b) suggest that knowledge of the census enterprise in general was very weak in Britain and did not improve substantially between January and March 1991 during which time the census information campaign had got underway; less than half the public knew that the census takes place every ten years, and only 14 per cent were aware that the census was one month away in March 1991. The information base in the US is also fairly weak; however, census day in the US was 1 April compared to 21 April in Britain, so the smaller number of 'don't knows' in the US in mid-March 1990 may just reflect increasing awareness as the census approached.

Three quarters of people in Britain (but less than half in the US) knew that participation in the census was compulsory. Yet they either did not know of, or failed to believe, the confidentiality guarantees given by the Census Offices, as the dismal results in answer to question (d) reveal: two in five of the public thought that the Census Offices might release data to other government departments. The level of disbelief in the US was somewhat lower, but still at a level capable of depressing Census Offices who had made these guarantees the centrepoint of a campaign to the general public.

Thus, both in Britain and in the US, public perceptions of the census enterprise do not correspond to the facts; many people believed that the Census Offices might hand out information to other government departments and do not honour the pledges

Table 5.2

Perceptions of census confidentiality

	USA 15–18 March 1990 (N=1225) (%)	GB 9–14 Jan 1991 (N=964) (%)	GB 12–18 March 1991 (N=1030) (%)

(a) The Government conducts a census, or a count of the country's population on a regular basis. Can you tell me if the census is taken every year, every five years, every ten years or every 20 years?

Every year	7	4	4
Every 5 years	21	24	29
Every 10 years	60	46	43
Every 20 years	2	4	3
Don't know	10	22	20

(b) Would you happen to know when the next census will be taken?

Jan-Mar this year	-	4	2
April this year	-	9	14
Right now, soon etc.	36	-	-
May-June this year	-	3	4
Later this year	30	8	11
Next year or later	7	14	15
Don't know	27	61	54

(c) To the best of your knowledge, is your participation in the census required by law or not?

Yes, required by law	47	63	76
No, not required	43	25	12
Don't know	10	12	12

(d) How confident are you that the Census Office will not release an individual's census information to other government agencies? Are you:

Very confident	23	15	17
Somewhat confident	44	30	27
Not at all confident	28	40	42
Don't know	5	15	14

Source: Data for Britain from personal interviews conducted in 1991 by Social Surveys (Gallup) Ltd, reported in *Gallup Political and Economic Index*, (368) April, 1991, reproduced here with their kind permission; data for US from telephone interviews conducted in 1990, reported in *The Gallup Poll News Service*, 22 March 1990, reproduced here by courtesy of the US Gallup Organization Inc.

they give of confidentiality. Similar work done in Australia in 1991 around the time of the census there produced very similar results; only at the height of the census advertising campaign, when confidentiality pledges were pressed home, did a bare majority of the population say it believed that census information would not be passed on to other government departments (Australian Bureau of the Census,1991).

The important thing is that people still cooperate despite the fact that they believe government departments exchange information in this way. It may be that the public simply do not feel that the subject matter of the census is sufficiently sensitive for them to care who knows this information; or they may care, but believe that in the global village of the late 20th century privacy can no longer be protected and thus view the collection of census data as a minor invasion of privacy in comparison to more worrying developments. A plausible third explanation for continued cooperation may be because they cannot see any detriment which has occurred through census information being passed on: not surprisingly if none has been passed on (Courtland, 1985). People may not believe the promises, but neither they nor, perhaps more importantly, the press would condone any breach in these assurances (Bouvard and Bouvard, 1975). Confidentiality and anonymity safeguards, therefore, remain an essential part of the cooperation given to the census enterprise.

6 The validation of census data

I — Post-enumeration survey approaches

Richard D. Wiggins

6.1 AN INTRODUCTION TO CENSUS EVALUATION

Earlier chapters have stressed the traditional role of the census as the most authoritative social accounting of people and housing in Britain. Because of this, great emphasis is placed upon complete coverage of the population. It is therefore important that there is an assessment of the extent to which the census achieves this goal and an estimate of where it falls short. One of the main checks on the completeness and coverage of the 1991 Census was provided by the Census Validation Survey (CVS), a survey conducted soon after the census in 1,200 Census enumeration districts. Another check, equally important in 1991, was provided by comparison with demographic estimates of the population and is discussed in part II of this chapter. The main focus of Part I of this chapter is on the role of post-enumeration surveys in validating the census, with a particular emphasis on the 1991 CVS. The methods of post-enumeration used in three other anglophone countries are also considered, particularly in terms of the increasing difficulty of achieving a complete enumeration. Part II of this chapter, by Catherine Marsh, examines in the context of more general problems with data quality in the census, how well the CVS worked, how and where it might have failed, the methods which OPCS use for checking the CVS, and, finally, some suggestions for those using the data.

6.2 WHAT IS POST-ENUMERATION?

6.2.1 Errors in the British census

The objects of a population census are to count the number of people in the country at a point in time, and to classify them according to a number of characteristics. Similarly, the census counts and classifies households, household spaces, families, dwellings, rooms and a number of other items (see chapter 2).

Two major types of error occur in the British census:

- Counting errors: people who should have been included but were omitted or people counted twice
- Classification errors: the wrong details, or no details at all, recorded about a person who was otherwise properly included in the census

Classification errors can, of course, produce the effect of a counting error. One subgroup of the population may appear to be undercounted simply because some members have been incorrectly classified and were therefore counted in another group.

One way to investigate such errors is to conduct a repeat enumeration on a sample basis and to compare the results with those obtained in the census. The first comprehensive attempt to check the quality of the census results in Britain was made by Gray and Gee (1972) following the 1966 sample census. The rigour of their methodology is both impressive and revealing. Trained interviewers uncovered fascinating insights on the extent to which households misunderstood or misinterpreted what was asked of them in the census. A less rigorous check was made following the 1971 Census but, in 1981, a full post-enumeration survey (PES) was conducted. The terminology was changed before the 1991 Census check because of confusion over the use of the abbreviation PES for the Public Expenditure Survey. All references to the 1991 survey will therefore be to the Census Validation Survey (CVS).

Post-enumeration surveys typically provide estimates of both types of error. Counting error is estimated by *coverage checks*; classification error is evaluated through *quality checks*. Quality checks may also reveal the reasons for any discrepancies that occur and should inform the design of future census forms. Post-enumeration surveys typically take place *immediately* after a population census using trained social survey interviewers or enumerators to re-enumerate a sample of census areas.

6.2.2 Counting errors

The most important function of a census is to provide an accurate population count for a particular moment in time. Britain has a tradition of enumerating people once and once only in the place where they happen to be on census night. By also recording the usual residents in a household, two different population bases can be compiled — the population present and the population usually resident (see chapter 2, section 2.3). The key role of a post-enumeration survey is to establish the accuracy of this count and to identify where any discrepancies may arise.

Despite careful training of enumerators and census officers, counting errors occur and population censuses invariably fail to count everyone. Errors may arise in a number of ways.

First, *enumerators* may fail to identify all residential accommodation, or fail to identify all households within the accommodation. Accommodation may be mistakenly classified as vacant or as containing 'wholly absent' households when it is vacant. Errors may be made in estimating the number of people living in 'wholly absent' households mistakenly assumed to be vacant. Second, *form-fillers*, within identified households and within communal establishments, may fail to enumerate all individuals present or resident, or make errors on other items. Other enumeration errors may occur when people are recorded as resident at more than one address or when babies born before census day are missed.

The *gross coverage error* represents the sum of all those in a population who are missed or wrongly counted. However, an enumeration of a person at the wrong address typically corresponds to a missed person at the correct address. Generally, the number of missed persons exceeds the number of erroneous enumerations and the difference is called the *net undercount*. Even if the number of missed persons was equalled by the number of people wrongly included, it is likely that the characteristics of the two groups would differ, leading to error in the counts for subgroups in the population.

Great weight is attached to the accuracy of population estimates derived from the census; in the US there has been much debate and, indeed, litigation on the issue of the census undercount. Post-enumeration surveys are one method of checking the accuracy of the census count. Alternative estimates of the population size can be obtained through the use of vital statistics and migration statistics in demographic analysis models although these estimates start from a previous census baseline (Fay, Passel, and Robinson, 1988; OPCS, 1992a) and are discussed in part II of this chapter. It is important to remember that the net undercount in the census, whatever method is used to estimate it, is subject to error.

6.2.3 Classification error

The second aspect of inaccuracy in the census is classification error and is typically assessed through post-enumeration surveys. Classification errors are mainly caused by incorrect entries made on the census form. These errors often occur because the form filler did not understand a question or did not follow instructions on the census schedule. Pre-census tests (see chapter 4) should minimise ambiguities in question wording but, invariably, in a full census there will be a small proportion of the population who misunderstand certain questions.

Sometimes a question may be perfectly understood by a form-filler but mistakenly recorded: for example, the form filler may hold incorrect information about the age or occupation of another household member or have been given wrong information by a member of the household. Although very little can be done to reduce this kind of error it may be revealed by a quality check. Occasionally, a form-filler may have deliberately entered wrong information. Finally, of course, the form-filler may have simply forgotten to answer a question or failed to realise that the question should be answered.

Errors and omissions may not be corrected when the enumerator collects and checks the forms, and errors may also be introduced by the enumerator. The basic task of an enumerator is to deliver and collect forms from households or communal establishments (see chapter 4), although they are instructed to help a household fill in a form if asked. However, Gray and Gee (1972) reported that enumerators often adopt the role of interviewer, although not trained to do so. The post-enumeration survey following the 1966 sample census found that enumerators had filled in the census form completely for some 3 per cent of households, rising to 6 per cent for multi-occupied addresses. There was evidence that individual questions may have been filled in by the enumerators on a much higher proportion of forms. Similar levels of enumerator intervention have been observed in subsequent tests and censuses. The enumerator is a key figure in a census, and, although instructions are carefully set out in the Enumerator's Handbook, we nonetheless know too little about his/her characteristics and the difficulties encountered when carrying out the task.

Although further classification errors may arise through the coding and editing process once the census forms arrive for office checking and processing, this is not subject to checks by the CVS. The CVS is confined to a check on information collected *before* any editing or processing. The CVS household interview is concerned with comparing the information recorded by form-fillers on their census schedules with that elicited by the CVS interview. However, as part of the coverage check, the CVS was able to assess the accuracy of imputation for wholly absent households.

In the rest of this part of the chapter the methods of post-census enumeration in Britain are described and then related to methods used in the US, Canada and Australia.

6.3 POST-ENUMERATION PRIOR TO 1991

Post-census validation surveys are a relatively recent development, but have an increasingly important role (Wormald, 1991; Barnes, 1989). Of the nine EC countries which conducted conventional censuses in 1991, Ireland was the only country not to carry out a post-census validation survey (Langevin, Begeot and Pearce, 1992). This section discusses the development of post-enumeration surveys in Britain prior to 1991 and is largely based on Barnes (1989).

6.3.1 Britain — a history of census validation prior to 1991

Some limited demographic checks, using birth and death registration records for instance, took place after the 1951 Census, but these were not as extensive, nor as preplanned, as those devised for subsequent censuses (GRO, 1958; 1968).

The first post-enumeration survey was carried out in England and Wales in 1961. Its aim was to check the coverage and quality of the 1961 Census. Although separate from the census, the checks were carried out by census personnel. The checks produced an estimate of net undercount of 0.2 per cent, but as stated in the General Report on the 1961 Census: 'the design of the enquiry was such that the quality of the result may be suspect but there is no information on this' (GRO, 1968).

The 1966 Census *quality* check of England and Wales (Gray and Gee, 1972) formed a significant milestone because it was carried out by the Social Survey Division of the Central Information Office — a separate department from the General Register Office which was responsible for the census itself. The 1966 *coverage* check was carried out by census officers. The 1966 quality check contained a number of key features which were to set the pattern for similar studies carried out in conjunction with future censuses. These are listed below:

(1) Whereas participation in the census was, and still is, compulsory, the post-enumeration survey was voluntary. Response to the 1966 quality check was 95 per cent.

(2) Whereas the census employed a large force of temporarily recruited enumerators, the survey used highly trained and experienced interviewers.

(3) The survey used detailed structured questionnaires to check answers to topics which in the census were covered by just one or two questions.

(4) Survey interviewers had copies of the informants' answers on the census form so that they could probe any discrepancies, partly to ensure that the check itself was not in error and partly to provide some reasons for the differences.

(5) The survey sought interviews from each adult in a household and so relied far less on proxy responses than did the census.

(6)   In order to avoid discrepancies arising through genuine change between the time of the census and the time of the survey, it was necessary that the survey took place soon after the census. In fact, the survey fieldwork was carried out between two and three months after the date of the census.

A check on both the coverage and quality of the 1966 Census in Scotland was carried out by census officers in selected areas and results published in the County Reports for that census.

Coverage and quality checks were again carried out on the 1971 Census. As before, the coverage check was conducted by census officers. Although the check showed a net undercount of only 0.23 per cent, the check was not considered entirely successful from a technical point of view. The General Report (OPCS, 1983a) stated, 'it was carried out by census officers some of whom would still have been busy with other work on the census. Some census officers might have viewed the check as a fault finding mission and in consequence would not have been fully motivated to ensure its success'.

The 1971 quality check (OPCS, 1983a) took the form of a post-enumeration survey of 5,000 addresses covering the whole of Great Britain. The check was again carried out by the Social Survey Division which had by now become part of the newly formed Office of Population Censuses and Surveys, responsible for conducting the census. As with the coverage check, there were unsatisfactory aspects about the quality check. The fieldwork did not start until two months after the census and was not completed until about five months after census night. Because of weaknesses in the design of the check and the delay in the completion of the fieldwork, a number of important aims of the check were not achieved. For example, there was no assessment of the accuracy with which questions on household tenure and amenities were answered.

Following the 1981 Census, coverage and quality checks were both carried out by the Social Survey Division of OPCS (Britton and Birch, 1985) and provided an integrated approach that set the scene for the 1991 CVS. After (unfounded) public concern about the confidentiality aspects of follow-up surveys linked to the 1971 Census, the 1981 Post-Enumeration Survey was announced in advance to Parliament and the public.

For the coverage check, roughly 1,000 EDs (around 1 per cent) were selected in England and Wales and all addresses in them were thoroughly relisted by trained interviewers to see if any had been missed by census enumerators. Additionally, separate coverage checks were carried out in Scotland by the Scottish General Register Office (GRO(S) 1982; 1983). The EDs were selected in blocks of four, adjacent to each other to enable enumeration boundaries to be checked. Different samples of addresses within selected EDs were taken to see whether people had been left off census forms or addresses otherwise correctly enumerated; whether anyone had been missed in addresses enumerated as vacant or non-residential; and to check the enumeration of multi-household addresses.

This was a much more rigorous approach than had been used in 1971. Moreover, in 1971 no attempt had been made in the field to check discrepancies. In 1981 interviewers were given copies of preliminary census address listings to check, by means of personal enquiry, numbers of people missed in non-enumerated addresses. Also in the 1981 Post-Enumeration Survey, unlike the previous checks, discrepancies in the number of people present in enumerated households were explored with the informant, thereby enabling the interviewer to reconcile any differences. There was one further way in which the 1981 check was superior to its predecessors: all EDs were graded on the basis of expected difficulty of enumeration (more detail is given in section 6.5). The design for the 1981 Post-Enumeration Survey oversampled, by a factor of two, these 'difficult' EDs, since it was hypothesised that such EDs would be likely to produce more errors.

However, in spite of the thoroughness with which the 1981 coverage check was carried out and the improvements made over previous studies, there are inherent difficulties in checking the coverage of a census using re-enumeration methods. Because of the cost of the approach, the samples have to be fairly small and the sampling errors are relatively large, especially at the subnational level. Also, in spite of the thoroughness of the methods, it is likely that some of the people missed in the census will, for similar reasons, also have been missed in the post-enumeration survey.

Therefore, in 1981 as in previous census evaluations, additional checks were made against independent administrative sources for particular subgroups of the population. These checks were primarily targeted at children under five years of age and school-age children, and were largely based on aggregate comparisons of census statistics with statistics derived from administrative records (OPCS, 1984).

Post-enumeration surveys in Britain have been confined to private accommodation. Institutions and other communal establishments have been excluded from most evaluation because of the highly transient nature of their population. Census evaluations have typically included checks on electoral registration commissioned by the Home Office (Butcher and Dodd, 1983).

Important lessons have been learned from past evaluations:

- fieldwork should be completed as soon as possible after the census
- field workers should be trained interviewers skilled in administering complex questionnaires
- the public should be informed in advance of the intention to carry out evaluations
- census evaluation studies should preferably be carried out by staff who were not directly involved with the census operation itself

6.3.2 1981 Census count of residents

The 1981 Census counted 48.52 million residents in England and Wales, present at their usual address or absent from a household at which someone else was present; this was the count used for most statistical output, and omitted residents of wholly absent households and residents absent from communal establishments. This was about 1 million people fewer than the estimate of 49.59 millions resident in England and Wales on 30 June 1981 (OPCS, 1982).

The 1981 Post-Enumeration Survey was used to assess the extent of under-enumeration; it found a net under-enumeration 0.452 per cent (214,000 people) of the population of England and Wales. The gross under-enumeration (0.62 per cent) was offset by 0.17 per cent people who were double-counted. However, there was a big difference between London (especially Inner London) and the rest of the country. Under-enumeration of persons in the Inner London area was estimated to be

Table 6.1

Under-enumeration of persons and households (as measured by the PES)
for sub-divisions of England and Wales, 1981

Area	Persons (net)		Households	
	Estimated rate of under-enumeration (%)	Confidence limits (%)	Estimated rate of under-enumeration (%)	Confidence limits (%)
Greater London				
Inner London	2.46	± 0.80	2.75	± 0.92
Outer London	1.01	± 0.54	0.42	± 0.26
Other metropolitan areas	0.24	± 0.23	0.37	± 0.18
Non-metropolitan areas	0.29	± 0.16	0.36	± 0.10
England and Wales (excluding inner London)	0.34	± 0.13	0.37	±0.08
England and Wales	**0.45**	**± 0.13**	**0.50**	**±0.11**

Source: Britton and Birch, 1985.

Table 6.2

Under-enumeration of persons (as measured by the PES) by selected causes;
Inner London and England and Wales contrasted, 1981

Selected causes	Inner London		England and Wales	
	(%)		(%)	
Misclassified as absent household	1.17	± 0.40	0.17	± 0.04
Misclassified as vacant	0.40	± 0.24	0.09	± 0.03
Building missed	0.32	± 0.21	0.05	± 0.02
Individual(s) missed in enumeration household	0.72	± 0.50	0.27	± 0.09
Gross under-enumeration†	**2.73**	**± 0.74**	**0.62**	**± 0.11**
Individuals enumerated more than once	- 0.27	± 0.31	- 0.17	± 0.07
Net under-enumeration	**2.46**	**± 0.80**	**0.45**	**± 0.13**

† Including causes not shown separately in the table.
Source: Britton and Birch, 1985.

around 2.5 per cent compared with 0.3 per cent outside London. It is, however, important to note the wide confidence intervals around these figures. Table 6.1 summarises the degree of under-enumeration by broad geographical areas reported by the 1981 Post-Enumeration Survey.

Table 6.2, also taken from Britton and Birch (1985), shows the four main causes of under-enumeration. The largest cause of gross under-enumeration of people in households was the number missed in enumerated households (although to some extent this was offset by the number of people whom the census counted twice).

Households misclassified by the enumerator as absent was the second most important cause. The final two major causes were the misclassifion of household spaces as vacant by the enumerator and missed property.

In the 1981 Census, households at which forms were delivered but not collected were usually regarded as absent. Households who were apparently away from their usual address on census night were *not* required to return a form for that address (this differed from 1971 when wholly absent households were requested to return a form with certain questions completed (Britton and Birch, 1985, section 4.1.6)).

In calculating the provisional mid-year estimates for 1981, the 1981 Census count of residents was taken as the base-line and then adjusted to take into account: 800,800 absent residents not recorded by the census; the natural change in the population between census day and 30 June; and the number of children aged 0–4. Additionally, the figures were adjusted by the 214,000 people whom the 1981 Post-Enumeration Survey estimated were missed from the census. (The second part of this chapter discusses these figures in more detail.) Revised mid-1981 population estimates were also adjusted for a processing error that affected the number of usually resident people in households but who were absent on census night (Britton and Birch, 1985).

In summary, the under-enumeration found by the 1981 coverage check, when added to the usually resident population count from the 1981 Census, provided a basis consistent with the Registrar General's mid-year estimates for 1981 based on the rolled-forward 1971 Census figures. As will later become evident, a similar reconciliation between rolled-forward mid-year estimates and the new census figures was not possible in 1991.

6.4 PRELIMINARY ESTIMATES FROM THE 1991 CENSUS

The 1991 Census Preliminary Report, based upon returns from enumerators, showed about 2 per cent fewer people than might be expected from estimates (Wormald, 1991). However, the preliminary count did not include people who returned their forms late, neither did it allow for the balance of visitors to Great Britain; additionally, it included no estimate of those whom the census had failed to count.

Census counts of the resident population, produced as part of the census processing (see chapter 4), differed from the preliminary count by including not only late returns from households where someone was present but also the voluntary returns from households where all members were absent on census night. Additionally, it included the imputation of persons in wholly absent households who did not make a voluntary return, and in other households where the enumerator could make no contact but where circumstantial evidence indicated that there were residents. These counts, made available during 1992, showed a total of 49,890,000 usual residents in England and Wales. This figure was still about 1 million lower than that expected from the Registrar General's mid-year estimates.

After taking into account natural change in population (births and deaths) and migration between 21 April 1991 (census day) and 30 June 1991 (the date of the Registrar General's estimates) and the adjustment necessary for students with a term-time address in England and Wales but not normally living there, it was expected that the remaining difference would be accounted for by the under-enumeration found in the CVS.

The preliminary results from the CVS — and its failure to identify the expected number of missing people — are discussed in section 6.6. The following section sets out the objectives and design of the 1991 CVS.

6.5 THE 1991 CENSUS VALIDATION SURVEY

The CVS was planned with the following aims:

- to check whether all persons present on census night in a household had been correctly enumerated by the census
- to verify the classification by census enumerators of unoccupied residential accommodation after editing and imputation to adjust for absent households
- to assess the quality of replies given to census questions

The CVS was confined to households and was carried out in England and Wales and Scotland. The CVS did not attempt to cover people in communal establishments or people sleeping rough. For practical reasons the CVS also excluded certain remote Scottish areas. The design was heavily based upon the 1981 Post-Enumeration Survey (Britton and Birch, 1985). An important procedural difference between 1981 and 1991 is that the 1981 Census processing did not include a procedure to impute for households classified by the enumerators as absent (Britton and Birch, 1985, section 4.1.6).

6.5.1 Design

The CVS was based on a nationally representative stratified cluster sample of over 1,200 EDs covering England, Wales and Scotland. Details of the method of sample selection are given below. The CVS was carried out by the Social Survey Division of OPCS and used trained interviewers both to check the classification of accommodation made by enumerators and also to conduct the interviews.

The degree of clustering and stratification

In England and Wales census geography databases (Clark and Thomas, 1990) provide an ideal population hierarchy of administrative units for multistage sampling. Data is held for each county, census district and ED. EDs are graded at the pre-fieldwork stage of the census in terms of the expected difficulty of enumeration based on five factors from the 1981 Census:

the percentages of:
- non-residential premises
- multi-occupancy
- persons in communal establishments
and also
- language difficulty
- area size

Each census district (see chapter 3, section 3.3.4 and chapter 4, section 4.4) was graded on the basis of the modal grade of its member EDs. Census districts were also clustered by census area manager districts in groups of around 20. Census area manager districts could be identified as local authority districts and thereby formed potential strata or clusters.

Thus, the principal stratification factors available were broad geographical areas, census district grading and ED grade. From the 1981 Census there was strong evidence to show that both geography and enumeration difficulty were related to the level of net undercount. The CVS design took these factors directly into account, either explicitly using areas or implicitly by ordering listings of districts by enumeration difficulty. However, it was also necessary to introduce some clustering into the design in order to keep down costs, despite any loss in precision. Broad geographical strata, corresponding to metropolitan areas (including Inner and Outer London), rural areas (the Shires) and a 'mixed' group containing part-rural and urban areas were defined. Within each stratum census districts were grouped by census area manager districts. These groupings deepened the geographical stratification. It is because some census area manager districts cover both former metropolitan and rural local authorities that the mixed strata were identified. Census districts were taken as the first stage sampling units (as in 1981). This provided a clustered sample, with one interviewer allocated to each census district, located in its parent census area manager district, with consequent reductions in fieldwork and administrative costs.

For sampling purposes Scotland formed a separate domain from England and Wales. Two geographical strata were formed, Glasgow City and the rest of Scotland. As in England and Wales, census districts were sampled as first-stage units.

Selection of first stage sampling units

Altogether 300 census districts were selected — 270 in England and Wales and 30 in Scotland (allocated proportionally to the estimated population size).

Within the broad geographical strata described above, census districts were listed by grade (within census area managers for England and Wales and by local authority district in Scotland) and selected with probability proportional to a measure of population size. The measure of size was calculated so that areas judged more difficult to enumerate had a relatively higher chance of selection. For example, within the metropolitan areas, those EDs deemed easiest to enumerate were given a double weighting; those hardest to enumerate, a four-fold weighting. EDs in the shire counties were given a weight of one, irrespective of grading difficulty (typically any grading difficulty was a function of area size alone). Thus, census district population sizes were adjusted accordingly before selection. In Scotland, all areas in the Glasgow City stratum were oversampled by a factor of two, and areas outside were unadjusted.

Selection of second stage sampling units

After the 300 census districts which were to be used in the CVS had been selected, the next step was to select the second stage sampling units — the EDs. Whilst the basic unit for census taking is an ED, in a few instances (about 5 per cent), an ED was combined with another to form an appropriate workload for an enumerator. Strictly, the second stage unit is an *enumeration workload*. These workloads were graded by the average grade of their member EDs. They were arranged by this grade to achieve some implicit stratification by enumeration difficulty within census districts. Four ED workloads were sampled independently with probability proportional to a measure of population size within each sampled census district.

Selection of third stage sampling units

Sampling of the third stage sampling units — enumerated housing units and unoccupied addresses within ED workloads — was carried out by the interviewers and is described below.

Within each ED workload, the CVS interviewer used the Enumerator's Record Book to draw separate samples of:

(a) households who had completed census forms and returned them to the enumerator;

(b) households which had not returned census forms to the enumerator either because of absence or because they could not be contacted;

(c) dwellings believed, by the enumerator, to be vacant;

(d) addresses believed, by the enumerator, to be non-residential.

The result was a national sample of 20,000 addresses, of which 6,000 were from sample (a) and 14,000 from which, for one reason or another, the enumerator had not collected census forms.

These 20,000 addresses, together with the visual listing of buildings made by the interviewer, provided the information used to make the *coverage check*. The preliminary results from the coverage check are given in section 6.6. The *quality check* was conducted from interviews with the 6,000 housing units from sample (a) above: households who had completed census forms and returned them to the enumerator.

The CVS interviews were carried out in June and July 1991, between six and twelve weeks after census day. The time gap was due to the work involved in selecting samples from the Enumerators' Record Books and in recording census data onto CVS documents to be checked with respondents during the interviews.

Details of exactly how interviewers sampled households within EDs are given in the following section. The sample drawn covered both the coverage and the quality check.

Selecting households within EDs

Interviewers implemented their fieldwork in two distinct stages. First, they were issued with Enumerators' Record Books. Chapter 4 describes how the Enumerator's Record Book was used during the census fieldwork. Figure 6.1 contains an entirely fictitious extract from an Enumerator's Record Book that was used in the Field Manual, issued to all enumerators. It therefore illustrates a selection of complex situations and is not typical of a completed page. The name and address of the household was recorded by the enumerator on the form (figure 6.1) during the delivery of census schedules. During this process Panel A (the codes are explained in chapter 4, figure 4.5 — see page 94) was completed in order to identify multi-occupied housing. Columns D and E (codes also explained in figure 4.5) confirm whether or not delivery and collection were made and the type of occupancy of the property (e.g. vacant accommodation, holiday accommodation, etc.). Each address formed a separate line in the Enumerator's Record Book.

The interviewer was asked to number the appropriate entries in the Record Book and then take a sample using a predetermined selection table. Once a sample was drawn, the interviewers made out address lists, obtained the Census H (house-

The 1991 Census User's Guide

Figure 6.1 Enumeration Record: Part 2, private residences and partly residential premises

Address (Location or Description of Premises - as required) A	Panel A Code Building Bracket† B	Name / No. of persons C	Del. D	Coll. E	Source F	No. of rooms G	Type of accomodation / Lowest floor* H	Notes I	ACO Completion of form check 1 2 3 4	Form No. J	Box 0 Ticked K	Boxes 1 or 2 Ticked L	Total on form K+L M
18 Colville Avenue	2	Stevens	√2	√2				Not Monday		1	6	1	7
20 " Flat above hairdressers	5	Carter	√+I	√+I				22/4 - 11am 24/4 - 5.30pm		2	4		4
22 " Basement Flat	7	Mrs Robinson	√SR	√				Collect after 6pm Envelope not used		3	3		3
" Ground Floor Flat	8	Evans	√(Q7)	√	3	5	4	No furniture or curtains Occupied from 20/4 Collect 24/4		4	2		2
" First Floor Flat	8	Allen	√ABS	√ABS	1	4	3	Entire household away 19/4 -22/4 - form completed anyway		5		3	3
24 "	3		V (IMP)	V (IMP)	2	8		Neighbour says property renovated throughout No change at Collection		6			
18 Colville Avenue Caravan in back garden	1	Anderson	√	√						7	2		2
Nelson House, Colville Avenue Flat 1	6	Burrows	√	√				5 people on form Mother-in-law arrived unexpectedly on 20/4		8	5		5
" Flat 2	6		SEC	SEC	2	5		Owner of property keeps 1 flat for own use and lets the others		9			
" Flat 3	6		STU	STU	2	5		Neighbour says students live in top flat during term time		10			
								Page Totals	For Use at Census Office		22	4	26

No. of persons (boxed): Stevens 7, Carter 4, Mrs Robinson 3, Evans 3, Allen 3, (24") 3, Anderson 2, Burrows 4

* Scotland only
† Multi-occupied only

Source: 1991 Census Field Manual, OPCS, 1990.

hold) forms for each household in their (a) sample, and then transcribed information relevant to the quality check from the census schedule onto specially designed CVS schedules.

In addition, interviewers conducted their own visual listing or enumeration of a sampled area using the same maps as issued to census enumerators. The purpose of this was to identify any missing or additional addresses when compared to entries made in Part 1 of the Record Book. Any discrepancies resulted in further field checks.

The coverage check sample consisted of:

- all addresses with 'absent' households (e.g. the Allen household in figure 6.1)
- a sample of half of the vacant addresses (e.g. 24 Colville Avenue in figure 6.1)
- a sample of half of the non-residential addresses (identified with a 5 in Panel A, e.g. 20 Colville Avenue)
- a sample of multi-occupied accommodation (limited to six selections per census district) (e.g. 22 Colville Avenue, identified with a bracket in Panel A)

Additionally, up to eight 'unresolved' entries in each census district were selected. These were entries in the Record Book without a concluding code in the collection column E.

For all addresses where the CVS found people in residence, a census form was completed. This was used to provide a check on the accuracy of imputed information for wholly absent households.

The quality check sample

The quality check sample (around five addresses per ED workload) was obtained from entries in the Enumerator's Record Book which contained a 'tick' in column E (figure 6.1). This signified that a census form had been collected and filed with the census officer.

6.6 PROVISIONAL RESULTS FROM THE 1991 CVS COVERAGE CHECK

Provisional results from the CVS were published in October 1992 as an appendix to *OPCS Monitor* PP1 92/1 which published the provisional mid-1991 population estimates for England and Wales. A revised and extended analysis, relating the results to the characteristics of the individuals and addresses missed, is due during 1993.

According to the provisional CVS results, the net effect, for Great Britain as a whole, of those enumeration errors which it detected was an estimated under-enumeration of the resident population in households of 299,000, or 0.56 per cent. This net effect was produced by several different kinds of error, which can be summarised under three main headings:

(1) errors at addresses from which the enumerator managed to collect forms (*enumerated addresses*);
(2) errors at addresses missed by the enumerator including those wrongly identified by the enumerator as vacant (*missed addresses*); and
(3) errors at addresses which the enumerator classified as occupied but from which no census forms were collected (*absent households*).

Table 6.3

Net enumeration error by source as measured by the CVS (Great Britain), 1991

Main source of error	Estimated error expressed as		
	Effect on total residents (000s)	Per cent of enumerated population	95 per cent confidence interval (per cent)
(1) Enumerated adresses	-178	-0.33	-0.54 -0.12
(2) Missed addresses	-216	-0.40	-0.51 -0.29
(3) Absent households	+94	+0.18	+0.05 +0.30
All sources	-299	-0.56	-0.82 -0.30

Source: *OPCS Monitor* PP1 92/1, October 1992.

Table 6.3 gives figures for each of these main headings. In the discussion that follows, it is important to take note of the confidence intervals given in the table which indicate the ranges between which the true value may lie, with a 95 per cent likelihood. The first line (error (1)) in table 6.3 refers to households who returned completed forms to the enumerator. The CVS identified a few instances in which non-residents had been counted as residents, and rather more cases in which residents had been missed. The net effect was an undercount of 178,000 residents in households.

Error (2) is the estimated undercount due to addresses being missed or wrongly identified as vacant. At 0.4 per cent of the enumerated population, this is slightly larger than error (1). Taken together, these two kinds of errors produced an estimated undercount of 394,000 residents, equivalent to 0.73 per cent of the enumerated population.

The overall estimate of the undercount is *less* than 394,000 because the CVS indicated that the data imputed for non-enumerated households produced an estimated *overcount* of 94,000 residents. This was because the census did not simply omit such households. In some cases the households did in fact return a census form late by post. In others the enumerators had managed to ascertain the number of residents, and the characteristics of such residents were imputed on the basis of information obtained about similar households in the area. In the remaining cases the number of residents itself was imputed.

In this situation, errors could arise because of mistakes made in completing those forms which were returned and because of biases in the imputation procedure. However, the most important single source of error was the misclassification of the address by the enumerator. On investigation by CVS interviewers it turned out that some of these addresses had been entirely vacant at the time of the census, and therefore should not have been classified as 'absent households'. The residents wrongly imputed to the addresses account for the overcount in error (3).

The preliminary results of the CVS give provisional estimates by four types of geographical area in England and Wales: Inner London, Outer London, other metropolitan counties in England and shire counties in England. Table 6.4 shows the estimated effect of net under-enumeration for each of these areas in both 1981 and 1991. Again, the very wide confidence intervals indicate that these results are likely to be subject to considerable sampling variation. It is, however, evident that in 1981,

Table 6.4

Geographic variation in net enumeration error in England and Wales in 1981 and 1991

	Estimated error expressed as per cent of enumerated population		95 per cent confidence interval (per cent)	
	1981	1991	1991	
Inner London	-2.46	-0.12	-1.60	+1.26
Outer London	-1.01	-0.33	-0.78	+0.08
Other metropolitan	-0.24	-0.98	-1.88	-0.11
Shire counties	-0.29	-0.53	-0.82	-0.25
All England and Wales	-0.45	-0.60	-0.88	-0.32
Scotland	-	-0.15	-0.87	+0.52

Source: 1981 figures: Britton and Birch, 1985.
    1991 figures: *OPCS Monitor* PP1 92/1, October 1992.

the post-enumeration survey estimated much higher levels of net under-enumeration in London than outside, whilst in 1991 this gradient was reversed. The figures for 1991 need to be understood in the context of the level of imputation for 'wholly absent household' which varied greatly by area and represented 8.85 per cent of households with residents in Inner London. This is discussed in more detail in the second part of this chapter.

It appears that the 1991 CVS, unlike its 1981 predecessor, failed to locate a sizeable proportion of people who did not complete a census form. It is estimated that the 299,000 net undercount represents only about one third of the estimated under-enumeration in the 1991 Census. Part II of this chapter discusses the issue of under-enumeration in more detail. Information on the accuracy of imputation of wholly absent households is not yet available.

6.7 THE QUALITY CHECK

The following section examines the role of the quality check which forms an integral part of the post-enumeration procedures. Examples are drawn from the 1981 Post-enumeration Survey as results from the 1991 CVS are not yet available.

In order to establish the accuracy with which responses are recorded on the census form, the interviewers who conduct the quality check repeat the census questions, as well as asking some additional background information. This method (criterion validation) assumes that the responses elicited by trained interviewers from the Social Survey Division, will establish a 'true' response against which responses recorded on the census form can be judged. High errors of reported misclassification on certain questions will indicate poorly answered questions.

The question on number of rooms serves as an example to illustrate this. This question has been asked since 1891 and, since quality checks began in 1961, has consistently had a high rate of misclassification. In order to check the answer given on the census form, the Post-Enumeration Survey interviewer followed a series of 11 questions (shown in figure 6.2) and, finally, entered the total number of rooms in the appropriate box. This was then compared with the number of rooms transcribed from

Figure 6.2 The 1981 PES questions on rooms

CARD B   ROOMS

		Census District	Enumeration District	Sample No.	H'hold No.

(1) Room No.	(2) Name/description (how used)	(3) Ineligible/unusable	(4) Storage only	(5) Business only	(6) Shared	(7) Let/sublet	(8) Included on Census Form
1		1	1	1	1	1	1
2		1	1	1	1	1	1
3		1	1	1	1	1	1
4		1	1	1	1	1	1
5		1	1	1	1	1	1
6		1	1	1	1	1	1
7		1	1	1	1	1	1
8		1	1	1	1	1	1
9		1	1	1	1	1	1
10		1	1	1	1	1	1
11		1	1	1	1	1	1
12		1	1	1	1	1	1
13		1	1	1	1	1	1
14		1	1	1	1	1	1
15		1	1	1	1	1	1

CHECK C.

1. Check against list below: are any of the rooms above ineligible, uninhabitable or unusable? IF YES, ring code 3 for each such room.

2. Enter total no. of rooms listed in cols. 1/2

3. Enter total no.of rooms coded as: Ineligible/unusable (col.3)   (a)
   DO NOT COUNT ANY ROOM TWICE
   Storage only (col.4)
   Business only (col.5)
   Let/sublet (col.7)

4. Subtract (b) from (a)   (b)

5. Enter total from (c) in the 'PES' box opposite CQ H1 on page 9.   (c)

6. Then go to CHECK D, page 9.

7. NOTE: If Census and PES disagree, ask which rooms form filler had in mind when completing Census Form, and ring code 1 in col.8 above for each such room.

INELIGIBLE/UNUSABLE ROOMS

Bathroom	Corridor	Lobby
Boiler room	Garage	Loft (if uninhabitable)
Cellar (if unusable/uninhabitable)	Garden shed	Outhouse
Clearoom	Kitchen or scullery under 6½ ft wide	Pantry (if uninhabitable)
Closet	Landing	

Passage
Recess
Storage room (if unusable)
Toilet
Unfit/derelict rooms

TO THOSE WITH 2 OR MORE ROOMS (see Q.2)

6. Can you tell me how many bedrooms you have. Please include any bedsitting rooms and spare bedrooms.
   Enter each bedroom on a separate line on CARD B.
   Then ask Q.7.

7. Do you have a kitchen, that is a separate room in which you cook (apart from bedsitters)?
   Yes ..... 1 → Enter on CARD B. then ask (a)
   No ..... 2 → (b)

   IF YES
   (a) Is the narrowest side of the kitchen less than 6½ ft from wall to wall?
   Less than 6½ ft . 1 **Ring code 1 at 'Ineligible/ unusable' on CARD B.** Then ask Q.8.
   6½ ft or more ... 2 → Q.8

   IF NO
   (b) Where do you cook? → Q.8

8. What other rooms do you have, for living or eating in?
   Enter on separate lines on CARD B. with informant's name for each room.
   Then ask Q.9

9. Do you have any rooms, other than those already mentioned, that are used for storing things?
   Yes ..... 1 (a) & (b)
   No ...... 2 → Q.10

   IF YES
   (a) **Add to list on CARD B; then ask (b) about each.**
   (b) Could this room be used for living accommodation?
   Yes ..... 1 → Q.10
   No ...... 2 → (i)

   IF NO
   (i) Why is this?

ROOM NO.	REASON

   Now ring code 1 at 'Storage only' on CARD B.
   Then go to Q.10

10. Apart from rooms you have already mentioned, do you have any extensions used as rooms, such as a sun lounge or conservatory?
    Yes .... 1 → Enter on CARD B. Then ask Q.11
    No .... 2 → Q.11

- 5 -

W1017 OPCS 2/81

Figure 6.2 – *continued*

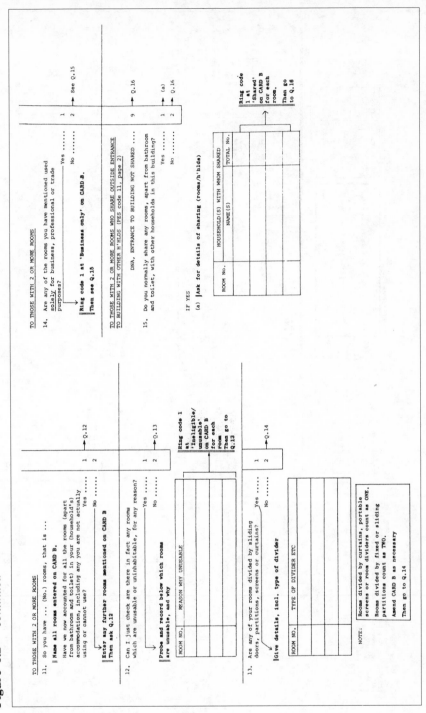

Figure 6.2 – *continued*

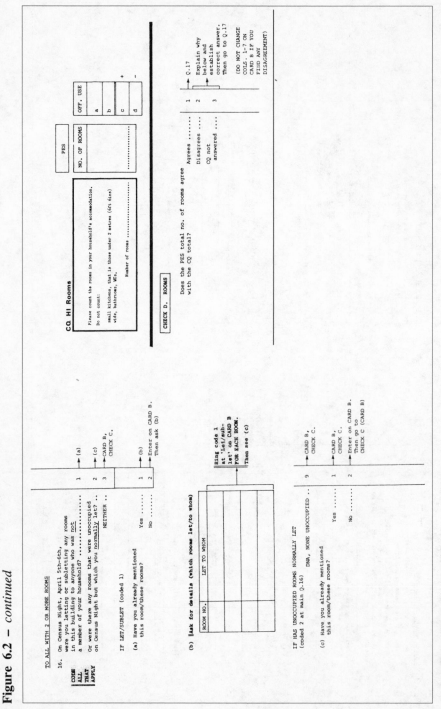

Source: Britton and Birch, 1985.

Table 6.5

Number of rooms: Gross percentage of census count found by PES, England and Wales, 1981

Number of rooms recorded by the PES	Number of rooms recorded by the Census								Sample numbers
	1	2	3	4	5	6	7/8	9 or more	
	%	%	%	%	%	%	%	%	
1	72.0	1.8	0.3	0.1	-	-	0.3	-	60
2	22.7	55.0	4.3	0.2	-	0.1	-	0.5	132
3	5.3	40.4	62.3	4.5	0.7	0.1	-	-	367
4	-	2.6	28.3	74.1	7.6	1.0	0.3	0.5	872
5	-	0.3	3.9	19.0	78.4	18.5	5.3	1.0	1,388
6	-	-	0.6	1.9	12.6	72.8	21.4	3.0	939
7/8	-	-	0.3	0.2	0.6	7.3	68.9	14.4	352
9 or more	-	-	-	-	0.1	0.2	3.9	80.6	98
Base (= 100%)	75	171	392	874	1,294	925	376	100	4,208
Non-response	10	26	38	83	109	88	30	10	394

Net distributions

Quality Check %	1.4	3.1	8.7	20.7	33.0	22.3	8.4	2.3
Census (PES) %	1.8	4.1	9.3	20.8	30.7	22.0	8.9	2.4

Gross error: Agree 71.4%; Disagree 28.6%
Sample size: 4,208 responding private households with usual residents

Source: Britton and Birch, 1985.

the census form. If there was a discrepancy, the interviewer tried to establish the reason. Table 6.5 shows the cross-classification of census responses by responses from the quality check for number of rooms, for those households in the 1981 Post-Enumeration Survey.

The most widely used measure of the extent of discrepancy between the census and the quality check is the *gross error rate* or *misclassification rate*. This represents the percentage of the total number of responses that differed for a particular question. From table 6.5 the gross misclassification rate was 28.6 per cent, made up of the proportion of off-diagonal elements in the table. The gross error rates indicate how well a particular census question worked and mainly reflect errors made by the form-filler.

When the marginal categories of a table are considered, it is often found that errors cancel out each other and therefore the *net error* rate may be much lower. For example, whilst only 78 per cent of households who recorded five rooms in the census also recorded five rooms in the quality check (table 6.5), the marginal difference in the number of households with five rooms was only 2.3 per cent. The net error rate is calculated as the difference between the marginal totals of the census and quality check, expressed as a percentage of the quality check population for the subgroup concerned. In the example in table 6.5, the total difference in each of the marginal totals sums to 210 which is 5 per cent of the total of 4,208. The error rates

Table 6.6

Selected reasons given for disagreement between 1981 Census (pre-processing) and PES classifications: Question H1 — Rooms

(i)   'I am rated as having three rooms, so I naturally thought that was the correct number to enter. I didn't read the form properly, or I'd have known not to include the bathroom.'

(ii)   'Kitchen omitted because not thought eligible and never even thought of scullery as a room. The scullery in fact was a utility room, i.e. washing machine, dry room/workshop.'

(iii) 'I only counted the bedrooms. I didn't think they wanted the kitchen and the living room.'

(iv)   'Enumerator counted with me and he recorded it for me as I get very shaky when I have to fill in forms and can't manage at all.'

(v)   'Counted the kitchen.'

(vi)   'Kitchen not included because I thought it was not big enough.'

(vii) 'Did not include shared dining room.'

(viii) 'Census man said 'put two rooms down'. Informant had no idea of size or what 6½ ft looked like!'

(ix)   'Kitchen was not included because lady thought it said 'not including kitchens'.'

Source: Britton and Birch, 1985, p.54.

are of course *estimates* subject to sampling variablility and, possibly, subject to some inherent errors of their own. No census count can be adjusted *precisely* on the basis of these rates.

How do these errors in number of rooms occur? The basic problem seems to be that every householder knows how many rooms they have according to some definition of their own, and therefore ignores the census definition! Table 6.6 casts some light on such instances.

6.7.1 Should the net or gross error rate be used?

Where users are concerned only with univariate statistics — for example the distribution of the number of rooms, then it is more appropriate to use the net error rate.

However, the compensating errors which give the net error rate may not occur evenly across categories of other variables. For example, misclassification of accommodation with only one room may be more likely amongst members of Social Class V but less likely amongst those in Social Class I. Therefore when the user is concerned with the relationship between variables, as is usually the case, it is appropriate to use the gross error rate.

Results for the 1991 CVS quality check will not be available until mid-1993. Hence the following section provides some information from the 1981 Post-Enumeration Survey and earlier quality checks for certain key variables. The results from the 1991 CVS are likely to be similar.

6.7.2 Variables with the highest gross error rate in 1981

Apart from the number of rooms, those 1981 Census variables with the largest gross error are briefly mentioned below. Economic activity recorded a gross error rate of 7.8 per cent (but 11.2 per cent for women and 4.1 per cent for men). For women in particular, major errors occurred in the distinction between full and part-time working, between part-time working and 'housewife', and between 'housewife' and 'retired'. Gross error rates approached 25 per cent for the full occupational codes used in the 1981 Census, although this was much lower (13 per cent) for social class. The gross error rate for employment status was 10 per cent, with 'foremen' and 'supervisors' being understated. Daily journey to work recorded a gross error rate of 8.6 per cent, with the proportion of people travelling by bus overstated and travelling by car understated (Britton and Birch, 1985).

Users should therefore be aware of the shortcomings of the census in providing reliable statistics for certain subgroups of the population.

6.8 STANDARD ERRORS IN THE 1981 POST-ENUMERATION SURVEY

Post-enumeration has now become an integral part of census taking in Britain. Its established status is closely linked to the increased use of census data in the formulation and execution of policies within local and national government, and the consequent need for users to be informed of the accuracy of census data.

Assessing the accuracy of census information depends on the existence of external criteria. There is no single criterion; various contenders exist. Demographic analysis is beset with problems such as inaccurate recording of net immigration. Nevertheless post-enumeration makes the assumption that follow-up survey interviews can act as arbiters of truth. How well do they perform? One important measure is the standard error.

Standard errors were calculated in 1981 for four geographical area: Inner and Outer London, and the metropolitan and non-metropolitan areas. Since the number of EDs selected in each of these areas was small, the estimates of variance are unstable.

Table 6.7

Values of design factors in the 1981 Post-Enumeration Survey

	England and Wales	Inner London	Rest
Under-enumeration			
Quality Check sample			
Multihousehold sample	1.0	1.0	1.0
Non-residential premises sample			
Visual list sample			
— persons missed	3.5	4.0	3.0
— households missed	3.0	3.5	2.5
Characteristics of:			
Persons within missed or misclassified households/household spaces	3.5	4.0	–
Persons in wholly absent households			
Missed or wholly absent households	3.0	3.5	–
Missed persons — gross undercoverage	2.5	–	–
Missed persons — net undercoverage	3.0	–	–
Missed or double-counted persons in enumerated households	1.0	1.0	–
Misclassification of households/ household spaces	3.0	3.5	–
Quality Check gross misclassification	1.0	–	–

– Not analysed.
Source: Britton and Birch, 1985 p.152.

This means that any subnational estimates from the CVS are fairly unreliable.

The 1991 CVS, by comparison with 1981, increased the sample taken of the Visual List and Vacant/Absent households in order to increase the precision of estimates. Details of the sample taken were given in section 6.5.

Table 6.7 provides a 'rough and ready' guide to the order of magnitude of the true standard error or design factor — the extent to which the design of the survey increases the standard error that would be obtained using a simple random sample. Thus, for some sources of net undercount at both national and subnational level, the design of the survey was likely to increase the estimates of standard error based on simple random sampling by a factor of 3 to 4. Estimates for the 1991 CVS are likely to be more precise as ED workloads were selected independently rather than in blocks as in 1981. Nonetheless, carrying estimates down beyond very broad geographical areas is likely to be misleading.

Whilst post-enumeration in Britain has been established relatively recently, there is a longer tradition in many other western countries. The following section provides an overview of the post-enumeration methods used in the US, Canada and Australia and also reviews the role played by these surveys in countries where an undercount is a familiar experience.

6.9 POST-ENUMERATION IN THE US, AUSTRALIA AND CANADA

In the US, Canada and Australia under-enumeration has been a familiar experience in recent censuses. In all three countries there have been often fierce debates over how to deal with the under-enumeration. These countries have also had more experience in developing methods to assess its extent. The following sections, therefore, discuss in some detail the methods of post-enumeration used in the US and, in less detail, those of Australia and Canada.

6.9.1 The US

According to the US Department of Commerce (1990, p.6): 'The Census shall be considered the most accurate count of the population of the United States... unless an adjusted count is shown to be more accurate'. These guidelines have given rise to a situation where, in order to challenge census figures, it is necessary not only to conduct a post-enumeration survey but also to demonstrate the superiority of its estimates over those from the census.

Statisticians from the US Census Bureau conducted a post-enumeration survey to estimate undercounts and to compute their best estimates of errors. Errors in the post-enumeration survey were compared with errors in the estimated undercounts, and with errors in the census. The method used is described below.

The US method of post-enumeration

The US post-enumeration attempts to match, for the same geographical areas, a sample of census enumerations against a sample from the population that has been drawn *entirely independently* of the census. In Britain, whilst the visual listing of buildings in the ED was independent of the enumerators records, all others elements of the CVS used the Enumerator's Record Book as the basis for sampling.

The US post-enumeration survey is composed of two samples: a sample of the population, known as the P sample, and a sample of census enumerations, the E sample. The two samples are independent but consist of the same local geographical areas, known as census blocks, and, within each census block, the same housing units.

The sample design for the 1990 post-enumeration survey was a stratified single stage cluster design with blocks or groups of blocks as the primary sampling units (Woltman, Alberti and Moriarty, 1988). Altogether 54 geographic areas served as major sampling strata; after selection, these areas were further subdivided into strata (poststrata) based on the concentrations of the population by race, age, sex and tenure groups within the same geographic strata.

The P sample is designed to estimate the number of people missed by the original census enumeration. The US Bureau of the Census interviews the occupants of the sample housing units to obtain their names, census day addresses, and other data necessary to match them to their census questionnaires. Depending upon how readily a match is made, the people in the P sample are assigned the status of match, non-match or unresolved. The P sample does not cover the institutional population, those living in shelters or homeless people.

The E sample is designed to estimate the number of census enumerations that are erroneous: that is, people who are counted twice or included but should not be, such as temporary visitors to the US or those born after census day. The E sample consists of the census enumerations at the same housing units as the P sample. The Census Bureau attempts to match each E sample person, (each person named on the census questionnaire from the sampled housing unit) to the P sample. If an E sample person is not matched to the P sample, a follow up interview is conducted to determine whether the person was correctly enumerated in the census. It is also possible that people enumerated in the census were, of course, missed by the P sample. If a follow-up interview is not possible, for example because the E sample household has moved outside the search area since census day, interviewers attempt to collect information from neighbours. Then the E sample person is classified as correctly enumerated, erroneously enumerated or unresolved.

Imputation procedures are then applied to all those with an unresolved status so that they can be classified as a correct enumeration (rather than an erroneous enumeration, if an E sample case; or a non-enumeration if a P sample case). It is important to resolve all uncertain cases before the next step when the number of people in or out of the E and P samples is used to calculate the estimated true population for each post-stratum.

The principles behind the calculation of the estimated true population can be explained by considering a 2 x 2 table which tabulates the number of people in an area who are in or out of the P sample by whether they are in or out of the E sample.

In table 6.8, cell a represents those people in both the E and P sample; cells b and c represent those in one but not the other, whilst cell d represents those in neither. If the numbers in cell d can be estimated, then the total of all four cells, $a + b + c + d$ provides an estimate of the true population for the area. This estimate is called the dual-system estimate (DSE).

It can be shown algebraically that $d = bc/a$, as long as the P and E samples are *independent*. Therefore, the estimate of the true population can be calculated as: $a + b + c + (bc)/a$. The difference between the estimated true population and the post-stratum census count estimates the net undercount. The ratio of the estimated

Table 6.8

The dual-system approach

		In E sample (original enumeration)	
		Yes	No
In P sample (population)	Yes	*a*	*b*
	No	*c*	*d*

true population to the census count is referred to as the *raw adjustment factor*.

Further information on this method, also known as the *dual-record system or capture-recapture approach* can be found in Bishop, Feinburg and Holland, (1975, pp.231-234). As with the dual-system estimate itself, adjustment factors are subject to sampling and non-sampling variability. Further refinements using regression models to 'smooth' these raw factors are described in Hogan (1990).

In order to achieve more accurate estimates the Census Bureau defined post-strata by those variables such as age and tenure known to be related to the undercount. Although the Census Bureau were able to supply this adjustment factor so that the 1990 Census could be corrected, in the event, and after considerable litigation, no adjustments were made.

The decision on adjustment is a matter of some considerable controversy in the US (Fienberg, 1990; Freedman, 1991). After the 1990 census the US Census Bureau resisted pressure from New York City and others to adjust the census estimates. One of the main reasons was that the post-enumeration survey itself had a high level of non-interviews and unresolved matchings with the census (about 9 per cent in total) (Keane, 1988: p.16). In 1990 it appears that this had been reduced to around 4 per cent. Had the 1990 US Census been adjusted on the basis of post-enumeration survey results, the official count of the resident population would have increased by 5.27 million. That would have made the official resident population of the US just under 254 million. Of the increase, 29 per cent would have been Black, 23 per cent Hispanic, 4.0 per cent Asian and Pacific Islander, and 1.9 per cent American Indian (Hogan, 1991).

6.9.2 Canada and Australia

Canada

In Canada, census counts between 1971 and 1981 were known to be subject to some undercoverage but felt to be acceptably small and fairly constant at 2 per cent nationally (Royce,1992). There was some concern, however, over variation in undercoverage between Provinces, particularly the persistently high undercoverage in British Colombia. The issue of adjusting the 1981 Census for measured undercoverage was raised in 1980, but after consultation and debate population estimates from census counts were not adjusted. In the 1986 Census of Canada, undercoverage increased substantially to around 3.2 per cent and there continued to be large geographical variation, as well as variation between males and females and between different age groups.

Traditionally, undercoverage in Canada has been estimated on the basis of four studies: a vacancy check on persons and households missed because their dwelling was misclassified as unoccupied; a temporary residents check on persons who were temporarily away from their usual place of residence; an overcoverage check to determine the number of residents who may have been enumerated twice and *a reverse record check.*

The reverse record check is the most important aspect of the study of undercoverage in Canada (Burgess, 1988) and is explained below. Essentially, a sample of persons who should have been enumerated is selected from sources independent of the current census and then located in the census. This provides a check from a population sample to the census. It reverses the direction in which checks are usually made. The reverse record check for the 1986 Census selected people from four sources: those enumerated in the 1981 Census; persons born between 3 June 1981 and 2 June 1986; landed immigrants who entered Canada between 3 June 1981 and 2 June 2 1986; and people missed in the 1981 Census (based on those selected for the 1981 reverse record check and classified as missed).

Statistics Canada has announced its intention to adjust estimates based on the 1991 Census, though a final decision will not be taken until after the reverse record check has been conducted. At the time of writing the outcome is not known.

Australia

In Australia, the need to make adjustment for under-enumeration was recognised when the 1976 Census count fell considerably below the population estimates. The 1976 post-enumeration survey also showed a high under-enumeration rate of 2.6 per cent compared with 0.5 per cent in 1966 and 1.3 per cent in 1971 and significant variation in enumeration between States and Territories, ranging from 4.2 per cent for the Northern Territory to 1.1 per cent for Tasmania. In 1986 the level of under-enumeration was estimated to be 1.9 per cent. Population estimates have been obtained from census counts, incorporating an adjustment for under-enumeration in 1976, 1981 and 1986. These adjustments are based on the results of the post-enumeration survey and demographic analysis (Choi, Steel and Skinner, 1988).

The basic approach in the 1986 post-enumeration survey was to select a sample of people independently of the census through a multistage sample of private dwellings. The information required of each person in the selected households was obtained by personal interview of any responsible adult by trained field staff. Census staff then matched post-enumeration survey and census records to determine whether each person in the sample should have been included in the census and whether or not the person was in fact included. The census post-enumeration survey was carried out within four to five weeks of census night.

Results of the post-enumeration survey were assessed by comparing them with estimates based on demographic statistics and other independent data such as statistics on school enrolments, on children whose parents receive government family allowances, and on persons registered with the government Medicare system. In Australia, school enrolments for children aged 6–15 are compulsory, and, until November 1987, family allowances were universally paid to mothers of all children aged less than 17. Medicare insurance is also compulsory for all residents. Although population estimates include an adjustment for under-enumeration, no adjustment is made for other census data.

6.10 CONCLUSION

Whilst the adjustment debate in the US and other countries is over for the current round of censuses there is still much work to be done to fully understand the causes and correlates of undercounts. If the demographic benchmark can be defined as an independent criterion of the quality of the British Census Validation Survey, then clearly the CVS is a victim of correlated bias (certain people missed in the census also appear to be missed by the CVS). Here the use of small scale ethnographic studies carried out by anthropologists (de la Puente, 1992) might provide interesting insights as to how and why people manage to avoid any attempts to enumerate them.

It is also important to evaluate the results of the various approaches to post-enumeration both within and between countries. Only then will it be possible to select and refine a method or combination of methods, to be used in future census validation in Britain.

In comparison with Britain, other countries have had to cope with the problems of under-enumeration much sooner, which perhaps explains why post-enumeration surveys in other countries, notably the US, have more sophisticated ways of assessing the undercount. What lessons should we be learning? A key issue in 1991 Census validation procedures is the extent to which the CVS uses independent or dependent re-enumeration. Certainly, social survey interviewers carry out independent visual listings of sampled areas but ultimately they use Enumerator Record Books in order to reconcile any discrepancies. These checks should be reconciled independently. Additionally, interviews with sampled housing units, to check on census enumerations and responses, are conducted so that each interviewer first transcribes the census data on to his/her quality check schedules. In this sense the interview checks are dependent. This is not the case with the approaches used in the US (section 6.9.1)

A further issue is the extent to which the CVS provides any reliable information on small area estimation. The sample size prohibits any adjustment information at subnational level from being particularly useful. There is a need therefore, to consider the most appropriate method for carrying down the estimate of net undercount to small area statistics.

The second part of this chapter examines in some detail the possible sources of the undercount which OPCS identified in the 1991 Census and the implications of the undercount for census users.

6 The validation of census data

II — General issues

Catherine Marsh

6.11 INTRODUCTION

Chapter 6 part I discussed the role of post-enumeration in validating both the coverage and the quality of the census. Part II of this chapter is concerned with providing the reader with some background information on the more general problem of under-enumeration in the 1991 Census which, as we have seen (section 6.6), the CVS only partially uncovered. We also provide some guidance on areas where caution is needed in using census data. Although the bulk of the discussion will focus on the problems associated with coverage and the undercount in the 1991 Census, this will be placed in context by, first, taking a more general view on the range of data issues of which the census user should be aware. None of these issues is new to the 1991 Census, but the ever-increasing use of census data, particularly at small area level, makes it important to call them to the attention of census users.

6.12 A GENERAL PERSPECTIVE ON DATA PROBLEMS IN THE 1991 CENSUS

6.12.1 Space

The first problem arises in deciding of where to draw fixed geographical boundaries. Chapter 3(II) discusses some of the factors that influence where boundaries are drawn. However, the fact there are an infinite number of ways of defining sets of areas into which to group people gives rise to the *modifiable areal unit problem*. The decision over where to draw area boundaries determines, at least partially, the summary measures of the characteristics of the areas. This is covered in detail in chapter 9.

A second problem related to space is the *ecological fallacy*. This is the assumption that, when a relationship is found by correlating data for areas, it also reflects a relationship at the level of individuals or households. The problems that may arise from making this erroneous assumption are also covered in chapters 3 and 9.

6.12.2 Time

Time interacts with space to produce changes, for example in boundaries between censuses, that make it almost impossible to compare results. Chapter 3(I) refers to the way in which ED boundaries are changed over time and to the use of census tracts to facilitate comparison between the 1971 and 1981 censuses.

Changes in definitions also occur over time; for example chapter 2 records the change in definition of a household between 1971 and 1981, and the additional categories added in 1991 to the question on relationship to head of household. Both these changes were made in order to reflect the reality of the situation in the field. But this nonetheless leaves unanswered the question of what meaning one should attach to the change in the number of, for example, households in privately rented accommodation between 1971 and 1991, or how one should make comparisons between cohabitation in the 1991 Census with earlier years.

6.12.3 Sampling

A stratified 10 per cent sample of households is drawn for all the hard to code (10 per cent coded) questions in the census (listed in chapter 4, table 4.2). Chapter 4 discusses the method used to draw the 10 per cent sample. When this is used as a sample of individuals, sampling error is increased because of the clustering effect obtained because people with similar characteristics (e.g. ethnicity) tend to live in the same household. An evaluation of the design effects, carried out by OPCS for 1981 is discussed in chapter 4, section 4.6, whilst chapter 11, section 11.4, on the Samples of Anonymised Records, (which are drawn from the 10 per cent sample), provides guidance on the likely design effects for both the individual and the household Samples of Anonymised Records.

6.12.4 Quality

All surveys, but particularly those that are self-completion, contain error caused by mistakes or misunderstandings made by respondents. The quality of census data has been the subject of a check since 1966 (Gray and Gee, 1972) and the procedures used to assess quality in the 1991 Census Validation Survey (CVS) have been discussed earlier. Additionally, of course, error is also introduced at the data entry and edit stages.

6.12.5 Modification

The modification of small area aggregate statistics in order to preserve confidentiality, first introduced into output from the 1971 Census, introduces small perturbations intentionally. Chapter 8, section 8.6.2, examines the effect of these modifications in small areas and also the cumulative effect produced by adding together a number of small areas, each of which contains some modification. The chapter also offers some guidance on precautions to take to ensure that modification effects do not lead to seriously misleading results.

6.12.6 Coverage

Finally, census data is subject to incomplete coverage. This forms the topic of the rest of this chapter, which, again, contains some guidance on compensating for its effects.

A follow-up survey, as discussed earlier in this chapter, is only one of the ways in which census coverage can be validated. Other methods include overall demographic checks in which the census total is compared with figures derived from the previous census, updated (or 'rolled forward') to allow for births, deaths and net migration, and comparisons with other figures for specific subpopulations using administrative sources, such as school rolls and the numbers of people receiving benefits of various kinds. For the 1991 Census, the level of undercount indicated by demographic checks came to over 1 million people in Great Britain, significantly higher than the 300,000 reported in the preliminary results from the CVS (see section 6.13 below). The former level of undercount was believed to be closer to reality and was adopted in producing the Registrars General's provisional mid-year population estimates for 1991 (OPCS, 1992b; GRO(S), 1992).

The degree of under-enumeration found in the 1991 Census (around 2 per cent of people in Great Britain, rising to 3.3 per cent if imputed persons in wholly absent households are also included, some of whom would have been enumerated as vistors elsewhere) is quite in line with under-enumeration found in other countries such as Australia, Canada and the US (Burgess, 1988; Fay, Passel and Robinson, 1988; Choi, Steel and Skinner, 1988). It is, however, much larger than experienced in recent decades in Britain. It therefore raises questions of how the extent of the undercount has been identified and estimated in Britain, and how users should take it into account in any data analysis. The rest of this chapter is concerned with these issues.

6.13 THE 'MISSING MILLION' IN THE PRELIMINARY COUNT

Three months after the census was taken, in July 1991, OPCS issued a preliminary count of the population of England and Wales. This was based on tallying the enumerators' count of people they had found present in their district on census night, before any correction for absent members had been made. The preliminary count of people present in England and Wales came to 49 million, and was considered to be about one million short of the number expected from an estimate based on updating a similar count in 1981 (OPCS, 1991b). This was, however, just a count of people present. Techniques for imputing absent households had been improved since 1981 (see chapter 2 and discussion below), some households absent on census night would return late forms, and it was hoped that the CVS would find further people who had been missed. There was a general expectation that most of this shortfall would eventually be accounted for (e.g. Wormald 1991). As we have seen, however, the CVS only found about 300,000 extra people in its preliminary estimate.

6.14 DEMOGRAPHIC CHECKS ON THE CENSUS

All modern societies require reliable headcounts of the population for a wide variety of administrative purposes, as we saw in chapter 1. This section examines how the Census Offices have come to the conclusion that the census count plus the numbers found to have been missed by the CVS, nonetheless still produce an undercount of the resident population of Great Britain. The arguments are of great and obvious interest to all those in local authorities, health authorities and elsewhere whose income derives from an estimated headcount of client populations. However, the reasoning about the general validity of the data is of interest to all census users; no social survey is subjected to greater scrutiny than takes place on the decennial census. It should be noted that the figures available at time of writing (January 1993) are provisional, and might change if further evidence or arguments come forward[1].

[1] See postscript on page 167.

Population estimates are rebased every 10 years using the new census results. The census is particularly important in rebasing the local population figures, for which the rolled forward estimates are less reliable than at the national level. The starting point for the new series is the census count of those usually resident. Three steps are then taken:

- adjustments are made for differences between the resident population as defined by the census and that as defined for the mid-year estimates;
- small adjustments are made to allow for time changes between census day and the mid-year;

Table 6.9

The steps in deriving (i) the provisional and (ii) final mid-1991 population estimate for England and Wales from the 1991 Census count

	Thousands of persons	
	(i)	(ii)
1991 Census count of usual residents for England and Wales (sum of totals shown in Table D of the 1991 Census County Monitors)	**49,890**	**49,890**
(a) *Adjustment for definitional difference*		
(1) Net student balance (the excess of students with term-time address in England and Wales over those with home address here)	*+ 58*	*+ 54*
(b) *Allowance for changes between census day (21 April) and mid-1991*		
(2) Natural change	+ 34	+ 34
(3) Net migration	+ 9	+ 9
	+ 43	*+ 43*
(c) *Allowance for under-enumeration in Census*		
(4) CVS adjustments		
Over-imputation in processing	- 85	- 115
Net under-enumeration arising from missed/misclassified dwellings	+ 200	+ 178
Net under-enumeration of persons in responding households	+ 177	+ 177
	+ 292	*+ 240*
(5) Enhancement of census count of infants using data from birth and death registrations and migration indicators	+ 21	+ 21
(6) Enhancement of census count of Armed Forces (and dependants of foreign force using MOD data)	+ 79	+ 42
(7) Enhancement of Census counts of persons aged 1–44 and 85+ to allow for under-enumeration additional to (4)-(6)	*+ 572*	*+ 465**
	+ 965	*+ 768*
(d) *Census visitors, with no usual address, omitted from usual resident count*		*+ 200*
Net adjustment to 1991 Census count of usual residents for England and Wales (a+b+c+d)	**+ 1,065**	**+1,065**
Rebased mid-1991 population estimate	**50,955**	**50,995**

* Includes 63 thousand elderly residents identified from DSS data.
Source: *OPCS Monitors* PP1 92/1 and PP1 93/1.

- allowance is made for under-enumeration in the census. It is the last step that is of most interest, but it is important to rehearse the first two as well.

Table 6.9 shows the detail of steps in moving from the 1991 Census count of usual residents to the provisional and final rebased mid-1991 population estimate for England and Wales. Summary figures for Great Britain are shown in Table 6.10 for the provisional estimates.

The basic count of usual residents in the Census was derived from those who were recorded as being normally resident in households on a completed form, whether they happened to be there on census night or not. To these were added the usual residents of communal establishments. If the whole household was absent on census

Table 6.10

Comparison of the 1991 Census with provisional mid-year population estimates: Great Britain

	1981	1991
1. *Residents counted in Census*	53,557	54,889
1(a) Resident population 1981 base	53,557	53,340
1(b) In wholly absent households — enumerated	n/a	680
1(c) In wholly absent households — imputed	n/a	869
2. *Coverage adjustments*	1,246	1,053
2(a) In wholly absent households	1,005	n/a
2(b) Net under-enumeration accounted for by CVS	215	299
2(c) Under-enumeration not accounted for by CVS	26	754
3. *Other adjustments*	12	113
3(a) Definition of residents — e.g. students	8	69
3(b) Timing changes — census day to 30 June	9	44
3(c) Other changes	-5	0
4. *Registrars General's mid-year estimates of residents**	**54,814**	**56,055**

Percentage of population missing from census tables for Great Britain in 1981 and 1991
(calculated from above)

Missing from census tables	1981	1991
in wholly absent households (2(a))	1.83	-
undercount explained by CVS (2(b))	0.39	0.53
undercount *not* explained by CVS (2(c))	0.05	1.35

Base = Registrars General's mid-year estimates of residents

Included in tables

wholly absent households (1(b)&1(c))	-	2.77

Base = residents counted in 1991 Census and estimates of under-coverage

* 1991 mid-year population estimate is provisional
Source: *1991 Census Great Britain National Monitor*, OPCS.

night, there was no legal compulsion to complete a return. Nonetheless, some house-holders still voluntarily filled in a form on return (see chapter 4, section 4.), and were thus added to the count. Finally, census enumerators used whatever local knowledge they could glean to provide an estimate of the number of people absent from addresses where they believed a household was usually resident; if these house-holds subsequently failed to fill in a voluntary return, these estimates of numbers in wholly absent households were used, and characteristics of their members imputed (see chapter 4, section 4.).

In England and Wales, this basic census count of usual residents came to 49,890,000 of whom 806,000 (1.6 per cent) were imputed members of wholly absent households who did not voluntarily complete a form on returning home after census night (OPCS, 1992b).

The first adjustment concerns the discrepancies of definition and coverage in the treatment of students. The main users of population estimates prefer students (including school children under 16) to be included as residents at their term-time addresses, whereas the parental home is treated as the usual residence for census purposes. In the 1991 Census there was a new question on students' term-time addresses to enable this distinction to be made.

In England and Wales as a whole in 1991 some 58,000[1] more students came to study than went overseas to study, so the net effect to the total was to increase the estimate by this amount. This factor played a larger part in the estimate of the mid-year population of individual local areas, where more precise estimates were made of student flows into and out of the area.

The second adjustment allows for differences in timing, since population esti-mates traditionally refer to the population as on 30 June. Small allowances (making a net addition of 43,000) were therefore made for the number of births, deaths and migrants in the intervening period and everyone's age was increased by ten weeks.

Thirdly, attempts were made to allow for deficiencies in the Census. We have already seen that, as a result of the CVS, a further 292,000[1] people were added to the estimated number of usual residents. This undercount was apportioned to local areas differentially according to the four main areas identified in the CVS: Inner London, Outer London, other metropolitan and other non-metropolitan.

Moreover, two administrative sources allowed further corrections for subgroups. The number of births registered in the previous year gives a good estimate of the number of infants aged less than 1 year who should appear in the census; historically there has always been a problem with the counting of infants. The second source for corrections comes from the Ministry of Defence records of members of the armed forces; these were used to correct estimates of their numbers. Making adjustments for these two sources added another 100,000 people to the count.

Perhaps the most important way of checking the accuracy of the headcount at the national level, however, is by comparing the 1991 Census with its predecessor. The number of people of a particular age and sex in one census ought to be con-sistent with the number who were ten years older in the following census, after making allowances for deaths and migration to and from Great Britain. This com-parison yields a large discrepancy. Component 7 in table 6.9 was derived in this way, and suggests a substantial shortfall, over and above that identified in the CVS, of an estimated 572,000[1]. Scrutiny of the age–sex profiles of the raw numbers recorded

---

[1] These figures refer to the provisional mid-year estimates. See Postscript on page 167.

Figure 6.3 Sex ratios (male:female) of various 1991 population counts for England and Wales

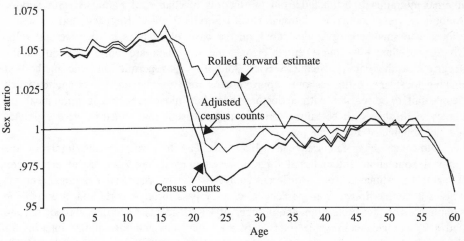

Source: *Population Trends* 1993, vol. 71 p. 23

by the 1991 Census for England and Wales (reproduced in figure 6.3) shows an implausibly high ratio of young women to young men, suggesting that the problem was particularly acute amongst young men and, more generally, arose among people aged 1–44 and 85+. Among the 45–85 year olds the Census and mid-year estimates corresponded pretty closely. This element of the undercount has therefore been apportioned to local districts, *pro rata* according to the age–sex distribution of the area, after making all the other adjustments shown in table 6.9 at the local level.

Whilst the rolled forward estimates gave a shortfall of 572,000[1] in England and Wales in the 1991 Census after adjustment, this could not be broken down by local area. Because of difficulties over migration figures at the local level, only national estimates are considered reliable. Therefore it is not possible by this means to establish with any reliability the extent of the undercount by local area. At the time of writing, various other demographic checks on the census subnational enumeration are being examined by the Census Offices and others (Simpson, Marsh and Sandhu, 1993). It is too early to say whether these will provide sufficiently strong evidence to change the provisional population estimates for subnational areas, in which the undercount of 572,000 is assumed to be spread evenly throughout the country[1], in accordance with the age–sex profiles of the area. This assumption means, for example, that areas with high concentrations of students or members of the Armed Forces will be allocated a rather higher proportion of the undercount than other areas.

6.15 METHODS USED IN ROLLING FORWARD ESTIMATES OF POPULATION

Because of the importance attached to the rolled-forward population estimates in establishing the estimated size of the 1991 Census undercount, it is important that the methods used to calculate them are made explicit. Each year the population is aged-on one year, deaths classified by age and sex are subtracted, new births are added, and adjustments are made for migration; the methods are fully explained in OPCS (1992a).

---

[1] A note on subsequent revisions to these numbers and assumptions about the geographical distribution of the undercount forms a postscript to this chapter.

The allowances for migration are the most problematic part of the procedure. Internal migration is estimated from the records of change of Family Health Service Authorities reported to the National Health Service Central Register, and these are allocated to smaller geographical units on the basis of changes in the electoral rolls. These procedures of course entail errors; the raw data are only as good as the accuracy of the Family Health Service Authority lists permit, and the method of making local area estimates only approximate. For example, to the extent to which people fail to re-register with a doctor when they move area, the geographical accuracy of the lists will be faulty. It is for these reasons that rolled-forward estimates are not reliable at the local level.

However, such faults are less likely to lead to errors in the totals of the national population. International migration is the most likely source of error here. It has to be estimated from a different source — the International Passenger Survey. This is a sample drawn from passengers as they pass through ports and airports. The sampling errors are quite high; the number of UK residents travelling abroad in 1984 had a 95 per cent confidence interval of ±1.7 per cent and the similar interval for the number of UK residents going to live abroad was ±9 per cent (Griffiths, 1988). Furthermore, the method of sampling cannot be very well controlled, since no precise lists are available for random selection purposes (Breeze and Butcher, 1988). Finally, there is scope for response error, since migrants are identified on the basis of a positive answer to a question about whether they intended to stay at their destination for more than a year. Those who went abroad during the 1980s intending a temporary stay but who ended up permanently emigrating will not have been so recorded in the International Passenger Survey. The increasing numbers of young people who spend some months travelling the globe will not be identified as emigrants by the International Passenger Survey, but many will have been out of the country on census night.

From this discussion it is clear that there is considerable scope for some error to creep into the rolled-forward population estimates, although the magnitude of any error would, in total, be very hard to estimate. On the assumption that the 1981 Census *and* the rolled-forward 1981 estimates are substantially correct, it is evident that the CVS has failed to identify all those missed by the Census and therefore the following section examines the scope for failing to identify people within that survey.

6.16 WHERE MIGHT THE CVS HAVE MISSED UNENUMERATED PEOPLE?

If one million people were missed from the census, this represents one in 50 people in the entire population, or, in terms of the census operation, about nine people missed by each enumerator covering a round of about 200 households. At the most extreme, it represents around 2,000 enumerators who recorded absolutely no population, not even any 'no contact'. How might the CVS have failed to locate up to two-thirds of people missed by enumerators?

The first focus for consideration is the design of the CVS, which aimed to quantify failures in coverage in three separate categories: at enumerated addresses, in wholly absent households and at missed addresses. We will consider each of these in turn:

Enumerated addresses: If enumerators missed people in enumerated households, this failure could have been repeated by CVS interviewers. To put this another way, if some people had avoided enumeration by the census — perhaps through misplaced fears that their presence would become known to other government departments — it is likely that they would also have evaded the CVS interviewer. Although the re-enumeration of persons is formally independent of the census enumeration, the interviewers had knowledge of the information reported at census, which could also have influenced their judgment.

Wholly absent households: The CVS interviewers decided that some of the addresses classified by enumerators as wholly absent households were in fact vacant, which led the provisional CVS figures to suggest that wholly absent households had been over-enumerated; that is, a dwelling was correctly identified but was considered to be vacant by the CVS interviewer. If in some cases the CVS interviewer was wrong, and the dwelling was occupied, then the CVS estimate of the number of cases of over-enumeration would be too high and its overall estimate of net under-enumeration would be too low.

Missed addresses: Finally, dwellings may have been missed by both the CVS interviewer and also the enumerator. The re-enumeration of dwellings is independent of the census enumeration; interviewers working on the CVS were instructed to do a visual listing of all the buildings in the ED and to include in the CVS sample any dwellings which had been missed by the enumerator. Whereas a trained interviewer from the Social Survey Division of OPCS would in the course of a personal interview be in a superior position to the householder to decide on the accuracy of the answers to various census questions with their precise definitions, it is less plausible that they would be any better equipped than the enumerator to check the buildings in their area. However, the number of household spaces reported in the Preliminary Report of the 1991 Census did not seem to be out of line with the number that most local authorities expected. Further evidence (Dorling, 1993) supports the supposition that missed addresses and household spaces were not a major cause of people missed by the Census and the CVS, and the cause lies *within* households — and, to a lesser extent, within communal establishments (see below).

The second general area focuses on the fact that the CVS did not attempt to check on the coverage of people who lived in communal establishments or who were homeless; therefore there is no available estimate of people missed from this source. It is, however, important to remember that this group comprise only about 2 per cent of the total population of Britain.

Those in charge of communal establishments had to make a return of all the people who spent census night in their establishment. There was a suggestion from census enumerators and area managers in their debriefing that problems had been encountered in the enumeration of communal establishments; many felt that the lists they had been given fell short of the total who had spent census night in the establishment (mentioned in Wormald, 1991; OPCS 1991b). Those in charge of some types of communal establishments also had to give a usual address for residents who had been there for less than six months; they were deemed to be visitors to the establishment and were excluded from the count of usual residents. However, it is possible that the householder filling in the form at this 'usual address' would no longer have agreed that the individual should be counted as usually resident in this household. Any such individual, even if correctly enumerated as a visitor to a communal establishment on census night, would not be included elsewhere in the count of usual residents.

There was no requirement on the people in charge to list any absent usual residents of their establishments. Moreover, it was assumed that there would not be any wholly absent communal establishments on a par with the 'wholly absent households', and no imputation was performed for people living in communal establishments. Thus people usually resident in communal establishments who happened to be away on census night will have been missed from the count of usual residents.

A category of people not living either in households or communal establishments were those sleeping rough. Whilst they are likely to have been difficult to enumerate (discussed in chapter 4), their numbers are sufficiently small that they are unlikely to account for much of the undercount.

At the time of writing we do not know whether all, or any, of these reasons lie behind the apparent undercount. Simpson, Marsh and Sandhu (1993) have argued that the apparent discrepancy between the adjusted census figures of 50,383,000 for England and Wales and the rebased mid-year estimates of 50,955,000 is unlikely to stem from any single factor and that all possible explanations should be examined. For example, over and above the demographic checks routinely conducted by OPCS and an examination of the possible reasons for the failure of the CVS, they explore the possibility that 'poll tax' effects may have led younger people — predominantly men — to conceal their presence. They also examine the possibility that the 1981 Census may have overestimated those who were absent from their usual address on census night, and they set out an agenda for further validation checks on the coverage of the 1991 Census. Whilst these issues are beyond the scope of this chapter, it is evident that, in the coming years, there will be a considerable amount of research effort aimed at providing a better understanding of the complex interactions that occur in the process of census taking. If it is concluded that the CVS did, indeed, fail to find 572,000 people in England and Wales, then there are likely to be calls to reconsider the design of this survey before the next census. There may be lessons to be learnt from the US, Canada or Australia where undercounts are the norm and post-enumeration is designed to allow adjustment of the census counts.

Having discussed the 1991 Census undercount in some detail, it is now important to provide the user with some guidance on how it should be dealt with in analyses.

6.17   HOW ARE CENSUS USERS AFFECTED BY THE UNDERCOUNT?

Any careful secondary data analyst should know the character of the data set he or she is working with, the likely sources of error and so on (Dale, Arber and Gilbert, 1988). In this section an attempt is made to summarise how such a careful user of census data should react to the increased undercount in 1991.

The first point is that the non-response rate on the Census is tiny compared to any other social survey. In total, only about 2 per cent of the population were not enumerated; an additional 1.6 per cent of the population were imputed, but may have been enumerated as vistors elsewhere. This figure compares favourably with the 15 per cent non-response to government continuous surveys such as the General House-hold Survey (GHS) which in the late 1980s was attaining a rate of between 84 per cent and 85 per cent, and extremely favourably with commercial surveys such as the National Readership Survey where the non-response rate is estimated to be 63 per cent. In short, by any comparison with survey data, the census is an overwhelming success and must continue to be used as the authoritative basis for denominators of rates, for constructing survey samples and so on. However, there are ways in which a prudent user may want to deal with specific features of the undercount when analysing 1991 Census results.

Next, it is important to understand how the 1991 Census figures compare with those for 1981. Table 6.10 shows the differences between 1981 and 1991 in moving from the residents counted in the Census to the Registrar General's mid-year esti-mates. The greatest differences are in the treatment of wholly absent households and in the level of under-enumeration not accounted for by the CVS. The lower part of the table shows the differences in the percentage of the population missing from census tables in 1981 and 1991.

Anyone for whom precise population figures, especially broken down by age and sex, are important must think carefully about using raw census results. Users who require absolute numbers in local government or health authority areas by age and sex should use the mid-year population estimates in preference to census figures (OPCS, 1992b). Such users must be aware that the definition of a usual resident is slightly different in the two sources, particularly for students, as explained above.

However, a broader group of users may be dealing with variables which are strongly related to age and sex and where relationships between variables might be biased by failing to take account of the missing 2 per cent. Users can check whether the relationships they are investigating could potentially be distorted by weighting the census results with a set of adjustment factors and seeing if this makes any difference. If it does, the weighted estimates are to be preferred. Table 6.11 shows the factors by which the Census counts of residents in England and Wales have been multiplied to allow for the estimated under-enumeration in compiling the mid-year estimates. These are the factors to use as weights. They account for the total esti-mated under-enumeration, including both that found by the CVS and that which the CVS failed to detect.

The factors shown in table 6.11 are for Great Britain, although it is assumed that they are sufficiently uniform across the country to apply to local areas, such as local or health authority areas (see Postscript on page 167). It is assumed that, when applying such correction factors, the distribution of census characteristics of those missed in particular age–sex groups is the same as those counted.

It is interesting to note that the undercounts in these particular age and sex categories are roughly similar to those discovered by the continuous government surveys such as the GHS. The 1989 GHS, for example, suggests that the GHS under-represents males aged 20–29, females 20–24 and females 75 and over. The GHS also under-represents people living in Greater London (Breeze, Trevor and Wilmot, 1992, p.278). If the 1991 Census therefore began to have difficulty in getting hold of the sorts of people that social surveys have traditionally considered hard to find, it is possible that there are census undercounts on other variables. Recent evidence from Britain suggests that the main categories for which low re-sponse is found in government surveys are households with no cars, young socially

Table 6.11

Adjustment factors for estimated under-enumeration in 1991 Census: Great Britain

Age	Persons	Males	Females
All ages	**1.02**	**1.03**	**1.01**
0–4	1.03	1.03	1.03
0–9	1.03	1.03	1.02
10–14	1.01	1.02	1.01
15–19	1.02	1.03	1.01
20–24	1.06	1.09	1.03
25–29	1.06	1.09	1.03
30–34	1.02	1.04	1.01
35–39	1.01	1.02	1.00
40–44	1.01	1.01	1.01
45–84	1.00	1.00	1.00
85 and over	1.05	1.09	1.03

Source: OPCS and GRO(S) *1991 Census, Sex, Age and Marital Status, Great Britain*, 1993.

active people, the widowed elderly, couples without children, households where no one is employed, people with no educational qualifications, the self-employed and single person householders (Barnes 1992). While we do not know whether non-response in the census is due to the same causes as non-response on the government surveys, it may be helpful for census users to be aware of the consistent patterns found in these social surveys. If users need to be particularly careful in their estimates, controlling for the variables in the above list in any analysis would be a prudent step.

It is ironic that, in the past, the way in which such response biases have been most convincingly demonstrated is by comparing the characteristics of non-respondents to government surveys such as the GHS and the Family Expenditure Survey with the census characteristics of the same people (e.g. Rauta, 1985; Redpath, 1986).

An understanding of the undercount problem needs to go hand-in-hand with an understanding of the extent of imputation for wholly missing households in order to get a meaningful picture of census coverage. It is only when we remember that 7.6 per cent (6.35 per cent net) of people in Inner London were imputed in 'wholly absent households', for example, that the low apparent undercount in Inner London (1 per cent) fits with our other knowledge about difficulties of enumeration in the capital. In other areas, for example West Glamorgan, the percentage of the apparent undercount was also low (0.5 per cent) but here only 1.4 per cent of people were imputed in wholly absent households. It is clear that there are very considerable area differences in the extent to which the population was successfully enumerated and these total differences in the level of non-enumeration (i.e. wholly absent imputed plus under-enumeration) must also affect the quality of the census data at area level. Table 6.12 shows the relationship between the imputed population, the undercount explained by the CVS and the undercount not explained by the CVS by broad geographical area.

This new problem with the 1991 Census poses a challenge to social researchers both inside and outside the Census Offices in coming to an understanding of how severe the problem is and whether there are any further steps that can be taken to correct any biases. It may provide a fruitful opportunity for a collaborative programme of enquiry undertaking further validation as new results become available.

Table 6.12

Imputation and under-enumeration in the 1991 Census, England Wales

	Percentages of total rebased population, 1991				
	Net* imputed in wholly absent households	Undercount explained by CVS			Undercount unexplained by CVS
		(1) Imputation of absent households	(2) Missed households	(3) Missed persons in enumerated households	
Inner London	6.35	- 1.23	0.54	0.82	1.34
Outer London	1.99	- 1.30	0.44	0.19	1.18
Other met. counties in England and Wales	1.57	0.16	0.39	0.40	1.13
Shire counties in England and Wales	0.91	- 0.18	0.37	0.31	1.09
England and Wales	1.42	- 0.17	0.39	0.35	1.12

* Based on the total percentage of people in wholly absent households minus the percentage over-imputed by the CVS, column (1).
Source: Simpson *et al* (1993) based on data from OPCS.

6.18   POSTSCRIPT

A final set of rebased mid-1992 population estimates from Census resident counts were published by OPCS on 24 June 1993 (*OPCS Monitor* PP1 93/1).

Although the final estimate of the population has not changed from the provisional estimate, there has been an additional allowance of 200,000 for Census visitors with no, or no identifiable, usual address, omitted from the usual resident count. There has also been an increase in the estimate of the extent to which the CVS over-imputed absent residents and a slight reduction in the estimated extent of under-enumeration arising from missed or misclassified dwellings. The extent to which the census count is enhanced for the Armed Forces has decreased whilst 63,000 elderly residents have been identified from DSS pensioner data. These revised figures are shown in column (ii) of table 6.9.

The allowance for under-enumeration amongst those aged 20-34 has, in the final mid-year estimates, been distributed between local authorities in such a way as to give plausible ratios of males and females in each area. Ten groupings of broadly similar local authorities were used for the distribution. For ages 1-19 and 35-44 sex ratios were not improved by differential distribution and the allowances have been distributed pro rata. DSS pensioner data provided a basis for adjusting for those aged 80 and over. The allowance for visitors and for net under-enumeration of people in responding households has been distributed between the 10 grouping of local authorities as for those aged 20-34. Broadly, the effect of this redistribution has been to give more than proportionate shares to city areas and smaller shares to less densely populated areas.

On 4 August 1993 OPCS announced that, following discussions with the Home Office concerning external migration statistics, they have concluded that the population of England and Wales should be 145,000 greater than the number given in *Monitor* PP1 93/1.

7   Output from the 1991 Census: an introduction

Chris Denham

7.1 INTRODUCTION

The statistical results of the Census are made available in two ways:

- in *printed reports* sold by HMSO bookshops (or directly from the Census Offices in a few cases); or
- in *statistical abstracts* available, on request and for a charge, from the Census Offices.

Reports cover either a topic at national level or the whole range of topics at county and local government district level. Statistical abstracts typically provide more detail than the reports, particularly in the form of Local and Small Area Statistics which are of unique value for the analysis of local populations.

The *reports* take three general forms:

- volumes containing substantial and detailed tables;
- *Key Statistics*, which give around 200 summary statistics for particular types of area throughout the country, with national and regional figures, laid out for easy comparison between areas; and
- *Monitors*, pamphlets which either give between 20 and 60 summary statistics for particular types of area in parts of the country, sometimes issued before main reports to give early results, or provide summaries for the country as a whole.

Statistical abstracts are supplied mainly in machine-readable form, although small quantities can be supplied as hard copies, and are generally:

- in a standard form, commissioned by a number of customers sharing costs, particularly to provide results for areas and populations smaller than those covered in reports; or
- specially designed output commissioned by individual customers - see section 7.5.

The Census Offices also supply supplementary products, for example to provide information on the geographical base of the Census, and documentation in a series of OPCS/GRO(S) *1991 Census User Guides*, available from Census Customer Services (see section 7.8).

There are two broad types of results:
*   *local statistics*, which cover the full range of census topics; and
*   *topic statistics*, which focus on particular census topics in more detail, mainly at national and regional level.

All the main statistical results and products are described in Prospectuses in the *User Guide* series. Those for reports and abstracts contain complete outlines of the tables produced.

All areas for which results are provided in reports and abstracts are as at the time of the 1991 Census unless otherwise indicated. Any major changes in the boundaries of statutory areas, such as happened with local government reorganisation in 1974/75, would probably be covered by the issue of new series of 1991 Census reports, although no decision had been made at the time of writing.

7.2 LOCAL BASE AND SMALL AREA STATISTICS

The *Local Base Statistics* are a set of tables designed to meet the needs for census information for a variety of areas upwards from the the census enumeration district (ED) (England and Wales) and Output Areas (OA) (Scotland). They cover all census topics and are standard throughout Britain to allow ready comparison between areas; they are issued both as reports and abstracts.

The 1991 tables are based on those produced for local areas from the 1981 Census, but, after extensive consultation, they were updated and expanded into two tiers. The new upper tier, called the Local Base Statistics (LBS), comprises about 20,000 statistical counts for each area. Users can, of course, manipulate and select from this large number of counts for their own information bases. The tables in the lower tier, the Small Area Statistics (SAS), were drawn entirely from those in the LBS for ease of comparison and comprise about 9,000 counts for each area. They are available only as abstracts. The 1991 SAS provide about twice as much data for each area as the 1981 SAS. Over half the increase is to cover new topics in the census; individual tables are generally not more complex. A further innovation is that SAS will be prepared for postcode sectors in England and Wales (as well as in Scotland). Full guidance on the LBS and SAS is given in chapter 8, and further information is available in *Prospectus/User Guide 3*.

The following paragraphs describe how results are made available for different types of local area, both in the form of reports and in the form of abstracts. Figure 3.1 in chapter 3(I) shows the relationship between different types of area.

7.2.1 Local authorities

Results for local authorities at county and district level in all parts of the country are available, with full comparability.

*   *County Reports* (England and Wales) and *Region Reports* (Scotland): issued separately in two parts for each county in England and Wales and for each region in Scotland (a 'part' may comprise of two physically separate volumes). They contain the LBS at local authority level.

- *Key Statistics* (Great Britain): a single report giving around 200 summary statistics drawn from the LBS and SAS, with some 1981/91 comparisons, for each local authority (see *Prospectus/User Guide 29*).

- *County Monitors* (England and Wales — bilingual in Wales) and *Region Monitors* (Scotland): pamphlets giving some 100 summary statistics issued separately for each county or region in advance of the main Reports.

- Local and Small Area Statistics are also available aggregated to local authority level.

7.2.2 Smaller areas within the local authorities

Results are available at two main geographic levels within local authorities throughout Great Britain, although the geographic base is different in Scotland.

Wards (England and Wales), Civil Parishes (England) and Communities (Wales), and Postcode sectors (Scotland)

Ward and Civil Parish Monitors (England) or *Ward and Community Monitors* (Wales) are pamphlets for each county in England and Wales which give some 30 statistics for each ward and civil parish/community, with figures for counties and districts/ boroughs for comparison (see *Prospectus/User Guide 32*).

LBS are available for wards above a minimum population size; SAS are available for wards (except for a handful in the City of London with very small populations) and for civil parishes/communities above a minimum population size.

Postcode sector Monitors are pamphlets for each region in Scotland, similar in content to Ward and Civil Parish Monitors. Pseudo sectors are created where postcode sectors cross local authority boundaries.

LBS are available for sectors and pseudo sectors above a minimum population size; SAS are available for all sectors and pseudo sectors.

In Scotland, SAS are also available aggregated to regional electoral wards, district wards, civil parishes and inhabited islands.

Enumeration districts (EDs) (England and Wales) and Output Areas (OA) (Scotland).

EDs and OAs — the minimum area 'building bricks' for output — are not used as such for the presentation of results in any reports, but SAS are available for all EDs (above a minimum population size) and for all OAs. Chapters 3 and 8 give more information about census geography and statistics respectively at these small area levels.

7.2.3 Health authority areas

Results are available for health authority areas in England, and to a lesser extent, for those elsewhere in Britain, although in Wales and Scotland health authority boundaries coincided with those of local authorities at the time of the 1991 Census.

- *Health Regions Report*: a single report, in the form of a County Report (see section 7.2.1), for regional health authorities in England.

- *Report for Health Areas*: gives a selection of tables for '100 per cent' topics for health administration areas in Great Britain.

- *Key Statistics*: a single report giving some 200 summary statistics drawn from the LBS and SAS for each health authority in Great Britain (see *Prospectus/User Guide 31*).

- *Health Authority Monitors*: pamphlets, in the form of County Monitors, for regional and district health authorities in England and Wales.

- LBS and SAS are also available aggregated to health authority level, and to FSHA areas in England and Wales. LBS and SAS are available for wards/postcode sectors and EDs/OAs within health authorities; EDs or OAs fit health area boundaries exactly.

7.2.4 Urban and rural areas

Results for urban and rural areas are available as *Key Statistics* which take the form of a single report for the larger urban areas and the rural areas in Great Britain, giving some 200 summary statistics drawn from the SAS for each area. There are also six 'regional' reports covering urban areas of all sizes and the rural areas in four parts of England and, separately, Wales and Scotland (see *Prospectus/User Guides 30*).

Urban and rural areas (urban 'localities' in Scotland) have been specially defined for both the 1981 and 1991 Censuses, and a further report will give measures of change over the decade. 'Urban areas' cover conurbations, cities and towns of all sizes defined on a land use basis ('bricks and mortar'), so, for example, Census results are available for smaller towns within the larger local authority areas. 'Rural areas' are all remaining parts of the country, presented in the reports as the rural 'remainders' of local government districts. SAS are also available aggregated to each urban and rural area.

7.2.5 Parliamentary and European Constituencies

Parliamentary Constituency Monitors are pamphlets, in the form of County Monitors, but with some additional '10 per cent' statistics, with results for each parliamentary constituency (with figures for Britain for comparison). There are separate Monitors for each standard statistical region in England, and for Wales and Scotland (see *Prospectus/User Guide 34*). A single pamphlet in the same form covers the European parliamentary constituencies in Great Britain.

7.2.6 Postcode areas

Postcode Sector Monitors are pamphlets for postal 'towns' or groups of postal 'towns' in England and Wales, giving some 20 '100 per cent' summary statistics at postcode sector level (see *Prospectus/User Guide 33*). SAS are also available for postcode sectors in England and Wales. The 1991 Census records for England and Wales, which were arranged initially in ED order, were processed again to give exact counts for postcode sectors.

Results are available for a wide range of postcode based areas in Scotland.

7.2.7 National versions of local results

Results for Great Britain, regions in England, and Wales and Scotland, and for these areas as a whole, are available in forms comparable with those for local authorities and other types of area described above.

- *National Reports:* issued in two parts, on the lines of a County Report, for Great Britain as a whole, including results for standard statistical regions in England and for Wales and Scotland. There is also a Report for Wales (bilingual in Welsh and English) with results at county level, and a Report for Scotland with results at regional level.

- *National and Regional Summary Monitors*: a pamphlet for Great Britain on the lines of a County Monitor, including results for standard statistical regions in England and for Wales and Scotland. There are similar summary Monitors for Wales (bilingual) and Scotland, including summary results at county/region level. A further Monitor brings together results for regional health authorities.

7.3 TOPIC STATISTICS

Results for particular census topics are available in a series of reports summarised in figure 7.1, which lists the reports in the approximate order of publication. The reports present results mainly at the national level, but the table shows those which have results at regional level, or at a county or district (or equivalent) level. An outline of the content of each report is given in the following paragraphs. A Prospectus is available for each report and should be checked for detailed information, if the reports themselves are not available.

The reports are published by HMSO and are available from HMSO bookshops. A report may comprise more than one physically separate volume. The *Prospectuses* (one per report) are issued in the OPCS/GRO(S) 1991 Census User Guide series, available without charge from Census Customer Services, and show all tables in outline. Each Prospectus also contains general notes on the Census, with particular notes and definitions for the topic concerned. Reference numbers of Prospectuses are given in the paragraphs below.

7.3.1 Geographic levels of tables in reports

The geographic levels at which tables are presented in reports are necessarily generalised in the outlines in paragraphs 7.3.4 to 7.3.11, and the following terms are used:

- Great Britain level: tables are aggregates for Britain as a whole.

- National level: tables are aggregates for England, Wales, Scotland, England and Wales and Britain as a whole.

- Regional level: tables are aggregates for standard statistical regions (including Wales and Scotland), and sometimes for the metropolitan counties and the remainder of the regions in which they are situated, as well as including national level aggregates.

- County/region and district level: tables are aggregates for local government areas, as well as regional and national level aggregates.

In addition, results are presented for a number of other types of appropriate geographical areas in particular reports. A fuller description of geographic levels is given in table 7.1.

7.3.2 Texts in the reports

Each report is introduced by a text, which follows a fairly standard pattern, with sections on: a brief background introduction to the 1991 Census results and how to obtain them; details of the census question(s) covered by the report; definitions of terms used in the output, together with any other information particular to a topic; notes on the conventions used in tables; notes on the interpretation of the 10 per cent sample where necessary; lists of table titles and a key word index.

Reports may also contain a brief commentary (Monitors are also issued to summarise the figures in most reports), and may contain any necessary guidance on the coverage and quality of the results (although the main results of the 1991 Census Validation Survey are published in a separate report, and summarised in Census Newsletters).

Each report also has brief guidance on the possibility of commissioning tables to provide more detailed statistics on a topic, or to give a more detailed geographical breakdown (see section 7.5.8 for more details).

7.3.3 Preliminary reports

These provide first results for a wide readership, later replaced by final results, but the commentary in the reports remains relevant.

The Preliminary report, England and Wales, published in July 1991, gives initial figures of the populations present in each local authority district, county, metropolitan county, regions and the country as a whole. Comparative populations for 1961, 1971 and 1981 are included, as well as the hectares in each area in 1991 and an initial count of the number of household spaces. Further tables give: the population of the country and intercensal change for every census since 1801; the population of the UK, and separately for its constituent parts, and also the Isle of Man, Jersey and Guernsey for each census from 1851, together with intercensal changes.

The report was compiled from summary returns made by the census field staff, and the text of the report explains the methods used and the qualifications to be placed on the results. There is also a commentary on the results and changes since 1981, illustrated by maps and diagrams.

The Preliminary report, Scotland, published in July 1992, gives information for local authority districts, Regions and Islands Areas in Scotland, and for censuses since 1801, comparable to that in the preliminary report for England and Wales. There are, however, some differences in the content of tables and in the accompanying text and commentary to suit the different circumstances in Scotland.

Table 7.1

Geographic levels in topic reports

Tables in topic reports for Great Britain are generally presented at one of five geographic levels. Each table outline in the Prospectuses indicates the level of geography for which the table will appear in the report. There are standard area levels for which results are presented, and also other geographic divisions. Figure 3.1 (see page 58) shows the relationship between area in diagrammatic form.

Geographic level	Standard areas presented (number of areas in parenthesis)
Great Britain	• Great Britain
National level	• Great Britain • England and Wales • England • Wales • Scotland
Regional level	• Great Britain • England and Wales • England • Standard regions (8) • Metropolitan counties (9) • Inner/Outer London • Regional remainders (5) (in the SE and other standard regions with metropolitan counties) • Wales • Scotland
County level	Same as regional level plus: • Non-metropolitan counties of England and Wales (55) • Regions and Islands Areas of Scotland (12)
District level	Same as regional level, plus: • London boroughs (33) • Non-metropolitan counties in England and Wales (55) • Districts in England and Wales (403) • Regions and Islands Areas in Scotland (12) • Districts in Scotland (53)

At the regional, county and district level, statistics for the remainder of the South East region are also presented for the Outer Metropolitan Area and Outer South East.

In topic reports for Scotland the standard geographic levels are:

- • Scotland
- • Regions and Islands Areas (12)
- • Districts (53)

Table 7.1 - *continued*

Other geographic divisions

In the Report for Health Areas, a selection of tables from the range of '100 per cent' topics is presented for the following health administration areas in Great Britain

Regional health authority level
- Great Britain
- England
- Regional health authorities in England (14)
- Wales
- Scotland

District health authority level
- Great Britain
- England
- Regional health authorities in England (14)
- District health authorities in England (191)
- Wales
- District health authorities in Wales (9)
- Scotland
- Health boards in Scotland (15)

In the National Migration and Regional Migration reports, 13 areas additional to the metropolitan counties, termed 'other main urban centres', are identified as areas of residence and of former residence in tables at the regional level. These areas are:

- North region — Cleveland county

- Yorkshire and Humberside region — Kingston upon Hull

- East Midlands region — Leicester
  Nottingham

- East Anglia region — Norwich

- South East region — Portsmouth–Southampton corridor, comprising: Eastleigh, Fareham, Gosport, Havant, Portsmouth, and Southampton

- South West region — Bristol
  Plymouth

- Wales — Cardiff

- Scotland — Aberdeen
  Dundee
  Edinburgh
  Glasgow

In Workplace and Transport to Work tables, areas of special interest for the analysis of travel to work are identified. These are:

- City centres — London (City and West End)
  Birmingham
  Leeds
  Liverpool
  Manchester/Salford
  Newcastle-upon-Tyne
  Sheffield

- Heathrow Airport, Gatwick Airport and London Docklands

7.3.4 Basic demographics

These reports provide historic analyses and information on population bases.

Sex, age and marital status, Great Britain (Prospectus/User Guide 2)
This contains three tables giving: marital status by sex and age in single years of age; similar figures with quinary age groups down to county/region level; and sex by single year of age 0-24 down to county/region level.

Usual Residence, Great Britain (Prospectus/User Guide 7)
This contains six tables down to local government district level which show the usual resident counts on which census results are based, together with figures of students and school children by area of usual residence and term time address, and visitors by country of usual residence.

Historic Tables, Great Britain (Prospectus/User Guide 4)
This contains six tables which show: persons present, and intercensal changes for Great Britain, England, Wales and Scotland for all censuses from 1801 to 1991; persons present down to county/region level from 1891 to 1991; the proportion of the total population in each area at each census, and intercensal change; and sex, age and marital status at national level from 1891 to 1991.

7.3.5 Subgroups in the population

These reports provide information on groups in the population with particular relevance to public policy, legislation and expenditure, and to commercial activities concerned with the groups. Variables in cross-tabulations are chosen specifically to highlight subjects, of interest.

Children and Young Adults, Great Britain (Prospectus/User Guide 13)
This contains eight tables, each down to regional level, giving breakdowns by age (up to the 29 years of age limit), covering: total numbers, migrants and long-term illness; marital status; economic activity; ethnic group; housing; family status of the child or young adult; social class of families; and higher educational qualification by ethnic group.

Persons aged 60 and over, Great Britain (Prospectus/User Guide 6)
This contains six tables, most down to regional level, covering: total numbers, age, sex and marital status; sex, age and long-term illness; persons not in households; 'earners' in households with elderly people; long-term illness in communal establishments; and housing.

Limiting Long-term Illness, Great Britain (Prospectus/User Guide 5)
This contains seven tables, mainly at the national level, each giving results by age groups on the long-term ill in: households; communal establishments by type; and ethnic groups; and also by economic activity, housing tenure and amenities, and household type.

Ethnic Group and Country of Birth, Great Britain (Prospectus/User Guide 9)
This contains 20 tables divided into '100 per cent' and '10 per cent' sections, mainly

at national level, but also with six at regional level, giving results, in the case of ethnic group, from information collected for the first time in the 1991 Census. Country of birth is tabulated by marital status, age, birthplace of household head, and migration. Ethnic group is tabulated by sex, age and marital status, birthplace, migration, economic position, housing characteristics, occupation, industry, social class and socio-economic group, higher qualification, and family composition. There is also a table giving counts of the full classification of 35 ethnic groups, based on the 'written in' answers to the question.

7.3.6 Welsh and Gaelic language

These reports provide information on Welsh speaking throughout Wales, and Gaelic speaking throughout Scotland (the information was not collected in England), and also on reading and writing the languages, with historic information and other data showing trends in the languages and factors relating to their use.

Welsh language in Wales (available in Welsh and English) (Prospectus/User Guide 10) This contains eight tables, mainly at Wales or county level (geographically detailed data are available in the LBS and SAS), covering: trends since 1921; speaking, reading and writing Welsh by age group; Welsh speaking migrants and other migrants; Welsh speakers by household and family composition; and Welsh speakers by economic position, occupation, social class and higher qualifications.

Gaelic language in Scotland (Prospectus/User Guide 18) This contains eight tables similar to those in the Welsh language report, except that trends since 1891 are shown, and results are given for more detailed geographical areas in the Gaelic speaking parts of Scotland than elsewhere.

7.3.7 Household and family composition; communal establishments

The first two of these reports provide information on people grouped in households and families — the latter based on '10 per cent' processing of the question on relationship to head of household. Such comprehensive information is one of the most valuable aspects of a census, in comparison to databases on individuals only or to data derived from small samples.

Household Composition (100 per cent) Great Britain (Prospectus/User Guide 11) This contains 18 tables, including seven at regional level, covering: dependent children; housing characteristics in a series of tables; 'earners' in households; ethnic group; composition in terms of dependents in the household; people caring for dependants ('carers'); and 'earners' and dependants.

Household and Family Composition (10 per cent), Great Britain (Prospectus/User Guide 23) This is a substantial report with 31 tables plus five subsidiary tables, with detailed breakdowns in many of the tables, primarily at Great Britain/national level. The results on households are extended to cover '10 per cent' variables such as social class, or are presented in combination with statistics on families. The results on families cover, for example, children in families, couples and lone parent families, multi-family households by ethnic group, and 'earners' and dependants in families.

Communal Establishments, Great Britain (Prospectus/User Guide 15)
This completes the picture with figures about people not in households on census night but present in establishments such as hospitals, hotels and prisons. The tables are mainly at regional level and cover the sex, age, marital condition, ethnic group, economic position, and long-term illness of the people in each type of establishment, together with figures on the number and size of each type of establishment.

7.3.8 Housing

These reports provide a picture of Britain's housing stock and the characteristics of the households in particular housing circumstances, summarising the national and regional position. This adds to the considerable amount of information on housing in the LBS and SAS. Characteristics of households with and without cars are provided.

Housing and Availability of Cars, Great Britain (Prospectus/User Guide 12)
This contains 22 tables, some down to district or county level, but most at regional or national level, which cover tenure, amenities, and number of rooms cross-tabulated by characteristics such as households with children and/or pensioners. Number of cars available to a household is similarly cross-tabulated. There are also figures on household spaces and dwellings.

A separate report for Scotland (also *Prospectus/User Guide* 12) covers characteristics of households by lowest floor level of accommodation (information collected in Scotland only) and by the derived variable 'occupancy norm' described in chapter 2, section 2.5.3, and also only available in Scotland.

7.3.9 Migration

These reports are based on information on address one year before the census, which is not necessarily representative of most recent moves but which provides a snapshot of migration in Britain — a topic for which there are few alternative sources of information. The reports also provide information on migrants leaving an area (origin) as well as arriving there (destination).

National Migration, Great Britain (Prospectus/User Guide 17)
This contains 12 tables based on '100 per cent' processing and eight tables based on '10 per cent' processing, published as two separate parts. In the first part there are tables of origins and destination down to the level of region and main urban centres (straight line distances of moves are also tabulated). Most other tables are at national level and cover, for example, the demographic characteristics of migrants and wholly moving households. These are tabulated by type of move, for example, 'moving within (local government) district'. The second part covers the socio-economic groups, occupations and industries of migrants, and also tabulates these variables by distance of move.

Regional Migration (Prospectus/User Guide 22)
There are two parts for each standard statistical region, Wales and Scotland and, like the national report, these contain tables (11) based on '100 per cent' processing, and tables (5) based on '10 per cent' processing, each set of tables with similar topic coverage to the national report, but with some figures down to (local government) district level.

7.3.10 Economic activity and workplace

These reports provide a uniquely comprehensive snapshot of Britain's workforce, both by area of residence and by area of workplace, together with the means of journeys to work. Because of the time needed to code 'written in' answers to the question on occupation and workplace, the reports are based predominantly on the '10 per cent' sample data.

Economic Activity, Great Britain (Prospectus/User Guide 16)
This is a sizeable report with 20 tables, plus three subsidiary tables, at regional or national level, covering: economic position and employment status; occupation (Standard Occupational Classification); industry; hours worked; and social class and socio-economic group.

Workplace and Transport to Work, Great Britain (Prospectus/User Guide 20)
This contains eight tables, with the some tables at regional level, and with figures for city centres and other major centres of employment. The tables cover: resident and working populations; area of workplace by area of residence; area of residence by area of workplace; means of travel to work; distance and means of travel to work; and car availability by means of travel to work.
There is a further separate report for **Scotland**, with the same table outlines, but with all figures given down to (local government) district level.

7.3.11 Higher qualifications

The report provides a profile, unavailable from any other source, of Britain's men and women with higher qualifications, data which are used in the planning of investment in education. The census measures current (census day) circumstances of the people who have gained a wide variety of qualifications from a wide variety of institutions. The information obtained in the 1991 Census was limited to degrees, professional and vocational qualifications, and does not cover school level qualifications. The written in answers are time consuming to code, and the report is based entirely on the 10 per cent sample data.

Qualified Manpower, Great Britain (Prospectus/User Guide 8)
This contains 19 tables, mainly at Great Britain level but with some at regional level, analysing the population aged 18 or over by higher qualifications. The qualified population is grouped into three levels of qualification and further analysed by such topics as occupation, subject of qualification, economic activity and industry. A further set of tables analyses men and women by subject of qualification by current occupation and industry.

7.4 OTHER STANDARD PRODUCTS

7.4.1 Workplace and migration statistics
The analysis of the census questions on address of workplace and usual address one year before the census gives results on journeys from residences to workplaces and on migration moves, together with figures on people with workplaces in an area and out-migrants from an area, not only for the larger areas covered by the reports (see

Figure 7.1 Topic statistics variables

The following variables are those which are included in one or more standard tables to be published in the reports on topic statistics from the 1991 Census. An indication is given of the individual topic reports in which each variable will be included.

SAM	Sex, Age and Marital Status
HT	Historical Tables
UR	Usual Residence
P60	Persons Aged 60 and Over
H	Housing and Availability of Cars
CE	Communal Establishments
HC	Household Composition (100 per cent)
LTI	Limiting Long-term Illness
WL	Welsh Language in Wales

GL	Gaelic Language in Scotland
EG	Ethnic Group and Country of Birth
NM	National Migration
RM	Regional Migration
EA	Economic Activity
WT	Workplace and Transport to Work
HFC	Household and Family Composition (10 per cent)
QM	Qualified Manpower
CYA	Children and Young Adults

	Topic Report																
	SAM	HT	UR	P60	H	CE	HC	LTI	WL	GL	EG	NM	RM	EA	WT	HFC	QM	CYA
Age																		
- dependants				✓			✓						✓					
- of persons present		✓	✓	✓		✓												
- of residents	✓	✓	✓	✓	✓		✓	✓	✓	✓	✓	✓	✓	✓		✓	✓	✓
- of head of household					✓		✓											
Absent residents			✓	✓		✓												
Amenities (use of)				✓	✓		✓	✓			✓	✓	✓					✓
Area (hectares)		✓																
Area of																		
- usual residence			✓									✓	✓	✓	✓			
- former usual residence												✓	✓					
- workplace														✓	✓			
Average annual change/of persons present		✓																
Average no of persons per room					✓													
Birthplace of head of household/family										✓	✓					✓		
Car availability					✓					✓					✓			
Communal establishments				✓		✓	✓			✓	✓		✓					✓
Country of birth											✓							
Date of census		✓																
Dependants				✓			✓									✓		
Dependent children					✓		✓	✓								✓		
Distance of move												✓	✓					
Distance to work															✓			

	SAM	HT	UR	P60	H	CE	HC	LTI	WL	GL	EG	NM	RM	EA	WT	HFC	QM	CYA
Topic Report (column group)																		
Dwellings					✓													
Dwelling type					✓													
Economic activity																		
- non dependants							✓											
- persons in households					✓		✓						✓	✓		✓		
Economic position																		
- of persons present						✓												
- of residents								✓	✓	✓	✓	✓	✓	✓		✓	✓	✓
- of head of household					✓		✓					✓	✓		✓			
Employment status																		
- of residents							✓				✓	✓	✓	✓				
- of head of household												✓	✓					
Ethnic group																		
- of persons present						✓				✓								
- of residents								✓		✓	✓	✓	✓	✓		✓		✓
- of head of household					✓		✓			✓	✓	✓				✓		
- of spouse/cohabitant																✓		
Family size																✓		
Family status																		✓
Family type									✓	✓	✓			✓		✓		
Floor level of accommodation *				✓	✓		✓	✓		✓								
Hours worked										✓				✓	✓			
Household space type					✓		✓	✓		✓	✓		✓					✓
Household size				✓	✓													✓
Household type				✓	✓		✓	✓	✓	✓		✓	✓			✓		
Industry										✓				✓	✓		✓	✓
Long-term illness				✓	✓	✓		✓				✓	✓	✓		✓		✓
Marital status																		
- of persons present		✓				✓												
- of residents	✓	✓		✓				✓			✓	✓	✓			✓		✓
- of head of household				✓														
Migrants						✓			✓	✓	✓	✓	✓					✓
No car					✓		✓	✓			✓	✓	✓					
No central heating					✓			✓			✓							
Non-dependants				✓			✓									✓		
Number of																		
- adults							✓										✓	
- cars					✓									✓				
- children under 5					✓													
- children under 16					✓													
- dependent children							✓	✓										

	Topic Report																	
	SAM	HT	UR	P60	H	CE	HC	LTI	WL	GL	EG	NM	RM	EA	WT	HFC	QM	CYA
- economically active					✓	✓												
- non-dependants							✓											
- pensioners				✓	✓													
- persons in communal establishments						✓												
- rooms					✓		✓	✓		✓								
Occupation									✓	✓	✓	✓	✓	✓	✓	✓		
Occupancy norm *					✓		✓											
Occupancy type					✓													
% of households with over one person per room					✓													
Persons per room				✓	✓		✓				✓	✓	✓					✓
Persons present	✓	✓		✓		✓		✓		✓								
Qualification level										✓							✓	✓
Residence type in households						✓												
Residents	✓		✓	✓	✓	✓	✓	✓	✓	✓	✓	✓	✓	✓	✓	✓	✓	
Rooms					✓		✓	✓		✓								✓
Rooms in hotels and boarding houses						✓												
Sex	✓	✓	✓	✓	✓	✓	✓	✓	✓	✓	✓	✓	✓	✓	✓	✓	✓	✓
Social class																		
- of family head									✓	✓	✓		✓	✓	✓			✓
Socio-economic group											✓	✓	✓	✓	✓			
Speaks/reads/writes																		
- Gaelic *										✓								
- Welsh †									✓									
Status in communal establishments						✓												
Students			✓															
Subject																	✓	✓
Tenure				✓	✓		✓	✓		✓	✓		✓					✓
Term-time address			✓															
Transport to work															✓			
Type of establishment				✓		✓	✓			✓	✓		✓					
Type of move												✓	✓					
Visitors			✓			✓												
Wholly moving households												✓	✓					
Working full/part time													✓	✓				

* Scotland only

† Wales only

Source: *1991 Census User Guide 14*

section 7.3.10) but also for smaller local areas. The latter are:

- Special Migration Statistics: providing information (in machine-readable form only) on migrants within and between local areas (see *Prospectus/User Guide 35*).

- Special Workplace Statistics: providing information (in machine-readable form only) on workforces in areas of workplace and residence for customer defined zones, and on journeys from residence to workplace between the zones (see *Prospectus/User Guide 36*).

Chapter 10 discusses the form and uses of these statistics.

7.4.2 Enumeration district/postcode directories

These directories link enumeration districts in England and Wales to postcodes. Directories are available, on magnetic media only, separately for each county. Alternatively, customers may purchase a national directory. Further details of the file specification, information on availability, cost and ordering are provided in *Prospectus/User Guide 26*.

The postcodes in the directories are, first, those for addresses of enumeration captured in the processing of the census forms, and, second, those merged in at a later stage for addresses such as business premises, where there was no census form. The different sources give some variation of geographical precision within the directories, but the 1991 Census directories are unique in providing a count of resident households in each unit postcode and counts of households in parts of a unit postcode split by ED boundaries. A user of the directories can create a 'best fit' of unit postcodes to an ED to compare non-census data referenced to postcodes with the Census statistics for the ED, or for other areas built up in the same way. The directories are discussed more fully in chapter 3 (I), section 3.3.3.

7.5 SPECIALLY COMMISSIONED ABSTRACTS

In addition to the output available as reports or standard statistical abstracts, it is possible for abstracts to be independently commissioned, and paid for, by customers. Commissioned output may take the form of either extension tables (that is standard tables for smaller areas than those presented in reports, or for expanded versions of standard distributions of variables) or new tables (that is tables to be specified by customers themselves). *Prospectus/User Guide 14* explains how customers may specify and order commissioned tables, and offers a guide to estimating costs.

The basis for the service is section 4(2) of the Census Act 1920, under which standard abstracts are also provided, which requires the Census Offices to recover the (additional marginal) cost of preparing a commissioned table. The output commissioned need not necessarily be confined to conventional 'tables', but it must comply with the Act's wording of "... abstracts ... containing any such *statistical* information ... as can be derived from the census returns".

A major development in the output commissioned from the 1991 Census is the Samples of Anonymised Records (SARs) which the Registrars General agreed to prepare at the request of the Economic and Social Research Council (ESRC). The SARs are two samples of the computer records of individual data from the Census

- sometimes called 'microdata' or 'public use samples' in other countries. One is a two per cent sample of individuals, the other is a one per cent sample of households. The data in each are anonymous and also subject to further confidentiality measures so that the chance of identification of any person or household in the samples and the disclosure of information about them is negligible. The SARs give users scope for preparing tables not otherwise issued or commissioned, and considerable scope for new techniques of statistical analysis. Chapter 11 gives a full description of the development of the SARs, and the data and services that are available from the Census Microdata Unit established by the ESRC at the University of Manchester to disseminate the SARs.

7.5.1 Information on output already available

Before commissioning any table, users should consult the set of prospectuses (see earlier sections of this chapter) to see whether the variables they require, or others very similar to them, are being produced as part of standard output. (A listing of variables so far identified as being included in the topic statistics volumes is given in figure 7.1.) Users may also contact the Census Microdata Unit at the University of Manchester to see if use of the SARs might meet their needs. If neither will meet the user's needs, contact should be made with Census Customer Services (see p 200), after considering the information given below.

7.5.2 Types of commissioned tables

There are four general types of table that users may wish to commission.

Extension tables: standard areas
These are versions of the same tables appearing in the topic reports but extended to lower area levels. For example, a cross-tabulation of Standard Occupational Classification Major Groups by employment status, hours worked and sex may only appear at the national level in the *Economic Activity* reports. A user may, however, wish to commission this table at local authority district level for particular counties. Such lower area levels are restricted to standard census areas (see the list of standard census areas in table 7.2), but exclude wards and EDs in England and Wales and Output Areas (OAs) and postcode sectors in Scotland to avoid risks of disclosure.

Extension tables: expanded variables
These are tables in which one or more distributions of variables are expanded from those appearing in the reports. For example, *Ethnic Group and Country of Birth* includes a table showing migrants by broad age group by country of birth, whereas a user might require information say, for single years of age for persons aged 16-45 by individual country of birth within the European Community. Such a table could be commissioned.

New tables: standard variables
These are tables where combinations of variables not otherwise cross-tabulated are requested. For example, a user might require an analysis of distance travelled to work by hours worked by ethnic group, which does not appear elsewhere.

Table 7.2

Census areas: statistical output

Type	Name (England and Wales (E & W), Scotland (S))	Head counts	SAS	LBS	Monitors	Key statistics	Local reports	Topic reports
Planning and operational	Postcode unit (S)	■						
	ED (S)							
	ED (E & W)	(1)	■					
	Census district							
Statutory	Civil Parish	(1)	■		■			
	Community (Wales)	(1)	■		■			
	Ward	(1)	■	■	■			
	Reg Elect. Div (S)		■	■				
	LA District		■	■	■	■	■	(2)
	County/Region		■	■	■	■	■	(2)
	England/Wales } Scotland/GB	■	■	■	■	■	(3)	■
	FHSA		■	■				
	DHA (E & W)		■	■	■	■		
	RHA (England)		■	■	■	■	(3)	
	HBA (S)		■	■				
	Parliamentary Constituency		■		■			
	European Constituency		■		■			
	New Town (S)		■	■				
Statistical	Postcode unit (E & W)	■						
	Output Area (S)		■					
	Postcode sector (S)		■	■	■			
	Postcode sector (E & W)		■		■			
	Urban area (E & W)		■			■		
	Locality (S)		■			■		
	Rural area (E & W)		■			■		
	Inhabited island (S)	(1)	■					
	Metropolitan county (Eng)		■	■	■	■	■	■
	Standard region (Eng)		■	■	■	■	(3)	■

Notes: (1) Headcounts if population is below threshold.   ■ Output available.
       (2) Included in a limited number of topic reports.
       (3) National versions of local reports.

New tables: customised variables

These are tables which are specified by users and contain variables not otherwise produced, in combination either with standard variables or with other user-specified variables. For example, there might be a requirement for details of: (i) people with limiting long-term illness living in households headed by a male aged 45-64 and working in the chemical industry by (ii) tenure of household. While (ii) is a standard variable appearing in other tables, (i) is a variable which does not appear elsewhere.

Output may also be commissioned for customised areas, that is non-standard areas to be defined in terms of either wards (in England and Wales) or postcode sectors (in Scotland), or of aggregations of EDs/OAs.

7.5.3 Confidentiality in commissioned tables

Generally, with any request for a commissioned table, the Census Offices will scrutinise the specified area(s) and/or variables so that confidentiality is maintained. Risks of disclosing information about identifiable individuals or households occur when the populations are too small (including situations in which customised areas differ only slightly from areas for which output has already been produced and/or variable categories are too detailed and/or too similar to those in other reports, standard abstracts or commissioned tables). A user is told if a requested table raises unacceptable risks, and would be told if risks could be reduced to an acceptable level.

7.5.4 Definitions

A user making a request for a commissioned table will need to check on existing definitions for the topic of interest. Definitions of some of the variables used in reports and abstracts are given in the Prospectuses, otherwise reference may be made to *1991 Census Definitions* (OPCS and GRO(S), 1992). But, if the output required is complex, early contact should be made with Census Customer Services (see p.200).

7.5.5 Media

Commissioned tables are supplied on magnetic tape or cartridge for both IBM and ICL environment mainframe computers. Tables can also be supplied to a publication standard through an electronic publishing system, at an additional cost. Alternatively, small quantities of tables can be supplied on paper.

7.5.6. Charges for commissioned output

At the planning stage of 1991 Census output, it was not possible for the Census Offices to give anything more than a general indication of costs for commissioned output. Indeed, firm costs cannot be quoted until the specification for any particular commissioned output is received. For users wishing to estimate expenditure, however, the following figures were offered as a guide when *User Guide 14* was issued in 1992:

Extension tables: standard areas
The additional cost of producing a version of an existing table for a lower geographic level was expected to range from about **£100** to **£450** depending on the number of cells in the standard tables and on the number and level of the areas.

Extended tables: expanded variables
The additional cost of providing a table with more detailed breakdowns of standard distributions was expected to range from about **£250** to **£750** depending on the number of cells in the standard table, on the degree of detail in the particular variable(s) required, and on the number and level of areas.

New tables: standard variables

Where a user requests cross-tabulations of variables not included in any existing standard table, the cost of providing such tables was expected to range from about **£550** to **£1,250** per table depending on the number and complexity of variables required and on the number and level of areas.

New tables: customised variables

For tables which are specified by a user and which might comprise combinations of standard and/or derived variables not otherwise produced in any other output, the cost was expected to start at around **£1,000** per table and rise depending on the range of factors influencing other types of commissioned tables.

Census Customer Services (see section 7.8) should be contacted about charges at an early stage. An estimate will be supplied without charge. The invoice for commissioned output is normally sent at supply, and VAT is charged.

7.5.7 Cost sharing

The charges for commissioned output may be shared by two or more customers ordering the same output, provided of course that such orders are received prior to processing. In addition, Census Customer Services identify similar orders and refer back to the customers involved, so that the potential for combining requirements and reducing costs is explored.

7.5.8 Ordering commissioned tables and timetable for production

Customers were initially requested to indicate requirements for commissioned tables by March 1992, and orders received by then formed the basis of the schedule for work. This does not, however, preclude further requests.

Extension tables for standard census areas are produced as soon as possible after the respective topic report. For other types of commissioned output, guidance should be sought from Census Customer Services on the availability dates. Provisional enquiries are without obligation, but, on confirmation of an order, customers are asked to enter into a formal agreement. However, the Census Offices have limited resources to devote to commissioned output, and it may not be possible to meet all requests.

7.6 TERMS FOR THE USE OF CENSUS OUTPUT

7.6.1 Census reports: copyright and reproduction of material

All text, statistical and other material in census reports and information of any kind derived from the statistics or other material in the reports is Crown copyright and may be reproduced only with the permission of the Census Offices.

The Census Offices are prepared to allow extracts of statistics or other material from reports to be reproduced without a licence provided that the statistics form part of a larger work not primarily designed to reproduce the extracts and provided that any extract of statistics represents only a limited part of a table or tables and provided that Crown copyright and the source are prominently acknowledged. The Census Offices reserve their rights in all circumstances, and should be consulted in any case of uncertainty. Enquiries about the reproduction of material should be directed to OPCS or GRO(S) as appropriate at the addresses given in section 7.8, and reproduction may require a licence and payment of fees.

7.6.2 Terms for the use of abstracts: charges and conditions of supply

Under the Census Act 1920, the Census Offices must recover the cost of producing statistical abstracts, that is the marginal additional cost beyond the basic cost of taking and processing the census which is met by the Government. The Census Offices can only produce abstracts when one or more customer has made a commitment to purchase and cover the cost. Where the abstracts have a standard form, such as the SAS, and are required by several customers, some of the costs can be shared between the customers and this reduces unit charges, although the customers may not then pass the data to third parties without the agreement of the Census Offices. A 'customer', in this sense, may comprise a large number of similar organisations, for example, local authorities or health authorities, where each covers part of the country, or the universities as a whole, which are treated as one for the purpose of setting charges. More guidance is given below.

Copies of abstracts are supplied by the Census Offices under a number of general conditions.

- The information in the abstracts remains Crown copyright.
- The purchaser obtains the use of standard abstracts within the authority or organisation as specified to, and agreed by, the Census Offices; or obtains use as otherwise agreed by the Census Offices.
- The purchaser must not transfer or publish the information in the abstracts (either in whole or part) or information of any kind derived from the abstracts, except as agreed, without first obtaining permission from the Census Offices.
- The abstracts incorporate safeguards against possible identification of any particular person or household, and the purchaser must not use abstracts to attempt to obtain or derive information relating specifically to an identified person or household, nor claim to have obtained or derived such information.

The customer accepts these conditions when completing an order form for abstracts. End user licences also repeat the conditions in circumstances where users may be remote from the original point of supply.

Customer sectors

Standard abstracts are supplied for use by specific authorities, organisations, companies, or persons agreed when the customer makes an order and accepts the conditions of supply. By so limiting the transfer of the abstracts to third parties, the Census Offices are able to charge any one customer only part of the total cost of the abstracts for any area. The 'customer sectors' for the 1991 Census abstracts are similar to those identified in 1981, and are, with conditions for their use of the abstracts, in summary, as follows:

Local authorities

A local authority may use the abstracts for its own activities or for activities which obtain at least half their resources or funds from the authority. This includes public use through libraries, for which special guidelines will be developed as necessary, and educational use through local education authorities. There is no restriction on the transfer of abstracts between departments in an authority. Higher tier authorities may purchase and use the abstracts in consortia with lower tier authorities regardless of funding arrangements between the tiers, and special inter-authority bodies may also purchase and/or use the abstracts in the same way, provided that all such arrangements have been specified at the time of ordering.

The Health Service

Central purchases of LBS/SAS were arranged for the health services in England, Wales and Scotland. Health authorities and other parts of the health service may use the abstracts for their own activities or for activities which obtain at least half their resources or funds from the National Health Service, or in any other way agreed with the funding government departments. There is no restriction on the transfer of the abstracts between different sections of an authority.

Universities and higher education establishments

The Economic and Social Research Council (ESRC) has purchased LBS and SAS for all areas in Great Britain, together with other abstracts, on behalf of all those in institutions qualifying to apply for ESRC funding. Terms of use have been agreed between the Census Offices and ESRC, and are made known to all users in this sector. The sector is being serviced from the Census Dissemination Unit at the University of Manchester Computing Centre (see chapter 8 section 8.8). The Census Microdata Unit at the University of Manchester distributes the Samples of Anonymised Records (see chapter 11, section 11.6).

Other users

The abstracts may be used only by the organisations, companies or persons specified by the customer on the order form, subject to the agreement of the Census Offices before supply of the abstracts. A similar arrangement applies to government departments and other Crown bodies. Where the purchasing organisation or company is part of a larger group of organisations or companies which may also wish to use the abstracts, full details must be given at the time of ordering.

User Guide 37 gives more details of the arrangements mentioned above. The Census Offices will, if neccessary, prepare further guidelines for customer sectors in consultation with the advisory groups representing the sectors. The Census Offices also reserve the right to modify the arrangements and terms for customer sectors if, for example, any are subject to large-scale reorganisation.

Transfer of abtracts

As mentioned above, the conditions of supply require a purchaser of standard abstracts to obtain permission from the Census Offices before transferring or publishing the abstracts in whole or part, or any material derived from them. In general, permission will normally be given for transfer between local authorities, between health authorities, and between a local and health authority where all concerned have purchased the abstracts for their area(s), or between other bodies in comparable circumstances, for example, to provide information about population in neighbouring areas, or to share information derived from the abstracts.

In other cases, a licence may be required from Census Customer Services for the transfer or publication of abstracts, which may require further payment to the Census Offices. Charges will not normally be made for the publication of information taken from the abstracts on a selective basis for inclusion, say, with other substantial textual matter as part of books, reports, commentary in the media, academic papers and so on, provided that Crown copyright and the source of the information is acknowledged. *User Guide 37* gives details of terms and charges for licences.

Specially commissioned abstracts
Whilst the general conditions of supply outlined above apply to specially commissioned abstracts, the limitations in transfer and use of standard abstracts do not generally apply, although specific arrangements may be subject to negotiation in making the agreement for the supply of abstracts.

7.7 REFERENCE MATERIAL, USER SERVICES, AND VALUE ADDED PRODUCTS

The growing significance of machine-readable output from the 1970s onwards, and the growth in variety and detail of statistics, has made the Census Offices aware of the market and the need for services to customers. A variety of means are now used to keep in contact with customers and to provide them with information. In addition, while the Census Offices have expanded their range of core products, the availability of machine-readable output has boosted the opportunities for intermediary bodies to process the raw statistics into value-added products.

7.7.1 The Census Newsletter

News of all developments on the Census is provided by the *Census Newsletter* produced by OPCS five or six times a year and distributed without charge. In the period after a census, the newsletter covers progress with output, and services and meetings of interest to census users. In the build-up to a census, the newsletter covers plans and consultation. Names may be added to the mailing list by contacting Census Customer Services (see section 7.8).

Interested organisations are also invited to contact OPCS Customer Services to be put on the *Register of Census Users*. This will ensure that they are consulted about future developments and are kept informed about the availability of census results. There is no charge for this service.

7.7.2 Reference material

Guidance for users

Definitions volume
The guide *1991 Census Definitions, Great Britain* was published in June 1992. This single comprehensive volume assists users in understanding and interpreting 1991 Census statistics, by providing detailed descriptions of, and explanatory notes on, many of the terms and categories used in the Census. The structure is similar to the volume produced for the 1981 Census to allow comparison of terms and definitions between the two censuses.

The first chapter describes briefly the legal basis for the Census, the topics included, how it was taken, how the forms were processed and what measures were taken to safeguard the confidentiality of census information. Subsequent chapters cover: the different types of population counts (chapters 2 and 3); the classification of communal establishments (chapter 4), household spaces (chapter 5), and types of dwellings (chapter 5); and definitions of the statistical terms used (chapters 6 and 7), with commentary on differences between 1981 and 1991 in the treatment of particular topics. Also included is a description of each of the various types of geographical area for which local and topic statistics are presented in published reports (chapter 8). Annexes list the full sets of census categories relating to country of birth, ethnic group, family composition, occupation, industry, socioeconomic group, and higher qualification subject groups.

The presentation of definitions and notes in a single volume reduces the amount of such material reproduced in individual reports. With the exception of the Key Statistics, census reports are not entirely free-standing, although each report contains general explanatory information and detailed notes necessary for a particular topic. Since the Definitions volume was published in 1992, a number of points have emerged where content needs to be improved or expanded. A revised edition of the volume is scheduled for publication in late 1993, and revisions are also issued through the Census Newsletter.

Standard Occupational Classification

The Standard Occupational Classification (SOC) is designed for use in the analysis of occupational data, and was developed by OPCS and the Employment Department Group with a technical contribution from the Institute for Employment Research of the University of Warwick. It provides an up-to-date, detailed and comprehensive classification for use by those who need to classify occupational information in as consistent a way as possible.

The SOC is described in a three part manual. Volume 1 sets out the structure of SOC, and the principles on which it is based. It also contains a description of typical job activities and a list of occupational terms and titles for each group of jobs in the classification. Volume 2 consists of an alphabetical index of about 20,000 different jobs titles used for allocating jobs to the SOC groups. Volume 3 shows how occupations, using SOC, can be arranged into other broad groupings such as social class groups or socioeconomic groups, which are both based on occupation.

Population Trends

Population Trends, first issued in 1975, is the quarterly house journal of OPCS, sold by HMSO bookshops, and includes articles on the methodology and results of the census, as well as related statistical output from OPCS.

Unpublished reference material

There are a very large number of working documents on the field and processing operations of the census. The material in these documents which is most helpful to census users is extracted and published elsewhere, but, if there is a special research interest, for example, in coding schemes for use in other surveys to produce data comparable to the census output, copies of working documents can normally be made available, and contact should be made through the professional staff of OPCS or GRO(S) Census Divisions (see section 7.8).

Guides to historic census sources

A general introduction to censuses from 1801 to 1966, and the output produced from them, is provided by *Guide to Census Reports: Great Britain 1801-1966* which is most likely to be found in libraries with series of census reports for all or part of that period.

The guide has not been up-dated to cover the 1971 and 1981 Censuses, but, to a limited extent for the 1971 Census, and to a much greater extent for the 1981 Census, the Census Offices issued 'user guides' which marked the shift to machine-readable output. The *1981 Census User Guides* are generally still available, some for a charge, from Census Customer Services (see section 7.8) and are listed in *The 1981 User Guide Catalogue*.

Guides to Census coverage and quality

The Census Office publish a series of documents giving the results of checks on the coverage and quality of the Census. The exact programme of documentation depends to some extent on the findings of the checks and there is, for example, more documentation on coverage in the 1991 Census than there was on the 1981 Census, but, as is pointed out elsewhere in this Guide, the findings allow only the most approximate adjustments to be made by users to census results for small areas.

The first results on coverage from the 1991 Census Validation Survey (CVS) were the subject of the leading article in *Census Newsletter 24* published in October 1992, and these were followed by a more complete account of coverage which was published in the Census report on *Sex, Age and Marital Status: Great Britain* in February 1993. This included adjustment factors for estimated under-enumeration of males and females in five year age groups for Great Britain as a whole. Versions of these two accounts have also appeared elsewhere as guidance with Census results.

Documentation on coverage scheduled to be published after this Guide had gone to press includes a *Monitor* on coverage, due in summer 1993, which will provide adjustment factors by age and sex at a regional level — most likely for metropolitan areas and remainders of regions. The Monitor may also include results from the CVS on the coverage of other key variables and populations such as number of usually resident households.

A *Monitor* with 'preliminary' results from the CVS on the quality of answers to Census questions is due in autumn 1993. A full report from the CVS on coverage is also due in autumn 1993, whilst the full report from the CVS on quality (similar to the 1981 report) is due in spring 1994. An overview of coverage and quality will be included in the *1991 Census General Report* (see below), in which it is planned to include any findings on coverage and quality drawn from demographic checks between the census and other sources. All documentation will be publicised, and summarised where appropriate, in the *Census Newsletter*.

The General Report

It has been customary for the Census Offices to complete the reports for each census by a *General Report* on the conduct of the census. The *1981 Census General Report*, for example, was published in 1990 and included sections on: planning and preparation; census pretests; legislation; security and confidentiality; fieldwork; processing and output; and a statistical assessment.

A report on similar lines is being prepared for the 1991 Census, and will be published towards the end of 1994.

7.7.3 User services

Advice and customer services from the Census Offices

The Census Offices welcome enquiries from users of the Census, particularly as this feedback helps improve products and, in the longer term, future censuses. Generally, enquiries relating to England and Wales, or to Great Britain, or the UK as a whole, should be directed to OPCS, and those relating to Scotland should be directed to GRO(S). Contact points are given at the end of this chapter.

Both Census Offices provide advice through their professional staff and through their Customer Services branches. The professional staff deal with enquiries about statistical aspects of the census, the interpretation and analysis of results and their application, international aspects, and census policy generally. There are also a number of topic specialists among the professional staff. Census Customer Services are the contact point for enquiries on specific 1991 Census products and those from previous censuses. They deal with orders for statistical abstracts and any technical problems arising, and issue documentation to describe, and support the use of, census products. Customer Services issue maps of census areas and will provide information about other geographic services available. They also promote census products through presentations and exhibitions. Customer Services have information about the intermediate agencies which also supply census statistics and value added products under agreements with the Census Offices (see section 7.7.7).

There is no hard-and-fast dividing line between the professional staff and Census Customer Services, and enquiries will be re-directed if necessary. But enquirers should mention all aspects of their queries and their interest in the Census wherever first contact is made. A list of named enquiry points is not included here, as staff numbers reduce in the intercensal period, but all functions remain allocated to staff.

Services elsewhere

While the Census Offices provide the first line of enquiry for census users, there are often experts in organisations which use large sets of census statistics who may be able to help others within the organisation with local problems. There are census units within a number of government departments. Typically, in shire counties and other local authorities, a research and intelligence (R and I) section, or another section with a central support function, will provide expertise. A number of county-wide services in the metropolitan counties provide expertise, with the London Research Centre as a leading example. The regional health authorities in England also usually have units that can provide help for users in the health service.

Users in higher educational institutes generally will find that the Census Dissemination Unit at the University of Manchester (see section 8.8) will provide a wide range of assistance, or direct enquirers to other experts covered by the ESRC Census programme (see chapter 14 for a central contact point).

Finally, for those requiring derived products and services, mainly but not exclusively for commercial applications, the census agencies (see section 7.7.7), and a number of further specialist consultants, will provide advice. Census Customer Services may be contacted for information about agencies.

7.7.4 OPCS Library

The OPCS Library at St Catherine's House in London holds copies of all 1991 Census reports, as well as complete sets of all previous census reports along with many series from overseas. The Library also holds the complete 1981 Census Small Area Statistics for England and Wales on microfiche, with reference maps of enumeration districts on microfilm. Users of the Library may extract material from the SAS, but copies are not supplied. The 1991 Census LBS and SAS will also be made accessible in the Library, and a decision in principle has been taken to make other abstracts available too.

The Library is open to visitors who should make an appointment at least a day in advance (see section 7.8 for contact point).

7.7.5 Software and analysis

Help in the computer processing and analysis of the census results is provided in two main ways. Both are currently provided by organisations outside the Census Offices, although with the Offices' agreement and assistance. First, there is purpose-built software for handling the statistics on mainframes or PCs which is designed for users wanting 'hands on' access. The SASPAC91 package, prepared on a consortium basis for census users, and the C91 package designed specifically for PCs are examples. More information is given in chapter 8. Second, licensed census agencies provide analyses and packages tailored to clients' specific needs. An intermediate type of service providing copies of statistics, perhaps with partially processed data together with software to manipulate them on PCs also seems likely to grow in the 1990s. More information is given below in section 7.7.7.

7.7.6 Value added products

The Census Offices have a programme, being undertaken in consultation with users, to facilitate products which add value to the 'core' of results in reports and standard abstracts. The programme is designed to implement policy stated in the 1988 White Paper on the Census. The scope of the programme includes all means by which value can be added, all media through which this may be done (including suitable new media), and the widest possible range of contributors. It is a rolling programme, with circulation of information so that census users can see what is being produced, by whom, and when, enabling products to be quickly identified and duplication of effort avoided. It may also provide information on users not being served by the census, and hence opportunities for new products. Further information is available from OPCS Census Customer Services (see section 7.8).

7.7.7 Census agencies and their products

Arrangements were made in the late 1970s and after the 1981 Census for intermediate agencies to hold 1971 and 1981 statistics (mainly SAS) under licence and supply extracts, generally to customers wishing to make only a small capital outlay, on payment of royalties to the Census Offices. A number of geodemographic firms began to operate as agencies. The trend has been to develop descriptive indicators such as area classifications and to offer value-added services rather than merely supply subsets of SAS.

The basis under which an intermediary agency operates is an agreement made with the Census Offices which *either* allows an organisation with statistical abstracts purchased at the standard charge for its own use to supply them to third parties *or* allows an organisation to hold statistical abstracts (without payment of a direct charge for the abstracts) specifically for the purpose of supply to of third parties. The agreement requires the payment of a fee whenever copies of all or parts of the abstracts, or material derived from the abstracts, are supplied to third parties. Such fees are based on the charges which would have applied if the Census Office had supplied the abstracts direct. Third parties supplied in this way are not permitted to pass on any of the Census material without the agreement of the Census Offices.

Agreements made so far for 1991 Census statistics cover the LBS and SAS. Further agreements to cover the dissemination of the Special Migration and Special Workplace Statistics will be available if required.

The first type of agreement mentioned above is generally known as a licence and mainly relates to the supply of copies of extracts of LBS/SAS. The second type of agreement relates to census agencies, and more details follow.

Arrangements for Licensees

At the time of writing, some six organisations have obtained quarterly licences as the basis of services to supply ad hoc copies and extracts of LBS and SAS. The organisations, with contact points are listed in figure 7.2.

The royalty fees paid by licensees to the Census Offices for ad hoc copies and extracts are standard, and are identical to the charges for direct purchases from the Census Offices, but a customer may find it convenient to deal with a local organisation and may also wish to obtain 'value added' services offered by the licensees. Some licensees may only offer data for the part of the country in which they operate, and it is also likely that the number of licensees will increase. Census Customer Services can supply up-to-date information.

A customer seeking a cost-effective source of copies and extracts of LBS and SAS should specify their complete requirements both to the Census Offices, and to appropriate licensees and to agencies, and should compare the total charges estimated by each potential supplier and other services offered by the suppliers.

Arrangements for agencies

A prospective agency has to satisfy the Census Offices of its intentions and ability to disseminate 1991 Census results beyond the boundaries of its own organisation. It is also required to show that no aspect of its activities could damage the reputation of the census operation, and, in particular, that no activity could threaten the confidentiality of census information or result in risks to confidentiality being perceived. Prospective agencies which meet the Census Offices' initial requirements are offered a standard agreement. Any subsequent revision of agreements, conditions or charges are offered equally to all agencies. Agreements can be terminated if any specified breaches occur and are not remedied within a given time.

An agency meets a basic initial charge to cover the cost of an agreement. There is a further initial charge to cover the cost of materials and copying required for the supply of the abstracts. Licences are renewed annually for a further fee.

The charges for census material which the agency passes to its customers, and will normally cover by charges to the customers, are based on the principle stated above that royalty fees relate to the charges which would have applied if the Census Offices had supplied the abstracts directly. For the purpose of calculating charges there is a standard royalty matrix which combines the number of LBS/SAS cells input and the number of output counts supplied per area. The charges in the matrix are disproportionately loaded on to the first few counts supplied, as these are held to have the highest value, and the matrix has a charge ceiling at the standard unit prices for LBS or SAS.

The matrix is typically used to calculate the royalties due when an agency supplies 'raw' statistics for unlimited use in a customer's organisation. But growth in the range of products which incorporate census material has resulted in the development of other options for the payment of royalty:

- an agency may opt to pay an annual lump sum in lieu of royalties due on certain types of product containing census material — typically where little or no re-usable raw statistics are provided, and typically a product for application by the client in marketing by targeting of small areas or by 'profiling' the client's own customers by area type. Other, non-census data are often included, and the price the customer pays to the agency will normally not be a direct reflection of the royalty to the Census Offices.

- an agency may develop a product containing raw statistics for hands on use by the customer at a single site or a limited number of sites not representing unlimited use in a customer's organisation. Such products are typically PC based, and a commensurate reduction of the royalty due under the standard matrix is made. The level of royalties will usually be clearly apparent to the customer.

- an agency may develop a value added product with sales potential among existing census customers, and in this case the Census Offices charge a fee which is a small percentage of the cover price of the product.

An agency, with the agreement of the Census Offices, may operate under one or more of these options to suit their range of products.

Some eleven organisations were confirmed as 1991 Census agencies by June 1993, and a very brief description of the products and services offered at that date is given in figure 7.2 (order of organisations is alphabetical).

7.7.8 Census on CD-ROM

The Census Offices, towards the end of 1991, circulated a discussion paper on the possibilities of the use of CD-ROMs or other high capacity media as a means of disseminating 1991 Census abstracts. This followed the successful issue of 1981 Census SAS on CD-ROM by Chadwyck Healey Ltd under licence from the Census Offices, and the successful use of CD-ROMs in other countries, most notably in Australia and the US. The discussion paper invited views on ways of using the new media to extend dissemination of Census results whilst making a fair contribution to the cost of the abstracts. The outcome of the consultation was a general welcome for the use of new media and confirmation that existing customers had a need for such alternatives.

Figure 7.2 Census agencies and licensees

Agencies

CACI, which has been a census agency since 1977, are applying 1991 Census data to develop a series of products and systems, as well as updating their existing datasets and the ACORN area classification systems. Contact: *CACI Ltd., CACI House, Kensington Village, Avonmore Road, London W14 8TS (tel: 071-602 6000).*

Capscan will be launching products that associate census data with postcoding, making links with the Postcode Address File on CD-ROM. Contact: *Capscan Ltd., Tranley House, Tranley Mews, London NW3 2QW (tel: 071-267 7055).*

CCN has acted as a census agency since 1987. The 1991 Census statistics will form a key ingredient in MOSAIC, CCN's geodemographic segmentation system, designed to address customer segmentation and local market planning. Contact: *CCN Systems Ltd., Talbot House, Talbot Street, Nottingham NG1 5HF (tel: 0602 410888) or CCN Systems Ltd., 39 Houndsditch, London EC3A 7DB (tel: 071-623 5551).*

Chadwyck-Healey, who have supplied 1981 Census SAS on CD-ROM, have announced the issue of the 1991 LBS and SAS on CD-ROM (including boundary mapping), in four versions designed for specific users — local authorities, health authorities, higher education, and schools. Contact: *Chadwyck Healey Ltd., Cambridge Place, Cambridge CB2 1NR (tel: 0223 311479).*

Claymore Services specialise in the provision of census data and related software for use on PCs. Both C91 and SASPAC91 produce files which can be read directly by Claymore's Map 91 census mapping package, which together with the ED91 or ED-LINE digitised boundaries enables the production of maps on a PC. Claymore have also produced the SCAMP CD-ROM schools' census and mapping package on CD-ROM. Contact: *Claymore Services Ltd., Station House, Whimple, Exeter EX5 2QH (tel: 0404 823097).*

The Data Consultancy, part of the URPI Group, continues to provide a range of census-related services, as it has done since the 1981 Census. A wide range of 1991 data are held, comprising the SAS at ED/Output Area level and the LBS at ward/postcode sector level. The Illumine for Windows system provides full PC-based census analysis, mapping and market analysis. Contact: *The Data Consultancy, 7 Southern Court, South Street, Reading, RG1 4QS (tel: 0734 588181).*

GMAP Ltd., owned by the University of Leeds, specialises in the development of market analysis and planning systems for retail-related markets. Its approach involves the use of predictive models which allow clients to evaluate markets and the competition. Contact: *GMAP Ltd., GMAP House, Cromer Terrace, Leeds LS2 9JU (tel: 0532 446164).*

Infolink offers geographic and topic extracts from the LBS and SAS, fully referenced to unit postcodes and other geographies. Products include a new version of DEFINE, Infolink's consumer and market segmentation system incorporating the 1991 Census, the Electoral Register, and data on financial behaviour. Contact: *Infolink Decision Services Ltd., Coombe Cross, 204 South End, Croydon CR0 1DL (tel: 081-686 7777).*

Pinpoint Analysis, which has supplied census-related data for ten years, offer a comprehensive range of services, including: supply of SAS; geodemographic classification systems; postcode-based data linkage to census data; market research sampling frames; and a variety of GIS and mapping systems. Contact: *Pinpoint Analysis Ltd., Tower House, Southampton Street, London WC2E 7HN (tel: 071-612 0568).*

SPA Marketing Systems are a consultancy focusing on geodemographics, modelling and market analysis. Census data will be available through PC-based market analysis software systems, or as separate data files, or through consultancy. Contact: *SPA Marketing Systems Ltd., 1 Warwick Street, Leamington Spa, Warwickshire CV32 5LW (tel: 0926-451199).*

Figure 7.2 - *continued*

Licensees (quarterly licences)

Organisations	*Telephone number*
Cumbria County Council	0228 812976
Essex County Council	0245 437576
Leeds City Council	0532 478122/348080
The London Research Centre	071 735 4250
Nottinghamshire County Council	0602 774541
Staffordshire County Council	0785 223121 ext 8306

Arrangements for existing and new customers

The Census Offices subsequently received proposals from organisations wishing to produce CD-ROMs containing complete or substantial sets of the 1991 Census LBS/SAS for Great Britain, together with various value-added elements. The arrangements made cover the supply of such CD-ROMs, first as an alternative medium to existing purchasers of LBS/SAS, and, second, as a primary medium to new customers.

Census CD-ROMs for existing purchasers of LBS/SAS

The conditions of supply of LBS/SAS necessarily vary between the customer sectors (see section 7.6.2) and do not automatically entitle all customers to obtain all LBS/SAS, although there are arrangements to cover the mutual exchange of data. In summary, permission for exchange of data from the LBS/SAS *within* a customer sector between parts of the sector which have made separate purchases may be obtained from the Census Offices for uses permitted under the conditions of supply when both parties have made purchases of the same type of data at the same geographic level; permission for exchanges *between* sectors may be similarly obtained when both parties have made purchases for the same geographic areas and levels. No charges are made by the Census Offices for these exchanges of data.

These arrangements continue, but, with complete purchase of the LBS/SAS for Great Britain, the Census Offices were able to introduce new arrangements to cover the supply, from any source, of complete or substantial sets of LBS/SAS on CD-ROM to any organisation covered by the existing customer sectors.

The Census Offices will licence any purchasing organisation to obtain, if necessary, the complete set of LBS/SAS from any source without further payment to the Census Offices, and will licence the supply of CD-ROMs containing sets of LBS/SAS by such a purchasing organisation to any organisation covered by the customer sectors, in return for the payment of a fee of 10 per cent of the cover price of the product containing the LBS/SAS in lieu of revenue lost to the Census Offices from their own direct sales of data on alternative media.

The Census Offices are also prepared to make arrangements with 1991 Census agencies (see section 7.7.8) to hold the LBS/SAS and supply sets on CD-ROM to any organisation covered by the existing customer sectors in return for the 10 per cent fee.

The effect of these new arrangements is to give, for example, to the users covered by a local or health authority, the benefit of access to the LBS/SAS for the entire country. Most public libraries and some schools are covered within the local authority sector, and are being served by specially developed CD-ROM products. The price of CD-ROMs depends, of course, on producers' own costs and the amount of value added material included, but the price is only like to be a fraction of the direct purchase price of the LBS/SAS from the Census Offices.

Census CD-ROMs for new customers

The Census Offices are prepared, in principle, to licence any purchasing organisation, or to make arrangements with a census agency, to cover the supply of complete or partial sets of LBS/SAS on CD-ROM to third parties not covered by the existing customer sectors. The arrangements cover substantial standard sets of LBS/SAS, limited to strictly defined uses and sites, in return for a payment to the Census Offices based on a commensurate reduction of the royalties due under the standard charging 'matrix' which governs the supply of LBS/SAS under licence or by agencies (see section 7.7.7). Introduction of such terms depends on the licensee or agency demonstrating that it has adequate measures to ensure the limitations on use. The reductions for limited use on CD-ROM range from one twentieth of the full royalty upwards to the full charge, and depend on the extent of the access required.

Subject to continuing measures to ensure limitations of use, these arrangements, in effect, create a sector for a new type of customer, attracted by the new terms but sharing a proportion of the cost of LBS/SAS in a similar way to existing customers.

7.8 FURTHER INFORMATION AND CONTACT POINTS

A summary of all developments relating to the census is provided by the *Census Newsletter* produced five or six times a year by the Census Offices and distributed without charge. Names may be added to the mailing list by contacting the Census Customer Services. Census Customer Services will supply details of all product *Prospectuses* and other *User Guides*

Interested organisations are also invited to contact OPCS Census Customer Services to join the *Register of Census Users*. This will ensure that they are consulted about future developments and are kept informed about the availability of census results. There is no charge for this service.

The **professional staff** of the Census Divisions of OPCS and GRO(S) may be contacted at

OPCS   General Register Office (Scotland)
St Catherine's House   Ladywell House
10 Kingsway   Ladywell Road
London WC2B 6JP   Edinburgh EH12 7TF
telephone 071-396 2008* (direct line) telephone 031 314 4217 (direct line)

* this is a general contact point and enquirers should state the nature of their query as fully as possible so that they can be directed to the appropriate member of staff.

The **OPCS Library** may be contacted at St Catherine's House, telephone 071 396-2235/2238.

Census Customer Services may be contacted at

OPCS
Segensworth Road
Titchfield
Fareham
Hampshire P015 5RR
telephone 0328 813800 (direct line)

General Register Office (Scotland)
(address as above)
telephone 031 314 4254 (direct line)

8 The 1991 Local Base and Small Area Statistics

Keith Cole

8.1 INTRODUCTION

The Local Base Statistics (LBS) and the Small Area Statistics (SAS) are a predefined set of cross-tabulations of two or more census variables which are made available by the Census Offices in a machine readable format for a wide range of different areal units throughout the whole of Great Britain, including areas smaller than those reported in the published volumes. In order to increase the amount of information displayed on a printed page and, in part, to provide continuity with the SAS for previous cenuses, these cross-tabulations have been grouped together into a series of tables. These summary tables cover all the 1991 Census topics and provide a uniquely detailed source of comparable statistics relating to demographic characteristics, housing conditions, household composition and economic activity. They also provide detailed information on specific groups in the population with particular needs, such as lone parent families and pensioner households.

The objective of this chapter is to provide a guide to those coming new to the 1991 LBS and SAS. Section 8.2 describes how the local statistics output in its current standardised format has developed since its introduction in 1961. Sections 8.3-8.5 describe the structure, content, format and geographical basis of the LBS and SAS and the various measures employed by the Census Offices to minimise the risk of inadvertent disclosure of information about identifiable households or individuals. Particular reference will be made to changes since 1981 and also to the differences between England and Wales and Scotland. A detailed description of some of the statistical and methodological problems associated with analysing and mapping SAS at a small spatial scale is provided in section 8.6. Sections 8.7-8.8 describe the dissemination arrangements for the LBS and SAS, the availability of access and manipulation software, and where to obtain further documentation, information and advice.

8.2 THE DEVELOPMENT OF THE LOCAL STATISTICS OUTPUT OVER FIVE CENSUSES

Although very simple statistics have been available in a published form for wards and civil parishes since 1871, the development of local statistics, output for small areas in a standardised format, began with the first computerised census in 1961

(Mills, 1987). From the 1961 Census, a standard set of statistics was made available for wards, civil parishes and, for the first time, enumeration districts (EDs). However, as the ED level statistics was only produced on demand, usually in response to requests from local authorities, national coverage at this level was incomplete. As noted by Whitehead (1983), the strength of demand for these local statistics came as a surprise to the General Register Office (predecessor to OPCS) which had only intended to produce one copy of each table on the assumption that only the local authority would be interested in the census data for the area of its jurisdiction. Complete national coverage at the ward, civil parish and ED level was achieved with the 1966 sample Census and then the full 1971 Census. At first these local statistics for small areas were referred to as the Ward Library, but for the 1971 and 1981 Censuses they were termed the Small Area Statistics (SAS). For the 1991 Census the local statistics output has been expanded into two tiers, the Local Base Statistics (LBS) and the SAS (see section 8.3).

Local statistics for small areas are produced under section 4(2) of the 1920 Census Act (see chapter 1). In theory, an almost infinite variety of tables for a wide range of different areal units could be requested. Consequently, the Census Offices have had to respond to the demand for local statistics from the census in two stages. Firstly, the Census Offices attempt to meet the majority of user's requirements for detailed local statistics by defining the LBS/SAS well in advance of the census through a process of consultation between the Census Offices and the potential users of the statistics. Secondly, after producing all the standard local statistics output, any unanticipated request for local statistics is met via a commissioned tables service (see chapter 7).

8.2.1 Increasing complexity and data volumes

The local statistics output for small areas has developed considerably since 1961 both in terms of its content and also in the range of different areal units for which the statistics are made available. These developments have been made possible by the increased use of computers to process and to analyse the census. The availability of specialised software packages for accessing and manipulating the SAS, such as SASPAC, has also given users the ability to handle the increasing volume of data with greater ease and flexibility (see section 8.7.2).

Table 8.1 illustrates the way in which the data volumes and complexity of the output has increased between 1971 and 1991 by comparing the number of questions asked on the census form (England only) with the number of tables (groupings of one or more cross-tabulations) and the total number of individual statistical counts contained in the SAS for areas in England.

Table 8.1

The increasing volume and complexity of local statistics output, 1971-1991

Census year	Number of questions	Number of tables	Number of counts	Count/table ratio
1971	30	28	1571	56.1
1981	21	48	4345	90.5
1991	25	82	8722	106.3

While the number of questions asked on the census form for England has fluctuated slightly between 1971 and 1991, the total number of tables, cross-tabulations and statistical counts contained in the SAS for each year has increased considerably. The 1991 SAS contained almost twice as much information for each area as the 1981 SAS. Over half the increase in the number of tables is to cover the new topics in the census, such as limiting long-term illness and ethnic group. The remainder of the increase reflects user requests for additional tables arising during the consultation process.

The complexity of the tables, as measured by the average number of counts per table, has almost doubled between 1971 and 1991. This increase is partly due to an increasing number of counts per cross-tabulation but also due to a greater number of cross-tabulations being grouped together to form tables. Indeed, it should be noted that the count/cross-tabulation ratio has increased less than the count/table ratio. The level of increase between 1981 and 1991 was not as great as that between 1971 and 1981. In part, this relects the unwillingness of the Census Offices to release tables for small areas which are too detailed, in case they result in the inadvertent disclosure of information about identifiable individuals or households. However it is worth noting that the maximum number of counts in any one 100 per cent table in the 1971, 1981 and 1991 SAS (England only) was 72, 224, and 400, respectively.

8.2.2 A developing geographical base

Since 1961, there has been a considerable increase in the range of different areal units for which the SAS have been made available. In addition to wards, civil parishes and EDs the standard SAS have been made available for a whole range of different administrative, political and statistical units, including district health authorities/health boards, Parliamentary constituencies, urban areas, new towns and postcode sectors (Scotland). A full list of all the different areal units for which the 1991 LBS and SAS are being released is contained in section 8.4.2.

There have also been a number of developments relating to the geographical base of the SAS. Although the enumeration district (ED) has remained the areal unit for collecting the census, a number of alternative geographical bases for output of the SAS have been used. In 1971 each census questionnaire was assigned an Ordnance Survey grid reference to 100 m in 'urban' areas and 1 km resolution elsewhere which enabled the Census Offices to generate the standard SAS for 1 km or 100 m grid squares (Denham and Rhind, 1983). Despite the advantages offered by grid squares, particularly for the analysis of intercensal change (see chapter 9), 1971 remains the only year for which grid square SAS was produced by the Census Offices for the whole of Great Britain. However, as the Ordnance Survey grid reference assigned to each ED/OA provides an invaluable link to the National Grid it is possible for users to generate their own pseudo-grid square SAS which can be used for both mapping and analysing intercensal change (Martin, 1989; Martin and Bracken, 1991).

Postcode areas

The other main innovation relates to the increasing use of postcode areas as an alternative geographical base for census output, particularly in Scotland (see chapter 3). One of the main advantages of using a postcode-based census geography is that it provides a powerful mechanism for linking SAS with postcoded data, such as health statistics, derived from other sources. In Scotland, GRO(S) first used unit postcodes, split when necessary to recognise local authority district boundaries, to define 1981 EDs. For 1991, GRO(S) has used postcodes to define output areas (OAs) for the SAS, which are different from the EDs used for collecting the census (Clark and Thomas, 1990; Raper, Rhind and Shepherd, 1992).

Although postcodes were not used in the planning of 1991 EDs in England and Wales, the capture of the unit postcode of the household from the census forms for the first time has enabled OPCS to generate the SAS for postcode-based areas, such as postcode sectors. During the consultation phase, there was a proposal to produce the SAS for a set of pseudo EDs which were aggregations of whole unit postcodes to form areas which closely approximated 1991 EDs. After careful consideration, this proposal was eventually rejected due to a lack of demand and also, importantly, because of the concern that the differencing of overlapping small areas with small populations based on different geographies might result in the indavertent disclosure of information about identifiable households and/or individuals (see chapter 9). As an alternative, separate postcode to ED directories for England and Wales have been issued which enable users to link ED level SAS to postcoded data from other sources and also to generate their own postcode based 'pseudo ED' SAS (see chapter 3(I)).

8.2.3 Analysing intercensal change

One of the major problems associated with the local statistics output over the last 30 years relates to the measurement and analysis of intercensal change. Differences between the censuses in terms of the topics covered, changes in the population base, variable definitions and classification systems, combined with changes in the geographical base of the census, make it extremely difficult to use the SAS to measure change at a small spatial scale (Norris and Mounsey, 1983). The Census Offices have made a number of attempts to rectify this problem. For England and Wales, OPCS generated the 1971-1981 Change File which contained a set of 452 generally comparable 100 per cent statistics for sets of geographically comparable areas. The smallest geographical unit for which the Change File was made available was the census tract or civil parish. Due to the methodological problems associated with analysing intercensal change, the 1971-1981 Change File was not widely used. A different approach to analysing 1971-1981 change was developed in Scotland where GRO(S) retrospectively postcoded 1971 Census records which were then reaggregated to 1981 EDs and retabulated, wherever possible, using 1981 table outlines. In addition, by continued use of postcodes, GRO(S) have been able to define a set of small areas which, when 1991 OAs are aggregated, give continuity between the 1971, 1981 and 1991 Censuses (see chapter 3(I).

8.2.4 Conclusion

The local statistics output in its current standardised format has developed considerably over the last 30 years to the point where, in 1981, it became the most widely used output from the census. However, the increasing data volumes and associated data duplication combined with the lack of flexibility offered by a standard set of cross-tabulations consisting of predefined variables and variable groupings have all been identified as negative features of the current format. The availability of true census microdata (see chapters 11 and 12) and the possible development of a secure, on-line tabulation system for the production of customised tables from the census (OPCS and GRO(s), 1988; Rhind *et al*, 1991) are all potential alternatives to the LBS/SAS.

8.3 UNDERSTANDING THE 1991 LBS AND SAS

A major innovation introduced with the 1991 Census has been the expansion of the local statistics output into two separate but interrelated tiers. The new upper tier is called the Local Base Statistics (LBS). The LBS forms the basis of the tables to be produced for each county (England and Wales)/region (Scotland) and local authority district which are published in full in the series of County/Region Reports. The LBS consist of 99 tables for Great Britain containing approximately 20,000 statistical counts and are available down to ward level in England and Wales and postcode sector level in Scotland.

The lower tier are the Small Area Statistics (SAS) which are an abbreviated version of the LBS and comprise 86 tables for Great Britain containing approximately 9,000 statistical counts. The SAS are available down to enumeration district (ED) level in England and Wales and output area (OA) in Scotland. As a result, the SAS are available for approximately 110,000 EDs in England and Wales and 38,000 OAs in Scotland.

It was not possible for the Census Offices to release the full LBS at ED/OA level as there was a risk that some of the detailed tables in the LBS might result in the inadvertent disclosure of information about identifiable housholds or individuals in those areas with very small populations. Therefore, by defining the SAS as an abbreviated version of the LBS it has been possible to lessen the risk of inadvertent disclosure whilst maintaining the maximum degree of comparability between those statistics published in the County/Region Reports and those available in a machine readable format at the ED/OA level. Of the 99 tables in the LBS, 36 are repeated in their entirety in the SAS. A further 50 are available only in a reduced form and 13 are omitted altogether. The reduction in the level of detail in an LBS table when produced as part of the SAS is accomplished by reducing the number of variable groups in one or both axes of the table. For example, the number of separate categories for ethnic groups in LBS table 9 is reduced from 10 to 4 when made available in the SAS.

8.3.1 Structure, content and format of the LBS/SAS

The LBS and SAS consist of a standard set of census statistics for areas. Very few of these statistics are one-dimensional counts, such as the total number of households or residents in an area. The majority of the statistics contained in the LBS/SAS are multivariate counts derived from the cross-tabulation of two or more census variables, with each cross-tabulation relating to a particular population base, such as residents in households, residents aged 16 and over, or persons aged 16 and over with limiting long-term illness. Consequently, the statistics in the LBS/SAS can provide extremely detailed pieces of information, such as the number of persons in an area with limiting long-term illness, aged 85 and over and living in a household with no central heating.

The cross-tabulated variables range from those derived from the easy to code questions on the census form, such as age, sex, tenure and numbers of cars and vans, to those more complex derived variables based on combinations of responses to two or more census questions, such as households with 'dependent children'; i.e. a person aged 0-15, or a person aged 16-18 who has never married, is in full-time education and is economically inactive. Similarly, many of the population bases used can have complex definitions and may also relate to specific groups of the population. For example, 'couple' households are defined as a household containing two persons aged 16 and over of the opposite sex with no other person aged 16 and over, with or without children aged 0-15. A brief guide to the definitions of the main terms used in the census, such as economically inactive, dependent child or lone parent family, together with notes on individual tables is provided in *User Guide 38*, which is issued free to each purchaser of the LBS/SAS. Further details about the construction of the different population bases from the census questions are contained in *1991 Census Definitions* (OPCS & GRO(S) 1992b) and are also summarised in chapter 2.

For ease of reference and also to increase the amount of information relating to a particular census topic displayed on a printed page, cross-tabulations which share common axes have been concatenated. As a large proportion of the tables in the LBS/SAS consist of two or more cross-tabulations, each of which may relate to a different population base, considerable care is required when analysing the content of each table. It is particularly important to be fully aware of the exact population base(s) of each table as this determines the extent to which statistics extracted from different tables in the LBS/SAS can be related or compared with each other or with those from earlier censuses or other data sources, such as the General Household Survey or Labour Force Survey.

All the table outlines for the LBS and SAS are contained in *User Guide 3*. In order to make the content of these tables as self-explanatory as possible, abbreviations in the row and column headings have been kept to a minimum and a number of standard conventions have been used in the construction of the margins and bodies of the tables. For example, where a table consists of two or more cross-tabulations, each separate cross-tabulation is delimited by a ruled line. Counts should not be summed across these ruled lines. Other table conventions are described in more detail in sections 3.6 – 3.9 of *User Guide 38*.

Some of the key features of the LBS/SAS are illustrated in figure 8.1 which displays the table layout for SAS table number 2. This SAS table contains a single, three dimensional cross-tabulation of age by sex by marital status for all residents in an area. The population base for this table (residents) is displayed in the banner heading at the top of the table. Nesting of variables within dimensions, such as sex by marital status, means that the table contains a number of detailed multivariate counts, such as the number of married male residents aged 20-24. Cross-tabulating age group (21 groups), by sex (2 groups) by marital status (2 groups) produces 84 different counts. If the row and column totals and subtotals are also included, the total number of counts in the table increases to 154. However, a number of these potential cross-tabulated variables may represent impossible combinations of variables, such as married females aged 0-4, and these cells are identified by XXXX in the table body.

Figure 8.1   Age and marital status layout from SAS table of demographic and economic characteristics

2. Residents							
Age	TOTAL PERSONS	Males			Females		
		Total	Single, widowed or divorced	Married	Total	Single, widowed or divorced	Married
ALL AGES							
0-4				xxxx			xxxx
5-9				xxxx			xxxx
10-14				xxxx			xxxx
15				xxxx			xxxx
16-17							
18-19							
20-24							
25-29							
30-34							
35-39							
40-44							
45-49							
50-54							
55-59							
60-64							
65-69							
70-74							
75-79							
80-84							
85-89							
90 and over							

Source: *1991 Census User Guide 3*

It is these individual multivariate counts (plus a few single variable counts) together with descriptive information about each output area, that are supplied when the LBS or SAS are distributed as machine readable data files. For each output area, the Census Offices have defined two different types of data record. The first set of data records for each area are the header records and these contain a variety of descriptive information relating to each output area, such as area identifier, area name(s), Ordnance Survey grid reference (ED/OA level only), area type, 1981 Census area identifier for comparable areas and indicators relating to whether the area has been subject to thresholding (see section 8.5.1). The header records for each area are followed by the table/counts records which contain the counts comprising each table in the LBS or SAS. Figure 8.2, which is the first 21 records from the 100 per cent ED level SAS data file for the Isle of Wight, shows how the LBS and SAS are supplied. Records 2 to 6 are the header records for ED KYFA01 in Cowes Castle ward in Medina local authority district. Records 7 to 12 and 13 to 21 are the table/counts records for SAS tables 1 and 2 respectively.

As the data files supplied by the Census Offices only contain the individual counts, any user wishing to print out the data as a complete LBS or SAS table as displayed in *User Guide 3, 24* or *25* will need to use a software package which

Figure 8.2   Example of supply format for ED level SAS

```
11OPCS  0013230/06/921991 SAS E290114P
210129KYFA01        422    446    182      SZ4872964611
22
3104Isle Of Wight
3203Medina
3302Cowes Castle
41001   00700071211
51001    407 347 178 169  60  18  42  14  14   9   5           9   9   5   4
51002             16  16   8   8              15   8   2   6   7   4   3  11
51003      8   2   6   3   1   2   4   0   0   0   4   3   1 422 355 180 175  67
51004     22  45 421 361 187 174  60  18  42 446 386 200 186  60  18  42
41002   01540071231
51001    448 219 102 117 229 115 114  12  10  10       2   2      18   8   8
51002     10  10      20   9   9          11  11       4   1   1   3   3       5
51003      4   4   0   1   1   0  12  10  10   0   2   2   0  15  10   9   1   5
51004      4   1  13  11  10   1   2   2   0  17  10   2   8   7   2   5  17   6
51005      4   2  11   0  11  25  12   2  10  13   1  12  36  18   2  16  18   4
51006     14  28  14   5   9  14   2  12  25  12   0  12  13   3  10  36  20   3
51007     17  16   5  11  40  16   4  12  24   8  16  32  16   7   9  16   7   9
51008     38  19   5  14  19  11   8  18   7   4   3  11   8   3  23   4   1   3
51009     19  18   1  14   2   2   0  12  11   1
```

Source: 1991 Census, Crown copyright

Figure 8.3   SAS table for ED KYFA01

```
1991 Census Small Area Statistics - 100%              Area Identifier - 29KYFA01        Grid reference - SZ48729646
   Cowes Castle                          Medina                                              Isle Of Wight
   PRODUCED USING SASPAC       ZONE 29KYFA01                              CROWN COPYRIGHT RESERVED
```

Table 2 Age and marital status: Residents

Age	TOTAL PERSONS	Males			Females		
		Total	Single widowed or divorced	Married	Total	Single widowed or divorced	Married
ALL AGES	448	219	102	117	229	115	114
0 - 4	12	10	10	xxxx	2	2	xxxx
5 - 9	18	8	8	xxxx	10	10	xxxx
10 - 14	20	9	9	xxxx	11	11	xxxx
15	4	1	1	xxxx	3	3	xxxx
16 - 17	5	4	4	0	1	1	0
18 - 19	12	10	10	0	2	2	0
20 - 24	15	10	9	1	5	4	1
25 - 29	13	11	10	1	2	2	0
30 - 34	17	10	2	8	7	2	5
35 - 39	17	6	4	2	11	0	11
40 - 44	25	12	2	10	13	1	12
45 - 49	36	18	2	16	18	4	14
50 - 54	28	14	5	9	14	2	12
55 - 59	25	12	0	12	13	3	10
60 - 64	36	20	3	17	16	5	11
65 - 69	40	16	4	12	24	8	16
70 - 74	32	16	7	9	16	7	9
75 - 79	38	19	5	14	19	11	8
80 - 84	18	7	4	3	11	8	3
85 - 89	23	4	1	3	19	18	1
90 and over	14	2	2	0	12	11	1

Source: 1991 Census, Crown copyright

provides access to a machine readable version of the table outlines. For example, figure 8.3 is SAS table 2 for ED KYFA01 and has been produced using SASPAC. Further details about the record format of the LBS/SAS supply files are contained in *User Guide 21*.

8.3.2 Table and topic identification

The LBS consist of 95, 96 and 99 tables for areas in England, Wales and Scotland respectively. The equivalent figures for the SAS, which are a subset of the LBS and

Table 8.2

Structure of the 1991 LBS/SAS

Section number	Table numbers	Subject area
I	1-18	Demographic and economic characteristics
II	19-27	Housing
III	28-53	Households and household composition
IV	54-66	Household spaces and dwellings
V	67-70	Scotland and Wales only tables
VI	71-99	10 per cent topics

available down to a lower areal level, are 82, 83 and 86 tables. For ease of comparison, each SAS table has the same reference number (see section 8.3.4) as its LBS counterpart. However, as some LBS are not included in the SAS, there are some gaps in the SAS table numbering sequence.

Each table has been given a short keyword title to provide a quick reference to the LBS/SAS. For example, table 21 which cross-tabulates numbers of cars per household by the number of persons aged 17 or over in each household, is given the descriptive keyword title 'Car Availability'. The full list of table titles is provided in appendix 8.1. In view of the complexity of many of the tables in the LBS/SAS the keyword titles should not be used as the sole criterion for selecting a table for further analysis.

Both the LBS and SAS tables are grouped together by subject area into six major sections as shown in table 8.2.

One of the major constraints to effective use of the 1981 SAS was the absence of an index to the tables. A potential user of the 1981 SAS had to scan the table layouts by eye, usually in conjunction with the explanatory notes, to identify which tables contained the required variables of interest. In order to deal with the problem created by the vastly increased number of tables, the Census Offices have responded to user requests and produced a basic keyword index for the 1991 LBS/SAS. This index can be used to locate tables relating to specific topics, such as tenure and ethnic group, and where particular topics are cross-tabulated, for example table 49 which contains tenure and ethnic group. The complete keyword index is reproduced in appendices 8.2 and 8.3.

8.3.3 National variations

National variations in the LBS/SAS take the form of additional tables for Wales and Scotland and different versions of particular tables for Scotland and/or Great Britain as a whole.

One additional LBS/SAS table (table 67) relating to the Welsh language question is available for areas in Wales. In Scotland, an extra four LBS/SAS tables (tables 67 to 70) have been defined. Tables 67 and 68 respectively relate to the Gaelic language and floor level of accommodation questions, asked only on the Scottish census form. Tables 69 and 70, which deal with occupancy norms in Scotland, have been retained in order to maintain comparability with the 1981 Census.

Some tables in the LBS/SAS, mainly those relating to migration and housing tenure, are released in different versions for Scotland or Great Britain as a whole.

There is one version for areas in England and Wales, a second for Scottish areas, and, where necessary, a further summary version for Great Britain as a whole. For example, renting from Scottish Homes is identified as a separate tenure category in many of the LBS/SAS tables for areas in Scotland. A full list of the LBS/SAS tables for which different versions have been defined is contained in section 88 of *User Guide 3* and section 3.10 of *User Guide 38*. Users should note that the table layouts contained in *User Guide 3* are those that relate to the Great Britain versions of the LBS/SAS tables only. The complete table layouts for the LBS and SAS (including national variations) are contained in *User Guides 24* and *25*, respectively.

8.3.4 Table and cell numbering system

The Census Offices have devised a table and cell numbering system which provides an index to the LBS/SAS. This system also provides a mechanism for accessing particular tables and/or counts from the machine-readable versions of LBS/SAS and also for conveying unambiguous definitions of derived variables to other users. Each LBS/SAS table has been assigned a unique identifier which consists of the table number (01 to 99) and a prefix. This prefix consists of a character (L or S) to indicate whether the table is LBS or SAS plus one or more optional characters (E, S, W or G) to identify tables which are specific to England and Wales, Scotland, Wales only and/or Great Britain. Table 8.3 illustrates how this coding system can be used to identify specific tables in the LBS or SAS.

Each LBS and SAS table comprises a number of counts. The number of counts in a table is a function of the number of variables and variable categories used in each cross-tabulation and also the number of row and column totals and subtotals produced. For reference purposes, each count in the LBS and SAS has been assigned a unique identifier comprising the table identifier and the cell number within the table. The cell number is in the range 0001 to 9999, although the highest number of valid counts in a single LBS/SAS table is 1305 (L08). Under this coding system, the cell identifiers comprise seven, eight or occasionally nine characters, for example S020050, SE200232 or SEG480001. This table-based coding system represents a significant change between 1981 and 1991. For the 1981 SAS, the cells in the 100 per cent and 10 per cent tables were simply numbered sequentially from 1 to 4345

Table 8.3

Examples of LBS/SAS table coding system

Table identifier	Description
L02	LBS table 2 (England and Wales, Scotland and Great Britain)
LE20	LBS table 20 (England and Wales only)
LS20	LBS table 20 (Scotland only)
LG20	LBS table 20 (Great Britain only)
LEG48	LBS table 48 (England and Wales and Great Britain only)
LW67	LBS table 67 (Wales only)
S02	SAS table 2 (England and Wales, Scotland and Great Britain)
SE20	SAS table 20 (England and Wales only)
SS20	SAS table 20 (Scotland only)
SG20	SAS table 20 (Great Britain only)
SEG48	SAS table 48 (England and Wales and Great Britain only)
SW67	SAS table 67 (Wales only)

(England and Wales tables only). The cell numbering system layouts for all the LBS/SAS tables are contained in *User Guides 25* and *24* respectively. By using *User Guides* 24 and 25 in conjunction with the Topic and Keyword Index (appendix 8.2) users will be able to determine the cell reference numbers for particular variables of interest. For the purposes of illustration, the cell numbering layout for SAS table 2 (S02) is reproduced as figure 8.4.

With reference to figure 8.4 the following section illustrates how the table and cell numbering system can be used to access and manipulate the LBS/SAS when supplied in a machine-readable format. All the cells in SAS table 2 have the prefix S02. Hence the full seven character identifier for cell number 1 (the total number of persons; all ages) is S020001. The identifiers for other example counts in table 2 are as follows:

S020008   Total number of persons aged 0-4

S020060   Total number of married males aged 25-29

By combining together individual cells it is possible to create new variables. For example, by adding together cells S020008 (total persons aged 0-4) and S020015 (total persons aged 5-9) it is possible to derive the total number of persons aged 9 or under. Similarly, by expressing S020008 as a ratio of S020001 (total persons) it

Figure 8.4   Cell numbering layout for SAS table 2

```
1991 Census Small Area Statistics — 100%
        Area Identifier —              :     Area Name —
        Table Prefix: S02
```

Table 2 Age and marital status: Residents

Age	TOTAL PERSONS	Males			Females		
		Total	Single widowed or div'ced	Married	Total	Single widowed or dĩv'ced	Married
ALL AGES	1	2	3	4	5	6	7
0 - 4	8	9	10	xxxx	12	13	xxxx
5 - 9	15	16	17	xxxx	19	20	xxxx
10 - 14	22	23	24	xxxx	26	27	xxxx
15	29	30	31	xxxx	33	34	xxxx
16 - 17	36	37	38	39	40	41	42
18 - 19	43	44	45	46	47	48	49
20 - 24	50	51	52	53	54	55	56
25 - 29	57	58	59	60	61	62	63
30 - 34	64	65	66	67	68	69	70
35 - 39	71	72	73	74	75	76	77
40 - 44	78	79	80	81	82	83	84
45 - 49	85	86	87	88	89	90	91
50 - 54	92	93	94	95	96	97	98
55 - 59	99	100	101	102	103	104	105
60 - 64	106	107	108	109	110	111	112
65 - 69	113	114	115	116	117	118	119
70 - 74	120	121	122	123	124	125	126
75 - 79	127	128	129	130	131	132	133
80 - 84	134	135	136	137	138	139	140
85 - 89	141	142	143	144	145	146	147
90 and over	148	149	150	151	152	153	154

Source: *1991 Census User Guide 24*

is possible to obtain the percentage of persons under 5 years of age. Certain tables (e.g. table 47) can be used to obtain 'hidden' counts, such as different types of pensioner households *with* cars as opposed to *without* cars, by subtracting particular counts from totals.

All the counts relating to a 1991 LBS/SAS table are displayed in the standard cell numbering layouts. For the 1981 SAS there were separate subsets of counts, such as row subtotals, which did not appear in the standard table layouts but were available in the machine readable versions (see 1981 *User Guides 48* and *49*).

8.4 GEOGRAPHICAL BASIS OF THE LBS AND SAS

One of the key features of the local statistics output is that it provides a set of comparable statistics for a wide range of different areal units which can be as small as EDs/OAs or as large as Great Britain as a whole. The primary geographical building block from which all other higher output areas are derived is the ED/OA. The major exception to this rule is the postcode sector level SAS for England and Wales which is based on aggregations of unit postcodes.

In England and Wales, EDs are used for the collection of the Census and for the output of the SAS. In Scotland, the 1991 ED was only used as a unit of collection and has not been used for the output of SAS (see chapter 3(I)). Instead, GRO(S) have defined output areas (OAs) which are aggregations of contiguous unit postcode zones, which have been mapped by GRO(S), to form areas which nest as closely as possible into 1981 EDs (Clark and Thomas, 1990; Raper, Rhind and Shepherd, 1992). To meet demands for statistics for small areas GRO(S) split 1981 EDs expected to have more than 80 households in 1991 into two or more postcode based areas each containing at least 40 households. The important point to note is that, as a consequence, OAs in Scotland are approximately one third the size of EDs in England and Wales. A more detailed description of the differences between England and Wales and Scotland in terms of the geographical base used for the collection and output of the 1991 Census is provided in chapter 3(I).

8.4.1 Different types of ED and OA

For census purposes three types of ED/OA have been defined for the output of 1991 SAS, standard EDs/OAs (as described in chapter 3(I)); special EDs/OAs (SEDs and SOAs); and shipping EDs/OAs. An indicator is provided in the header record to enable users to differentiate between these three different types of EDs/OAs.

SEDs and SOAs have been defined for those large communal establishments that were expected to contain 100 or more persons on census night. Examples of large communal establishments that have been defined as SEDs/SOAs include psychiatric hospitals, children's homes, prisons, educational establishments and hotels. These types of establishments are frequently characterised by populations which are significantly different from those in the surrounding area and sometimes by an absence of resident households. Therefore, in order to prevent these large communal establishments from distorting the SAS for the ED/OA in which they are located, they are treated as separate both for enumeration, and in certain cases (see section 8.5.1), for the output of statistics. The estimated number of SEDs for England and Wales is 3,269 (*User Guide 3*). Although no boundaries have been defined for these SEDs/SOAs an Ordnance Survey grid reference (see section 8.4.3) is supplied in the header record for each SED/SOA which can be used to locate the establishment.

Shipping EDs/OAs are a separate category of SEDs/SOAs. Apart from house-boats in inland waters, which are enumerated as households, vessels are treated in a similar way to communal establishments. For the output of statistics for people enumerated on vessels, a separate shipping ward/postcode sector, which contains one shipping ED/OA, has been defined for each local authority district in Great Britain, although no data may be present.

8.4.2 Area levels for output

During the first phase of processing the 1991 Census, the LBS/SAS are made available in a machine readable format for a nested hierarchy of primary output areas (see table 8.4). However, the LBS and SAS are only released for an area if it exceeds certain population thresholds. A full description of these population thresholds is provided in section 8.5.

Initially, the smallest geographical unit for which the LBS are available is the electoral ward in England and Wales and the postcode sector in Scotland. OPCS will also make the LBS available for user defined subdivisions of wards. To avoid the problems associated with differencing of overlapping areas only one set of ward subdivisions will be made available and these must cover the whole population/area of the wards. In addition, each subdivision must exceed the minimum population thresholds set for the release of the LBS (see section 8.5). Similarly, in Scotland, LBS will be made available for subdivisions of postcode sectors.

After the completion of the 10 per cent processing, the Census Offices have released the LBS and SAS (100 per cent and 10 per cent) for a variety of different area levels, such as Parliamentary and European constituencies and Great Britain as a whole. Once again, there are a number of differences between England and Wales and Scotland in terms of the area levels for which the LBS and SAS are available. For example, in order to avoid the problems associated with differencing, the LBS is not being released for postcode sectors in England and Wales. Tables 8.5 and 8.6 summarise the additional area levels for which the LBS and SAS will be made available.

After the second phase of processing, the LBS and SAS may be made available for other statistical areas. At the time of writing, the Census Offices have no plans to release the LBS/SAS for travel-to-work-areas (TTWAs) defined on the basis of journey to work patterns revealed by the 1991 Census, although such output may be produced by intermediaries. The 1981 SAS for TTWAs was generated for the Department of Employment by the Centre for Urban and Regional Development Studies (CURDS) at the University Newcastle (Department of Employment, 1984).

Table 8.4

Nested hierarchy of primary output areas for Great Britain

Area level	LBS	SAS
County/region	✓	✓
Local authority district	✓	✓
Ward (England and Wales)/ postcode sector (Scotland) *	✓	✓
ED/OA		✓

* Aggregates of Output Areas which approximate postcode sectors.

Table 8.5

Additional output areas for England and Wales

Area level	LBS	SAS
National level	✓	✓
Standard regions of England	✓	✓
Regional and district health authorities	✓	✓
Parliamentary and European consituencies	✓	✓
Postcode sectors		✓
Civil parishes in England/communities in Wales		✓
Urban and rural areas		✓

Table 8.6

Additional output areas for Scotland

Area level	LBS	SAS
National level	✓	✓
Health boards	✓	✓
Parliamentary and European constituencies*	✓	✓
Sottish regional electoral divisions*		✓
Wards*		✓
Civil parishes*		✓
Scottish new towns *		✓
Inhabited islands *		✓
Localities		✓

* Aggregates of Output Areas which approximate to the higher level output level.

Area Index files

The Census Offices have produced two machine readable index files called the Area Master File (England and Wales) and the Output Area to Higher Area Index File (Scotland) which list the EDs/OAs comprising each higher output area. These index files will be of particular value to those users wishing to obtain the area constitutions of those higher output areas which do not form part of the nested hierarchy of primary output areas, such as district health authorities/health boards and Parliamentary constituencies. For example, these index files will be essential for any user wishing to undertake an ED or ward level analysis of spatial variations in particular census variables, such as unemployment rates within Parliamentary constituencies.

8.4.3 Geo-referencing the LBS/SAS

A number of spatial indexes have been built into the header records for each output area. These spatial indexes include the unique area identifier, area name(s) (where applicable) and the Ordnance Survey grid reference (ED/OA only). As these indexes are an integral part of the machine readable data supplied for each output area they can be used by software packages to access, manipulate and extract the LBS/SAS in a variety of different ways. In addition, the Census Offices have also generated a set of separate machine readable index files, such as the Postcode to ED Directory

(England and Wales) or the Output Area to Postcode Index File (Scotland), which can also be used for linking postcoded data to the ED/OA level SAS (see chapter 3 (I)).

The area identifier is the primary spatial index for the LBS and the SAS. Each areal unit for which the LBS and SAS are issued is assigned a unique identifier. For areas which form part of the primary output hierarchy (ED/ward/district/county in England and Wales) a hierachical coding system, which is similar to that adopted for the 1981 SAS, has been devised. One of the main advantages of having a hierarchically structured identifier is that software packages can use the different levels for the flexible selection and manipulation of areas. For example, it can be used implicitly to select all the EDs within a ward without having to specify the identifier for each ED.

England and Wales

In England and Wales, each county is given a two digit code, which is the same as that used for the 1981 Census, in the range 01 to 55. For census purposes, Inner and Outer London are treated as two separate counties (01 and 02 respectively). Each local government district (including each London borough) is assigned a two character code in the range AA to TT. The letters I, O and V together with the combinations CD, CP, EA, ED, LA and LB are not used. For the majority of local authority districts, the district level identifiers are the same as those used for the 1981 Census.

Within each district, the wards are sorted alphabetically by ward name (or numerically where the wards have not been named) and then assigned a two character code in the range FA to ZZ. Thus the first ward in each district will be coded FA and subsequent wards FB, FC onwards. As with the district level identifier, certain characters or combinations of characters are not used. These codes are different to those used for the 1981 Census where the wards within each district were coded in sequence from AA onwards. As a result, wards that are unchanged between 1981 and 1991 will have different ward level identifiers, for example AA and FA.

Within each ward, EDs are given a two digit number in sequence from 01 onwards, although there may be occasional gaps where an ED was abolished at a late stage of census planning. The ED number, when used in conjunction with the county, district and ward level identifiers, provides a unique eight character identifier for each ED in England and Wales. For example:

03BSFR14 where:

03	:	is the county code for Greater Manchester.
BS	:	is the district code for Stockport.
FR	:	is the ward code for North Marple
14	:	is ED number 14 within the ward.

Chapter 3, section 3.3.1 also provides an example of the way in which the ED identifiers are constructed.

Where the boundaries of an ED or ward in England and Wales have remained unchanged between the 1981 and 1991 Censuses, the 1981 area identifier for that ED or ward will be supplied in the header records.

Scotland

In Scotland, each region is given a two digit code in the range 56 to 67. Each local government district or Islands area is assigned a two digit code in the range 01 to 56. In Scotland, the census equivalent of the ward is the postcode sector. These are not necessarily true postcode sectors as they may have been split to recognise local government district boundaries. Within each local government district, each pseudo postcode sector is assigned a two character code in the range AA to FG. For ease of reference, pseudo postcode sectors are called postcode sectors.

In Scotland the 1991 ED was used only as a unit of collection and has not been used for the output of SAS (see chapter 3 (I)). Instead, GRO(S) have used subdivisions of 1981 EDs, or sometimes whole 1981 EDs, as the output units for 1991 SAS. These 1991 OAs are aggregations of contiguous unit postcodes, or, rarely, single unit postcodes, to form areas which nest as closely as possible into 1981 EDs. The codes assigned to OAs consist of two digits and an alphabetic character, for example 01A. The first two digits are the 1981 ED code and the character suffix is used to identify each separate OA within a subdivided ED. For example, if a 1981 ED (01) has been subdivided into two OAs, the codes will be 01A and 01B respectively. Where 1981 EDs are not subdivided, the character code suffix is not used. This code, when used in conjunction with the region, district and postcode sector level identifiers provides a unique eight or nine character hierarchical identifier for each output area in Scotland, for example 5601AB03A. The first eight characters of the OA code will correspond to the code used for the 1981 ED except in parts of the Aberdeen (AB) postal area where postcode sectors were reorganised between the censuses by the Royal Mail.

Shipping wards/postcode sectors have been assigned special identifiers (SS) which can be used to distinguish them from standard areas. For example the area identifier for the shipping ED in district 03BS is 03BSSS01.

The area coding systems used for the 1981 and 1991 Censuses require printed or machine readable index files in order for the user to obtain the census code for the required area. For the 1991 LBS/SAS, these index files are the Area Master File (England and Wales) and the Output Area to Higher Areas Index File (Scotland).

Details of the area coding system used for each other area level for which the LBS and SAS are issued, such as Parliamentary constituencies and district health authorities/health boards, are provided in the relevant User Guide.

Names

The names of the areas forming the different consituent parts of the area identifier are also stored in the header record for each area. For example, for each ED/OA and ward/postcode sector, the header record contains the names of the ward/postcode sector, district and county/region. In the case of Scotland, the postcode sector level area name record contains the postcode sector identifier, for example: TD3 6 (Part). As this textual information is stored in the header record for each area it can be used by computer software to provide access to the LBS/SAS by area name (Manchester) rather than by area identifier (03BN).

As described in chapter 3, the location of each ED/OA in Great Britain is identified by an Ordnance Survey grid reference (OSGR) which is stored in the header record for each area. In England and Wales this OSGR is the residentially weighted centroid that has been defined by OPCS for each ED. The OSGR is at 10 m resolution where ED planning was based on 1:1250 or 1:2500 scale OS maps and 100 m resolution elsewhere. This represents a significant improvement over 1981 when the centroid was only available at 100 m resolution. In Scotland, the OSGR for each OA is the residentially weighted centroid of the unit postcode within the OA which contains the largest number of households. It is available to a 10 m resolution as in 1981. Unlike 1981, no OSGRs are being made available for wards/postcode sectors.

As the OSGR is stored in the header record for each area it can be used by software to geo-reference and manipulate the LBS/SAS in a variety of different ways. For example, it is possible to select and aggregate all the EDs/OAs which have centroids falling within a given distance of a particular location, such as a school. Further discussion of the applications of the OSGR is provided in chapter 10.

8.5 PREVENTING INADVERTENT DISCLOSURE OF DATA ABOUT IDENTIFIABLE HOUSEHOLDS/INDIVIDUALS IN THE LBS AND SAS

In the section on confidentiality in the White Paper on the 1991 Census (OPCS and GRO(S) 1988), an assurance was given that all possible steps would be taken to prevent the release of statistical abstracts from the census which might result in the inadvertent disclosure of information about identifiable households or individuals. Releasing the LBS/SAS for geographical areas with large populations, such as local authority districts, is not considered a risk. For areas which may have very small populations, such as EDs/OAs and wards/postcode sectors, there is a small risk that some of the very detailed tables in the LBS/SAS might inadvertently reveal information about identifiable households or individuals. As with the 1971 and 1981 SAS, the two procedures adopted by the Census Offices to lessen the risk of inadvertent disclosure are the modification of the 100 per cent statistics produced for EDs/OAs and wards/postcode sectors *and* the suppression of statistics for those EDs and wards/postcode sectors falling below particular population thresholds. This section describes the rules in force; for a discussion of the place of these rules in census confidentiality as a whole, the reader is referred to chapter 5.

8.5.1 Population thresholds and data suppression

Although the vast majority of EDs in England and Wales have more than 100 households with residents, a small proportion, about 8%, have smaller populations (see figure 8.5). One of the main reasons for this is the recognition of all civil parishes in England (communities in Wales) as EDs, however small their population.

In order to deal with the disclosure risk presented by areas with small populations, the Census Offices have defined a set of minimum population thresholds below which the LBS and/or SAS for a particular area level will not be released. These population thresholds, together with the procedures for dealing with the suppressed statistics, are different in a number of respects to those used for the 1981 SAS.

1991 SAS thresholds

In **England and Wales**, the 1991 SAS are only released for those EDs and wards with 50 or more usually resident persons *and* 16 or more resident households. With the exception of a few wards in the City of London, all wards exceed this threshold. The SAS for those areas failing to pass the minimum population thresholds will not be released with the exception of three basic counts (total persons present, total residents and total resident households). The SAS for a suppressed ED or ward will be amalgamated with those of a contiguous area following procedures described below. The only exception to this rule is for those EDs or wards with true zero populations which will not be subject to amalgamation.

In **Scotland**, the SAS have been released for all OAs. This was made possible because all provisional OAs which did not pass the minimum population thresholds were amalgamated with a predetermined contiguous area in the final stage of creating OAs (chapter 3(I)). All amalgamations are with areas within the same statutory boundary, and, whenever possible, within the same 1981 ED.

LBS thresholds

In view of the greater detail of some of the tables in the LBS, much higher minimum population thresholds have been set. The full LBS have only been released for those wards with 1,000 or more residents *and* 320 or more resident households. In Scotland, the same arrangements apply for the release of the LBS for postcode sectors, with the exception that the tables on ethnic group (i.e. the whole of LBS tables 6, 9, 17, 43, 49, 51, 85 and 93, and part of tables 4 and 5) have not been released as standard for any postcode sector; although the SAS versions are available. However, LBS tables on ethnic groups will be made available for those sectors which pass additional thresholds, such as the sector must contain at least 50 non-white residents. The LBS for those wards/postcode sectors failing either population threshold will be amalgamated with those of a contiguous area. However, the SAS are available for those wards/postcode sectors which fall below the thresholds for the LBS, but are above the thresholds for the release of the SAS. This is an important feature of the two-tier output model as over one third of the LBS tables are repeated in their entirety when made available in the SAS. Therefore, in those areas where wards have small populations, such as some of the Welsh counties, it may be necessary to use the LBS and SAS in tandem.

1981 SAS thresholds

It should be noted that the minimum population thresholds used for the 1981 SAS were 25 usually resident persons and eight resident households. The reason why the minimum population thresholds have been doubled for the 1991 SAS is to reflect increased concerns about the risk of inadvertent disclosure combined with the greater number of cross-tabulations available in the 1991 SAS (see section 8.2.1).

For the 1981 SAS, the person and household thresholds were used separately which resulted in partial suppression of the SAS. For instance, if the number of usually resident persons was over 25 but the number of resident households was under eight, tables counting persons would be released but tables relating to households would be suppressed. The problems associated with the differential suppression of statistics are avoided with the 1991 SAS as the population thresholds, with the exception of SEDs/SOAs, are not applied separately.

Suppressed EDs

The SAS for a suppressed 1991 ED in England and Wales are amalgamated with those of a contiguous ED, provided that the combined total number of persons and households exceeds the minimum population thresholds. The SAS for the importing ED will always be for the two EDs combined. The contiguous ED selected to be amalgamated with a suppressed ED will generally be that with the fewest people, including an ED which also falls below the minimum population thresholds. Other factors that will also be taken into consideration include ensuring that all amalgamations are kept within statutory boundaries unless the statutory areas are themselves at or near the population thresholds. Similar procedures are also adopted in England and Wales when amalgamating the statistics from suppressed wards, including shipping wards, with those of an adjoining ward. It should be noted that for the 1981 SAS, only the 10 per cent data from suppressed EDs were amalgamated with those of an adjoining area. The failure to redistribute the 1981 100 per cent data from suppressed EDs resulted in the under-reporting of totals when one or more suppressed EDs were aggregated with other EDs by users to form larger output areas, such as wards and local authority districts. The aggregate 1981 SAS supplied by the Census Offices for these higher output areas were based on the total populations.

Special EDs and OAs

Slightly different procedures have been adopted for dealing with SEDs/SOAs. Three basic counts (total persons present, total residents and total resident households) are released for all SEDs/SOAs. All the SAS are released for a SED/SOA with 50 or more residents *and* 16 or more resident households. In England and Wales, the SAS for a SED which has failed both population thresholds are suppressed and not amalgamated with those of the containing ED. However, the populations from all wholly suppressed SEDs are included in the SAS at ward level and above. In Scotland, different procedures are used and the SAS for a SOA which has failed both population thresholds are merged with those of its surrounding OA rather than being suppressed.

SAS tables counting residents are also issued for a SED/SOA with 50 or more residents but less than 16 resident households. The tables and parts of tables which are not issued are suppressed but are included in the SAS at ward/postcode sector level and above.

As described above, the full or partial suppression of the SAS for SEDs/SOAs may result in the under-reporting of population totals when aggregating EDs/OAs to form larger output areas, such as wards or local authority districts, which contain numbers of wholly and/or part suppressed SEDs or part suppressed SOAs.

The header record for each area contains information in the form of indicators which will enable users to distinguish between different area types, such as standard, special and shipping EDs, and also to identify those areas which have been subject to suppression. For suppressed areas, the header record contains the area identifier of the area to which the counts have been imported. Similarly, the header record for an importing area contains the area identifier of the area(s) from which the counts have been exported. (For the 1981 SAS, the identifier of the adjacent ED to which the suppressed 10 per cent data were amalgamated was not stored in the header record but was made available as a separate list.) For each county in England and Wales, OPCS have issued *User Guide 43* which contains a list of all the 1991 EDs and wards which have been suppressed together with the identifier of the ED or ward to which the statistics have been exported, the identifiers of all the restricted SEDs and shipping EDs and their level of restriction, the identifiers of all those EDs and wards with zero populations and any other errors or anomolies.

8.5.2 Data modification

In addition to suppression, a data modification technique is used to ensure that no information in the released LBS/SAS can be related to any identifiable household or individual with any degree of certainty. Non-zero counts in the SAS based on the 100 per cent data at ward/postcode sector level and below are modified by the addition of +1, 0 or -1 in quasi-random patterns. In the LBS the data modification procedure is applied twice with the result that each non-zero cell count will have been modified by the addition of a number between +2 and -2. All counts are modified, with the exception of the basic population counts in tables 1, 27 and 71 and the counts of establishments in table 3 where modification would impair the usefulness of the tables. The counts in the 10 per cent tables are not modified as sampling is regarded as providing sufficient protection against inadvertent disclosure.

A full description of the data modification technique is provided in chapter 5. A detailed discussion of some of the statistical problems associated with this technique is contained in section 8.6.

8.6 STATISTICAL AND METHODOLOGICAL PROBLEMS

8.6.1 Introduction

The availability of the ED/OA level SAS in a machine readable format will inevitably mean that a large number of users will be undertaking computer-based analysis and mapping of 1991 Census statistics at this area level. However, there are a number of statistical and methodological problems associated with attempting to analyse and map SAS at such a small spatial scale. The four main problems associated with the ED/OA level SAS which will be discussed in this section are related to data modification, variations in population size, imputation, and sampling error. A user should be aware of the potential impact of these problems as they may in some cases severely affect the reliability of any results based on an analysis of the SAS at ED/OA level.

8.6.2 Effect of data modification

As described in section 8.5, the 100 per cent LBS/SAS at ward/postcode sector and below are subject to blurring in order to prevent the inadvertent disclosure of information about identifiable individuals or households. All the non-zero cell counts with the exception of a few basic counts in a number of tables, are modified in the SAS by the addition of 1, 0 or -1 in a quasi-random pattern such that there is a higher probability of leaving the count unmodified. In the LBS this procedure is operated twice, so that each count is altered by the addition of a number between -2 and +2.

In a table consisting of a single cross-tabulation, such as LBS/SAS table 2 (see figure 8.1), the row and column totals and subtotals are the sum of all modified counts. This means that the overall table total, such as the total number of residents, will be the same regardless of whether the row or column totals are added together.

A number of the tables in the LBS/SAS comprise two or more cross-tabulations concatenated together, such as table 49, but only contain one total row or column which is common to the table as a whole. In these tables, each separate cross-tabulation was modified independently, then the row or column totals from only *some* of the cross-tabulations were used to obtain the common total row or column for the table. As a result, adding together the counts from the other cross-tabulations in the table may produce totals which are inconsistent with those reported in the common total row or column.

In the case of SAS tables 20, 22, 58 and 67, different procedures were used to obtain the common total row or column. In these tables the totals and subtotals were derived as separate counts and modified independently of the cross-tabulations. A consistent set of totals and subtotals for these tables can be obtained by summing the counts in some of the cross-tabulations. However the totals obtained by this method will have a larger standard error than those in the common total row or column which have been modified independently.

Data modification can thus introduce two different types of perturbation into the SAS. Firstly, each non zero cell will have been subject to the possible addition of +1 or -1. The effect of this data adjustment will be greatest when the value of the count is small which is also when the risk of disclosure would be greatest. For example, adding or subtracting 1 from a value of 5 has a far greater proportionate effect than it does on values of 50 or 500. Therefore the effects of data adjustments on individual cell counts is most severe in areas with small populations and/or for those census variables with a low frequency of occurrence, and/or distributed over a large number of categories, such as single years of age.

Secondly, as the table totals, with the exceptions noted above, and subtotals are the sum of all the modified cell counts within a cross-tabulation they are also subject to the effects of data modification. Adding the modified cells together to form a table or subtotal also has the effect of summing the individual random adjustments to produce a net error term. This net error term will be the difference between the modified and unmodified table totals or subtotals. For example, if a table total consists of five cell counts which have been modified through the addition of the following sequence of random errors (1, 0, -1, -1, -1) then the net error term for that table total will be -2. (It should be noted that, for the purposes of illustration, a more extreme sequence of data modification than normally occurs in practice has been used.) Similarly, any user defined variables based on the aggregation of a series of individual counts will also be subject to net error.

In the 1981 and 1991 SAS, a small number of tables containing basic population counts, such as the total number of households and the total number of residents in each area, are not subject to any modification. By comparing these basic counts from modified and unmodified tables it is possible to illustrate the extent to which net error affects table totals. Using 1991 SAS, the following two cell totals

(S010065 and S350001) were extracted for all the 1991 EDs in England and Wales (excluding shipping, special and restricted EDs):

S010065   Total number of residents in households.
          Unmodified total (table S01)

S350001   Total number of residents in households
          Modified total (table S35)

The difference between the two population totals was calculated. The frequency distribution of the net error term revealed that, although the maximum difference between the modified and unmodified number of total households was ±6, 71 per cent of the EDs had totals which were within ±1 of the unmodified total, and only 1.7 per cent of the EDs had net error terms greater than ±4. However, the extent to which the net error term will have a distorting effect will depend on the size of the total.

Similar frequency distributions can be obtained for other population bases, such as the number of households with residents, where the modified and unmodified totals are both recorded in the SAS. These frequency distributions confirm that the statistical likelihood of a large net error term tends to increase as the number of cell counts comprising each table total increases.

Net error terms do not automatically cancel out when EDs/OAs are aggregated; unfortunately, aggregating EDs/OAs may actually result in the error terms cumulating. This can be demonstrated by using the 1991 ED level SAS for the Isle of Wight. For all EDs (excluding shipping EDs) in Medina (KY) and South Wight (KZ) local authority districts, the modified and unmodified total number of residents in households (S350001 and S010065 respectively) were aggregated to obtain ward level totals. The difference between these two totals represents the net error term. Table 8.7 illustrates the way in which net errors may cumulate when EDs are aggregated by users to obtain ward and/or district level statistics.

Individually, none of the EDs has an aggregate error term which exceeds ±3. However, due to the distorting effect that the distribution of true zero cell counts within tables and supressed EDs have on the allocation of random errors to individual cells, the net error terms may cumulate rather then cancel themselves out when EDs are aggregated within wards. For example, wards KYFA and KYFP have net errors of +23 and -19 persons respectively.

Similarly, the errors may also cumulate when ED level totals are aggregated up to district level. For instance, the aggregate errors for districts KY and KZ are minus 6 and plus 40 persons respectively. This is entirely due to the effect of data modification since none of the special EDs on the Isle of Wight has been subject to partial suppression (see section 8.5.1).

Caution is therefore required when aggregating ED/OA level SAS to obtain totals for larger areas, such as wards/postcode sectors, districts, counties/regions or countries, since these totals will not necessarily be the same as those reported in the SAS or Census Reports for those area levels. For example, the total number of residents in households in the Isle of Wight (S350001) obtained by a user aggregating all the EDs in the county is 120,346 compared to 120,439 reported in the county level SAS and County Report. The difference between these two totals (-93 persons)

Table 8.7

Effect of aggregation on the cumulative net error term for SAS table S35

Ward ID	Number of EDs	S010065	S350001	Net error
Medina District				
KYFA	9	3519	3542	23
KYFB	5	2514	2522	8
KYFC	7	3157	3154	-3
KYFD	9	3678	3676	-2
KYFE	7	3831	3831	0
KYFF	10	5106	5096	-10
KYFG	5	1719	1718	-1
KYFH	7	3106	3099	-7
KYFJ	8	4333	4348	-15
KYFK	10	3476	3488	12
FYFL	14	6102	6099	-3
KYFM	6	2917	2915	-2
KYFN	14	5624	5626	2
KYFP	14	5515	5496	-19
KYFQ	12	3943	3935	-8
KYFR	11	4894	4885	-9
KYFS	13	5499	5497	-2
KY	161	68933	68927	-6
South Wight District				
KZFA	8	3502	3505	3
KZFB	11	3383	3396	13
KZFC	5	2063	2066	3
KZFD	7	2411	2414	3
KZFE	8	2321	2322	1
KZFF	7	2747	2747	0
KZFG	15	5081	5087	6
KZFH	6	2539	2538	-1
KZFJ	10	4341	4350	9
KZFK	16	4930	4934	4
KZFL	11	3872	3871	-1
KZFM	11	3516	3519	3
KZFN	6	2431	2431	0
KZFP	14	5723	5725	2
KZFQ	4	1642	1639	-3
KZFR	3	877	875	-2
KZ	142	51379	51419	+40

is due to the combined effect of data adjustment (+34 persons) and the suppression of statistics for Special EDs (-127 persons) (see section 8.5.1). While the differences between totals may appear small, their effect can be severe, particularly if rigid cut off points are used for classifying areas. For example, the ward level deprivation index used by the Department of Health was originally based on aggregated 1981 ED level SAS (Senior, 1991). When the deprivation index was recalculated using 'true' ward level SAS it was discovered that 19 out of 8,465 wards in England had been misclassified, which cost the Department of Health an extra £190,000 in deprivation payments in 1991. This illustrates one of the problems of attributing a spurious level of accuracy to SAS, particularly to out-of-date figures.

As a guideline, the ED/OA level SAS should not be aggregated to obtain population totals for area levels which form part of the standard output, such as wards, districts, district health authorities or Parliamentary constituencies where the user has access to such output. In addition, when aggregating the LBS/SAS to form user defined new zones which do not form part of the standard output, the highest possible area level(s) should be used as the basic building blocks for the aggregation.

Moreover, using 100 per cent SAS tables to calculate ratio measures requires even more caution as both the numerator and the denominator may have been subject to data modification, particularly if these are based on the aggregation of a number of counts. For areas with small populations the combined effect of data adjustment on individual counts and table totals can have a highly distorting effect on ratio measures. For instance, the following counts have been extracted for ED ELFA05 in Cheshire:

	HHLDS	S420001	S420020
ELFA05	22	27	2

S420020   Number of households lacking or sharing use of bath/shower and/or inside WC containing one adult of pensionable age

S420001   Total number of households with residents— modified total (table 42)

HHLDS   Total number of households with residents—unmodified total (table 27)

Firstly, as S420020 has been subject to data modification, the unmodified count of the number of households lacking or sharing use of a bath/shower and/or inside WC and containing one adult of pensionable age must be either 1, 2 or 3. Using HHLDS as the denominator, the 'true' percentage of households lacking or sharing use of bath/shower/ and/or inside WC and containing one adult of pensionable age will be either 4.5 per cent, 9.1 per cent or 13.6 per cent. However, when S420020 is expressed as a ratio of the table total S420001 a further distorting influence is introduced. Using the table total, which is 5 greater than the unmodified total, produces a percentage figure of 7.4 per cent. Conversely, had the table total been 5 less than the unmodified total a percentage figure of 11.7 per cent would have been produced.

These wide variations (4.5 per cent to 13.6 per cent) clearly illustrate the distorting effect that data modification can have on the calculation of ratios for areas with very small populations. While this may be an extreme example, it does illustrate how it can be very difficult to decide whether a high or low concentration is real or the result of a statistical accident. It also makes it extremely difficult to identify areas of disadvantage solely by looking at the extremes of distributions since the amount of error at the extremes of the distribution may be greater than in the middle.

A further complication arises as a result of the considerable duplication of counts that exists within the SAS which means that it is possible to calculate the same ratio measures, such as the percentage of households in council tenure, using a number of different tables. As the combined effect of data modification on individual cell counts and the table totals may vary from table to table, it is possible that a wide range of different results may be obtained depending on which table is used. Unfortunately, it is not possible to measure the extent of the net error term for all tables, as only a small percentage of unmodified population bases are reported in the SAS. Similarly, due to the differential effect that data modification may have on different tables, users should be wary of using numerators and denominators from different tables to avoid the potential problem of obtaining percentage values greater than 100.

8.6.3 Variations in population size

As figure 8.5 reveals, there is considerable variation in the size of 1991 EDs in England and Wales (excluding shipping EDs, special EDs and restricted EDs) as measured by the number of households with residents. Some 1.9 per cent of 1991 EDs had less than 50 households and 8.1 per cent had less than 100 households. The comparable figures for the 1981 Census were 5.2 per cent and 15.0 per cent, respectively. In Scotland, the average size of an OA is approximately 52 households which is significantly smaller than the average size of an ED in England and Wales.

Figure 8.5 Size of EDs in 1991 as measured by the number of households with residents, England and Wales

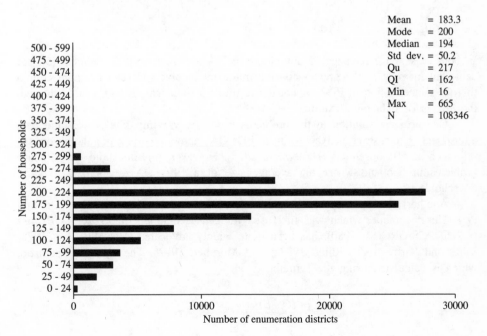

For the 1991 Census, Scotland differs from England and Wales in terms of the size of the smallest unit for which the SAS are released. Whereas the Census Offices reduced the number of smaller EDs for enumeration purposes, the number of small output areas in Scotland increased as OAs became separate from enumeration areas (see chapter 3 (I)). It is estimated that OAs in Scotland will have population sizes averaging only one third the size of EDs in England and Wales. As will be described below, such a pronounced national variation may have a significant effect on any analysis of the ED/OA level SAS, such as an area classification or the identification of deprived areas, undertaken for Great Britain as a whole. OAs could be aggregated together to form larger, more comparable sized intermediate units, such as 1981 EDs, but, as described above, the resultant SAS would contain aggregate net errors.

The SAS are supplied as a series of counts for geographical units which may vary considerably in population size. In order to be able to compare areas in terms of their census characteristics, it may be necessary to take account of this variation. The standard method used to control for variations in population size is to express a count as a percentage of a particular population base. Using such percentages to identify areas with high or low concentrations of particular characteristics, such a male unemployment, is a widely used technique. For example, the DoE (1983) used Z-scores based on percentages to identify deprived areas using 1981 SAS. As described above, data adjustment can severely affect ratio measures calculated for EDs/OAs with small populations. As a result, using percentages to identify areas with high or low concentrations can produce misleading results. For example, consider the following two hypothetical EDs (ED01 and ED02):

	Total council-owned households	*Total households*
ED01	8	16
ED02	100	200

In both EDs, the percentage of households in council ownership is identical (50 per cent) but in view of the greater absolute numbers involved we can be more certain that the concentration in ED02 is not the result of a statistical artifact, caused through the effects of data modification.

One possible solution to the problems posed by varying ED/OA size and data adjustment is to restrict analysis to those EDs/OAs above a certain population threshold, such as 50 households (Holterman, 1975). However, this threshold would cause problems in Scotland where the average size of a 1991 OA is approximately 52 households.

Another alternative approach is the use of the signed chi-square transformation (χ^2). This technique, which was first used for census mapping in *People in Britain* (CRU/OPCS/GRO(S), 1980), has been quite widely advocated (Visvalingham, 1978; Jones and Kirby, 1980; Rhind 1983a; and Morphet, 1992). The signed χ^2 statistic, which is calculated using the formula

$$\chi^2 = \sum \frac{(O - E)^2}{E}$$

(where O and E are the observed and expected numbers respectively), can be used to identify areas which have high or low concentrations based on the expected and observed number within an area. The χ^2 statistic is given a positive or negative value depending on whether the observed value is greater or less than the expected number. A value of zero indicates that the observed and expected values are identical. The main advantage of the signed χ^2 statistic over percentages is that it takes into account both relative and absolute values. Consequently, it provides a useful technique for compensating for the distorting effect that data adjustment can have on the calculation of ratio measure for EDs with small populations. For example, consider the following two hypothetical EDs:

	Economically active males	Unemployed males	Percentage unemployed	Signed χ^2
ED01	20	6	30.00	2.69
ED02	224	69	30.80	33.66

These EDs have almost identical percentage male unemployment rates but the much larger positive χ^2 statistic value for ED02 reflects the greater numbers in that ED. An ED with a small population must have extremely large concentrations in order to have a high χ^2 value. Details about how to calculate the signed χ^2 statistic are contained in Visvalingam (1978) and Morphet (1992).

Any ranking of EDs based on the χ^2 statistic may be substantially different to that based on percentage figures. Therefore, the decision whether to use percentages or the signed χ^2 statistic could have an important effect on the outcome of exercises which use ED/OA level SAS to identify where the most deprived EDs/OAs in Great Britain are located. Any ranking of EDs/OAs based on percentages may give greater weighting to those areas of Great Britain, such as Scotland, with higher proportions of small EDs/OAs. Conversely, a ranking based on the signed χ^2 statistic may tend to put areas with higher populations at the extremes.

Both the percentage and the signed χ^2 statistic are techniques that can be used to identify those EDs/OAs with the highest concentrations of particular groups, such as unemployed males or lone parent families. However, they may not be effective in identifying where the majority of the members of a particular group live. For example, most of the unemployed males in Great Britain in 1981 (approximately 70 per cent) did not live in the 10 per cent of EDs with the highest levels of male unemployment. Therefore, for certain purposes, such as targeting resources to areas on a *per capita* basis, it may be more appropriate to identify the absolute numbers of particular individuals and/or households in an area. Similarly, by ranking EDs/OAs by absolute numbers it is possible to identify the extent to which particular groups, such as lone parent families or pensioner households lacking central heating, are spatially concentrated (Jones and Moon, 1987).

8.6.4 Imputation

As described in chapter 4, imputation has been used to obtain 100 per cent data for households which were considered to be usually resident but were not enumerated. At the time of writing, very little is known about the effect that variation in imputation rates has on the reliability of the ED/OA level SAS. Preliminary investigations reveal that in some local authority districts there are considerable variations between EDs/OAs in terms of the level of imputation. For example, within one ward in Manchester, the imputation rates by ED for residents in households vary from 1 per cent of total residents to 53.2 per cent. Although this is an extreme example, it does illustrate how users need to be aware of variations in imputation rates when analysing ED/OA level SAS and, in particular, when making estimations of the 100 per cent population from the 10 per cent sample statistics (see section 8.6.5). In this context, tables 1, 19 and 71 in the SAS can be used to obtain the number of imputed absent households and residents in each ED/OA. Further details about imputation procedures are provided in chapter 4 and the *1991 Census Definitions* volume (OPCS and GRO(S), 1992b).

8.6.5. Sampling error

Statistics in section VI of the LBS/SAS are based on a 10 per cent sample of households (excluding imputed households) and a 10 per cent sample of persons in communal households. Further details about how the 10 per cent sample was created are provided in chapter 4 and section 5 of *User Guide 38*.

Due to sampling error, statistics derived from the 10 per cent sample can only provide estimates of the 100 per cent figures. The reliability of these estimates may also be affected both positively and negatively by the fact that it is not a simple random sample. As described in chapter 4, the 10 per cent sample is a geographically stratified sample of households (excluding imputed households) which are in turn clusters of individuals. Whilst a stratified sample of households will tend to reduce the degree of sampling error, this may be offset by the effect of clustering within households. It is known that people with similar characteristics, such as ethnicity or educational level, tend to cluster together within households. Consequently, clustering within households usually increases the sampling error, particularly for groups of the population with rare characteristics.

An investigation into the sampling errors associated with the 1981 Census (OPCS, 1983c; OPCS, 1985) provided little evidence of bias in the sample and confirmed that the 10 per cent sample statistics could be grossed up by a factor of 10 to provide reliable estimates of the 100 per cent population for large areas such as local authority districts. However, for areas with small populations such as wards, parishes and EDs the 10 per cent statistics were subject to large sampling errors. Therefore, it is not advisable to gross up the 10 per cent statistics into estimates for small populations.

The 1991 10 per cent sample statistics can be similarly grossed up, but not by a simple factor of 10, since imputed households have been excluded from the sample. Using a grossing factor of 10 will only provide an estimate of the enumerated population. Therefore due to the effect of imputation, the grossing factor for the 1991 10 per cent sample will be over 10 and may vary from area to area.

The 1991 grossing factor for basic population counts (total residents, total residents in households and total households) can be determined by using table 71 to calculate the ratio of the 100 per cent count to the 10 per cent sample count. In terms of the LBS table and cell numbering system (see section 8.3.4), the grossing factor for total residents in households can be calculated using the following formula:

$$\frac{(L710003 + L710004)}{L710009}$$

This method of calculating the grossing factor for the 10 per cent sample statistics does not take into account any variations in sampling errors which result from the clustering effect of particular variables. To do this it is necessary to calculate grossing factors for specific subpopulations. This can be achieved where the 10 per cent tables contain statistics for a subpopulation for which comparable 100 per cent counts are available. For example, suppose an estimate of the 100 per cent count of all the male corporate managers and administrators aged 30-44 (table 74), which is a group within the subpopulation of male employees and self-employed, is required for a particular area. The most accurate grossing factor for this subpopulation can be obtained by calculating the ratio between the 100 per cent count of all male employees and self-employed aged 30-44 from table 8 and the corresponding sample count from table 74.

In those tables for which no comparable 100 per cent subpopulation count is available (tables 80, 86, 88, 89, 96 and 97), the total residents, total residents in households or total households grossing factors should be used. Alternatively, a close approximation of the subpopulation could be used. For example, the grossing factor for residents in employment (derived from tables 8 and 72) could be used for armed forces (table 96), or, for counts of families in tables 80, 86, 88 and 89, household grossing factors could be used.

The evaluation of the sampling errors associated with the 1981 10 per cent sample (OPCS, 1983c) revealed that, with one or two exceptions, users could assume that the standard error (SE) of a 10 per cent count was the square root of the number of observations ($\sqrt{n}$). For example, if a cell in one of the 10 per cent tables has a value of 25 it would have a standard error of 5 ($\sqrt{25}$). This means that 95% of the time the true value of the count would be in the range 15-35 (that is $25\pm$ 2SE).

Table 8.8 shows standard errors for particular critical values. The standard errors have also been expressed as a percentage of the sample value.

The existence of potentially large sampling errors in the ED/OA level 10 per cent SAS means that unreliable results may be produced when the data are analysed or mapped at such a small spatial scale. The ED/OA level 10 per cent SAS must always be aggregated to form much larger areas in order to produce more reliable

Table 8.8

Standard errors for sample values in 10 per cent SAS

Sample value (a)	Standard error $=\sqrt{}$ sample value (b)	Percentage error (b)* 100/(a)
10,000	100.0	1
2,500	50.0	2
1,111	33.3	3
625	25.0	4
400	20.0	5
204	14.3	7
100	10.0	10
25	5.0	20
4	2.0	50

Source: *1991 Census User Guide 38.*

estimates of the 100 per population. As the 10 per cent SAS are *not* modified, aggregations are free from this source of variability. *The 10 per cent SAS have only been released at ED/OA level to provide users with a primary building block which can be used as a basis for flexible area aggregations.*

Table 8.8 can be used as a guideline to decide how many EDs/OAs should be aggregated together in order to produce reliable estimates of the 100 per cent population. For example, a count in a 10 per cent table would require a value of 400 before the user could be reasonably confident that the count was within 5 per cent of its true value (68 per cent confidence level). In order to satisfy this accuracy criterion it may be necessary to aggregate large numbers of EDs/OAs. For example, using 1981 10 per cent SAS it was necessary to aggregate together all the 363 EDs in Macclesfield District to produce a sample value of 434 for the number of households where the economically active head of household was in Social Class I.

As table 8.8 reveals, extremely large increases in the size of the sample value are required to bring about small improvements in the level of percentage error. Therefore in order to retain any level of geographical detail in the data, such as wards or local authority districts, it may be necessary to accept lower accuracy levels.

Users should also be aware of how sampling errors can affect the reliability of percentage figures obtained using the 10 per cent sample statistics. The following formula (Weis and Hassett, 1991; Butcher and Elliot, 1986) can be used to calculate the standard error (SE) of a percentage obtained from sample data:

$$SE\ (p) = \sqrt{\frac{p\ (100 - p\ )}{n}}$$

where p is the percentage and n is the sample size. The important point to note from this formula is that the standard error is based on the value of the percentage as well as the sample size. Thus for a given sample size, the standard error of a percentage is greatest when it has a value of 50 per cent and lowest for values of 0 per cent and 100 per cent.

The table 8.9 shows the standard errors for particular percentages (10 per cent and 50 per cent) and different sample sizes. For example, for a percentage value of 50 per cent based on a sample size of 25 the user can be confident 95 per cent of

Table 8.9

Standard errors for percentages obtained from sample data

Sample size	Percentages	Standard error	95% confidence interval
10	10%	9.5%	0% - 29%
10	50%	15.8%	18% - 82%
25	10%	6.0%	0% - 22%
25	50%	10%	30% - 70%
100	10%	3.0%	4% - 16%
100	50%	5.0%	40% - 60%
400	10%	1.5%	7% - 13%
400	50%	2.5%	45% - 55%

the time that the true percentage figure is in the range 30 per cent to 70 per cent (that is, $50 \pm 2SE$).

8.7 DISSEMINATION OF THE LBS AND SAS

8.7.1 Dissemination media

With the increasing use of computers to process and analyse the census, magnetic media has tended to replace printed output either in the form of paper or microform, as the principal means of disseminating the local statistics output. The Census Offices will supply A4 paper copies of all the 1991 SAS tables, but this is restricted to a maximum of five areas. Microfilm and microfiche, which were available for the supply of 1981 SAS, have been discontinued as a standard supply format, but are available on request.

The magnetic media used by the Census Offices for the supply of the LBS/SAS during the first phase of output processing are open reel or cartridge tape (IBM or ICL format) which can be accessed by mainframe computers. This initial supply format reflects the hardware configuration (Amdahl 5990 (IBM MVS) and ICL 3965 (ICL VME)) used for processing the 1991 Census. The 100 per cent and 10 per cent LBS/SAS for the nested hierarchy or primary output areas (see section 8.4.2) comprise 10 files per County/Region with each file being supplied on a separate magnetic tape/cartridge. Any organisation purchasing the 100 per cent and 10 per cent LBS/SAS for the whole of Great Britain will therefore have received approximately 675 magnetic tapes/cartridges.

A user ordering the LBS/SAS on magnetic media must be aware of the potential data volumes involved, especially for the ED/OA level SAS. Table 8.10, which shows the number of kilobytes required for the 100 per cent and 10 per cent LBS/SAS per area when supplied in a fixed format, can be used to calculate the potential size of the supplied data files. For example, the size of the computer disk files required for the 100 per cent and 10 per cent ward level LBS for the whole of Hampshire (280 wards) is approximately 24.6 megabytes (280 * 90 kilobytes) and 8.2 megabytes (280 * 30 kilobytes) respectively. Similarly, the 100 per cent and 10 per cent ED/OA level SAS for the whole of Great Britain will occupy approximately 7 gigabytes of disk space.

In addition to magnetic tape/cartridge, a wide variety of different magnetic media can be used for the dissemination of the 1991 LBS/SAS in a digital form including on-line access, network file transfer, optical disc (CD-ROM), high density floppy

Table 8.10

Approximate number of kilobytes of computer storage required for each   area

	100 per cent Area level			10 per cent Area level		
	ED	Ward	Other	ED	Ward	Other
SAS fixed format	31	35	58	20	23	38
LBS fixed format	-	90	144	-	30	48

Source: *1991 Census User Guide 21.*

disks, and high capacity tape (Exabyte and DAT). As described in chapter 7, the Census Offices have made arrangements for the use of alternative high capacity media, such as CD-ROM, for the future distribution of the LBS/SAS. Significantly, many of these alternative supply media will have been used by the different customer sectors for the internal transfer of the LBS/SAS.

As described in chapter 7, agreements made at the purchase of the LBS and SAS mean that there is no restriction on the transfer of the LBS/SAS within the health service and higher education. Local authorities in effect constitute a third sector in which transfer between purchasing authorities has been permitted by the Census Offices. A variety of different procedures have been set up within these customer sectors for the dissemination of the LBS/SAS. Many local authorities are receiving the LBS/SAS direct from the Census Offices and are making their own arrangements for handling the data. A number of higher tier authorities, such as regional health authorities and county councils, which have purchased the data on a consortium basis, are providing a census data service for lower tier authorities. For example, the London Research Centre (LRC) is providing on-line access to the LBS/SAS at ED level and above for London and the rest of the South East Region to all the London boroughs. The LRC has also supplied each London borough with the ED and ward level LBS/SAS for its own area, together with the district level LBS/SAS for the whole of London, on IBM-compatible high density floppy disks in SASPAC-PC system file format.

For the academic sector, the Economic and Social Research Council (ESRC) has funded the establishment of a Census Dissemination Unit at the University of Manchester Computing Centre (MCC) to supply census data for the purposes of teaching and academic research. This unit is providing a national on-line 1991 Census data service as well as using network file transfer to supply the LBS/SAS to those institutions, such as the Universities of Edinburgh and Newcastle, who are holding national or regional subsets of the data. The Census Dissemination Unit has also transferred a copy of the 1991 LBS/SAS to the ESRC Data Archive at the University of Essex which also holds archival copies of the 1961, 1966, 1971 and 1981 SAS in machine readable format.

Users, outside of the major purchasing consortia described above, with limited data requirements, can obtain subsets of data either from the Census Offices or from those organisations acting as census agencies (see chapter 7, section 7.7.7).

8.7.2 Software for handling the LBS/SAS

The last decade has seen a significant move away from paper to computer based analysis of the census. This has been facilitated by a number of developments in computing technology which has opened up a whole variety of new opportunities for the computer based analysis and mapping of census data.

The lack of suitable software for handling the large volumes of data associated with the 1971 SAS was one of the main reasons why the 1971 Census was relatively under-utilised. Researchers at the Census Research Unit at the University of Durham, for example, had to write their own software for compacting, storing and accessing the 1 km grid square SAS for Great Britain (Visvalingham, 1975). In order to overcome some of the problems associated with the increasing data volumes, a consortium comprising mainly local authorities commissioned the Universities of Durham and Edinburgh to develop a standard software package (SASPAC) for handling the 1981 SAS. SASPAC was one of the most portable software packages of its time and was designed to run in batch mode on a range of mainframe and mini-computers under a variety of different operating systems. SASPAC was used by nearly 200 different public and private organisations and was responsible for introducing large numbers of users in a wide variety of organisations to computer based census analysis (Rhind, 1984).

Since SASPAC was developed in the late 1970s and early 1980s there has been a number of significant developments in computing technology, such as the advent of the IBM personal computer (PC) in 1981. The increasing data storage capabilities and processing power of PCs, combined with the development of software packages with easy to use graphical user interfaces, has made it possible to provide interactive desk-top facilities for the access and analysis of census data thus freeing many users from dependence on central mainframes. The feasibility of using PCs to provide flexible access to the SAS was clearly demonstrated in 1989 when Northern Software Technology released a menu driven version of SASPAC (SASPAC4/386) for a high performance 80386 PC. Similarly, Powys County Council also developed a package to handle the 1981 SAS which ran on a PC. A wide variety of PC based menu driven systems have been developed to handle the SAS, ranging from simple view data systems containing subsets of SAS in the form of area profiles to more sophisticated systems, such as InSite (CACI), which combined SAS with other spatially referenced datasets, such as ward level unemployment data and standardised mortality ratios.

At the same time, improvements in the local and wide area networking of computers also made it possible to access and analyse census data held on remote systems. For example, a consortium of University Computer Centres (Manchester, Edinburgh, London, Bath, Newcastle and Aberdeen) in conjunction with the ESRC Data Archive at the University of Essex were reponsible for providing the UK academic community with on-line access to the 1981 SAS and related datasets over the Joint Academic NETwork (JANET). Similarly, the National On-line Manpower Information System (NOMIS), based at the University of Durham, provides national on-line access to a variety of different government statistics, including the 1981 SAS, and to a number of organisations, including central and local government (Townsend, Blakemore and Nelson, 1987).

The development of optical disc technology in the form of CD-ROMs (Compact Disc - Read Only Memory), which can be accessed using CD-ROM drives attached to personal computers, has also been exploited as an alternative dissemination media for census data in a number of different countries including Australia, Canada and the US. The 1981 SAS for Great Britain on CD-ROM was published by Chadwyck Healey in March 1991. This product consists of three CD-ROMs, each containing approximately 540 megabytes of data in a compressed format, and combines the full 1981 SAS with digital boundary data down to ward level in England and Wales and postcode sector level in Scotland together with retrieval software (Supermap for Windows). This software, which was originally developed for the 1980 Australian Census, can be used to access, manipulate, display and map 1981 Census data down to ED level. CD-ROM products using 1991 Census data are described in chapter 7.

The 1980s also saw the emergence of geodemographic systems which synthesised the conventional SAS into proprietary area classification or market segmentation systems, particularly in the private sector. A number of organisations have exploited the multivariate nature of the SAS to develop national classifications of 1981 EDs. These geodemographic systems include ACORN (CACI), PiN (Pinpoint), MOSAIC (CCN), Super Profiles (CDMS) and DEFINE (Infolink). These systems vary in terms of the number and range of census and non-census variables used, the clustering method used and the number of clusters/area types produced by the classification. For example, Super Profiles used 55-65 census variables combined with 19 non census variables to produce a neighbourhood classification system comprising 11, 37 and 150 clusters. Many of these classifications have been made available in specialised software packages for specific commercial applications, such as retail site analysis, credit rating and target marketing. A more detailed review of the development and applications of geodemographics is provided in Brown (1991).

At the time of writing, two specialised software packages (SASPAC and C91) are available for handling the 1991 LBS/SAS as supplied by the Census Offices. Following the success of the 1981 version of SASPAC, a consortium consisting mainly of public sector organisations was formed to fund the development of similar software for handling the 1991 Census. The development of SASPAC has been managed on behalf of the Local Government Management Board by the London Research Centre (LRC) and the software has been written by MVA Systematica in partnership with Salford University Computing Services. SASPAC runs on a range of different hardware platforms including mainframes, minis, Unix workstations and PCs and is being used by over 290 organisations. In addition to the LBS/SAS, SASPAC can also be used to acccess the Special Workplace Statistics (Sections A and B) and the 1981 SAS. SASPAC, which stores the LBS/SAS in a highly compressed format (to 20 per cent the size of the original data files), can be used for area selection, data manipulation, the creation of new zones and for the extraction of statistics in a range of different formats, including the standard LBS/SAS tables and data files suitable for input into statistical or mapping packages. C91, which has been developed by Powys County Council, runs on PCs and provides similar functionality. Further details about the availability of these these two packages can obtained from the developers (see section 8.8).

It should be noted, however, that SASPAC and C91 are not mandatory in order to handle the LBS/SAS as supplied by the Census Offices. The structured format of the data files (see *User Guide 21*) means that a wide variety of different software packages can be used for the storage, access, manipulation and analysis of the LBS/SAS, although the level of data compression achieved will depend on how each package stores data. Undoubtedly, Geographic Information Systems (GIS) applications will be developed to provide an easy-to-use graphical interface to the LBS/SAS and other spatially referenced datasets.

Finally, at the time of writing, two organisations have announced plans to suppply the entire 1991 LBS/SAS for the whole of Great Britain on CD-ROMs in software specific formats. Chadwyck-Healey have concluded an agency agreement with the Census Offices and will publish the 1991 Census on CD-ROM. This product will combine the 1991 Census LBS/SAS and digital boundary data down to ED/OA level together with the Supermap retrieval software. The London Research Centre (LRC) are acting under license from the Census Offices in partnership with MVA Systematica and will be producing CD-ROMs containing the 1991 LBS/SAS for ED/OA area level and above in SASPAC-PC system file format initially for distribution within the main 100 per cent purchasing consortium described above. A third organisation, Claymore Services, have concluded an agreement with the Census Offices, and have produced a CD-ROM for use in schools under the name of 'SCAMP-CD' (Schools Analysis and Mapping Package) which combines an extract of SAS for EDs, digital boundary data, related non-census information, together with software for analysis and mapping.

8.8 CONTACT POINTS

Further documentation, information and advice can be obtained from the following organisations. Information about agencies supplying census data and related services can be obtained from the *Census Newsletter*. See also figure 7.2 on page 197.

(a) ESRC-funded census dissemination and support units:

Census Dissemination Unit
Census Dissemination Unit
Manchester Computing Centre
University of Manchester
Oxford Road
Manchester
M13 9PL

Tel: 061 275 6066
Fax: 061 275 6040

ESRC Data Archive
User Services
ESRC Data Archive
University of Essex
Wivenhoe Park
Colchester
C04 3SQ

Tel: 0206 872001
Fax: 0206 872003

(b) Suppliers of specialist computer software for handling 1991 SAS/LBS:

SASPAC91
Hywel Davies
SASPAC91 Project Officer
London Research Centre
Parliament House
81 Black Prince Road
London
SE1 7SZ

Tel: 071 627 9696
Fax: 071 627 9606

C91
Jon Simonds
Powys County Council
Powys County Hall
Llandrindod Wells
Powys
LD1 5LG

Tel: 0597 826380
Fax: 0597 826231

(c) Suppliers of 1991 SAS/LBS on CD-ROM:

Chadwyck-Healey
Paul Holroyd
Chadwyck-Healey Ltd
Cambridge Place
Cambridge
CB2 1NR

Tel: 0223 311479
Fax: 0223 66440

London Research Centre
Rob Lewis
London Research Centre
Parliament House
81 Black Prince Road
London
SE1 7SZ

Tel: 071 627 9652
Fax: 071 627 9606

Claymore Services
Chris Witt
Claymore Service Ltd
Station House
Whiple
Exeter
EX5 2QH

Tel: 0404 823097
Fax: 0404 823030

APPENDIX 8.1 SAS AND LBS KEYWORD INDEX

(Source: OPCS *User Guide 38*)

Keyword titles

All tables are included in the LBS Tables 18, 45, 52, 64, 65, 72, 85, 88, 93, 96, 97, 98, 99 are omitted from the SAS.

I Demographic and economic characteristics

1 Population bases
2 Age and marital status
3 Communal establishments
4 Medical and care establishments
5 Other establishments

6 Ethnic group
7 Country of birth
8 Economic position
9 Economic position and ethnic group
10 Term-time address

11 Persons present
12 Long-term illness in households
13 Long-term illness in communal establishments
14 Long-term illness and economic position

15 Migrants
16 Wholly moving households
17 Ethnic group of migrants
18 Imputed residents

II Housing

19 Imputed households
20 Tenure and amenities
21 Car availability
22 Rooms and household size
23 Persons per room

24 Residents 18 and over
25 Visitor households
26 Students in households
27 Households: 1971/81/91 bases

III Households and household composition

28 Dependants in households
29 Dependants and long-term illness
30 'Carers'
31 Dependent children in households
32 Children 0-15 in households
33 Women in 'couples': economic position
34 Economic position of household residents
35 Age and marital status of household residents
36 'Earners' and dependent children
37 Young adults

38 Single years of age
39 Headship
40 Lone 'parents'
41 Shared accommodation
42 Household composition and housing

43 Household composition and ethnic group
44 Household composition and long-term illness
45 Migrant household heads
46 Households with dependent children: housing
47 Households with pensioners: housing

48 Households with dependents: housing
49 Ethnic group: housing
50 Country of birth: household heads and residents
51 Country of birth and ethnic group
52 Language indicators
53 'Lifestages'

IV Household spaces and dwellings

54 Occupancy (occupied, vacant, and other accommodation)
55 Household spaces and occupancy
56 Household space type: rooms and household size
58 Household space type: tenure and amenities

59 Household space type: household composition
60 Dwellings and household spaces
61 Dwelling type and occupancy
62 Occupancy and tenure of dwellings

63 Dwelling type and tenure
64 Tenure of dwellings and household spaces
65 Occupancy of dwellings and household spaces
66 Shared dwellings

V Scotland and Wales only tables

67 Welsh language
67 Gaelic language
68 Floor level of accommodation
69 Occupancy norm: households
70 Occupancy norm: residents

VI 10 per cent topics

71 Comparison of 100% and 10% counts
72 Economic and employment status (10% sample)
73 Industry (10% sample)
74 Occupation (10% sample)
75 Hours worked (10% sample)

76 Occupation and industry (10% sample)
77 Industry and hours worked (10% sample)
78 Occupation and hours worked (10% sample)
79 Industry and employment status (10% sample)

80 Working parents: hours worked (10% sample)

81 Occupation and employment status (10% sample)
82 Travel to work and SEG (10% sample)
83 Travel to work and car availability (10% sample)
84 Qualified manpower (10% sample)
85 Ethnic group of qualified manpower (10% sample)

86 SEG of households and families (10% sample)
87 Family type and tenure (10% sample)
88 'Concealed' families (10% sample)
89 Family composition (10% sample)
90 Social class of households (10% sample)

91 Social class and economic position (10% sample)
92 SEG and economic position (10% sample)
93 SEG, social class and ethnic group (10% sample)
94 Former industry of unemployed (10% sample)
95 Former occupation of unemployed (10% sample)

96 Armed forces (10% sample)
97 Armed forces: households (10% sample)
98 Occupation orders: 1980 classification (10% sample)
99 Occupation: Standard Occupational Classification (10% sample)

APPENDIX 8.2 SAS AND LBS TOPIC AND KEYWORD INDEX: 100 PER CENT ITEMS

(Source OPCS: *User Guide 38*)

The numerical and alpha references in this index refer to county report and summary tables respectively

Absent residents
  in households *1*

Absent residents - *continued*
  students *10*
  imputed *18, 19*

Absent households *19*

APPENDIX 8.3 SAS AND LBS TOPIC AND KEYWORD INDEX:
10 PER CENT ITEMS

(Source OPCS: *1991 Census County Report, Part 2*)

9 Mapping and spatial analysis

Robert Barr

9.1 INTRODUCTION

In chapter 3 the geographical base for the census was discussed. This chapter provides an overview and critique of a number of issues faced by the census user when analysing the geographical patterns in census data and presenting them through maps. An important effect of the geographical framework adopted is the opportunities that it offers for mapping census data and for relating it to other data sources. However, it is important to remember that the geographical base chosen, one of fixed areal units, is an abstraction and is subject to the modifiable areal unit problem.

9.1.1 Modifiable areas

The modifiable areal unit problem arises because there is an infinite number of ways to define sets of areas into which to group people (see Openshaw, 1984; Openshaw and Taylor, 1981). The definition itself, at least partially, determines the characteristics of those areas. If an alternative set of boundaries were to be chosen, of approximately equal size, the characteristics of the second set of areas would almost certainly differ from the characteristics of the first. For example if there were an area of public housing adjacent to an owner occupied estate and the two collectively were large enough to require two enumerators to distribute and collect census forms, the area might be divided in many ways. If it were divided into one enumeration district (ED) that was composed almost entirely of public housing and a second almost entirely of owner occupied housing, the characteristics of the two EDs would contrast strongly. If, on the other hand, a boundary was drawn in such a way as to include about half the public and half the owner-occupied housing in each district, the adjacent districts would appear to be similar areas of mixed housing. It would not be clear whether this mixture was due to the sale of public sector housing, or the local authority buying up private housing (possibly for redevelopment), or a mismatch between the social boundary on the ground and the census boundary.

The boundaries of the EDs were defined largely for operational reasons and were only one of many ways in which the population might have been divided into a set of workable areal units for enumeration. While the set of units is designed to fit into the administrative boundaries of the country, it does not necessarily reflect many other possible geographies such as the travel to work pattern, where people shop or postal geography (except in Scotland where census geography is based, as far as possible, on postal geography).

In chapter 3 the output geography of the census was discussed and in chapters 11 and 12 the availability of census microdata has been covered. In order to help ensure confidentiality and achieve a manageable data set, the characteristics of individuals and individual households are aggregated and published as the characteristics of areas or, in the case of microdata, are made available with only a geographical reference to a relatively large area (see chapter 5). Geographers, and other social scientists, have frequently used area based aggregated census data to investigate the relationship between the social characteristics of an area and other occurrences such as the incidence of crime or unemployment. Unfortunately such analysis can fall foul of the 'ecological fallacy'.

9.1.2 Ecological fallacy

The ecological fallacy is the assumption that when a relationship is found by correlating data for *areas* it reflects a relationship at the level of the *individual* or household. This is not necessarily the case. For example, a correlation exists at the area level between car ownership and owner occupation. While it is true that in predominantly local authority owned housing areas, car ownership tends to be low and in exclusively owner occupied areas it is usually high, it is not necessarily the case that in areas of mixed housing the owner occupiers, perhaps at the bottom of the housing ladder, are more likely to own cars than tenants who may have had the advantage of relatively cheap housing. For many census variables the required cross-tabulations are available (for example, Table 20 in the LBS cross-tabulates tenure and car access); however, the ecological fallacy can be particularly acute where non-census data are combined with the social variables from the census. Crime figures for particular areas are commonly related to the social characteristics of those areas derived from the census. If a correlation is found, for example, between the presence of a particular ethnic minority and violent crimes against the person, what may one conclude? Without additional evidence, very little. It may be true that members of that ethnic minority are the perpetrators of the crime. However, they may equally well be the victims or they may find themselves living in an area, perhaps of marginal housing, where members of the majority ethnic group perpetrate violent crimes against each other not involving the minority at all. At the ecological level all these situations lead to the same statistical outcome which must be interpreted with great caution.

Both these problems are important for anyone wishing to do any detailed analysis of census data and they are dealt with pragmatically by census takers, but need it necessarily be like this? Since the 1960s the Census Offices have been under pressure from some users to give almost total geographical flexibility in the census. Could we imagine a totally flexible dataset that could respond to all the calls placed upon it? While it would not, at present, be technically feasible, nor socially desirable, to monitor the characteristics of the population in real time, it may be helpful to conduct a speculative exercise in what would constitute a complete geographical and statistical replacement for the present census. Let us imagine a Utopian (or perhaps a Dis-Utopian) situation where we have complete access to all the census characteristics of the whole population all of the time. What might such a hypothetical all-pervasive system look like?

First, we could imagine that we have a computerised map displayed on a large screen. This map is scaleless and seamless. That means that it is possible to zoom in on the map so that individual buildings and streets are identifiable, or zoom out until the whole of the United Kingdom can be viewed. Individuals might be represented by coloured dots, these might normally be red to signify women and blue to signify men. The dots would have a border which could be switched to a contrasting colour. The border would tell us if the individual was at home (border kept the same colour as the dot), at their usual place of work or education or elsewhere. By selecting a dot the remainder of the individual's census characteristics such as age, marital status, position in household, economic status and occupation could be revealed in a form that appeared on the screen. These characteristics and the person's location would be plotted in real time. By selecting buildings, or living-spaces, it would be possible to reveal the collective characteristics of the household, or, in workplaces, the employees. Where an individual was not at their usual address an actual, or probable route might be displayed. Although the system would operate in real time, it could be wound back to show the situation at any previous point in time, allowing daily, weekly and longer term patterns to be animated.

In addition to its ability to wind back and compress time, the system would allow any spatial aggregation to be carried out. It would already be programmed with all known sets of current (and historical) statutory, administrative, commercial and operational boundaries. The aggregate characteristics of the population of any of these areal units could be calculated and displayed either in tabular form or by using an appropriate shading on the display. In addition areal units based on proximity to roads, buildings, sources of pollutants or dangerous facilities could be defined. The proximity could be based on straight line, road or time based measures of distance.

In short, such a system would provide us with a complete picture of the social and the spatial characteristics of the population while sacrificing totally both privacy and, almost certainly, confidentiality. It is not suggested that such a system would ever be politically feasible or desirable (even though technology may permit it one day). However, such a system would be the only way to satisfy all the demands that are placed on the present census. It is a problem that many potential census users appear to imagine that the present census already has some of these properties. Unfortunately this is not the case and much of the effort that goes into mapping and analysis of census data is necessary because of its inherent limitations.

The biggest limitation of the contemporary census is its extreme infrequency. An operation that enumerates the population on a single night every decade is extrapolated and updated (admittedly using additional sources) in order to project the pattern of the population over the following 10 years, including daily, weekly and seasonal migrations. In the UK a mid-term census was taken in 1966. Proposals for a mid-term census have been considered, and rejected on cost grounds, in each decade since. The temporal problem is dealt with in some countries, for example Denmark and Sweden, by systems of compulsory registration. In the UK, there is no formal system to record population change between censuses, though the registration of births, marriages and deaths, and changes of address notified to the Family Health Service Authorities, provide a basis for updating official statistics. However, this chapter is concerned with a slightly less heroic endeavour, that is to represent the distribution of the population cartographically for the census based geographic units, and to construct, and display, the census characteristics of other geographic units.

Census maps, and related data, are used for three purposes: to locate census areas in relation to other places; to display census data in an effective and parsimonious way; and, to carry out analytical operations such as calculating the population characteristics of the catchment population of a major store.

9.2 LOCATION

Chapter 3 discussed the process of defining ED boundaries. An output of that process is the collection of hand marked Ordnance Survey maps at various scales, which are used in the field during the census enumeration and which, in turn, define the output areas for which data are made available. Prior to 1991, these maps and photocopied, microfilmed or microfiched facsimiles of them, made up the principal tool for locating census areas. Anyone wishing to relate streets, villages or neighbourhoods to the ED framework had to examine the original enumerators' and census officers' maps (see figures 3.1-3.3). Many local authorities produced their own redrawn versions of the maps for their own internal use, and would also usually have ward maps available for elected members, officers and the general public. The relatively high cost of the original maps from OPCS meant that most census users who wanted to retrieve census data for places identified by local names, or sets of addresses, needed to contact a number of organisations in order to obtain the relevant maps. While it would be theoretically possible to use the Ordnance Survey (OS) base maps to create an address to ED directory, such an undertaking would be very costly and time consuming. However, there is considerable demand for such a translation table, so what substitutes can one use?

9.2.1 Grid references

Two additional locational references are available. Since 1971 an Ordnance Survey grid reference that represents the centre of the populated part of each enumeration district, as identified visually from the original enumerators' maps, has been available as part of the Small Area Statistics. A second, more generally used, dataset which has assumed great importance in identifying census areas, is the 100 m resolution grid reference that is available for every unit postcode in the country. Unfortunately this reference is often misunderstood, and assumed to be more accurate and reliable than is actually the case.

Originally these grid references for unit postcodes were commissioned by the Department of Transport in 1976 for use in travel surveys. These references were based on the location of the first address in each unit postcode (defined as the first address to appear in the Post Office's official list of postal addresses). They were recorded with limited precision (100 m), and relatively poor accuracy which varied in different parts of the country. Precision refers to the resolution of the measurement system; in this case, the grid references refer to the south west corner of a square with 100 m sides — the same reference will be given to any point occurring anywhere within the square; in densely populated urban areas several postcodes may share the same reference. Accuracy refers to the extent to which addresses have been located in the correct 100 m grid squares; given that some postcodes have appeared in the sea, there were clearly some problems with accuracy.

A check on the 1986 version of the Central Postcode Directory found that only 72 per cent of the grid references given fell within the 100 m range, 92 per cent fell within 400 m and 95 per cent within 900 m leaving one postcode in 20 misplaced by a kilometre or more (Neffendorf and Hamilton, 1987). Why should this matter? For the original purpose of calculating trip distances such levels of accuracy were acceptable; however, once the grid references in the Central Postcode Directory are used together with the OPCS population weighted centroid grid references for EDs to generate a postcode to ED conversion table, the accuracy of that table is critically dependent on the accuracy of the original grid references. If neither the grid references for the postcodes nor the grid references for the EDs are sufficiently accurate, that table will be highly error prone. This has been the case for most 1981-based postcode to ED translation tables.

Efforts have been made over the years to improve the accuracy of the grid reference allocated to each postcode; the most promising approaches are those of Pinpoint Analysis and, more recently of the proposed Address Point product from Ordnance Survey. Each of these has as its objective the grid referencing, to 1 m precision, of each building with a postal address. Pinpoint reference the equivalent of the letterbox, that is the centre of the frontage of each building. Ordnance Survey will use a building centroid. These products, neither of which can yet provide national coverage, offer the potential of improving the grid reference associated with each postcode very significantly. A question remains as to whether a postcode should be represented by the grid reference of the first house, the middle house, or the geometric centre of all the houses within a unit postcode. It is also feasible, as has been demonstrated in Scotland and elsewhere, to represent a postcode as a space-filling polygon or as a line joining properties acting as a partial analogy to the postman's walk.

9.2.2 Postcode to ED links

Despite the problems of representing a postcode or an ED by a single point recorded with limited precision, several organisations have related postcodes to EDs. This computationally trivial, though time-consuming, task involved calculating the distances between the postcodes, as reflected by their grid references and the EDs represented by the references of their centroids. The ease of this operation encouraged the creation, after the 1981 Census, of directories that related each postcode to an ED. These directories were particularly widely used by geodemographic companies to assist clients in profiling the characteristics of populations whose home postcodes were known. Enumeration districts were classified into a number of 'life-style' categories by companies such as CCN, CACI, Pinpoint and Infolink.

Any client wishing to profile their customer list simply needed to ensure that the addresses on the list were postcoded. Then, by relating address to postcode, postcode to ED and ED to life-style category, life-style categories could be attached to the original customer records. The accuracy of this process is dependent on the accurate referencing of the locations of the clients, a reliable postcode to ED table, and a reliable social area classification. (It should be remembered that chapter 3 (II) discussed the factors that might affect the population statistics obtained for an ED, and that the way an ED was defined could strongly influence its aggregate character.) While little is known about the reliability of much of this conversion process, Gatrell (1989) has shown that relating the postcode-based references to EDs is highly unreliable with up to 40 per cent of addresses being allocated to the wrong ED. The pessimistic view would be that such inaccuracies make any attempts to relate address-based data to ED level census data, or derived products, such as sociodemographic classifications, useless. The optimistic view is that the value of census data is so great, and that no other source of data even approximates it, that even an imprecise locational match provides valuable information.

The 1991 data will be very much better referenced than ever before. In England and Wales the possibility of constructing the entire ED base from unit postcodes was explored, but considered too costly and complicated to put into practice. However, the decision was taken to enter the postcode associated with each census form into the census computer. This provided two opportunities, one was to produce an accurate postcode to ED look-up table. Where a postcode is broken between EDs the number of households in each ED is given. This means that any address can be matched to an ED perfectly, or with a known probability of being correct. Postcodes change over time, and it is important to ensure that when 1991 Census data are being matched, only the frozen April 1991 Central Postcode Directory or Postal Address File is used.

Secondly, a proposal was considered to release data for pseudo EDs, composed of the nearest fitting whole unit postcodes, if there was a demand. These EDs would not have had a mapped, or even an easily mappable, geographic base. They may have been broken, or, might have crossed administrative boundaries, but they would only have been constituted of complete postcodes. The pseudo EDs would have then ensured a complete and accurate match between any other address based, or postcoded data and the census output areas. However, concern over confidentiality led to a reconsideration of pseudo EDs. It was feared that some postcode-based pseudo EDs might only differ from the actual EDs by one or a few addresses. The possibility then arose that by taking the difference between the two sets of statistics the characteristics of an individual household could be revealed. Rather than risk such an occurrence, OPCS decided not to make pseudo ED-based data available for 1991. (For further details on the use of postcodes see Raper, Rhind and Shepherd, 1992 and Martin, 1992).

The use of census maps, and look-up tables to locate the areas for which statistics are available and to relate these to other data is very important, and perhaps the most important use of spatial references. It is not, however, the most obvious, which is the use of the spatial base of the census to display census data in map form rather than as tables of statistics.

9.3 DISPLAY

Perhaps the most famous social map of all time is Dr John Snow's map of deaths in two months near Broad Street during the London cholera outbreak in 1854 (reproduced in Tufte, 1983; Monmonier, 1991, see map 9.1). It records a vital event, death. However, it represents an obvious way (provided confidentiality is not considered important!) of representing many social distributions, and one which would be considered routine given our 'ideal' information system postulated above. Such a disaggregated way of displaying social phenomena is appropriate for certain, usually rare, events such as the occurrence of particular diseases, the locations of crimes or social delivery points. Social scientists other than geographers often query the validity of the map as a display device for social information. They argue that it places undue emphasis on a single independent variable, location, at the cost of many other variables which may be equally important. The geographers' response is that, while location in itself is relatively unimportant, space and spatial relationships are important.

Map 9.1 Dr John Snow's dot map of cholera deaths in Central London in September 1854

Source: Gilbert, 1958

Where something occurs in absolute space seldom matters, what is important is where it occurs *relative* to other places or events.

The location of any individual death on Dr Snow's map tells us nothing. However, the spatial clustering of deaths, and the proximity of those events to the Broad Street pump leads to a hypothesis that there may have been a connection between the two. This interpretation is also based on information that does not exist in the map. It is necessary to know that there was no piped water and that water is heavy and difficult to carry so that it will usually be collected from the nearest source. Aspects of disease aetiology and social behaviour must also be known, or assumed. So the importance of a map depends critically on the additional information that those interpreting the map bring with them.

There are certain important generalisations about socio-spatial relationships which those interpreting a map displaying social data will often take for granted, but which cannot be so easily interpreted from tabular output. Places which are close to each other will generally have similar social characteristics, gradients of social change across a city are much more common than sudden shifts. When using services, particularly health and social services, which are used by the least mobile members of the community, such as the elderly or women with young children, the nearest facility is likely to be used. When interpreting maps the reader will also have a mental image of the location of major town centres, the location of areas of public or owner-occupied housing, or the major transport routes through a city. On a census map, few if any of these may actually be depicted yet they provide an important background to the way the map is interpreted. Concepts such as the 'inner city' are most easily interpreted when particular social characteristics are identified with the wards or EDs surrounding a city centre. Patterns associated with poverty and affluence such as the distribution of unemployment, low car ownership, owning two or more cars and dominant owner occupation soon become 'imprinted' on the user of census maps and are used to interpret other factors such as economic activity, or family structure. Such relationships could, of course, be explored using other statistical techniques. However they would usually require appropriate hypotheses to be formulated beforehand. Tufte has discussed, in both his classic books on the display of social information (1983, 1990) the power of the map as an exploratory and hypothesis formulating device. He admires the power of maps to handle large quantities of data in a parsimonious and elegant way. It is for this reason that a dataset as rich and complex as the census, with a geographic base should be displayed and explored in maps.

Unfortunately, any powerful tool is open to abuse! Monmonier's provocatively entitled book *How to lie with maps* (1991) and Evans's (1977) quotation, where '... intuition, inspiration, legerdemain, and predetermined ideas ...' were cited as the basis of selecting class intervals, should warn the aspiring census mapper that all may not be as easy as it seems.

A large number of options exist when mapping census data. The cartographic representation must be chosen. Theoretically, and in our 'ideal' situation postulated above, this choice can be very open. In practice the choice is constrained by the geographic base of the census and the locational data that are available. There are three main 'families' of representations that can be used — point, line and area. Space filling area based maps, the familiar 'choropleth' map where areas based on census output boundaries are shaded or coloured according to the value of the variable being mapped, are the most common. The very familiarity of such maps often distracts census users from the possibility of alternative, perhaps more appropriate representations. Some of these alternatives are discussed below.

9.4 POINT MAPPING

Given the absence of individual census data and the incompleteness and high cost of address based grid references from Pinpoint or Ordnance Survey, point mapping in the most detailed sense would seldom appear to be an option in the United Kingdom. However, the two point locational references that were discussed above, the population centroid for EDs, and the postcode reference, can be used for mapping. Using symbols located on the population centroids of wards or EDs to represent the population of that area is an effective method. The Census Offices used a variety of the method to produce maps from the 1981 Census data. Data from ED centroids were laid over a mesh of grid squares, and aggregated before mapping where there were more than two EDs per square. Circular symbols were then mapped in any square with one or more ED centroids. A complex version of a point map, with age-sex pyramids located at the centres of the London boroughs, was used in the *Social atlas of London* (See map 9.2; Shepherd, Westway and Lee, 1974). Similar maps have been drawn which have included ward outlines, and have had symbols

Map 9.2 A point symbol map with age sex pyramids located at the centres of the London boroughs (1971 Census)

Source: Shepherd *et al.*, 1974

proportional to some characteristic of the populations of individual EDs located within them. Such a device goes some way towards overcoming the cartographic difficulty posed by the densest populations occupying the smallest areas on the map and the areas with the least dense population visually dominating the map. Pseudo-point distributions are available as options in some cartographic packages which will fill an area with a known boundary with a random pattern of dots whose density is proportional to a given variable. While the maps in such a case do not represent the location of individuals, or multiples of individuals, they give the impression of the point distribution that all census maps represent.

Point mapping can also be used in combination with area based mapping to represent a rare phenomenon, diagnoses of a particular illness for example, against an area-filled map representing some potentially explanatory social variable. The home address of the mothers of underweight babies, translated into a postcode and mapped using the postcode grid reference may be superimposed on a map showing car ownership (or some other proxy for affluence). Such a point map should be used with care. While the postcode grid reference is unlikely to identify an individual address, and thus breach confidentiality, it may appear to do so. In a rural area a 100 m postcode reference may be in close proximity to only one household; while that may or may not be the address where the particular event (e.g. birth, death illness or crime) took place, it may be interpreted as a breach of confidentiality by the occupants of that household. It is also usually the case that the data that is compared to the census, and is often available at the level of the individual address, is often very much more sensitive than the census data itself and its confidentiality must be protected. Point mapping can either breach that confidentiality, or appear to breach it. In either case great care must be taken in deciding what is publishable.

9.5 LINE MAPPING

While point and area based mapping may seem appropriate for population data, line mapping may appear a rather unusual way of presenting population patterns. It should be remembered however that point, line and areal patterns are all usually based on generalisations and aggregations of the underlying point pattern discussed above. The most obvious use of line maps in census mapping is to represent travel to work and other migratory patterns which are best represented by a directional line symbol linking the origin and the destination. The usual cartographic device is to make the width of the line proportional to the size of the flow, though this can cause difficulties where there are large flows into small, congested areas. Another original use of the line as a symbol was demonstrated by the Experimental Cartography Unit, Royal College of Art, 1971. Unit postcodes were represented by a line joining the properties that shared the postcode. The lines were then colour coded according to the value of some other variable, such as average rateable value. It would be possible to map census data in a similar way by colouring or symbolising streets, rather than complete areas. This is easy to do in the US because of the availability of the TIGER data (see chapter 3(II)). While such symbolism is seldom used for census data, it *is* used to show the catchment areas of schools and other facilities.

Another type of line map that was used for a pioneering social atlas (Rosing and Wood, 1971) is the isoline map, better known as a contour map. While, strictly speaking, a contour map can only display the shape of the land, isolines can be used to join any points with an equal quantity of anything being measured. Map 9.3

Map 9.3 An isoline representation of the concentration of council housing in Birmingham (1966 sample census) produced with SYMAP

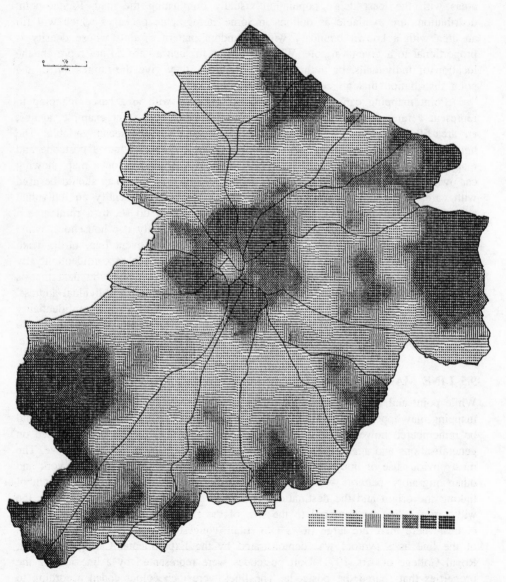

Source: Rosing and Wood, 1971

shows the concentration of council housing in Birmingham in 1966. It has the virtue that it can be constructed from a set of point values (in this case the ED centroids and the percentage of houses within each ED that were rented from local authorities). It shows general patterns very well, the concentration of public housing in the inner city and on 'overspill' estates at the edge of the city is clearly seen. The effect is one of an area based map, although the program (SYMAP) used to construct the map calculated the path of the contours and then shaded the area between the contour lines. Bracken and Martin (1989) have proposed similar methods for constructing three-dimensional population 'surfaces' to be used both for display and for further analysis of patterns related to the population.

There are many arguments for using such methods of displaying population distributions. The main advantage is that they can synthesise a spatial distribution from a very limited set of spatial references, a set of centroids. There is also a tendency to rationalise such a choice of method by extolling the virtues of representing population patterns as continuous over space, rather than broken artificially at boundaries as is the case with more conventional area-filled maps. This is less convincing; the distribution that we are trying to represent is one of discrete individuals, grouped into households which are laid out along streets and in largely urban parcels of land. Individual housing estates, be they public or private, tend to be relatively homogeneous in social terms. Individual streets will usually have a common standard of housing, unless they are being gentrified or are falling into decay. Much urban land and most rural land is in fact not populated and any adequate representation of the population should take account of this. Unfortunately most space filling techniques, be they isoline-based or areal-unit based, take little account of these characteristics of population. Dasymetric approaches, that involve overlaying a map of unpopulated spaces and excluding them from shaded or plotted populated area, have been recommended by cartographers for many years; unfortunately, because of the cost and difficulty of constructing such maps, they are seldom used. However, the technique was used in the wall chart maps produced from 1971 and 1981 Census data by the Census Offices and a variant of this technique has been used to construct an original map of population change between 1981 and 1991 (see Map 9.5) discussed below.

9.6 AREA BASED MAPPING

The most common way of displaying census data is by area. Polygons corresponding to census or administrative units are shaded according to a scale devised to categorise a continuous census variable (such as proportion of households lacking or sharing the use of a bath, Map 9.4). Producing such a map appears to be a childishly easy 'colouring by numbers' exercise. Why in that case does it warrant consideration? and why are so many choropleth maps so bad?

There are a number of areas of choice open to anyone who has decided to produce such a map, with or without the use of a computer. The first is the selection of an appropriate area to map; if both extensive sparsely populated rural areas and densely peopled urban areas are to appear on the same map, the contrast in sizes may make it difficult to shade each in an interpretable way, particularly if line or point symbols are used as in Map 9.2. It may be necessary to produce an inset at a larger scale to accommodate the most densely populated areas. The choice of areas

Map 9.4 A choropleth map showing percentage of households lacking or sharing a bath (1981 Census) for counties in England and Wales

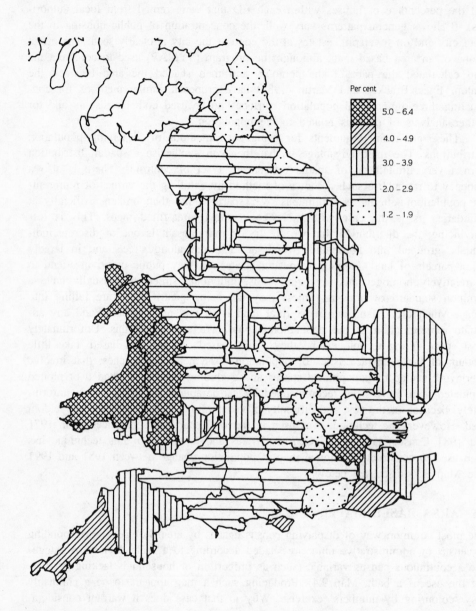

Source: Champion 1983

Map 9.5 Population in Britain 1991 and change since 1981

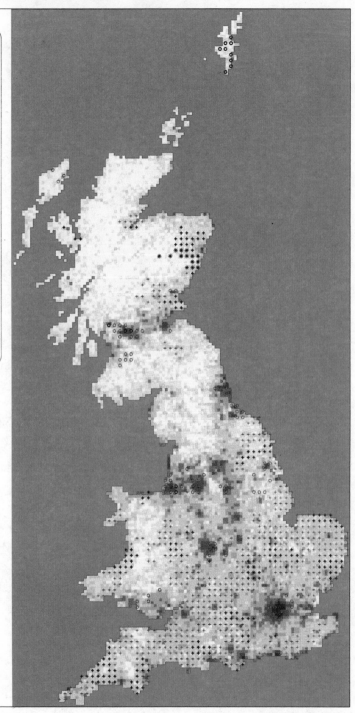

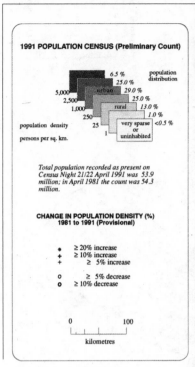

1991 POPULATION CENSUS (Preliminary Count)

population distribution

6.5 %
25.0 %
urban 29.0 %
rural 25.0 %
13.0 %
1.0 %
very sparse or uninhabited <0.5 %

5,000
2,500
1,000
250
25
1

population density
persons per sq. km.

Total population recorded as present on Census Night 21/22 April 1991 was 53.9 million; in April 1981 the count was 54.3 million.

**CHANGE IN POPULATION DENSITY (%)
1981 to 1991 (Provisional)**

∗   ≥ 20% increase
+   ≥ 10% increase
+   ≥ 5% increase

o   ≥ 5% decrease
O   ≥ 10% decrease

0   100
kilometres

Notes

Population density is based upon the count of population present in census night.

This map uses a modified form of the 'dasymetric' choropleth technique and was produced using GRIDMAP mapping software written at the University of Edinburgh as part of the research programme of RRL Scotland.

Source: Data Library and Computing Services, The University of Edinburgh. The University of Edinburgh and Crown Copyright 1991. All rights reserved.

The map, including details of how it has been constructed and data sources, is available from Data Library and Computer Services.

262

Map 9.6 A choropleth map, produced using simplified boundaries, to show the percentage of households renting their home from a local authority for each ward in Greater London (1971 Census)

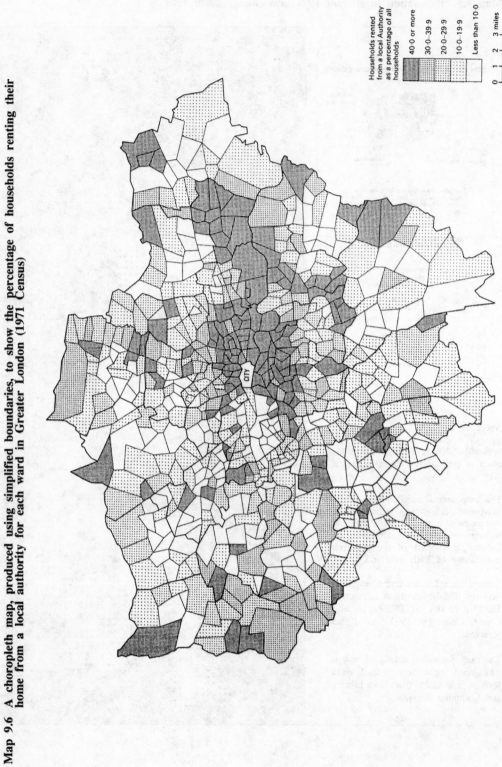

Households rented
from a local Authority
as a percentage of all
households

40·0 or more
30·0–39·9
20·0–29·9
10·0–19·9
Less than 10·0

CITY

0 1 2 3 miles

Source: Shepherd et al., 1974

to map may be constrained by a lack of boundary maps to trace, or, in digital form, to use on a computer. This may be overcome in a number of ways, one of which is to use a contoured surface as discussed above. More recently two other methods have been used, the most novel and interesting was perhaps the grid square technique used for the *People in Britain* atlas produced using 1971 Census data (CRU/OPCS /GRO (S), 1980). 1971 Census records were tagged with a 100 m grid reference in urban areas and with 1 km references elsewhere, which allowed the census data to be reaggregated into 1 km grid squares nationally. The usual confidentiality constraints led to the suppression of data for very sparsely populated squares, however, the boundary-independent maps that were produced in this atlas gave one of the most interesting views of British population patterns ever seen. Japanese census data is geocoded and displayed in this way (Tufte, 1990) and each address in that country is grid referenced for statistical purposes.

A variant of this technique on a rather coarser scale has been employed by a team from the ESRC Regional Research Laboratory for Scotland (Map 9.5). They have used 1991 population data for districts, mathematically apportioned to 1981 EDs assuming a proportionate increase or decrease in population across the whole of the district. The centroid grid references available for the 1981 EDs were then used to reaggreagate both the 1981 and the 1991 data to 5-km grid squares. This allows the dual purpose map, which displays both 1991 population density and the change in population since 1981, to be displayed using a combination of shading and symbol mapping. The advantage of this technique is that two aspects of a very large and complex dataset have been displayed in an easily understood way using relatively standard software and a modern medium priced printer.

Another common way of creating area-based maps in the absence of detailed boundary data is to manually, or automatically, create a simplified boundary. This was the choice taken by Shepherd, Westway and Lee (1974) (see map 9.6), for the *Social atlas of London*, before detailed digitised ward boundaries were available. The manual version used here maintained approximate area and shape, without producing excessively complex (but, realistic) boundaries.

An alternative approach is to use the ED or ward centroids to generate 'Theissen' polygons. These are space-filling simplified polygons, which have the characteristic that every point within the polygon is closer to that polygon's centroid than the centroid of any other polygon. Theissen polygon-based ED boundaries have been used for certain applications with 1981 ED data. While a neat solution to the problem of not having boundaries, this solution has probably been chosen because such polygons can be produced automatically as a function of several Geographical Information System (GIS) packages, rather than because of its inherent merits. More complex 'weighted' Theissen polygons can be produced which have boundaries adjusted to give centroids a larger or smaller catchment area depending on some attribute of that centroid; unfortunately this procedure often produces complex broken polygons that poorly represent ED boundaries or even simplifications of them. Such synthetic methods are likely to be unnecessary for the 1991 Census because high quality digitised boundaries are available at ED level in England and Wales and at unit postcode level in Scotland (see chapter 3 (I)).

After the choice of area, the second important decision that has to be taken is the choice of variables to be mapped, and their denominators. Area-based maps cannot be legitimately used to map absolute values because these are an artefact of the boundaries chosen. An appropriate denominator has to be found for each variable; for many variables at the household level, the proportion of households with a particular characteristic such as the percentage of owner-occupied households, is appropriate. For other variables, such as the number of single-parent families, the purpose of the map becomes important. If one is examining health or school services then single-parent families as a proportion of all families with children may be more appropriate than the number of single parent-families as a proportion of all households. The spatial patterns, and the interpretation of these two maps could be very different.

A problem with mapping rates, as opposed to absolute values, is that areas with very small populations can show great variability in the rates for particular variables due only to the value of the denominator being very small. The significance of a rate will depend on the size of the population involved. Visvalingham (1978) devised a measure based on the chi-squared statistic which takes account of this problem (see chapter 8, section 8.6.3). The measure was used in the *People in Britain* atlas, where the populations of individual kilometre grid squares varied greatly (very much more than the populations of EDs which are defined with a target population figure in mind). It has since been used by a number of other studies to good effect. Unfortunately few automated mapping packages offer a chi-square based classification for mapping purposes.

Once a variable and a denominator have been chosen it becomes important to decide how the variable will be classified into a number of discrete classes. There has been a controversy since computerised mapping, and in particular continuous map shading, techniques became available, as to whether classification was necessary at all. The balance of opinion suggests that continuous scales on maps are difficult to interpret and that it is part of the cartographer's task to make data understandable; the choice of an appropriate classification is part of that task. Evans (1977) offers a comprehensive review of classification techniques and Monmonier (1991) warns of the very different results that may be obtained by choosing different classification schemes for the same variable. Many choices need to be taken including: the number of classes; whether that number should be odd or even; the treatment of outliers, the treatment of highly skewed distributions; whether class boundaries fall on 'round' values, and the extent to which 'natural breaks' in data should be exploited. It is beyond the scope of this chapter to deal with these issues in detail; however, it is important to warn users of simple automated mapping packages that the 'default' options offered for classifying data will almost never be the most appropriate for any particular data set. Anyone wishing to produce maps to be used for policy making should refer to both Evans and Monmonier before deciding on a classification scheme, and should experiment with a range of options.

The appropriate use of colour and a particular classification scheme can help to deal with some of these issues. The design of choropleth maps involves a great many cartographic judgments that involve both art and science as well as a critical awareness of the census data itself and the way in which it relates to particular research or policy objectives. It is because there are so many difficult judgments, that there are so many poor maps and so few really good ones.

9.7 MAPPING TOOLS

In the same way that a word processor does not turn the average person into a great author, nor the CAD (computer aided design) program turn the doodler into an engineer or architect, mapping programs do not create cartographers. One-off maps are almost always produced more easily manually by tracing outlines and using press down lettering and shaded or coloured film to fill areas. Most cartographers wishing to produce the highest quality maps for publication still rely on manual methods, particularly when each map requires a slightly different design. Computers come into their own when a series of similar maps is to be produced; however, it is not always necessary to use specific mapping programs.

In the 1970s, before graphics displays and output devices were commonly available on computer systems, much effort went into the design of computer packages (notably SYMAP from the Harvard Computer Graphics Laboratory), which could produce maps on line printers that printed only characters. While no one would suggest using a word processor to 'type' maps made up of discrete characters, the use of such methods in the early days of computer mapping serves to illustrate the extent to which the method can become more important than the objective — to produce a clear readable map.

Perfectly acceptable maps can be produced, however, using the simple 'paintbrush' drawing programs distributed with many computer systems that run the Microsoft Windows environment. An advantage of such programs is that they do not require a particularly detailed boundary and can work with a scanned or roughly traced set of boundaries. It is up to the user to choose appropriate shading and shade each area using a 'fill' tool which allows a fill pattern to be selected from a 'palette' and applied evenly within a boundary. Better results can be obtained using more sophisticated drawing or CAD packages such as Corel Draw or AutoCAD. Such packages allow much more detailed boundaries to be used than is usually feasible with a simple drawing package. In each of these cases the computer 'knows' nothing about the identity of each area or the data related to it. The user makes the match between the data, the class it falls in and the appropriate symbol or shading pattern to represent it. These tools simply assist the drawing and the editing of a map rather than its overall construction.

Mapping packages such as GIMMS or MapViewer are graphically much less sophisticated than the more advanced drawing packages discussed above, but do take 'responsibility' for identifying the geographical areas that make up a map. Mapping programs need a set of digitised boundaries in a suitable format that identifies each boundary as belonging to a particular area. They also require a set of data which are either ordered to allow them to be matched to the boundaries, or are identified with the same codes as the boundaries. Care must be taken to ensure that this matching is correct; the most reliable methods match an area code in the data file with the same code in the boundary file. Methods based on an assumed order of data items or boundaries are more error prone.

Typically, mapping programs will have a number of preset classification routines for the data, and will allow user-defined classifications. Once the data has been classified, they will automatically match the appropriate area shading to the appropriate boundaries.

Mapping programs require a detailed set of digitised boundaries in a strict format specified by the authors of the particular program. Because of this, digitised boundaries usually need to be reformatted before they can be used in a different mapping package. The high cost and the lack of digitised boundaries has constrained census mapping in the past. In 1981 a set of ward boundaries commissioned by the

Department of Environment was sold to a wider community. For 1991 ED boundaries are available from at least two sources, the ED-Line Consortium and Graphical Data Capture Ltd, in formats suitable for a range of popular mapping packages (see chapter 3(I) section 3.5). ED boundaries and unit postcode boundaries will be available in Scotland. The availability of boundaries will not only encourage mapping of census data but will also encourage analysis using GIS software. Chapter 3(I) discusses 1991 Census boundary products in more details and provides contact points.

9.8 ANALYSIS

Many claims have been made, and expectations raised, concerning the analysis of census data using GIS software. In order to understand the issues it is important to understand how a GIS differs from a simpler mapping package. Like a mapping package, GIS software has increasingly sophisticated facilities for plotting maps comprising points, lines, areas and annotation. However, unlike mapping packages, which usually have a simple one-way link between a data file and the display of that data on a map, GIS software includes a more sophisticated database. The database can store attribute data that describes the points, lines and areas in the map. These attributes can be a range of data values associated with the items on the map, they can also be topological characteristics of those items. For example, the data in the database for a line segment would typically include the start point, the end point, the area to the left and the area to the right of the line. If the line represented a road the data may also include its classification, and traffic levels at different times of day. In addition to holding more data for the objects on the map, a GIS not only allows the way the object is displayed to reflect data values associated with it, it also allows an object to be selected on a graphical computer display and its characteristics to be queried, appearing as a data form on the screen. All objects with a particular characteristic may be chosen; for example, if an ED map is being displayed, all EDs with male unemployment rates above 15 per cent may be highlighted, or an individual ED might be selected and its unemployment rate queried.

The sophisticated two way link between map and underlying database is an important characteristic of a GIS, but for many commentators it is not enough to change a mapping package into a GIS. A range of analytical functions are required. These are of two sorts, the first is based on spatial search and the analytical combination of existing objects in the GIS maps to create new geographical objects. The second type of analysis (an area where GIS are still thought to be weak) is the statistical modelling of spatial relationships within the data in the GIS. An example of the former would be polygon overlay. Given a set of ED boundaries for which census data is available, and a second set of boundaries, for example police-beat boundaries, for which census data is not available, a GIS can overlay the two. The resulting smaller polygons have the characteristic that they fall entirely in a single beat and a single ED. The census characteristics of these can be estimated by calculating their area and apportioning the data from their EDs in proportion to the part of the ED that makes up each of the smaller beat/ED areas. Once these characteristics have been calculated, the partial ED areas can be reassembled to make up the beats, the apportioned data can be summed and hey presto, census data is available for new geographical areas. Is there a snag? Of course there is. The entire process presumes that the population and its characteristics were evenly spread across the

ED, a very unlikely assumption. If the assumption is not correct, the data calculated for each beat will be incorrect and, more seriously, the extent of that error can neither be calculated nor estimated reliably. Polygon overlay, a process that virtually defines a piece of software to be a GIS, was designed for applications using natural environmental data which is less likely to suffer from the probable uneven distribution of census data.

Another simple analytical benefit of GIS systems, which has been exploited for electoral redistricting applications, particularly in the US, is the ease with which areas and their data can be aggregated and reaggregated. A major advantage of the digitised census boundaries being made available for the 1991 Census is the fact that they record the census area on each side of any boundary line. As a result it becomes computationally easy to 'dissolve' boundaries and build larger units, with known characteristics from existing sets of boundaries. Until now SASPAC has offered facilities for building new census areas, but no file has existed which shows which EDs share common boundaries, so new areas have needed to be defined by looking up the ED maps. The digital boundaries have this contiguity information built into them and will also allow a contiguity table to be built up which will list each ED's neighbours. The generation of census data for new areas which comprise a complete set of EDs is much more reliable than the polygon overlay method, but still subject to the accumulated randomisation error discussed in chapter 8, section 8.6. Of course, once the contiguity table is available the region-building operation can be carried out without recourse to the maps or the graphical analysis facilities of the GIS; it becomes a table look up, or a database operation. In fact few of the graphical operations feasible in a GIS are going to be appropriate for census data. A GIS can carry out other types of searches against a set of polygons, it can search for points that fall in the polygon or for lines that cross the polygon, for example. However, given the absence of reliable and affordable point references for addresses at present, and the lack of a digitised street network, neither of these facilities will be exploitable early in the life of the 1991 data in much of the country.

Another characteristic of GIS is their ability to model areas on the basis of a 'buffering operation'. At smaller scales these offer the prospect of calculating the approximate characteristics of the population within a certain distance of a major road, for example (the buffer being a corridor either side of the road); or within a certain distance of a dangerous facility (a buffer around a point marking out a circular, or a series of circular, zones around that facility). In each case the resulting buffers are overlaid on census boundaries using the polygon overlay technique discussed above. If the zones are large in relation to the size of the EDs (unlike the police beats which were quite small in relation to EDs) the amount of error in the process, due to the incorrect inclusion or exclusion of parts of the population on the boundary of the zone, is likely to be relatively small and more reliable estimates can be obtained.

Statistical analysis facilities for such operations as spatial correlation, regression, autocorrelation and the estimation of distance decay functions, are not yet available in most GIS software. Data have to be extracted from the GIS and analysed in other packages. Unfortunately the weakness of the non-graphical analytical capabilities of GIS and the frequently inappropriate nature of the graphical analysis, lead to GIS often being used, and seen, primarily as a mapping tool. This is a job that is usually done better by simpler mapping packages or other graphics programs.

What GIS *does* contribute is a realisation that given appropriate data structures (such as the ED contiguity table or the postcode-to-ED lookup table), most of the analysis that one is likely to want to do using census data is better done using a conventional relational database.

This is not to say that GIS has no future in this area: once better point references for addresses, and digitised street maps are available, it will become possible to use GIS to integrate data from a range of sources more reliably. Further research is also required (such as the work of Flowerdew and Green, 1989) on the accuracy of a range of analytical operations on zonal data, before census data can be used reliably for areas other than those for which it was collected and simple aggregations of them.

9.9 CONCLUSION

The 1991 Census data, and the associated digitised boundary information, marks an important incremental step in the geographical referencing of the census and the opportunities offered for mapping and analysis. The opportunity to draw maps and to analyse data at a finer level of resolution can lead to pitfalls as well as successes and the current generation of mapping and GIS tools offer little or no protection against these.

Important research areas remain to be explored concerning how census data is actually used and the way in which the cartographic presentation and analysis of census data influences policy makers. Only once those questions are answered will we be able to assess the adequacy of our present tools and methods and the accuracy of estimation that we should be aiming for.

The mapping of census data is not as simple as it may at first appear; the best rule of thumb for those working with census data for the first time is to keep presentations and analysis as simple as possible, and seek expert advice from cartographers, spatial statisticians and practitioners in the given field, before embarking on a time-consuming and possibly costly exercise.

10 Migration, transport and workplace statistics from the 1991 Census

Robin Flowerdew and Anne Green

10.1 INTRODUCTION TO MIGRATION, TRANSPORT AND WORKPLACE STATISTICS[1]

The 1991 Census included questions for each respondent about place of residence one year before the Census date and, for those aged 16 and over who had a paid job, about the address of the workplace. These questions are slightly different from the others in the census in that they are concerned with mobility and they allow linkage to be made between two places (current and previous residence, or home and workplace). Most other questions are specific to one place, the respondent's home, but these questions relate to movement or flow between an origin and a destination. A full analysis of these origin-destination flow data is thus more complicated than the analysis of the other place-specific census questions. Accordingly, OPCS and GRO(S) provide tabulations in the form of large matrices connecting places of origin and places of destination. These matrices are referred to as the Special Migration Statistics (SMS) and the Special Workplace Statistics (SWS), and their special nature raises special problems (and special opportunities) for people wishing to use them. These problems are discussed in this chapter, along with some suggestions for the types of analysis which they will permit.

Place-to-place flow data of this kind have been produced since the 1966 Census, although the way in which the output is presented has changed considerably between 1981 and 1991 (see Denham and Rhind (1983) for a discussion of the 1981 datasets). They are time-consuming to produce because of the necessity to examine workplace address or previous home address and to relate the postcode to census geography; in some cases, missing or incorrect postcodes, or addresses incomplete in other ways, make this process harder. In this respect, SMS and SWS data involve much more processing effort, and hence have more 'value added' than most other census products, and are usually relatively late in making their appearance.

In addition to the SMS and SWS, however, census data on migration, transport (including car availability) and workplace are reported in other census output, including published reports and the Small Area (SAS) and Local Base Statistics (LBS).

---

[1] The Special Workplace and Special Migration Statistics will not be available until some months after this book has been published. However, to avoid later confusion they are referred to in the past tense.

Although the main focus of the chapter is on SMS and SWS, these other forms of output are discussed in the early sections of the chapter. This is followed by a discussion of how the origin-destination flow matrices are generated; by some points to bear in mind when using these flow statistics, and by some research issues and applications, especially the use of the SWS for deriving travel-to-work areas.

For simplicity, the names of the areal units used by the census in England and Wales are normally given in the text; references to wards in the chapter are normally applicable also to postcode sectors in Scotland, and references to counties are normally applicable also to regions in Scotland.

10.2 MIGRATION DATA IN THE PUBLISHED REPORTS AND SAS

Question H9 of the 1991 Census (see appendix A) asked the form-filler whether the address of each person in the household was the same as one year ago. If it was not, the address and postcode on 21 April 1990 were requested. Children born since that date were indicated using a tick box.

10.2.1 Definition of migration

The term 'migration' has been defined in different ways by different investigators (see Lewis, 1982), often involving the crossing of a boundary between settlements or administrative areas. The census takes the simplest possible approach, defining a *migrant* as: 'a person with a different usual address one year ago to that at the time of the Census' (OPCS and GRO(S), 1992b). Thus a migrant may have moved half-way round the world or just next door.

A *migrant household* is defined as a household whose head is a migrant (the *head of household* is the first usually resident adult mentioned on the census form). A *wholly moving household* is a household all of whose resident members aged one year and over were migrants with the same postcode of usual residence one year before the census (OPCS and GRO(S), 1992b; see also chapter 2).

It should be noted that, in cases where a person moved more than once during the year preceding the census date, only the net result of these moves is recorded. Thus people moving during the year before the census but returning to their original address before enumeration would not be recorded as migrants. People resident at A one year before the census who moved from A to B and then from B to C before the census date would be recorded as migrants from A to C.

Different *types of move* may be distinguished based on the importance of the boundaries that have been crossed; thus for certain purposes migrants may be distinguished according to whether they have migrated within or between wards, districts, counties, standard regions and countries. It should be borne in mind that the census includes internal migrants within Great Britain and immigrants to Great Britain, but it cannot of course include emigrants from Great Britain, who will not have been enumerated by the census. It should also be pointed out that these boundaries may be somewhat arbitrary and artificial; sometimes a move wholly within an administrative unit may be longer and far more significant for the person concerned than a very local move which happens to cross a county boundary.

Migrants may also be distinguished on the basis of the *distance moved* (based on National Grid references for the previous and current postcodes as given in the Central Postcode Directory (chapter 3 (I)). Tabulations exist of the number of migrants of all these types, disaggregated for various types of areal unit, and broken down according to various categories of age, sex, economic activity, occupation, and many other variables.

10.2.2 National and Regional Migration Reports: tables available

A series of published reports are issued on migration; their structure and composition are broadly similar to those issued for the 1981 Census, but there are a number of significant new tables. A *National Migration Report* for Great Britain is issued in two parts, the first containing tabulations relating migration to those (easy to code) topics that are coded for 100 per cent of households, and the second containing tabulations involving topics that are harder and thus more expensive to code, based on a 10 per cent sample. The second part contains tables relating migration to socioeconomic group (SEG), employment status, standard occupational classification and industry division.

In addition, a series of *Regional Migration Reports* are produced, one for each standard region of Great Britain. Like the *National Migration Report*, each *Regional Migration Report* is issued in two parts, Part 1 based on 100 per cent data and Part 2 based on 10 per cent sample data. Outlines of the tables are given in *User Guides 17* (National) and *22* (Regional).

The tables in Part 1 of the *National Migration Report* record the number of migrants by a series of different variables. These include:

- age
- sex
- marital status
- economic position
- household amenities
- car availability

- persons per room
- tenure
- household composition
- limiting long-term illness
- ethnic group
- residence in communal establishments

Some of these variables are recorded for migrant households as well as, or instead of, individual migrants. In all cases, these tables are supplied for Great Britain and separately for England, Scotland and Wales. In the case of age, sex, marital status and ethnic group, they are also provided for regions and for conurbations. The units for which these data are available are:

- Great Britain
- England and Wales
- England
- Regions
- Metropolitan counties
- Inner London
- Outer London
- Main urban centres (other)

- Regional remainders
- Wales
- Cardiff District
- Wales remainder
- Scotland
- Scotland (main urban centres)
- Scotland remainder

In addition, a table is provided showing the numbers of males and females migrating from each of these units to each of the other units, allowing the construction of an inter-regional or inter-conurbation migration matrix. Another table provides this information broken down by age group (normally five-year bands).

Certain tables disaggregate migration according to the type of move. The categories used for defining the type of move are not the same for all tables, but in general they allow the user to distinguish between intra-district, inter-district, inter-county, inter-regional and international migrants. The number of out-migrants from an area may also be available, provided they have not left Great Britain. Type of move can be related to all the variables mentioned above, though not to area of origin.

Lastly, distance of move is available for each of the areas listed above, further disaggregated by age group. Six distance categories are available measured in kilometres: 0–4, 5–9 10–19, 20–49, 50–79, and 80 and over.

Part 2 of the *National Migration Report* contains tables relating type of move to SEG, employment status, occupation and industry for England, Wales and Scotland. For the regions and conurbations, distance of move is related to SEG, occupation and industry. All these tables are disaggregated by sex, and the table showing type of move by SEG is also disaggregated by age group.

The *Regional Migration Reports* contain information on migration at the county and district level within the region concerned. Part 1 includes a district-level migration matrix (for moves within the region only), disaggregated by sex. For each district, it also includes figures on the number of migrants from each region and conurbation (as given in the list above). A similar table is available at the district level giving the destinations of out-migrants, again disaggregated by sex. There is also a table giving the sex, age, employment status and type of move for in-migrants to each district.

Other tables in the *Regional Migration Reports* (Part 1) are available only at the level of the region, metropolitan counties (if any), other main urban centres, and regional remainders. At these levels, type of move is cross-tabulated with age, sex, economic position, household amenities, car availability, persons per room, tenure, household composition, limiting long-term illness, ethnic group and residence in communal establishments. The *Regional Migration Reports* (Part 2) contain tables relating type of move to economic position, employment status, occupation and industry. They also include data on the SEG of both in-migrants to, and out-migrants from, each of the other regions.

10.2.3 Migration data from the SAS and LBS

Chapter 8 discusses the nature and format of the SAS and LBS, which supply a vast amount of information for areal units down to the level of the enumeration district (SAS) or ward (LBS). Some data on migration are available in this form, considerably more than was the case for the 1981 Census. This section describes the data available in the LBS, a subset of which is also included in the SAS (details are given in *User Guide* 3).

For each small area, the numbers of male and female migrants are recorded, split according to age group (five-year bands) and the type of move. Six categories of move are used: intra-ward, inter-ward, inter-district, inter-county, inter-regional, and international (i.e. from outside Great Britain). In addition, because moves between neighbouring districts and between neighbouring counties may be short-distance flows which happen to cross a boundary, these are separately recorded. A similar breakdown is also available for wholly moving households, which are themselves disaggregated by household type. The ethnic group of migrants is also tabulated.

Another table (in LBS only) shows the number of households with migrant heads according to the age of the household head, his or her economic activity and tenure. Additional tabulations give the number of households with migrant heads according to the number of rooms, persons usually resident, persons per room and household composition. The number of migrants in communal establishments of different types is also recorded. At the 10 per cent level, a breakdown of migrants by SEG and household composition is available. Lastly (in LBS only), migrants in the armed forces are enumerated according to age group and marital status.

10.2.4 Migration data from the OPCS Longitudinal Study and the Samples of Anonymised Records

Census data on migration are also available at the individual level from the OPCS Longitudinal Study (LS) and the Samples of Anonymised Records (SARs). Both datasets are described elsewhere in this book (chapters 11 and 12).

A good deal of work has already been accomplished using the migration data in the LS (e.g. Congdon, 1989; Fielding, 1989; Grundy, 1989). In addition to the data in each census linking address at the census date to address one year before, it is of course possible to derive migration indicators based on changes in region of residence between the censuses. OPCS derived an indicator to record whether an LS member changed address between the 1971 and 1981 Censuses and are considering the possibility of deriving a similar indicator of migration between 1981 and 1991. This latter indicator would be based on a comparison of the LS member's postcode of usual residence in 1981 with that given in 1991.

Creeser (1991) has shown how migration data in the LS can be used to analyse the relationship between migration and tenure. Congdon (1992) reviews the potential of the LS for migration studies, with particular reference to the analytical techniques that can be employed. As he points out, the main disadvantage of the LS is that the size of the sample prevents data being released for small areas because of confidentiality constraints; however, he suggests that inter-county flows should be obtainable in most cases.

The SAR data contain information on migration for the samples of individuals and households, along with a vast range of other information. They are available only for large districts or combinations of districts (with a minimum resident population of 120,000). In both the LS and the SAR, the distance of move in kilometres (for migrants within Great Britain) is available, offering the potential of cross-tabulating migration distance against a wide range of other variables.

10.3 TRANSPORT AND WORKPLACE DATA IN THE PUBLISHED REPORTS, SAS AND SPECIAL WORKPLACE STATISTICS (SWS)

10.3.1 Journey-to-work data

Question 18 of the 1991 Census (reproduced in appendix A) asked, for people aged 16 years or over and in employment, the *mode* by which the longest part, by distance, of the daily journey to work was normally made. Those using different means on different days were asked for the means most often used. Ten categories were identified on the census form: British Rail train, underground/tube/metro, bus/minibus/coach (public or private), motorcycle/scooter/moped, driving a car or van, passenger in a car or van, pedal cycle, on foot, other (with space to enter details) and a category 'working mainly at home'.

10.3.2 Car availability data

Question H5 of the 1991 Census asked respondent households to indicate the *number of cars and vans* normally available for use by members of the household (excluding visitors). Cars and vans provided by employers were to be included if normally available for household use, but those used only for carrying goods were to be excluded. Four categories were identified on the census form: none, one, two, and three or more.

10.3.3 Workplace data

Question 17 of the 1991 Census asked, for persons aged 16 years or over and in employment (excluding those on a government employment or training scheme), the *full address and postcode* of their *workplace*. Persons employed on a site for a long period were requested to give the address of the site, while those not working regularly at one place but reporting daily to a depot or other fixed address, were asked to give details of that address. Individuals not reporting daily to a fixed address or working mainly at home were shown by a tick in the relevant boxes. Members of the Armed Forces were instructed to leave question 17 blank.

10.3.4 Tables available in published reports

Tables on *workplace and transport to work* (see *User Guide 20* for details of the table outlines) are based on a 10 per cent sample processing of the census information on people in households and in communal establishments from the SWS. They are published in two volumes: one for Great Britain and the other for Scotland (in 1981 there were publications for England and Wales, and for Scotland). In the Great Britain volume Scotland is treated as a region, and no analyses at lower area levels within Scotland are provided. In addition to the standard national, regional and local authority areas normally identified in the census volumes, the *Workplace and Transport to Work Report* includes nine city centre areas: London West End and City, Manchester and Salford, Liverpool, Sheffield, Newcastle upon Tyne, Birmingham, Leeds, Edinburgh, and Glasgow, and three special areas (for the first time) covering Heathrow airport, London docklands and Gatwick airport. Those resident outside Great Britain but with workplaces in Great Britain are also shown separately.

Eight tables on *workplace and transport to work* appear in the national reports of the same name (see table 10.1 for details of the three main *workplace type* categories and their subcategories):

(i) *Resident and working populations*: a cross-tabulation of residents aged 16 and over economically active by sex; (for the first time in 1991) hours worked weekly for females (15 hours and under, 16–30 hours, and 31 hours and over); economic position (in employment and unemployed); and employees and self-employed persons aged 16 and over by sex and hours worked for females by residence/workplace type.

(ii) *Area of workplace*: a cross-tabulation of employees and self-employed persons aged 16 and over by area of residence by area of workplace by sex.

Table 10.1 Details of workplace types, 1991 Census

Main category	Detailed category	Description
	1	Total residents (economically active)
	2	In employment
	3	Unemployed
	4	Working in the area
I	5	Resident and working in the area
	6	Workplace at home
	7	No fixed workplace
	8	Workplace not stated - armed forces
	9	Workplace not stated - other
II	10	Working in area, resident outside
	11	Resident outside Great Britain
III	12	Resident in area, working outside
	13	Workplace outside Great Britain
Notes	I + II	Total population working in the area
	I + III	Total employed population resident in the area

Source: Topic Statistics — Workplace and Transport to Work Prospectus. *1991 Census User Guide 20.*

(iii) *Area of residence*: a cross-tabulation of employees and self-employed persons aged 16 and over by area of workplace by area of residence by sex.

(iv) *Occupation and industry*: a cross-tabulation of employees and self-employed persons aged 16 and over by sex by Standard Occupational Classification major and submajor groups and industry divisions by workplace type.

(v) *Social class and socioeconomic group*: a cross-tabulation of employees and self-employed persons aged 16 and over by sex by social class and SEG by workplace type.

(vi) *Mode of transport*: a cross-tabulation of mode of transport to work by workplace type, sex and hours worked weekly for females, for employees and self-employed persons aged 16 and over.

(vii) *Distance and transport to work*: a cross-tabulation of mode of transport to work by sex and hours worked weekly for females by distance to work (less than 2, 2–4, 5–9, 10–19, 20–29, 30–39, and 40 km and over, measured as a straight line between the postcode of residence and the postcode of workplace) by means of transport to work for employees and self-employed persons aged 16 and over (see figure 10.1 showing layout). In interpreting *distance* statistics it is worth noting that anomalies in addresses of residences (e.g. persons having a temporary residence near their workplace with a usual residence elsewhere, such as weekly commuters) would result in an incorrect distance to work and a seemingly implausible means of transport to work over a long distance.

(viii) *Car availability:* a cross-tabulation of transport to work mode by number of cars available to household (none, one, two, and three or more) by sex with hours worked weekly for females, for employees and self-employed persons aged 16 and over.

The topic report on *Housing and availability of cars*, based on 100 per cent of the census information, is published in two volumes: one for Great Britain and a

Figure 10.1 Outline of a published table on workplace and transport to work, 1991

Table 7 Distance and transport to work

Great Britain, England and Wales, England, regions, metropolitan
counties, Inner London, Outer London, regional remainders, Wales,
Scotland, resident outside Great Britain

PERSONS AGED 16 AND OVER IN EMPLOYMENT											10% sample
Sex and distance to work in kilometres	TOTAL PERSONS	Transport to work									
		British Rail train	Under-ground train	Bus	Car		Motor cycle	Pedal cycle	On foot	Other	Not stated
					Driver	Passenger					
TOTAL PERSONS											
Workplace stated											
Distance to work											
Less than 2 km											
2- 4km											
5- 9km											
10-19km											
20-29km											
30-39km											
40km and over											
Workplace at home		xxxx	xxxx	xxxx	xxxx	xxxx	xxxx	xxxx	xxxx	xxxx	xxxx
No fixed workplace					Scottish volume areas to include:-						
Workplace outside GB					Scotland						
Workplace not stated					regions						
Males					districts						
Workplace stated					Islands Areas						
Distance to work					resident outside Great Britain						
Less than 2 km					(workplace in Scotland)						
2- 4km											
5- 9km					Stub repeats for females						
10-19km					Working 15 hours and under						
20-29km					Working 16-30 hours						
30-39km					Working 31 hours and over						
40km and over					Working hours not stated						
Workplace at home		xxxx	xxxx	xxxx	xxxx	xxxx	xxxx	xxxx	xxxx	xxxx	xxxx
No fixed workplace											
Workplace outside GB											
Workplace not stated											
Females											
Wordplace stated											
Distance to work											
Less than 2 km											
2- 4km											
5- 9km											
10-19km											
20-29km											
30-39km											
40km and over											
Workplace at home		xxxx	xxxx	xxxx	xxxx	xxxx	xxxx	xxxx	xxxx	xxxx	xxxx
No fixed workplace											
Workplace outside GB											
Workplace not stated											

Source: *1991 Census User Guide 20*, Table 7.

separate volume for Scotland. Four tables in the published reports include information on car availability (see *User Guide 12* for table outlines):

(i) *Cars and housing*: a cross-tabulation for households of number of cars by tenure, household space type and amenities.

(ii) *Household size and cars*: a cross-tabulation for households and persons in households of number of cars by household size (number of persons in household) and number of rooms.

(iii) *Cars and dependent children*: a cross-tabulation for households and persons in households of number of cars by household composition (children), number of dependent children in households and age of dependent children.

(iv) *Cars and pensioners*: a cross-tabulation for households and persons in households of number of cars by household composition (pensionable age) and number of persons of pensionable age in households.

10.3.5 Transport and workplace data from the SWS

Nine standard SWS tables provide transport and workplace information (see table 10.2). The tables are produced in three sets:

Table 10.2

Standard SWS Tables, 1991

Table no.	Description	Cell count
1	Economic position and age *(Set A, B & C)*	54
2	Hours worked by family position *(Set A & B)*	60
	Hours worked *(Set C)*	10
	Family position *(Set C)*	12
3	Type of workplace: *Set A*	18
	Set B	16
	Set C: not required as categories covered in columns of matrix	0
4	Distance to work *(Set A, B & C)*	16
5	Transport to work *(Set A, B & C)*	22
6	Cars available in households *(Set A, B & C)*	10
7	Occupation (sub major groups) *(Set A, B & C)*	48
8	Social class and socio-economic group *(Set A, B & C)*	54
9	Industry divisions and classes: *Set A*	292
	Set B	288
	Set C	48
Aggregate of cells:	*Set A*	574
	Set B	572
	Set C	274

Source: Special Workplace Statistics. *1991 Census User Guide 36.*

Set A: for employees or self-employed residents in each zone (i.e. a customer specified area) of residence;

Set B: for employees or self-employed persons with a workplace in each workplace
zone;

Set C: for employees or self-employed persons with residence to workplace trips
between residence and workplace zones, between residence zones to areas
outside the workplace zones, and into workplace zones from areas outside the
residence zones.

10.3.6 Transport data from the LBS and SAS

Two tables in the 10 per cent LBS and SAS provide information on transport to
work. The first is *travel-to-work and socioeconomic group* (with nine SEG categories
identified), providing a cross-tabulation of the full travel-to-work mode disaggregation
by SEG for all resident employees and self-employed aged 16 years and over, and
for residents and self-employed residents in households with no car, one, two, and
three or more cars. The second is *travel-to-work and car availability*, providing a
cross-tabulation at the household level of car availability (no car, one car, and two
or more cars) by number of resident employees or self-employed aged 16 or over

277

(one, two, and three or more) by travel-to-work mode (various categories involving combinations of use of car and public transport).

10.3.7 Transport and Workplace data from the LS and the SARs

The following data from the 1971 and 1981 SAS are available in the OPCS Longitudinal Study (LS) for the ward of enumeration: *one-car households*, *two-car households*, proportion of workers *walking to work*, and proportion of workers *travelling to work by bus or train*. For 1991 the LS also includes information on all 10 per cent variables (including *place of work*, *mode of transport to work* and *distance to work*) for the LS member, the LS member's spouse, and for other family or household members. Although in 1991 *place of work* information has been postcoded and computerised, the need to maintain confidentiality means that postcodes are not available for analysis, but can be used to provide a linkage to other geographical areas (Creeser, 1991). In 1981, the workplace and transport to work variables were not coded; although other variables, including car availability, were coded. In 1971, all variables were fully coded; workplace and transport to work are present for the LS member and, if female, her spouse. Workplace is coded to the local authority level.

The SAR individual and household samples contain variables relating to *number of cars*, *distance to work* and *transport to work mode*. In addition there is a *workplace* variable (the *usual workplace* variable referred to in chapter 2) including the following major categories: working at home (including no fixed workplace), working inside district of usual residence, working outside district of usual residence but within Great Britain, and working outside Great Britain.

10.4 GENERATION OF ORIGIN–DESTINATION FLOW STATISTICS

10.4.1 Postcoding of statistics

Transport and workplace statistics: those filling in 1991 Census forms were requested (as in 1981) to provide the address and postcode (if known) of the place of work of each person who was aged 16 years or over and in a job the previous week. For those respondents providing no postcode or an incomplete postcode, lists of workplace establishments from the 1989 Census of Employment were searched in order to obtain the postcode. Where a full postcode was not obtained, the case was treated as *not stated*. Members of the Armed Forces were also assigned to the *not-stated* category for security reasons. Persons working on off-shore installations were treated as if working outside Great Britain.

Migration statistics: question 9 in the 1991 Census, on usual address one year ago, was used in the derivation of migration statistics. A person whose former address and current address were different was classified as a one-year migrant. As with the workplace data, the postcode of the former address was used to assign the address to a ward. Only about 45 per cent of respondents in 1981 supplied the postcode for their former address; for the remainder, OPCS attempted to impute the data (Manchester Computing Centre, 1989). Non-responses to question 9 were assigned a non-migrant code or a migrant (origin not stated) code by the edit/imputation system. If there was no postcode given and the address was too incomplete for a postcode to be assigned, the response was coded as migrant (origin not stated).

10.4.2 Geographical organisation of the data sets

The geographical organisation of the SWS (Set C) origin–destination flow statistics is relatively straightforward. The main options for specifying residence/origin zones (i) and workplace/destination zones (j) are:

England and Wales
(a) i and j local authority wards or districts
(b) i and j postcode sectors
(c) EDs (England and Wales) for residence (i) and aggregations of postcodes for workplace (j)

Scotland
(a) i and j local authority wards (based on best-fit of output areas) or districts
(b) i and j postcode sectors
(c) i and j output areas or aggregations of output areas

(Three additional destination categories are identified for workplace destination: no fixed workplace, not stated or inadequately described, and outside Great Britain.)

It is possible to use the origin–destination matrix to identify movements within a zone, movements out of zone i to zone j, and movements into zone i from zone j.

The geographical organisation of the 1991 Special Migration Statistics (SMS) has been substantially changed from that used in the 1981 SMS. The SMS for the 1981 Census had a complicated geographical organisation, because of the need to observe confidentiality constraints. One set of data, known in 1981 as SMS(2), were straightforward in that all data were available as ward-to-ward flows, with additional categories for countries outside the United Kingdom and for 'origin not stated'. However, they were not disaggregated except by sex.

Another 1981 set, SMS(1), included data disaggregated by age, marital status, economic position and tenure. Five types of movement could in principle be iden-tified: within ward, from ward to district, from district to ward, from countries outside Great Britain to ward, and from origins not stated to ward. Any of the five types of movement, however, could have been 'thresholded up' to the next highest geographical level (i.e. produced only for a larger geographical area), if the total number of recorded movements was less than or equal to 25 (Manchester Computing Centre, 1989). These confidentiality measures and the associated complexity of the geographical zoning system meant that most of the flows between wards were not in practice available, greatly restricting the value of the data set as a research tool below the county level.

Because of these problems, the geographical organisation of the SMS was re-vised for the 1991 Census. For 1991, SMS Set 1 includes all inter-ward flows which are subject to no confidentiality restrictions, with disaggregation available by sex and age group only. The same disaggregations are available for intra-ward moves, from any ward to all destinations, to any ward from all origins, to any ward from indi-vidual countries outside Great Britain, and to any ward from origins not stated.

SMS Set 2 for 1991 is not offered as standard at the ward level, but is available for all district-to-district flows (though in modified form if confidentiality requirements are not met). Users of the 1981 SMS data should note that SMS(1) in 1981 corresponds with SMS Set 2 in 1991 and SMS(2) in 1981 corresponds with SMS Set 1 in 1991!

SMS Set 2 for 1991 contains inter-district migrant flows disaggregated by sex and five-year age groups; it also contains the numbers of wholly moving households making up each flow. If there are at least 10 migrants between any two districts, inter-district flows are also given disaggregated by marital status, ethnic group, limiting long-term illness, economic position and Gaelic and Welsh speaking (only in Scotland and Wales respectively and only in and between areas within Wales and Scotland respectively). If there are at least 10 wholly moving households, disaggregation by tenure and economic position of the household head is also available. The majority of inter-district flows are likely to be affected by these limitations (based on 1981 experience) but most flows between districts reasonably close to each other and most flows between large cities will not be affected.

In addition to data for district-to-district flows, SMS Set 2 is available (subject to the thresholds given above) for intra-district migration, from any district to all destinations, to any district from all origins, to any district from individual countries outside Great Britain and to any district from origins not stated.

A third data set, SMS Set 3, is also available. The information in SMS Set 3 is identical to that in SMS Set 2 except that flows are available for groups of districts specified on the basis of contiguity. The flows for which Set 3 are provided are as follows:

(i)   within each district;
(ii)   from each district to every other district in the same county and contiguous counties;
(iii)   from each district to each non-contiguous county;
(iv)   from each district to all destinations (total outflow);
(v)   to each district from every other district in the same county and contiguous counties;
(vi)   to each district from each non-contiguous county;
(vii)   to each district from individual countries outside Great Britain;
(viii) to each district from origins not stated; and
(ix)   to each district from all origins (total inflow).

The advantages of Set 3 are that the threshold criteria are more likely to be met for these aggregated flows, and hence disaggregated data can be provided.

The discussion so far has identified the standard SMS output geography. However, for 1991 data, census users can define their own areas of origin and destination, which can be any aggregations of wards. If the user-defined areas have 25,000 residents or more, confidentiality restrictions are the same as for SMS Sets 2 and 3. If they have less than 25,000 residents and less than 10 migrants, they will be amalgamated with neighbouring areas until one of these constraints is satisfied. No statistics will be produced for user-defined areas which will allow flows below these thresholds to be calculated by comparison with other statistics available. The objective of this service is to allow users to obtain SMS data for such areas as functional

Figure 10.2   Tables outlines from the Special Migration Statistics

Table 1

All migrants		
Age	Sex	
	Male	Female
1-15		
16-29		
30-44		
45-Pens.age		
Pens.age+		

Table 2

Wholly moving households; residents in wholly moving households	
Wholly moving households	Residents in wholly moving households

Table 3

All migrants		
Age	Sex	
	Male	Female
1-4		
5-9		
10-14		
15		
16-19		
20-24		
25-29		
30-34		
35-39		
40-44		
45-49		
50-54		
55-59		
60-64		
65-69		
70-74		
75-79		
80-84		
85+		

Table 4

All migrants			
Sex	Marital status		
	Single	Married	Widowed/ divorced
Male			
Female			

Table 5

All migrants			
Ethnic group			
White	Black groups	Indian, Pakistani and Bangladeshi	Chinese and Other

Table 6

All migrants		
	With limiting long-term illness	Without limiting long-term illness
In households		
Not in households		

Figure 10.2 - *continued*

Table 7

Migrants aged 16 and over						
Economic position						
Self employed	Other employed	Unemp- loyed	Retired	Student (inact)	Other inactive	Student (active)

Table 8 (England and Wales version)

Wholly moving households		
Tenure		
Owner occupied	Rented from LA / New Town	Other rented

Table 8 (Scotland version)

Wholly moving households			
Tenure			
Owner occupied	Rented from LA	Rented from NT / Scottish Homes	Other rented

Table 9

Wholly moving households						
Sex of head of household		Economic position of head of household				
Male	Female	Self employed	Other employed	Un- employed	Retired	Other inactive

Table 10

Residents in wholly moving households						
Sex of head of household		Economic position of head of household				
Male	Female	Self employed	Other employed	Un- employed	Retired	Other inactive

Table 11 (Scotland version)

Migrants resident in Scotland who speak Gaelic

Table 11 (Wales version)

Migrants resident in Wales who speak Welsh

Source: Special Migration Statistics *1991 Census User Guide 35*.

regions, travel-to-work areas, health areas, and other units for which they were not produced in 1981. Proposals for such output areas should be sent to Census Customer Services, who will refer the proposals back to the customer if the original suggestions contain sub-threshold flows. OPCS Census Customer Services at Titchfield will also provide details on any user-defined SMS already ordered and/or available (see chapter 3(I) for information).

10.5 CHARACTERISTICS OF MIGRANTS AND COMMUTERS

The 1991 SMS and SWS tables will allow researchers to find out fairly detailed information about the people who have migrated or who commute between specific local areas. In figure 10.2, tables 1 to 11 from *User Guide 35* are reproduced to illustrate this for SMS.

10.5.1 Migrants

The tables show the information in the SMS data sets. SMS Set 1 (ward-to-ward flows) provides the information shown in tables 1 and 2 (using the numbering system of *User Guide 35*). Tables 3 to 11 are available for SMS Sets 2 and 3 (district-to-district flows) subject to the constraints outlined above. The information available is considerably more detailed than was the case in 1981, and there are many opportunities for analyses of specific migration flows. The availability of migrant flows disaggregated according to the new census questions on ethnic group and limiting long-term illness will be particularly exciting.

10.5.2 Commuters

As indicated in figure 10.3, the SWS (Set C) tables cover journey to work by persons in employment — men and women separately — by employment status (employees, self-employed) and age group (16–19, 20–29, 30–39, 40–49, 50–54, 55–59, 60–64, 65 and over); hours worked by family type (hours worked: 1–15, 16–30, 31 and over, not stated); family position (family head/partner, lone parent, non-dependent child, not in family, not in household); mode of transport to work; cars available in households; occupations (sub-major group); social class/SEG; and industry (division) by employment status (employee, self-employed). The disaggregation of the journey to work matrix by number of cars in household is a new feature of the 1991 Census, as is the employee/self-employed distinction, the hours worked and family type distinctions. Hence, it is possible to contrast journeys to work for commuters of different ages, working in different industries and occupations, in part-time and full-time jobs.

10.6 USING THE ORIGIN-DESTINATION FLOW STATISTICS

10.6.1 Characteristics of the flow matrices

The amount of information available in the SMS and SWS data sets is vast, and its size in itself presents problems to the user. There are 9,135 wards in England and Wales and 1,152 postcode sectors in Scotland, so the potential number of ward-to-ward flows, including intra-ward flows, is the square of the sum of these two numbers (10,287). This number is over 100 million and, even for SMS Set 1, twelve different counts are available for each flow. In practice, the vast majority of these flows are zero; in 1981, there were only 1,916,522 ward pairs for which migration was recorded, and only 882,760 connected by journey-to-work flows (Manchester Computing Centre, 1989). However, this still represents a huge amount of data. This means, first of all, that inspection or analysis of even a small fraction of the data is a mammoth task requiring major inputs of time, expertise and computing power. It has also meant that software has been developed just for the purpose of helping

Figure 10.3 Table outlines from the SWS

Table 1 Economic position and age

EMPLOYEES AND SELF-EMPLOYED		10% sample	
		Economic position	
Age	TOTAL EMPLOYEES AND SELF-EMPLOYED	Employees	Self-employed
TOTAL EMPLOYEES AND SELF-EMPLOYED			
16-19			
20-29			
30-39			
40-49			
50-54			
55-59			
60-64			
65 and over			

Table 2 Hours worked and family position

EMPLOYEES AND SELF-EMPLOYED					10% sample
Family position	TOTAL EM-PLOYEES AND SELF-EMPLOYED	Hours worked			
		15 and under	16-30	31 and over	Not stated
TOTAL EMPLOYEES AND SELF-EMPLOYED					
Family head/partner in couple family					
Lone parent					
Non dependent child					
Not in family					
Not in household					

Table 2(1) Hours worked [Set C]

EMPLOYEES AND SELF-EMPLOYED	10% sample
Hours worked	
TOTAL EMPLOYEES AND SELF-EMPLOYED	
15 and under	
16-30	
31 and over	
Not stated	

Table 2(2) Family position [Set C]

EMPLOYEES AND SELF-EMPLOYED	10% sample
Family position	
TOTAL EMPLOYEES AND SELF-EMPLOYED	
Family head/partner in couple family	
Lone parent	
Non dependent child	
Not in family	
Not in household	

Table 3 Type of workplace [Set A]

EMPLOYEES AND SELF-EMPLOYED	10% sample
Type of workplace	
TOTAL EMPLOYEES AND SELF-EMPLOYED	
Workplace postcoded - working in zone	
Workplace postcoded - working outside zone	
Workplace at home	
No fixed workplace	
Workplace not stated - armed forces	
Workplace not stated - other	
Workplace outside GB - offshore installations	
Workplace outside GB - other	

Table 3 Type of workplace [Set B]

EMPLOYEES AND SELF-EMPLOYED	10% sample
Type of workplace	
TOTAL EMPLOYEES AND SELF-EMPLOYED	
Workplace postcoded - residence in zone	
Workplace postcoded - residence outside zone	
Workplace at home	
No fixed workplace	
Workplace not stated - armed forces	
Workplace not stated - other	
Residence outside GB	

Table 4 Distance to work

EMPLOYEES AND SELF-EMPLOYED WITH A WORKPLACE POSTCODED	10% sample
Distance to work	
TOTAL EMPLOYEES AND SELF-EMPLOYED WITH A WORKPLACE POSTCODED	
Less than 2 km	
2-4 km	
5-9 km	
10-19 km	
20-29 km	
30-39 km	
40 km and over	

For set C the categories shown in table 3 are incorporated into the trip matrix

Table 5 Transport to work

EMPLOYEES AND SELF-EMPLOYED	10% sample
Transport to work	
TOTAL EMPLOYEES AND SELF-EMPLOYED	
British Rail train	
Underground	
Bus	
Car - Driver	
Passenger	
Motor cycle	
Pedal cycle	
On foot	
Not stated	
Works at home	

Table 6 Cars available in households

EMPLOYEES AND SELF-EMPLOYED IN HOUSEHOLDS	10% sample
Cars available in households	
TOTAL EMPLOYEES AND SELF-EMPLOYED IN HOUSEHOLDS	
0 cars	
1 car	
2 cars	
3 or more cars	

Figure 10.3 - *continued*

Table 7 Occupation (sub-major group)

EMPLOYEES AND SELF-EMPLOYED	10% sample
Occupation (sub-major group)	

TOTAL EMPLOYEES AND SELF-EMPLOYED

Managers and Administrators
1 (a) Corporate Managers and Administrators
1 (b) Managers/Proprietors in Agriculture
    Services

Professional Occupations
2 (a) Science and Engineering Professionals
2 (b) Health Professionals
2 (c) Teaching Professionals
2 (d) Other Professional Occupations

Associate Professional and Technical Occupations
3 (a) Science and Engineering Associate Professionals
3 (b) Health Associate Professionals
3 (c) Other Associate Professional Occupations

Clerical and Secretarial Occupations
4 (a) Clerical Occupations
4 (b) Secretarial Occupations

Craft and Related Occupations
5 (a) Skilled Construction Trades
5 (b) Skilled Engineering Trades
5 (c) Other Skilled Trades

Personal and Protective Service Occupations
6 (a) Protective Service Occupations
6 (b) Personal Service Occupations

Sales Occupations
7 (a) Buyers, Brokers and Sales Reps.
7 (b) Other Sales Occupations

Plant and Machine Operatives
8 (a) Industrial Plant and Machine Operators, Assemblers
8 (b) Drivers and Mobile Machine Operators

Other Occupations
9 (a) Other Occupations in Agriculture, Forestry and Fishing
9 (b) Other Elementary Occupations

Occupation not stated

Table 8 Social class and socio-economic group

EMPLOYEES AND SELF-EMPLOYED	10% sample
Social class and socio-econmic group	

TOTAL EMPLOYEES AND SELF-EMPLOYED

Social class
I Professional, etc., occupations
II Intermediate occupations
III(N) Skilled occupations - non-manual
III(M) Skilled occupations - manual
IV Partly skilled occupations
V Unskilled occupations

Socio-economic group
    Employers and managers in central and
    local government, industry, commerce,
    etc., - large establishments
1.1 Employers
1.2 Managers

Employers and managers in industry,
commerce, etc., - small establishments
2.1 Employers
2.2 Managers
3 Professional workers - self employed
4 Professional workers - employees

Intermediate non-manual workers
5.1 Ancillary workers and artists
5.2 Foremen and supervisors - non-
    manual
6 Junior non-manual workers
7 Personal service workers
8 Foremen and supervisors - manual
9 Skilled manual workers
10 Semi-skilled manual workers
11 Unskilled manual workers
12 Own account workers (other than
    professional)
13 Farmers - employers and managers
14 Farmers - own account
15 Agricultural workers
16 Members of armed forces
17 Inadequately described and not
    stated occupations

Table 9 Industry divisions and classes [Sets A and B]

EMPLOYEES AND SELF-EMPLOYED	
Industry division and class	

Employees

0 Agriculture, Forestry and Fishing
  01 Agriculture and horticulture
  02 Forestry
  03 Fishing

1 Energy and Water Supply Industries

(continue for industry divisions and classes)

Industry not stated or not adequately described
Workplace outside GB (Set A only)

(Stub repeats for self-employed)

Table 9 Industry divisions [Set C]

EMPLOYEES AND SELF-EMPLOYED	10% sample
Industry division	

Employees

0 Agriculture, Forestry and Fishing

1 Energy and Water Supply Industries

2 Extraction of mineral and ores other than fuels

3 Metal goods, Engineering and Vehicle Industries

4 Other manufacturing industries

5 Construction

6 Distribution, Hotels and catering; repairs

7 Transport and Communication

8 Banking, Finance, Insurance, Business services and leasing

9 Other services

Industry not stated or not adequately described

(Stub repeats for self-employed)

Figure 10.3 - *continued*

Set C Trip Matrix

SET C TRIP MATRIX: EMPLOYEES and SELF-EMPLOYED

Tables in SET C will be produced for trips between zones of residence and zones of workplace as shown in the matrix below:

Zones for residence and workplace will normally be symmetrical.
For non-symmetrical zones the residence zones may not cover the same areas or be the same number of zones as those for workplace.
For areas outside the totality of customer specified zones the trips into and out of these zones will be shown by local authority districts, counties and regions covering the rest of Great Britain.

RESIDENCE AREA	WORKPLACE AREA			
	1 2 3	4 CUSTOMER'S ZONES W1 W2 ......Wm	5 REST OF GB (districts, counties,regions as thresholded)	6 OUTSIDE GB
1 2 3 Special counts for asymmetrical zones orders only	Not applicable	These counts will only be produced if non-symmetrical zones apply	Not applicable	Not applicable
4 Customer's zones R1 R2 . . Rn		Trips (Rn x Wm) within area covered by zones	Trips from customer's zones to areas in rest of GB	Trips to outside GB
5 Rest of GB (districts, counties and regions as thresholded)	Not applicable	Trips into customer's zones from areas outside	Not applicable (Trips unrelated to customer's zones and not included in analyses)	
6 Outside GB		Trips into customer's zones from outside GB		

1 Persons working at home

2 Persons with no fixed workplace

3 Persons with workplace not stated

4 Customer zones (Rn and Wm zones shown, Rn = Wm for symmetrical zones)

5 Rest of Great Britain (Districts, counties, regions as thresholded)

6 Outside GB

Source: Special Workplace Statistics *1991 Census User Guide 36.*

non-expert users gain access to the data. The MATPAC package, which fulfils this role, is discussed in section 10.6.2.

In addition to their large size, the data in both the SMS matrices and (especially) the SWS are exceedingly sparse. In his study of inter-ward migration in Hereford and Worcester, Boyle (1991) found that 34,271 of the 39,006 pairs of wards in the county had no migration between them recorded in the 1981 Census; many other pairs had only one or two migrants, although a few contiguous pairs of wards had large flows (the biggest was 299). In general, the size of the flows is related to the population and distance variables used in spatial interaction models, with flow size declining much more rapidly with distance in the case of SWS than SMS. However, there are many cases of both migrants and commuters travelling long distances, often where there is some degree of functional linkage between origin and destination.

These features of the data sets may have implications for analysis of migration and journey-to-work data. For many purposes, it may be useful to aggregate the SMS or SWS data into larger zones to ensure there is a reasonable number of cases for analysis. Small numbers raise many problems in the interpretation, mapping and analysis of data, reviewed for example by Kennedy (1989). In particular, much standard statistical methodology is based on the assumption that observations are drawn from a normal distribution, which is most implausible when count data with small values are being considered. Stillwell (1991), Flowerdew (1991) and Congdon (1991) discuss methods which may be more appropriate in the context of migration analysis.

10.6.2 Software for using the origin-destination flow statistics

As suggested above, the large and complex nature of the SMS and SWS data sets makes it difficult for non-expert users to access the data effectively. A package called MATPAC (MATrix analysis PACkage) was developed for this purpose for the 1981 data and an updated version, MATPAC91, was produced to handle the SMS and SWS data from the 1991 Census. MATPAC91 was produced by MVA Systematica in association with the London Research Centre. MATPAC91 is written in portable FORTRAN77 and can run on a wide range of mainframe systems; Unix and PC (386 and above) versions are also available.

The facilities available in MATPAC were described in a manual issued by Manchester Computing Centre (1989), which also includes an excellent discussion of the SMS and SWS data sets for the 1981 Census. MATPAC provides the following facilities:

(i) reformatting of the OPCS-supplied data sets to a more compact form;
(ii) extraction of zone count data;
(iii) ability to redefine by aggregation the zones to which the data relate;
(iv) arithmetic operators to calculate new variables on the basis of those supplied;
(v) a variety of output facilities providing printed reports and files suitable for input into other packages (MATPAC itself has no graphics or mapping facilities and very little capability for statistical analysis).

MATPAC91 has improved facilities for data management and output, including the production of histograms.

Although MATPAC greatly facilitates use of the SMS and SWS, it is still quite complicated for an inexperienced user. Successful extraction of data via MATPAC involves several distinct operations, each of which requires the mastery of a set of MATPAC commands. New users will need to study a manual carefully, or to obtain expert guidance, though the procedure is reasonably straightforward once some experience has been acquired.

For many academic users, access to SMS and SWS is through Manchester Computing Centre (the data and MATPAC91 have been purchased by the Economic and Social Research Council on behalf of the academic community). This has the major advantage that users at other sites can draw on the expertise available at Manchester, but it has the disadvantage that such users must learn the rudiments of the Manchester operating system (currently CMS) and file transfer protocols, in addition to MATPAC91 itself. Contact points for further information are given at the end of this chapter.

10.7 RESEARCH ISSUES AND APPLICATIONS

10.7.1 Migration

The census is the most complete and detailed source of information on migration in Great Britain. Rees (1977; 1989) provides a discussion of census migration data and their interpretation, and Bulusu (1991) has produced a recent review of migration data sources. In many respects, the 1991 Census offers data that have not been available in previous censuses. For example, there are new tabulations in the National and Regional Migration Reports, in the LBS and SAS, and a much wider range of information is available in the SMS. The potential for individual-level analysis using the Longitudinal Study and the Samples of Anonymised Records is particularly striking.

Migration is a lively interdisciplinary research area, and Champion and Fielding (1992) have published a set of reviews of current work with an agenda for future priorities. These reviews raise a great many issues, both theoretical and applied, which the further study of migration can shed light on, and many of the contributors draw attention to the potential of the 1991 Census for increasing our understanding of the migration process and its effects. Some current issues where it may be useful are outlined in the next few paragraphs.

Owen and Green (1992) review current knowledge of the *characteristics of migrants* and how they differ from the non-migrant population. Questions concerning the propensity to migrate for different parts of the population are of intrinsic interest, but also are highly relevant to economic and social policy, and to local and regional planning. New information is available in the 1991 Census which will allow further development of our ideas on the impact of age, employment status, socioeconomic group, housing tenure and many other variables on migration. In certain cases, such as long-term illness and ethnic group, it will become possible for the first time to study the relationships between these variables and migration for the population of Great Britain. For many variables, the new SMS data sets will allow researchers to investigate the nature of well known migration differentials at a more localised level than has previously been possible. Individual-level data in the LS and SARs will permit insights into the joint effects of these differentials.

Studies of the *spatial pattern of migration* can also be conducted at a more disaggregated level. For the first time, it will be possible to get reasonably accurate data on migration for small areas. Planning authorities will be able to assess whether migrants to certain areas are local or have come a long distance. Educational, health and welfare authorities will be able to measure migration flows for specific population groups and hence to plan more effectively for future needs.

Comparisons of 1991 data with earlier census results will of course make it possible to assess how *migration trends* are changing, and to make this assessment at the local level. The main source of data used to monitor migration patterns between censuses is the National Health Service Central Register, and Stillwell, Rees and Boden (1992) have recently produced a collection of papers on migration in the

United Kingdom using this source. Migration data from the 1991 Census will act as a check on the validity of this data source and the generalisations made using it, and will also allow us to investigate how the county and regional level trends discussed by Stillwell and colleagues are manifested at the district and ward levels.

10.7.2 Commuting

The Census of Population is the only comprehensive source of data on commuting in Great Britain collected on a consistent basis, and is therefore widely used by researchers.

One of the key research issues relates to *characteristics of commuters*. In particular there is an interest in comparing the characteristics of residents and workers within an area. What are the occupational and industrial profiles of employment within an area (as shown by the SWS Set B data) compared with the characteristics of residents of that area (from the SWS Set A data)? What proportion of jobs in an area are filled by in-commuters? (These types of issue are of importance to labour market and policy analysts seeking to identify the likely impact of job creation policies in specific areas.) To what extent are certain subgroups (e.g. women, young people, the semi-skilled and unskilled) more reliant on public transport for their journeys to work than other subgroups? Are such restrictions reflected in shorter journeys to work?

Turning to the *spatial pattern of commuting*, several important questions may be posed. Where are in-commuters coming from? Where are residents commuting to? Is there scope for encouraging local people to work locally, so that investment in skills is not lost from home areas, so as to reduce congestion on roads or to relieve environmental pressures arising from commuting? Perhaps of even greater interest are questions such as: what spatial form do contemporary patterns of commuting take? what are the differences between subgroups in spatial patterns of commuting? to what extent do journey lengths vary for different subgroups? and what are the policy implications of these differences?

Finally, turning to *changes over time*, is there evidence of a continuation in the long-term trends towards longer journeys to work (Coombes, Green and Openshaw, 1985)? Are flows becoming more disparate as car availability increases? How much impact have major infrastructure projects (e.g. completion of the M25) had on spatial patterns of commuting flows? In attempting to answer such questions it is necessary to remember that the Census of Population merely provides a decennial snapshot of continually evolving commuting patterns, and that major construction projects, together with subsequent closures and openings of workplaces, may have a substantial impact on current commuting patterns at the local level.

10.8 DERIVATION OF TRAVEL-TO-WORK AREAS

In the past one of the major uses of the commuting data available from Set C of the SWS has been in the derivation of travel-to-work areas (TTWAs) by the Employment Department. TTWAs are relatively self-contained local labour market areas within which the majority of residents work (supply-side self-containment) and the majority of jobs are filled by local residents (demand-side self-containment). In 1981 the requirement set was that a minimum of 75 per cent of the journey-to-work trips to or from any TTWA both started and ended in the area. The minimum size of

Map 10.1   Key stages in the derivation of Travel-To-Work Areas: the example of the Lincolnshire Wolds and Marshes

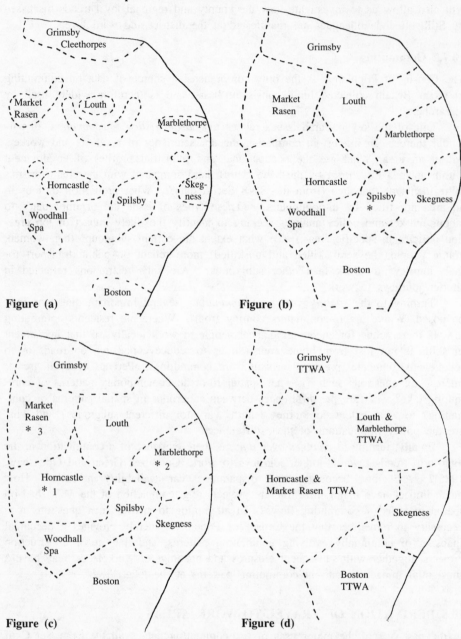

The asterisks indicate which areas do not meet statistical criteria necessary to qualify as TTWAs.

Figure (a) shows *proto TTWAs*. The expansion of *proto TTWAs* into *provisional TTWAs* is illustrated in figure (b). Spilsby *provisional TTWA*, marked by an asterisk, is the weakest of the areas not satisfying the statistical criteria, so it is dismembered and the component wards re-allocated, mainly to Woodhall Spa *provisional TTWA*, as displayed in figure (c). Horncastle, Mablethorpe and Market Rasen *provisional TTWAs*, marked by asterisks, do not satisfy the statistical criteria to qualify as TTWAs, so are in turn dismembered and the component wards re-allocated. Eventually, all meet the statistical criteria to qualify as TTWAs, as illustrated in figure (d).

each TTWA was specified as a resident workforce of 3,500 (10 per cent sample grossed up). A limited size/self-containment trade-off was allowed so that large areas with a resident workforce in excess of 20,000 could have a self-containment of 70 per cent. In 1981 and in previous years, TTWAs were mutually exclusive (i.e. non-overlapping) and were defined to exhaust the whole country. The significance of TTWAs stems from the fact that they are the smallest areas for which local unemployment rates are officially calculated (published in the *Employment Gazette* and available on the National Online Manpower Information System *(NOMIS)* at the University of Durham — see Townsend, Blakemore and Nelson, 1987), and for which the unemployment rate can be calculated as an indicator of local economic prosperity, rather than social deprivation.

In 1981 TTWAs were defined by the application of a complex statistical algorithm incorporating minimum size and self-containment thresholds to the journey-to-work flow matrix from the SWS (Set C) (Department of Employment, 1984; Coombes, Green and Openshaw, 1986). A number of key stages in the process may be identified: individuation, consolidation, (re)allocation, and implementation. *Individuation* involved identification of *foci* (or job centres) around which to build; foci being wards characterised either by a high *job ratio*, i.e. the ratio of jobs to employed residents (e.g. city centres), or high supply-side self-containment (e.g. rural areas). In the *consolidation* stage, the foci were expanded, individually or in combination, into *proto TTWAs* covering the most interdependent hinterland areas. In the *(re)allocation* stage all remaining territory was allocated to a *proto TTWA* to produce a set of *provisional TTWAs* which met specified statistical criteria; this involved a reallocation procedure in which the least self-contained TTWAs were dismembered and their component wards reallocated to other *provisional TTWAs* until all *provisional TTWAs* satisfied the objective statistical function set by the algorithm. Finally, in the *implementation* stage comments made by local authorities and central government departments in response to the *provisional TTWAs* produced using the first three steps were assessed and any adjustments were made as appropriate, and any non-contiguous wards were reallocated. (See map 10.1 for an illustration of various stages in this process in part of Lincolnshire.)

The availability of journey-to-work data from the 1991 Census provides an opportunity for revision of TTWAs. Definition of TTWAs based on 1991 Census data will begin after the release of the SWS, which is scheduled for the end of September 1993; draft TTWAs are planned to be circulated six to nine months after that. A Working Group was set up by the Department of Employment in 1991 to discuss and make proposals for a review of TTWAs. Topics covered by the group include: geographical building blocks, criteria for self-containment, systems for categorising TTWAs, and the relationship of TTWAs to administrative boundaries. Proposals informed by a Eurostat study of *employment zones* (Eurostat, 1992) for use in the support of the structural policies of the EC (particularly for the revision of the regulations concerning the structural funds) may have an impact on future TTWA reviews, in recognition of the benefits of harmonising the key statistical criteria used for defining such areas; this might involve imposition of different minimum/maximum population and self-containment criteria.

Apart from the issues identified above, there are a number of other research questions relating to TTWAs. For example, as noted in section 10.7.2, it is widely recognised that different subgroups of the population have different commuting patterns, raising several questions. Does a definition of TTWAs based on commuting data for all subgroups represent a gross *averaging out* of dramatic differences in commuting flows of different subgroups? How different are TTWAs for different subgroups, and what is the range of variation in subgroup TTWAs? Research on the application of the algorithm used for the 1981 TTWA regionalisation exercise to commuting flow data for different subgroups indicates that in absolute terms there are fewer local labour market areas (LLMAs) for males than for females (see map 10.2), and for managerial, professional and intermediate non-manual workers than for semi-skilled and unskilled workers (Green, Coombes and Owen, 1986; Coombes, Green and Owen, 1988). In qualitative terms, the most dramatic differences between the LLMAs for different subgroups are in the metropolitan areas. Hence, in any

Map 10.2   Male and female travel-to-work areas in the London metropolitan region

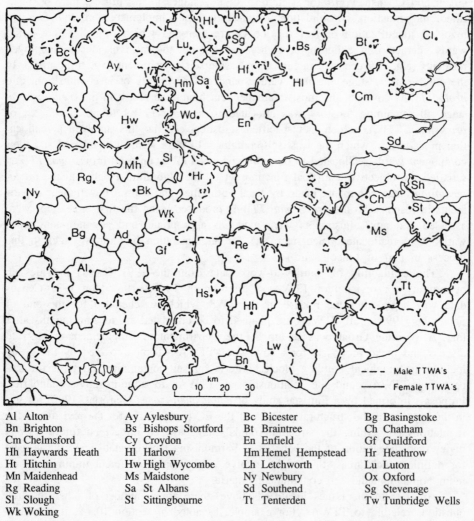

Al	Alton	Ay	Aylesbury	Bc	Bicester	Bg	Basingstoke
Bn	Brighton	Bs	Bishops Stortford	Bt	Braintree	Ch	Chatham
Cm	Chelmsford	Cy	Croydon	En	Enfield	Gf	Guildford
Hh	Haywards Heath	Hl	Harlow	Hm	Hemel Hempstead	Hr	Heathrow
Ht	Hitchin	Hw	High Wycombe	Lh	Letchworth	Lu	Luton
Mn	Maidenhead	Ms	Maidstone	Ny	Newbury	Ox	Oxford
Rg	Reading	Sa	St Albans	Sd	Southend	Sg	Stevenage
Sl	Slough	St	Sittingbourne	Tt	Tenterden	Tw	Tunbridge Wells
Wk	Woking						

Source: Green, A.E. *et al*, 1986

locality there is unlikely to be a single *local* labour market area; rather there are overlapping gender-, occupation-, industry-, and age-specific LLMAs. TTWAs defined using aggregate commuting data represent the outcome of a process of *averaging* across all these subgroups.

Other research has been undertaken on the theme of defining two-tier TTWAs, sometimes termed 'dominants' (centres of in-commuting) and 'subdominants' (areas with strong out-commuting links to the associated 'dominants') in metropolitan areas. The related issue of devising alternative systems for classifying TTWAs, in order to aid generalisation and comparison, enable use of 'sparse' data (perhaps from 'national' surveys) at the subregional level, and enhance the relevance of subnational spatial coding by devising alternative coherent subnational classification systems to regions, has also been addressed. There is no single classification method; rather there are a variety of classification methodologies, which may be more or less appropriate to different circumstances. Two contrasting methodologies which have been used in categorising TTWAs are *a priori* classification (Green and Owen, 1990) and *cluster analysis* classification (Green, Owen and Hasluck, 1991). There is considerable scope for applying similar or new methodologies to classification of TTWAs based on 1991 commuting data.

10.9 CONCLUSION

The SMS and SWS data report on movements between places, and are thus rather different in nature from most of the rest of the census output. The information they provide on migration and commuting behaviour is exceedingly rich and its availability for small areal units provides some excellent opportunities for researchers and practitioners with interests in these topics. The flow data should be seen as complementary to the data tabulated in the census reports; the SMS and SWS offer detailed spatial disaggregation but relatively little topical disaggregation; the published reports provide the opposite mixture. Almost any social or economic survey can be enriched by consideration of how its findings vary geographically, and these data sets facilitate such insights. In addition, the reports (and the SAS) offer detailed information on the state of affairs at *one end* of the journey (the origin in the case of commuting, the destination in the case of migration); but SMS and SWS provide information on origins *and* destinations, and can also show what sort of people are making what sort of move.

The SMS and SWS data sets are large and unwieldy. Software has been developed to make them easier to use, but there are still problems for new users in learning how to access and to manipulate the data. Nevertheless, these data sets have the potential to tell us a great deal about migration and commuting in contemporary Britain.

Some of the applications possible with the SMS and SWS have been reviewed. For both data sets, it is interesting and important to look at the characteristics of the people involved, at the spatial patterns, and at changes over time. It is possible to construct and test models of spatial interaction using these data, and it is possible to use them to build new sets of areal units, such as the travel-to-work areas discussed above. Many other applications have been suggested, and new and innovative ones will doubtless emerge over the next few years.

10.10 DOCUMENTATION, KEY PUBLICATIONS AND CONTACTS

For further information about SMS or SWS, contact Census Customer Services (telephone 0329 813800), OPCS, Segensworth Road, Titchfield, Hampshire PO15 5RR (England and Wales) or Census Customer Services (telephone 031-314 4254), GRO(S), Ladywell House, Ladywell Road, Edinburgh EH12 7TF (Scotland).

SWS are expected to become available around the end of November 1993 and SMS are expected to follow by December 1993. Information on charges for the two data sets is given in *Census Newsletter* No. 25, February 1993.

More detailed information about the data sets referred to in this chapter is available in the relevant *1991 Census User Guides*, which include:

3 *Local and Small Area Statistics - Prospectus*
12 *Housing and Availability of Cars - Prospectus*
17 *National Migration - Prospectus*
20 *Workplace and Transport to Work - Prospectus*
22 *Regional Migration - Prospectus*
35 *Special Migration Statistics - Prospectus*
36 *Special Workplace Statistics - Prospectus*

These are obtainable from OPCS or GRO(S) at the addresses given above.

For further information about MATPAC91, contact Keith Dugmore, MVA Systematica, MVA House, Victoria Way, Woking, Surrey GU21 1DD, or Rob Lewis, London Research Centre, Parliament House, 81 Black Prince Road, London SE1 7SZ. At the time of writing, MATPAC91 was scheduled to be ready for testing with live data in March 1993, with general distribution following as soon as testing is completed.

Practical advice on the use of the data sets described in this chapter, and on software available for using them, can be offered by the Census Dissemination Unit, Manchester Computing Centre, University of Manchester, Oxford Road, Manchester M13 9PL (Director: Keith Cole).

For information on the *TTWA Review Group* contact Mr Glenn Everett, Statistics B, Department of Employment, Caxton House, London SW1H 9NF.

For information on the *National Online Manpower Information System (NOMIS)* contact the NOMIS Team, Unit 3P, Mountjoy Research Centre, University of Durham, Stockton Road, Durham DH1 3SW.

11   The Sample of Anonymised Records

Catherine Marsh

11.1 BACKGROUND

For the first time in a British census, the 1991 statistical output includes Samples of Anonymised Records (SARs). Known as census microdata or public use sample tapes in other countries, SARs differ from traditional census output of tables of aggregated information in that abstracts of individual records are released. The released records do not conflict with the confidentiality assurances given when collecting census information since they contain neither names or addresses nor any other direct information which would lead to the identification of an individual or household. Essentially 3 per cent of records are being released in two samples (see section 11.3).

Other special samples have been drawn from the census. The most well known of these is probably the OPCS Longitudinal Study (LS) which is a 1 per cent sample of the population of England and Wales (see chapter 12 for full details). All the individual LS records are kept confidential, however, and analysis of them must be performed on the OPCS computer. The Census Offices also run a customised table service from the census, but neither of these mechanisms offer users the freedom to import individual-level census records into their own computing environment. The SARs offer a flexible database through which users have such access to anonymised individual records. They gain the ability to produce their own tables or run analyses which are not possible using aggregated statistics.

Other countries have successfully released SARs from their censuses. In the USA, SARs were released retrospectively for the 1960 Census and have become part of the routine census output ever since. Canada followed in the 1970s and Australia in the 1980s. Census offices in most European countries have so far not released full SARs, although some (such as France) have released a limited set of variables and cases, and others (such as Italy) have made SARs available to regional offices.

Requests have been made for SARs to be released from previous censuses in Great Britain. The principal stumbling block in the past has been an argument as to whether SARs could be considered a statistical abstract for release under section 4.2 of the Census Act 1920 at the request and expense of user(s). Furthermore, in the past, requests for SARs had failed to reach a compromise between those (often geographers) wanting fine grain areal detail and those (often sociologists and demographers) wanting fine grain detail on other variables such as occupation.

The 1991 Census White Paper (OPCS and GRO(S),1988), however, announced: 'The Government intends that results from the 1991 Census should wherever practicable be made available in a convenient form to meet users' needs'.

Following the receipt of legal advice that SARs could be deemed statistical abstracts, the White Paper went on to say: 'Requests for abstracts in the form of samples of anonymised records for individual people and households ... would also be considered, subject to the overriding need to ensure the confidentiality of individual data'.

The Economic and Social Research Council (ESRC) set up a working party to negotiate with the Census Offices and present a formal request. Their report, presented to the census offices in 1989 (subsequently published as Marsh *et al.*, 1991) concentrated on the benefits of releasing SARs, the uses to which they would be put, and also an assessment of the confidentiality risks involved in releasing SARs.

The request was mentioned by Ministers during the debate on the Census Order in Parliament at the end of 1989. Having considered the request, the Registrars General for England and Wales and for Scotland announced in July 1990 that they had agreed in principle to the release of SARs from the 1991 Census. There then followed detailed work by the Census Offices and ESRC in developing the statistical specification. An independent technical assessor, Professor Holt (University of Southampton), was appointed to advise the Registrars General on the confidentiality aspects and to write a report to Ministers. Following receipt of the report, it was announced in March 1992 that two SARs from the censuses in England and Wales and in Scotland would be produced and released to the ESRC. At the time of writing a contract to purchase Northern Ireland SARs is being negotiated and the data should be available by January 1994. The Census Microdata Unit will be producing harmonised SARs for the whole of the United Kingdom.

11.2 USES

In previous censuses, users who found that the preplanned tables did not give them precisely what they wanted had two choices: either to settle for the way the data was presented in the published volumes or the small area statistics, or to commission a special table, a process which could be both expensive and time-consuming. From 1991, the SARs offer a useful intermediate route. Users can explore relationships on the sample data, interacting until they reach the table that they feel gives the best information. They may still then decide to commission a special tabulation, perhaps to get data to a level of geographical specificity not available in the SAR or because small numbers demand a 100 per cent run, but they will be much more confident than in the past that they will be getting what they want.

Many kinds of analysis are possible with the SAR data that are not possible from the published census tables. Having access to individual-level records allows non-tabular forms of analysis such as analysis of variance and regression. It is possible, for example, to take the occupational detail as recorded on the 1 per cent household SAR, and to assign to each occupation a social status score, thus creating an ordered metric of social prestige. One can use regression techniques to compare the occupational destinations of different ethnic groups, or men and women, holding constant their educational qualifications and their age. Such analyses would take the debate about discrimination a lot further than the usual descriptive comparisons that are made about the absolute attainment levels of both groups. Readers interested in getting a richer flavour of the use of microdata to explore such issues should consult Li (1988) and Breton *et al.* (1990).

The sheer size of the file makes some forms of research possible on the SARs which cannot be undertaken on the smaller continuous surveys. The file is large enough, for example, to extract groups defined by detailed census characteristics, such as those holding a doctorate in physics; these can be selected for profiling or analysis, perhaps comparing characteristics of all with PhDs in physics with the population of university teachers who have doctorates in physics. Similarly, one can construct reliable detailed measures of occupational segregation by gender or ethnic group in each of the 350 occupational groups identified.

Having access to the full hierarchical detail of the household SAR also opens up interesting possibilities. Exploration can be done with alternative forms of household classifications, lifestyle stages, and so on. There are research questions where it makes sense to choose the head of household by different criteria from that used in standard census output, e.g. by economic position or by gender. The SARs enable one to search for specific household types: households in which there are elderly dependents and no other household members in employment; households with cohabiting couples; or lone parent families. One can also create a new household typology that can be cross-tabulated with any number of other census variables.

The existence of a large sample of the long-term residents of communal establishments will make possible more detailed analysis of the population of residential homes, long-stay hospitals and so on, and enable very detailed profiles of the inhabitants to be given. Such research will help focus attention on a group of people who form one of the most deprived groups in society and who are often neglected by other social research endeavours.

In the final analysis, however, the value of the SARs lies in the fact that, in contrast to tabulations produced by the Census Offices, we do not have to plan in advance all the useful ways in which the data can be presented. Although the amount of information supplied in tabular form is vast, it is still a very tiny fraction of the total number of possible ways in which census variables can be combined. Almost every census user will have experienced the frustration of finding that the table they required was slightly different from the one they had in the end to use: they wanted to know a particular characteristic of the electorate and found the 16–19 year age group banded together or they wanted to know how many people lived in a household containing members with a particular characteristic and could only find out how many households contained members with this particular characteristic, and so on.

11.3 DETAILS OF THE SARS

Two SARs have been extracted from the GB censuses:

(1) a 2 per cent sample of individuals in households and communal establishments; and
(2) a 1 per cent hierarchical sample of households and individuals in those households.

As we shall see, the 2 per cent SAR has finer geographical detail and the 1 per cent SAR has finer detail on other variables, thus providing a solution to the conflict between users' demands discussed above.

The 2 per cent individual SAR contains some 1.1 million individual records (a 1 in 50 sample of the whole population enumerated in the census). Details are given as to whether or not the person was a usual resident of the household, and if so (and enumerated in a household) whether they were present or absent on census night. The following other information is given for each sampled individual:

- details about the individual ranging from their age and sex to so-called derived information such as social class;
- details about the accommodation in which the person is enumerated (such as the availability of a bath/shower and the tenure of the accommodation) or, if they were in a communal establishment, the establishment type (hotel, hospital, etc.);
- information about the sex, economic position (in employment, unemployed, etc.), and social class of the individual's family head; and
- limited information about other members of the individual's household (such as the number of persons with long-term illness and numbers of pensioners).

In effect, all the census topic variables (listed in table 1.1) are on the file, and the possibility exists to create almost every derived census variable. The only exceptions are variables either suppressed or grouped to maintain the confidentiality of the data; these are listed below in section 11.5 (and justified more fully in chapter 5). In all, there are about forty pieces of information about each individual, and the size of the raw data file, before any new variables have been derived and before any data compression techniques have been applied, is around 80 megabytes.

The 1 per cent household SAR contains some 240,000 household records together with sub-records, one for each person in the selected household. Information is available about the household's accommodation together with information (similar to the 2 per cent sample) about each individual in the household and how they are related to the head of the household. The data have been supplied as a hierarchical file in non-software specific character format (one line of information about housing and household, followed by one line of information about each individual in the household), and users will have complete freedom to hold the data in any software package they decide; some standard software platforms are available from Manchester, and are described more fully in section 11.6 below. This file is smaller than the individual level file in its raw form (about 45 megabytes), but could expand if inefficient methods are used to turn it into a rectangular data set with equal numbers of records for each household.

The full details of the information provided in both SARs is given in the SARs statistical specification (Teague and Marsh, 1992). Table 11.1, however, provides summaries by describing the information collected on the census form, the detail of coding of that information on the census database, and in how much detail that information is released in the SARs.

11.4 SAMPLING

Census data go through two separate coding processes. As explained in chapter 4, the easy to code information such as housing details, sex, date of birth, and country of birth is processed for all forms (100 per cent). The harder to code information such as occupation and industry is only processed for 10 per cent of forms. Both

Table 11.1

Details of the information to be supplied in the two Samples of Anonymised Records from the 1991 Census of Great Britain

Item	Household (1%) sample		Individual (2%) sample	
	No. of categories (maximum*)	Other details	No. of categories (maximum*)	Other details
Geographical area of enumeration	12	Standard regions of England (with split of South East into Inner London, Outer London and Rest), Wales and Scotland	278	Local authority districts over 120,000 population. Others amalgamated to form areas over 120,000
Housing/household information				
Accommodation type	14 (14)	Detached, semi-detached or terraced house; purpose built flat in a commercial or residential building; converted or not self-contained accommodation in a shared house or flat	As household sample	
Availability of amenities				
• bath/shower	3 (3)	Exclusive, shared or no use	As household sample	
• inside WC	3 (3)	Exclusive, shared or no use	As household sample	
• central heating	3 (3)	Full, part or none	As household sample	
Cars (number of)	4 (4)	0, 1, 2, 3 or more	As household sample	
Floor level (lowest), of accommodation (Scotland only)	7 (101)	Basement, ground, 1st/2nd, 3rd/4th, 5th/6th, 7th to 9th 10th or higher	As household sample	
Number of household (accommodation) spaces in dwelling	4 (35)	Top coded: 4 or more	Not included	
Number of persons (enumerated) in household	12 (99)	Top coded: 12 or more	Not included	
Number of residents in household		Derivable	4 (99)	0, 1, 2 to 5, 6 or more
Number of dependent children in household		Derivable	2 (99)	0, 1 or more
Number of pensioners in household		Derivable	2 (99)	0, 1 or more
Number of persons with long-term illness in household		Derivable	2 (99)	0, 1 or more
Number of persons in employment in household		Derivable	3 (99)	Top coded: 2 or more
Number of rooms	15 (19)	Top coded: 15 or more	Not included	

* The maximum number of categories as available on the full census database.

Table 11.1 - *continued*

Item	Household (1%) sample		Individual (2%) sample	
	No. of categories (maximum*)	Other details	No. of categories (maximum*)	Other details
Number of persons per room		Derivable	5	Ranging from less than 0.5 to more than 1.5
Tenure	10 (10)	Owner occupier or rented (public sector or private)	As household sample	
Wholly moving household indicator	2 (2)	Yes (all resident household members are migrants from the same address) or No	Not included	
Individual information				
Age	94 (111)	Single years 0 to 90, 91/92, 93/94, 95 and over	As household sample	
Status in communal establishment		Not applicable	3 (7)	Visitor, resident staff or resident non-staff
Type of communal establishment		Not applicable	15 (35)	Hotel, hospital, nursing home etc.
Country of birth	42 (102)		As household sample	
Migrants — distance of move (km)	13	5, 10, 20 and 50 km bands; top coded above 200 km	As household sample	
Distance to work (km)	8	10 km bands; top coded above 40 km; 0–9 km band split 0-2, 3-4 and 5-9	As household sample	
Economic position primary	10 (12)	Employee, self-employed, unemployed, student, retired etc.	As household sample	
secondary	7 (10)		As household sample	
Economic position of family head		Derivable	3 (12)	Employed, unemployed or inactive
Ethnic group	10 (10)		As household sample	
Family head indicator	2 (2)	Yes or no	Not included	
Family number	5 (5)	Used to identify individual's family	Not included	
Family type	8 (8)	Married or cohabiting couple family with or without children or lone-parent family	As household sample	
Gaelic language (Scotland only)	5 (8)	Ability to speak, read or write Gaelic	As household sample	
Hours worked weekly	72 (99)	Single hours 0–70, 71 to 80, 81 or more	As household sample	

* The maximum number of categories as available on the full census database.

Table 11.1 - *continued*

Item	Household (1%) sample		Individual (2%) sample	
	No. of categories (maximum*)	Other details	No. of categories (maximum*)	Other details
Industry of employees and self-employed	185 (334)	Mainly third digit (groups) of 1980 SIC	60 (334)	Mainly second digit (classes) of 1980 SIC
Limiting long-term illness	2 (2)	Yes (individual has illness) or no	As household sample	
Marital status	5 (5)		As household sample	
Migrant - geographical area of former residence	13	Standard regions of England (with split of South East), Wales, Scotland, outside GB	As household sample	
Occupation	358 (371)	Mainly unit groups of 1990 SOC	73 (371)	Mainly minor groups of 1990 SOC
Number of higher educational qualifications	3 (7)	0, 1, 2 or more	As household sample	
Level of highest qualification	3 (3)	Higher degree, first degree, above GCE A-level	As household sample	
Subject of highest qualification	88 (108)	Mainly third digit of Standard Subject Classification	35 (108)	Mainly second digit of Standard Subject Classification
Relationship to household head	17 (17)		8 (17)	
Resident status	3 (3)	Present resident, absent, resident, visitor	As household sample	
Sex	2 (2)		As household sample	
Sex of family head		Derivable	2 (2)	
Social class	8 (8)		As household sample	
Social class of family head		Derivable	8 (8)	
Socioeconomic group	19 (20)		As household sample	
Term-time address of students and school children	4	Inside or outside region of usual residence	As household sample	
Transport to work (mode)	10 (10)		As household sample	
Visitor — geographical area of residence	13	Standard regions of England (with split of South East), Wales, Scotland, outside GB	As household sample	
Welsh language (Wales only)	5 (8)	Active use of (speak, read or write)	As household sample	
Workplace	5	Inside or outside region of usual residence	5	Inside or outside SAR area of usual residence

* The maximum number of categories as available on the full census database.

SARs were drawn from the 10 per cent sample so that they contain information from the whole of the census form. In order to consider the sampling scheme for the SARs it is therefore first necessary to consider the sampling scheme for the 10 per cent sample.

The 10 per cent sample was selected by first forming separate 'census processing units', each containing 50 consecutive enumeration districts (EDs) within a county (or within a region and output area in Scotland). Each processing unit was then split into groups of 10 households or 10 persons in communal establishments. One household or one person from a communal establishment was then selected at random from each group to form the 10 per cent sample for full coding. The sample is thus a stratified simple random sample with strata of size 10 and one household or person selected per stratum. Further details of the comparable 1981 sampling scheme are given in OPCS (1983c).

The 1 per cent household SAR was the first of the SAR samples to be selected. The households selected in the 10 per cent sample were ordered by ED within county and then formed into groups of 10 (persons from communal establishments are excluded from the household SAR). One household was then selected at random from each group to form the 1 per cent household SAR. This SAR may thus be viewed as a stratified simple random sample of households, with strata each of size 100 from which one household was selected. The last stratum in each county may contain fewer than 100 households.

The 2 per cent SAR is comprised of both individuals in private households and individuals in communal establishments. The sample of people in private households was selected from those households in the 10 per cent sample which remained after the household SAR had been selected, thus ensuring that there was no overlap between the two samples. Individuals in these remaining households were formed into groups of nine, and two individuals were selected from each group by simple random sampling. Individuals in communal establishments selected in the 10 per cent sample were then formed into groups of five and one individual was selected at random from each group. The 2 per cent individual SAR may thus be viewed roughly as a stratified simple random sample of individuals with two types of strata. The first type of stratum, from which two individuals are sampled, contains 100 people who each live within a household. The second kind of stratum, from which one individual is sampled, contains 50 people who each live in a communal establishment. However, the 2 per cent SAR is not precisely a stratified simple random sample of individuals since there are two possible sources of clustering which arise in the sample selection process. First, individuals are clustered into households in the selection of the 10 per cent sample and second, the removal of the household SAR from the 10 per cent sample implies a further minor clustering into households.

Users of the SARs will need to take sampling errors into account in their analyses. Standard errors and significance tests computed from conventional statistical software are usually based on the assumption of simple random sampling. Strictly, the presence of stratification and clustering in the selection of the SARs invalidates this assumption. The effect of these sampling schemes on sampling errors for the SARs will be investigated by the Census Microdata Unit at the University of Manchester, in collaboration with a researcher at the Department of Social Statistics at the University of Southampton. Before this work takes place, it is still possible, however, to offer some broad advice to users.

Analyses of the 1 per cent household SAR, which take a household as the unit of analysis and assume simple random sampling, are unlikely to be greatly affected. At worst the stratification of the sample may mean that the sampling errors tend to be overestimated. Whilst most users of the 1 per cent SAR are likely to take the household as the unit of analysis, some users may want to treat the file as a sample of individuals because of its finer grained information on many variables. Analyses of this file, which take the individual as the unit of analysis and assume that the SAR is a simple random sample of individuals could, however, be very misleading in the sense that sampling errors might be seriously underestimated. This problem would be expected to be most acute for variables which tend to be similar for individuals in the same household, for example ethnic group, and especially for variables which are constant across a household, for example persons living in a single-parent household. The effect of household clustering could, however, probably be ignored for estimates for population subgroups of which there is usually no more than one per household. For example, sampling errors for estimates of the characteristics of women aged 80+ living in households could reasonably be calculated based on the assumption of simple random sampling, if it is the case that such women rarely live together in the same household. For individual-based analyses, for which such an argument for ignoring household clustering is not available, it will generally be preferable to calculate sampling errors on the assumption that the sample was selected by cluster sampling with households as clusters, using standard formulae (e.g. Barnett, 1991, chapter 6). Wolter (1985, appendix E) gives details of several software packages which can be used to calculate such sampling errors. Alternatively the effect of the clustering of individuals into households might be handled by some form of multilevel modelling (Goldstein, 1987).

For analyses of the 2 per cent individual SAR it seems likely that the stratification will usually compensate for the minor sources of clustering and that users are not likely to go far wrong if they assume that this SAR is a simple random sample of individuals. Cases where this approach would be most suspect are where, just as for individual-based analyses of the household, variables are constant across households and the relevant subpopulation of interest includes all individuals within relevant households, for example in the estimation of the proportion of all individuals in London living in a single parent household, or living in accommodation with no bath. The effect of household clustering in the individual SAR may however be expected to be much less than for individual-based analyses of the household SAR because individuals in the households selected in the 10 per cent sample are subsampled at a rate of 1 in 5. Hence, only for the larger households selected in the 10 per cent sample would one expect to find more than one member appearing in the individual SAR. This subsampling will tend to reduce the effect of clustering considerably. Thus, in OPCS (1983c) it was found that the largest design effect for individual-based analyses of the 10 per cent sample from the 1981 Census was 5.24 for variables that were constant across households and 1.88 for other variables. With 1 in 5 subsampling one might expect these figures to be reduced to 1 + 0.2*4.24 = 1.85 and 1 + 0.2*0.88 = 1.18 respectively, based on the following formula from Skinner, Holt and Smith (1989, section 3.3.2):

$$\text{design effect for SAR sample} = 1 + 0.2 \left(\text{design effect for 10\% sample} - 1 \right)$$

where 0.2 is the fraction by which the individual SAR is subsampled from the 10 per cent sample.

Thus one might reasonably expect that sampling variances for analyses of the individual SAR will not be increased by more than 85 per cent for household-based variables and not more than 18 per cent for individual-based variables. The corresponding factors for a standard error (square root of sampling variance) are 36 per cent and 9 per cent. For analyses for which sampling errors are critical these rough factors might be applied to err on the cautious side. Sampling errors will usually be most critical when studying small subgroups and we note again that if these subgroups tend to cut across households, for example if they are defined at least partially by gender and age group, then these factors are likely to be over-cautious and sampling errors calculated on the assumption of simple random sampling are likely to provide a reasonable approximation.

The 10 per cent sample and hence the SARs, do not contain wholly absent imputed households. The extent of imputation shows considerable geographical variation (see chapter 4) and also varies with sociodemographic characteristics. Additionally, of course, and in common with all data from the 1991 Census, the SARs are subject to the effects of the undercount (see chapter 6 (II)).

11.5 CONFIDENTIALITY PROTECTION

The census offices in most European countries have so far not released microdata because, on the basis of research such as that conducted by Paass (1988) and Bethlehem, Keller and Pannkoek (1990), they have doubts about the risk of disclosing respondents' identities. Much of this work is concerned with how many people have unique combinations of census characteristics which would make them open to identification. The Economic and Social Research Council Working Party which negotiated the release of the SARs took the view that uniqueness was only one part of a four-stage process of disclosure: data in the microdata file would have to be recorded in a compatible way to that in an outside file; the individual in an outside file would have to turn up in a SAR; the individual would have to have unique values of a set of key census variables; and the matcher would need to be able to verify this uniqueness. Rough estimates of the size of risk at each stage were made; when cumulated, the risks of disclosure appeared negligible; multiplying the various probabilities together, the working party concluded that the risk of anyone in the population being identifiable from their SAR record was extremely remote; their best estimate was something of the order of 1 in 4 million. (For more details of such calculations, consult Marsh, *et al.*, 1991; Marsh, Dale and Skinner, forthcoming; and Skinner *et al.*, 1992.) The arguments put forward were important in persuading the Census Offices to release the SARs suitably modified to protect anonymity where this was felt at risk. In this section the various disclosure protection measures taken are described.

11.5.1 Sampling

The low sampling fractions offer a major degree of protection against disclosure, as discussed above. In order to protect the anonymity of respondents further, some alterations are nevertheless being made to the information available in the full census database before its release in the SARs.

11.5.2 Restricting geographical information

One of the key considerations which may affect the possibility of disclosure of information about an identifiable individual or household is the geographical level to be released (i.e how much detail is given about where the person was enumerated). The full census database holds information at ED level (about 200 households or 500 persons in each ED) and even at unit postcode level (about 15 households). If released, such detailed geography would obviously pose a confidentiality risk. Empirical work and comparisons with SARs released in other countries showed that a sensible level for release would be areas equivalent to large local authority districts for the individual (2 per cent) SAR.

To be separately identifiable, the decision was taken that an area had to have a population size of at least 120,000 in the mid-1989 estimates. The primary units used were local districts; only one geographical scheme was permitted, otherwise smaller areas could be identified in the overlap, say between a local district and a health district. A population size of 120,000 is slightly higher than the lowest level of geography permitted in the US SARs (100,000), but it still has the advantage of allowing all non-metropolitan counties in England and Wales, most Scottish regions, all London boroughs (bar the City of London), and all Metropolitan districts to be separately identified.

Smaller local authority districts (under 120,000 population) were grouped to form areas over 120,000. Several rules were used to decide how districts should be amalgamated where this was necessary. First, the integrity of county/Scottish region geography was maintained where possible. Second, districts which achieved the minimum population threshold on their own were left intact, where possible; and smaller areas were grouped with each other. Third, grouping was done on the basis of contiguity. Finally, if there was a choice left once the above criteria had been met, areas were grouped on the basis of their apparent social and historical similarity. The resulting list of areas is shown in map 11.1.

The 1 per cent household SAR, because of its hierarchical nature (i.e. statistics about the household and all its members), poses a greater disclosure risk. For this reason it was decided that, for this SAR, the lowest geographical level would be the Registrar General's Standard Regions, plus Wales and Scotland. The only exception is that the South East is split into Inner London, Outer London, and the Rest of the South East Region. The full list is therefore as follows:

- North Region
- North West Region
- Yorkshire and Humberside Region
- East Midlands Region
- East Anglia Region
- West Midlands Region

- Inner London
- Outer London
- Rest of South East Region
- South West Region
- Wales
- Scotland

It should be noted that the order of records in both SARs was rearranged before the Census Offices released them. This was to prevent any possible deduction of the geographical location of individuals or households within a region or district.

11.5.3 Suppression of data and grouping of categories

Some alterations have been made to the data to reduce the number of rare and possibly unique cases. The extent to which the variables on the local base have been either suppressed entirely or modified by grouping small categories before release in SARs is shown in table 11.1.

Map 11.1   Geographical areas for the 2 per cent individual SAR

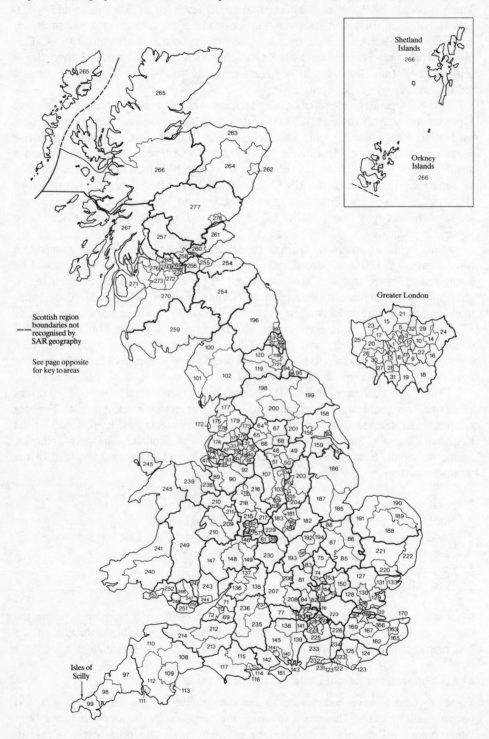

Scottish region
boundaries not
recognised by
SAR geography

See page opposite
for key to areas

Greater London

Shetland
Islands
266

Orkney
Islands
266

Isles of
Scilly

Source: *Population Trends* 1992, vol. 69, pp 20-22

Key to Map 11.1 – Geographical areas for two per cent individual SAR

Local authorities/London boroughs

Inner London
1 City of London; City of Westminister
2 Camden
3 Hackney
4 Hammersmith and Fulham
5 Haringey
6 Islington
7 Kensington and Chelsea
8 Lambeth
9 Lewisham
10 Newham
11 Southwark
12 Tower Hamlets
13 Wandsworth

Outer London
14 Barking and Dagenham
15 Barnet
16 Bexley
17 Brent
18 Bromley
19 Croydon
20 Ealing
21 Enfield
22 Greenwich
23 Harrow
24 Havering
25 Hillingdon
26 Hounslow
27 Kingston upon Thames
28 Merton
29 Redbridge
30 Richmond upon Thames
31 Sutton
32 Waltham Forest

Greater Manchester
33 Bolton
34 Bury
35 Manchester
36 Oldham
37 Rochdale
38 Salford
39 Stockport
40 Tameside
41 Trafford
42 Wigan

Merseyside
43 Knowsley
44 Liverpool
45 St Helens
46 Sefton
47 Wirral

South Yorkshire
48 Barnsley
49 Doncaster
50 Rotherham
51 Sheffield

Tyne and Wear
52 Gateshead
53 Newcastle upon Tyne
54 North Tyneside
55 South Tyneside
56 Sunderland

West Midlands
57 Birmingham
58 Coventry
59 Dudley
60 Sandwell
61 Solihull
62 Walsall
63 Wolverhampton

West Yorkshire
64 Bradford
65 Calderdale
66 Kirklees
67 Leeds
68 Wakefield

Avon
69 Bath; Kingswood; Wansdyke
70 Bristol
71 Northavon
72 Woodspring

Bedfordshire
73 Luton
74 Mid Bedfordshire; South Bedfordshire
75 North Bedfordshire

Berkshire
76 Bracknell Forest; Slough
77 Newbury
78 Reading
79 Windsor & Maidenhead
80 Wokingham

Buckinghamshire
81 Aylesbury Vale
82 Chiltern
83 Milton Keynes
84 Wycombe

Cambridgeshire
85 Cambridge; South Cambridgeshire
86 East Cambridgeshire; Fenland
87 Huntingdonshire
88 Peterborough

Cheshire
89 Chester; Ellesmere Port and Neston
90 Congleton; Crewe and Nantwich; Vale Royal
91 Halton
92 Macclesfield
93 Warrington

Cleveland
94 Hartlepool; Stockton-on-Tees
95 Langbaurgh-on-Tees
96 Middlesbrough

Cornwall & Isles of Scilly
97 Caradon; North Cornwall
98 Carrick; Restormel
99 Kerrier; Penwith; Isles of Scilly

Cumbria
100 Allerdale; Carlisle
101 Barrow-in-Furness Copeland
102 Eden; South Lakeland

Derbyshire
103 Amber Valley; North East Derbyshire
104 Bolsover; Chesterfield
105 Derby
106 Erewash; South Derbyshire
107 High Peak; The Derbyshire Dales

Devon
108 East Devon; Mid Devon
109 Exeter; Teignbridge
110 North Devon; Torridge
111 Plymouth
112 South Ham; West Devon
113 Torbay

Dorset
114 Bournemouth
115 Christchurch; East Dorset North Dorset
116 Poole
117 Purbeck; West Dorset; Weymouth and Portland

Durham
118 Chester-le-Street; Durham
119 Darlington; Teesdale
120 Derwentside; Wear Valley
121 Easington; Sedgefield

East Sussex
122 Brighton
123 Eastbourne; Hove; Lewes
124 Hastings; Rother
125 Wealdon

Essex
126 Basildon
127 Braintree; Uttlesford
128 Brentwood; Epping Forest; Harlow
129 Castle Point; Maldon; Rochford
130 Chelmsford
131 Colchester
132 Southend-on-Sea
133 Tendring
134 Thurrock

Gloucestershire
135 Cheltenham; Cotswold
136 Forest of Dean; Stroud
137 Gloucester; Tewkes'bury

Hampshire
138 Basingstoke & Deane
139 East Hampshire; Havant
140 Eastleigh; Fareham; Gosport
141 Hart; Rushmoor
142 New Forest
143 Portsmouth
144 Southampton
145 Test Valley; Winchester

Hereford and Worcester
146 Bromsgrove; Wyre Forest
147 Hereford; Leominster; South Herefordshire
148 Malvern Hills; Worcester
149 Redditch; Wychavon

Hertfordshire
150 Broxbourne; East Hertfordshire
151 Dacorum
152 Hertsmere; Welwyn Hatfield
153 North Hertfordshire; Stevenage
154 St Albans
155 Three Rivers; Watford

Humberside
156 Beverley; Boothferry
157 Cleethorpes; Great Grimsby
158 East Yorkshire; Holderness
159 Glanford; Scunthorpe
160 Kingston-upon-Hull

Isle of Wight
161 Medina; South Wight

Kent
162 Ashford; Tunbridge Wells
163 Canterbury
164 Dartford; Gravesham
165 Dover; Shepway
166 Gillingham; Swale
167 Maidstone
168 Rochester upon Medway
169 Sevenoaks; Tonbridge & Malling
170 Thanet

Lancashire
171 Blackburn
172 Blackpool
173 Burnley; Pendle
174 Chorley; West Lancashire
175 Fylde; Wyre
176 Hyndburn; Rossendale
177 Lancaster
178 Preston
179 Ribble Valley; South Ribble

Leicestershire
180 Blaby; Oadby & Wigston
181 Charnwood
182 Harborough; Melton; Rutland
183 Hinckley & Bosworth; North West Leicestershire
184 Leicester

Lincolnshire
185 Boston; South Holland
186 East Lindsey; Lincoln; West Lindsey
187 North Kesteven; South Kesteven

Norfolk
188 Breckland; South Norfolk
189 Broadland; Norwich
190 Great Yarmouth
191 Kings Lynn & West Norfolk

Northamptonshire
192 Corby; Kettering
193 Daventry; South Northamptonshire
194 East Northamptonshire; Wellingborough
195 Northampton

Northumberland
196 Alnwick; Berwick-upon-Tweed; Castle Morpeth; Tynedale
197 Blyth Valley, Wansbeck

North Yorkshire
198 Craven; Hambleton; Richmondshire
199 Ryedale; Scarborough
200 Harrogate
201 Selby; York

Nottinghamshire
202 Ashfield; Mansfield
203 Bassetlaw; Newark & Sherwood
204 Broxtowe; Gedling; Rushcliffe
205 Nottingham

Oxfordshire
206 Cherwell
207 Oxford; Vale of White Horse; West Oxfordshire
208 South Oxfordshire

Shropshire
209 Bridgnorth; Shrewsbury & Atcham
210 North Shropshire; Oswestry; South Shropshire
211 The Wrekin

Somerset
212 Mendip; Sedgemoor
213 South Somerset
214 Taunton Deane; West Somerset

Staffordshire
215 Cannock Chase; South Staffordshire
216 East Staffordshire; Staffordshire Moorlands
217 Lichfield; Tamworth
218 Newcastle-under-Lyme; Stafford
219 Stoke-on-Trent

Suffolk
220 Babergh; Ipswich
221 Forest Heath; Mid Suffolk; St Edmundsbury
222 Suffolk Coastal; Waveney

Surrey
223 Elmbridge; Epsom & Ewell
224 Guildford
225 Mole Valley; Waverley;
226 Reigate & Banstead; Tandridge
227 Runnymede; Spelthorne
228 Surrey Heath; Woking

Warwickshire
229 North Warwickshire; Nuneaton & Bedworth; Rugby
230 Stratford-on-Avon; Warwick

West Sussex
231 Adur; Worthing
232 Arun
233 Chichester; Horsham
234 Crawley; Mid Sussex

Wiltshire
235 Kennet; Salisbury
236 North Wiltshire; West Wiltshire
237 Thamesdown

Clwyd
238 Alyn & Deeside; Delyn; Wrexham Maelor
239 Colwyn; Glyndwr; Rhuddlan

Dyfed
240 Carmarthen; Dinefwr; Llanelli
241 Ceredigion; Preseli Pembrokeshire; South Pembrokeshire

Gwent
242 Blaenau Gwent; Islwyn
243 Monmouth; Torfaen
244 Newport

Gwynedd
245 Aberconwy; Arfon; Dwyfor; Meirionnydd; Ynys Mon - Isle of Anglesey

Mid Glamorgan
246 Cynon Valley; Rhondda
247 Merthyr Tydfil; Rhymney Valley; Taff-Ely
248 Ogwr

Powys
249 Brecknock; Montgomeryshire; Radnorshire

South Glamorgan
250 Cardiff
251 Vale of Glamorgan

West Glamorgan
252 Lliw Valley; Neath; Port Talbot
253 Swansea

Borders and Lothian
254 Berwickshire; East Lothian; Ettrick & Lauderdale; Mid Lothian; Roxburgh; Tweeddale
255 Edinburgh City
256 West Lothian

Central
257 Clackmannan; Stirling
258 Falkirk

Dumfries & Galloway
259 Annandale & Eskdale; Nithsdale; Stewarty; Wigtown

Fife
260 Dunfermline
261 Kirkcaldy; North East Fife

Grampian
262 Aberdeen City
263 Banff & Buchan; Moray
264 Gordon; Kincardine & Deeside

Highland and Islands Areas
265 Caithness; Sutherland; Ross & Cromarty; Skye & Lochalsh; Western Isles
266 Badenoch & Strathspey; Inverness; Lochaber; Nairn; Orkney Islands; Shetland Islands

Strathclyde
267 Argyll & Bute; Dumbarton; Inverclyde
268 Bearsden & Milngavie; Clydebank; Strathkelvin
269 Cumbernauld & Kilsyth; Monklands
270 Clydesdale; Cumnock & Doon Valley; Kyle & Carrick
271 Cunninghame
272 East Kilbride; Hamilton
273 Eastwood; Kilmarnock & Loudon
274 Glasgow City
275 Motherwell
276 Renfrew

Tayside
277 Angus; Perth & Kinross
278 Dundee City

Information which is unique in itself, such as names and addresses, has been omitted altogether; technically these variables have not been suppressed since they were never put on the computer. Precise day and month of birth have been suppressed.

As explained in chapter 5, the degree of detail permitted on other variables was the subject of a thresholding rule which ensured that the expected value of any category at the lowest level of geography on any file was at least 1. The threshold, when operationalised, dictated that a category must have 25,000 cases in it in the GB file before it could be released on the individual SAR, or 2,700 cases before it could be released on the household SAR.

When expected frequency counts fell below the threshold, categories were grouped. With some variables, grouping was only required at one end of the distribution: thus rooms were top-coded above 14 and the number of persons in the household was top-coded above 12. Two variables were both grouped and top coded; with age, 91 and 92 were grouped, 93 and 94 were grouped and 95 and over was top-coded; with hours of work, 71–80 hours per week was grouped and the rest top-coded above 81.

When variables were not measured on a numeric scale, judgments had to be made about which categories to put together. Classifications for census data are often hierarchical. For example, for the Standard Occupational Classification there are 371 unit groups, 77 minor groups, 22 sub-major groups, and 9 major groups. In cases such as these, small categories could be amalgamated to the next level in the hierarchy. In other cases, detailed advice was sought from subject experts about how the groups should be formed.

In the case of three variables in the 2 per cent individual SAR, it was deemed necessary to further group categories, even though they contained numbers which fell above the threshold: occupation, industry, and subject of qualification. As a result of advice received from the Technical Assessor, occupation was reduced from the 220 categories proposed (out of a possible 371) to 73; similarly industry was cut from a possible 334 to 60 and subject of educational qualification from a possible 108 to 35. (Almost full occupational detail remains on the 1 per cent household SAR, however.) The full list of all variables is given in Teague and Marsh (1992).

There were other factors which determined the detail to be released:

(1) Categories of occupations and industries in the public eye were grouped further than mathematically necessary to guard against disclosure; for example, actors/ actresses and professional sportsmen/women.

(2) Large households were seen as a disclosure risk in the household sample. Applying the frequency rule to size of household, a large household in the 1981 Census was estimated to be one of 12 persons or more. Consequently, only housing information is given for households containing 12 or more persons. No information about the individuals in the household is given.

(3) Geographical information for such items as workplace and migration (address one year before census) has been heavily grouped. This is because of the high likelihood of uniqueness of such information when used in conjunction with area of residence.

11.6 DISSEMINATION

The ESRC combined forces with the Joint Information Services Committee of the Universities Funding Council to buy the data on behalf of the academic community. The sponsors have paid the full marginal cost of developing the SARs and have been granted sole licence to the data for a period of five years from the date of supply. They have the right to pass on the data to others, either free (in the case of academic research) or for a charge (in other cases), to enable them to recoup some of the costs of their investment.

The sponsors have contracted the University of Manchester to house a Census Microdata Unit, where a programme of research based on the microdata is being conducted, and to handle all aspects of data distribution to the academic community and elsewhere.

All end users have to give binding undertakings to respect confidentiality. Specifically, users have to guarantee not to use the SARs to attempt to obtain or derive information about an identified individual or household, nor to claim to have obtained such information. Furthermore, they have to undertake not to pass on copies of the raw data from the SARs without permission, and the user registration undertaking gives the Census Microdata Unit authority to audit their use of the data. They must sign a statement that they understand that the consequences of any breach of the regulations on the part of any user in a specific institution can lead to the withdrawal of all copies of the data from that institution.

The Census Microdata Unit is responsible for documenting the data set, and for calculating and disseminating sampling errors where possible and necessary. A preliminary version of the codebook containing marginal frequencies is available with the data. A more complete version will be released early in 1994, containing information on sampling errors, on further derived variables and on the SARs for Northern Ireland. The Census Microdata Unit provides training half-days and full-days on the SARs, run both at the University of Manchester and as roadshows in any institution which requests it. A user newsletter keeping people informed of the latest developments is being produced. Information on all these dissemination activities is available from the Census Microdata Unit, Faculty of Economic and Social Studies, University of Manchester, Oxford Road, Manchester M13 9PL.

The Census Microdata Unit provide three different sorts of dissemination service.

(1) *An on-line service:* the data have been mounted on the Manchester Computing Centre's mainframe, currently running under CMS, and are available nationally over the Joint Academic Network or by a dial-up service. Various software platforms are available for the data, including statistical packages such as SPSS and SAS. Database management packages such as SIR and tabulators such as Quanvert are also being evaluated for use as a platform for the SARs (see Roberts *et al.*, (1992) for more details); although the strengths and weaknesses of these packages are well-known among social researchers, the problems encountered when these packages are used to handle data files with one million records are not. The Census Microdata Unit provides advice on handling the data using a variety of software packages.

(2) *Distribution of raw SAR data*: the Census Microdata Unit either distribute copies of the entire data set, or specific subsets of cases or variables to suit individual

requirements, together with any necessary documentation and set-up programs to run the data in different software environments. For the reasons given in the previous section, the supply of data is only for users' own use; they are not allowed to pass it on to others without obtaining the prior approval of the Census Microdata Unit at Manchester. Data are supplied in different formats. Most demand is expected for magnetic tapes, exabyte tapes and floppy disks to run on DOS, Apple Macintosh, or Unix machines. The progress of CD-ROM technology for handling data will also be kept under review.

(3) *A customised tables service*: for most social researchers, the census forms a supplementary data source, more often supplying denominators than numerators. It is therefore desirable to be able to provide occasional census users with one or two tables, instead of insisting that they learn to manipulate the data themselves. While priority will be given to other aspects of the service, it is hoped that there will be sufficient capacity to run a fast customised tables services for those who require it.

The data are free for the purposes of academic research; to get the data free the researcher must in an institution qualified to receive an ESRC award, and the research must be funded either by the Higher Education Funding Council or one of the Research Councils. When the data are used either by those outside the academic sector or by researchers in universities for sponsored research, a charge is made. In order to encourage a high volume of usage of a product whose advantages may not yet be well appreciated in Britain, these charges are being kept extremely low; an entire national SAR can be bought for £1,000 + VAT, and subsets of one SAR area for £500.

11.7 CONCLUSION

The demand by users to extract ever increasing amounts of value from the census perhaps finds its logical outcome in the provision of raw data in anonymised form. Users of the SARs have a large flexible database, the like of which has never been previously available in Britain.

12   The OPCS Longitudinal Study

Angela Dale

12.1 BACKGROUND

The OPCS Longitudinal Study (LS) represents an unusual and distinctive research resource which has developed within the OPCS for England and Wales over the last 15 years. (A comparable study in Scotland was discontinued at about the time of the 1981 Census.) In essence, the LS is a 1 per cent sample of records drawn from the 1971, 1981 and 1991 Censuses, to which are linked information on certain vital events, e.g. births, deaths and cancer registration, for the *same individuals* (figure 12.1). The basis for selection is having one of four birthdates in the year. The original rationale for the LS was to provide better statistics on occupational mortality by using occupation recorded at census linked to subsequent information from death registration, for the same people. No new data collection is involved; the LS uses solely those data which are already available, within OPCS, from census and administrative records. Because of the confidential nature of such data the LS is held under very secure conditions within OPCS. Nonetheless, tabulations and summary data from statistical analyses can be made available to both the academic and public sector. With the addition of 1991 Census records, the majority of LS members now have census information for three time points over a 20-year period. OPCS welcomes and encourages the exploitation of this very rich resource.

Figure 12.1   Diagrammatic representation of the OPCS Longitudinal Study

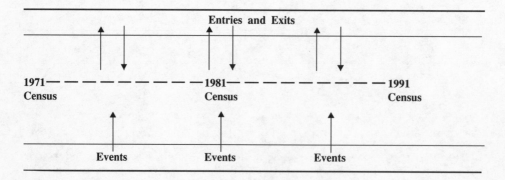

The LS therefore differs considerably from most other census products. First, it allows analysis of individual-level data; prior to the release of the Samples of Anonymised Records from the 1991 Census the LS was the only means by which individual-level information could be accessed for analysis. Second, it provides a unique longitudinal dimension to census data which adds considerably to the range and scope of analysis. Thirdly, it allows data collected at census to be related, *prospectively,* to vital events which are routinely collected by OPCS. The structure and analysis potential of the LS is discussed in further detail below.

12.1.1 The wider context of the OPCS Longitudinal Study

A number of other countries have studies which link census and vital registration data, although the LS is unique in the extent of data that can be linked and in the arrangements that have been made for access under secure conditions. The Scandinavian countries, notably Denmark and Finland, have pioneered linkage of census information to mortality records to enable the analysis of occupational mortality. In Norway, linkage of census records for the same individuals can be made between 1960, 1970, 1980 and 1990, but only on a one-off basis for particular research purposes. The French Institut National de la Statistique et des Etudes Economiques (INSEE) has constructed linkages between census data and vital registration records - the Echantillon Démographique Permanent (EDP) which has many similarities to the LS. In these examples which involve *linkage* of records, methods to allow analysis by those outside the census office are generally embryonic or unformalised. The LS stands out as distinctive in providing *both* linked microdata across successive censuses *and* linkage to vital registration with a formalised strategy to provide access to any bona fide user within a secure and regulated setting. The research potential of the LS clearly goes well beyond that of any of its individual components. The rest of this chapter provides a fuller description of the LS and explains the methods of access available to potential users.

12.1.2 Why the OPCS Longitudinal Study was set up

Planning for the LS started in the late 1960s when there was serious concern with the adequacy of the social statistics that were then available to government. Mortality was a topic on which existing information was particularly poor. Statistics on occupational mortality were known to be unreliable because they used information on occupation given at death registration. The link to information given at an earlier census offered the prospect of improved figures on occupational mortality (see section 12.6.4). Other linkages, for example between census information and birth registration, extended the range of fertility data available, whilst linkage between census records and cancer registration provided a socioeconomic dimension to the analysis of recorded cancer. Linking successive censuses added a new time dimension to census analyses. Thus, without the need for new fieldwork, information could be derived that was not previously available and greater use could be made of existing data.

The LS, therefore, allows analysis of longitudinal individual-level data from the census, as well as analyses which relate information from vital registration to that from census. This means that all the standard multivariate analysis techniques are appropriate, as well as survival analysis and methods used to calculate standardised mortality ratios.

The addition of records from the 1991 Census now offers the prospect of longitudinal analyses over three time points for a range of topics that include migration, household formation and dissolution, educational achievement and occupational status, mortality and fertility. As time goes by, more data become linked into the study and the research potential increases enormously.

12.2 CONFIDENTIALITY

A data source such as the LS cannot be released as individual records to researchers who wish to analyse it. The LS is governed by both the 1920 Census Act and the Census (Confidentiality) Act 1991 and also the 1938 and 1960 Population (Statistics) Acts. OPCS has responsibility to preserve the confidentiality of the data and for this reason the LS is held in secure conditions within OPCS. All analysis of individual records must take place on the OPCS computer and only statistical abstracts or tabulations can be released to the user (see chapter 5). To ensure confidentiality there are limits on the amount of detail that is permitted in a table either in the number of cells, the size of the population to be analysed, or the size of the geographical area.

However, because the LS is not released to users as individual-level data, no alterations — top coding, grouping of small categories — are made to the data as held on the OPCS computer. The only absolute constraints are that date of birth is not available to researchers (although it can be used to generate exact age and person-years-at-risk) and tabulations and analyses cannot be conducted below the level of local district, although ward-level aggregate data can be attached to individual records by OPCS. This means that detailed analyses can be run on the OPCS computer, as long as all output meets the confidentiality requirements. For example, a multivariate analysis may use full details of age, household composition, spouse's characteristics and area of residence to predict the level of overcrowding recorded. Overcrowding (the number of people per room) can be used as a continuous variable because the LS retains the component variables on number of rooms and number of persons in the household. Output can be released in the form of regression coefficients and standard errors, and thus poses no threat to confidentiality. Where tabulations are required, these are subject to rules to protect confidentiality.

OPCS monitors both requests to use the LS and the resulting output and, for this reason, formal channels have been established for requests to use the LS for research purposes. Details on the procedures for accessing the LS and the ways in which data can be made available are given in section 12.9.

12.3 THE STRUCTURE AND CONTENT OF THE LS

Initially, all people born on each of four dates each year were selected from information given in the 1971 Census. This produced a sample of 4/365, slightly over 1 per cent. From census day 1971 additional members, having one of the four LS birth dates, joined the LS from two sources:

- new births
- people who enter the country as immigrants and register with the National Health Service

Figure 12.2 The structure of the OPCS Longitudinal Study

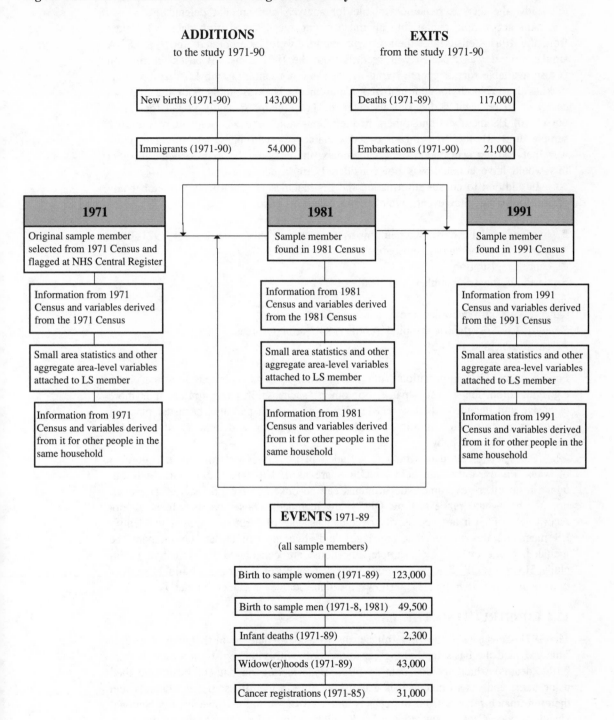

Similarly, deaths and emigrants are also recorded. Although these are 'exits' from the study, the records remain available for analysis and are not deleted.

Another sample comprising all those giving the selected birth dates was taken from the 1981 Census and their Census records were incorporated into the LS. A similar process was repeated with records from the 1991 Census. Census information is also available for all people living in the same household as the LS member, thus making the LS both longitudinal *and* hierarchical. The LS holds both the 100 per cent and 10 per cent coded Census data, the latter being specially coded for (the 9 out of 10) LS members and others in their household who are not part of the 10% sample. In 1981, the 10 per cent coded variables for workplace and travel to work were not 100 per cent coded for LS members; the case for the extra expenditure that this would have entailed was not considered strong enough.

In addition to census information the LS includes for each sample member any of the following vital events which have occurred since 1971:

- live and still births to women (births to men are only recorded for 1971-78)
- infant mortality among those births
- cancer registration
- death of the LS member and death of a spouse

Other events also recorded are:
- entry to a psychiatric hospital (until 1984), armed forces
- emigration and re-entry

For all events, full information from the relevant form is recorded. In some cases, e.g. emigration, this is very sparse. For others, such as birth registration, it is more extensive and includes whether registered by one or both parents, the usual place of residence, place of birth of mother and father, occupation and industry of parent(s), and birth weight of baby.

The selection of data which is included in the LS is determined in a number of ways. Firstly, only data held by OPCS are used. No data about individuals obtained from other government departments can be linked to the LS records. However, not all the events processed by OPCS are included. Those events which do not record date of birth are necessarily excluded as date of birth is essential to identify LS members; this means that marriages and divorces cannot, at the moment, be included. Some events, for example, abortions, are considered too sensitive to include. However, OPCS regularly review the feasibility of including additional sources of data in the LS. Figure 12.2 shows the data sources included in the LS.

12.4 CONSTRUCTING THE LS

The 1971 Census was the first full census to ask for date of birth rather than age. This provided the basis for linking census records with vital registration records (e.g. births, deaths) which include date of birth. By selecting on date of birth, and then using name and sex to match, it is usually possible to identify someone uniquely and therefore match records from the census and vital registration. However, the National Health Service Central Register (NHSCR) plays a crucial part in ensuring the accuracy of linkage and in maintaining the LS sample. The NHSCR, located at Southport, is part of OPCS. It maintains a computerised register of all NHS members. All deaths are recorded in the Register, as well as new births and immigrants joining the NHS or emigrants leaving the country. All LS members drawn from the 1971 Census were 'traced' in the NHSCR to locate their NHS number and 'flagged' or marked in the Register. As new members enter the LS, either through being born on an LS date or through having an LS birth date and registering with a GP, or appearing in subsequent censuses, they are also traced and flagged in the NHSCR.

The NHSCR entry is used to ensure the correct linkage to LS members of routinely recorded events, for example deaths or cancer registrations. A record of emigration is also obtained through notification to the Register although it is known that this is subject to considerable under and late-reporting.

The NHSCR holds the unique number allocated to each LS member, which is crucial in making the link between new and existing census records. The 1981 Census was sampled for all persons with the four LS birth dates and the extracted sample was matched with the existing sample. In 1981 the method of linkage was entirely manual and is fully described in the *OPCS Longitudinal Study User Manual* (SSRU, 1990). If a record could not be matched against a pre-existing one, then attempts were made to trace that person in the NHSCR. Where there were uncertainties over linkage, additional information on change of name and geographical location was obtained from the NHSCR; the marriage index was searched, and further information sought from the census schedules of other household members and from the most recent Electoral Register.

A similar process was repeated with records from the 1991 Census. The 1991 linkage process gained from the computerisation of the NHSCR, which made it much quicker to locate the LS member's existing LS number. However, because names and addresses from the 1991 Census were not entered onto computer, the full potential of computerisation could not be realised. Early indications of the 1991 Census link suggested that 95 per cent of potential LS members enumerated in England and Wales in the 1991 Census had been linked to a member of the existing LS sample. This means that much less supplementary searching is needed in order to maximise linkage than was needed for the 1981 link.

12.5 QUALITY OF LS DATA

The quality of the LS depends upon three components:

- the quality of census data
- the quality of data from event registration
- the quality of linkage

12.5.1 Quality of data sources

The quality and coverage of census data is assessed by post-enumeration surveys, although the 1971 coverage check was generally considered to be inadequate (Barnes, 1989). Full details for 1971 and 1981 are given in OPCS (1983a) and Britton and Birch (1985), respectively, and are summarised in the *OPCS Longitudinal Study User Manual* (SSRU, 1990).

The quality of event registration data varies with the source and the year. Notification of births and deaths in England and Wales is statutory and, as a result, recording of these is almost complete. The National Cancer Registration Scheme is based on a system of voluntary notification and there is known to be temporal and regional variation in the completeness of registration. Other events (entry to the country, leaving the armed forces or leaving a psychiatric hospital), are only picked up when the LS member registers with a general practitioner thereby alerting the NHSCR and, in turn, the LS Unit, to the event. There may be a considerable delay, which will vary with age and stage of lifecycle, before a general practitioner is consulted. Other events also depend upon notification to the NHSCR. The Armed Forces Medical Services notify the Register of enlistments, as do psychiatric hospitals after a patient has been in their care for more than two years. People leaving the country (embarkations) who are known to the Department of Social Security are automatically notified to the Register, although other embarkations may only be picked up after considerable delay or not at all. An assessment of the completeness and quality of each source of event data is given in the *OPCS Longitudinal Study User Manual* (SSRU, 1990).

12.5.2 Quality of data linkage

One of the strengths of the LS is its ability to relate information from census to that from vital registration and, also, to provide longitudinal data by linking census records from 1971, 1981 and 1991. The quality of data linkage is therefore of the utmost important to the success of the LS.

Quality of tracing at the NHSCR

Accuracy of linkage in the LS depends, firstly, upon success in tracing the LS member at the NHSCR. Once the NHS number of the LS member has been located, and the entry in the register flagged, then the chances of accurate linkage are greatly improved. A considerable amount of research has been carried out on the quality of tracing rates (Fox and Goldblatt, 1982; SSRU, 1990; Goldblatt, 1990). Of the sample drawn from the 1971 Census, 96.8 per cent were successfully traced initially. The 'not-traced' rate was 2.82 per cent for men, 2.77 per cent for single women, 4.08 per cent for married women and 6.89 per cent for divorced women. These figures immediately highlight one of the problems in establishing linkage — changing names on marriage or divorce and the delay in notifying any changes to the NHSCR. Not-traced rates are higher for members of communal establishments, and also higher for LS members born outside England and Wales. Because all linkage of events uses the NHSCR entry, it is crucial that LS members have been traced in the register. For this reason, research which uses the events data should be confined to LS members who have been traced at the Register and therefore flagged as LS members.

It is important for LS users to know the extent to which the 'no trace' rate for a particular group introduces bias into analyses. One way of looking at this is to establish the sampling fraction that results from comparing the traced LS population with the 1971 Census population. Fox and Goldblatt (1982) describe in detail the sampling fractions obtained for different groups. One of their more important findings was that people from the New Commonwealth and Pakistan had sampling fractions considerably higher than expected, despite the fact that there was difficulty in tracing them in the Register. This is explained by a higher than expected proportion of people born in these countries who gave one of the LS birth dates. Further details are available in Fox and Goldblatt (1982) and SSRU (1990). The effect is that over-sampling from the 1971 Census has compensated for the high no-trace rates in the

Register. Some comparisons of the ethnic minority population identified in the LS with that obtained from the 1971 Census are given in Stuart (1990).

Even for the traced population, there is variation in the success of linking events to LS members. The computerisation of the NHSCR has meant that a number of events, missed under the manual system, have recently been linked. For both deaths and cancer registration, linkage rates are near 100 per cent, in part because of a dual method of ensuring linkage into the main sample. Firstly, as with all events, weekly routine notification to the NHSCR results in the Register being updated and, as the LS member is flagged in the Register, this generates notification of the event to the LS Unit. This method means that if a date of birth as reported at death registration differs from that which selected the person into the LS, the death will, nonetheless, be recorded. Secondly, an annual search is made of both the deaths and cancer registration files for entries with the LS dates of birth. These are checked against the routine notifications and, if additional deaths are found for LS members, these are recorded.

Linkage of new births to LS members depends upon identifying the parents' dates of birth in the OPCS annual births file. If this date of birth is inconsistent with that given at census, then the birth will not be linked. It is estimated that about 15 per cent of births are missed in this way. The *OPCS Longitudinal Study User Manual* summarises OPCS research on the variation of linkage rates by socioeconomic characteristics for births to LS members in 1970. However, a special exercise carried out by OPCS identified a high proportion of these missing births between 1972–80 resulting in a final linkage rate of 94 per cent for 1971–81. Babb and Hattersley (1992) have demonstrated the impact of missed births for 1980–88. A similar exercise to that following the 1981 Census link is planned to follow the 1991 Census link and this should, similarly, improve linkage rates.

Linkage between censuses depends upon consistency in recording date of birth and name at each census. Generally, linkage rates between the 1971 and 1981 Censuses were good; about 92 per cent of the LS members found in the 1971 Census were *either* alive and found in the 1981 Census (80 per cent) *or* were known to have died (11 per cent) *or* known to have emigrated (1 per cent) (OPCS, 1988). The remaining 40,000 (8 per cent) could not be found. Further research (OPCS, 1988) showed that date of birth discrepancies and a failure to record the person on the census form accounted for over two thirds of the linkage failures. Other reasons included the person being abroad on census night and an emigration not notified to, or recorded in, the NHSCR. Of all failures to link, only 8 per cent were estimated to be due to clerical error.

There is, of course, considerable variation in linkage rates by sociodemographic characteristics. Linkage rates were considerably lower for those born overseas, the elderly, and those in communal establishments in 1971. Details can be found in the OPCS report of the linkage results (OPCS, 1988). Some of the consequences of non-linkage between censuses and a failure to trace the LS member in the NHSCR is discussed further in section 12.6.2. An OPCS LS Technical Report is planned for publication by HMSO in 1994. It will contain information on linkage rates and sampling fractions for the entire period of the LS, including the 1991 Census link. Preliminary information will be published as soon as it becomes available. As mentioned in section 12.4.1, the 1991 Census link has been greatly facilitated by the computerisation of the Register, and linkage rates should be at least as good as between 1971 and 1981.

12.6 THE RESEARCH POTENTIAL OF THE LS

This section outlines those research areas where the LS is uniquely placed to provide data. Because of its restricted access (section 12.2) it is usually advisable to concentrate on using the LS for those purposes for which there is no alternative data source. In earlier years the LS has been used for cross-sectional research, for example to derive new, non-standard, household classifications for the 1971 and 1981 Census. Cross-sectional work on 1991 Census data will now be easier to undertake with the Samples of Anonymised Records (see chapter 11) rather than the LS, although users may well wish to extend comparisons backwards to 1981 and 1971 using the LS. The way in which the LS is structured (section 12.4.1) means that it can be used to provide a number of different samples, depending on the research requirement. Some of these are briefly outlined below.

12.6.1 Selecting samples from the LS

The LS represents a continuously updated sample of the population of England and Wales, even though census records are only added at 10-year intervals. This is because the study records the death and emigration of existing members, as well as the entry of immigrants and new births with the LS dates of birth. Bias in the sample comes from under-enumeration in the census, or failure to link into the LS, and from the imperfect recording and linkage of exits and entries to the study.

Depending on the research use, the LS can provide a number of different samples. These include:

(1) *A 4/365 quasi-random sample of individuals drawn from the census of popu lation for England and Wales at 1971, 1981 or 1991.* The sample is unclustered except by date of birth. The four selected dates of birth are equally spaced throughout the year, thereby avoiding any seasonal effects. The selected sample represents a 1.1 per cent cross-section of the population of England and Wales at the date of the particular census.

(2) *A cross-sectional sample of households present in the census for England and Wales.* To obtain an equal probability sample of households, those LS members categorised as 'head of household' at the relevant census should be selected. This sample is appropriate for analyses of household-level characteristics. If household-level data (e.g. tenure, size of household) are analysed by individual LS member, two problems arise: large households are over-represented (because sampling is individual-based) and there is a small chance that two LS members will be present in the same household. These issues are discussed in more detail in *Update* (LS User Group, 1992), the Newsletter of the LS User Group.

(3) *A sample of LS members present at two or more censuses, e.g. 1971 and 1981; 1981 and 1991.* This sample allows the analysis of change between two or three censuses. By confining the sample to those present at two (or three) time points, the population selected is not representative of the population of England and Wales at either time point taken separately. This can be explained by considering the sample present in the LS in *both* 1971 and 1981. Those LS members present in 1981 but who had not been born, or had not entered the country in 1971, are excluded. Conversely, all those present in the 1971 Census

but who died or emigrated before the 1981 Census are eliminated. Additionally, there will be a small number of LS members — about 8 per cent (OPCS, 1988) — enumerated in the 1971 Census, with no record of either death or emigration, who could not be linked to a 1981 census record. The reasons for this are discussed in section 12.5 on data quality.

It is possible to define age cohorts of LS members, grouping together several years, and to compare change between cohorts between censuses. The potential for longitudinal inter–cohort comparisons is discussed in section 12.7. Where one is interested in change between censuses, then the sample should be based on all LS members in the defined cohort who were in, for example, the 1971 *and* the 1981 census. The limitations of this sample are the same as those discussed in the preceding paragraph.

(4) *A continuously updated cohort sample.* For some analyses it is important to ensure that the sample remains representative of the population over time. Calculations of age specific fertility rates for different age cohorts, for example, will be affected by whether or not the sample has been adjusted for immigration and emigration (Babb and Hattersley, 1992). In this example, the composition of the cohort will change over time, offsetting selection effects through migration and mortality. The following paragraphs highlight some of the topic areas where the LS can provide data unavailable from other sources.

12.6.2 Mortality

The main reason for establishing the LS was to improve the availability of data on occupational mortality. Whilst regular mortality statistics are published by OPCS in the Decennial Supplements (e.g. OPCS, 1978) it is acknowledged that the method by which mortality rates are calculated has a number of shortcomings. The number of deaths (the numerator) occurring in a calendar year is divided by an estimate of the size of the population on 30 June of that year (the denominator). Deaths are characterised by information on the death certificate whilst estimates of the mid-year population come from the latest census, updated to take account of subsequent births, deaths and migrations. Whilst this is satisfactory for annual mortality statistics, it leads to biases in calculating occupation-based mortality rates — termed numerator-denominator bias. This arises if there are biases in recording occupation at death which are greater or different from those biases arising from occupational recording at census. Because the LS links occupation recorded at census to the subsequent death of the same individual, any numerator-denominator bias is removed, although any bias within the census data remains. Bias in occupation recorded at death is well established: there may be a tendency to 'promote' the deceased person by giving a rather higher status occupation than the most recent one; also the person registering the death may have very limited information on the last occupation of the dead person (Heasman and Lipworth, 1966). Also, the last occupation may be different from that in which the person spent most of their working life. The LS is able to avoid most of these problems by using occupation given at census. Additionally, by restricting deaths to those occurring five or more years after census, the selection effects which occur when prior ill health influences choice of occupation are greatly reduced.

The LS can also be used to measure health inequalities based on a variety of alternative measures of social class (e.g. availability of cars, tenure) which may be particularly appropriate for some subgroups of the population, for example, women with no recent employment. A great deal of work has already been done (Fox and Goldblatt, 1982; Goldblatt, 1990) and a programme of research is continuing at OPCS and at the London School of Hygiene and Tropical Medicine.

When using any LS data that come from event registration it is important to restrict the population to those traced in the NHSCR (see section 12.5.2). By doing so, there is a much greater likelihood that the death, or other event, will have been correctly linked to the LS member. If a death is not correctly linked, then the LS member is assumed to remain alive and therefore biases the calculation of death rates. This becomes particularly important amongst the small group of very old people. Fox and Goldblatt (1982) and Goldblatt (1990) discuss a number of other methodological issues associated with using the LS for the analysis of mortality.

The LS provides a unique resource for mortality analyses. When new software currently being developed by OPCS becomes available, there will be greatly expanded opportunities for research involving person-year-at-risk calculations: this is, where one needs to know the exact length of time that an LS member is exposed to risk of death, or cancer. Until then, scope for such analyses is very limited and those interested should contact the LS Unit at St Catherine's House (see below). However, alternative software, SPSSX, GLIM and SAS can be used for many purposes and these provide some alternative routes into the mortality data (Weatherall, 1992).

12.6.3 Fertility

The analysis of fertility data was a further reason behind setting up the LS in the early 1970s when it became evident that such data were difficult to collect in a census. (The 1971 Census question on children born to married women was not repeated in either the 1981 or 1991 Census.) Because the LS collects information on successive births from registration, it is able to provide data not only on age at first birth but also on the interval between births and birth outcomes such as birth weight, single or multiple births and live or still births. Information is available on whether a birth is inside or outside marriage and registered by one or both parents. Again, the availability of linked census data enables analysis by such variables as housing tenure, ethnic group and social class of mother. OPCS has recently derived a subset of data from the LS for the analysis of both fertility and infant mortality which contains a considerable number of specially derived variables (LS Medical Analysis Section, 1992; Creeser, 1992) whilst another specially prepared data set on births to young mothers is described by Penhale (1990a).

Section 12.5.2 discussed the quality of linkage of birth data in the LS. For further work on quality of the LS fertility data see Babb and Hattersley (1992).

12.6.4 Geographical and occupational mobility

The LS offers considerable scope for analyses of migration and of area-based differences. Because the LS sample is drawn using date of birth alone, there is no geographical clustering built into the sample. Both the census and vital registration record area-based information to a very fine level and, although the analyst cannot work at this level of detail, fine geographical areas can be recoded to non-standard areas, or can be used as linking variables to attach area-level indicators to individuals.

Census returns for LS members in 1971 and 1981 recorded ward and enumeration district. In the 1991 Census, postcodes (each containing about 15 addresses) have been recorded for all addresses. Many of the vital events recorded by the LS contain geographical locality at the level of the postcode. Although confidentiality constraints preclude user access to data below county district level, OPCS have added to individual records a number of area-based variables, for example Acorn-type and Craig-Webber classifications, ward-based deprivation scores and travel to work areas (see chapter 10). A selection of ward-level variables from the Small Area Statistics for 1971 and 1981 have also been added. From 1994, following the 1991 Census link, it will be possible for users to supply aggregate level variables that have the appropriate ward or local authority identifiers (including 1991 SAS) which can be linked to individual LS records using these identifiers. This provides considerable scope for analyses that incorporate areal effects, included multilevel modelling (Ward and Dale, 1992), provided that confidentiality requirements are met.

Occupation is recorded in the census and is available for the LS member and others in the household. Occupation is coded to the full OPCS classification (in 1991, there are 371 Occupational Unit Groups) which, with employment status, allows the derivation of a number of different social class schema. As part of the occupational coding for the 1991 Census, it is also possible to obtain the Classification of Occupations used with the 1981 Census, thereby providing some consistency between the 1981 and 1991 occupational information. The LS has already been used very effectively to demonstrate the relationship between occupational mobility and geographical mobility (Fielding, 1989).

Migration and area-level data from the census

The linkage of individual records *between* censuses provides migration data which extends well beyond that available from any one census; usual residence is recorded at 1966, 1970, 1971 (from the 1971 Census one- and five-year migration questions), 1980, 1981 (1981 one-year migration), 1990 and 1991 (1991 Census one-year migration). The usual address is available at the level of local district, county and region for each of these time points. Data from the 1971 Census is also coded to one of 15 hospital regions, whilst that from the 1981 and 1991 Censuses is available at district health authority level. Address of enumeration in the 1971 Census is coded to both pre- and post-1974 boundaries, although usual address is only available for the pre-1974 boundaries.

The LS also holds the census-derived variables on migration for each of the censuses, for example, the wholly moving household indicator,[1] the extent of one-year movement and, for 1971, the extent of five-year movement. Additionally many of the migration variables are available for others in the LS member's household.[2]

---

[1] A 'wholly moving household' is a household where all members have moved together since one year before the census.

[2] Until the end of 1993 these additional variables for other household members are only available on a very restricted basis. By the beginning of 1994, following the 1991-LS link and the move to Model 204, relationships between the LS member and other household members should be much easier to establish.

Migration and area-level data from vital registration

Further area-based information can be obtained from that recorded at vital registration. Area of birth is available for births to LS members and new births since 1971; and usual address for deaths and cancer registrations. This enables migration between successive events to be tracked, as well as between census and an event. Through the NHS number, OPCS has also derived area of birth, coded to post-1974 county and county district, for all LS members born before 1971 but after September 1939. Area of residence in 1939 is also available for a high proportion of LS members alive in 1939 and living in England and Wales. For further information see Creeser, (1991). Information from the National Health Service records and from census can be combined to provide additional migration indicators, for example variables which categorise extent of movement between two time points: between 1939 and 1971, between birth and 1971 or from 1971 to death.

The availability of mortality and cancer registration details in the LS provides an opportunity to investigate the relationship between migration and health. Research of particular interest includes the impact of internal migration of elderly people from London to popular retirement areas and the associated resource implications which stem from the differential propensity of the healthy elderly to migrate (Grundy, 1987).

Shortcomings of LS migration and area-based data

The shortcomings of using the LS for migration also need to be identified. The LS represents a sample of individuals enumerated in England and Wales only; it does not cover Scotland. In 1981 the 10 per cent coded variables for workplace and travel to work were not coded for the LS. Workplace and travel-to-work data are available for 1971, and all 10 per cent variables will be fully coded for 1991. Census information on migration between geographical locations is collected only for discrete points in time with no information for the intervening periods. Nicholson (1992) highlights some of the problems that arise from this, for example there is no information on the total number of moves within a time period; only net migration can be recorded.

The census asks for no information on reasons for moving. Therefore it is not possible to distinguish job-related from housing mobility. Whilst it may be possible to infer that housing-related mobility is confined to moves within a local authority, this pays no regard to that fact that one might move two miles across a local authority boundary, or move 50 miles whilst still remaining within the same authority.

12.6.5 Ethnicity

The LS contains an indicator of ethnicity derived using the 1971 Census information on place of birth of both the LS member and his/her parents (Stuart, 1990). Until the ethnic group question was asked in the 1991 Census, the LS provided a unique source of longitudinal, nationally representative data on ethnic groups.

With the linked 1991 Census data, a range of both methodological and substantive analyses become possible. Firstly, for those LS members for whom there are linked census records for 1971, 1981 and 1991, the LS allows changes in occupation, household structure and family formation, housing tenure and geographical mobility to be tracked over a 20-year time period. For those LS members with both

1971 and 1991 Census records, the comparability of information derived from the two sources — LS ethnic indicator and 1991 Census — can be established. Whilst it will not be possible to know which is 'correct' (and, of course, they are based upon different information), the LS may be able to shed some light on those enumerated as 'other' in the 1991 Census and, conversely, the 1991 Census variable will provide a check on the validity of the 1971-based indicator.

Section 12.5.2 pointed to the fact that linkage rates are considerably lower for LS members born overseas. This represents a problem both in the depletion of numbers and in the bias that is introduced to the sample. This, together with the fact that the LS is only a 1 per cent sample, makes it difficult to distinguish more than the largest five or six ethnic groups living in England and Wales. Nonetheless, as with all census variables, the full codings of the variable (36 categories) are available (chapter 2, section 2.6.5). In summary, despite some limitations, the LS can shed considerable light on the variation between ethnic groups in social and geographical mobility over a 20-year period.

12.6.6 Housing and household change

The census is one of the key sources of data on housing in Britain. It also provides extensive information on household structure and the relationship between household size and housing amenities. The availability of census records on all members of the LS person's household allows new and complex household and family composition variables to be derived. For example, the LS has been used to derive a family definition that is comparable to that used in the French census of 1982. This allows comparisons to be made between household composition in France and England and Wales using a standardised classification (Penhale, 1990a, 1990b; Wall, 1990).

The LS has also been used as a source of data on household formation and dissolution and the effect that this has on housing needs. Holmans, Nandy and Brown (1987) estimated that, for every 100 marriages dissolved, there were 153 successor households. They showed that this generated a demand for rented accommodation both from the ex-partners of owner-occupiers and also from the ex-partners in tenant households. However, remarriage was also associated with change in housing tenure resulting in movement into owner-occupation. The increase in household formation through divorce, net of remarriages, was estimated at around 55,000 a year at divorce rates current at the time of the research.

Indicators of housing deprivation can be constructed from census data and analysed by ethnic group, household composition and stage of life-cycle. Using linked census data one can show that the factors associated with improvements or deterioration in housing amenities between censuses and the way in which these vary with the kind of amenity under consideration, for example, overcrowding versus shared accommodation (Williams and Dale, 1991).

The census has a number of readily identified shortcomings as a source of information on housing; there is no information of the quality of housing, for example dampness, structural problems, and no information on the age of housing. Changes in definitions over time, for example the change in definition of a household between 1971 and 1981, and changes in measures of self-containment, cause major problems of comparison over time, although the extent to which form-fillers read and implement definitions given on census schedules must be open to question. The difficulty in recording accurately the number of rooms available to a household (see chapter 6 (I) also leads to problems in establishing levels of overcrowding, measured as number of people per room. Failure to link between censuses is particularly likely amongst those living in rented accommodation in large urban areas.

12.7 NEW OPPORTUNITIES BASED ON THE 1991 CENSUS LINKED DATA

The availability of three time points (1971, 1981 and 1991) allows *longitudinal* comparisons to be made between separate cohorts between the same age ranges, but across different time periods (Plewis, 1990). The sample size of the LS is such that cohorts, covering perhaps a five-year age group, can be identified. For example, it is possible to distinguish two birth cohorts, one aged 20–25 in 1971 and the other aged 20–25 in 1981. Longitudinal, individual-level comparisons can be made for members of each cohort over the 10 year period, between the age of 20–25 and 30–35. For the older cohort this will be from 1971-1981; for the younger cohort from 1981-1991. The considerable differences in the economic climate (for example in the labour market and the housing market) between these 10-year periods opens the way for some valuable comparative analyses.

The addition of data from the 1991 Census will open up some important new research areas within the LS. First, new questions will extend the scope of the LS. The extent of limiting long-term illness provides a much needed indicator of health status. The question on ethnic group asked in the 1991 Census can be linked to earlier LS data, for example, to identify how migration patterns vary with ethnicity and how changes in occupational and social mobility are associated with migration. This was discussed in section 12.6.4.

The LS also records up to three of the possible answers on economic activity given at question 13 in the 1991 Census. It thereby provides valuable information on the extent to which certain categories of the population hold alternative economic statuses.

12.8 THE STRUCTURE OF THE LS DATABASE AND METHODS OF ACCESS

By early 1994, the 1991 Census records will have been added to the LS, and the entire database will be held in a powerful database system known as Model 204 on the OPCS Amdahl mainframe computer. The way in which LS data are structured within Model 204 allows any LS record to be accessed and linked to any other. Linkages can be determined by users to meet their research requirements, within the constraints of confidentiality.

Census records are held for each person in the LS member's household and algorithms used to determine the relationship of the LS member to each person in the household. Once relationships are established, linkages between individuals can be made so that, for example, the characteristics of the LS member's spouse, child or parent can be associated with the LS member. Similarly, summary variables describing the characteristics of the LS member's household can be derived. The database structure will facilitate linkage between censuses and also between census and events.

The structure of the database means that there is ready access to its various components. This gives greatly increased flexibility and speed of access by comparison with the system of fixed datastreams (rectangular subsets of data) used prior to completion of the 1991 Census link.

Once the variables needed by the user have been located and linkages between data files established, a subset of data can be written to a SAS system file for analysis. The use of SAS as the preferred analysis package on the OPCS machine allows a much greater range of analyses than were previously possible. Although analysis of all data still has to take place on the OPCS computer, this new structure and the associated software open up much greater possibilities than hitherto existed.

It is OPCS' policy that the LS should be used as widely and easily as is consistent with maintaining the confidentiality of the data. This latter constraint means that access within OPCS to linked data for individuals is tightly controlled.

For this reason channels have been developed to facilitate access whilst ensuring the confidentiality of the data. For academic users, the LS Support Programme, based at the Social Statistics Research Unit, City University, provides advice, documentation and assistance with computing. For other users, the LS Unit at St Catherine's House provides a similar service. This is explained further below.

The LS Support Programme at the Social Statistics Research Unit (SSRU) receives funding from two sources. With OPCS funding, the SSRU provide academic users with an interface to the LS and ensures that the procedures laid down by OPCS for using the LS are followed. The SSRU also receive funding under the joint ESRC/Information Systems Committee Initiative on the 1991 Census to provide support to academic users of the LS. Both sources of funding enable the SSRU to provide continuing documentation on the LS and training workshops. Therefore academics interested in using the LS should initially approach the LS Support Programme at the SSRU. A User Pack is available which contains complete information on documentation, methods of access and further contact points. The LS Support Programme does not, however, extent to analyses which require the calculation of person–years–at–risk. At the moment these analyses require specialised and very time-consuming in-house software that goes beyond the SSRU remit and are carried out by the LS Unit at OPCS. All non-academic users should approach the LS Unit at OPCS directly. Addresses and telephone numbers are given below.

The LS Support Programme at the Social Statistics Research Unit makes no charge to academic users, unless they are being funded by government or by industry. However, a charge is made if analyses are conducted by the LS Unit at OPCS; all users who are serviced by OPCS are charged for the computing and staff time incurred. No LS users are charged for data. More detailed information on charges is available on request.

12.8.1 Methods of access

All potential users must sign an undertaking form stating that they will use the data supplied only for the approved project; that they will not seek to identify any individuals, or claim to have done so; they will return data if requested by OPCS. Proposals to use the LS must be submitted in writing and approved by OPCS.

Because individual records cannot be released, access to the LS is via either the Social Statistics Research Unit (for academic users) or OPCS (for all others).

The LS Support Programme,	The LS Unit,
Social Statistics Research Unit,	OPCS,
City University,	St Catherine's House,
Northampton Square,	Kingsway,
London	London
C1V 0HB	WC2B 6JP
Tel: 071 477-8586	Tel: 071 396-2090 or 071 396-2031

Until January 1994: analysis is restricted to a number of 'datastreams' or large rectangular subsets of data, each containing several hundred variables. There are three main methods of access:

(1) To set up an SPSSX system file that resides on tape at OPCS, but which the user can analyse remotely by sending SPSSX command files to the Social Statistics Research Unit over the JANET system or, alternatively, on disk. Output can be returned either as paper copy, on floppy disk or sent over the JANET network.

(2) To extract a large machine-readable table that can be downloaded onto floppy disk or tape and sent to the user for further analysis at the user's home site. Guidelines on the table dimensions permitted are given in the LS User Pack. Generally a table should contain no more than seven variables and fewer than 250,000 cells. Restrictions on the amount of detail permitted vary with the geographical level. Below the level of region, the same restrictions apply as on the 2 per cent individual Sample of Anonymised Records (see chapter 11).

(3) A table service, where the user requests the extraction of a printed table.

From January 1994: the LS will be held in a Model 204 database as a series of linked files representing the various sources of the data (e.g. census, events) and the different types or levels within each. Users will be able to extract the variables of their choice from the entire database and output them to a SAS system file, subject to the usual confidentiality restrictions. The SAS system file will reside in filestore on the OPCS computer. It should also be possible to write data to an SPSSX system file. Academic users will be able to send a SAS or SPSSX command file to the Social Statistics Research Unit; non-academic users will work in a similar way through OPCS. Output will be returned either as paper copy, on floppy disk or sent over the JANET network. Large machine-readable tables will also be available, subject to the guidelines outlined above.

12.9 DOCUMENTATION AND TRAINING AVAILABLE

The *OPCS Longitudinal Study User Manual* (SSRU, 1990) brings together information on the content of the LS, methods of linkage and quality of the data. This is available from the LS Support Programme, at the SSRU, with a machine readable Data Dictionary. An *LS Technical Report* is being produced, due for publication by HMSO in 1994, which will replace the current *LS User Manual*. Detailed information on methods of access, derived variables and similar will be covered in separate *LS User Guides*.

The *LS User Guide* series focuses on particular aspects of the LS, for example the area-based data, the fertility data, and on methods of analysis appropriate to the LS. User Guides are available free of charge from the LS Support Programme, at the SSRU.

A twice-yearly *LS Newsletter* is produced by OPCS in collaboration with the SSRU. Order forms are contained in the LS User Pack.

The LS Support Programme also runs a User Support Group. The Group holds an annual meeting and has its own newsletter distributed to all users three times a year. In addition regular two-day workshops are held to provide intensive training in using the LS.

Through this programme of support, documentation and training the SSRU and OPCS are working together to maximise the potential of a unique research resource.

13   Population censuses in Northern Ireland: 1926–1991

Paul A. Compton

13.1 INTRODUCTION

The objective of this chapter is to provide users with a general guide to the population censuses that have been conducted in Northern Ireland, with particular emphasis on the 1991 enumeration. The chapter is divided into four sections. These consist
of a resumé of census taking in Northern Ireland before 1991 in which the principal
changes in content from census to census and comparisons with Britain are discussed. Other sections deal with census geography, census reliability and the 1991
enumeration itself. Samples of Anonymised Records (SAR) and Small Area Statistics
(SAS) information will form part of the output for 1991 but there are no plans to
produce longitudinal data.

Of the three censuses in the UK, least is known about Northern Ireland. This
is partly because of the province's small size (just over 1.57 million people were
enumerated in 1991 — approximately the same number as in Merseyside), which
means that comparatively little information is lost by ignoring the province altogether
and treating Great Britain as a UK surrogate. However, the reason is also partly
historical; up to 1972 Northern Ireland had its own devolved administration with
wide powers of internal decision-making. Censuses were authorised by the Stormont
as opposed to Westminster Parliament giving the Northern Ireland authorities, in
theory at least, complete discretion over census timing, logistics and content. In
practice, of course, there has always been a large degree of coordination between
Belfast, Edinburgh and London, but this notwithstanding, important differences exist
between censuses in Northern Ireland, particularly the earlier ones, and the remainder
of the UK.

Although the institution of direct rule after 1972 and loss of local autonomy
has brought the Northern Ireland census more into the mainstream, the last enumeration in 1991 still differed from Great Britain in a number of respects. These differences, of course, highlight the fact that the information required for administration
and policy formation in Northern Ireland is not always the same as the needs of the
rest of the UK. The division of census responsibilities between Belfast, Edinburgh
and London is, therefore, perfectly logical in that it mirrors the fundamental administrative structure of the country, but equally this fragmentation does frustrate the
presentation of a UK-wide view and it is to be regretted that a UK general report

has never been part of published census output. It is hard to think of another country where census material is not aggregated to the level of the national territory. A final comment that should be made at the outset concerns the unique difficulties that have confronted recent Northern Ireland censuses as a result of the political unrest in the province. Terrorist groups and their allies set about disrupting the fieldwork stage of both the 1971 and 1981 Censuses in protest at the 'British presence' in Ireland. In 1981 this resulted in wide-spread non-cooperation and localised non-enumeration and raises fundamental doubts about the reliability of that census. Fortunately, the 1991 Census has been free from disruption and appears to have been a *comprehensive enumeration* of the population. The problems that have confronted recent censuses will be discussed in greater detail in a later section of the chapter.

13.2 A RESUMÉ OF CENSUS-TAKING IN NORTHERN IRELAND BEFORE 1991

Following the secession of the Irish Free State in 1921, Northern Ireland was established as a separate governmental entity within the UK. Census information for the territory of Northern Ireland before this date is contained in the various censuses of Ireland, the first of which was conducted in 1821 and thereafter decennially up to 1911. To date, eight censuses have been conducted in Northern Ireland itself — in 1926, 1937, 1951, 1961, 1966, 1971, 1981 and 1991.

13.2.1 Legislative basis

Up to 1966, each census undertaken in Northern Ireland was authorised by separate Act of the Parliament of Northern Ireland. The Acts are printed in The Public General Acts Northern Ireland (HMSO, various dates) and are known as Census Act (Northern Ireland) 1925, Census Act (Northern Ireland) 1936, Census Act (Northern Ireland) 1951, Census Act (Northern Ireland) 1960, and Census Act (Northern Ireland) 1965.

The substance of each Act up to 1966 was identical. The Ministry of Finance was designated to superintend the census and the Registrar General to make the arrangements and prepare and issue the necessary forms and instructions. The persons for whom census returns were to be made were listed in a first schedule and the particulars to be stated in the returns, i.e. the topics to be covered, in a second schedule. Other matters specified were: the census date; enumeration districts and enumerators; preparation and filling of forms and making returns; collection of forms and returns by enumerators; the Registrar General's obligation to prepare abstracts of returns and reports; statutory declaration by enumerators; penalties for offences by persons employed under the Act, or by those obliged to make a return, and provision for the collection and publication of statistics until the taking of the next census. Each Act authorised the Registrar General to draw up enumeration districts and prescribed the duties of superintendents, enumerators and other persons employed to execute the census. Officers and men of the Royal Ulster Constabulary, not civilians, were specified as enumerators, continuing the tradition followed in the earlier censuses of Ireland when members of the Royal Irish Constabulary had been used as enumerators.

The 1971, 1981 and 1991 enumerations were carried out under the authority of the Census Act (Northern Ireland) 1969. The 1969 Act makes provision for taking

Table 13.1

Matters into which a Northern Ireland census may enquire as specified in the 1969 Census Act

1.	Names, sex, age
2.	Occupation, profession, trade or employment
3.	Nationality, birthplace, race, language
4.	Place of abode and character of dwelling
5.	Condition as to marriage, relation to head of family, issue
6.	Education, professional and technical qualifications
7.	Religion
8.	Any other matters relating to the social condition of the population for which statistical information is required

a census in Northern Ireland from time to time by Order in Council. It further specifies that no census may be taken unless five years have elapsed since the previous census. An Order prescribes the date on which the census is to be taken, the persons by whom and with respect to whom the census returns are to be made, and the particulars to be stated in the returns. Unlike earlier censuses, officers of the Royal Ulster Constabulary are no longer specified as enumerators. Other provisions in the Act are broadly the same as before. It names the Ministry of Finance as superintending a census (a responsibility since passed on to the Department of Health and Social Services) and the Registrar General as making the necessary arrangements and preparing and publishing abstracts of and reports on the returns.

Calling a census through Order in Council as opposed to full Act of Parliament brought the province more in line with practice in England and Wales and Scotland, with clear advantages by way of streamlining and creating a more flexible procedure. This applies particularly to the matters of inquiry because, in contrast to earlier Acts in which these were precisely specified, the 1969 Act lays down seven broad areas into which inquiry can be made plus an eighth category which authorises the gathering of statistical information about any other aspect of the social condition of the population (table 13.1). Since the term 'social condition' is not defined by the Act, in effect this makes it lawful to inquire into any matter deemed necessary by Government, although Parliamentary scrutiny of draft Orders provides a measure of public accountability and should prevent abuse of this provision.

The Act gives the Registrar General considerable discretion concerning the census information he is able to release, within the broad constraint that it 'shall not be used otherwise than in accordance with this Act'. It also expressly prohibits him from granting access to any forms of return, enumeration books or other confidential documents (not defined) unless lawful authority has been granted. In other words, the Act denies access to individual returns in Northern Ireland indefinitely and is significantly different from the position in England and Wales where the 100-year rule applies. However, the Registrar General may release to any person abstracts 'containing statistical information that can be derived from the census returns but is not supplied by the census abstracts or reports' provided he is satisfied that their requirement is reasonable. At no point does the Act deal with the matter of computer-held records, although these may be deemed to fall into the categories of 'abstracts' or 'confidential documents'. To close a gap caused by the repeal of section 2 of the Official Secrets Act 1911, the Census Confidentiality (Northern Ireland) Order 1991 was enacted. The Order made it unlawful to release personal census information, i.e. census information that relates to an identifiable person or household.

13.2.2 Census contents and coverage, and comparisons with Britain

The areas of inquiry at each enumeration since 1926 are summarised in table 13.2. Elements common to all include relationship to head of household, age, sex, birthplace and marital status. Most censuses have also enquired into current residence, religion, employment/occupation and education although the emphasis in the case of the last mentioned has changed from school attendance in the early enumerations, to qualifications obtained, in more recent censuses. Although a topic may be covered in successive censuses variations in the wording of questions or response categories may still render temporal comparison difficult. A characteristic feature, particularly since 1961, has been the extension of the scope of successive censuses to include information on dwellings, migration, fertility, journey to work, car ownership, long-term illness and the Irish language.

Following the practice in the rest of the UK, Northern Ireland censuses are conducted on a *de facto* basis. Individuals present in Northern Ireland at midnight on census date plus those who arrive in Northern Ireland after midnight and before the returns are completed, are covered by the enumeration. It includes individuals in private households and communal establishments (hotels, clubs, boarding houses, hospitals, prisons, military establishments, ships in in-land waters, etc.). Since 1981, the returns have also sought information on persons usually living in a household but present elsewhere on census night to give a better representation of the usually resident population.

Census of 1926

The reorganisation of government in Ireland led to the cancellation of the 1921 Census and chronological consistency in census taking between Northern Ireland and the rest of the UK was not restored until 1951. Preparation for the census of 1926 began with the formation of a committee comprising representatives of each Ministry in Northern Ireland, whose main function was to determine the nature and extent of the information to be sought from the public on the census forms. Eventually a schedule basically similar to that used at the 1921 Census of England and Wales was recommended but containing additional questions relating to religion, school, national health insurance and infirmities. In so far as certain questions were omitted which had been asked in the 1911 Census of Ireland, the 1926 Census was brought more into line with decennial censuses taken in Great Britain. Regarding the form of reports, the course followed was largely determined by precedent and the practice adopted in England and Wales. Accordingly, the idea of topic reports — 'occupations', 'birthplaces', 'religions', etc — was not used, and county volumes with a general report and topographic index published instead (see bibliography). Each report contains a commentary summarising the principle results.

Census of 1937

It had been the intention to hold the next census in 1941 at the same time as the usual decennial census in Great Britain. However, the results of the 1926 Census had been unsatisfactory in terms of age mis-statement and it therefore seemed that there

Table 13.2

Summary of content of Northern Ireland censuses - 1926–91

	Census year							
	1926	1937	1951	1961	1966	1971	1981	1991
1 Full name	yes	yes	yes	yes	yes	yes	yes	yes
2 Relation to H. of H.	yes	yes	yes	yes	yes	yes	yes	yes
3 Sex	yes	yes	yes	yes	yes	yes	yes	yes
4 Age (years and months or date of birth)	yes	yes	yes	yes	yes	yes	yes	yes
5 Marital status	yes	yes	yes	yes	yes	yes	yes	yes
6 Place of birth	yes	yes	yes	yes	no	yes	yes	yes
7 Religion	yes	yes	yes	yes	no	yes	yes	yes
8 Usual address	no	yes	yes	yes	yes	yes	yes	yes
9 Nationality	yes	no	yes	yes	no	no	no	no
10 Whereabouts on census night	no	no	no	no	no	no	yes	yes
11 Long-term illness	no	no	no	no	no	no	no	yes
12 Term-time address of students	no	no	no	no	no	no	no	yes
13 Irish language	no	no	no	no	no	no	no	yes
14 Employment or trade								
Nature of job or occupation	yes	no	yes	yes	no	yes	yes	yes
Whether working, retired etc.	yes	no	yes	yes	no	yes	yes	yes
Business of employer	yes	no	yes	yes	no	yes	yes	yes
Name of employer	yes	no	yes	yes	no	yes	yes	yes
Employment status	no	no	yes	yes	no	yes	yes	yes
Hours worked	no	no	no	no	no	yes	no	yes
Occupation a year ago	no	no	no	no	no	yes	no	yes
Address of place of work	no	no	no	no	yes	yes	yes	yes
Whether worked in last 10 years	no	no	no	no	no	no	no	yes
Means of journey to work	no	no	no	no	yes	yes	yes	yes
Time journey to work starts	no	no	no	no	no	no	yes	no
15 Education:								
Attendance at school/college	yes	no	yes	no	no	no	no	no
Age finishing full-time education	no	no	no	yes	no	no	no	no
Qualifications in science or technology	no	no	no	yes	no	no	no	no
A-levels and equivalent	no	no	no	no	no	yes	no	yes
Degrees, professional and vocational qualifications	no	no	no	yes	yes	yes	yes	yes
O-levels and equivalent	no	no	no	no	no	no	no	yes
16 The household and dwelling								
Number of rooms	no	no	yes	yes	no	yes	yes	yes
Tenure and amenities (various)	no	no	no	yes	no	yes	yes	yes
Dwelling type	no	no	no	yes	no	no	no	yes
Sharing	no	no	no	no	no	yes	yes	no
Wholly residential or not	no	no	no	yes	no	no	no	no
Number of cars	no	no	no	yes	no	yes	yes	yes
Garaging of cars	no	no	no	no	no	yes	no	no
17 Migration								
Foreign born residence 1 year ago	no	no	no	yes	no	no	no	no
Usual address 5 years ago	no	no	no	no	yes	yes	no	no
Usual address 1 year ago	no	no	no	no	yes	yes	yes	yes
18 Fertility								
Children born in year before census	no	no	no	yes	no	no	no	yes
Date of birth of live-born children	no	no	no	no	no	yes	no	yes
Date of marriage	no	no	no	yes	no	yes	no	no
Termination of marriage	no	no	no	yes	no	yes	no	no
Number of live-born children	no	no	no	yes	no	no	no	yes
19 From early censuses								
For foreign born - resident or visitor	yes	yes	no	no	no	no	no	no
For married men, widowers and widows: living children under 16	yes	no	no	no	no	no	no	no
Deaf, dumb, blind, crippled or mentally afflicted	yes	no	no	no	no	no	no	no
Entitlement under National Health Insurance Acts when ill	yes	no	no	no	no	no	no	no
For children under 16: parents alive or dead	yes	no	no	no	no	no	no	no

might be real advantages in familiarising the population with the process of census taking if an enumeration with a request for the minimum of information were to be held in some intervening year. Accordingly, it was decided to conduct a limited census in 1937 with the intention of launching a complete enumeration in 1941 in conjunction with the rest of the UK. The 1937 Census was therefore restricted to place of residence, age, sex, marital status, birthplace and religion. In the event the outbreak of war prevented the issue of a normal general report; instead publication was restricted to booklets for each county containing brief summary tables, without statistical notes or commentary (see bibliography).

Census of 1951

Since the war also made it impracticable to hold the enumerations planned for 1941, it was considered desirable that the 1951 Census in Northern Ireland should be as wide in scope as was reasonably possible. It was also agreed that the programme adopted in Britain should be accepted in principle but with differences reflecting local circumstances and that the enumeration should be on the same day. In the event, the deviations were substantial. Topics covered in Great Britain but omitted in Northern Ireland included household arrangements for water supply etc., date of marriage of women under 50 years of age, fertility, age at which full-time education ceased and employer's address. Offsetting these omissions, the Northern Ireland return enquired into religion and length of residence of those born outside Northern Ireland. The form of the results also differed in one important respect from Great Britain in that 1 per cent sample tables were not produced in view of the small size and distribution of the province's population; this has continued to be the practice in later censuses. Nine reports were published — preliminary report, general report, six county reports, and a report for Belfast and its environs (see bibliography). Each report contains a commentary summarising the principal results.

Census of 1961

The content of the 1961 Census was drawn up in close collaboration with the census authorities in Great Britain. Apart from relatively small changes to meet local requirements, the programme adopted for Great Britain was applied in Northern Ireland, which ensured a higher degree of comparability of census information across the whole of the UK than had been possible before. As a result, the 1961 Census was wider in scope than its predecessors. A range of personal questions identical to those in Great Britain covering: age at which full-time education ceased, academic and professional qualifications in science and technology and the marriage and number of children of ever-married women, was asked for the first time. Another innovation was the introduction of questions seeking information about private households and dwellings, again broadly in line with Great Britain. These explored tenure and the availability of piped water, cooking and toilet facilities. In addition, enumerators indicated the number of rooms occupied by the household, the number of households occupying the premises, the type of accommodation occupied and whether the building was wholly residential or not. The only information collected in Great Britain but not sought in Northern Ireland was address of work place and particulars about persons normally resident in the household but absent on census night. As before religion was sought in Northern Ireland but not in Britain. The results were published as 10 reports — preliminary report, general report, six county reports, a report for Belfast County Borough and a fertility report (see bibliography). Each report contains a commentary summarising the principal results.

Census of 1966

The 1966 Census is the only mid-term enumeration to have been held in Northern Ireland. Consideration was given to whether it should be based on a sample of the population, as in Great Britain, but this was rejected on the grounds that sampling errors would seriously hinder the subsequent use of the census, given the small population sizes of many administrative districts. Instead, the census covered every household but the range of questions asked was limited. In an effort to improve accuracy, age was ascertained by asking date of birth instead of age in years and months, which had previously been the practice. Questions that had been asked in 1961 but which were omitted in 1966 were place of birth, religion, fertility, education, occupation, tenure and household arrangements. On the other hand, questions about migration (address one and five years ago), place of work and means of transport to work were added for the first time. The results were published in a single census report (see bibliography). The report contains a commentary summarising the principal results.

13.2.3 The 1971 and 1981 Censuses

The trend towards greater uniformity with England and Wales has continued with the three most recent censuses. They also mark a substantial watershed compared with previous enumerations in terms of range of content, geographical coverage (see section 13.3), a shift from area to topic-based reports, and the inclusion since 1981 of household members absent on census day.

Census of 1971

In 1971 questions were asked for the first time about hours worked, occupation in the previous year, educational, professional and vocational qualifications of A-level standard and above; cars and garaging and sharing of dwellings. Subjects that had been covered in 1961 but which were dropped from the 1971 Census included nationality; the previous residence of foreign born individuals; age at which full-time education ceased; qualifications in science and technology and dwelling type. In addition to these changes, the scope of the fertility enquiry was widened to include dates of birth of all live born children but restricted to ever-married women under the age of 60. In addition, the information collected about household amenities was widened and made more explicit.

Questions that were asked in Britain but not in Northern Ireland were country of birth of mother and father (the small overseas ethnic presence in the province made this enquiry irrelevant); information about individuals normally living in the household but absent on census day (the resident population estimates are incomplete as a consequence), and the audit of students in full-time education. The traditional enquiry about religion was the one question not asked in Britain but the results were of doubtful value due to the high non-response rate (see section 13.5). Regarding published material, county reports were produced initially, but were subsequently overtaken by the local government reform of 1973 when new topic-based reports containing information for the new local government districts were produced (table 13.3, appendix 13.1 and bibliography).

Table 13.3

Published census reports for 1971 and 1981 and availability with publication date for 1991

	1971	1981	1991
Preliminary	yes	yes	7/91
Summary	yes	yes	10/92
Belfast urban area	no	no	12/92
Religion	yes	yes	2/93
Economic activity	yes	yes	4/93
Workplace and transport to work	yes	yes	9/93
Housing and household composition	yes	yes	9/93
Migration	yes	yes	10/93
Education	yes	yes	11/93
Irish language	no	no	12/93
Fertility	yes	no	no
County reports	yes	no	no
Belfast local government district	no	yes	no

Census of 1981

A departure in 1981 from the previous practice of only enumerating individuals present was the inclusion of persons usually living in a household who were absent on census night. The purpose of this innovation was to capture usual residents who happened to be either elsewhere in Northern Ireland or outside the province at the time of the enumeration and brought the enumeration fully into line with Great Britain in this regard. In common with Britain, specific instructions were given about how new babies should be treated in order to eliminate a common reason for under-enumeration and to improve accuracy. In the event, these refinements were sabotaged by a substantial amount of non-cooperation and the 1981 enumeration turned out to be the least satisfactory Northern Ireland census up to that time (see section 13.5).

Otherwise, to reduce costs more questions were dropped than included afresh compared with 1971. Omitted were the questions on hours worked; occupation the previous year; the garaging of cars; usual address five years ago and fertility. In addition, the question into educational, professional and vocational qualifications was restricted to degrees and equivalents, i.e. the enquiry about GCE A-levels and equivalents was dropped. Included for the first time were whereabouts on census night and the time of starting the journey to work. The differences with Britain were minor and, apart from the enquiry in Northern Ireland about religion, concerned the scope of certain questions. For instance, in addition to the availability of bath and toilet facilities, the Northern Ireland question on amenities also sought information about water supply, domestic sewage disposal, central heating and heating insulation. The topics covered in the published reports for 1981 are listed in table 13.3 and the contents summarised in appendix 13.1.

13.3 CENSUS GEOGRAPHY

Northern Ireland's census geography comprises three components: the delimitation of areas to facilitate field work; the geographical information collected as part of the census return; and the definition of the areas for which census results will be available.

337

13.3.1 Field work areas

Like the rest of the UK, the enumeration district (ED) is the basic areal unit for field work in Northern Ireland. Fresh EDs are delimited for each enumeration and, in consequence of this, spatial consistency is not maintained from census to census at the ED level. Up to 1971, it was also customary to group EDs into census districts. The number of EDs delimited was reasonably constant up to 1966 but has grown in number since then as the census has become more complex and population size increased. The area covered by individual EDs varies inversely with household density, and rural EDs therefore cover larger areas than their urban counterparts, although they contain fewer households. EDs also vary widely in shape but are defined so as never to violate administrative area boundaries. The ED location of each census return has been coded since 1961.

13.3.2 Census returns and geography

The nature of the geographical information collected about the locations of census returns has varied in response to changes in local government structure. Only two items of geographical information have featured in all eight enumerations — the postal address of the household making a return and the townland (roughly equivalent to the English parish) in which the dwelling is situated. The 1926, 1937 and 1951 Censuses have a decidedly historic ring to them in relating information to Poor Law Unions and medical dispensary districts. These also corresponded to superintendent registrar and registrar districts for the registration of marriages, births and deaths. Otherwise addresses were coded for county or county borough, urban or rural district, county or district electoral division or ward, and parliamentary division in the case of county boroughs. Electoral divisions, wards and parliamentary divisions were the territorial units used in local, Stormont and Westminster elections and nested into the administrative hierarchy. These, with the addition of EDs and census districts after 1961, constituted the basic geographical data recorded on each return up to and including 1971.

The reform of local government in Northern Ireland on 1 October 1973, swept these areas away, however. Counties, county boroughs, and urban and rural districts were abolished and replaced by a single tier of 26 local government districts (LGDs), nesting into regions for the purposes of administering health (four regions) and education (five regions). The electoral divisions, parliamentary divisions and wards were also scrapped and superseded by a uniform set of 526 electoral wards. Accordingly, addresses have been coded by district and ward identifiers since 1981. The 1971 returns were also subsequently recoded on this basis. In addition to these, ED and townland identifiers continue to be used. Returns have also been regularly geocoded since 1971 (unlike Britain, this practice was not dropped after 1971) but postcodes were only introduced in 1991. The use of six-figure grid references in built-up areas theoretically yields information down to the level of 100 m squares, whereas in rural areas, where a four-figure reference is used, the maximum resolution is the 1 km square. Geocoding in Northern Ireland is based on the Irish National Grid. Specific requirements have also led to the occasional designation of other areal codes — planning codes in 1981 and a Belfast urban code in 1991. The geographical identifiers used since 1971 are summarised in table 13.4.

Census users quickly become familiar with the frustrations caused by the lack of spatio-temporal comparability from one census to another arising from constant

Table 13.4

Geographical identifiers used on private household returns since 1971

	1971	1981	1991
Address	yes	yes	yes
District council	yes	yes	yes
Ward	yes	yes	yes
Enumeration district	yes	yes	yes
Grid reference	yes	yes	yes
Townland (parish)	yes	yes	yes
Postcode	no	no	yes
Planning code	no	yes	no
Belfast urban area code	yes	no	no
Census district	yes	no	no
Urban or rural district	yes	no	no
Electoral divisions/old wards	yes	no	no

modifications to the administrative area base. In the case of Northern Ireland, the reform of local government in 1973 had the effect of inserting a major discontinuity into the statistical time series. It destroyed geographical consistency below the level of Northern Ireland itself and has created two distinct time series — 1926 to 1971 and 1971 to the present. For the user interested in spatio-temporal patterns, there is no easy way in which pre-1971 Census information can be reconciled with later data. The new districts do not nest into the former counties and although still very much alive in the minds of the population, the counties no longer exist in any demographic sense. The pre- and post-1973 administrative bases are summarised in map 13.1.

Yet, there are a number of ways in which the two distinct parts of the time series might be reconciled. Conversion of 1981 and 1991 data to the pre-1973 framework could be accomplished by the appropriate aggregation of grid square and ED level data, although conversion of pre-1971 information to the current 26 LGDs would be of more value. In the latter case, the linkage would have to be via townlands. As we have already seen, apart from actual address, the townland is the one geographical identifier that has appeared on each Northern Ireland census return since 1926. Also, townlands are unique in two other important respects. They have not undergone boundary changes, and also nest exactly into the pre-1973 administrative framework and into the post-1973 districts with relatively minor adjustments. The one serious drawback is that townland information, although collected on the enumeration schedule, has not been tabulated since 1951.

One should also note that the post-1973 areas, in turn, have been subject to change. Electoral wards underwent a substantial revision in 1984 (their number was increased from 526 to 566), when the LGD boundary of Belfast was also subject to minor change. Thus, whereas 1971 and 1981 Census data are identical and directly comparable at these scales, the 1991 Census is not, although the population effect of the changes to Belfast LGD will be minimal. Furthermore, the most recent 1992 recommendations of the Northern Ireland Boundary Commission, with yet more ward and LGD modifications, will effect the comparability of the census that will presumably be held in 2001. To complicate matters still further, the basic ED framework has been redefined at each of the last three censuses.

Map 13.1 Local government districts in Northern Ireland pre-and post-1973 reform

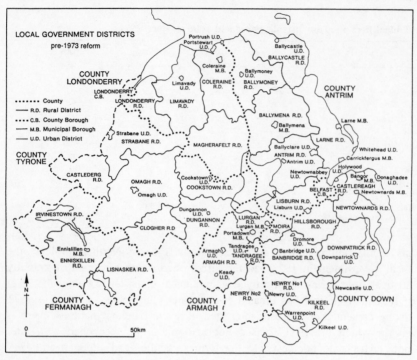

13.3.3 Geographical breakdowns used in census reports and abstracts

The geographical breakdowns used in the published census reports, by and large, have been combinations of administrative and/or electoral areas. As we have already shown, these have come in a wide variety of forms over the decades and usage in . the different censuses is summarised in table 13.5. Many of the areas have long since disappeared but even during their existence boundary changes made spatial comparison somewhat problematic.

Before the 1973 reform, quite detailed information is available by county, county borough and urban and rural district aggregates. In addition, the principal findings about population, households, economic activities, etc are also broken down by individual urban and rural districts. Otherwise, only summary population data were prepared for individual towns, townlands, electoral districts and parliamentary constituencies. Since the reform, only the summary reports have been oriented towards LGDs. Information for wards and individual towns is restricted to basic demographic data — total population, males, females and number of households. The topic reports generally deal with Northern Ireland as a single unit. In addition, a flexible facility has existed since 1971 for the provision of small area statistics by grid squares tailored to the specific needs of the individual user. ED-based data are not available

Table 13.5

Summary of the availability of published census information by geographical area

	Census year							
	1926	1937	1951	1961	1966	1971	1981	1991
Regions	no	no	no	no	no	yes	yes	yes
District council areas	no	no	no	no	no	yes	yes	yes
Wards	no	no	no	no	no	yes	yes	yes
Grid squares	no	no	no	no	no	yes	yes	yes
Towns (1,000 or more population)	no	no	yes	yes	yes	yes	yes	yes
Belfast urban area	no	no	yes	no	no	no	no	yes
Counties	yes	yes	yes	yes	yes	yes	no	no
County boroughs	yes	yes	yes	yes	yes	yes	no	no
Municipal boroughs	no	yes	yes	yes	yes	yes	no	no
Urban district	yes	yes	yes	yes	yes	yes	no	no
Rural districts	yes	yes	yes	yes	yes	yes	no	no
Urban district aggregates	yes	no	yes	yes	no	no	no	no
Rural district aggregates	yes	no	yes	yes	no	no	no	no
Parliamentary constituencies	no	yes	yes	yes	yes	yes	no	no
County electoral divisions	yes	yes	yes	yes	no	no	no	no
District electoral divisions	yes	yes	yes	yes	no	no	no	no
County borough wards	yes	no	yes	yes	yes	no	no	no
Towns (no population limit)	yes	no	yes	yes	no	no	no	no
Townlands	yes	no	yes	no	no	no	no	no
Poor Law Unions or Superintendent registrar districts	yes	yes	no	no	no	no	no	no
Medical dispensary or registrar districts	yes	yes	no	no	no	no	no	no
Education areas	yes	no	no	no	no	no	no	no

for any previous census although ED-based data may become available for 1991. There are no specific plans at the moment to produce postcode-based output for 1991, notwithstanding the obvious commercial value of such output. However, it is understood that consideration will be given to users' demand for such data, subject to the satisfaction of confidentiality criteria.

13.4 THE 1991 CENSUS

13.4.1 Fieldwork

The preparatory work for this census began in 1989 with consultations about question content. In the event, it was decided to follow the programme adopted in Britain with some exceptions to allow for local needs and to hold it on the same day, 21 April 1991. The differences with Britain are set out in the section that follows. For the purposes of fieldwork, the province was divided into 3,729 enumeration districts in recognition of the wide-ranging scope of the 1991 Census, the increase in the number of households and to speed up the enumeration process, especially in rural areas. This may be compared with 2,800 EDs in 1981 and 1,070 EDs in 1926. In urban areas, EDs were delimited so as to cover between 120 and 200 households and in rural areas between 60 and 80 households. There were approximately seven EDs to each electoral ward and between 120 and 180 to each LGD. The resulting increase in spatial resolution will clearly be of value in view of plans to produce an ED-based SAS (see section on SAR, SAS, postcodes and wards).

Just under 4,000 field staff were employed — 3,800 enumerators with reserves, 160 Census Officers and 7 Census Area Managers. All field staff, recruited via job centres, advertisements in the press, etc., were given intensive training. For the first time in Northern Ireland, a census validation test was carried out on 2,000 randomly selected households, the findings of which were deemed to be satisfactory. As for the actual enumeration, in contrast to the problems encountered in 1981, cooperation from the general public was good and the enumeration is considered to have been comprehensive. (Enumerators were instructed to return to addresses until an enumeration form was received.) Following the pattern in the rest of the UK, separate enumeration forms were used for private households and communal establishments (including ships), the latter comprising a form L listing the names of persons in the establishment and a form I for the detailed information on each person.

13.4.2 Content and comparison with Britain

The content of the 1991 Census in Northern Ireland was identical in virtually all respects to the content in Britain. The question on ethnic group was considered to be of limited applicability to the province and therefore omitted. Included, however, were two questions concerning the fertility of ever-married women, i.e. total number of live-born children and number of children born alive in the year preceding the census. The same questions had appeared in the 1961 Census when they yielded valuable information about trends and patterns in family size. Their usefulness this time round, however, will be more limited. One fifth of Northern Ireland births now occur outside marriage and a substantial section of the population's fertility will not have been captured because of the restriction to ever-married women. The other areas investigated exclusively in Northern Ireland were knowledge of the Irish language (equivalent to the Gaelic and Welsh language questions in Scotland and Wales), educational qualifications obtained at secondary school (post-school qualifications were sought in Britain) and religion. In view of the high non-response rates in 1971 and 1981 and the clear non-acceptability of the question to a large section of the population, there were strong grounds for dropping the religion question in 1991; however, set against this, the 'fair employment' legislation on the province's statute books — outlawing religious discrimination in the field of employment, requires the monitoring of religion and has made the census question of direct policy relevance. Specifically, census data are of considerable theoretical use in determining the religious composition of the economically active population in employment catchment areas. These data can then be compared with the religious composition of employers' labour forces to pinpoint the imbalances that might exist. This latter consideration, coupled with the hope of a better response in 1991, would appear to have outweighed doubts about the wisdom of persevering with an inquiry that has yielded incomplete data of questionable usefulness in previous censuses. One may also note that the enquiry into household amenities was a little wider than in Britain, water supply and method of domestic sewage disposal being included. In addition, the tenure categories were different on some points of detail and 'unpaid work' was included as a response to the general question on work because of the relatively large size of the agricultural sector in Northern Ireland.

Otherwise, enquiries were made for the first time in Northern Ireland into term time addresses of students, work experience during the last 10 years, the Irish language and long term illness. It is worth noting that knowledge of the Irish language was regularly covered in the censuses of Ireland up to 1911 and that enquiries were made about 'health infirmities', i.e. something akin to long-term illness, in 1926. The latter was not asked again, however, on the grounds that it was not possible to obtain accurate and uniform information about infirmities through the medium of the census. It will therefore be interesting to see how successful the long-term illness question has been. Information about lower level qualifications — CSEs, O-levels etc. — was also collected in 1991 giving a full qualifications profile of the population from a census source for the first time. (This information will not be available for Britain). Other questions covered in 1991 but not in the 1981 Census were hours worked, dwelling type, and A-level and equivalent qualifications. Time of start of journey to work was the one topic included in 1981 to be omitted in 1991. The topics covered in the 1991 Census are listed in table 13.2, the reports planned with likely dates of publication in table 13.3 and the report contents summarised in appendix 13.1.

13.4.3 Population bases

When interpreting census results, it is important to know precisely what has been counted: the population base. Following the practice adopted in Britain (see chapter 2), three separate population bases have been defined for Northern Ireland for 1991.

(a) *The population present* is the count of all individuals spending census night in a given area regardless of whether this was their usual residence. This base will be used for the determination of intercensal population change.

(b) *The usually resident* population on a present/absent basis is the count of all persons recorded as usually resident in a given area even if they were present elsewhere on census night. It is derived from the usual address question. Since the census returns contain full information for absent residents in households and since the present/absent base can be produced area by area and does not have to await the processing of all areas, this is the base that is most commonly used in census reports and small area statistics. It is, however, ambiguous in the treatment of HM Forces as responses to the question about usual address can produce inconsistencies even though guidance was given to military personnel about the completion of census forms.

(c) *The usually resident population on a transfer basis* for a given area is the count of the present residents in an area, plus a transfer count of visitors elsewhere in Northern Ireland, Great Britain or in the Irish Republic back to their area of residence. Since this base cannot be calculated until all areas have been processed it is not used for census reports or small area statistics. However, it has been used for the production of the mid-year population estimate for 1991. For the purposes of the mid-year estimate, HM forces *present* in Northern Ireland are treated as *residents*. Students are allocated to their term-time addresses. The Northern Ireland home population is defined as the usually resident population plus HM Armed Forces.

13.4.4 Sample of Anonymised Records (SAR), Small Area Statistics (SAS), and Local Base Statistics (LBS)

Northern Ireland will be included in the UK SARs as part of the ESRC Census Initiative. A 1 per cent sample of households and a 2 per cent sample of individuals will be drawn from population aggregates of at least 120,000. The Northern Ireland SAR should thus comprise roughly 30,000 records broken down by 13 areas although in practice its availability is likely to be limited to fewer areas. Access will be governed by the procedures agreed between the ESRC and the Northern Ireland Census Office, and distribution will be by the Census Microdata Unit, University of Manchester (see chapter 11). The Northern Ireland SARS should be available early in 1994.

As happened in 1971 and 1981, the Northern Ireland Census Office will produce grid-square based statistics for 1991. These will be available for 100 square metres in built-up areas and kilometre squares in rural areas but subject to aggregation and/or blurring for squares with less than eight households or 25 persons to preserve confidentiality. Grid-square based data have the advantage of providing detailed spatial information for a consistent set of areas (in this case the Irish National Grid) through time but are also subject to limitations. First, the range of census material available will be restricted to around 1,500 items of information; second, accessibility will be by special request to the Census Office; and third it will be relatively expensive.

A 1991 ED-based SAS and LBS consistent with Great Britain was not originally planned by the Northern Ireland Census Office and the production of UK-wide SAS would again have been frustrated if this decision had been adhered to. However, there is now a decision to produce a Northern Ireland ED-based SAS and LBS within the framework of the ESRC Census Initiative. The form that these data sets are likely to take is already reasonably clear although the means of implementation still await finalisation. The SAS will consist of approximately 9,000 counts arranged

Table 13.6

Geographical frameworks for Small Area Statistics and Local Base Statistics for Northern Ireland, 1991

Areas	Number	SAS	LBS
Enumeration districts	3,729	yes	no
Grid-square aggregates	c1,500	yes	no
Postcode sectors	c400	yes	no
Wards	566	yes	yes
Districts	26	yes	yes
Paliamentary constituencies	17	yes	yes
Education and library board areas	5	yes	yes
Health board areas	4	yes	yes
Belfast urban area	1	yes	yes
Northern Ireland	1	yes	yes

in up to 99 tables. As far as possible, the counts will be modelled on the specifications for the SAS and LBS for GB, although there will be differences reflecting the specifically local questions in the Northern Ireland census. Hence, the Northern Ireland SAS/LBS will feature religion instead of ethnicity; include tables on Irish language, equivalent to the Welsh language in Wales and Gaelic in Scotalnd; contain tables on the fertility of ever-married women and children born the year preceding the census; and modifications reflecting the wider range of the enquiry into educational qualifications in Northern Ireland.

The probable geographical framework for a Northern Ireland SAS/LBS is summarised in table 13.6. It draws on the three basic building blocks available — enumeration districts, postcode areas and grid squares. EDs, of course, nest into the administrative and electoral geographies of the province. The provision of postcode sector data will bring Northern Ireland into line with England and Wales. The grid-square aggregates are designed to provide consistent areal data for 1971, 1981 and 1991 at a sensible spatial scale. The criteria for protecting confidentiality are similar to those adopted by OPCS (see chapter 5 and chapter 8, section 8.5) but thresholds for both the LBS and SAS are double those used in GB. A blurring procedure of adding 0, +1 or -1 to each count in quasi-random patterns is also applied.

The SAS/LBS data sets are being purchased by the ESRC for dissemination among the academic community, and will be deposited with the Census Dissemination Unit at Manchester Computing Centre. Academic use will be governed under a User Registration System. The SAS/LBS will be available to other users from the Northern Ireland Census Office.

13.5 CENSUS RELIABILITY

Judging from the published comments of the time, there were no particular problems about the completeness of each enumeration up to and including the census of 1966. Fieldwork was performed by members of the Royal Ulster Constabulary and cooperation from the general public was good. The one area of concern was the high level of age mis-statement in 1926 and 1937 which resulted in heaping at most ages terminating with the digits 0 and 5. Although this problem was subsequently less evident, an element of age heaping was still present in 1951, 1961 and 1966, particularly amongst females. Otherwise the only other matter of record was the reluctance of a small section of the population to answer the voluntary question on religion. In 1961, for example, this amounted to just under 2 per cent of the resident population. Of these, a portion would have been individuals of no religious persuasion, with the remainder, presumed mainly to be Protestants, not answering on conscientious grounds. It may also be noted that these early enumerations were conducted on a population present basis, and there is therefore no need for the user to take particular note of the population base being used when making comparisons between them.

The 1971 and 1981 enumerations were more problematic. The 1971 Census was the target of a deliberate campaign of disruption by paramilitary groups. The most tangible evidence of this was the jump in the non-response rate to the question on religion to over 9 per cent of the population, compared with less than 2 per cent 10 years earlier. Although it is generally thought that the enumeration was satisfactory otherwise, one cannot be categorical about this, since no post-census validation survey was undertaken and some degree of non-enumeration cannot be ruled out.

The situation in 1981 was even more difficult. The census coincided with the IRA hunger strikes which created considerable tension in nationalist areas in the province. This time the campaign of disruption extended to direct intimidation, and one enumerator was shot dead in Londonderry. Many returns were not collected; others were burned and the Registrar General had to resort to encouraging householders to return by post or by hand. In the event, a comparison of information derived in the field with the number of actual returns received suggested an eventual under-enumeration of just under 6,000 households, or 1.4 per cent of the total, which may be considered a remarkable achievement in the circumstances, especially since in Britain, without these problems, under-enumeration was put at 0.4 per cent. On the assumption that the mean size of non-enumerated households was equal to the Northern Ireland average of 3.2 persons, the population present on census night was adjusted upwards from 1,488,077 to 1,507,065. However, upon publication, this 'corrected' figure, along with the corrected estimates of the populations of local government districts considered to be affected by non-enumeration, was immediately attacked. A number of district councils argued that the upward revision for their own areas was too low and, given the implications for rate support, appealed to the Department of the Environment (Northen Ireland).

There followed a thorough investigation of the matter by the Department of Finance and Personnel which revealed larger than expected discrepancies between the results of the school census and the number of child benefit payments on the one hand and the corresponding groups as enumerated in the decennial census on the other. This was seen as confirming that non-enumeration had been higher than first estimated (now put at 74,000) and the total population was revised upward for a second time to 1,561,696. This, however, was not the end of the matter and once the extent of emigration to the Irish Republic during the 1970s became apparent a third revision was undertaken which this time brought the 1981 estimate down to 1,532,619, with non-enumeration put at 44,500 or 3 per cent of the enumerated population. (The detailed arguments surrounding the question of non-enumeration in 1981 are presented in Morris and Compton, 1985). A level of non-enumeration amounting to just over 3 per cent of the population might not be regarded as particularly serious, but the fact that it was concentrated in certain localities and affected some subgroups more than others rather than being spread uniformly within the population casts a shadow over the reliability of 1981 Census data especially when used in time series. Against this, it also follows that for the majority of localities in the province, as opposed to Northern Ireland as a unit, it may be accepted at face value.

In addition, the 1981 Census was accompanied by an 18 per cent non-statement rate to the religion question which, when non-enumeration is also taken into account, translates into a Catholic non-statement rate of around 30 per cent, compared with an estimated 15 per cent non-statement rate among Protestants (Compton and Power, 1984). Hence, whereas the enumerated breakdown of the population by religion in 1981 was 27 per cent Catholic, 52 per cent Protestant, and 21 per cent 'other and non-stated', after correction the breakdown becomes 38 per cent Catholic, 61 per cent Protestant and 1 per cent 'other'. While a preoccupation with the matter of religious composition may appear rather abstruse, it is never the less of significance in the Northern Ireland context where the percentage of Catholics and Protestants within the population is a demographic fact of constitutional importance.

With the recent publication of the Summary Report, it is now confirmed that the 1991 Census has been more successful than either of the two previous enumerations. Non-enumeration was not a problem as it was in 1981 and although the Preliminary Report refers to returns not being received from around 1 per cent of dwellings, multiple home ownership is the main explanation for this. There was also a greater level of cooperation with the question about religious denomination, and the non-response rate was down to 7.4 per cent. Since Catholic politicians and other representatives urged compliance with the census, there are grounds for thinking that Protestant refusals account for most of the non-statement this time round. This would seem to be confirmed by the fact that the rate of non-statement was substantially higher in predominantly Protestant LGDs than in predominantly Catholic LGDs, and represents a return to the situation experienced at censuses prior to 1971 when those withholding their religion were mainly Protestants who did so on conscientious grounds. Although an assessment must await the analysis of small area data, the 1991 findings are consistent with Catholics comprising 40–41 per cent of the Northern Ireland population.

The returns with regard to the percentage of the population claiming some knowledge of the Irish language also lent credence to the reliability of the enumeration. Given the obvious temptation to inflate this figure for political reasons, the 5.3 per cent recorded as being able to speak, read and write Irish is within the expected range. One further point: when the preliminary report for 1991 was published, some district councils and area health boards, in a repetition of 1981, queried the population totals for their areas on the grounds that they were lower than the 1990 mid-year estimates. The explanation for such discrepancies does not, however, lie in under-enumeration, as the councils and area boards were implying, but in inaccuracies in the mid-year estimates arising from the over-correction of some population totals in 1981 (i.e. actual non-enumeration was lower than assumed) and/or an underestimation of the rate of net out-migration. Unlike England and Wales and Scotland, there was no imputation for 'wholly abent households'.

Set against this background of persistent difficulties, it is encouraging to be able to report that the third revision of the 1981 population total (1,532,619) equates very well with the resident population as enumerated on a present/absent basis in 1991 (1,577,836) and is consistent with what is known from independent sources about net migration over the intercensal period. The calculation produces a net outflow of population amounting to 69,420 between 1981 and 1991 against a natural increase of 115,060, but it still needs to be stressed that the results of the 1971 and 1981 Northern Ireland censuses should be treated with considerable circumspection, particularly when used in time series.

13.6 CONTACT ADDRESS

Users interested in the Northern Ireland census should contact:

Census Office
Castle Buildings
Stormont
Belfast
BT4 3RA
Tel: 0232 520000

APPENDIX 13.1 SUMMARY OF CONTENTS OF NORTHERN IRELAND CENSUS REPORTS: 1971, 1981 AND 1991

Preliminary report (for 1971, 1981 and 1991): contains provisional figures of population and private households for each local government district with brief statistical summary.

Summary report (for 1971, 1981 and 1991): for Northern Ireland and each of the 26 local government districts, this report covers population change, age distribution, sex, marital status, birthplace, religion, households, tenure, amenities, density of occupation and private cars and vans. In addition, ward level information is given listing area in hectares, total population, and numbers of males, females, private households unoccupied dwellings and rooms together the summary statistics for towns with a minimum population of 1,000. For 1991, new tabulations will present information for long-term illness and students' term-time address.

Belfast urban area report (for 1991 only): information is available at ward level about age distribution, sex, marital status, birthplace, religion, households, tenure, amenities, density of dwelling occupation, availability of cars, communal establishments, economically active population and employment status.

Religion report (for 1971, 1981 and 1991): the population is tabulated by detailed religious denomination. The main denominations (Presbyterian, Church of Ireland, Methodist, Roman Catholic and others) are broken down by age, sex, marital status, occupation, industry, socioeconomic group and household characteristics. Most tabulations are for Northern Ireland but some contain information for local government districts.

Economic activity report (for 1971, 1981 and 1991): data are given on economically active and inactive populations. The economically active are analysed by industry and occupational groupings broken down by age, marital status, employment status, socioeconomic groups and area of work place. Most tabulations are for Northern Ireland but others contain information for local government districts.

Workplace and transport to work report (for 1971, 1981 and 1991): these reports detail the economically active population by area of residence and area of workplace. The main workplace movements are given at the level of local government districts (a geographical breakdown of limited value) and include main means of transport to work, socioeconomic group and occupation and industry classifications. Time of journey to work is also given in 1981.

Housing and household composition report (for 1971, 1981 and 1991): these reports provide information on the composition and social and economic characteristics of households. Topics covered include tenure, housing density, car availability, sex, age and marital status. The majority of tabulations are for Northern Ireland.

Migration report (for 1971, 1981 and 1991): migrant characteristics are broken down by age, sex and marital status. Flow matrices for local government districts showing current residence by residence one year ago (also five years ago in 1971) are given, also detailing intra-LGD moves and migrants from outside Northern Ireland. Care is needed when interpreting these tables as civilian and military moves are not distinguished separately.

Education report (for 1971, 1981 and 1991): this report gives details of educational, professional and vocational qualifications by age, sex, occupation and industry. In 1971, the report was concerned with qualifications equating with A-level standard and above, in 1981 with qualifications of degree standard, and in 1991 with qualifications of at least GCSE standard.

Irish language report (for 1991 only): the content of this report is likely to include tables on spoken, written and reading knowledge of Irish with cross-tabulations by age, sex, marital status, occupation, industry and socioeconomic group.

Belfast local government district (for 1981 only): information is given at ward level about age distribution, sex, marital status, birthplace, religion, households, tenure, amenities, density of dwelling occupation, availability of cars, communal establishments, economically active population and employment status. In being restricted to the local government area, however, the report excludes about two fifths of the population living within the built-up area of Belfast.

County reports (for 1971 only): these contain the same information as appeared in the summary report for 1971. Separate reports were published for each county (Antrim, Armagh, Down, Fermanagh, Londonderry, Tyrone) and Belfast County Borough. Londonderry County Borough was included within the Co. Londonderry report. The tabulations give data for counties, urban and rural districts, wards, district electoral divisions and towns and villages with 50 or more dwellings.

Fertility report (for 1971 only): the report deals with the fertility of ever married women under the age of 60. Cohort information by year of marriage and date of birth is given but the value of these data is limited because of the upper age limit imposed. Linkage with the fertility data from the 1961 Census allows completed family size to be traced back to the beginning of the century.

BIBLIOGRAPHY

Census Act (Northern Ireland) 1925. In *Northern Ireland - The Public General Acts of 1925*, chapter 21, 117-123, HMSO, Belfast

Census Act (Northern Ireland) 1936. In *The Public General Acts of 1935-1936*, chapter 25, 144-149, HMSO, Belfast

Census Act (Northern Ireland) 1951. In *The Public General Acts of 1951*, chapter 6, 67-74, HMSO, Belfast

Census Act (Northern Ireland) 1960. In *The Public General Acts 1960*, chapter 8, 47-55, HMSO, Belfast

Census Act (Northern Ireland) 1965. In *Northern Ireland - The Public General Acts 1965*, chapter 5, 28-34, HMSO, Belfast

Census Act (Northern Ireland) 1969. In *The Public General Acts 1969*, chapter 8, 143-147, HMSO, Belfast

Department of Health and Social Services Registrar General Northern Ireland, *The Northern Ireland Census 1981*;

    (1982) *Belfast Local Government District*, HMSO, Belfast

    (1983) *Summary Report*, HMSO, Belfast

    (1983) *Household and Household Composition Report*, HMSO, Belfast

    (1983) *Workplace and Transport to Work Report*, HMSO, Belfast

    (1983) *Migration Report*, HMSO, Belfast

    (1983) *Economic Activity Report*, HMSO, Belfast

    (1984) *Education Report*, HMSO, Belfast

    (1984) *Religion Report*, HMSO, Belfast

Department of Health and Social Services Registrar General Northern Ireland, The Northern Ireland Census 1991;

    (1991) *Preliminary Report*, HMSO, Belfast

    (1992) *Summary Report*, HMSO, Belfast

Government of Northern Ireland, Census of Population of Northern Ireland 1926:

    (1928) *Belfast County Borough*, HMSO, Belfast

    (1928) *County of Antrim*, HMSO, Belfast

    (1928) *County of Armagh*, HMSO, Belfast

    (1928) *County of Down*, HMSO, Belfast.

    (1928) *County of Fermanagh*, HMSO, Belfast

    (1928) *County and County Borough of Londonderry*, HMSO, Belfast

    (1928) *County of Tyrone*, HMSO, Belfast

    (1929). *General Report*, HMSO, Belfast

    (1929). *Topographic Index*, HMSO, Belfast

Government of Northern Ireland, Census of Population of Northern Ireland 1937:

    (1937) *Preliminary Report*, HMSO, Belfast

    (1938) *Belfast County Borough*, HMSO, Belfast

    (1938) *County of Antrim*, HMSO, Belfast

    (1938) *County of Armagh*, HMSO, Belfast

    (1938) *County of Down*, HMSO, Belfast

    (1938) *County of Fermanagh*, HMSO, Belfast

    (1938) *County and County Borough of Londonderry*, HMSO, Belfast

(1938) *County of Tyrone*, HMSO, Belfast

(1939) *Supplement to 1926 Topographic Index,* HMSO, Belfast

(1929) *Topographic Index*, HMSO, Belfast

Government of Northern Ireland, Census of Population of Northern Ireland 1951:

(1951) *Preliminary Report*

(1953) *Belfast County Borough*, HMSO, Belfast

(1953) *Belfast County Borough*, HMSO, Belfast

(1954) *County of Antrim*, HMSO, Belfast

(1954) *County of Armagh*, HMSO, Belfast

(1954) *County of Down*, HMSO, Belfast

(1954) *County and County Borough of Londonderry*, HMSO, Belfast

(1954) *County of Tyrone*, HMSO, Belfast

(1955) *General Report*, HMSO, Belfast

(1951) *Topographic Index*, HMSO, Belfast

Government of Northern Ireland - General Register Office, Census of Population of Northern Ireland 1961:

(1962) *Topographic Index*, HMSO, Belfast

(1963) *Belfast County Borough*, HMSO, Belfast

(1964) *County of Antrim*, HMSO, Belfast

(1964) *County of Armagh*, HMSO, Belfast

(1964) *County of Down*, HMSO, Belfast

(1964) *County of Fermanagh*, HMSO, Belfast

(1964) *County and County Borough of Londonderry*, HMSO, Belfast

(1964) *County of Tyrone*, HMSO, Belfast

(1965) *Fertility Report*, HMSO, Belfast

(1965) *General Report*, HMSO, Belfast

Government of Northern Ireland: General Register Office, Census of Population of Northern Ireland 1966:

(1967) *Preliminary Report*, HMSO, Belfast.

(1968) *General Report*, HMSO, Belfast.

Northern Ireland - General Register Office, Census of Population of Northern Ireland 1971:

(no date) *Belfast County Borough*, HMSO, Belfast

(no date) *County of Antrim*, HMSO, Belfast

(no date) *County of Armagh*, HMSO, Belfast

(no date) *County of Down*, HMSO, Belfast

(no date) *County of Fermanagh*, HMSO, Belfast

(no date) *County and County Borough of Londonderry*, HMSO, Belfast

(no date) *County of Tyrone*, HMSO, Belfast

(1973) *Summary Tables*, HMSO, Belfast

(1975) *Household and Household Composition Tables*, HMSO, Belfast

(1975) *Education Tables*, HMSO, Belfast

(1975) *Religion Tables*, HMSO, Belfast

(1975) *Workplace and Transport to Work Tables*, HMSO, Belfast

(1976) *Migration Tables*, HMSO, Belfast

(1976) *Fertility Tables*, HMSO, Belfast

(1976) *Supplement to '61 Topographic Index*, HMSO, Belfast

(1977) *Economic Activity Tables*, HMSO, Belfast

Statutory Instruments, 1991 No. 760 (N.I.5) Northern Ireland, *The Census (Confidentiality) (Northern Ireland) Order 1991*, 1-3, HMSO, London

14　WHITHER THE CENSUS?

Angela Dale

Earlier chapters in this book have reviewed the administrative basis for the census, the way it was conducted in 1991 and the different kinds of output from the 1991 Census. In this concluding chapter we take a brief look back at the 1991 Census to consider some of the lessons to be learnt from it, and then look forward to what the future might hold, particularly in the light of practice in other western countries. It is important to emphasise that this discussion is not intended to be comprehensive and does not necessarily reflect the views or future plans of the Census Offices.

14.1 LESSONS FROM THE 1991 CENSUS

One of the most discussed aspects of the 1991 Census has been the estimated undercount of about 2 per cent (discussed in chapter 6 (II)) which, although low by the standard of the US, Canada and Australia, and very low by comparison with voluntary surveys, was, nonetheless, considerably higher than in previous UK censuses.

It is likely that this level of undercount will not prove to be a freak occurrence and, as in other countries, will continue in future censuses. Therefore future censuses will probably use more extensive procedures for estimating the level and distribution of any undercount than were used in 1991. In 1991, the Census Validation Survey (CVS) used a methodology unchanged in principle from the mid-1960s and was, perhaps, better equipped to deal with the quality of census responses than selective non-enumeration and even deliberate avoidance of enumeration. Further, it was not designed to provide estimates of the extent of coverage error below broad geographical areas — such as Inner London, Outer London, other metropolitan counties and non-metropolitan counties. This means that results from the CVS are of only limited value in estimating variation in the level of under-enumeration at a local authority level and below.

Chapter 6 reported that provisional results from the CVS suggested that it had failed to locate a substantial proportion of the estimated undercount. Work still underway on the results of the CVS will help to identify how parts of the undercount were missed by the CVS and this, in turn, will inform developments for future post-enumeration methods. Chapter 6 (II) reviewed some of the ways in which people could have been missed by the CVS and, in this respect, the methods being used by the US and Canada will be of interest because these countries have had longer in which to develop methods of post-enumeration geared to an expected undercount of several per cent of the population (chapter 6 (I)). One area where there may be scope for exploring alternative approaches is in the degree to which the post-enumeration survey is independent of the census. In Britain, CVS interviewers transcribed details of the households to be interviewed from the census form to the CVS interview schedule. The effect of this may be that, if the CVS interviewer obtains information consistent with that on the census form, there is little incentive to query its accuracy. This could be one of the factors contributing to the failure of the CVS to locate additional household members; thus, if householders were consistent in failing to report the more transitory members of their household, then there was little reason to query the accuracy of the information supplied.

Some of the difficulties experienced by enumerators in the 1991 Census — for example, making contact with households who were reluctant to answer the door, or who were away from home a great deal — are likely to increase over time. It is also likely that, with an increase in the numbers of young people moving into higher education, and also the growing trend towards spending some months travelling overseas, this group, in particular, will become even harder to enumerate. Registers such as the National Health Service Central Register may, in future censuses, be able to provide supplementary information on overall numbers within certain age and sex groups. As we shall see later, a number of European countries are making increasing use of registration-based information to supplement and, in some cases, replace, census data.

The option for a mid-term census in 1996, which might have been able to recover from some of the problems caused by the 1991 Census undercount, was ruled out in a Parliamentary answer on 12 October 1992, and so it will be 2001 before there is another opportunity to count the population. It is therefore important to provide users with the fullest information on likely problems caused by under-enumeration. Whilst chapter 6 (II) has provided some specific guidance for census analysts, the following section provides a brief general discussion.

14.2 HOW TO DEAL WITH THE UNDERCOUNT IN THE 1991 CENSUS

Table 6.11 provided the weights issued by OPCS and GRO(S) by which individual age groups can be adjusted to compensate for the estimated undercount. These do not provide any variation between geographical areas, and vary only with age and sex. At the time of writing it is not known exactly how the Census Offices will issue weighting factors by type of area but the most likely sub-division is into metropolitan and non-metropolitan parts within standard statutory regions (see *OPCS Monitor* PP1 93/1, 1993 for further information).

Levels of imputation of wholly absent households (who did not make a voluntary return) are known to show considerable geographical variation — for example levels are considerably higher in London and other metropolitan areas than in non-metropolitan counties (chapter 6 (I)). There is also considerable variation at the ED and ward level, within districts (chapter 4). The CVS will be providing information on the overall level of accuracy of the imputed data for wholly absent households. However, it would never be possible to provide an indication of the level of accuracy of imputation within EDs, wards, or districts. It is therefore important that users of ED and ward-level data, in particular, are aware of the level of imputation in the data they are using. Chapter 8, section 8.6.4, has highlighted the possible effects of modification of aggregate data at ED and ward level.

For census data that are based on the 10 per cent sample, there is no imputation of wholly absent households. Overall, a net figure of about 1.4 per cent of people were in imputed wholly absent households. This has a more significant effect on particular kinds of output. Data from the 10 per cent sample have an *effective* undercount about 60 per cent higher than the 100 per cent data. Apart from the 10 per cent SAS and LBS, the Samples of Anonymised Records are drawn from the 10 per cent sample. Additionally, the OPCS Longitudinal Study (chapter 12) omits people in imputed wholly absent households not because it is drawn from the 10 per cent sample but because its method of sampling is based on four birth dates. Whilst age is imputed, date of birth is not.

Some characteristics of imputed wholly absent households and the people living in them are available from SAS and LBS tables 18 and 19. Apart from geographical distribution, these tables give values for wholly absent households on: tenure, housing amenities, car, presence of children under 16 and, for the individuals in such households: age, marital status, long-term illness, economic activity, whether white or non-white. This can provide some information on the characteristics of one section of the population omitted from the 10 per cent sample data.

14.3 VALUE ADDED TO THE 1991 CENSUS: THE ESRC AND JISC PROGRAMME

The 1991 Census promises to have the most extensive range of census-related products of any census so far. The census is one of the most widely used of all datasets and the additional products associated with it reflect the fundamental role which it plays in providing benchmark data for the entire country.

The Economic and Social Research Council (ESRC) and the Joint Information Systems Committee (JISC) of the Higher Education Funding Council and the Department of Education, Northern Ireland have financed a £3.12 million programme of training, development and research based on the 1991 Census, the full details of which programme are available from the coordinator, Professor Philip Rees, at the address below:

Professor Phil Rees
School of Geography
University of Leeds
Leeds LS2 9JT

In this section we highlight some of the key parts of the programme that will provide additional products to census users. Although aimed primarily at the academic sector, most of the products are available to non-academics for appropriate charges.

Topics already discussed in this book and covered by the ESRC/JISC programme include: the purchase of the SAS, the LBS and SASPAC91 (chapter 8); the establishment of the Census Dissemination Unit at the University of Manchester (chapter 8); the purchase of the Samples of Anonymised Records and the establishment of the Census Microdata Unit at the University of Manchester (chapter 11); financial support for the Longitudinal Study Support Programme (chapter 12); the purchase of digitised ED boundaries and locational reference data for Great Britain (chapters 3(I) and 9); the purchase of ED to postcode directories (chapter 3(I)); the purchase of Special Migration Statistics and Special Workplace Statistics and MATPAC91 (chapter 10); and the production of small area statistics in Northern Ireland (chapter 13).

The SAS and LBS will also be available from the ESRC Data Archive which has the additional responsibility of cataloguing and archiving the data. The Archive also holds the small area statistics from the 1966, 1971 and 1981 censuses; these are available to users who wish to analyse change over time.

The ESRC/JISC programme has also funded a series of training workshops on the 1991 Census, the production of training materials such as sample datasets, and the development of a teaching resource pack. A number of other products funded within this programme and not specifically covered elsewhere in this Guide are discussed below.

14.3.1 The 1991 Census Development Programme

The innovative work funded by this programme provides an excellent example of the valuable relationships that can develop between government and academia. The outputs from the programme will add considerable value to the 1991 Census, greatly increasing the return on the investment made by government in conducting the Census.

Dr David Martin, University of Southampton and Dr Ian Bracken, University of Wales College of Cardiff are conducting an analysis of social change using spatial models of census data. The project has developed methods of examining socioeconomic change between 1981 and 1991 using the small areas statistics for the two censuses. The technique allows models to be constructed directly from centroid and population data to form a geographical database without the use of any digital boundary data. The method is outlined in Martin (1989) and Bracken and Martin (1989). For each ED in the 1991 Census it uses the 'population-weighted' centroid provided by OPCS as a single grid reference representing the centre of the residential part of that zone. These centroids represent local summary locations for the distribution of the population and its characteristics. In 1981, locations were provided as 100 m Ordnance Survey grid references. The 'surface generation' technique uses these centroid locations in order to redistribute the population associated with each ED into the cells of a regular grid. The technique is able to provide an analysis of population change over time where the areal units are not compatible — for example in the case of the 1981 and 1991 Census areal units. For those EDs which cannot be directly matched between 1981 and 1991 (the majority), 1981 data are reapportioned to the nearest 1991 centroid location using a distance function which preserves all population and variable totals. A fuller description is available in Martin (1993).

Two projects are concerned with aggregation issues in census data analysis. Professors Holt and Wrigley, of the University of Southampton, are developing a technique for adjusting the outcomes of analyses based upon spatially aggregated areal data to yield estimates of the underlying individual level parameters. Professor Openshaw at Leeds University is carrying out an empirical study of the magnitude of scale and zoning effects on the inference of individual associations from spatially aggregated data, identifying the types of area and methods of analysis most affected. Best practice advice to ameliorate or avoid the problems will be offered, along with a set of tools to reduce the effects of aggregation on census analysis. Both projects are using the SAS and also the SARs.

The programme is also supporting work by Professor Stan Openshaw and Dr Ian Turton at Leeds to develop a UNIX-based tabulation package customised for use with the Samples of Anonymised Records. Called 'USAR', the software should require virtually no prior training by users and should cater for both the new and the more experienced census user. It differs from most tabulation packages by enabling a high degree of interactive table design, allowing the easy creation of pseudo SAS/LBS formatted tables, a degree of intelligent data interpretation (for example, by detecting very small cell sizes in tables), and having the ability to formulate 'fuzzy' data queries. A prototype of the software is due to be available by autumn 1993. It is planned that the software will be distributed over the Joint Academic NETwork (JANET) to any UNIX workstation.

Other projects within the development programme include the production of a source book of occupational detail from the 1981 and 1991 Censuses, particularly in relation to changes in coding between the two censuses. For example, it will contain a series of tables showing the cross-classification of the occupational structure of employment in 1981 and 1991 by both the classification used in 1981 and that used in 1991. The project is being run at the University of Warwick by Professor Peter Elias, in close collaboration with the Occupational Information Unit of OPCS.

A team of researchers at the University of Leeds is conducting two further projects. The first is concerned with migration flows. A systematic comparison is being made between the migration data of the 1991 Census and migration data on flows between Family Health Service Authorities produced by the National Health Service Central Register. Linkage between these two kinds of migration data is of considerable value in population estimation and projection and in the use of migration data at local authority and small area level. A further project is designed to simulate whole populations and add income attributes to this population. A model is being developed to construct a simulated, synthetic population for of a major city, giving that population characteristics contained in the 1991 Census, based on probability distributions computed from SAS and SAR tabulations. Information on household income and consumption patterns will be added from the General Household Survey and Family Expenditure Survey by linking census characteristics with income and consumption attributes. One of the outcomes of this project will be the ability to evaluate the usefulness of individual-level income and consumption variables versus area-based geodemographic classifications. The methodology and software will be made available to the academic community.

Professor Phil Rees at the University of Leeds has created a machine readable data set from the published data in the County and Region Monitors for Great Britain, for all 67 county/regions in GB and all 459 districts in GB and from the Summary Report for Northern Ireland. The files are available to members of the academic community through the Census Dissemination Unit at Manchester University or from Professor Rees.

14.4 POLICY EVALUATION AND REAPPRAISAL (PEAR)

Soon after one census has been taken the planning and preparative work begins for the next one. However, as part of a more radical forward look, in spring 1992 the UK Census Offices issued a consultation paper, *Statistical information on population and housing 1996-2016: an invitation to shape future policy,* to a wide range of census users. The paper invited users to predict their future needs and to give views on how these needs might best be met. It outlined some possible options for meeting needs, and a set of criteria that would be used to assess the relative merit of each option.

Options reviewed for providing census-type information included:

- a conventional census, including sub-options such as reducing the content and sampling;
- a rolling census;
- population or housing registers; and
- making use of data held in administrative records

A report of the PEAR review (OPCS, 1993) summarised the following views which were submitted with a high degree of unanimity:

(1) Users in all sectors will continue to need census-type information for the foreseeable future. They stressed the key role of census statistics in planning, in needs assessment, in resource allocation, and in targeting services.

(2) Users are generally satisfied with the traditional form of census as the *primary* source for providing this information.

(3) Users expressed the need for supplementary census-type information for the years between censuses, particularly for annual subdistrict population figures and for annual statistical indicators for areas smaller than standard regions.

(4) Users wished data to continue to be collected by a central government organisation, in order to retain consistency, integrity and continuity of relevant expertise.

In October 1992 the government announced that the evaluation and reappraisal was to conclude and planning would be based on the assumption that there would be a census on conventional lines in 2001. It had been concluded that there was little chance of a cost-effective alternative to the census being developed before 2001, and therefore a decision was taken not to give further consideration to alternative primary data sources but to concentrate on ways of improving the conventional census. However, because of the widely stated requirement for information during the years between censuses, it was stated that sources of supplementary data would be sought. Possible sources of data include the government sample surveys, administrative records and registers. Developments to be considered include:

- combining data from existing surveys, thereby increasing the effective sample size sufficiently to give information for small areas;
- using synthetic estimation to derive estimates for small areas from data (for example from surveys) for larger areas;
- extracting relevant data from administrative records or registers.

In the light of these conclusions, it is worth examining further some of the options mentioned above, particularly in the light of the experience of other countries, and also to consider ways in which the next census might be more cost-effective.

357

14.5 WAYS OF MAKING THE CENSUS MORE COST-EFFECTIVE

OPCS regularly review procedures for conducting the census and assess ways in which changes may be introduced to increase its cost-effectiveness. Whilst it is premature to speculate on decisions that might finally emerge over the conduct of the next census, it is appropriate to consider some of the options available. The following discussion is based on the premise that the cost of the 2001 Census will not, in real terms, exceed that of the 1991 Census.

Sampling

Sampling in the field or sampling at the processing stage is widely used as a means of reducing census costs — although when it was first used in Britain in the 1951 Census it was as a means of speeding up the production of census output rather than cutting costs. A 1 per cent sample was drawn from the full census of 1951, and the results were laid before Parliament only 15 months after census day. In 1961, with the introduction of computerised processing, it was assumed that this early sample was not needed and a 10 per cent sample of households was taken *in the field*. When sampling in the field is used, a short form is usually completed by the majority of households whilst a longer form is given only to the sample selected to receive it — typically 10 per cent. In the 1961 Census in Britain, enumerators were asked to give a long form to every tenth household and, as discussed in chapter 1, this turned out to produce a biassed sample because of enumerator selection. The sample was found to under-represent the elderly, the widowed, divorced people of all ages, and single people over 25. Immigrants from the New Commonwealth were particularly under-represented, with about 20-25 per cent under-enumeration of West Indians (Whitehead, 1983).

If a prior sampling frame exists, then the danger of enumerator selection bias can be overcome by pre-sampling and thereby removing from enumerators the scope for any influence over who is given a long form. However, in Britain, there is no entirely comprehensive sampling frame that can be used. It is the preliminary round of the census enumerator which establishes a listing of addresses in each ED. The 1966 10 per cent sample census used the 1961 Census to provide a sampling frame of addresses, topped up for new housing since 1961. However, this was not entirely successful as some property recorded as vacant in 1961 was occupied in 1966, and not included in the sampling frame.

The 1971 Census began the practice of drawing a 10 per cent sample of the 'hard to code' items at the *processing stage* and this has been continued in subsequent censuses. Whilst this measure was introduced to limit the cost of fully coding those items that were time consuming to code, it has the disadvantage that it places an unnecessary burden on 90 per cent of households from whom unused data are collected. Although the cost of all coding is much reduced by restricting part of it to a 10 per cent sample, the cost of coding the 10 per cent items is much more than one tenth of the cost of fully coding the items. Britain has a very short census form by comparison with most other western countries (Redfern, 1981); if the 'hard-to-code' questions were *asked* of only a 10 per cent sample of households, it might be feasible to extent the number of questions included in the form used for this sample without imposing an undue burden on the respondents.

However, for pre-sampling to be effective, a prior sampling frame is needed and, as already indicated, this is not readily available in the UK. The US draws a sample prior to the census (chapter 3 (II)) and has developed a comprehensive address register to facilitate this. Nonetheless, enumerators are still needed to update this register prior to a census and this method has the disadvantage that it cannot distinguish more than one household living at the same address. In time, the Ordnance Survey Address Point product (chapter 3 (I)) may provide a basis for pre-sampling addresses in Britain.

Alternatively, if coding costs could be reduced sufficiently, all the data currently collected on census forms could be used in processing and the error introduced by taking a 10 per cent sample could be eliminated. One possibility is to increase the level of automation, for example capturing written answers by keying or by scanning, and using a computerised system programmed to code all but the rarest of categories. Such a system has been successfully used for some of the written-in answers to the Canadian Census, with cost-saving over conventional coding methods (Ciok, 1993).

One of the largest costs of the census is the field-force; could this cost be reduced by a mail-out and/or mail-back system? The US, Canada and Australia have now largely moved to this method. However, like pre-sampling, this also requires the availability of an accurate and complete address list. Whilst North America and Australia have moved in the direction of sampling and mail-out/mail-back in order to reduce respondent burden and processing costs, many European countries have sought to achieve this by linking alternative data sources, particularly from population registers, to census data.

Before discussing the use of population registers it is first important to draw attention to the way in which the introduction and development of large-scale sample surveys in Britain has influenced, and been influenced by, the content of the census of population and housing.

14.6 THE RELATIONSHIP OF SAMPLE SURVEYS TO THE CENSUS OF POPULATION AND HOUSING

The key difference between a census of population and a sample survey is that the former should be a complete enumeration of 100 per cent of the population whilst the latter may well be nationally representative but is typically designed to sample at most 0.5 per cent of the population. This has two immediately obvious effects. Firstly, the size of the survey (and sometimes also the design of it) means that it cannot provide reliable estimates for small geographical areas. Typically, national surveys do not provide reliable data below the level of standard region. Related to this, all figures from surveys are subject to sampling errors. Secondly, the voluntary nature of the sample survey, by comparison with the compulsory census, means that the former has a non-response rate of at least 15 per cent and often higher and often has an associated bias. The effects of this may be particularly acute for small sub-groups of the population.

Nonetheless, it is evident that the availability and content of survey data has been one of the factors taken into consideration when deciding topics for inclusion in the decennial census (Redfern, 1981, 1987; Whitehead, 1983). The first continuous government survey was the Family Expenditure Survey, introduced in 1957. Initially, this was small (about 3,000 households), with a response rate of about 70 per cent. It was not until the introduction of the General Household Survey in 1971 that government had a consistent source of annual information on the households and people of Great Britain. The Labour Force Survey (LFS) was introduced in 1973, with a rather larger sample size and was specifically geared to employment issues. The LFS was, in part, a response to the requirement of the Statistical Office of the European Community (SOEC) for such a survey to be conducted biennially by all member states.

Whitehead (1983) recalls that during the middle 1970s consideration was given to the best overall package of censuses and surveys for the 1980s. It was assumed that a decennial census would continue but that there were alternative strategies for intercensal years. OPCS tested the feasibility of a continuous 1 per cent multi-purpose household survey, with its own field force and using optical mark reading documents to speed processing. Although shown to be feasible there was, apparently, little support for the idea, particularly because of overlap with the LFS which SOEC required to be carried out during the spring of the relevant year.

Despite the newly available GHS, a mid-term census was planned for 1976, but cancelled at very short notice. Its cancellation, however, increased pressure for survey data on housing, in order to update the 1971 Census. The result of this was the National Dwelling and Housing Survey which covered about 1 million (6 per cent) of the housing units in England and Wales and was conducted in 1977-78. It is interesting to note that this survey included the ethnic question that had been tested but was eventually not used in the 1981 Census. The survey was therefore able to provide valuable information on the housing conditions, household composition and employment of ethnic minorities. The 1979 LFS also introduced a direct question on ethnic group as a result of government's wish to obtain this information — but from voluntary surveys, rather than from the 1981 Census (Whitehead, 1983).

The National Dwelling and Housing Survey had another interesting feature — it broke new ground in the way in which it was conducted. Although planned by the Department of Environment with advice from OPCS, field work was contracted out to a consortium of private firms, clerical processing was carried out by the Research and Planning Unit of the Greater London Council, and computing was contracted to a commercial bureau.

In order to update the housing information in the National Dwelling and Housing Survey, additional housing questions were included in the 1981 LFS. However, the LFS was not able to produce results at a local authority level.

The topic of fertility (number and spacing of children born to women) provides another example of the relationship between the content of the decennial census and social surveys. The availability of information on fertility in the GHS, and the linkage of fertility information into the OPCS Longitudinal Study, were clearly relevant to a decision not to include in the 1981 Census the fertility questions asked in post-war censuses prior to 1981 (Redfern, 1981).

Income is another topic which has never been asked in a British census. It has been included in a number of pre-census tests and in a voluntary survey linked to the 1971 Census, but subsequently rejected for inclusion in a census (see chapter 5). Although there is considerable pressure from many census users to have income data at small area level, the presence of detailed income questions in the GHS from 1979 to 1992 and in the Family Resources Survey from 1992 onwards, must obviously influence the decision over whether to include an income question in the census.

The preceding discussion has highlighted the relationship between the content of government surveys and the census. In the intercensal period of the 1990s social surveys, and in particular the LFS, are likely to play an important role in providing updated figures. In 1992 the LFS moved to an unclustered sample design in order to increase the precision of its estimates.[1] The LFS provides an annual cross-sectional sample of about 96,000 households in Great Britain, representing a 0.43 per cent sample. The sample includes students in halls of residence or boarding schools and resident staff in NHS hospital accommodation, for example in nurses homes. Because of the unclustered design, sampling errors can be readily calculated using standard formulae, although if individual level data are used there is obviously an element of clustering within households, particularly on characteristics such as ethnic group. Confidentiality constraints preclude the release of micro-data with geographical identifiers below the level of standard region. However, if pre-planned tabulations were available at the local authority level it might provide an important step towards meeting one of the major needs of census users identified in the PEAR review: for better local area statistics between censuses (section 14.4). The recent introduction of a question on income for employees in the LFS is also likely to be of considerable interest to those seeking to impute income information to census data.

14.7 USE OF REGISTER-BASED SYSTEMS TO PRODUCE CENSUS-TYPE DATA

Another way of providing intercensal data at subregional levels is through the use of administrative registers. This was a topic on which views were sought in the PEAR review. This section discusses the use of register-based systems in other countries and the scope for using such information in Britain.

In a review of alternative approaches to the census of population, Redfern (1987) provides a valuable discussion of the way in which registers are used in different European countries. All countries keep administrative registers for a variety of purposes, at very least to record births and deaths. However, only some countries keep a population register that provides complete current coverage, records migration accurately, and is kept up-to-date.

The most notable example of a country where such a register exists is Denmark and, in the 1991 round of censuses, Denmark's census was entirely register based, drawing on a variety of computer files to obtain information on individuals and also dwellings (Langevin, Begeot and Pearce, 1992). The Netherlands uses a variety of sources, including municipal population registers and information from the continuous Labour Force Survey to provide census-type information, and has not held a census since 1971. In Belgium, the national register was used in 1991 to produce pre-printed census questionnaires containing certain basic information. These were then posted out and the people completing the forms were asked to correct and update the information where necessary. This information was then used to update the national register. In relation to the discussion in section 14.5, the availability of

---

[1] In the design of the LFS introduced in 1992, twelve thousand *new* addresses are sampled each quarter and then re-interviewed on each of the next four quarters, so that each household is interviewed five times, with the fifth and last quarterly interview on the anniversary of the first. All first interviews are face to face, but 70 per cent of recall interviews are by phone. For reasons of costs, the sample in Scotland north of the Caledonian Canal is drawn from the published phone book and conducted by telephone; this will obviously introduce some additional response bias for this area.

an accurate and up-to-date national register provides the potential for using a longer form for a sample of the population. Although the Belgian 1991 Census was mailed out, enumerators were used to collect forms — and were therefore able to track down anyone not recorded in the population register. However, because the individual identity number is widely used in many everyday aspects of life in Belgium, the National Register is believed to provide very effective population coverage.

In the former Federal Republic of Germany, the census had also been used as a means of updating and correcting population registers maintained by local communities. However, shortly before the census planned for April 1983, a campaign was mounted to challenge the legality of using census data in this way. A final court ruling accepted the need for a conventional census, but ended the practice of using census data to update local population registers. A conventional census was finally taken in May 1987. However, Germany also takes an annual micro-census of 1 per cent of households and persons in institutions and this information was used to provide 1991 census-type data, in place of a full census.

In Britain there is no population register containing lists of residents and their addresses as there is in Denmark and Belgium. However, the National Health Service Central Register (NHSCR), discussed in chapter 12, provides a near-complete computerised register of the population, compiled from individual registration with Family Health Service Authorities (FHSA). All new births are automatically allocated NHS numbers and added to the register, irrespective of whether there is a registration with the FHSA. The register does not, however, hold information on immigrants to the country unless and until they register with a National Health Service doctor. The NHSCR holds the surname and forename, sex and date of birth of each patient, as well as the code for the FHSA in which the patient is registered. (There are 98 FHSAs in England and Wales with boundaries contiguous with counties; in Scotland, the Area Health Board is the equivalent of the FHSA.) For the majority of the population this provides information on area of residence; however, a move to another area is only recorded when the individual changes registration to a doctor within a different FHSA. How quickly a person re-registers when they change address varies considerably with age and stage of life-cycle; mothers with young children and elderly people are most likely to register quickly, and young, single people least likely. Those who do not use the NHS will have no moves recorded. Also, people who emigrate, or simply leave the country for 6 months or a year, do not always notify their doctor or any other official body and therefore may remain on the register. For these reasons the NHSCR cannot, as it stands, provide an alternative to census data. However, the NHSCR should be able to provide an estimate of the population of Great Britain by age and sex, although there is likely to be some inflation of numbers, particularly of unrecorded emigration. Other registers, for example the electoral register and school enrolments, provide information for certain age groups in the population and are routinely used by local authorities to update intercensal estimates. However, a recent survey (Smith, 1993) shows that, in 1991, 7% of eligible Britons who completed the census were not on the electoral register and, in Inner London, this rose to 20 per cent.

14.8 COMPARABILITY OF CENSUSES IN EUROPE AND BEYOND

Although in recent decades the United Nations and the European Community have actively promoted the harmonisation of census information across countries, the concept of international comparability is not new. As long ago as 1872, the International

Statistical Institute, at a meeting in St Petersburg, agreed that a census should take place every ten years and that it should be completed within 24 hours. A list of topics for inclusion was also drawn up (Brown, 1978). Although the aim of a 'world census', proposed at a later meeting in 1890, has not been achieved, there has been a steady movement towards greater uniformity in census taking world-wide. This has been promoted by the United Nations Statistical Commission with world wide recommendations for each decennial round of censuses, and the European variant of the recommendations, compiled by the UN and the Conference of European Statisticians working under the auspices of the UN's Economic Commission for Europe. Joint recommendations have been regularly published and have informed the 1960, and subsequent, round of censuses.

The Statistical Office of the European Community drew up plans for a set of 100 tables from the 1970 round of censuses to give harmonised output in the six member countries, although differences in timing and in definitions impeded the implementation of this plan (Brown, 1986). In November 1973 an EC directive proposed synchronised census reference dates by specifying that the census should be carried out between 1 March and 31 May 1981. It also proposed a set of statistical tables covering basic topics in a standardised format for all member states (Langevin, Begeot and Pearce, 1992). However, the production of harmonised tabulations from the 1981 Censuses has been greatly delayed by a variety of different factors, including the postponement of the Federal Republic of Germany's census until 1987 (discussed above). A Council directive adopted in May 1987 required that information should be collected or compiled by member states between 1 March and 31 May (with exceptions for France and Italy) for a programme of statistical tables covering demographic, economic and social characteristics of individuals, households and families at national and regional level which would be completed and forwarded to the Commission. The recommendations of the 1990 Censuses of Population and Housing in the Economic Commission for Europe Region prepared by the UN were used as the basis for putting together the programme of statistical tables. The topics were divided into basic and additional ones. Table 2.1 in chapter 2 showed which countries excluded basic topics. The complete synchronisation of information is hampered by the fact that member states can obtain derogations on timing and content. In fact, most of the nine countries carrying out conventional censuses in the 1991 round included all the basic topics. However, it remains to be seen how successfully, and within what time scale, the proposed set of harmonised tables become available.

14.9 CONCLUSION

There is every indication that the decennial census will retain its position as the most important and widely used of all the UK data sources. All the evidence suggests that the use made of census data is increasing steadily and that more, rather than less, information is being demanded by users. Whilst social surveys and administrative records play an essential role in supplementing and updating the decennial census, they are unlikely to be able to offer an alternative that provides comparability at small geographical areas across the entire country. It is this ability to provide comparability on key social and demographic variables at very fine geographical areas that makes the UK decennial census unique and which is of such importance to local and central government and to academic researchers.

Appendix A The 1991 Census forms

The forms are shown at reduced size. Each H form allows for details of up to six people to be recorded on it, across a double-page spread. For reasons of space, only the first side of each double-page spread is shown here, for persons 1 and 2. The opposite side is identical and is used for persons 3 to 6.

H form for private households, England

**1991 Census
England**

H form for Private Households

To the Head or Joint Heads or members of the Household aged 16 or over

Please complete this form for all members of the household, including children, and have it ready for collection on Monday 22nd April. Your census enumerator will call to collect it then or soon afterwards and will help you with the form if you have any difficulties. The enclosed leaflet explains why the Census is necessary and how the information is used.

Completion of the form is compulsory under the Census Act 1920. If you refuse to complete it, or give false information, you may have to pay a fine of up to £400.

Your answers will be treated in strict confidence and used only to produce statistics. Names and addresses will not be put into the computer; only the postcode will be entered. The forms will be kept securely within my Office and treated as confidential for 100 years.

Anyone using or disclosing Census information improperly will be liable to prosecution. For example, it would be improper for you to pass on to someone else information which you had been given in confidence by a visitor to enable you to complete the Census form.

If any member of the household aged 16 or over does not wish you, or another member of the household, to see their information, please ask the enumerator for an individual form with an envelope.

After completing the form, please sign the declaration on the last page.

Thank you for your co-operation.

P J Wormald

P J Wormald
Registrar General
Office of Population Censuses and Surveys
PO Box 100 Fareham PO16 0AL.
Telephone: 0329 844444

Please read these instructions before filling in this form

A Household:

A household comprises either one person living alone or a group of people (not necessarily related) living at the same address with common housekeeping — that is, sharing at least one meal a day or sharing a living room or sitting room.

People staying temporarily with the household are included.

▶ If there is more than one household in this building, answer for your household only.

▶ First answer questions **H1 and H2** on **this page** and H3 to H5 on the **back page** about your household and the rooms which it occupies.

▶ When you have answered the household questions, answer the questions on the **inside pages** about each member of your household.

▶ If a member of the household is completing an Individual form please still enter their name and answer questions 5 and 6 on this form.

▶ Then complete **Panel B** and **Panel C** on the back page.

▶ *Answer each question by ticking the appropriate box or boxes* ☑ *where they are provided.*

▶ *Please use ink or ballpoint pen.*

To be completed by the Enumerator

Census District	Enumeration District	Form Number

Name

Address

Postcode ☐☐☐ ■ ☐☐☐   **ABS** ☐

Panel A
To be completed by the Enumerator and amended, if necessary, by the person(s) signing this form.

Tick one box to show the type of accommodation which this household occupies.

A caravan or other mobile or temporary structure	☐ 1
A whole house or bungalow that is — detached	☐ 2
— semi-detached	☐ 3
— terraced (include end of terrace)	☐ 4
The whole of a purpose built flat or maisonette — in a commercial building (for example in an office building or hotel or over a shop)	☐ 5
— in a block of flats or tenement	☐ 6
Part of a converted or shared house, bungalow or flat — separate entrance into the building	☐ 7
— shared entrance into the building	☐ 8

H1 Rooms

Please count the number of rooms your household has for its **own** use.

Do not count: small kitchens, under 2 metres (6 feet 6 inches) wide
bathrooms
toilets

Do count: living rooms
bedrooms
kitchens at least 2 metres (6 feet 6 inches) wide
all other rooms in your accommodation

The total number of rooms is ☐

H2 Accommodation
If box 7 or box 8 in Panel A is ticked, tick one box below to show the type of accommodation which your household occupies.

A one roomed flatlet
with private bath or shower, WC and kitchen facilities. ☐ 1

One room or bedsit, not self-contained
(to move from your room to bathroom, WC or kitchen facilities you have to use a hall, landing or stairway open to other household(s)). ☐ 2

A self-contained flat or accommodation with 2 or more rooms,
having bath or shower, WC and kitchen facilities all behind its own private door. ☐ 3

2 or more rooms, not self-contained
(to move between rooms or to bathroom, WC or kitchen facilities you have to use a hall, landing or stairway open to other household(s)). ☐ 4

Please turn to the back page and answer questions H3 to H5 ▶

H form for private households, England — *continued*

1-3	**Name, sex and date of birth of people to be included**	**Person No. 1**	**Person No. 2**

Important: please read the notes before answering the questions.

In answering the rest of the questions please include:

▶ every person who spends census night (21-22 April) in this household, **including anyone staying temporarily.**

▶ any other people who are usually members of the household but on census night are absent on holiday, at school or college, or for any other reason, even if they are being included on another census form elsewhere.

▶ anyone who arrives here on Monday 22nd April who was in Great Britain on the Sunday and who has not been included as present on another census form.

▶ any newly born baby born before the 22nd April, even if still in hospital. If not yet given a name, write BABY and the surname.

Write the names in BLOCK CAPITALS starting with the head or a joint head of household.

Person No. 1

Name and surname

Sex — Male ☐ 1 / Female ☐ 2

Date of birth — Day / Month / Year

Person No. 2

Name and surname

Sex — Male ☐ 1 / Female ☐ 2

Date of birth — Day / Month / Year

4	**Marital status**

On the 21st April what is the person's marital status?
If separated but not divorced, please tick 'Married (first marriage)' or 'Re-married' as appropriate.
Please tick one box.

Person No. 1
Single (never married) ☐ 1
Married (first marriage) ☐ 2
Re-married ☐ 3
Divorced (decree absolute) ☐ 4
Widowed ☐ 5

Person No. 2
Single (never married) ☐ 1
Married (first marriage) ☐ 2
Re-married ☐ 3
Divorced (decree absolute) ☐ 4
Widowed ☐ 5

5	**Relationship in household**

Please tick the box which indicates the relationship of each person to the person in the first column.

A step child or adopted child should be included as the son or daughter of the step or adoptive parent.

Write in relationship of 'Other relative' — for example, father, daughter-in-law, niece, uncle, cousin.

Write in position in household of an 'Unrelated' person for example, boarder, housekeeper, friend, flatmate, foster child.

Person No. 2 — Relationship to Person No.1
Husband or wife ☐ 1
Living together as a couple ☐ 2
Son or daughter ☐ 3
Other relative ☐
please specify

Unrelated ☐
please specify

6	**Whereabouts on night of 21-22 April 1991**

Please tick the appropriate box to indicate where the person was on the night of 21-22 April 1991.

Person No. 1
At this address, out on night work or travelling to this address ☐ 0
Elsewhere in England, Scotland or Wales ☐ 1
Outside Great Britain ☐ 2

Person No. 2
At this address, out on night work or travelling to this address ☐ 0
Elsewhere in England, Scotland or Wales ☐ 1
Outside Great Britain ☐ 2

7	**Usual address**

If the person usually lives here, please tick 'This address'. If not, tick 'Elsewhere' and write in the person's usual address.

For students and children away from home during term time, the home address should be taken as the usual address.

For any person who lives away from home for part of the week, the home address should be taken as the usual address.

Any person who is not a permanent member of the household should be asked what he or she considers to be his or her usual address.

Person No. 1
This address ☐ 1
Elsewhere ☐
If elsewhere, please write the person's usual address and postcode below in BLOCK CAPITALS

Post-code ☐☐☐☐ ☐☐☐

Person No. 2
This address ☐ 1
Elsewhere ☐
If elsewhere, please write the person's usual address and postcode below in BLOCK CAPITALS

Post-code ☐☐☐☐ ☐☐☐

8	**Term time address of students and schoolchildren**

If not a student or schoolchild, please tick first box.

For a student or schoolchild who lives here during term time, tick 'This address'.

If he or she does not live here during term time, tick 'Elsewhere' and write in the current or most recent term time address.

Person No. 1
Not a student or schoolchild ☐
This address ☐ 1
Elsewhere ☐
If elsewhere, please write the term time address and postcode below in BLOCK CAPITALS

Post-code ☐☐☐☐ ☐☐☐

Person No. 2
Not a student or schoolchild ☐
This address ☐ 1
Elsewhere ☐
If elsewhere, please write the term time address and postcode below in BLOCK CAPITALS

Post-code ☐☐☐☐ ☐☐☐

H form for private households, England — *continued*

1-3 **Name, sex and date of birth of people to be included**	**Person No. 1**	**Person No. 2**

Important: please read the notes before answering the questions.

In answering the rest of the questions please include:

► every person who spends census night (21-22 April) in this household, **including anyone staying temporarily.**

► any other people who are usually members of the household but on census night are absent on holiday, at school or college, or for any other reason, even if they are being included on another census form elsewhere.

► anyone who arrives here on Monday 22nd April who was in Great Britain on the Sunday and who has not been included as present on another census form.

► any newly born baby born before the 22nd April, even if still in hospital. If not yet given a name, write BABY and the surname.

Write the names in BLOCK CAPITALS starting with the head or a joint head of household.

Person No. 1

Name and surname

Sex   Male ☐ 1
       Female ☐ 2

Date of birth
Day   Month   Year

Person No. 2

Name and surname

Sex   Male ☐ 1
       Female ☐ 2

Date of birth
Day   Month   Year

---

9   Usual address one year ago

If the person's usual address one year ago (on the 21st April 1990) was the same as his or her current usual address (given in answer to question 7), please tick 'Same'. If not, tick 'Different' and write in the usual address one year ago.

If everyone on the form has moved from the same address, please write the address in full for the first person and indicate with an arrow that this applies to the other people on the form.

For a child born since the 21st April 1990, tick the 'Child under one' box.

Person 1:
Same as question 7 ☐ 1
Different ☐
Child under one ☐ 3

If different, please write the person's address and postcode on the 21st April 1990 below in BLOCK CAPITALS

Post-code ☐☐☐ ☐ ☐☐☐

Person 2:
Same as question 7 ☐ 1
Different ☐
Child under one ☐ 3

If different, please write the person's address and postcode on the 21st April 1990 below in BLOCK CAPITALS

Post-code ☐☐☐ ☐ ☐☐☐

---

10   Country of birth

Please tick the appropriate box.

If the 'Elsewhere' box is ticked, please write in the present name of the country in which the birthplace is now situated.

Person 1:
England ☐ 1
Scotland ☐ 2
Wales ☐ 3
Northern Ireland ☐ 4
Irish Republic ☐ 5
Elsewhere ☐

If elsewhere, please write in the present name of the country

Person 2:
England ☐ 1
Scotland ☐ 2
Wales ☐ 3
Northern Ireland ☐ 4
Irish Republic ☐ 5
Elsewhere ☐

If elsewhere, please write in the present name of the country

---

11   Ethnic group

Please tick the appropriate box.

If the person is descended from more than one ethnic or racial group, please tick the group to which the person considers he/she belongs, or tick the 'Any other ethnic group' box and describe the person's ancestry in the space provided.

Person 1:
White ☐ 0
Black-Caribbean ☐ 1
Black-African ☐ 2
Black-Other ☐
please describe

Indian ☐ 3
Pakistani ☐ 4
Bangladeshi ☐ 5
Chinese ☐ 6
Any other ethnic group ☐
please describe

Person 2:
White ☐ 0
Black-Caribbean ☐ 1
Black-African ☐ 2
Black-Other ☐
please describe

Indian ☐ 3
Pakistani ☐ 4
Bangladeshi ☐ 5
Chinese ☐ 6
Any other ethnic group ☐
please describe

---

12   Long-term illness

Does the person have any long-term illness, health problem or handicap which limits his/her daily activities or the work he/she can do?

Include problems which are due to old age.

Person 1:
Yes, has a health problem which limits activities ☐ 1
Has no such health problem ☐ 2

Person 2:
Yes, has a health problem which limits activities ☐ 1
Has no such health problem ☐ 2

H form for private households, England — *continued*

1-3	**Name, sex and date of birth of people to be included**

Important: please read the notes before answering the questions.

In answering the rest of the questions please include:

► every person who spends census night (21-22 April) in this household, **including anyone staying temporarily.**

► any other people who are usually members of the household but on census night are absent on holiday, at school or college, or for any other reason, even if they are being included on another census form elsewhere.

► anyone who arrives here on Monday 22nd April who was in Great Britain on the Sunday and who has not been included as present on another census form.

► any newly born baby born before the 22nd April, even if still in hospital. If not yet given a name, write BABY and the surname.

Write the names in BLOCK CAPITALS starting with the head or a joint head of household.

Person No. 1

Name and surname

Sex   Male ☐ 1   Female ☐ 2

Date of birth
Day   Month   Year

Person No. 2

Name and surname

Sex   Male ☐ 1   Female ☐ 2

Date of birth
Day   Month   Year

Answers to the remaining questions are not required for any person under 16 years of age (born after 21st April 1975)

13	**Whether working, retired, looking after the home etc last week**

Which of these things was the person doing **last week**?

Please read carefully right through the list and **tick all the descriptions that apply**.

Casual or temporary work should be counted at boxes 1, 2, 3 or 4. Also tick boxes 1, 2, 3 or 4 if the person had a job last week but was off sick, on holiday, temporarily laid off or on strike.

Boxes 1, 2, 3 and 4 refer to work for pay or profit but not to unpaid work except in a family business.

Working for an employer is **part time** (box 2) if the hours worked, excluding any overtime and mealbreaks, are usually 30 hours or less per week.

Include any person wanting a job but prevented from looking by holiday or temporary sickness.

Do not count training given or paid for by an employer.

Person No. 1

Was working for an employer full time (more than 30 hours a week) ☐ 1

Was working for an employer part time (one hour or more a week) ☐ 2

Was self-employed, employing other people ☐ 3

Was self-employed, not employing other people ☐ 4

Was on a government employment or training scheme ☐ 5

Was waiting to start a job he/she had already accepted ☐ 6

Was unemployed and looking for a job ☐ 7

Was at school or in other full time education ☐ 8

Was unable to work because of long term sickness or disability ☐ 9

Was retired from paid work ☐ 10

Was looking after the home or family ☐ 11

Other ☐
please specify

Person No. 2

Was working for an employer full time (more than 30 hours a week) ☐ 1

Was working for an employer part time (one hour or more a week) ☐ 2

Was self-employed, employing other people ☐ 3

Was self-employed, not employing other people ☐ 4

Was on a government employment or training scheme ☐ 5

Was waiting to start a job he/she had already accepted ☐ 6

Was unemployed and looking for a job ☐ 7

Was at school or in other full time education ☐ 8

Was unable to work because of long term sickness or disability ☐ 9

Was retired from paid work ☐ 10

Was looking after the home or family ☐ 11

Other ☐
please specify

H form for private households, England — *continued*

1-3	**Name, sex and date of birth of people to be included**	**Person No. 1**	**Person No. 2**

Important: please read the notes before answering the questions.

In answering the rest of the questions please include:

▶ every person who spends census night (21-22 April) in this household, **including anyone staying temporarily.**

▶ any other people who are usually members of the household but on census night are absent on holiday, at school or college, or for any other reason, even if they are being included on another census form elsewhere.

▶ anyone who arrives here on Monday 22nd April who was in Great Britain on the Sunday and who has not been included as present on another census form.

▶ any newly born baby born before the 22nd April, even if still in hospital. If not yet given a name, write BABY and the surname.

Write the names in BLOCK CAPITALS starting with the head or a joint head of household.

Person No. 1

Name and surname

Sex — Male ☐ 1 / Female ☐ 2

Date of birth — Day / Month / Year

Person No. 2

Name and surname

Sex — Male ☐ 1 / Female ☐ 2

Date of birth — Day / Month / Year

Please read A below, tick the box that applies and follow the instruction by the box ticked.

A	Did the person have a paid job last week (any of the boxes 1, 2, 3 or 4 ticked at question 13)?	YES ☐ Answer questions 14, 15, 16, 17 and 18 about the main job last week, then go on to question 19 NO ☐ Answer B	YES ☐ Answer questions 14, 15, 16, 17 and 18 about the main job last week, then go on to question 19 NO ☐ Answer B
B	Has the person had a paid job within the last 10 years?	YES ☐ Answer questions 14, 15 and 16 about the most recent job, then go on to question 19 NO ☐ Go on to question 19	YES ☐ Answer questions 14, 15 and 16 about the most recent job, then go on to question 19 NO ☐ Go on to question 19

14	**Hours worked per week**		

How many hours per week does or did the person usually work in his or her main job?

Do not count overtime or meal breaks.

Number of hours worked per week ☐

Number of hours worked per week ☐

15	**Occupation**		

Please give the full title of the person's present or last job and describe the main things he/she does or did in the job.

At a, give the full title by which the job is known, for example: 'packing machinist'; 'poultry processor'; 'jig and tool fitter'; 'supervisor of typists'; 'accounts clerk'; rather than general titles like 'machinist'; 'process worker'; 'supervisor' or 'clerk'. Give rank or grade if the person has one.

At b, write down the main things the person actually does or did in the job. If possible ask him/her to say what these things are and write them down.

Armed Forces — enter 'commissioned officer' or 'other rank' as appropriate at **a**, and leave **b** blank.

Civil Servants — give grade at **a** and discipline or specialism, for example: 'electrical engineer'; 'accountant'; 'chemist'; 'administrator' at **b**.

a Full job title

b Main things done in job

a Full job title

b Main things done in job

16	**Name and business of employer (if self-employed give the name and nature of the person's business)**		

At a, please give the name of the employer. Give the trading name if one is used. Do not use abbreviations.

At b, describe clearly what the employer (or the person if self-employed) makes or does (or did).

Armed Forces — write 'Armed Forces' at **a** and leave **b** blank. For a member of the Armed Forces of a country other than the UK — add the name of the country.

Civil Servants — give name of Department at **a** and write 'Government Department' at **b**.

Local Government Officers — give name of employing authority at **a** and department in which employed at **b**.

a Name of employer

b Description of employer's business

a Name of employer

b Description of employer's business

H form for private households, England — *continued*

1-3 **Name, sex and date of birth of people to be included**	Person No. 1	Person No. 2
Important: please read the notes before answering the questions. In answering the rest of the questions please include:	**Name and surname**	**Name and surname**

Important: please read the notes before answering the questions.

In answering the rest of the questions please include:

▶ every person who spends census night (21-22 April) in this household, **including anyone staying temporarily**.

▶ any other people who are usually members of the household but on census night are absent on holiday, at school or college, or for any other reason, even if they are being included on another census form elsewhere.

▶ anyone who arrives here on Monday 22nd April who was in Great Britain on the Sunday and who has not been included as present on another census form.

▶ any newly born baby born before the 22nd April, even if still in hospital. If not yet given a name, write BABY and the surname.

Person No. 1

Name and surname

Sex — Male ☐ 1 / Female ☐ 2

Date of birth — Day / Month / Year

Person No. 2

Name and surname

Sex — Male ☐ 1 / Female ☐ 2

Date of birth — Day / Month / Year

17 Address of place of work

Please give the full address of the person's place of work.

For a person employed on a site for a long period, give the address of the site.

For a person not working regularly at one place who reports daily to a depot or other fixed address, give that address.

For a person not reporting daily to a fixed address, tick box 1.

For a person working mainly at home, tick box 2.

Armed Forces — leave blank.

Person No. 1: Please write full address and postcode of workplace below in BLOCK CAPITALS

Post-code ☐☐☐☐ ■ ☐☐☐

No fixed place ☐ 1
Mainly at home ☐ 2

Person No. 2: Please write full address and postcode of workplace below in BLOCK CAPITALS

Post-code ☐☐☐☐ ■ ☐☐☐

No fixed place ☐ 1
Mainly at home ☐ 2

18 Daily journey to work

Please tick the appropriate box to show how the longest part, by distance, of the person's daily journey to work is normally made.

For a person using different means of transport on different days, show the means most often used.

Car or van includes three-wheeled cars and motor caravans.

For both Person No. 1 and Person No. 2:

British Rail train ☐ 1
Underground, tube, metro ☐ 2
Bus, minibus or coach (public or private) ☐ 3
Motor cycle, scooter, moped ☐ 4
Driving a car or van ☐ 5
Passenger in car or van ☐ 6
Pedal cycle ☐ 7
On foot ☐ 8
Other ☐ 9
please specify

Works mainly at home ☐ 0

19 Degrees, professional and vocational qualifications

Has the person obtained any qualifications after reaching the age of 18 such as:

-degrees, diplomas, HNC, HND,

-nursing qualifications,

-teaching qualifications (see * below),

-graduate or corporate membership of professional institutions,

-other professional, educational or vocational qualifications?

Do not count qualifications normally obtained at school such as GCE, CSE, GCSE, SCE and school certificates.

If box 2 is ticked, write in all qualifications even if they are not relevant to the person's present job or if the person is not working.

Please list the qualifications in the order in which they were obtained.

If more than three, please enter in a spare column and link with an arrow.

*For a person with **school teaching qualifications**, give the full title of the qualification, such as 'Certificate of Education' and the subject(s) which the person is qualified to teach. The subject 'education' should then only be shown if the course had no other subject specialisation.

For both Person No. 1 and Person No. 2:

NO — no such qualifications ☐ 1
YES — give details ☐ 2

1 Title
Subject(s)
Year
Institution

2 Title
Subject(s)
Year
Institution

3 Title
Subject(s)
Year
Institution

H form for private households, England — *continued*

H3 Tenure

Please tick the box which best describes how you and your household occupy your accommodation.

If buying by stages from a Council, Housing Association or New Town (under shared ownership, co-ownership or equity sharing scheme), answer as an owner-occupier at box 1.

As an owner-occupier:

-buying the property through mortgage or loan ☐ 1

-owning the property outright (no loan) ☐ 2

By renting, rent free or by lease:

-with a job, farm, shop or other business ☐ 3

If your accommodation is occupied by lease originally granted for, or extended to, more than 21 years, answer as an owner-occupier. For shorter leases, answer 'By renting'.

-from a local authority (Council) ☐ 4

-from a New Town Development Corporation (or Commission) or from a Housing Action Trust ☐ 5

-from a housing association or charitable trust ☐ 6

A private landlord may be a person or a company or another organisation not mentioned at 3, 4, 5 or 6 above.

-from a private landlord, furnished ☐ 7

-from a private landlord, unfurnished ☐ 8

In some other way:

-please give details below ☐

H4 Amenities

Does your household — that is, you and any people who usually live here with you — **have the use of:**

a A bath or shower?

Yes — for use only by this household ☐ 1

Yes — for use also by another household ☐ 2

No — no bath or shower available ☐ 3

b A flush toilet (WC) with entrance inside the building?

Yes — for use only by this household ☐ 0

Yes — for use also by another household ☐ 1

No — flush toilet with outside entrance only ☐ 2

No — no flush toilet indoors or outdoors ☐ 3

c Central heating in living rooms and bedrooms (including night storage heaters, warm air or under-floor heating), whether actually used or not?

Yes — all living rooms and bedrooms centrally heated ☐ 1

Yes — some (not all) living rooms and bedrooms centrally heated ☐ 2

No — no living rooms or bedrooms centrally heated ☐ 3

H5 Cars and vans

Please tick the appropriate box to indicate the number of cars and vans normally available for use by you or members of your household (other than visitors).

Include any car or van provided by employers if normally available for use by you or members of your household, but **exclude** vans used only for carrying goods.

None ☐ 0

One ☐ 1

Two ☐ 2

Three or more ☐ 3

◀ **Please turn to the first inside page**

Panel B

Was there anyone else (such as a visitor) here on the night of 21-22 April whom you have not included because there was no room on the form?

No ☐
Yes ☐

If **yes** ticked, please ask the Enumerator for another form.

Have you left anyone out because you were not sure whether they should be included on the form?

No ☐
Yes ☐

If **yes** ticked, please give their names and the reason why you were not sure about including them.

Name

Reason

Name

Reason

Name

Reason

Panel C

Before you sign the form, will you please check:

▶ that all questions which should have been answered have been answered for every member of your household

▶ that you have included everyone who spent the night of 21-22 April in your household

▶ that you have included everyone who usually lives here but was away from home on the night of 21-22 April

▶ that no visitors, boarders or newly born children, even if still in hospital, have been missed

It would help the Enumerator to be able to telephone you if there is a query on, or an omission from, your form.

If you have no objection, please write your telephone number here.

Telephone number

Declaration

This form is correctly completed to the best of my knowledge and belief.

Signature(s)

Date   April 1991

H form for private households, Scotland — opening page only

**1991 Census
Scotland**

H form for Private Households

For
office
use

☐ 1
☐ 2
☐ 3

To the Head or Joint Heads or members of the Household aged 16 or over

Please complete this form for all members of the household, including children, and have it ready for collection on Monday 22nd April. Your census enumerator will call to collect it then or soon afterwards and will help you with the form if you have any difficulties. The enclosed leaflet explains why the Census is necessary and how the information is used.

Completion of the form is compulsory under the Census Act 1920. If you refuse to complete it, or give false information, you may have to pay a fine of up to £400.

Your answers will be treated in strict confidence and used only to produce statistics. Names and addresses will not be put into the computer; only the postcode will be entered. The forms will be kept securely within my Office and treated as confidential for 100 years.

Anyone using or disclosing Census information improperly will be liable to prosecution. For example, it would be improper for you to pass on to someone else information which you had been given in confidence by a visitor to enable you to complete the Census form.

If any member of the household aged 16 or over does not wish you, or another member of the household, to see their information, please ask the enumerator for an individual form with an envelope.

After completing the form, please sign the declaration on the last page.

Thank you for your co-operation.

C. M. Glennie

CM Glennie
Registrar General for Scotland
Ladywell House, Ladywell Road, Edinburgh EH12 7TF
Telephone: 031-316 4172

To be completed by the Enumerator

Census District	Enumeration District	Form Number

Name

Address

Postcode	☐☐☐ ☐ ☐☐	ABS ☐

Panel A
To be completed by the Enumerator and amended, if necessary, by the person(s) signing this form.

Tick one box to show the type of accommodation which this household occupies.

A caravan or other mobile or temporary structure ☐ 1

A whole house or bungalow that is
- detached ☐ 2
- semi-detached ☐ 3
- terraced (include end of terrace) ☐ 4

The whole of a purpose built flat or maisonette
- in a commercial building (for example in an office building or hotel or over a shop) ☐ 5
- in a block of flats or tenement ☐ 6

Part of a converted or shared house, bungalow or flat
- separate entrance into the building ☐ 7
- shared entrance into the building ☐ 8

Please read these instructions before filling in this form

A Household:

A household comprises either one person living alone or a group of people (not necessarily related) living at the same address with common housekeeping — that is, sharing at least one meal a day or sharing a living room or sitting room.

People staying temporarily with the household are included.

▶ If there is more than one household in this building, answer for your household only.

▶ First answer questions **H1, HL and H2** on **this page** and **H3 to H5** on the **back page** about your household and the rooms which it occupies.

▶ When you have answered the household questions, answer the questions on the **inside pages** about each member of your household.

▶ If a member of the household is completing an Individual form please still enter their name and answer questions 5 and 6 on this form.

▶ Then complete **Panel B** and **Panel C** on the back page.

▶ *Answer each question by ticking the appropriate box or boxes* ☑ *where they are provided.*

▶ *Please use ink or ballpoint pen.*

H1 Rooms

Please count the number of rooms your household has for its **own** use.

Do not count: small kitchens, under 2 metres (6 feet 6 inches) wide
bathrooms
toilets

Do count: living rooms
bedrooms
kitchens at least 2 metres (6 feet 6 inches) wide
all other rooms in your accommodation

The total number of rooms is ☐

HL Floor level of household's living accommodation

Which is the lowest floor on which any of your household's living accommodation is situated?
Tick box **B** or **G** or write number of floor

Basement ☐ **B**
Ground floor ☐ **G**
Floor number ☐

H2 Accommodation
If box 7 or box 8 in Panel A is ticked, tick one box below to show the type of accommodation which your household occupies.

A one roomed flatlet
with private bath or shower, WC and kitchen facilities. ☐ 1

One room or bedsit, not self-contained
(to move from your room to bathroom, WC or kitchen facilities you have to use a hall, landing or stairway open to other household(s)). ☐ 2

A self-contained flat or accommodation with 2 or more rooms,
having bath or shower, WC and kitchen facilities all behind its own private door. ☐ 3

2 or more rooms, not self-contained
(to move between rooms or to bathroom, WC or kitchen facilities you have to use a hall, landing or stairway open to other household(s)). ☐ 4

Please turn to the back page and answer questions H3 to H5 ▶

H form for private households, Wales — opening page only

1991 Census
Wales

W form for Private Households

This form is available in English and Welsh. If you have not received the version you require, please telephone 0329 844444

Mae'r ffurflen hon ar gael yn Gymraeg ac yn Saesneg. Os na chawsoch y fersiwn y mae ei eisiau arnoch, ffoniwch 0329 844444

For office use

☐ 1
☐ 2
☐ 3

To the Head or Joint Heads or members of the Household aged 16 or over

Please complete this form for all members of the household, including children, and have it ready for collection on Monday 22nd April. Your census enumerator will call to collect it then or soon afterwards and will help you with the form if you have any difficulties. The enclosed leaflet explains why the Census is necessary and how the information is used.

Completion of the form is compulsory under the Census Act 1920. If you refuse to complete it, or give false information, you may have to pay a fine of up to £400.

Your answers will be treated in strict confidence and used only to produce statistics. Names and addresses will not be put into the computer; only the postcode will be entered. The forms will be kept securely within my Office and treated as confidential for 100 years.

Anyone using or disclosing Census information improperly will be liable to prosecution. For example, it would be improper for you to pass on to someone else information which you had been given in confidence by a visitor to enable you to complete the Census form.

If any member of the household aged 16 or over does not wish you, or another member of the household, to see their information, please ask the enumerator for an individual form with an envelope.

After completing the form, please sign the declaration on the last page.

Thank you for your co-operation.

P J Wormald
P J Wormald
Registrar General
Office of Population Censuses and Surveys
PO Box 100 Fareham PO16 0AL
Telephone: 0329 844444

Please read these instructions before filling in this form

A Household:

A household comprises either one person living alone or a group of people (not necessarily related) living at the same address with common housekeeping — that is, sharing at least one meal a day or sharing a living room or sitting room.

People staying temporarily with the household are included.

▶ If there is more than one household in this building, answer for your household only.

▶ First answer questions **H1 and H2** on **this page** and H3 to H5 on the **back page** about your household and the rooms which it occupies.

▶ When you have answered the household questions, answer the questions on the **inside pages** about each member of your household.

▶ If a member of the household is completing an Individual form please still enter their name and answer questions 5 and 6 on this form.

▶ Then complete **Panel B** and **Panel C** on the back page.

▶ *Answer each question by ticking the appropriate box or boxes* ☑ *where they are provided.*

▶ *Please use ink or ballpoint pen.*

To be completed by the Enumerator

Census District	Enumeration District	Form Number

Name

Address

Postcode | | | | | | | ABS ☐

Panel A

To be completed by the Enumerator and amended, if necessary, by the person(s) signing this form.

Tick one box to show the type of accommodation which this household occupies.

A caravan or other mobile or temporary structure	☐ 1
A whole house or bungalow that is detached	☐ 2
semi-detached	☐ 3
terraced (include end of terrace)	☐ 4
The whole of a purpose built flat or maisonette in a commercial building (for example in an office building or hotel or over a shop)	☐ 5
in a block of flats or tenement	☐ 6
Part of a converted or shared house, bungalow or flat separate entrance into the building	☐ 7
shared entrance into the building	☐ 8

H1 Rooms

Please count the number of rooms your household has for its **own** use.

Do not count: small kitchens, under 2 metres (6 feet 6 inches) wide
  bathrooms
  toilets

Do count: living rooms
  bedrooms
  kitchens at least 2 metres (6 feet 6 inches) wide
  all other rooms in your accommodation

The total number of rooms is ☐

H2 Accommodation

If box 7 or box 8 in Panel A is ticked, tick one box below to show the type of accommodation which your household occupies.

A one roomed flatlet
  with private bath or shower, WC and kitchen facilities. ☐ 1

One room or bedsit, not self-contained
  (to move from your room to bathroom, WC or kitchen facilities you have to use a hall, landing or stairway open to other household(s)). ☐ 2

A self-contained flat or accommodation with 2 or more rooms,
  having bath or shower, WC and kitchen facilities all behind its own private door. ☐ 3

2 or more rooms, not self-contained
  (to move between rooms or to bathroom, WC or kitchen facilities you have to use a hall, landing or stairway open to other household(s)). ☐ 4

Please turn to the back page and answer questions H3 to H5 ▶

Language questions for Scotland and Wales and tenure question for Scotland (extracts from H forms)

Scottish Gaelic

This question is for all persons aged 3 or over (born before 22nd April 1988)

G	**Scottish Gaelic**

Can the person speak, read or write Scottish Gaelic?

Please tick the appropriate box(es)

Can speak Gaelic ☐ 1
Can read Gaelic ☐ 2
Can write Gaelic ☐ 4
Does not know Gaelic ☐ 0

Can speak Gaelic ☐ 1
Can read Gaelic ☐ 2
Can write Gaelic ☐ 4
Does not know Gaelic ☐ 0

Welsh language

This question is for all persons aged 3 or over (born before 22nd April 1988)

W	**Welsh language**

Does the person speak, read or write Welsh?

Please tick the appropriate box(es)

Speaks Welsh ☐ 1
Reads Welsh ☐ 2
Writes Welsh ☐ 4
Does not speak, read or write Welsh ☐ 0

Speaks Welsh ☐ 1
Reads Welsh ☐ 2
Writes Welsh ☐ 4
Does not speak, read or write Welsh ☐ 0

Tenure, Scotland

H3 Tenure

Please tick the box which best describes how you and your household occupy your accommodation.

If buying by stages from a Council, Housing Association or New Town (under shared ownership, co-ownership or equity sharing scheme), answer as an owner-occupier at box 1.

If your accommodation is occupied by lease originally granted for, or extended to, more than 21 years, answer as an owner-occupier. For shorter leases, answer 'By renting'.

A private landlord may be a person or a company or another organisation not mentioned at 3, 4, 5 or 6 above.

As an owner-occupier:

-buying the property through mortgage or loan ☐ 1

-owning the property outright (no loan) ☐ 2

By renting, rent free or by lease:

-with a job, farm, shop or other business ☐ 3

-from a local authority (Council) ☐ 4

-from a New Town Development Corporation (or Commission) or from a Housing Action Trust ☐ 5

-from a housing association or charitable trust ☐ 6

-from a private landlord, furnished ☐ 7

-from a private landlord, unfurnished ☐ 8

In some other way:

-please give details below ☐

I form for making an individual return, England

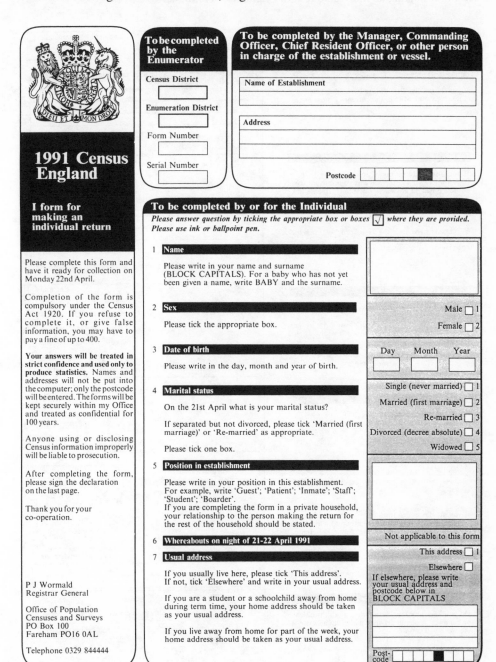

1991 Census England

I form for making an individual return

Please complete this form and have it ready for collection on Monday 22nd April.

Completion of the form is compulsory under the Census Act 1920. If you refuse to complete it, or give false information, you may have to pay a fine of up to 400.

Your answers will be treated in strict confidence and used only to produce statistics. Names and addresses will not be put into the computer; only the postcode will be entered. The forms will be kept securely within my Office and treated as confidential for 100 years.

Anyone using or disclosing Census information improperly will be liable to prosecution.

After completing the form, please sign the declaration on the last page.

Thank you for your co-operation.

P J Wormald
Registrar General

Office of Population Censuses and Surveys
PO Box 100
Fareham PO16 0AL

Telephone 0329 844444

To be completed by the Enumerator

Census District

Enumeration District

Form Number

Serial Number

To be completed by the Manager, Commanding Officer, Chief Resident Officer, or other person in charge of the establishment or vessel.

Name of Establishment

Address

Postcode

To be completed by or for the Individual

Please answer question by ticking the appropriate box or boxes ☑ where they are provided. Please use ink or ballpoint pen.

1 **Name**

Please write in your name and surname (BLOCK CAPITALS). For a baby who has not yet been given a name, write BABY and the surname.

2 **Sex**

Please tick the appropriate box.

Male ☐ 1
Female ☐ 2

3 **Date of birth**

Please write in the day, month and year of birth.

Day   Month   Year

4 **Marital status**

On the 21st April what is your marital status?

If separated but not divorced, please tick 'Married (first marriage)' or 'Re-married' as appropriate.

Please tick one box.

Single (never married) ☐ 1
Married (first marriage) ☐ 2
Re-married ☐ 3
Divorced (decree absolute) ☐ 4
Widowed ☐ 5

5 **Position in establishment**

Please write in your position in this establishment. For example, write 'Guest'; 'Patient'; 'Inmate'; 'Staff'; 'Student'; 'Boarder'.
If you are completing the form in a private household, your relationship to the person making the return for the rest of the household should be stated.

6 **Whereabouts on night of 21-22 April 1991**

Not applicable to this form

7 **Usual address**

If you usually live here, please tick 'This address'.
If not, tick 'Elsewhere' and write in your usual address.

If you are a student or a schoolchild away from home during term time, your home address should be taken as your usual address.

If you live away from home for part of the week, your home address should be taken as your usual address.

This address ☐ 1
Elsewhere ☐

If elsewhere, please write your usual address and postcode below in BLOCK CAPITALS

Postcode

Please turn over ▶

375

I form for making an individual return, England — *continued*

8 **Term time address of students and schoolchildren**

If not a student or schoolchild, please tick first box.

If you are a student or schoolchild and you live here during term time, tick 'This address'.

If you do not live here during term time, tick 'Elsewhere' and write in the current or most recent term time address.

Not a student or schoolchild ☐
This address ☐1
Elsewhere ☐

If elsewhere, please write your term time address and postcode below in BLOCK CAPITALS

Postcode ☐☐☐☐■☐☐☐

9 **Usual address one year ago**

If your usual address one year ago (on the 21st April 1990) was the same as your current usual address (given in answer to question 7), please tick 'Same'. If not, tick 'Different' and write in your usual address one year ago.

For a child born since the 21st April 1990, tick the 'Child under one' box.

Same as Question 7 ☐1
Different ☐
Child under one ☐3

If different, please write your address and postcode on the 21st April 1990 below in BLOCK CAPITALS

Postcode ☐☐☐☐■☐☐☐

10 **Country of birth**

Please tick the appropriate box.

If the 'Elsewhere' box is ticked, please write in the present name of the country in which your birthplace is now situated.

England ☐1
Scotland ☐2
Wales ☐3
Northern Ireland ☐4
Irish Republic ☐5
Elsewhere ☐

If elsewhere, please write in the present name of the country

11 **Ethnic group**

Please tick the appropriate box.

White ☐0
Black-Caribbean ☐1
Black-African ☐2
Black-Other
please describe ☐

If you are descended from more than one ethnic or racial group, please tick the group to which you consider you belong, or tick the 'Any other ethnic group' box and describe your ancestry in the space provided.

Indian ☐3
Pakistani ☐4
Bangladeshi ☐5
Chinese ☐6
Any other ethnic group
please describe ☐

12 **Long-term illness**

Do you have any long-term illness, health problem or handicap which limits your daily activities or the work you can do?

Include problems which are due to old age.

Yes, I have a health problem which limits activities ☐1
I have no such health problem ☐2

I form for making an individual return, England — *continued*

Answers to the remaining questions are not required for anyone under 16 years of age (born after 21st April 1975)

13 **Whether working, retired, looking after the home etc last week**

Which of these things were you doing **last week**?

Please read carefully right through the list and **tick all the descriptions that apply**.

* Casual or temporary work should be counted at boxes 1, 2, 3 or 4. Also tick boxes 1, 2, 3 or 4 if you had a job last week but were off sick, on holiday, temporarily laid off or on strike.

Boxes 1, 2, 3 and 4 refer to work for pay or profit but not to unpaid work except in a family business.

Working for an employer is **part time** (box 2) if the hours worked, excluding any overtime and mealbreaks, are usually 30 hours or less per week.

† Includes wanting a job but prevented from looking by holiday or temporary sickness.

$ Do not count training given or paid for by an employer.

* Was working for an employer full time (more than 30 hours a week) ☐ 1
* Was working for an employer part time (one hour or more a week) ☐ 2
* Was self employed, employing other people ☐ 3
* Was self employed, not employing other people ☐ 4

Was on a government employment or training scheme ☐ 5

Was waiting to start a job already accepted ☐ 6

† Was unemployed and looking for a job ☐ 7

$ Was at school or in other full time education ☐ 8

Was unable to work because of long term sickness or disability ☐ 9

Was retired from paid work ☐ 10

Was looking after the home or family ☐ 11

Other ☐
please specify

Please read A below, tick the box that applies and follow the instruction by the box ticked. This will tell you which questions to answer.

A Did you have a paid job last week (any of the boxes 1, 2, 3 or 4 ticked at question 13)?

Yes ☐
No ☐

If **yes** ticked, answer questions **14, 15, 16, 17** and **18** about the main job last week, then go on to question **19**. If **no** ticked, answer **B**.

B Have you had a paid job within the last 10 years?

Yes ☐
No ☐

If **yes** ticked, answer questions **14, 15** and **16** about the most recent job, then go on to question **19**. If **no** ticked, go on to question **19**.

14 **Hours worked per week**

How many hours per week do or did you usually work in your main job?

Do not count overtime or meal breaks.

Number of hours worked per week ☐

15 **Occupation**

Please give the full title of your present or last job and describe the main things you do or did in the job.

At a, give the full title by which the job is known, for example: 'packing machinist'; 'poultry processor'; 'jig and tool fitter'; 'supervisor of typists'; 'accounts clerk'; rather than general titles like 'machinist'; 'process worker'; 'supervisor' or 'clerk'. Give rank or grade if you have one.

At b, write down the main things you actually do or did in the job.

Armed Forces - enter 'commissioned officer' or 'other rank' as appropriate at **a** and leave **b** blank.

Civil Servants - give grade at **a** and discipline or specialism, for example: 'electrical engineer'; 'accountant'; 'chemist'; 'administrator' at **b**.

a Full job title

b Main things done in job

Please turn over ▶

I form for making an individual return, England — *continued*

16 Name and business of employer (if self-employed give the name and nature of business)

At **a**, please give the name of your employer. Give the trading name if one is used. Do not use abbreviations.

At **b**, describe clearly what your employer (or yourself if self-employed) makes or does (or did).

Armed Forces - write 'Armed Forces' at **a** and leave **b** blank. For a member of the Armed Forces of a country other than the UK - add the name of the country.

Civil Servants - give name of Department at **a** and write 'Government Department' at **b**.

Local Government Officers - give name of employing authority at **a** and department in which employed at **b**.

a Name of employer

b Description of employer's business

17 Address of place of work

Please give the full address of your place of work.

If employed on a site for a long period, give the address of the site.

If not working regularly at one place but reporting daily to a depot or other fixed address, give that address.

If not reporting daily to a fixed address, tick box 1.

If working mainly at home, tick box 2.

Armed Forces - leave blank.

Please write full address and postcode of workplace below in BLOCK CAPITALS

Postcode

No fixed place ☐ 1

Mainly at home ☐ 2

18 Daily journey to work

Please tick the appropriate box to show how the longest part, by distance, of your daily journey to work is normally made.

If using different means of transport on different days, show the means most often used.

Car or van includes three-wheeled cars and motor caravans.

British Rail train ☐ 1
Underground, tube, metro ☐ 2
Bus, minibus or coach (public or private) ☐ 3
Motor cycle, scooter, moped ☐ 4
Driving a car or van ☐ 5
Passenger in car or van ☐ 6
Pedal cycle ☐ 7
On foot ☐ 8
Other ☐ 9
please specify

Work mainly at home ☐ 0

19 Degrees, professional and vocational qualifications

Have you obtained any qualifications after reaching the age of 18 such as:

- degrees, diplomas, HNC, HND,
- nursing qualifications,
- teaching qualifications (see * below),
- graduate or corporate membership of professional institutions,
- other professional, educational or vocational qualifications?

Do not count qualifications normally obtained at school such as GCE, CSE, GCSE, SCE and school certificates.

If box 2 is ticked, write in all qualifications even if they are not relevant to your present job or if you are not working.

Please list the qualifications in the order in which they were obtained.

* If you have **school teaching qualifications,** give the full title of the qualification, such as 'Certificate of Education' and the subject(s) which you are qualified to teach. The subject 'education' should then only be shown if the course had no other subject specialisation.

NO - no such qualifications ☐ 1
YES - give details ☐ 2

1 Title	2 Title
Subject(s)	Subject(s)
Year	Year
Institution	Institution

3 Title	4 Title
Subject(s)	Subject(s)
Year	Year
Institution	Institution

Declaration

This form is correctly completed to the best of my knowledge and belief.

Signature

Date

April 1991

L form for communal establishments, HM Ships or other vessels, England and Wales

1991 Census England/Wales
L Form for Communal Establishments, HM Ships or other vessels

To the Manager, Chief Resident Officer, Commanding Officer or other person in charge of a communal establishment:

To the Captain, Master, Commanding Officer or other person in charge of a vessel or HM Ship:

I am seeking your help in conducting the Census. Under the Census Act 1920 you have a legal obligation to list the names of the people in your establishment or on your vessel, to distribute forms to them and to collect the forms on completion. In a communal establishment you must also complete the 'type of establishment' panel. If you refuse to complete this form, or give false information, you may have to pay a fine of up to 40 0. The instructions opposite tell you what to do and should be followed carefully.

The Individual forms with which you have been supplied are for the returns to be made by or for each person who spends the night of **21-22 April** at this establishment or on board this vessel. To assist you in issuing and collecting the individual forms, spaces have been provided overleaf for listing those people.

The answers given will be treated in strict confidence and used only to produce statistics. Names and addresses will not be put in the computer; only the postcode will be entered. The forms will be kept securely within my Office and treated as confidential for 100 years.

Anyone using or disclosing census information improperly will be liable to prosecution. For example, it would be improper for you to pass on to someone else, information which you have been given in confidence on, or for completion of, an individual form.

Thank you for your co-operation.

P J Wormald
Registrar General

Office of Population Censuses and Surveys
PO Box 100 Fareham PO16 0AL

Telephone 0329 844444

For Enumerator/Census Office use

CD No.	ED No.	Form No.

Instructions

Listing of names

List the names of all people present, as instructed overleaf.

You may start drawing up the list in advance of Census day, but before collection or despatch you must bring it up to date.

Distribution

An Individual form (I form) must be completed for each person listed. Where a person is incapable of making a return, you must arrange for a form to be completed on his or her behalf.

Before you issue each form, enter the name of the establishment or vessel in the panel at top right hand corner on the front of the Individual form (a rubber stamp may be used).

Please issue an envelope to any person who wishes to make a return under sealed cover.

For communal establishments, please give the type of establishment below.

When you have completed this form please fill in and sign the declaration overleaf.

Collection of forms

Communal Establishments

Please have all the completed forms ready for collection by the Enumerator, who will call on Monday 22nd April or soon afterwards.

Vessels other than HM Ships

Please have all of the completed forms ready for collection by the Enumerator who will call on Monday 22 April, or return them to the Enumerator in accordance with the instructions issued at delivery.

HM Ships

Please despatch the completed forms as soon as possible after 21st April to:

Office of Population Censuses and Surveys,
PO Box 100 Fareham PO16 OAL

To be completed by the Enumerator or Customs Officer

Name of Establishment/Vessel/HM Ship

For communal establishments: address of establishment

Postcode

For vessels other than HM Ships: port of registry

Place at which the form is delivered, that is: name of town or port and of harbour, dock, wharf, mooring etc.

Name of master or person in charge of vessel

Communal establishments : type of establishment

Please give a full description of the type of establishment and if the establishment caters for a specific group or groups, please describe; *for example mentally ill or handicapped, physically disabled, elderly, children, students, nurses.*

Hospitals, homes and hostels only

- **Please specify type of management:** *private, voluntary (charitable), central government, local authority, housing association, health authority etc.*

- **Please indicate if the establishment is registered** with a local authority or health authority

Hotels or boarding houses only

Please enter the number of rooms in the establishment, including any annexes in which meals are not provided. Do not count kitchens, bathrooms, WCs, rooms used as offices or stores.

L form for communal establishments, HM Ships or other vessels, England and Wales — *continued*

List the names of all people present, that is:
everyone who spends Census night **21-22 April 1991** in this establishment or on board this vessel; and everyone who arrives in this establishment or on board on **Monday 22 April** before the forms are collected by the Enumerator (or despatched in the case of HM Ships) and who was in Great Britain on Sunday but has not been included as present on another Census form.

In communal establishments do not list the names of any non-resident personnel who happen to be on duty on the premises on Census night.

Please put a tick in the appropriate column when you issue each form and when you collect it.

Name	Individual form		Name	Individual form	
	Issued	Collected		Issued	Collected
1			31		
2			32		
3			33		
4			34		
5			35		
6			36		
7			37		
8			38		
9			39		
10			40		
11			41		
12			42		
13			43		
14			44		
15			45		
16			46		
17			47		
18			48		
19			49		
20			50		
21			51		
22			52		
23			53		
24			54		
25			55		
26			56		
27			57		
28			58		
29			59		
30			60		

Enter the number of **Individual** forms collected on this L form. ☐

Declaration - If more than one 'L' form is used, only complete this panel on the first form

Enter the total number of 'L' forms completed for this establishment/vessel. ☐   Signature

Enter the total number of **Individual** forms collected (sum of all L forms). ☐

Date   April 1991

References

Australian Bureau of the Census (1991) Australian census of population and housing: public attitudes on confidentiality issues, *Diffusion, 9*, December, 1-5

Babb, P. and Hattersley, L. (1992) *The Quality of the Fertility Data in the OPCS Longitudinal Study*, LS User Guide No. 10, London: Social Statistics Research Unit, City University

Banfield, F. (1978) 1971 Census: voluntary survey on income, *Population Trends, 12,* 18-21

Barnes, R. (1989) Post censal surveys in Great Britain *Population Trends, 57,* 35-38

Barnes, R. (1992) The second international workshop on household survey non-response, *OPCS Survey Methodology Bulletin, 3,* 25-27

Barnett, V. (1991) *Sample Survey Principles and Methods*, London: Edward Arnold

Benjamin, B. (1970) *The Population Census*, London: Heinemann

Bennett, R.J. (1980) *The Geography of Public Finance: Welfare under Fiscal Federalism and Local Government Finance,* London: Methuen

Benzeval, M. and Judge, K. (1993) *The 1991 Census Health Question*, Discussion Paper, London: The King's Fund Institute

Bethlehem, J. G., Keller, W. G. and Pannekoek, J. (1990) Disclosure control of microdata, *Journal of the American Statistical Association, 85,* 38-45

Bishop, Y. M.M., Fienberg, S.A. and Holland, P.W. (1975) *Discrete Multivariate Analysis: Theory and Practice*, Cambridge, Mass: MIT Press

Bouvard, M. G. and Bouvard, J. (1975) Computerised information and effective protection of individual rights, *Society, 12* (6): 62-67, in G. S. McClellan (ed) *The Right to Privacy*, New York: The H W Wilson Co: pp. 25-40

Boyle, P. J. (1991) A theoretical and empirical examination of local level migration: the case of Hereford and Worcester, unpublished Ph.D. thesis, Department of Geography, Lancaster University

Bracken, I. and Martin, D. (1989) The generation of spatial population distributions from census centroids, *Environment and Planning A, 21,* 307-325

Brant, J.D. and Chalk, S.M. (1985) The use of automatic editing in the 1981 Census, *Journal of the Royal Statistical Society A, 148,* Part 2, 126-146

Breeze, E. and Butcher, B. (1988) Sub-sampling in the field - an illustration from the International Passenger Survey, *Survey Methodology Bulletin, 23,* 5-9, London: OPCS

Breeze, E. , Trevor, G. and Wilmot, A. (1992) General Household Survey 1989, OPCS Series GHS No. 20, London: HMSO

Breton, R., Isajiw, W., Kalback, W. and Reitz, J. (1990) *Ethnic Identity and Equality*, Toronto: University of Toronto Press

Britton, M. and Birch, F. (1985) *1981 Census Post-Enumeration Survey: an enquiry into the coverage and quality of the 1981 Census in England and Wales,* London: HMSO

Brown, A. (1978) 'Towards a world census', *Population Trends, 14,* 17-19

Brown, A. (1986) Family circumstances of young children, *Population Trends, 43,* 18-23

Brown, P. J. B. (1991) Exploring geodemographics, in I. Masser and M.J. Blakemore (eds), *Handling Geographic Information: Methodology and Potential Applications* (Harlow: Longman)

Bryant, B.E. (1990) Asian or Pacific Islanders in the 1990 Post-Enumeration Survey, Memorandum for M.R.Darby, 24 Sept. 1990, Washington, DC: US Bureau of the Census

Bulmer, M. (1979) Parliament and the British Census since 1920, in M. Bulmer (ed), *Censuses, Surveys and Privacy*, London: Macmillan, pp. 158-169

Bulusu, L. (1991) *A Review of Migration Data Sources,* Occasional Paper 39, London: OPCS

Burgess, R. (1988) Evaluation of reverse record check estimates of undercoverage in the Canadian census of population, *Survey Methodology, 14,* (2), 147-167

Butcher, R. and Dodd, P. (1983) The Electoral register — two surveys, *Population Trends, 31,* 15-19

Butcher, R. and Elliot, D. (1986) *A Sampling Errors Manual,* London: OPCS

Castles, I. (1991) *How Australia Takes a Census,* Australian Bureau of Statistics, Catalogue No. 2903.0

Champion, A. G. (1983) *England & Wales '81,* Sheffield: The Geographical Association

Champion, A. G. and Fielding, A. J. (1992) *Migration Processes and Patterns, Volume 1: Research Progress and Prospects,* London: Belhaven

Choi, C.Y., Steel, D.G. and Skinner, T.J. (1988) Adjusting the 1986 Australian Census Count for under-enumeration. *Survey Methodology, 14,* (2), 173-189

Ciok, R. (1993) (forthcoming) 'The results of Automated Coding in the 1991 Canadian Census of Population', US Bureau of the Census, Proceedings of the 1993 Annual Research Conference

Clark, A. M. (1992) 1991 Census: data collection, *Population Trends, 70,* 22-27

Clark A.M. and Thomas F.G. (1990) The geography of the 1991 Census, *Population Trends, 60,* 9-15

Committee of Enquiry into the Handling of Geographic Information (1987) *Report to the Secretary of State for the Environment of the Committee into the Handling of Geographic Information,* London: HMSO

Compton, P.A. and Power, J. (1984) Estimates of the religious composition of Northern Ireland local government districts in 1981 and change in the geographical pattern of religion between 1971 and 1981, *The Economic and Social Review, 17,* 87-105

Congdon, P. (1989) Modelling migration between areas: an analysis for London using the Census and OPCS Longitudinal Study, *Regional Studies, 23,* 87-103

Congdon, P. (1991) An application of general linear modelling to migration in London and South East England, in J. Stillwell and P. Congdon (eds), *Migration models: macro and micro approaches,* London: Belhaven, pp. 113-136

Congdon, P. (1992) The potential of the Longitudinal Study for migration studies, *Update - News from the LS User Group,* (1) 11-14

Coombes, M. G., Green, A. E. and Openshaw, S. (1985) Britain's changing local labour market areas. *Employment Gazette, 93,* (1) 6-8

Coombes, M. G., Green, A. E. and Openshaw, S. (1986) An efficient algorithm to generate official statistical reporting areas: the case of the 1984 travel-to-work areas revision in Britain, *Journal of the Operational Research Society, 37,* 943-953

Coombes, M. G., Green, A. E. and Owen, D. W. (1988) Substantive issues in the definition of 'localities': evidence from sub-group local labour market areas in the West Midlands, *Regional Studies, 22,* 303-318

Courtland, S. (1985) Census confidentiality: then and now, *Government Information Quarterly, 2* (4), 407-418

Cox, L.H., McDonald, S-K, and Nelson, D. (1986) Confidentiality issues at the United States Bureau of the Census, *Journal of Official Statistics, 2,* (2), 135-160

Creeser, R. (1991) *An Introduction to the Area Based Variables in the OPCS Longitudinal Study,* LS User Guide No.7, London: Social Statistics Research Unit, City University

Creeser, R. (1992) *An Introduction to the Fertility and Infant Mortality Datastream,* LS User Guide No. 9, London: Social Statistics Research Unit, City University

CRU/OPCS/GRO(S), (1980) *People in Britain — a census atlas,* London: HMSO

Cushion, A.A. (1969) Population Census pre-test 1968, *Statistical News,* No.4, 4.20-4.22, February

Dale, A., Arber, S. and Gilbert, G. N. (1988) *Doing Secondary Analysis,* London: Unwin Hyman

de la Puente, M. (1992) An analysis of the under-enumeration of Hispanics: evidence from Hispanic concentrated small area ethnographic studies, paper presented to US Bureau of the Census Annual Research Conference, Washington: 1992

Denham, C. (1992) An introduction to the 1991 Census, *MRS Census Briefing,* 24 June 24

Denham, C. and Rhind, D. (1983) The 1981 Census and its results, in D.Rhind (ed) *A Census User's Handbook*, London: Methuen, pp. 17-88

Department of Employment (1984) Revised travel-to-work areas, *Employment Gazette, 92*, Occasional Supplement 3, September

Department of Environment (1983) Urban Deprivation, *Information Note 2*, London: Inner Cities Directorate, Department of Environment

Dorling, D. (1993) 'The 1991 Census and Housing Tenure', *BURISA Newsletter*, May 1993, 5-7

Drake, M. (1972) The census, 1801-1891, in E. A. Wrigley (ed.) *Nineteenth Century Society: Essays in the Use of Quantitative Methods for the Study of Social Data*, Cambridge: Cambridge University Press, pp.7-46

Employment Gazette Occasional Supplement, (1984) No.3, September

Eurostat (1992) *Regional Statistics and Accounts: Study on Employment Zones*, Document E/LOC/20, Luxembourg: Eurostat

Evans, I.S. (1977), The selection of class intervals, *Transactions of the Institute of British Geographers*, New Series, *2*, (1), 98-124

Experimental Cartography Unit Royal College of Art (1971), *Automatic Cartography and Planning*, London: Architectural Press

Fay, R., Passel, J.S., and Robinson, J.G., with assistance from C.D. Cowan (1988) The coverage of population in the 1980 Census, *1980 Census of Population and Housing, Evaluation and Research Reports PHC80-E4*. Washington, DC: US Department of Commerce

Fellegi, I. P. (1975) Controlled random rounding, *Survey Methodology, 1*, 123-135

Fellegi, I. P. and Holt, D. (1976) A systematic approach to automatic edit and imputation, *Journal of the American Statistical Association, 71*, 17-35

Fielding, A.J. (1989) Inter-regional migration and social change: a study of South-East England based upon data from the OPCS Longitudinal Study, *Transactions of the Institute of British Geographers Transactions, 14*, (1), 24-36

Fielding, A.J. and Halford, S. (1993) Geographies of opportunity: a regional analysis of gender-specific social and spatial mobilities in England and Wales 1971-81 *Environment and Planning A, 25*, 10

Fienberg, S.E. (1990) An adjusted census in 1990? An interim report, in *Chance: New Directions for Statistics and Computing*, New York: Springer-Verlag Inc.

Flowerdew R. (1991) Poisson regression modelling of migration, in J. Stillwell J and P. Congdon (eds), *Migration Models: Macro and Micro Approaches*, London: Belhaven, pp. 92-112

Flowerdew, R. and Green, M. (1989) Statistical methods for inference between incompatible zonal systems, in M. Goodchild and S. Gopal (eds), *Accuracy of Spatial Databases*, London: Taylor and Francis

Fox, J. and Goldblatt, P.O. (1982) *1971-1975 Longitudinal Study Socio-demographic mortality differentials*, LS Series No. 1, London: HMSO

Freedman, D.A. (1991) Adjusting the 1990 Census. *Science, 252*, 1233-1236

Gatrell, A.C. (1989), On the spatial representation and accuracy of address-based data in the U.K., *International Journal of Geographical Information Systems, 3*, (4), 335-348

Gilbert, E.W. (1958) Pioneer maps of health and disease in England, *Geographical Journal, 124*, 172-183

Glass, D (1973) *Numbering the People: the eighteenth-century population controversy and the development of census and vital statistics in Britain*, Farnborough, Hants: Saxon House

Goldblatt, P.O. (ed.) (1990) *Mortality and Social Organisation*, LS Series No.6, London: HMSO

Goldstein, H (1987) *Multilevel Models in Educational and Social Research*, London: Charles Griffin and Company

Gray, P. and Gee, F. (1972) *A Quality Check on the 1966 ten per cent Sample Census of England and Wales*, London: HMSO

Green, A. E., Coombes, M. G. and Owen, D. W. (1986) Gender-specific local labour market areas in England and Wales, *Geoforum, 17*, 339-351

Green, A. E. and Owen, D. W. (1990) The development of classification of travel-to-work areas, *Progress in Planning, 34*, 1-92

Green, A. E., Owen, D. W. and Hasluck, C. (1991) *The Development of Local Labour Market Typologies: Classifications of Travel-to-Work Areas*, Department of Employment Research Paper 84, London: Employment Department

Griffiths, D. (1988) Sampling errors on the International Passenger Survey, *OPCS Survey Methodology Bulletin*, (23) July, 3-4

GRO (1958) *Census 1951, General Report, England and Wales*, London: HMSO

GRO (1968) *Census 1961, General Report, Great Britain, Part II*, London: HMSO

GRO (Scotland) (1982). Census Memorandum 2220, Assessment of coverage (re-enumeration), Edinburgh: HMSO

GRO (Scotland) (1983), *Census 1981, General Report*, Edinburgh: HMSO

GRO (Scotland) (1991) *1991 Census Preliminary Report for Scotland*, Edinburgh: HMSO

GRO (Scotland) (1992) Provisional mid-1991 population estimates, GRO(S), Edinburgh: HMSO

Grundy, E.M.D. (1987) Retirement migration and its consequences in England and Wales, *Ageing and Society, 7*, (1), 57-82

Grundy, E.M.D. (1989) *Women's Migration: Marriage, Fertility and Divorce*, OPCS Longitudinal Study Series No. 4, London: HMSO

Harley, J. B. (1975) *Ordnance Survey Maps: a descriptive manual*, London: Ordnance Survey

Heasman, M.A. and Lipworth, L. (1966) *Accuracy of certification of cause of death*, Studies on Medical and Population Subjects, no.20, London: HMSO

Hewitt, P. (1977) *Privacy: The Information Gatherers*, London: National Council for Civil Liberties

History of the Census of 1841, manuscript in the library of the OPCS

HMSO (1979) *The Standard Industrial Classification (Revised)*, London: HMSO

HMSO (1991) The 1991 Census of Great Britain, *Social Trends 21*, 16, London: HMSO

Hogan, H. (1990) The 1990 Post-Enumeration Survey: an overview. *Proceedings of the Section on Survey Methods Research*, American Statistical Association, pp 518-523

Hogan, H. (1991) The 1990 Post-Enumeration Survey: operations and results, paper presented to the *1991 Annual Meetings of the American Statistical Association*

Holmans, A.E., Nandy, S. and Brown, A.C. (1987) Household formation and dissolution and housing tenure: a longitudinal perspective, *Social Trends, 17*, 20-28

Holterman S. (1975) Areas of urban deprivation in Great Britain: an analysis of 1971 census data *Social Trends 6*, 33-47

International Statistical Institute (1992) *Proceedings of a Conference on Data Protection*, Dublin

Jones, H. J. M., Lawson, H. B., Newman, D. (1973) Population census: some recent British developments in methodology, *Journal of the Royal Statistical Society (A), 136*, 505-538

Jones, K. and Kirby, A. (1980) The use of chi-square maps in the analysis of census data *Geoforum 11*, 409-417

Jones, K. and Moon, G. (1987) *Health, Disease and Society*, London: Routledge

Keane, J. G. (1988) Testimony before the House of Representatives Committee on Post Office and Civil Services, Subcommittee on Census and Population, 3 March, 1988

Kennedy, S. (1989) The small number problem and the accuracy of spatial databases, in M. Goodchild and S. Gopal (eds), *The Accuracy of Spatial Databases*, London: Taylor & Francis, pp. 187-196

Langevin, B., Begeot, F. and Pearce, D. (1992) Censuses in the European Community, *Population Trends, 68*, 33-36

Lewis, G. J. (1982) *Human Migration*, London: Croom Helm

Li, P. (1988) *Ethnic Inequality in a Class Society*, Toronto: Wall and Thompson

LS Medical Analysis Section (1992) Fertility and infant mortality in the OPCS Longitudinal Study, *Population Trends, 68*, 1-6

LS User Group (1992) Technical issues: sampling issues in the LS, Update no.2, p.9-11, London: Social Statistics Research Unit, City University

Mahon, B. (1992) 1991 Census — the story so far, *Population Trends, 68*, 30-36

Mahon, B. and Pearce, D. (1991) The 1991 Census of Great Britain, *Social Trends*, 21, HMSO

Manchester Computing Centre (1989) *MATPAC User's Manual*, Manchester: Manchester Computing Centre

Marsh, C. (1985) Informants, respondents and citizens , in M Bulmer (ed) *Essays in the History of British Sociological Research*,Cambridge: Cambridge University Press

Marsh, C., Arber, S., Wrigley, N. Rhind, D., and Bulmer, M. (1988) The view of academic social scientists on the 1991 UK Census of Population: a report of the Economic and Social Research Council Working Group, *Environment and Planning (A), 20*, 851-889

Marsh, C., Dale, A. and Skinner, C. (forthcoming) Safe data versus safe settings: access to microdata from the British census, *International Statistical Review*

Marsh, C., Skinner, C., Arber, S., Penhale, B., Openshaw, S., Hobcraft, J., Lievesley, D. and Walford, N. (1991) The case for samples of anonymised records from the 1991 Census, *Journal of the Royal Statistical Society (A), 154*, (2), 305-340

Martin, D. (1989) Mapping population data from zone centroid locations, *Transactions of the Institute of British Geographers NS 14*, 90-97

Martin, D. (1991) *Geographic Information Systems and their Socioeconomic Applications*, London: Routledge

Martin, D. (1992) Postcodes and the 1991 Census: issues, problems and prospects, *Transactions of the Institute of British Geographers, 17*, 350-57

Martin, D. (1993) 'Modelling Change: 1991 Surface of Population', paper presented at the Annual Conference of the Institute of British Geographers, January 1993

Martin, D. and Bracken, I. (1991) Techniques for modelling population related raster databases, *Environment and Planning A 23*, 1069-1075

Mills, I. (1987) Developments in census-taking since 1841, *Population Trends 48*, 37-44

Mills, I. and Teague, A. (1991) Editing and imputing data in the 1991 Census, *Population Trends 64*, 30-37

Monmonier, M. (1991) *How to Lie with Maps*, Chicago: The University of Chicago Press

Morgan, C. and Denham, C. (1982) Census Small Area Statistics (SAS): measuring change and spatial variation, *Population Trends, 28*, 12-17

Morphet, C. (1992) The interpretation of small area census data, *Area 24.1*, 63-72

Morris, C. and Compton, P.A. (1985) Non-enumeration in the 1981 Northern Ireland census, *Population Trends, 40*, 16-20

Mulry, M.H. and Spencer, B.D. (1991) *Journal of the American Statistical Association, 86*, (416), 839-863

Müller, W., Blien, U., Knoche, P. and Wirth, H. (1991) *Die faktische Anonymität von Mikrodaten*, Band 19 der Schriftenreihe Forum der Bundesstatistik herausgegeben vom Statistischen Bundesamt, Stuttgart: Metzler-Poeschel

National Research Council (1979) *Privacy and Confidentiality as Factors in Survey Response*, Assembly of Behavioural and Social Sciences, Committee on National Statistics, Washington DC: National Academy of Sciences

Navarro, A., Florez-Baez, L. and Thompson, J.H. (1988) Results of data switching simulation, US Department of Commerce Bureau of the Census Statistical Support Division, paper presented to the American Statistical Association and Population Statistics Advisory Committee

Neffendorf, H. and Hamilton, D. (1987) Locational referencing applications — The Central Postcode Directory Review, in *Applications of Postcodes in Locational Referencing*, London: LAMSAC

Newman, D. (1978a) *Techniques for Ensuring the Confidentiality of Census Information in Great Britain*, OPCS Occasional Paper 4, 20-30

Newman, D. (1978b) *Practical Problems of Sampling in the Census of Population*, OPCS Occasional Paper 4, 1-19

Nicholson, B. (1992) The Longitudinal Study and migration: a cautionary comment, *Update -News from the LS User Group*, no.2, London: SSRU, City University

Nissel, M. (1987) *People Count: A History of the General Register Office*, London: HMSO

Norris, P. and Mounsey, H. M. (1983) Analysing change through time, in Rhind, D. (ed) *A Census User's Handbook*, London: Methuen

Office of the Data Protection Registrar (1989) *Data Protection Act 1984: The Data Protection Principles, Guideline 4*, ODPR, Springfield House, Water Lane, Wilmslow, Cheshire SK9 5AX

OPCS (1978) *Occupational Mortality: Decennial Supplement 1970-72*, Series DS No.1, London: HMSO

OPCS (1980) *The Government's Decision on an Ethnic Question in the 1981 Census*, OPCS Monitor CEN 80/3, April

OPCS (1981) *1981 Census Definitions, Great Britain*, London: HMSO

OPCS (1982) Provisional mid-1981 population estimates for England and Wales and local government areas, *OPCS Monitor PP1 82/2*, London: OPCS

OPCS (1983a) *Census 1971 General Report Part 3, Statistical Assessment, Coverage Checks England and Wales, Quality Check Great Britain*, London: HMSO

OPCS (1983b) Provisional mid-1982 population estimates and revised mid-1981 population estimates for England and Wales and local government areas. *OPCS Monitor PP1 83/3*, London: OPCS

OPCS (1983c) Evaluation of the 1981 Census: the 10 per cent sample, *OPCS Census Monitor CEN 83/6*, 20 December

OPCS (1984) Evaluation of the 1981 Census: demographic comparisons, *OPCS Monitor* CEN *84/1*, London: OPCS

OPCS (1985) Evaluation of the 1981 Census: the 10 per cent sample (bias check), *OPCS Census 1981 Monitor, CEN 85/1*, 25 June

OPCS (1987) *Census of Population England and Wales — The Geographic Base*, London: OPCS

OPCS (1988) *Census 1971-1981 The Longitudinal Study: linked census data, England and Wales*, London: HMSO

OPCS (1990) *Census 1981 General Report England and Wales*, London: HMSO

OPCS (1991a) *Census geography — an Information Paper on Geography in the 1991 Census and its Antecedents*, Census Division, May 1991, London: OPCS

OPCS (1991b) *1991 Census: Preliminary Report for England and Wales*, London: HMSO

OPCS (1991c) *1991 Census: Preliminary Report for England and Wales* (Supplementary Monitor on people sleeping rough), London: OPCS

OPCS (1992a) *Making a population estimate in England and Wales*, OPCS Occasional Paper No. 37

OPCS (1992b) Provisional mid-1991 population estimates for England and Wales and constituent local and health authorities based on 1991 Census results, *OPCS Monitor PP1, 92/1*, 16 October

OPCS (1992c) OPCS Statement of Policies on Confidentiality and Security of Personal Data, Titchfield: OPCS

OPCS (1992d) *The Labour Force Survey 1990-91* , HMSO: London

OPCS (1992e) *An Introduction to the 1991 Census and its output*, Census Division, 1 September 1992, London: OPCS

OPCS and Employment Department Group (1990a) *The Standard Occupational Classification, Volume 1: Structure and definition of major, minor and unit groups*, London: HMSO

OPCS and Employment Department Group (1990b) *The Standard Occupational Classification, Volume 2: Coding Index*, London: HMSO

OPCS and Employment Department Group (1991) *The Standard Occupational Classification,Volume 3: Social Classification and Coding Methodology*, London: HMSO

OPCS and GRO(S) (1988) *1991 Census of Population*, White Paper, Cmnd 430, London: HMSO

OPCS and GRO(S) (1990a) The census order 1990, *Statutory Instruments 243*, London: HMSO

OPCS and GRO(S) (1990b) The census regulations 1990, *Statutory Instruments 307*, London: HMSO

OPCS and GRO(S) (1991a) *1991 Census of Population: Confidentiality and Computing*, Cmnd 1447, London: HMSO

OPCS and GRO(S) (1991b) *1991 Census Field Manual*, London: OPCS

OPCS and GRO(S) (1992a) 1991 *Census Great Britain, National Monitor, CEN 91 CM56*

OPCS and GRO(S) (1992b) *1991 Census Definitions*, Great Britain London: HMSO

OPCS and GRO(S) and CO (NI) (1993) *Report on review of statistical information on population and housing (1996-2016)*, London: OPCS

Openshaw, S. (1984), The modifiable areal unit problem, *CATMOG 38*, Norwich: Geo Books

Openshaw, S. (1989), Computer modelling in human geography, in B. Macmillan, *Remodelling Geography*, Oxford: Basil Blackwell

Openshaw, S. and Taylor, P.J. (1981), The modifiable areal unit problem, in N. Wrigley and R.J. Bennett (eds), *Quantitative Geography, 60-69*, London: Routledge & Kegan Paul

Owen, D. and Green A. (1992) Migration patterns and trends, in A. G. Champion and A. J. Fielding (eds), *Migration Processes and Patterns, Volume 1: Research Progress and Prospects*, London: Belhaven, pp.17-38

Paass, G. (1988) Disclosure risk and disclosure avoidance for micro data, *Journal of Business and Economic Statistics*, 6(4): 487-500

Pearce, D., Clark, A. and Baird, G. (1988) The 1987 census test, *Population Trends, 53*, 22-26

Pearce, D. and Thomas, F. (1990) The 1989 census test, *Population Trends, 61*, 24-30

Penhale, B. (1990a) *Households, Families and Fertility*, LS User Guide No. 1, London: Social Statistics Research Unit, City University

Penhale, B. (1990b) *Living Arrangements of Young Adults in France and England*, LS Working Paper No.69, London: Social Statistics Research Unit, City University

Pickering, W.S.F. (1967) The 1851 religious census — a useless experiment?, *British Journal of Sociology, 18*, 382-407

Plewis, I. (1990) *The Analysis Potential of the LS*, LS User Guide No.3, London: Social Statistics Research Unit, City University

Priest, G. (1987) Considerations for the definitions and classification of households and families and related variables for the 1990 round of censuses, *Statistical Journal of the United Nations Economic Commission for Europe, 4,* 3, 271-303

Raper, J., Rhind, D. and Shepherd, J. (1992) *Postcodes: the New Geography*, London: Longman

Rauta, I. (1985) A comparison of the census characteristics of respondents and non-respondents to the 1981 GHS, *Statistical News, 71*, 12-15

Redfern, P. (1981) Census 1981 — an historical and international perspective, *Population Trends, 23*, 3-15

Redpath, B. (1986) Family Expenditure Survey: a second study of differential response, comparing census characteristics of FES respondents and non-respondents, *Statistical News, 72*, 13-16

Rees, P. H. (1977) The measurement of migration, from census data and other sources, *Environment and Planning A, 9*, 247-272

Rees, P. H. (1989) How to add value to migration data from the 1991 Census, *Environment and Planning A, 21*, 1363-1379.

Rhind, D. (ed) (1983) *A Census User's Handbook*, London: Methuen

Rhind, D. (1983a), Creating new variables and new areas, in Rhind, D. (ed), *A Census User's Handbook*, London: Methuen, pp. 151-169

Rhind, D. (1983b), Mapping census data, in Rhind, D., *op. cit.*, pp.171-198

Rhind, D. (1984) The SASPAC story, *BURISA 60*, 8

Rhind, D. (1990), *An On-Line Secure and Infinitely Flexible Database System for the National Population Census*, Working Paper 13, South East Regional Research Laboratory, Department of Geography, Birkbeck College, University of London, 7-15 Gresse Street, London

Rhind, D., Cole, K., Armstrong, M., Chow, L. and Openshaw, S. (1991) An online, secure and infinitely flexible database system for the national census of population Working Paper 14, South East Regional Research Laboratory, London: Birkbeck College, University of London

Rickman, J (1800; 1973) Thoughts on the utility and facility of ascertaining the population of England, *The Commercial and Agricultural Magazine*, Vol 2, London, June, 391-399; reprinted in David Glass (1973). op. cit.

Roberts, J., Middleton, E., Campbell, M., Cole, K. and Marsh, C. (1992) Software solutions for samples of anonymised records, paper presented to the 21st Anniversary Conference of the Study Group on the *Use of Computers in Survey Analysis*, University of Bristol, September

Rosing, K.E. and Wood, P.A. (1971), *Character of a Conurbation — a computer atlas of Birmingham and the Black Country*, London: University of London Press

Royce, D. (1992) Incorporating estimates of census coverage error into the Canadian Population Estimates Program, paper submitted to the 1991 Conference on the Census Undercount, US Bureau of the Census, Washington DC

Senior M. (1991) Deprivation payments to GPs: not what the doctor ordered, *Environment and Planning C, 9*, 79-94

Sharp, L. M. and Frankel, J. (1983) Respondent burden: a test of some common assumptions, *Public Opinion Quarterly 47*, 36-53

Shepherd, J., Westaway, J. and Lee, T. (1974), *A Social Atlas of London,* Oxford: Oxford University Press

Shils, E. (1979) Privacy in modern industrial society, in M. Bulmer (ed), *Censuses, Surveys and Privacy*, London and Basingstoke: Macmillan, pp 22-36

Sillitoe, K. (1987) Developing questions on ethnicity and related topics for the census, *Occasional Paper 38*, London: OPCS

Sillitoe, K. (1987) Questions on race/ethnicity and related topics for the Census, *Population Trends, 49*, 5-11

Sillitoe, K. and White, P. (1992) Ethnic group and the British census: the search for a question, *Journal of the Royal Statistical Society, 155*, 141-164

Simpson, S., Marsh, C. and Sandhu, A. (1993) 'Measures of local population in 1991: census versus other indicators', paper presented at the Annual Conference of the Institute of British Geographers, January 1993

Singer, E. (1978) Informed consent: effects on response rate and response quality in social surveys, *American Sociological Review, 43*, 144-162

Skinner, C.J., Holt, D. and Smith T.M.F. (eds)(1989) *Analysis of Complex Surveys,* New York: Wiley

Skinner, C., Marsh, C., Openshaw, S. and Wymer, C. (1992) *Disclosure Control for Census Microdata,* University of Southampton, mimeo

Smith, S. (1993) *Electoral registration in 1991,* London: HMSO

Smyth, M. and Browne, F. (1992) *General Household Survey 1990*, OPCS, London: HMSO

Social Statistics Research Unit (1990) *OPCS Longitudinal Study User Manual*, London: Social Statistics Research Unit, City University

Stillwell, J., Rees, P. and Boden, P. (eds) (1992) *Migration processes and patterns. Volume 2: Population Redistribution in the United Kingdom*, London: Belhaven

Stillwell J. (1991) Spatial interaction models and the propensity to migrate over distance, in J. Stillwell and P. Congdon P (eds), *Migration Models: Macro and Micro Approaches*, London: Belhaven, pp. 34-56

Stuart, A. (1990) *The measurement of ethnicity*, LS User Guide No.2, London: Social Statistics Research Unit, City University

Taylor, A.J. (1951) The taking of the census, 1801-1951, *British Medical Journal,* 7 April, 715-720

Teague, A. and Marsh, C. (1992) *1991 Census Samples of Anonymised Records Statistical Specification,* Census Microdata Unit, University of Manchester

Thompson, D. M. (1978) The religious census of 1851, in R.Lawton (ed), *The Census and Social Structure,* London: Frank Cass: pp.241-286

Todd, J. and Griffiths, D. (1986) *Changing the Definition of a Household,* London: HMSO

Townsend, A. R., Blakemore, M. J. and Nelson, R. (1987) The NOMIS database: availability and uses for geographers, *Area 19.1,* 43-50

Tufte, E.R. (1983), *The Visual Display of Quantitative Information,* Cheshire, Connecticut: Graphics Press

Tufte, E.R. (1990), *Envisioning Information,* Cheshire, Connecticut: Graphics Press

US Department of Commerce (1990) *Final guidelines for considering whether or not a Statistical Adjustment of the 1990 Decennial Census of Population and Housing should be made for Coverage Deficiencies resulting in an overcount or Undercount of the Population,* Washington DC: US Bureau of the Census

Visvalingham, M. (1975) Storage of the 1971 UK Census data: some technical considerations, *Census Research Unit Working Paper 8,* University of Durham

Visvalingham M (1978) The signed chi-square measure for mapping, *Cartographic Journal 15,* 93-98

Wall, R. (1990) *English and French households in Historical Perspective,* LS Working Paper, No.67, London: Social Statistics Research Unit, City University

Ward, C. and Dale, A. (1992) Geographical variation in female labour market participation: an application of multilevel modelling, in *Regional Studies, 26* (3), 243-256

Weatherall, R. (1992) *A Comparison of Mortality Measures in the LS,* LS User Guide No. 8, London: Social Statistics Research Unit, City University

Weis, N.A. and Hassett, M.J. (1991) *Introductory Statistics,* third edition, Addison-Wesley

White, P. (1990) A question on ethnic group for the census: findings from the 1989 census test post-enumeration survey, *Population Trends, 59,* 11-20

Whitehead, F. (1983) Micro-censuses and large-scale surveys: the British experience, *Population Trends, 32,* 21-24

Whitehead, F. (1988) How the 1991 census should improve government statistics, *Population Trends, 53,* 18-21

Williams, M. and Dale, A. (1990) *The Measurement of Housing Deprivation in the LS,* LS Working Paper, No.72, London: Social Statistics Research Unit, City University

Williams, R. (1976) *Keywords: a Vocabulary of Culture and Society,* London: Fontana

Wolter, K.M. (1985) *Introduction to Variance Estimation,* New York: Springer Verlag

Woltman, H., Alberti, N., and Moriarty, C. (1988) Sample design for the 1990 Census Post Enumeration Survey, *Proceedings of the Section on Survey Research Methods,* American Statistical Association, pp. 529-534

Wormald, P. (1991) The 1991 census — a cause for concern? *Population Trends, 66,* 19-21

Index

Aspects of the 1991 Census are to be found under their specific terms e.g. geography, population base, planning *etc; aspects of previous censuses are under* British censuses *and those of foreign censuses under their specific country, e.g.* French census. *Numbers in* **bold** *indicate tables or boxed entries; numbers in* italics *indicate figures or maps. The 10% sample is to be found under* ten.

Printed in the United Kingdom for HMSO.
Dd.0297078, C30, 10/93, 3396/4, 5673, 261419.